FOREIGN AFFAIRS STRATEGY

This is a book on how to think – strategically – about foreign policy, especially American foreign policy. Strategy is about the application of resources to achieve objectives, about the relationship, in thought and action, between ends and means. In the realm of *ends* this book explores the concept of the national interest and describes how to select objectives that will take advantage of opportunities to promote interests while protecting them against threats at reasonable cost and risk. On the *means* side it discusses national power and influence, as well as the political, informational, economic, and military instruments of state power. It also surveys the contemporary international environment for foreign affairs strategy, as well as the domestic context in which strategy must be formulated and executed. Based on a graphic model that illustrates strategic logic, the book uses examples from recent American statecraft, and it ends with an extended critique of current American foreign policy, outlining an alternative strategy better suited to the problems of the twenty-first century.

Terry L. Deibel is a graduate of Ohio Wesleyan University, the Institute of Advanced International Studies, in Geneva, Switzerland, and the Fletcher School of Law and Diplomacy. In Washington he has served in the International Programs Division of the Office of Management and Budget, Executive Office of the President of the United States, and in the Politico-Military Affairs Bureau of the Department of State, as well as at the Center for Strategic and International Studies and the Carnegie Endowment for International Peace. In the 1970s Dr. Deibel taught at the School of Foreign Service, Georgetown University, and since then he has been on the faculty of the National War College, where for many years he directed the teaching of foreign affairs strategy to mid-career foreign service, intelligence, and military officers.

Foreign Affairs Strategy

LOGIC FOR AMERICAN STATECRAFT

Terry L. Deibel

The National War College

CAMBRIDGE
UNIVERSITY PRESS

CAMBRIDGE UNIVERSITY PRESS
Cambridge, New York, Melbourne, Madrid, Cape Town, Singapore,
São Paulo, Delhi, Dubai, Tokyo, Mexico City

Cambridge University Press
32 Avenue of the Americas, New York, NY 10013-2473, USA

www.cambridge.org
Information on this title: www.cambridge.org/9780521692779

© Terry L. Deibel 2007

First published 2007
Reprinted 2010

A catalog record for this publication is available from the British Library.

Library of Congress Cataloging in Publication Data

Deibel, Terry L.
Foreign affairs strategy : logic for American statecraft / by Terry L. Deibel.
    p.   cm.
Includes bibliographical references and index.
ISBN-13: 978-0-521-87191-4 (hardback)
ISBN-10: 0-521-87191-3 (hardback)
ISBN-13: 978-0-521-69277-9 (pbk.)
ISBN-10: 0-521-69277-6 (pbk.)
1. United States – Foreign relations administration. 2. United States –
Foreign relations – 1989– I. Title.
JZ1480.D45 2007
327.730068'4 – dc22 2006034605

ISBN 978-0-521-87191-4 Hardback
ISBN 978-0-521-69277-9 Paperback

To the students and faculty

of the National War College,

strategists all.

Contents

Contents ix

Preface and Acknowledgments

More than three decades ago, in a graduate class I was teaching at Georgetown University, there occurred one of those little epiphanies that later turn out to have much greater significance than initially appears. I was expounding on the foreign policy of one or another nineteenth-century American president – probably James K. Polk – and concluded my peroration by labeling it an example of a *good* foreign policy. A hand shot up. "Professor, *why* was it good?" What had seemed self-evident to me obviously was not. I doubt the answer I gave that day was at all satisfactory from the student's point of view. But the question began an intellectual odyssey on my part, a search for standards by which to judge the quality of foreign policy, that has ultimately led me to write the following pages.

In a sense, this is a book about one of the ingredients that makes for a good foreign policy, as well as a book about how one ought to define the term "good" with regard to the nation's external affairs. It is a book, in the broadest sense, about how to think productively about foreign policy. And its thesis is that effective thinking in this realm is necessarily strategic in nature: that is, consciously concerned with means as well as ends of policy, and with the relationship between them. It argues, in short, for a strategic approach to foreign policy, using the term "strategic" not in a military sense but as a kind of shorthand for the ends-means relationship and all that it implies.

This is not, then, a book that argues for any *particular* foreign affairs strategy, although it does end with a critique of current American foreign policy and a proposed alternative. It was not written so much to provide answers as to suggest questions, to offer guidelines that might help structure the search for effective policy. At the same time, this is very much a book about *American* foreign affairs strategy. Although I believe that the strategic logic discussed in these pages is applicable to any nation's (or even a nonstate actor's) foreign policy, the examples I use to illustrate it are exclusively American, and the book is animated by the range of choice available to the world's only superpower and by the importance of the choices it makes to all the world's people.

It has been said that professors are people who see that something works in practice and wonder whether it would work in theory. Nevertheless, the

reader will discover that this book is not one of international relations theory. It is in the broader and I hope more useful tradition of international
affairs, written empirically as much as *a priori*, and rests its logic more
on the tradition of self-evidence than close theoretic reasoning.[1] Its purpose is to provide a guide to systematic thinking, and to the strategic logic
that underpins it, that will be useful both to students and practitioners.
I will be more than satisfied if these chapters record in an ordered way
some of what successful statesmen already know from experience and
intuition.

The concept of foreign affairs strategy as I use it has two very important
limitations that should also be noted at the outset. First, it will tell us very
little about how foreign policy is actually formulated by the government.
This is not, in other words, a book about the policy *process* but about
policy *substance*. It hopes to provide a useful intellectual framework for an
individual's thinking about foreign policy, but policy in our democracy is of
course a product of a complex process involving compromise among many
people in the public at large, the Congress, and the Executive branch. If it
succeeds, this book might help the various players in the process with their
own policy thinking, but it will do nothing to ameliorate the predictable
clash of divergent strategic visions.

Second, readers will find that this book has little to say about what
happens *after* the policy process works its magic. It does not deal with
foreign relations, with what the United States does in executing its foreign
policy. Although the prospect of successful execution is certainly critical to
the strategist's work, foreign affairs strategy itself is rather an intellectual
conception, existing on paper or in someone's head. It is a plan for action
that will usually require continuous adjustment once it gets into the hands
of practitioners and runs into the real world.

Still, an essential requirement for success in foreign affairs, as well as
within the policy process, is a firm sense of what one wants to do and
how one expects to get it done. Faced with the end of the Cold War and
with terrorist assaults on its homeland, the United States must urgently
refashion its foreign policies for a new era, and this book contends that that
process must begin with individuals who can think strategically about the
whole range of foreign affairs. The pages that follow provide one view of
what such thinking entails.

[1] See Daniel J. Boorstin, *The Americans: The Colonial Experience*, Book II, Part V
(New York: Random House, 1973), for a description of this peculiarly American approach to philosophy. On "international relations" versus "international
affairs" as terms of art, the former refers to the international branch of the traditional academic discipline of political science, whereas the latter denotes a multi-
disciplinary academic approach to foreign affairs drawing on diplomatic history,
international economics and law, security studies, and the international slices
of other disciplines in addition to political science.

Acknowledgments

As would necessarily be true of a decades-long effort, many people since my Georgetown graduate students have contributed to the thinking exhibited here. Most important among them are the extraordinary diplomats, policymakers, and military officers who have come to learn and grow at the National War College since I began teaching there in 1978. Beginning in 1986 I created and have since more often than not directed the College's core course on national security strategy and statecraft, and many of these ideas were born and refined in that crucible. More directly, the College contributed a year's sabbatical in 1993 during which an early draft of much of this book was written, and then a decade later some additional release time from teaching duties and a second sabbatical in 2005–06 to allow its completion. Thanks are also due to David Abshire and the Center for Strategic and International Studies, which provided a stimulating and congenial home while the initial writing was in progress. Needless to say, the views expressed in these pages are only my own, and do not represent the policies of any administration, agency, or department, in or out of government.

The work of so many scholars and practitioners has been important to my own education in strategic thinking over so many years that I can only acknowledge here those whose contributions were outstanding or directly related to the production of this manuscript. First, I am most particularly in the intellectual debt of John Lewis Gaddis, not only for his penetrating insights about the logic of strategy, but also because his legitimization of historical "lumpers" and frank recognition that "to remain broad you've got to retain a certain shallowness" may help excuse many of the errors of omission and understanding in what follows.[2] Thanks are also due to a broader array of scholars whose writings, as will be apparent in the pages to follow, have had the most profound impact on my conceptualization of foreign affairs strategy, especially Thomas Schelling, Joseph Nye, Robert Gilpin, David Baldwin, K. J. Holsti, Donald Puchala, and Robert Art. I am grateful to Richard Melanson of the NWC faculty and Ambassador Steve Mann of the Department of State, who read and commented upon the entire manuscript, as well as Marcelle Wahba, John Tefft, Mary Kilgore, Mark Clodfelter, Elaine Grigsby, Michael Mazarr, Karen Wilhelm, Robert Gallucci, Susan Watters Steel, Theresa Sabonis-Helf, and Jack Leonard, who have given me the benefit of their counsel or commented on sections of the manuscript. Special thanks is also due to Harvey Rishikof,

---

[2] On lumpers, see *Strategies of Containment*, Rev. & Expanded Edition (New York: Oxford University Press, 2005), p. vii; on the inevitable shallowness of grand strategy, see "The Past and Future of American Grand Strategy," *Charles S. Grant Lecture, Middlebury College* (April 21, 2005).

the department chairman who gave me the time and encouragement to press this project to conclusion; Peter Laundy, who clarified and enriched the graphic model for foreign affairs strategy on which this book is based; and John Berger of Cambridge University Press, who along with Peter Katsirubas of Aptara, Inc., found easy solutions to every problem. I would also thank my wife Carolyn for putting up with and supporting me through the many years this project absorbed, but that would so ludicrously underrate her importance to everything in my life as to offend reality. Alas, despite all this help, it is evidently only I who bear responsibility for a book not better than this one is. Happily, there is always more to learn.

Washington, D.C.
September, 2006

1

Introduction: Defining Strategy

Rarely if ever in American history has systematic thinking about foreign affairs been more important than it is today. For in the past decade and a half, two extraordinary shocks from abroad have thoroughly unsettled traditional patterns of American statecraft. First, in the fall of 1991, the collapse of the Soviet Union ended the Cold War. Then, in the fall of 2001, coordinated terrorist attacks against the American homeland killed thousands in a single morning.

Taken together, these two shocks radically altered the environment for American foreign policy both at home and abroad. For nearly five decades after World War II the antagonism between Washington and Moscow had structured the world along bipolar lines, setting the parameters of foreign policy for all nation-states. The two superpowers focused on building and defending their alliance systems, while many so-called Third World countries struggled to remain "nonaligned." Generations of Americans accepted Moscow's threat to the very existence of their country, if not to humanity itself, as a permanent fact of life. Indeed, the Soviet threat was so overwhelming and so widely recognized in the United States that it automatically performed the most essential function of strategic thinking: to set priorities. Containing Soviet power was accepted as the primary objective, the central organizing principle of foreign policy; debate was mostly about how best to implement it. And in that debate, because the threat was ultimately a military one, military means were always a prominent and often the dominant part of the answer.

All that changed with the demise of the Soviet Union. The end of bipolarity meant a revolution in world politics, although the new distribution of world power was at first obscure. Certainly the United States had no principal adversary once the USSR was gone, but in the early 1990s its lagging economy and persistent federal budget deficits hardly seemed to herald an era of American global preponderance. Indeed, in a manner eerily reminiscent of the 1920s, the salience of economic issues, combined with the apparent lack of an external threat, tended to focus American attention inward. Foreign affairs and defense budgets fell by more than 40 percent from Cold War levels, interest in foreign news rapidly dissipated, and politics was dominated by domestic issues like health care, welfare reform, crime, and abortion.

1

Meanwhile, the question of basic priorities in U.S. foreign policy remained unsettled, along with the utility of military power in an environment without apparent military threats. Analysts explained that geopolitics would be replaced by geoeconomics, and pundits argued over what should replace containment as the new primary objective of American statecraft: human rights, assertive multilateralism, commercial promotion, humanitarian intervention, enlargement of market democracy, political retrenchment abroad, or the maintenance of American primacy.[1] The Clinton administration succeeded in righting the fiscal equation and in expanding trading opportunities, and it ended the 1990s presiding over an economic boom that appeared to establish American global power for decades to come. But as it intervened in Somalia, Haiti, and the former Yugoslavia, attempted to mediate the Middle East conflict, and pursued cooperative diplomacy with adversary nations like North Korea and China, the administration's foreign policy became a matter of bitter partisan controversy.[2] President Clinton was never able to establish a widely accepted strategic construct as the new central organizing principle of post–Cold War statecraft, and the United States entered the twenty-first century without any clear idea of the use to which its enormous power ought to be put.

Then came 9/11. When George W. Bush took office, Americans thought only 7 percent of their country's biggest problems were foreign related; after the attacks, they thought 41 percent were.[3] Foreign policy was back, and with it a threat that, although less serious than nuclear war with the Soviets, seemed more likely· to materialize. The Bush administration quickly launched a war against terrorists of global reach and then expanded it into a global war on terrorism (GWOT) and on rogue states that might support them or directly attack the United States with weapons of mass destruction (WMD).[4] Spending on military forces and other

[1] Representative samples of these views can be found in Edward N. Luttwak, "From Geopolitics to Geo-economics," *The National Interest* 20 (Summer 1990): 17–24; Jeffrey E. Garten, "Business and Foreign Policy," *Foreign Affairs* 76 (May/June 1997): 67–79; Anthony Lake, "From Containment to Enlargement," (Washington, DC: SAIS/Johns Hopkins University, September 21, 1993); Eugene Gholz, Daryl G. Press, and Harvey M. Sapolsky, "Come Home, America: The Strategy of Restraint in the Face of Temptation," *International Security* 22 (Spring 1997): 5–48; Charles Krauthammer, "The Unipolar Moment," *Foreign Affairs: America and the World, 1990/91* 70 (1990–91): 23–33. For an overview of the debate, see Barry Posen and Andrew L. Ross, "Competing U.S. Grand Strategies," Chapter 5 in Robert J. Lieber, *Eagle Adrift* (New York: Longman, 1997), pp. 100–134.

[2] For an overview of these policy controversies, see Terry L. Deibel, *Clinton and Congress: The Politics of Foreign Policy*, Headline Series No. 321 (New York: Foreign Policy Association, Fall 2000).

[3] Marshall M. Bouton and Benjamin I. Page, *Worldviews 2002: American Public Opinion and Foreign Policy* (Chicago, IL: Chicago Council on Foreign Relations, 2002), p. 11. The referenced polls were done in 1998 and 2002.

[4] George W. Bush, "Address to a Joint Session of Congress and the American People," Washington, DC: White House Press Office, September 20, 2001.

instruments of foreign policy again began to rise, helping (against the background of Bush tax cuts) to return the federal budget to substantial deficit. The new war differed from the Cold War in being partly hot (in Afghanistan and Iraq), in lacking negotiations or any modus vivendi with the adversary, and in aiming at victory rather than coexistence. But like the Cold War threat from Moscow, the terrorist threat was serious enough that other foreign policies began to be shaped around it, conforming to its requirements rather than more diverse interests. Cooperation against terrorism, for example, radically altered U.S. relations with Russia and China, while the United States muted its concerns about human rights and democratization in order to construct new anti-terrorist alliances with Pakistan and across Central Asia.

Despite its current importance, however, it is far too soon to tell whether the objective of defeating global terrorism will endure as the new central organizing principle of American statecraft. The future may well turn out to be an age of counter-terror, but the features of the post–Cold War era are still very much in evidence. Either way, the increased importance of strategic thinking about foreign affairs seems assured. To the extent that combating and protecting against terrorists becomes all-encompassing, the United States will need strategic logic to help it design policies that will frustrate its enemies while protecting its liberties and advancing its interests in an ever more globalized world. To the extent that counterterrorism becomes just one goal among many, on the other hand, foreign affairs strategy will need to show the United States a route through the complexities of the post–Cold War era that policymakers failed to discover in the 1990s. Indeed, the utility of strategic thinking is even more fundamental than this dichotomy would seem to suggest: it is needed to help determine where the terrorist threat *ought* to fit in American statecraft, to guide the decisions that will partly determine what shape the future holds.

Whatever tomorrow brings, then, it is likely that the nation will need citizens and officials who can think strategically about foreign affairs, people who are able to understand strategic concepts and their interrelationships and to apply them systematically to the world statesmen confront. The purpose of this chapter is to define foreign affairs strategy, to discuss its characteristics, and to introduce the approach to strategic logic taken in the rest of the book.

What Is Strategy?

Reduced to its essentials, strategy is *how* something is done; it is a plan for action. The plan need not be put in writing, but it must be kept in mind. Thus, one has a strategy for – a sense of how to go about – buying a car, writing a book, investing one's assets, or serving the nation's interests. More precisely, *strategy is a plan for applying resources to achieve objectives*; it is thus inseparable from, indeed it is, the relationship in thought and action between means and ends, resources and objectives, power and purpose, capabilities and intentions in any sphere of human activity.[5]

Considered in this way, the term "strategy" has both a larger and smaller scope. It can be used narrowly to refer to the plans or courses of action that prescribe specific objectives, the instruments needed to pursue them, and the ways those instruments will be applied, leaving consideration of all the factors that lie behind those choices of ends and means to a realm explicitly outside that labeled strategy. Or strategy can be seen more broadly as including the interests and threats that justify objectives, the power and influence that support them, and external factors like the international and domestic context within which the strategic plan must operate. This book begins, as any strategist ought, with the broader view but moves steadily toward the more specific.

Writing about strategy has so long been confined to military subjects that many people naturally think of military matters when they see the word, and many writers use the term without modification when they really mean *military* strategy. Similarly, although it has gained widespread acceptance in the corporate world to designate long-range planning departments, the adjectival form "strategic" is often thought to have military connotations.[6] The premise of this book, however, is that strategic thinking is far too useful to be limited to military subjects. Therefore, "strategy" and "strategic" most definitely will not mean *military* strategy in the discussion that follows unless that modifier is used.[7] Still, since the roots of strategic thinking lie in military thought, it makes sense to begin developing a concept of foreign affairs strategy with a look at the way the term has been used in military parlance, along with its recent application to the related yet broader domain of national security affairs.

To the extent that describing foreign affairs strategy is a semantic exercise, precision requires that two somewhat conflicting guidelines be employed. First, terms should be defined rigorously and in ways useful to strategic analysis. Second, however, definitions ought to relate as closely as possible to a word's usage by scholars, practitioners, and the public. Unfortunately, this second task is highly problematic; the wide range of definitions in common usage and in the literature (illustrated by Appendix A) means that choices among several plausible meanings often have to be

---

[5] In *Strategies of Containment*, historian John Lewis Gaddis describes it as "the process by which ends are related to means, intentions to capabilities, objectives to resources." (New York: Oxford University Press, 1982), p. viii.

[6] During the Cold War, in fact, it was usually applied even more narrowly within the international affairs community to characterize a particular class of weapons with intercontinental capabilities.

[7] Indeed, although military strategy is a subset of foreign affairs strategy, war fighting is a specialized subject with an extensive literature of its own; hence, this book will not deal with military strategy.

made. But since it does little good to reinvent words for one's own purposes, what follows sticks as closely to accepted usage as strategic utility allows.

From Military Strategy to National Security Strategy

Military strategy, of course, is about the application of military means to achieve military objectives and, if one adopts Clausewitzian logic, higher political ends. The U.S. Joint Chiefs of Staff (JCS) define it as "the art and science of employing the armed forces of a nation to secure the objectives of national policy by the application of force or the threat of force."[8] Three aspects of this definition are worth noting. First, the only means addressed are military ones, "the armed forces of a nation." Second, military strategy is made subservient to a higher "national policy" that, as will be seen below, should be viewed as reflecting higher-level strategic thought. Third, and interestingly, the definition is not limited to outright warfare but entertains the possibility of achieving national objectives via the threat of force alone, without fighting. Military strategy has commonly been distinguished from tactics, which deals with the optimal order, arrangement, and maneuver of units in or in preparation for combat, and from operational art, which focuses – *between* military strategy and tactics – at the theater or campaign level of war.[9] Military strategy thus deals with the employment of military force at the highest, broadest, and most general level.

Modern commanders, of course, are well aware that even defeating the enemy on the field of battle – to say nothing of success in terms of the political goals of the nation-state – depends on the effective use of more than military power. The realization that the use of military force in war, if it is to be fully successful, must be a component of a broader strategy encompassing many nonmilitary instruments leads to the notion of "grand strategy," a concept used with much less consistency among writers than is military strategy.[10]

One of the narrower definitions of grand strategy is that of political scientist Robert J. Art, who includes in it the full range of U.S. foreign policy *ends*, both security and nonsecurity in nature, but restricts the *means*

---

[8] Department of Defense, *Dictionary of Military and Associated Terms*, JCS Pub. 1–02 (June 10, 1998), p. 287.

[9] Definition of tactics also based on JCS Pub. 1–02; definition of operational art from JCS, *Doctrine for Unified and Joint Operations*, Pub 3–0, January 1990.

[10] Paul Kennedy sketches the broadening of strategy from a strictly military definition in "Grand Strategy in War and Peace: Toward a Broader Definition," Chapter 1 in Kennedy, ed., *Grand Strategy in War and Peace* (New Haven, CT: Yale University Press, 1991), pp. 1–7. He does not, however, transcend its connection with war and the military to recognize that strategic thinking is applicable to all of foreign relations.

considered to purely military ones.[11] His definition is so narrow that it appears to differ little from the JCS definition of military strategy quoted above, except that it encompasses and itself deals with those national political objectives that the military strategist merely accepts as handed down from higher authority. The opposite and somewhat more common approach to grand strategy in the narrow sense is that of B. H. Liddell Hart, who wrote that "the role of grand strategy – higher strategy – is to coordinate and direct all the resources of a nation, or band of nations – towards [sic] the attainment of the political objective of the war – the goal defined by fundamental policy."[12] Here, as in the JCS definition of military strategy, political objectives are seen as outside the realm of grand strategy, having been defined at a higher level of authority; but all the means of state power, nonmilitary as well as military, are included within grand strategy. Liddell Hart's sense of grand strategy is more restrictive than the JCS definition, however, in making the assumption that grand strategy is of use only in time of war.

Today, most writers using the term grand strategy discard this limitation and argue for the application of strategic thinking to peacetime security as well as in planning for or fighting a war. "Strategy is not merely a concept of wartime," writes historian Edwin Meade Earle, "but is an inherent element of statecraft at all times."[13] Such thinking certainly includes the idea that grand strategy should be concerned with the transition from peace to war and with how the conduct of a war will affect the peace to follow. From there is but a short step to the thought that a really clever grand strategy might avoid war altogether; as the Chinese military strategist Sun Tzu wrote some 2,500 years ago, "to subdue the enemy without fighting is the acme of skill."[14] Indeed, writers like Earle and John Collins emphasize that a successful grand strategy "alleviates any need for violence," that it "so integrates the policies and armaments of the nation that the resort to war is either rendered unnecessary or is undertaken with the maximum chance of victory."[15]

---

[11] Robert J. Art, *A Grand Strategy for America* (Ithaca, NY: Cornell University Press, 2003), pp. 1–2; also "A Defensible Defense: America's Grand Strategy after the Cold War," *International Security* 15 (Spring 1991): 6–7. Art defines foreign policy as this book defines foreign affairs strategy, thereby allowing no distinction between policy and strategy (see note 28). David Baldwin specifically objects to defining grand strategy, as Art does, in terms of only one instrument as if that were the preeminent or most important one. David A. Baldwin, "Force, Fungibility, and Influence," *Security Studies* 8 (Summer 1999): 175.

[12] B. H. Liddell Hart, "The Theory of Strategy," from *Strategy*, 2nd rev. ed. (New York: Meridian, 1991), p. 322.

[13] Edwin Mead Earle, *Makers of Strategy* (Princeton: Princeton University Press, 1971), p. viii.

[14] Sun Tzu, *The Art of War*, Samuel B. Griffith, trans. (London: Oxford University Press, 1963), p. 77.

[15] "Alleviates" is John M. Collins, *Grand Strategy: Principles and Practices* (Annapolis, MD: Naval Institute Press, 1973), p. 15; "so integrates" is Earle, *Makers of Strategy*, p. viii.

But many writers on grand strategy go even further, putting the connection of strategy with war in second place and arguing that strategic thinking should be applied to the whole field of national security. This was the approach used in John Lewis Gaddis's path-breaking study, *Strategies of Containment*, which examined the strategies used by administrations since Harry Truman's for containing the expansion of the Soviet Union. All the instruments of state power were included, and the analysis focused on how the choice of instruments and the way they were used was derived from the administration's concepts of the national interest, the international system and the threats it posed, and the domestic context, including perceived trends in resources available for defense. In Gaddis's hands, grand strategy thus became nearly synonymous with a much newer term, "national security strategy," defined by a congressional panel as "the art and science of employing and using the political, economic, and psychological powers of a nation, together with its armed forces, during peace and war, to secure national objectives."[16] Today, in fact, most writers on *grand* strategy use that term in ways that cannot be distinguished from that definition of *national security* strategy. Christopher Layne, for example, writes that

> 'Grand Strategy'...is the process by which a state matches ends and means in the pursuit of security. In peacetime, grand strategy encompasses the following: defining the state's security interests; identifying the threats to those interests; and allocating military, diplomatic, and economic resources to defend the state's interests.[17]

But Gaddis, as fit the era of the Cold War, still employed a relatively narrow concept of security, and his book looked only at strategies directed toward the attainment of a single, all-important goal: containment of Soviet power. Simultaneously with the broadening of the use of strategic thinking described above, however, concepts of security were undergoing their own evolution. Beginning in the 1970s with the rise of global interdependence and the growth of concern about transnational problems like narcotics trafficking, world food shortages, uncontrolled migration, planetary pollution, climate change, and terrorism, the term security was itself broadened to include a variety of areas beyond that of the nation's protection from military attack.[18] This trend was naturally much accelerated by the collapse

---

[16] U.S. Congress, House of Representatives, *Report of the [Skelton] Panel on Military Education of the One Hundredth Congress of the Committee on Armed Services*, April 21, 1989 (Washington: GPO, 1989), p. 26. The report uses the JCS Pub. 1–02 definition for "national strategy," simply renaming it national security strategy.

[17] Christopher Layne, "Rethinking American Grand Strategy," *World Policy Journal* (Summer 1998): 8.

[18] The classic text, of course, is Robert O. Keohane and Joseph S. Nye, *Power and Interdependence: World Politics in Transition* (Boston: Little Brown, 1977).

of the Soviet Union and the end of the Cold War.[19] The result today is a view of grand or national security strategy that is very broad indeed. As the president of Washington's largest foreign affairs think tank wrote in the late 1980s:

> Today more than ever, security is both military and economic, and the two must be interrelated in a grand strategy. Western grand strategy, however, must do even more. It must embrace political and diplomatic, technological, and even cultural and moral factors. It must be a comprehensive way to deal with all the elements of national power, matching ends and means, relating them to commitments and diplomacy, and ensuring that they work in harmony.[20]

The Many Meanings of Strategy

As the analysis above demonstrates, the evolution of thought on any subject is rarely a neat or tidy affair. Today, the meanings of grand strategy and national security strategy are so fuzzy that each scholar must (and usually does) begin his analysis by defining the terms anew.[21]

This study argues that the term "grand strategy" should be reserved for the use to which Liddell Hart put it, that is, to represent the broadest planning for and the conduct of war; encompassing all the policy instruments, nonmilitary as well as military; tailoring them to meet the political goals of the state; and considering how the conduct of hostilities will affect the peace to follow. This definition of grand strategy is not in accord with its usage in much recent literature, however, because it deliberately excludes the efforts of a nation to maintain security while at peace. Those will be included here in the term "national security strategy," limited to goals that have mainly to do with the protection of the nation's physical security against attack – presumably the most important area of the national interest, but far from the only one with which strategic thinking should deal.[22] National security strategy would thus include grand strategy properly defined, with the latter operating within the former when the nation is at war and the two becoming less and less distinguishable to the extent that the war becomes total (see Figure 1.1).[23] Finally, the term "national

---

[19] See, for example, Jessica Tuchman Mathews, "Redefining Security," *Foreign Affairs* 68 (Spring 1989): 162–177, and Theodore Sorenson, "Rethinking National Security," *Foreign Affairs* 69 (Summer 1990): 1–18.

[20] David M. Abshire, *Preventing World War III: A Realistic Grand Strategy* (New York: Harper and Row, 1988), p. 13.

[21] See Appendix A for a compilation of such definitions.

[22] See the national interest taxonomy developed in Chapter 4.

[23] In World War II, for example, it is hard to imagine any foreign policy matter that was not related to the war, so national security strategy and grand strategy can be said to have been virtually synonymous. In the Persian Gulf War of 1990–91, however, many important national security concerns continued almost without reference to the war (*e.g.*, the fate of nuclear missiles in the disintegrating Soviet Union). Here, then, national security strategy had a life of its own and the grand strategy used in prosecuting the war was only one part of it.

National Strategy:
    domestic as well as foreign
Foreign Affairs Strategy:
    all foreign policy related
National Security Strategy:
    foreign, but security interest only
Grand Strategy:
    broadest conduct of war with all tools
Military Strategy:
    use of military instrument only

Figure 1.1: A hierarchy of strategies.

strategy," often used interchangeably with grand or national security strategy, should be reserved for strategic thinking applied to the *whole* range of public policy, domestic as well as international.[24]

But national security strategy as defined above still leaves a considerable area of foreign affairs outside its scope that needs the clarity and precision of strategic thought. Political scientist Hans Morgenthau prefigured this broader kind of strategy when he wrote:

> The conduct of a nation's foreign affairs by its diplomats is for national power in peace what military strategy and tactics by its military leaders are for national power in war. It is the art of bringing the different elements of national power to bear with maximum effect upon those points in the international situation which concern the national interest most directly.[25]

Clearly, Morgenthau was going beyond national security strategy to a broader concept that we shall call "foreign affairs strategy." Instead of stretching the term "national security" far beyond its traditional meaning of protection against military attack, this concept accommodates any goal, security related or not, that serves the nation's interests in its external relations.[26] As to means, it considers military power as merely one policy instrument among many, to be used or not in coordination with the others

---

[24] As noted above, the Skelton Panel defined national security strategy exactly as the JCS define national strategy, obliterating the difference between them.

[25] Hans J. Morgenthau, *Politics Among Nations: The Struggle for Power and Peace*, 5th ed., Rev. (New York: Alfred A. Knopf, 1973), p. 146.

[26] Although he defines the term strategy as if he meant military strategy – "as a plan for using military means to achieve political ends" – Richard K. Betts also makes clear that the term can have wider application: "strategies are chains of relationships among means and ends that span several levels of analysis, from the maneuvers of units in specific engagements through larger campaigns, whole wars, grand strategies, and foreign policies.... the logic at each level is supposed to govern the one below and serve the one above." "Is Strategy an Illusion?" *International Security* 25 (Fall 2000): 6.

as strategy might demand. Foreign affairs strategy might be briefly defined, then, as *an evolving written or mental plan for the coordinated use of all the instruments of state power to pursue objectives that protect and promote the national interest.*[27]

This definition is only a start; we will need to look much more extensively at the nature of strategic thinking before its meaning can be fully understood. But first there is an important distinction to be made between strategy in all its meanings and "policy." Policy is best defined as *the statements and actions of government*; it is the *output* of what is often called the "policy process," which takes place within and among the departments and agencies of the Executive branch of the federal government and between it and the Congress. Strategy, as used here, should be thought of as an *input* to that process, a guiding blueprint whose role is to direct policy, to determine what the government says and does.[28]

It is extraordinarily rare for a coherent strategy to be produced by a bureaucracy of any sort, rarer still for it to emerge from the contest between the executive and the legislative branches of a democratic government. Strategic thinking is therefore best thought of as a tool used by an individual or a small policy planning staff in its effort to decide what kind of output it *wants* from the policy process.[29] In a democratic government, these individuals will then have to contest with others (who may well have different strategic visions) in a seemingly endless struggle to make their preferred

---

[27] This definition is very close to some given for grand strategy, which Paul Kennedy defines as "the capacity of the nation's leaders to bring together all of the elements, both military and nonmilitary, for the preservation and enhancement of the nation's long-term (that is, in wartime *and* peacetime) best interests." *Grand Strategies in War and Peace*, p. 5.

[28] Ignoring this functional distinction between strategy and policy, Robert Art tries to distinguish grand strategy from foreign policy by limiting the former to the military instrument and defining the latter much as I have defined foreign affairs strategy. "Grand strategy ... differs from foreign policy in one fundamental respect. To define a nation's foreign policy is to lay out the full range of goals that a state should seek in the world and then determine how all of the instruments of statecraft – political power, military power, economic power, ideological power – should be integrated and employed with one another to achieve those goals. Grand strategy, too, deals with the full range of goals that a state should seek, but it concentrates primarily on how the military instrument should be employed to achieve them. It prescribes how a nation should wield its military instrument to realize its foreign policy goals." *A Grand Strategy for America*, pp. 1–2.

[29] Such staffs exist at several places in the U.S. Executive branch but are often not used for the purpose. The State Department's Policy Planning Staff has often been a trouble-shooting, fire-fighting and speech-writing arm of the Secretary's office; the Undersecretary for Policy in the Pentagon is fully engaged in the day-to-day activities of the Department of Defense; and the National Security Council staff at the White House – the most centrally located and potentially powerful strategic entity in Washington – has often been managed by officials who lack either the skills or the access to the President needed for successful strategic efforts.

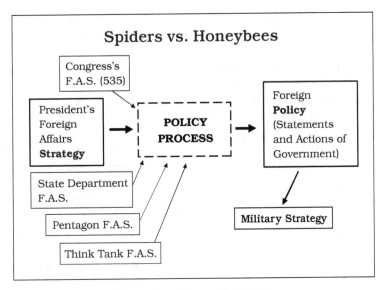

Figure 1.2: Policy and strategy.

strategy prevail in that process and, by so doing, determine the statements and actions – the policies – of the government in all its branches and departments.[30] Some of these competing visions are generated in think tanks or universities representing the intellectual elite; some are the products of special interests in society at large; some come from the Congress, which controls the federal budget and sets the laws under which the president must operate; and some are formulated by the departments and agencies of the Executive branch, which control the instruments of statecraft through which the government acts in foreign affairs.

General John Galvin, former Supreme Allied Commander, Europe, used the images of spiders and honeybees to point out that strategists must not merely spin consummate webs of logic in splendid isolation but also build consensus into their schemes by cross-pollinating ideas and gathering support (see Figure 1.2).[31] Naturally, some blueprints will be more

[30] This, of course, is what distinguishes foreign affairs strategy from what has been dubbed the "rational actor model" of governmental decision making. See Graham Allison, "Conceptual Models and the Cuban Missile Crisis," *American Political Science Review* 63 (September 1969): 689–718. Strategy is not a model of decision making at all but a structured thinking process that takes place before the policy process begins to work its distinctive magic. The strategist is not so naïve as to think that his musings will become policy; he merely understands that unless he knows where he wants to go, and how to get there, and with what, that he has little chance of pushing the policy process in his preferred direction.

[31] Testimony before the National Defense University Transition Planning Committee (the Long Committee), Center for Naval Analysis, 1 June 1989. Used by permission.

acceptable than others to key players in the process; and since an unexecutable strategy is all but useless, the prospects for success in the struggle to determine policy should certainly affect the strategist's designs. *But this book is about spiders, not honeybees; it is about how strategists spin their webs, not about how decision makers prevail in the policy process.* Policy should reflect strategy, of course, but often it does not, or does so only partially. When things go wrong in foreign affairs, it is always worth asking whether the fault lies with poorly conceived strategies or with their translation into policy, that is, whether the spiders or the honeybees are to blame.

To characterize strategies as inputs to the policy process and foreign policies as outputs should not be taken to imply that strategies are never subsidiary to policies. Rather, the question of precedence varies in each case according to the level of government on which the strategies and policies are formulated. Though foreign affairs strategies and national security strategies belong to the highest levels of government, other strategies are constantly being devised by officials at lower levels to execute the *policy* decisions of their superiors. This is what is meant when the Joint Chiefs define *military strategy* as employing the armed forces "to secure the objectives of *national policy*:" the Chiefs design military strategy to execute objectives which are the outputs of the policy process at a higher level, *outputs which themselves ought to reflect the guidance of higher level foreign affairs strategy.* And the objectives set by JCS military strategy will then be executed through the strategies, operational plans, and tactical decisions of commanders down the line.[32] The same kind of interaction between strategy formulation and policy decision takes place (or ought to) in the State Department and other agencies of the civilian government that are in charge of executing nonmilitary elements of the nation's foreign and national security policies. But unlike the proverbial chicken and egg, strategy should definitely come first at each level – especially at the highest levels of government.[33]

Finally, it should be noted that the strategic concepts discussed in this book need not be relegated exclusively to the use of the national government, or indeed of government at all. Though the point can be easily

[32] This distinction between strategy and policy is the key to the clarity Richard K. Betts seeks when he complains that "what is called national strategy in the Pentagon and grand strategy by many historians and theorists so overlaps policy that it is hard to distinguish them." The confusion goes away if one sees strategy as an input to the policy process and policy as its output. "The Trouble with Strategy: Bridging Policy and Operations," *Joint Forces Quarterly* 29 (Autumn/Winter 2001–02): 23–30.

[33] As Gregory Foster notes, "The natural inclination is to view strategy as supporting policy, rather than the reverse. ... But strategy is more than this: it is the grand design, the overall mosaic into which the pieces of specific policy fit. It provides the key ingredients of clarity, coherence and consistency over time." Gregory D. Foster, "Missing and Wanted: A U.S. Grand Strategy," *Strategic Review* 13 (Fall 1985): 14.

exaggerated, it is often noted that in today's more interdependent world both local and municipal governments, as well as a number of private and intergovernmental nonstate actors, are engaged in international activities that encroach on what was once exclusively national turf.[34] The skills of strategic reasoning presented here are quite adaptable to these groups, assuming that they have their own interests to pursue and means to execute their own policies. Because the range of their foreign affairs would seem by definition less encompassing than that of a national government, their strategic equations should be less complex, but the need for systematic thought in the areas of their concern may be no less intense. All organizations and individuals have many desirable goals, limited means, and competing interests; strategic logic provides a way of sorting them out to best effect.

The Characteristics of Foreign Affairs Strategy

The discussion above establishes the scope of foreign affairs strategy, the boundaries of what it includes and excludes, and its place in the more commonly discussed world of foreign policy. But as yet we have only begun to inquire as to its nature and characteristics. What is it that makes strategic thinking different, and more useful, than other ways of thinking about foreign affairs? We have noted that all strategies deal with the relationship between ends and means, with how resources are to be applied to achieve objectives. Within that broad description, six characteristics of strategy are worth exploring. Like any strategy, foreign affairs strategies are comprehensive, long-range, concerned with the means necessary for their execution, purposeful, internally coordinated and coherent, and interactive.

1. Comprehensive

Foreign affairs strategy tries to look at the whole picture, to be inclusive rather than exclusive, structured and systematic rather than random, episodic, or piecemeal in approach. The natural temptation of policymakers, confronted with crisis after crisis, is simply to jump into the problem of the day and try to solve it, or at least deal with it. By contrast, foreign affairs strategy makes a conscious effort to consider the whole range of issues in the nation's external relations, those relating to functional concerns (like population, the environment, proliferation, or trade) as well as those relating to all the regions and countries of the world.[35]

---

[34] See for example Michael Clough, "Grass Roots Policymaking," *Foreign Affairs* 73 (January–February 1994): 2–7; also Jessica Tuchman Mathews, "Power Shift," *Foreign Affairs* 76 (January–February 1997): 50–66.

[35] John Gaddis's list of grand strategy's characteristics begins with breadth: it "requires taking information from a lot of different fields, evaluating it intuitively rather than systematically, and then acting," in the process tolerating "a certain shallowness" in the effort to remain broad. "The Past and Future of American Grand Strategy," *Charles S. Grant Lecture*, Middlebury College (April 21, 2005).

Then, with the whole range of statecraft in mind, decision makers are better able to weigh possible responses to the day's crises for their effects, not just on the crisis itself, but on all the other foreign and domestic issues in which the nation is engaged. "A strategically focused policy," wrote Zbigniew Brzezinski, President Carter's National Security Advisor, "is one that... develops a broader approach – combining strategy and tactics – with regard to specific regional or functional objectives."[36]

Foreign affairs strategy is also comprehensive in its need for control; in this sense, it embodies the breadth that the term "grand" strategy captures so well. As John Collins puts it,

> Military strategy is mainly the province of generals. Grand strategy is mainly the purview of statesmen. Grand strategy *controls* military strategy, which is only one of its elements.[37]

As defined in this study, foreign affairs strategy is even more "grand" than grand strategy, for it seeks to direct all public policy relating to foreign relations, not just those aspects having to do with war and security. If it is to be effective, it must be on the highest level, controlling all policy having to do with the nation's external relations, including all the policies and strategies beneath it (as represented in Figure 1.1).

2. Long-Range

Strategic breadth applies not only across subjects but also over time. Strategy tries to look well into the future, and thus to help refocus decision makers from the urgent to the important. Indeed, successful foreign affairs strategies often need to look out five, ten, fifteen, twenty or more years. Henry Kissinger, National Security Advisor and Secretary of State to Presidents Nixon and Ford, warned that "[i]n foreign policy the most important initiatives require painstaking preparation; results take months or years to emerge."[38] And when former Secretary of State George Shultz asked himself "'Where are we trying to go, and what kind of strategy should we employ to get there?'" he did so "recognizing that results would often be a long time in coming."[39]

The need for continuity and persistence, and hence for future-sightedness, arises from the inherent difficulty of trying to change the behavior of other sovereign states or even affect the international system itself. It also relates to the way strategists often must get things done: gradually, over time, and by using the forces they find in the environment around them at home and abroad. Shultz argued that foreign affairs

---

[36] "The NSC's Midlife Crisis," *Foreign Policy* 69 (Winter 87–88): 96.
[37] Collins, *Grand Strategy: Principles and Practices*, p. 15.
[38] *White House Years* (Boston: Little Brown, 1979), p. 130.
[39] Shultz lamented that "while the economist is accustomed to the concept of lags, the politician likes instant results." George P. Shultz, *Turmoil and Triumph: My Years as Secretary of State* (New York: Charles Scribner's Sons, 1994), p. 31.

strategies often work like fiscal or monetary policy, taking actions on the margins that play out slowly and whose effects are often difficult to distinguish from natural forces.

> Economic policies are partially anticipated and continue to affect the economy long after they have been put in place. Results occur, but with a lag. The key to a successful policy is often to get the right process going . . . .
>
> So the economist is by training a strategist who will try to understand the constellation of forces present in a situation and try to arrange them to point toward a desirable result.[40]

In fact, the great strategic successes of the United States in the postwar era have all been long-range efforts of several administrations and both political parties. The still incomplete American effort to limit the potential for Arab-Israeli war in the Middle East runs from the Kissinger disengagement shuttles following the 1973 October war to Carter's Camp David Accords, the Israeli–Egyptian peace treaty, the historic Oslo Accords reached during the Clinton administration, and the Bush administration's "road map" to Middle East peace. The strategic rapprochement with the People's Republic of China – which revolutionized world politics in the post-Vietnam era – was begun by Nixon and Kissinger, completed by Carter and Brzezinski, and renewed (after a brief hiatus) by Ronald Reagan, George H. W. Bush, Bill Clinton, and (after another hiatus) by George W. Bush. Most notable, of course, was the decades-long American effort to contain Soviet power, running from the Truman Doctrine to the Eisenhower Doctrine to the Carter Doctrine to the Reagan Doctrine, the fall of the Berlin Wall, and the collapse of the Soviet state. Most recently, the "long war" on terrorism is quite properly expected by the current Bush administration to outlast its time in office.[41]

This is not to argue that each administration had the *same* strategy on each of these issues; in the area of containment, for example, Gaddis finds that each successive administration had a different strategy, some more than one. Though continuity is essential to strategy, the ability to change course when appropriate is also vital, lest policy succumb to the sort of creeping and eventually massive obsolescence that was typical of the Eastern bloc during the Cold War. In any case, the politics of American presidential elections seem to put a premium on dramatic changes at least in declaratory policy, illustrating how difficult strategic continuity is in a democracy. With authoritarian systems likely to sacrifice relevance for

[40] Shultz, *Turmoil and Triumph*, pp. 30–31.
[41] "This campaign may not be finished on our watch, . . ." George W. Bush, State of the Union address, cited in *Washington Post* (January 30, 2002): A16. By 2006, officials had adopted the term "Long War" to describe the struggle against terrorism. See Bradley Graham and Josh White, "Abizaid Credited With Popularizing the Term 'Long War'," *Washington Post* (February 3, 2006): A8.

stability and democratic ones prone to constant strategic revisions, the best any political system can probably do is to strike a balance between persistence and change – attempting equally to avoid ineffectiveness via inconsistency or collapse through stagnation.

3. Means-Sensitive

The characteristic that may best distinguish strategic thinking from policy thinking is the focus on means, on the instruments of policy, the various forms of the resources or power of the state. While policymakers all too often fall into the habit of assuming that their declarations are determinative, strategists never assume that something will happen simply because an official says or writes it. There have to be tools for implementing what is to be done, and their husbanding and management is no trivial task. It is in fact the major preoccupation of "statecraft," which can be generally thought of as the implementation of foreign affairs strategy or used more precisely to denote the *ways* in which instruments are applied to pursue objectives.[42] As political scientist David Baldwin writes,

> Statecraft...refers to the selection of means for the pursuit of foreign policy goals....
>
> To study statecraft...is to consider the instruments used by policy makers in their attempts to exercise power, *i.e.*, to get others to do what they would not otherwise do.[43]

As we have seen, although some grand and national security strategists still focus on military instruments, most stress the entire range of policy tools at the statesman's command. Foreign affairs strategy as defined here continues and extends this trend, including armed force among the instruments within its purview but focusing as much on its use for diplomatic purposes as on its employment in combat. Moreover, foreign affairs strategy is at least as concerned with economic and military assistance, international law and organizations, trade and investment policies, economic sanctions, information and cultural programs, diplomacy and negotiations, and other nonviolent means. Foreign affairs strategists are concerned to learn the strengths and weaknesses of these various policy instruments in the field, to understand what sorts of goals they can help achieve overseas and under what circumstances their use is appropriate and successful. Moreover, in addition to knowledge bearing on their use, foreign affairs strategy must be concerned with a quite different set

---

[42] See Chapter 7.

[43] David A. Baldwin, *Economic Statecraft* (Princeton: Princeton University Press, 1985), pp. 8–9.

of decisions on their acquisition and maintenance, with the conditions affecting the optimal balance among the instruments the statesman has on hand.[44]

But foreign affairs strategy is also concerned with the means of state-craft in a deeper sense, with the underlying power of the nation-state and how it is husbanded and maintained. Its focus on creating and sustaining the national power needed to underpin acquisition of policy tools means that foreign affairs strategy must worry about a variety of issues which otherwise might seem to be purely domestic in nature, that is, issues one might think belong to the realm of *national* strategy rather than *foreign affairs* strategy (these kinds of strategy are differentiated in Figure 1.1). Many of these issues have to do with economics, including interdependence with the world economy (especially energy dependence); macroeconomic fiscal and monetary policies and their impact on consumption, investment, and growth; the trade and budget deficits; the role of government in fostering competitiveness and technological development; the effectiveness of educational systems; and so forth. Others have to do with demographics, immigration policies, and political cohesion. Indeed, virtually any factor that can affect national power and therefore the resources available to conduct foreign relations is properly a concern of foreign affairs strategy.

4. Purposeful

Of course, strategists do not concern themselves with state power and the instruments of statecraft for their own sake. The use of policy tools is to pursue and (one hopes) to achieve certain ends; it is to accomplish specified national goals or objectives relating to the state's external environment. John Gaddis listed "setting an objective and sticking to it" as the second of five characteristics of grand strategy, while Gregory Foster put objectives at the heart of his definition: "the coordinated direction of all the resources, military and nonmilitary, of a nation ... *to accomplish its objectives.*"[45]

Paradoxically, in spite of its stress on means, the whole point of foreign affairs strategy is to put purpose into policy, to bring intentionality into statecraft by infusing in decision makers' minds ways of thinking about foreign affairs and a sense of direction that will help them gain some control over the avalanche of events. Henry Kissinger once wrote that "the public life of every political figure is a continual struggle to rescue an element

---

[44] Indeed, among the most difficult of strategy's tasks is to balance the acquisition of these instruments against one another. Paul Kennedy captures the dilemma nicely in *Grand Strategy in War and Peace*, p. 169 (see quote on p. 173 below).

[45] Gaddis, "The Past and Future of American Grand Strategy"; Foster, "Missing and Wanted," p. 15. Italics added.

of choice from the pressure of circumstance," and strategy is the essential intellectual tool for doing so.[46] First, the discipline of strategic thought forces the statesman to plan ahead, to set goals he wants to achieve over the long run and think through how they can be accomplished; as noted earlier, he can thus try to avoid merely reacting to day-to-day events or drifting along with them.[47] Second, foreign affairs strategy can help the statesman turn unexpected but inevitable crises into opportunities for getting where he wants to go instead of letting them derail his progress. As Secretary Shultz once said:

> Say there's a fire. You have to get the fire out...[but] there are various ways you can do it. If you don't have any strategy you just get the fire out. Now if you have a strategy you say to yourself, "Well, all right, I'm going to get this out, but I'm going to do it in...a way that...is compatible, or at least not incompatible, with my general thrust." So what you try to build is the implementation of your strategy by these incremental little things.[48]

As will be seen in the chapters to follow, goal setting in foreign affairs strategy is no easy task, for strategic objectives must be both desirable *and* feasible. "Desirable," of course, means that at a minimum the goal must be in accord with the nation's values. "Statecraft," as Harold and Margaret Sprout defined it, "embraces all the activities by which statesmen strive *to protect cherished values and to attain desired objectives* vis-à-vis other nations...."[49] But values are exceedingly difficult to capture, so strategists tend to use the term "national interest" as a more manageable way of defining the nation's values in foreign affairs, both in general and with regard to specific countries and circumstances. Political scientist Robert Osgood characterized grand strategy as "the nation's plan for using all its instruments and resources of power *to support its interests most effectively*," and foreign affairs strategy is very much about defining the national interest and then setting objectives to defend and advance it.[50]

"Feasible" means that the state must have the power, must possess and be able effectively to employ the instruments of statecraft necessary to achieve its goals, a requirement that recalls the means-sensitive nature of strategy and brings us directly to the fundamental nexus of ends and

---

[46] Kissinger, *White House Years*, p. 54.

[47] "What, then, is strategy? Strategy is *structure* – it provides an intellectual framework for the development of policy. Strategy is *direction* – it affords a guiding path through the welter and maze of international events. Strategy is *purpose* – it is tied to ultimate, global objectives rather than to the exigencies of the moment. Finally, strategy is *continuity*...." Foster, "Missing and Wanted," p. 15.

[48] Quoted in Jim Naughton, "George Shultz, in Myriad Detail," *Washington Post* (March 19, 1989): F1, F4.

[49] Harold and Margaret Sprout, *Towards a Politics of the Planet Earth* (New York: Van Nostrand Reinhold Co., 1971), p. 135.

[50] Robert E. Osgood, "American Grand Strategy: Patterns, Problems, Prescriptions," *Naval War College Review* (September–October 1983): 5.

means. Simply defined, "strategy involves a process of reconciling what we want (objectives) with the resources available (capabilities) to meet these wants."[51] The relationship between ends and means is the all-important center, the iron linkage of strategic thought. In fact, John Gaddis argues that strategy "is nothing more than the calculated relation of ends and means," with the adjective "calculated" meant to imply "a deliberate as opposed to an accidental, inadvertent, or fortuitous connection" between the two.[52] The concern with ends, the focus on purpose, is what gives form to the strategist's calculations.

5. Coherent

The importance of the relationship between ends and means points to the fifth characteristic that distinguishes strategic thinking. It is not only comprehensive – taking account of everything relevant – but integrated. It hangs together, relating things logically, both in thought and action. As Kissinger puts it in his memoirs, "Good policy depends on the patient accumulation of nuances; care has to be taken that individual moves are orchestrated into a coherent strategy."[53] And Christopher Layne writes,

> In concrete terms, the debate over U.S. grand strategy is being played out almost daily with respect to NATO enlargement, China, U.S.-Japan relations, Bosnia, U.S. policy with respect to the proliferation of weapons of mass destruction, trade policy, and the defense budget. These are not discrete issues. The function of grand strategy is to weave them into a coherent framework.[54]

At the level of action, the use of all the instruments of statecraft naturally leads to a need for coordination, organization, integration, and direction of these instruments for maximum efficiency and effectiveness. In a presidential-style democracy like that in the United States, there are at least two dimensions of such coordination. First, the successful strategist must be able to coordinate the Executive branch of government, since the instruments of policy are parceled out among various departments and agencies (the Pentagon has military forces, the State Department handles diplomacy, the Agency for International Development manages foreign assistance, trade policy is in the Commerce Department and Office of the U.S. Trade Representative, and so forth). As students of bureaucratic politics know well, each of these entities can be counted on to have an agenda of its own which may or may not comport with the nation's foreign affairs

[51] Charles M. Fergusson, Jr., "Statecraft and Military Force," *Military Review* 46 (February 1966): 70.

[52] John Lewis Gaddis, "Containment and the Logic of Strategy," *The National Interest* 10 (Winter 1987–88): 29.

[53] Kissinger, *White House Years*, p. 415.

[54] Layne, "Rethinking American Grand Strategy," p. 8.

strategy. As if this were not enough, the strategist must remember that policy instruments are provided to foreign affairs agencies by the Congress, raising the equally vexing problem of coordination between the executive and the legislative branches. The Congress not only controls through its power of the purse the amount of each instrument granted to the Executive (and therefore the mix of instruments available to pursue any range of foreign policy objectives). It also often surrounds its grants of funds with elaborate restrictions on the *use* of the tools of policy, limiting the strategist's flexibility even more.

The importance as well as the difficulty of coordinating the instruments of policy across the government led Brent Scowcroft, National Security Advisor to Presidents Gerald Ford and George H. W. Bush, to remark that "the hallmark of a successful administration is the extent to which its strategic concept can integrate the government."[55] Scowcroft's comment points to a level deeper than simply orchestrating policy instruments, suggesting that strategic coherence is first and foremost a matter of intellectual dominance. Certainly the strategist's prospects for success in "integrating the government" will be enhanced if he knows his objectives, has a plan, and can mentally get hold of the situation, showing his colleagues a path toward mastering events. Coordination and integration of the instruments of statecraft must therefore begin with the intellectual coordination and integration of concepts, with logical coherence. The proper relationships between interests and threats, ends and means, costs and risks must be appreciated and applied. The whole strategic concept must fit together.[56]

Strategic coherence is essential in the first instance because of the enormous complexity of modern foreign relations. As Kissinger put it, "To ignore the interconnection of events was to undermine the coherence of *all* policy."[57] Without it, the statesman is likely to take actions on one issue that contradict his objectives on another, to try to use the same instruments for multiple goals, or to field policies that contradict and undercut each other. With it, there is at least the chance that policies will reinforce each other, so that the state can achieve more than the strict allocation of its power across its interests might seem to make possible.

In attempting to achieve such intellectual coherence the strategist will find it essential to make choices, to set priorities. The reasons are at least three. First, although the ideal is to integrate the whole range of issues,

[55] Remarks to National War College Class of 1989, November 1988. Used by permission.
[56] "Grand strategy represents a road map delineating our most important foreign policy goals and the most effective instruments and policies for achieving those goals. It contains a vision for America's role in the world based in part on America's domestic needs and in part on the international challenges the country faces. It thus establishes priorities and gives focus to an otherwise volatile foreign policymaking process...." Sherle R. Schwenninger, "Revamping American Grand Strategy," *World Policy Journal* 20 (Fall 2003): 25.
[57] *White House Years*, p. 129. Italics in original.

regions, and countries, intellectual capacities rarely match the ideal. Prior-itization then becomes the only shortcut through complexity. Second, there are always more desirable objectives than available resources, yet a lack of correspondence between ends and means is a critical strategic failure. Perhaps the most necessary and most difficult challenge for the statesman is to choose the two or three most important and doable goals, rather than dissipating energy and resources on a myriad of worthwhile efforts, only to see none of them succeed.[58] Finally, even if one's power seems overwhelm-ingly preponderant, reality often manifests objective conflicts that cannot be overcome, which is merely to say that everything is not always possible in an interdependent world. Strategic coherence then requires that choices be made, that priorities be established.

6. Interactive

The final element common to all strategic thinking is the need to deal with what might be called intelligent resistance to the strategist's designs. *Military* strategy naturally places a great deal of emphasis on the enemy and the threat he represents, and the concentration of *national secu-rity* strategy on protecting the nation's physical security against attack also directs its primary attention to military dangers. But while foreign affairs strategy may not need to be so focused on threats, some form of resistance to the statesman's designs is assumed – otherwise, wish-ing alone would suffice to make things happen, and there would be no need for strategy at all. Political scientist K. J. Holsti defines statecraft as "the organized action governments take to *change the external environ-ment in general, or the policies and actions of other states in particular,* to achieve the objectives set by policy makers."[59] Such change probably means frustrating some other state's objectives, and its strategists can be expected to resist.

In game theory this characteristic of intelligent resistance distinguishes games of strategy from those of skill or chance. Strategic games are those in which the best course of action for each participant depends on what he *expects* the other players to do, because the outcome of the game depends substantially on what they *actually* do.[60] Military strategist Edward N. Luttwak has pointed out that this makes the logic of strategy paradoxical. If the strategist wants to get from A to F, he does not go in a straight line B-C-D-E, since his opponent will throw up obstacles; instead, an indirect or even devious approach is called for, one which takes into account how

---

[58] Zbigniew Brzezinski felt that Carter's over-ambition was a major reason for his foreign policy failures. *Power and Principle* (New York: Farer, Straus, Giroux, 1983), p. 57.

[59] K. J. Holsti, "The Study of Diplomacy," in James N. Rosenau, Kenneth W. Thompson, and Gavin Bond, eds., *World Politics* (New York: Free Press, 1976), p. 293.

[60] See Thomas C. Schelling, *The Strategy of Conflict* (Cambridge, Mass.: Harvard University Press, 1960), pp. 3–5.

the opponent is likely to forecast one's actions and what steps he will take to counter them.[61] Strategy is thus interactive.

The fact that the subject of the game is another strategist means that a large part of the statesman's job, just like the soldier's, has to do with assessing the capabilities and intentions of those in a position to frustrate his purposes. What the other actor is capable of doing, what he wants to do, what power we have relative to him, and how we can influence his behavior – all are essential judgments a strategist has to make. Moreover, while the soldier necessarily thinks in terms of enemies, the statesman has to deal with a much broader range of relationships. As Nobel laureate Thomas Schelling put it in his classic *The Strategy of Conflict*,

> "winning" in a conflict does not have a strictly competitive meaning; it is not winning relative to one's adversary. It means gaining relative to one's own value system . . . .
>
> Thus, strategy . . . is not [only] concerned with the efficient *application* of force but with the *exploitation of potential force*. It is concerned not just with enemies who dislike each other, but with partners who distrust or disagree with each other. It is concerned not just with the division of gains and losses between two claimants but with the possibility that particular outcomes are worse (better) for *both* claimants than certain other outcomes.[62]

Foreign affairs strategy deals, then, not just with enemies, but with allies and partners and all kinds of relationships in between. It is as much, perhaps even more concerned with U.S.-Japanese and U.S.-European relations as with U.S.-Iranian or U.S.-North Korean relations, as much with U.S.-Russian relations today as with U.S.-Soviet relations during the Cold War. It is usually what political scientists call a "mixed-motive" game, in which the players simultaneously have goals both in common and in conflict (as when Europe and the United States are security partners but economic competitors or, within the economic sphere, involved in both highly cooperative relationships like joint ventures and very conflictual ones like high-tech competition or trade negotiations).

Whatever the issues or actors, strategic situations are those "involving two or more participants, each trying to influence, to outguess, or to adapt

---

[61] Edward N. Luttwak, *Strategy: The Logic of War and Peace* (Cambridge, MA.: Belknap Press of Harvard University Press, 1987). At many points in his book, Luttwak argues that paradoxical logic applies only when the use or threat of force is present and when there is no restraining force of law or custom to keep competition within bounds. Elsewhere, however, he argues that it applies "in all that is characterized by the struggle of adversary wills" (p. 18) and that "diplomacy, propaganda, secret operations, and economic controls are all subject to the logic of strategy, as elements in the adversarial dealings of states with one another" (p. 65). I would contend that it applies anywhere there is intelligent resistance to the strategists' designs, certainly throughout the anarchy of international politics, and probably even (for example) between companies competing for market share.

[62] Schelling, *The Strategy of Conflict*, pp. 4–5.

to the decisions or lines of behavior that others have just adopted or are expected to adopt."[63] As a result, much of strategic analysis has to do with the *choices* that other strategists will make, and strategists must pay attention to how people formulate alternatives and decide among them, as much to improve their own decision abilities as to better understand those of their strategic partners. As Schelling defined it, strategy is initially about vicarious problem solving:

> We figure out what a person might do by putting ourselves into his position ... and deciding what he ought to do ..., what he should decide in accordance with his own aims, values, and objectives, given the alternatives that he faces. The supposition is that he has a choice to make, can reflect on that choice, ... and will decide ... in a way that suits his apparent purposes. If we have some clue as to what his purposes are, and some appreciation of the alternatives he faces, we anticipate his choice by figuring out what one would do in that situation with those aims and values.[64]

However, strategy is not only about figuring out and anticipating others' choices but also about changing them. As Schelling continues, "people have choices to make and must weigh the consequences. The structure of the situation can affect what those consequences are; and often one or both parties are trying to restructure the situation" in order to affect those choices.[65]

After the Cold War and before 9/11, U.S. objectives often appeared to be shifting toward cooperative goals like cleaning up the environment or combating world hunger, areas in which the primary resistance to the strategist's designs might seem to be inanimate rather than intelligent, to be the problem itself rather than other strategists. But even if this shift deepens in the decades to come, there will continue to be conflict at both the inter- and intra-national levels, if only about the distribution of costs and benefits from cooperative efforts to deal with common problems. For example, even though it is clear that reduced impediments to international trade will result in a more productive world economy from which the majority will benefit, American labor unions and many working Americans opposed the loss of present-day jobs to North and Central American Free Trade Areas despite their promise of more, higher-wage jobs in the future.[66] Thus, although it may not always be as easy to see as in a hostile entity bent on military attack, the phenomenon of intelligent resistance to the strategist's objectives is very likely to be a continuing feature of international politics.

---

[63] Thomas C. Schelling, "Strategic Analysis and Social Problems," in Schelling, ed, *Choice and Consequence* (Cambridge, MA: Harvard University Press, 1984), p. 198.

[64] Schelling, "Strategic Analysis," pp. 205–206.

[65] Schelling, "Strategic Analysis," p. 198.

[66] Thomas B. Edsall, "'New Democrat' Bloc Opposes Trade Pact," *Washington Post* (May 21, 2005): A4.

Thinking about Foreign Affairs Strategy

The picture that emerges from this discussion of foreign affairs strategy, then, is of an intellectual activity that takes place in the minds of people who are determined to influence or keen to evaluate the direction of the nation's foreign relations. As applied to government, it is an analytical and planning function that must be done at the highest levels, in the United States by the president and his top subordinates for foreign and national security affairs. It has to do with the conscious coordination, orchestration, and control of all the instruments of statecraft – political, informational, and economic, as well as military – with a view to attaining specified objectives or goals that in some way serve the nation's values as seen by decision makers and embodied in their concept of the national interest. Indeed, foreign affairs strategy pays very explicit attention to the relationship between means and ends, between instruments of state power and the objectives they seek. Moreover, it recognizes that success depends largely upon influencing the behavior of other governments or nonstate actors, themselves directed by strategists, who range from partners and allies through the nonaligned to outright adversaries, and doing so in conditions running from friendship to hostility to full-scale warfare.

The heart of the strategist's work is to see clearly the extraordinarily complex interrelationships among the elements of strategy – to grasp, as it were, the logic of strategic thought – and then to apply that understanding to the real world, making the choices and setting the priorities that strategy demands. Those relationships – between ends and means, interests and threats, costs and benefits, to name a few – exhibit no simple linear cause-and-effect relationship. Their correlations are like those in gestalt psychology, or field theory in physics, or macroeconomics, in that every variable is a dependent one; everything is connected to and affects everything else. Hence, if one element of a strategic design changes, all the others must change, too.

Although books are unavoidably linear, this kind of tight conceptual system is best portrayed in a graphic framework or model of strategic logic, which attempts to capture visually the principal interrelationships in foreign affairs strategy.[67] Such a model would need to include ends like interests and objectives, and means like power and instruments. It would also need to represent the international environment in which threats and opportunities originate, as well as the domestic environment that sets the purposes of and generates the power behind a nation's strategy. It should show statecraft, or the ways in which instruments are used to serve

---

[67] There is a dilemma here, for although everything cannot be explained at the same time, knowledge of each element of strategy is essential to understanding each of the others. In the pages that follow there is no avoiding looking at the same problem from different angles, but repeated turning of the kaleidoscope should eventually produce a clear picture of strategic logic.

Figure 1.3: The real world.

objectives, along with the relationship of planned courses of action to the policy process. And it should make clear that what the nation says and does has feedback effects on the international and domestic contexts of the future. Such a graphic model should orient the reader to the conceptual landscape, provide a skeleton on which to hang the discussion of concepts that might otherwise seem unrelated, and help strategists order their own strategic thinking.[68]

Since strategic thinking begins with and ends in the real world, such a model for foreign affairs strategy must have the real world as its background. The real world is first of all the *environment* for strategy (as shown at the top of Figure 1.3). Even though international and domestic affairs are increasingly interrelated, these two components of the strategic environment should be kept conceptually distinct, for there are significant differences in how they affect strategy. But the real world, or at least the international environment, is also the destination of foreign affairs strategy, the realm on which strategy intends to have its effect through the foreign policies it generates (as shown at the bottom of Figure 1.3). Thus, foreign

[68] Readers who prefer a linear approach should see the five-level framework reproduced in Appendix B.

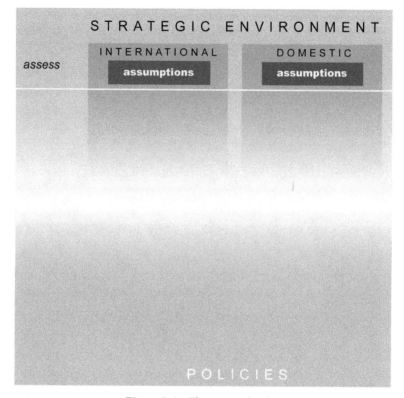

Figure 1.4: The assess level.

affairs strategy departs *from* the real world, abstracting from its problems and concerns, and then returns *to* it in the form of foreign policies.

It is against the background of the strategic environment, then, that foreign affairs strategy is modeled in the center of this graphic. It is shown on three levels, each representing a set of tasks that strategists must perform. The most fundamental task (if not necessarily the first in sequence) is to *assess* one's assumptions about the strategic environment, both international and domestic (see Figure 1.4). These assumptions, the foundation of all strategic thought, are so critical that the following two chapters are devoted to them: Chapter 2 deals with assumptions about "The International Strategic Environment," and Chapter 3 with those concerning "The Domestic Context for Strategy."

The next two levels of strategic thinking each deal with the bedrock concepts of ends and means, as represented in Figure 1.5. Here the strategist is working at farther remove from the real world than on the first level, manipulating abstractions in an attempt to capture the ends to be accomplished and the means to be applied to them.

On the second level, the strategic task is to *analyze* concepts that lie at the heart of strategic thinking (see Figure 1.6). On the ends side these

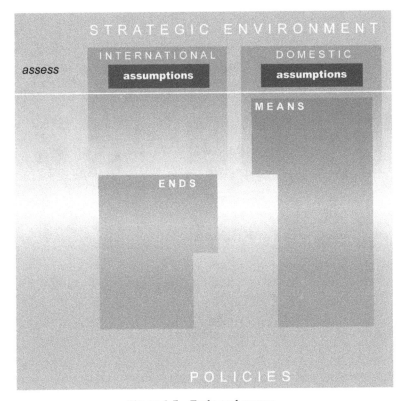

Figure 1.5: Ends and means.

include the concept of *national interests,* as well as the *threats* to them that come out of the international environment and the *opportunities* for advancing them that may be found in both the international and domestic environments; these are the subjects of Chapter 4, "Interests, Threats, and Opportunities." On the means side strategists must analyze the *power and influence* that come from the domestic environment and are available to serve those interests, protecting them against threats and taking advantage of opportunities to advance them; these concepts are the subject of Chapter 5, "Power and Influence."

The task strategists face on the third level is to make these concepts explicit and actionable, that is, to *plan* for what they want the government to say and do (see Figure 1.7). To do so they must distill from their concept of the national interest a set of actionable *objectives* to form the specific ends of their strategy; select an instrument or *instruments* of state power that will constitute the means through which those ends will be pursued; and determine the *statecraft* with which those instruments will be used, that is, the ways in which they will be applied to achieve objectives. Chapter 6, "The Instruments of State Power," defines and surveys the characteristics of nine specific instruments of statecraft,

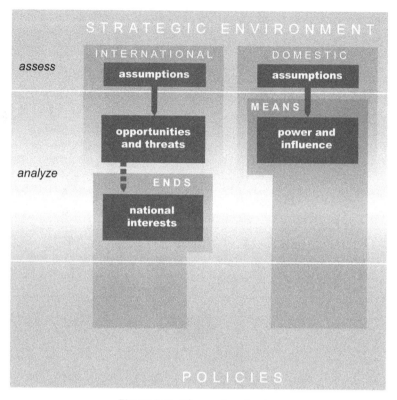

Figure 1.6: The analyze level.

describing their strengths and weaknesses; Chapter 7, "Linking Ends and Means," explains how to set objectives, link them with instruments, and use statecraft to apply instruments to objectives; and Chapter 8, "Evaluating Courses of Action," considers how strategists can refine objective-instrument packages based on their likely cost, risk, impact, and success.

Once complete, these courses of action will be the outward expression of the foreign affairs strategy as it competes in the policy process to determine the statements and actions of government, or foreign policies (see Figures 1.2 and 1.8). And as the feedback arrow running along the right side of the model in Figure 1.8 from its bottom to its top indicates, those policies will influence the international and domestic environment for future strategy, affecting on the second, analytical level the opportunities and threats future strategists will face along with the power and influence they will have to deal with them. As an illustration of how assessments of the strategic environment and analysis of strategic concepts relate to such specific plans, Chapter 9 looks at "American Foreign Affairs Strategy Today," critiquing the strategy of the George W. Bush administration and offering an alternative foreign affairs strategy for the United States. Its purpose is to offer an extended application of strategic logic.

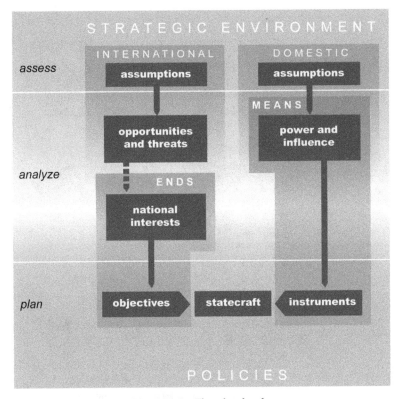

Figure 1.7: The plan level.

Learning how to think strategically about foreign affairs is really a two-part process. Without question, it is important to *understand* the concepts that make up strategic logic and how they relate to one another. Therefore this book takes care to define these terms in considerable detail, especially in this chapter for strategy and policy; Chapters 2 and 3 for the international and domestic environments; Chapter 4 for the national interest, threats, and opportunities; and Chapter 5 for power and influence (see Figure 1.9). At the same time, it is necessary to know how to *apply* the concepts to real-world cases. Attention to this practical side of strategic thinking is given throughout the book, but especially in Chapters 6 through 9. Readers should note that these two aspects of strategic learning, the conceptual and the practical, are both sequential and simultaneous; that is, although more than a rudimentary understanding of strategic logic is required before strategic analysis and planning can begin, it is only by *using* the concepts that one can really come to understand their meaning. Similarly, strategic application cannot be done in a strictly linear fashion. Although one has to start somewhere, it is only by moving repeatedly between ends and means while continuously reassessing assumptions; further analyzing interests, threats, opportunities, power and influence; and planning more effective

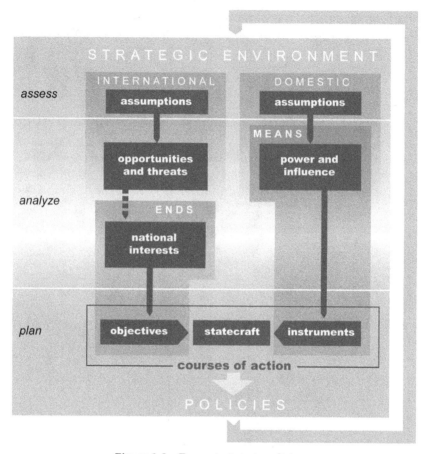

Figure 1.8: From strategy to policies.

and efficient courses of action that the strategist can arrive at clarity of thought about the issue at hand and a solid approach to dealing with it.

Although foreign affairs strategy is necessarily an exercise in abstract thought, then, its utility lies in the use of carefully defined concepts and the strategic logic that interrelates them to discipline thinking about real-world cases. In order to illustrate these concepts and logic, this book draws on many examples from the last four decades of American foreign affairs.[69] Why use this slice of American history? First, it offers enough material to do the job, and enough variety in foreign affairs strategies to illustrate the

[69] That I am drawing selective examples from this history to illustrate points of strategic logic, rather than doing numerical analysis of carefully encoded historical data sets, may bother some of a more "scientific" bent. My defense, again, is that my purpose is not to construct scientific theory, which I believe to be all but impossible for realms of human interaction like foreign affairs. I do, however, draw on such research where it seems useful to illuminate issues of strategic logic.

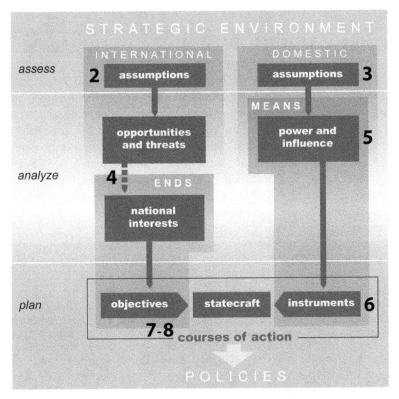

Figure 1.9: Concepts with chapter numbers.

range of strategic choice. Second, it shows how statesmen reacted to major shifts in the international context as the United States moved from the high threat environment of the late Cold War, to the more relaxed strategic circumstances of the 1990s, and back to the dangers of the post-9/11 world. Third, it also shows how statesmen dealt with continuing challenges, for the 1970s and 1980s moved beyond the Cold War even as it continued, bringing into play a series of factors that continue to shape American foreign affairs today: oil and energy shortages, economic globalization, weapons proliferation, the rise of nonstate actors, budget and resource stringencies, popular distrust of government, and radical differences among Americans on how to deal with it all. Finally, the prominence of the United States in world affairs means that readers should be familiar with much if not all of this recent history, allowing succinct treatment of illustrations that might otherwise require long explanation.

Before beginning our detailed look at the elements of strategy, one final word of introduction may be in order. The portrait of strategy offered here is obviously and admittedly an ideal one. No foreign affairs strategy will be completely comprehensive, totally purposeful, fully coordinated. Strategy is a tool, and useful tools are often dirty – and occasionally, broken. But neither is it correct to maintain that strategies are only invented after the fact to justify actions taken in the heat of battle, that the best statesmen can or should expect to do is react to events, or that no "strategic logic transcending time and circumstance" even exists.[70]

Rather, our historical experience lies somewhere in between the ideal and the cynical. It indicates that real strategies grow up alongside the real world in the minds of observers or practitioners witnessing and grappling with events. They often draw on existing policy while at the same time shaping it, giving policies justification and meaning they would not otherwise possess but also showing statesmen the way ahead. They are adopted by governments because of their explanatory power and because of the sense of direction they offer.[71] And in the end they rest not on the prospect of flawless performance but on faith: that the statesman can push events in some preferred direction, however slightly, and that the only hope for doing so is to have an idea of where the country should go in its foreign relations and how to make the logic of strategy work to move it forward.

[70] See Whittle Johnson, "The Containment of John Gaddis," *National Interest* 6 (Winter 1986–87): 85–94.

[71] This certainly is the conclusion one reaches from two detailed accounts of the origins of containment. See Melvin P. Leffler, *A Preponderance of Power: National Security, the Truman Administration, and the Cold War* (Stanford, CA: Stanford University Press, 1992), and Wilson D. Miscamble, *George F. Kennan and the Making of American Foreign Policy, 1947–1950* (Princeton, NJ: Princeton University Press, 1992).

Part I

Assess

2. The International Strategic Environment
3. The Domestic Context for Strategy

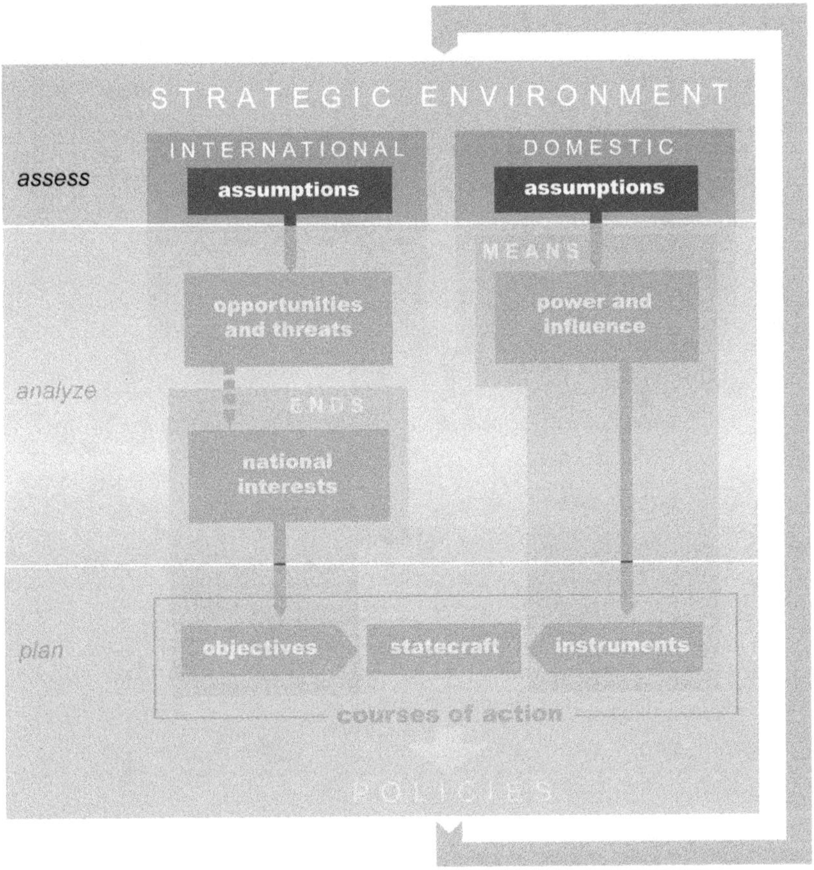

2

The International Strategic Environment

Successful strategy for foreign affairs ends – and therefore must begin – in the real world of international relations. If successful, it ends by influencing other global actors or changing the international environment in ways favorable to the nation's interests. To do so it must begin with an accurate mental picture of domestic and international reality, an understanding of the politics and economics of foreign policy at home and of how the world works abroad.

Such knowledge is not easily acquired. For most decision makers it is a product of years of experience and learning, heavily influenced by deeply ingrained habits of mind and by value preferences of which the individual may only be dimly aware. Much of the most useful knowledge relates to how other strategists are likely to think and react, demanding a kind of empathy with foreign mentalities and cultures that few Americans, at least, possess. During the months preceding the U.S. 2003 invasion of Iraq, for example, even Western observers with the most impressive experience of the Arab world and of Iraq itself were far from agreement as to how Saddam Hussein might respond to American pressures. When it comes to the broader vistas of foreign affairs strategy, "knowing" involves such a vast universe and comes at such remove from it in time, space, and cognition that the task may seem virtually beyond human capacity. Drawing on the specialized knowledge of experts where they can, strategists have no choice but to seek refuge in generalization, judicious simplification, and their own well-developed intuition based on experience – the "intellectual capital" developed over a lifetime.[1]

As a result, the strategist's knowledge of the nation and the world should be seen less as a set of facts than of perceptions or "assumptions" that must be assessed and reassessed as reality changes or new evidence comes to light (see Figure 2.1).[2] All foreign affairs strategists have such assumptions

---

[1] As Henry Kissinger writes, "...the convictions that leaders have formed before reaching high office are the intellectual capital they will consume as long as they continue in office." *White House Years* (Boston, MA: Little, Brown & Co., 1979), pp. 27, 54.

[2] Note that the strategic model in Figure 2.1 applies "assumptions" only to the environment for strategy, because only at this level does the model presume to

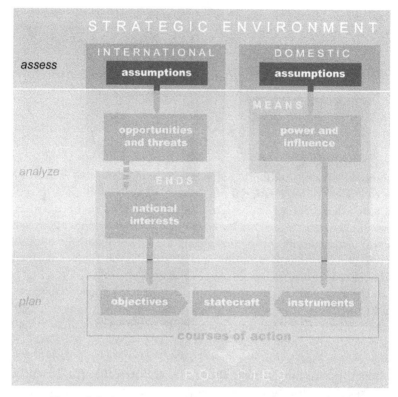

Figure 2.1: Assumptions about the strategic environment.

in mind whether they know it or not; the trick (to paraphrase Plato) is not to lead an unexamined life, but to expose one's assumptions and be ready repeatedly to reevaluate them. But cultivating a mental stance of provisional agnosticism is no easier than acquiring useful strategic knowledge in the first place, for perceptions of external reality are central to the whole edifice of strategic thought. They are the background reference points, the field of strategy, the ocean (intellectually speaking) on which the ship of state sails. They go a long way to give the strategist a sense of the possible, an idea of the constraints on and opportunities for action in the world. They are of primary importance to the outcomes of strategic analysis. Changing them therefore requires the most wrenching kind of change in every other aspect of the strategist's thinking.

The importance of such assumptions means that the battle for sound strategy can often be lost right here, at the very beginning. Decision makers may come to office with a flawed, inconsistent, or badly distorted view of

replicate reality. Other concepts in the model – like interests, threats, or influence – are really artifacts of strategic analysis and planning, even though they may appear to reflect real-world phenomena.

the world and spend years learning from their mistakes. Worse, they may spend years *not* learning if, unable to tolerate the cognitive dissonance between their perceptions and the evidence presented to their senses, they screen out contrary indicators. Either way, foreign affairs strategy that does not start with realistic assumptions about the strategic environment or that fails to alter them as reality changes has little hope of success. It will remain a detached intellectual exercise, likely (if given the chance) to do more harm to policy than good.

American experience over the past three decades amply demonstrates both the importance of assumptions to strategic outcomes and the dangers when they are out of line with reality. In 1981, for example, Ronald Reagan took office believing that the world that mattered was bipolar, rigidly divided into two alliance systems headed by the United States and the Soviet Union. The USSR was seen as posing a direct military threat to the United States, creating a "window of vulnerability" which might invite outright military blackmail or worse by the early 1980s; indeed, Soviet leaders were believed to be driven by Communist ideology, bent on expansion, and implicated in every disturbance to the status quo worldwide. The Third World of developing countries was an important battlefield for the superpower struggle but otherwise (aside from the oil-rich Persian Gulf) of little intrinsic importance, basically not worth the trouble its mostly hostile leaders caused at the United Nations and elsewhere.

The worldview held by Jimmy Carter when he took office four years earlier could hardly have been more different. For Carter, the international system was becoming multipolar, with the East-West alliance systems already loosening and with power more and more diffuse and more and more economic in nature. The Soviet Union was seen as an essentially status quo nation, run by an aging gerontocracy and with severe economic problems that demanded a respite from overseas adventures, and whatever military threat the United States might face was at least as much a result of the existence of huge arsenals of nuclear weapons on both sides as of any malevolent Soviet intent. The country did, however, need to worry about economic threats from abroad, as the Organization of Petroleum Exporting Countries (OPEC) had demonstrated by forcing Americans to wait in long lines to gas up their cars. In this regard the Third World was vitally important as a source of raw materials and markets for American goods; problems there were largely due to indigenous social, political, and economic conditions rather than Soviet machinations.[3]

These radically different assumptions about the external environment had dramatic effects on the two administrations' foreign affairs strategies.

---

[3] These brief sketches of the Reagan and Carter worldviews are more fully elaborated in my *Presidents, Public Opinion, and Power*, Headline Series #280 (New York: Foreign Policy Association, April 1987) and in "Reagan's Mixed Legacy," *Foreign Policy* 75 (Summer 1989): 34–55.

Ronald Reagan, for example, initiated a crash buildup of U.S. military forces, while Jimmy Carter set out to make annual 5 percent reductions in military spending. Reagan turned away from serious arms control discussions with the Soviets, while Carter eagerly sought a treaty with Moscow embodying deep cuts in nuclear weapons. Where Carter focused foreign assistance for the Third World on basic human needs, Reagan reallocated funds from development to security assistance and restricted American support for the international financial institutions (IFIs) that help Third World economies. Reagan insisted that Arabs and Israelis set aside their differences to join in a "strategic consensus" against the Soviet threat to the Middle East and sent Jean Kirkpatrick to the UN to confront Third World pretensions; Carter worked hard to defuse Third World conflicts by ratifying the Panama Canal treaty and negotiating a treaty of peace between Israel and Egypt, and he sent an African-American former mayor of Atlanta, Andrew Young, to the UN to demonstrate American understanding for Third World aspirations.

Since only four years elapsed between these two presidents' terms in office, it would seem unlikely that such contrasting sets of assumptions could both have been accurate. In fact, neither man's worldview comported very well with international reality. The result was that each administration wasted valuable months, even years, pursuing ill-conceived policies. After eighteen months Ronald Reagan abandoned "strategic consensus" in the Middle East in favor of a serious proposal on Palestinian autonomy, but his administration never really recovered momentum toward an Arab-Israeli peace; Reagan's disdain for arms control had to be replaced by at first the appearance, then the reality of serious negotiations after it helped create a trans-Atlantic peace movement that complicated U.S. efforts at military containment; and the 1982 Mexican debt crisis forced an about face in his administration's attitude toward the IFIs by demonstrating the damage that Third World debt could do to the American banking system. Carter, for his part, found his arms control efforts frustrated by Soviet adventurism. He wound up extending military protection to the Persian Gulf via the Carter Doctrine, embarking on a broad expansion of American alliances backed by military aid, and developing major new strategic weapons systems as well as the Rapid Deployment Joint Task Force (later to become Central Command) for Third World contingencies. Though they started on the political extremes, the Carter and Reagan administrations thus moved dramatically toward the center, driven there as experience forced their assumptions into closer alignment with the real world.

Just as erroneous assumptions can generate faulty strategies and lead to wrenching change, accurate assumptions about how the world works have great power to sustain a coherent strategy. Far more experienced in foreign affairs than its two successors, the Nixon administration provides a case in point. It saw the international system as essentially bipolar in nature and the Soviets as the major threat to American security and world peace. But it also anticipated the gradual replacement of bipolarity with a pentagonal world order, and perceived the USSR not as a ferocious "evil empire" but as a dangerous superpower that could be controlled through a complex set of inducements and pressures. Such perceptions were far more centrist and pragmatic than either Reagan's or Carter's, and they proved durable enough to sustain a coherent foreign affairs strategy for eight tumultuous years – even in the face of a change in presidents.

A similar, more recent contrast between accurate and flawed assumptions can be seen in the administrations of the Bush father and son. Coming to the oval office after a lifetime of experience in foreign affairs, George H. W. Bush fielded a pragmatic statecraft that skillfully recognized and responded to the major changes in world politics accompanying the demise of the Soviet Union. Indeed, the elder Bush's policy was so pragmatic that he was often accused of failing to do more than preside over American foreign affairs, of lacking a vision of where to lead the country after the Cold War's end.[4] George W. Bush, on the other hand, took the presidency with no prior foreign policy experience, and he surrounded himself with neoconservative advisors who saw enemies of the United States everywhere and demanded that the U.S. confront them with military power.[5] Although the younger Bush proved adept at rallying the country against Al Qaeda and its Taliban sponsors in Afghanistan, the administration's thinking served it less well as it decided how to handle Iraq. Instead of using intelligence – however flawed – to validate its assumptions, the administration manipulated it to support claims about Saddam Hussein's pursuit of nuclear weapons and his ties to Al Qaeda that it felt were needed to justify war.[6] Worse, the administration was so certain that Iraqis would welcome Americans as liberators and spontaneously create democracy that it deliberately ignored all contrary predictions, no matter how thoroughly grounded.[7] These mistaken assumptions led to the use of insufficient troops to control the postwar situation, facilitating the growth of an

[4] See Terry L. Deibel, "Bush's Foreign Policy: Mastery and Inaction," *Foreign Policy* 84 (Fall 1991): 3–23.
[5] James Mann, *The Rise of the Vulcans* (New York: Viking, 2004).
[6] For failures in pre-war intelligence, see Dana Priest and Walter Pincus, "U.S. 'Almost All Wrong' on Weapons," *Washington Post* (October 7, 2004): A1, A34; Dafna Linzer, "Panel: Work of U.N. Arms Inspectors Was Ignored by U.S. Before Iraq War," *Washington Post* (April 3, 2005): A6; and Kenneth M. Pollock, "Spies, Lies, and Weapons: What Went Wrong," *Atlantic Monthly* (January/February 2004): 78–82, 84–86, 88, 90, 92. Colin Powell told Barbara Walters that he had seen no credible evidence while in office that Saddam had ties to Al Qaeda. *20/20* television show, broadcast September 9, 2005.
[7] See James Fallows, "Blind into Baghdad," *Atlantic Monthly* (January/February 2004): 52–54, 56–58, 60, 62–66, 68–70, 72–74; also David Rieff, "Blueprint for a Mess," *New York Times Magazine* (November 2, 2003).

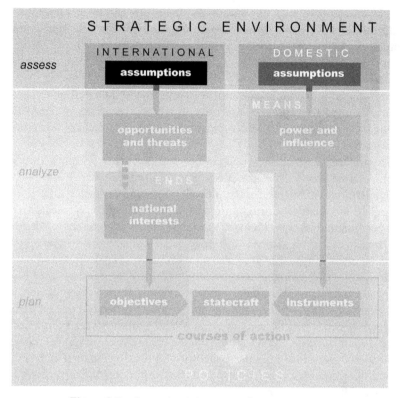

Figure 2.2: Assessing international assumptions.

insurgency that cost thousands of American casualties and compromised the entire effort.[8]

As these examples demonstrate, few factors are as important to the formulation of foreign affairs strategy as the strategist's assumptions about the international environment. Given its focus on that environment, this chapter looks at the factors that determine *foreign* strategists' actions (and thereby constitute the primary resistance one's own strategy meets). It is developed along two simultaneous axes. First, the chapter moves inward along classical levels of analysis, beginning with pressures on foreign state or nonstate actors from the international environment, moving to those produced by their domestic circumstances, and concluding at the level of the foreign strategist's own ideas. Second, it simultaneously moves progressively deeper into that strategist's mind, beginning with perceptions that are likely to be on the surface of his analysis, then moving to

---

[8] "We didn't have enough troops on the ground," said Colin Powell. "We didn't impose our will. And as a result, an insurgency got started, and...it got out of control." Quoted in Monifa Thomas, "Powell: U.S. made 'serious mistakes' in Iraq," *Chicago Sun Times* (April 9, 2006).

assumptions that are conscious in most cases if often inexplicit, and ending with deep and possibly unconscious habits of mind. Given this structure, it will hardly strike the reader as accidental that the chapter also moves steadily from power toward principle as the motive force in world politics.

The discussion that follows relates to the "international environment" section on the first level of the graphic model for foreign affairs strategy, the place to take note of features of the strategic context that are not directly applicable to other conceptual categories but that condition or influence the whole strategic situation (see Figure 2.2). Strategists should be sure to include here assumptions about actors other than those that are the targets of their strategies, about the likely effects of strategies other than the one they are working on, about how the international system is structured and operates, and about future trends in all these key features of the environment. At the same time, this section should be kept spare and directly relevant to the strategic problem being analyzed. In particular, one should get a sense of constraints and possibilities for American action here; factors that create opportunities or that augment American power and influence should be listed under those categories on the model's second level, where they will more directly assist analysis.

Actors, System, and Structure

By far the most numerous of the assumptions a strategist must make about the global context, and those likely to be at the surface of strategic analysis, have to do with the motives and power of other global actors. The strategist will naturally want to know which are friendly and which hostile to the United States, how other governments and nonstate actors stand on various issues of importance to America, and what motivates their positions on those issues. Decision makers also must form opinions about the power of other actors, what policy tools they command (from UN votes to foreign aid to suicide bombers), and how they might deploy those to affect the United States. As one world politics textbook put it:

> Before we can understand the ways in which nations treat each other, there are two things that we must know about each nation: what does it want to do, and what is it capable of doing? In other words, we must know its goals, and we must assess its power.[9]

As they puzzle out these issues of foreign intention and capability, ends and means, American strategists will have at their disposal the enormous analytical resources of the intelligence community and the reporting of U.S. embassies abroad, organized to track developments in individual countries and regions around the world as well as various functional issues of

---

[9] A. F. K. Organski, *World Politics*, 2nd ed. (New York: Alfred A. Knopf, 1968), p. 61.

importance.[10] Such data should be eagerly sought, for even the most sophisticated understanding of strategic logic is no substitute for factual data on the world in which strategies operate, or for the judgments of regional and country specialists who have spent decades building their knowledge and understanding. However, such specific information will assume its shape and significance based on the deeper assumptions strategists hold about how the international system is structured and operates. The standards upon which they judge the importance of country- or issue-specific information, and the uses they make of it, will depend largely on how they believe the world works and how, as a consequence, the United States can most effectively act to influence its workings and shape its future.

Indeed, the very idea that some kind of a system exists in international politics and economics opens worlds of strategic possibilities.[11] For "system" means "interconnection;" a system is defined, after all, because the interactions among its constituent elements are more significant to the observer than those between them and outside entities. Moreover, one can conceptualize a system only if the interactions are regularized and therefore somewhat predictable. If strategists can learn what the key interconnections and linkages are and how a change in one part of the system will affect other parts, they may be able to manipulate some elements of the system through others.

There is always room for debate, of course, as to how tight the linkages in any system are. During the Cold War this question often divided analysts into so-called "globalist" and "regionalist" ways of thinking. Globalists like Reagan argued that the international system was tightly connected by the actions of the Soviet Union, that problems in southern Africa, the Middle East, Southeast Asia, or Latin America had a common cause in Soviet machinations. The way to deal with these was obviously to "go to

---

[10] This is not to say that strategists can have whatever information they deem necessary about the external context. In fact, a great deal of what they most urgently need to know will be simply unavailable, often in spite of spending millions of dollars to find out – as, for example, American leaders' inability to determine the true level of the Soviet military budget during the Cold War years or the correct status of Iraq's WMD programs before the 2003 invasion.

[11] In his widely-used text on international politics, K. J. Holsti defines an international system "as any collection of independent political entities – tribes, city-states, nations, or empires – that interact with considerable frequency and according to regularized processes." He lists five important characteristics that define international systems: (1) boundaries, or where the system begins and ends; (2) the characteristics of individual units making up the system, in this case mainly nation-states but also sub- or nonstate actors; (3) the structure and stratification of the system, based on power differentials; (4) characteristic patterns or interactions of the system, from diplomacy to war; and (5) rules or customs that regulate system behavior. See *International Politics: A Framework for Analysis*, 6th ed. (Englewood Cliffs, N.J.: Prentice Hall, 1992), p. 15–17.

the source" in Moscow.[12] Regionalists like Carter countered that problems in each area of the world had distinct roots in local political, social, and economic conditions; the Kremlin might fish in troubled waters, but the way to counter Moscow was to deny it opportunities by ameliorating those local conditions.[13] It was ironic that the rapid and simultaneous solution of hitherto intractable conflicts in Central America, Southern Africa, and Central Asia as the Cold War ended seemed to validate the globalists' position, even as the demise of the Soviet Union simultaneously eliminated the linkage on which Cold War globalists depended.[14]

Today, many believe that economic and technological changes may be tightening other connections that strategists must increasingly take into account. Certainly the rapid increase in the availability and decrease in the cost of communications and transportation links people and nations as never before. One result may be an increase in so-called "demonstration effects," as the 24-hour news cycle beams events around the world in vivid real time. The spate of popularly-driven regime changes in states of the former Soviet Union and Central Asia in the early twenty-first century may be an example, although it also seems obvious that democratic governments had a hand in encouraging the linkages between resistance groups and in increasing their capabilities. Another may be the similarity of successive terrorist attacks in various parts of the world, although organizations like Al Qaeda are again directly helping make such events happen.

Linkages, of course, are between entities, so a first set of assumptions about any international system has to do with the nature of the units or actors included in it. Traditionally, only nation-states have been considered as possessing sufficient power to concern the strategist, power being defined as centralized control over the kind of wealth needed to equip and field military forces.[15] For several decades now, however, there has been a debate over the future viability of the nation-state and its sovereignty, loosely defined as a government's autonomous control over its territory and citizens.[16] On the one hand, the post–Cold War era has seen dramatic

---

[12] The phrase is Alexander Haig's, *Caveat* (New York: Macmillan, 1984), pp. 117–137.

[13] For a sketch of the differences between regionalists and globalists, as well as a defense of the regionalist position, see Peter Jay, "Regionalism as Geopolitics," *Foreign Affairs: America and the World 1979* 58 (No. 3, 1980): 485–514.

[14] Nicaragua/El Salvador, Afghanistan, and southern Africa (Angola, Namibia, Mozambique) are the most obvious examples, although it is noteworthy that both in Afghanistan and Angola the local conflicts underlying U.S.-Soviet rivalry took a decade and much additional blood to resolve.

[15] George F. Kennan, for example, argued in the late 1940s that only five major countries or regions possessed significant industrial power: the U.S., USSR, Japan, UK, and Europe's Ruhr valley. See Chapter 5 for a complete discussion of power.

[16] Stephen D. Krasner, "Sovereignty," *Foreign Policy* 122 (January/February 2001): 20–30.

increases in the number of nation-states, and nationalism seems as strong a force as ever in world politics.[17] But there are also a variety of more or less failed states, where government is too corrupt or weak to provide basic services or security to its citizens, or even to prevent terrorists from gathering – a phenomenon that has made nation-building a central preoccupation of American statecraft.[18] And even within the most capable of states there is concern that sovereignty is at risk, as economies become more and more interdependent, illegal migration swells, international law applies increasingly to individuals, transnational threats bypass perimeter security, and actors above and below the state grow in power.[19]

Indeed, an increasing number of entities other than nation-states are now active internationally, and some can materially affect the fortunes of states. A few are powerful individuals, like multibillionaire Bill Gates, financier George Soros, or terrorist Ayman al-Zawahiri. Others are transnational private organizations, whether religious (such as the Catholic Church), business (multinational corporations like IBM), charitable (nongovernmental organizations, or NGOs, such as Oxfam), professional (Rotary International), or criminal (various Latin American narcotics cartels). Above the state are public international organizations like UN agencies and supranational bodies such as the European Union, to which member states have granted some sovereign powers. After 9/11, few would deny that these so-called "nonstate actors" also must be included in any meaningful structural portrait of the modern international system.

Whatever units are included, the next task is to categorize them in some meaningful way. Strategists use terms like "the great powers" or "the Third World" to try to impose some mental order on the chaos of nearly 200 unique countries. Or they may rely for a sense of order on characteristics such as geographical location, ideological stance, religious or cultural

---

[17] Pascal Boniface, "The Proliferation of States," *The Washington Quarterly* 21 (Summer 1998): 111–127; Samuel P. Huntington, "Robust Nationalism," *National Interest* 58 (Winter 1999/2000): 31–40.

[18] See particularly the work of Robert I. Rotberg, including "The New Nature of Nation-State Failure," *The Washington Quarterly* 25 (Summer 2002): 85–96; "Failed States in a World of Terror," *Foreign Affairs* 81 (July/August 2002): 127–140; and *State Failure and Weakness in a Time of Terror* (Cambridge, MA: World Peace Foundation, 2003).

[19] On the negative effects of globalization on state power, see Susan Strange, "The Defective State," *Daedalus* 124 (#2, 1995): 55–74 and "The Erosion of the State," *Current History* (November 1997): 365–369, along with Martin Van Creveld, "The Fate of the State," *Parameters* 26 (Spring 1996): 4–18 and James Rosenau, "Security in a Turbulent World," *Current History* 94 (#592, 1995): 193–200. For a contrary view championing the state see Kenneth N. Waltz, "Globalization and American Power," *National Interest* 59 (Spring 2000): 46–56 and Martin Wolf, "Will the Nation-State Survive Globalization?" *Foreign Affairs* 80 (January/February 2001): 178–190. On international law see Jeremy Rabkin, "International Law *vs.* the American Constitution," *National Interest* 55 (Spring 1999): 30–41.

orientation, economic development, or how states are governed internally. Ray S. Cline borrowed the image of tectonic plates from modern geology to group states into geographically cohesive "polytechtonic zones."[20] Harvard's Samuel Huntington uses civilizations to divide the world into Western, Confucian, Japanese, Islamic, Hindu, Slavic-Orthodox, Latin American and African groups, arguing that "[i]t is far more meaningful now to group countries not in terms of their political or economic systems or in terms of their level of economic development but rather in terms of their culture and civilization."[21] Such mental pictures provide a shorthand way of dealing with what would otherwise be an almost overwhelming complexity, helping the strategist make preliminary decisions about how various classes of states are likely to act, what effects their actions will have on the United States, and how to influence them.

Grouping can also be based on actors' relative power, leading to assumptions about the international system's structure.[22] As noted earlier, the tightness of the bipolar hierarchy was in some dispute during the long years of the Cold War, but the Soviet Union's demise dramatically widened the debate over the shape of the new international system.[23] Most observers agreed that power would be diffused more broadly in the post–Cold War world, with oil producers and newly industrialized countries garnering increased economic clout, and the spread of high-technology weaponry giving relatively poor states and nonstate adversaries the capacity to cause serious international trouble. Some argued that the result would be a violent new anarchy, particularly in the southern hemisphere, as failing Third World governments lost control to poverty, corruption, disease, population growth, rampant urbanization, and various armed warlords – a tapestry of medieval chaos.[24] Simultaneously, however, they expected a peaceful concert of powers among the developed, northern states, resulting in a world divided between zones of peace and zones of turmoil.[25] But that dark vision was countered by others who believed that the spread of western technology, culture, and economic interdependence would eventually create a

---

[20] *U.S. Power in a World of Conflict*, Significant Issues Series, Vol. II, No. 7 (Washington, DC: Center for Strategic and International Studies, 1980), p. 4.

[21] "The Clash of Civilizations?" *Foreign Affairs* 72 (Summer 1993): list on p. 25, quote from p. 23.

[22] First, of course, one has to decide what attributes of power are most important: military forces, economic productivity, or various softer sources of influence like prestige or ideology. See the later material in this chapter on transnationalism, as well as Chapter 5.

[23] The indispensable guide to this debate is Robert E. Harkavy, "Images of the Coming International System," *Orbis* (Fall 1997): 569–590.

[24] Robert D. Kaplan, "The Coming Anarchy," *Atlantic Monthly* (February 1994): 44–76.

[25] For concert of powers, see Richard Rosecrance, "A New Concert of Powers," *Foreign Affairs* 71 (Spring 1992): 64–82. For zones, see Max Singer and Aaron Wildavsky, *The Real World Order* (Chatham, NJ: Chatham House Publishers, 1993).

prosperous and stable Third World that could be integrated with the North into a kind of global village.[26]

Nor was there consensus among analysts about what kind of structure would obtain among the most powerful nations. One view was that the demise of bipolarity would lead to a multipolarity similar to the nineteenth century European balance of power, with four or five great powers balancing each other, perhaps leading to new hegemonic wars like those that plagued the first half of the twentieth century.[27] Those focused on economic power tended to see the development of a three-bloc system, centered around the dollar, the deutschmark (or euro), and the yen, led by the United States, Germany (or Europe), and Japan, as these three reserve currencies pulled nations around them into monetary alliances buttressed by regional trade pacts.[28] Other analysts even saw the return of bipolarity, with the United States opposed to either a revived Russia or, more likely, a rising China.[29]

As the first decade of the post–Cold War era came to an end, however, more and more analysts accepted columnist Charles Krauthammer's characterization of the international system as unipolar, with the United States as the unchallenged (and unchallengeable) superpower or even hyperpower.[30] With the flexing of American muscle in the war against terrorism, this image has now become the dominant one, cemented into the Bush administration's national security strategy.[31] However, as the images of

---

[26] Richard Barnet and John Cavanagh, *Global Dreams* (New York: Simon and Schuster, 1994). Also Thomas L. Friedman, *The Lexus and the Olive Tree* (New York: Farrar, Straus, Giroux, 1999).

[27] For this realist view see John Mearsheimer, "Back to the Future: Instability in Europe After the Cold War," *International Security* 15 (Summer 1990): 5–56; Christopher Layne, "The Unipolar Illusion: Why New Great Powers Will Rise," *International Security*, 17 (Spring 1993): 5–51; Christopher Layne and Benjamin Schwarz, "A New Grand Strategy," *Atlantic Monthly* (January 2002); "The Next Balance of Power," *Economist* (January 3, 1998): 17–19.

[28] For examples of this tripolar thinking, see Jeffrey Garten, *A Cold Peace* (New York: Times Books, 1992); Edward Luttwak, *The Endangered American Dream* (New York: Simon and Schuster, 1993); Lester Thurow, *Head to Head: The Coming Economic Battle Among Japan, Europe, and America* (New York: Murrow, 1992).

[29] Hans Binnendijk, "Back to Bipolarity," *Washington Quarterly* 22 (Autumn 1999): 7–14.

[30] Charles Krauthammer, "The Unipolar Moment," *Foreign Affairs: America and the World 1990/91* 70 (No. 1, 1991): 23–48, as well as "The Unipolar Moment Revisited," *National Interest* 70 (Winter 2002/03): 5–17. For data and arguments supporting U.S. unipolarity, see William C. Wohlforth, "The Stability of a Unipolar World," *International Security* 24 (Summer 1999): 5–41, and Stephen G. Brooks and William C. Wohlforth, "American Primacy in Perspective," *Foreign Affairs* 81 (July/August 2002): 20–33. "Hyperpower" is the appellation of Herbert Vedrine, French foreign minister.

[31] "The United States possesses unprecedented, and unequaled, strength and influence in the world." George W. Bush, *The National Security Strategy of the United States* (Washington, DC: The White House, September 2002): 1.

the international system sketched above demonstrate, the reality is probably more complex. One prominent political scientist separated the military, economic, and transnational dimensions of power into a three-tiered image of the international system's structure, agreeing that it is unipolar in military power but arguing that economic power is multipolar and that power in transnational relations – those in which nonstate actors play a prominent role – is simply diffuse.[32] Whether one accepts the reigning view of U.S. dominance or not, it is obvious that the kind of shape one attributes to the international hierarchy of power is another vital strategic assumption.

How the World Works

Even more critical than static images of the system's structure, though, are assumptions about its dynamic operation. For centuries, analysts have searched for generalizations or rules governing world politics that could help the statesman make sense out of the daunting variety of state behavior. It is possible, of course, that no such rules worth knowing exist, that there is no coherent system beyond the observer's imaginings. But it is probably not by mere coincidence that statesmen from completely different historical and cultural backgrounds have often shared remarkably similar ideas about how the world works.[33]

Most begin from the proposition that the international system is what Hedley Bull called an anarchical society, in that (unlike the situation within most nation-states) there is no legitimate authority at the top holding a monopoly of force.[34] This condition requires that states try to accumulate power in their own self-defense, and that quest is often cited as the first rule of state conduct.[35] In fact, to ensure its own security each state must attempt to be stronger than all the others, or at least than all likely adversaries or combinations thereof, an effort at which (since we are speaking of relative power) only a few at most can be successful. Indeed, the

---

[32] Joseph S. Nye, Jr., has variously called this a layer cake or three-dimensional chessboard. See his "What New World Order?" *Foreign Affairs* 71 (Spring 1992): 83–96, and *The Paradox of American Power* (New York: Oxford University Press, 2002), p. 39.

[33] Henry Kissinger found this to be true when he met Chou En-Lai to arrange the U.S. rapprochement with China after more than two decades of mutual hostility. See *White House Years*, pp. 780–781.

[34] Hedley Bull, *The Anarchical Society* (New York: Columbia University Press, 1977).

[35] Indeed, the most widely used textbook on international politics in the United States since World War II was based on the simple proposition "that statesmen think and act in terms of interest defined as power." Hans J. Morgenthau, *Politics Among Nations*, 5th ed., revised (New York: Alfred A. Knopf, 1978), p. 5. Morgenthau's remarkable identification of means with ends, of interests with power, is however a fundamental strategic error; as will be seen in Chapter 5, power in all its forms is a means of serving interests; equating the two destroys the very heart of strategic logic.

paradoxical logic of strategy can be expressed in this realm by the tru-
ism that absolute security for any state means absolute insecurity for all
the others. Given the interactive nature of strategy, a state's becoming too
powerful – as some argue the United States has in the early twenty-first
century – can be expected to concentrate the minds and efforts of other
strategists, making the task of maintaining its power advantage doubly
difficult.[36] And yet states have no choice but to seek power; the lack of a
sovereign authority at the top of the system condemns them to a continual
struggle for advantage.

Statesmen can accumulate power in two basic ways. First, they can do
so internally, by the "natural" method of economic growth and by converting their expanding wealth into whatever tools of statecraft they consider
most useful, from trained diplomats to military forces.[37] Such growth may
or may not include territorial expansion to secure raw materials, skilled
workers, and other economic assets. Second, especially if they lack the time
or resources needed for internal economic or external territorial expansion, statesmen can increase their power through the "artificial" means of
alliances with other states to aggregate capabilities for whatever purposes
the resulting coalition can agree on.[38]

This process of alliance and alignment has seemed to many observers to
follow its own set of rules, and assumptions about these are often expressed
in terms of the spatial relationships of states across the globe. More than
2,200 years ago the Indian philosopher Chanakya Kautilya noticed that
territorial neighbors are generally hostile, while the country on the other
side of a neighbor is a state's natural ally.[39] As a territorial application of the
old adage, "the enemy of my enemy is my friend," these simple rules create
a kind of "sandwich system" in international politics.[40] British political
scientist Martin Wight suggested as an alternate metaphor that the pattern
of power resembled a "chequer-board of alternating colours," except that
all regularity is distorted by various peculiarities of geographic position:
states obviously are not square, while topographical features like oceans,
deserts, and mountain ranges provide spatial separation and protection.[41]
Still, during the Cold War one analyst found that a simple computer model

---

[36] See Edward N. Luttwak, *Strategy: The Logic of War and Peace*, Chapter 2. This
problem was defined as the "security dilemma" long ago by John Herz.

[37] See Chapter 2.

[38] For the "natural-artificial" distinction, see Inis L. Claude, Jr., *Power and International Relations* (New York: Random House, 1962), p. 89. On alliances as tools of
statecraft, see Chapter 6.

[39] R. Shamasastry, trans., 3rd ed. *Arthashastra* (Mysore: Wesleyan Mission Press,
1929). Kautilya's wisdom was echoed by Alexander Hamilton in Federalist Paper
No. 6: "It has...become a sort of axiom in politics that vicinity, or nearness of
situation, constitutes nations natural enemies," p. 33.

[40] The term is Sir Lewis B. Namier's, in *Conflicts* (London: Macmillan, 1942), p. 14.

[41] Martin Wight, "The Pattern of Power," in Wight (Hedley Bull and Carsten
Holbraad, eds.), *Power Politics* (New York: Holmes and Meier, 1978), p. 159.

based on Kautilyan principles required only basic data on national power and geography to reproduce an uncannily accurate portrait of the pattern of alliances in South Asia.[42]

Geopolitics and the Balance of Power

However, the classical geopoliticians who wrote in Germany, England, and the United States in the late nineteenth and early twentieth century feared that technology might permit powerful states to override these rules of alignment, progressively forcing weaker countries into their orbits until they became strong enough to dominate the globe. As the most famous geopolitical formulation put it:

Who rules East Europe commands the Heartland;

Who rules the Heartland commands the World Island;

Who rules the World Island commands the World.

Sir Halford MacKinder's 1919 triad was really a statement about the impact of technology on the projection of power across geography. In straightforward terms, MacKinder was predicting that the advent of railroads would enable one political center to control so much of Eurasia that it might be capable of building, and deploying to the maritime littoral, sufficient naval power to challenge British and American control of the seas. The American naval historian, Alfred Thayer Mahan, doubted MacKinder's premise and countered that sea powers could always maintain their dominance, while his compatriot Nicholas Spykman focused on the areas contiguous to the Eurasian heartland – which he called the rimland – as the real key to world power.[43] "Who controls the Rimland rules Eurasia," he wrote; "Who rules Eurasia controls the destinies of the world."[44]

Whatever the precise formulation, these sorts of assumptions about world politics did seem validated during the Cold War. Whether in Korea (1950–53), Quemoy/Matsu (1954 and 1958), Vietnam (1965–73) or Afghanistan (1980–89), the most prominent struggles between the superpowers were precisely in the rimland, the area between the Soviet heartland power and American sea power. In fact, it is hardly an exaggeration to say that the struggle between the United States and the Soviet Union for control of the rimland was until 1990 the struggle of modern world politics. Yet during the first half of the twentieth century, the challenge posed by

---

[42] For this computer run and for alerting me to the relevance of Kautilya to geopolitical thinking I am indebted to former U.S. Foreign Service Officer John Tkacik, "Soviet Geopolitical Strategy and the Kautilyan Model," unpublished NWC paper, April 1989.

[43] "Geopolitical Perspectives," Chapter 2 in Saul B. Cohen, *Geography and Politics in a World Divided*, 2nd ed. (New York: Oxford University Press, 1973), pp. 40–51.

[44] Nicholas Spykman, *The Geography of the Peace* (New York: Harcourt, Brace & Co., 1944), p. 43.

Germany in two world wars found the nation dominating the heartland (Russia and then the USSR) *allied to* the Western sea powers rather than fighting against them. In this earlier period Germany may be seen geopolitically either as a power aiming at control of the heartland (MacKinder's view) or as a rising rimland power along with Japan (Spykman's interpretation).[45] Such ambiguity about key categorizations points up the difficulty involved in using geopolitical assumptions for strategic analysis, but it hardly invalidates the logic they represent. The lesson that political predominance is a matter not just of raw power but also "of the structure of the field within which that power is exercised" remains valuable.[46]

Fundamentally, though, geopolitical thinking is simply a territorially based expression of an even deeper set of assumptions about how the world works that can be grouped under the phrase "the balance of power." This term is often used in a purely descriptive way to portray the existing distribution or configuration of power in the world, whether balanced or unbalanced (though it may also imply an evenness or equality of power across the international system.)[47] But for many strategists balance of power is a much richer concept that connotes a whole series of assumptions about the operation of the international system, a model of how the world works which argues that an even distribution of power is not only a good thing but that the international system operates more or less automatically to produce it. Both of these assumptions remain controversial, however, since most analysts believe that they are closely related to the causes of major or "hegemonic" wars – wars fought over who will dominate the international system.

The idea that an approximate equilibrium of power is desirable seems obvious at first glance, given the interest of every state in seeing that no other state or coalition of states becomes powerful enough either to endanger its interests or in the worse case (as the geopoliticians warned) to control the world. Many analysts argue that as long as states can maneuver to maintain such an even balance, aligning and realigning as changes in their relative power occur, the world can also remain peaceful; only when such re-equilibration fails will states have to resort to war to prevent any state or

---

[45] For commonly overlooked differences between MacKinder and Spykman, see Michael P. Gerace, "Between Mackinder and Spykman: Geopolitics, Containment, and After," *Comparative Strategy* 10 (No. 4, 1991): 347–364.

[46] G. R. Sloan, *Geopolitics in United States Strategic Policy, 1890–1987* (New York: St. Martin's Press, 1988), p. ix.

[47] The term balance of power has been shown to have a wide variety of meanings that can make this analytical tool as confusing as it is helpful. Martin Wight lists nine; Inis Claude lists three, each with subvariants. The argument here draws heavily on their analysis. Wight, "The Balance of Power," in Herbert Butterfield and Martin Wight, *Diplomatic Investigations* (Cambridge, MA: Harvard University Press, 1966), p. 151; Inis L. Claude, Jr., "The Balance of Power: An Ambiguous Concept," Chapter 2 in *Power and International Relations* (New York: Random House, 1962).

coalition of states from becoming too powerful. As Richard Nixon once put it, "The only time in the history of the world that we have had any extended period of peace is when there has been balance of power. It is when one nation becomes infinitely more powerful in relation to its potential competitor that the danger of war arises. . . ."[48] But other observers assert the opposite assumption: that a clear imbalance or hierarchy of power is what makes for peace, and that it is precisely when a large number of states are of relatively equal strength that miscalculations of power and challenges leading to war are most likely to occur.[49] Robert Gilpin injects time into the equation, arguing that the risk of serious conflict increases as differential rates of economic growth distort the power relationships that were codified in law and institutional arrangements after the last hegemonic war. Gradually the hierarchy of power gets out of alignment with this "hierarchy of prestige," and newly powerful states feel they must fight to secure the status to which they believe they are now entitled.[50] What is needed to preserve the peace, then, is the system's ability to accommodate inevitable shifts in power relationships.

The issue of whether the international system actually tends toward an even distribution of power is at least as much in doubt as whether such a balance is desirable. Balance of power assumptions hold that states tend naturally to balance against concentrations of power, so powerful coalitions tend to beget powerful anti-coalitions. Just as the striving of each individual for maximum economic wealth produces the greatest good for the greatest number in a free market system through the invisible hand of Adam Smith, so in this view the striving of each state for maximum power in conditions of anarchy automatically produces a relatively even distribution of power. But many analysts also admit that certain conditions are needed for such a system to operate – conditions that may not always be present. Among these are a fairly large number of more or less equally powerful states; a willingness of states to align and realign with each other regardless of ideology or other constraints; and the ability of statesmen accurately to estimate their own and other states' power and to act skillfully on their assessments. It is also frequently asserted that the system

[48] Quoted in John Lewis Gaddis, *Strategies of Containment*, Revised and Expanded ed. (New York: Oxford University Press, 2005), p. 278.

[49] See "power transition" theory, popularized by A.F.K. Organski and Jacek Kugler, *The War Ledger* (Chicago, IL: University of Chicago Press, 1980). Geoffrey Blainey also argues that the idea that an even balance of power promotes peace is wrong; what promotes peace is clear agreement among statesmen of many nations about their relative power, and that is most likely when there is a clear hierarchy. See *The Causes of War* (New York: Free Press/MacMillan, 1973), pp. 109–114. For a more recent argument that the unipolar international system currently headed by the United States is inherently peaceful, see Wohlforth, "The Stability of a Unipolar World," pp. 23–28.

[50] Robert Gilpin, *War and Change in World Politics* (London: Cambridge University Press, 1981), pp. 9–49.

needs a major power willing to play the role of balancer, to realign itself as needed to offset power shifts produced by other states as they maneuver for advantage.[51]

Other observers, in fact, deny that there is any self-equilibrating tendency at all in the international system, that states are more likely to align themselves *with* a major power than attempt to balance against it. Today some analysts believe that such a phenomenon could appear in Asia as China achieves dominant power, giving states on its periphery no choice but to accommodate its preferences. Obviously, deciding whether states generally balance or bandwagon has a lot to do with whether the international system is assumed to be in stable or unstable equilibrium, that is, whether the system itself operates to check the ambitions of the powerful, or whether a strengthening state or coalition might rapidly become unstoppable.[52] Such assumptions determine how much room the statesman has for maneuver, whether his vigilance needs to be unending or whether he can tolerate some adverse developments with equanimity.

Stephen Walt argues that states will balance or at least attempt to maintain neutrality as long as they have the option of doing so. More important, he suggests that states balance not so much against power as against threat, that is, against capability *combined with* hostile intent.[53] During the Cold War, for example, the Soviet Union threatened all of the many states on its borders, whereas the United States had only two immediate neighbors and showed relatively benign intent toward them. Most of the states in the world, then, and particularly those in the geopolitical rimland, were so positioned as to fear the USSR and sought American help to balance against it. Thus, Walt concluded, the Cold War balance of power was not only strongly in America's favor but also remarkably stable.[54]

Today's power realities make the United States the obvious country against which states will balance, and some analysts argue that the run up to the 2003 Iraq war demonstrated a kind of soft balancing on the part of France, Russia, and Germany.[55] If states do balance against power, the United States may inevitably have troubled relationships with other great powers and might be expected to find common interests with

---

[51] For a recent restatement of the realist view of power sketched above, see John Mearsheimer, *The Tragedy of Great Power Politics* (New York, NY: W.W. Norton, 2001).

[52] Stable equilibrium can be envisioned as a ping pong ball in the bottom of a large bowl; if disturbed, it will gradually return to its position of rest at the bottom of the bowl unless the disturbance is so great that the ball is forced over the side. Unstable equilibrium is akin to a ping pong ball on the top of an upside down bowl; here the results of any but the mildest disturbances would be catastrophic.

[53] See the discussion of threat in Chapter 4.

[54] Stephen M. Walt, "Alliance Formation and the Balance of World Power," *International Security* 9 (Spring 1985): 36.

[55] For example, see Josef Joffe, "Continental Divides," *The National Interest* 71 (Spring 2003): 157–160. Also William Pfaff, "The Question of Hegemony," *Foreign Affairs* 80 (January/February 2001): 221–232.

secondary regional powers in trying to limit their local dominance. And the world's pattern of alignments in the twenty-first century does indeed find the U.S. more or less loosely allied with Japan and India against China, with Pakistan against India, with Britain against Europe, with Ukraine against Russia, and with Saudi Arabia against Iran.[56] But if states tend to balance against threats rather than against power alone, the world's sole superpower may have an opportunity to minimize the balancing against it by making sure that its current primacy appears as benign as possible to other great powers. According to some analysts, the United States did so the last time its power was overwhelmingly predominant, in the years after its victory in World War II, by offering its partner nations opportunities to influence its policies, by enmeshing itself in a web of international institutions that limited arbitrary use of its power, and by being a transparent, predictable, and cooperative leader.[57] It can, if it wishes, do so again.[58]

At the same time, a variety of changes may be weakening the basic anarchy of the international system and with it the security dilemma states face. The growth of international organizations and law may be creating a kind of weak global governance on which states can rely for at least some of the help they formerly had to provide themselves. Economic ties between nations are broader and deeper than ever before, while wealth increasingly depends not on territorially based factors of production that can be acquired by conquest but on the education, skill, and motivation of people. Rapid, inexpensive transportation and communication is creating an international elite of highly-skilled individuals, and the spread of democracy is creating security communities whose members consider war with each other unthinkable. Indeed, much of what follows in this chapter describes trends that may now be changing the way the world has worked since the state system began 350 years ago.

As a result, the extent to which these assumptions about the impact of power on state behavior still apply in the world of the twenty-first century is one of the key puzzles that must be solved by modern strategists. But if one believes that states remain the primary units of the system and that international anarchy still essentially prevails, then there is every reason to suppose that statesmen must continue to worry about power relationships.[59] Regionally, at least, the logic of power will continue to apply

---

[56] Samuel P. Huntington, "The Lonely Superpower," *Foreign Affairs* 78 (March/April 1999): 47.

[57] G. John Ikenberry, "Getting Hegemony Right," *National Interest* 63 (Spring 2001): 7–14.

[58] William Pfaff, on the other hand, argues that "it is in the nature of a hegemonic system to generate opposition," "because its objective, however 'benevolent,' is seen by other nations as a threat." Pfaff, "The Question of Hegemony," pp. 230, 224.

[59] For a skillful argument to this effect, see Robert J. Lieber, "Existential Realism After the Cold War," *Washington Quarterly* 16 (Winter 1993): 155–168.

anywhere American interests demand involvement, from the Persian Gulf to Northeast Asia. Globally, the present-day lack of a nation-state strong enough to threaten the United States may reduce the need for immediate vigilance, but American foreign affairs strategies to shape the international system of the future should keep the avoidance of such a threat very clearly in mind.[60]

Newton, Darwin, and Chaos

Based as they are on power, all the perceptions of the international system discussed above are essentially mechanical in nature, envisioning a universe of objects on which force acts and reacts. They are "deterministic, linear, concerned with the predictable interaction of objects and forces, and oriented toward sequential change."[61] This may be due to a real correspondence between patterns of political and mechanical interaction, or it may merely reflect the fact that most of our notions of how the world works originated in an era when scientific thinking was dominated by Newtonian concepts and persist because they are easily understandable and offer a reassuring view of change. Whichever the case, it is worth noting that at least two non-Newtonian sets of assumptions might be made about international political processes, each with strikingly different implications for foreign affairs strategy.

The most obvious alternative to a mechanistic worldview is an organic one, which treats international politics as more akin to a living organism than a machine. Such a model would imply a greater role for change in the system over time, implying cycles of growth and decay both in the units of the system and in the system itself. Certainly nation-states, like cells in a plant or animal, can seem to share this quality, rising and falling in vitality, being born and dying while the broader system continues to function, but capable of altering the contours of the system itself in cases of dramatic change (for example, when superpowers form as during the mid-twentieth century or die as did the Soviet Union in 1991, or when nonstate actors assume a role on a par with some nation-states). And although the fundamentals of the broader system may not yet have changed sufficiently to

[60] In 1991 Huntington argued that preventing "the emergence of a political-military hegemonic power in Eurasia" is one of the three principal strategic interests in the post–Cold War world. "America's Changing Strategic Interests," *Survival* 33 (January/February 1991): 11–13. The next year, the Pentagon's draft defense guidance reportedly adopted such a goal: Patrick E. Tyler, "U.S. Strategy Plan Calls for Insuring No Rivals Develop," *New York Times* (March 8, 1992): 1, 14; and it was made explicit in the Bush administration's 2002 National Security Strategy, which pledged on page 30 that "[o]ur forces will be strong enough to dissuade potential adversaries from pursuing a military build-up in hopes of surpassing, or equaling, the power of the United States."

[61] Steven R. Mann, "Chaos Theory and Strategic Thought," *Parameters* (Autumn 1992): 55.

produce a different world order, there is little question that gradual developments like economic integration and the communications and transportation revolutions have altered its functioning.

Perhaps the best-known application of organic thinking to international politics grew out of social Darwinism around the turn of the twentieth century. Its most prominent disciple was Theodore Roosevelt, a naturalist as well as president who believed that the struggle for power among nation-states was very much like that in nature, exhibiting the same positive evolution through processes of natural selection and the survival of the fittest.[62] Strategists thinking in organic terms about international politics might, like Roosevelt, see conflict as the natural order of things, something instinctive quite apart from any clash of power or interests; indeed, they might well consider the challenge of conflict as good for a society, forcing it to sharpen its strength and hone its values.[63]

Certainly strategists holding organic assumptions would expect less of statecraft, setting aside the confidence of mechanics and engineers, who can build or fix any machine, in favor of the cautious hopefulness of doctors, who know that they can only intervene on the margins to promote healing. Indeed, they would probably be particularly attentive to causes of national and international pathology that lie outside the political economy, like religious fervor, social divisions, or cultural shifts.[64] Instead of conceptualizing terrorism as a politico-military phenomenon to be countered by war, for example, they might consider Islamist extremism as akin to a metastasizing cancer or virus, infecting new terrorists with its beliefs, spreading through complex interactions with people and the environment, and capable of control (if not eradication) by classic counter-epidemic measures like quarantine and containment, immunizations of vulnerable populations, and remediation of key environmental conditions.[65]

But in addition to seeing international problems as akin to disease, strategists with an organic mindset might also have more faith in the possibilities of evolution, seeing in the post–Cold War world hope for the kind of intense functional specialization and cooperative, interdependent relationships that are characteristic of higher level organs in living systems. In this

---

[62] See John Morton Blum, *The Republican Roosevelt* (Cambridge, MA: Harvard University Press, 1954), Chapters 3 and 8.

[63] George Kennan clearly took this view of the postwar contest with the Soviet Union, thanking Providence for providing the American people with a challenge that "has made their entire security as a nation dependent on their pulling themselves together and accepting the responsibilities of moral and political leadership that history plainly intended them to bear." "Sources of Soviet Conduct," *Foreign Affairs* 25 (July 1947): 582.

[64] On international pathology see Davis R. Bobrow, "Complex Insecurity: Implications of a Sobering Metaphor," *International Studies Quarterly* 40 (December 1996): 442–448.

[65] Paul Stares and Mona Yacoubian, "Terrorism as Virus," *Washington Post* (August 23, 2005): A15.

respect, certainly, organic models seem better suited to an international system much more fully evolved than the anarchy we now experience. It is possible, in fact, that the recent spread of democratic systems of government is a survival of the fittest phenomenon, representing this kind of evolution. Because they are better economic producers, popular motivators, and information processors, democracies may not only be a better form of government for their citizens but also more powerful and therefore likely to win in any struggle with authoritarian states – an encouraging prospect.[66]

A different non-Newtonian set of assumptions about the international environment with equally dramatic impacts on strategy comes from the chaos theory of modern physics. Chaos theory deals with what researchers call dynamical systems, those composed of very large numbers of component parts, whose interaction may seem totally random and disorderly but upon careful analysis shows recurrent if non-periodic patterns. To illustrate: a satellite revolving around the earth follows Newtonian laws of motion, predictable with great accuracy; smoke swirling upward or the movement of water in a stream is chaotic, regular but unpredictable except within wide parameters. Many of these systems display a behavior known as self-organizing criticality, meaning that the system reaches a critical state on its own, breaks down, and then continues to evolve through successive catastrophes from one metastable state to the next. Not only is the system a self-contained disaster successively happening, but the same internal mechanisms and initial conditions that most of the time have minor and benign effects will occasionally have major and cataclysmic impacts. A sand pile, to which grains are steadily added without noticeable effect until one of them triggers an avalanche, is the researchers' favorite model of self-organizing criticality, but evidence of the same kind of behavior is found across systems as diverse as earthquakes, forest fires, ecosystems, population dynamics, natural evolution, traffic on a highway, and economic markets.[67]

Could the international system, composed as it is of large numbers of interacting units and subsystems, be a chaotic system exhibiting self-organizing criticality? And if so, what difference should it make to

---

[66] Bruce Russett, *Controlling the Sword* (Cambridge, MA: Harvard University Press, 1990), p. 150. See also David C. Gompert, "Right Makes Might: Freedom and Power in the Information Age," Chapter 3 in Zalmay Khalilzad, John P. White and Andrew W. Marshall, eds. *Strategic Appraisal: The Changing Role of Information in Warfare* (Washington, DC: RAND Report MR-1016-AF, 1999), pp. 45–73.

[67] Fractals are a scientific shorthand for describing "the distribution of objects such as mountains, clouds, galaxies and vortices in turbulent fluids." Flicker noise – "an erratic signal that has features of all durations" – may result "when a dynamic system in the critical state produces chain reactions of all sizes and durations." The ubiquity in nature of fractal structures and flicker noise – "the spatial and temporal fingerprints, respectively, of self-organized criticality" – is one of the signs of how widespread these chaotic systems may be. Per Bak and Kan Chen, "Self-Organized Criticality," *Scientific American* (January 1991): 46–53.

strategic analysis? Certainly our experience with the catastrophe of war indicates that seemingly minor events can randomly produce dramatic reorderings of the system: think of the way the assassination of an archduke in Sarajevo triggered World War I.[68] Moreover, historians and political scientists are increasingly telling us that history is path-dependent, that small changes in events decades ago would have made revolutionary differences today, mirroring the chaotic system's exquisite sensitivity to initial conditions.[69] At the very least, the exponential growth of policy influences and the increasing complexity of contemporary world affairs cut against any mechanistic reduction of international reality to political, economic, and military variables and exclusively state actors. Rather like the Ptolemaic view of the universe in Galileo's time, Newtonian theory may no longer be the most parsimonious, effective explanation of observed reality. Chaos, in other words, may not be just a metaphor for international reality; as a system of interacting systems, the international environment may actually *be* chaotic in a scientific sense.[70]

If international politics is a chaotic system, the strategist should expect that weak states or nonstate actors, or events that are normally of no consequence, may randomly trigger effects out of all proportion to their importance, and that major changes may occur in the system even without external shocks. Prediction over the long term may be next to impossible. Whereas strategy has traditionally suggested "a capability . . . to identify the factors that will be relevant for the future, and eventually to shape that future,"

> the idea that an individual or a human community could determine long-term goals and develop a strategy to attain them may become increasingly unrealistic: too many factors are beyond our control, and there are too many unknowns. . . . Under these circumstances, strategy's goal becomes, not identifying the best outcome and finding the means to attain it, but keeping as many options open for as long as possible to provide maximum tactical flexibility.[71]

[68] The correlates of war project claims to find regularity in peaks of global violence about 20 years apart, while other researchers link periodicity in conflict with long cycles of world leadership or the Kondratieff wave cycle of economic growth and depression. See J. David Singer and Melvin Small, *The Wages of War, 1816–1965* (New York: John Wiley, 1972), pp. 215, 375; William R. Thompson, *On Global War* (Columbia, SC: University of South Carolina Press, 1988).

[69] "The flow of international politics is, in significant measure, contingent or path-dependent. History matters. Particular events can send world politics down quite different paths." Robert Jervis, "The Future of World Politics: Will It Resemble the Past?" *International Security* 16 (Winter 1991/92): 42. See also David Jablonsky, "Time's Arrow, Time's Cycle: Metaphors for a Period of Transition," *Parameters* (Winter 1997–98): 4–27.

[70] Mann, "Chaos Theory and Strategic Thought," p. 62. I owe a great debt to Ambassador Steve Mann for exposing me to chaos theory and sketching out many of its implications for foreign affairs strategy; this section draws heavily on his insights.

[71] Jean-Marie Guehenno, "The Impact of Globalisation on Strategy," *Survival* 40 (Winter 1998–99): 5–19.

At the very least, the control that strategy aims for will be more problematical if the international system is chaotic. "*Effective* treaties and compacts
can slow the progress of a system toward criticality, but we indulge in illusion if we believe absolute stability is attainable. In international affairs, all
stability is transient. . . . We should therefore be wary of incurring immediate policy costs to achieve a future stability: odds are that we will not get
what we bargained for."[72] On the other hand, relatively minor but properly targeted efforts – for example, like aid in the 1980s to the mujahhedin
in Afghanistan – may have the potential to push the system through a
reordering that could dramatically serve the nation's interests – like the
end of the Soviet Union.

> How then to use criticality to our advantage? The true aim of national
> strategy is shaping the broad context of security affairs, achieving the
> desired end state with the mildest upheaval. There are times when we
> will wish to delay formation of a critical state; there are times when we
> will wish to encourage it and will seek to shape the reordering.[73]

Interdependence, Globalization, and
the Information Revolution

One need not, of course, go so far as to see the international system as
akin to a living organism or a sand pile in order to recognize that dramatic
changes have been occurring in recent decades in international affairs that
must be taken into account by the foreign affairs strategist. After all, traditional worldviews not only have little to say about the role of nonstate
actors; they also tend to assume away any outside interference in the *internal* processes of nation-states and see relations between them as consisting
of the single issue of relative politico-military power. States in this view are
like billiard balls, colliding on the one-dimensional surface of the table,
protected by their hard outer shells, with the game unaffected by their
internal composition.[74]

Beginning in the 1970s, one group of analysts, first labeled "transnation-
alists" or the "interdependence" school, began arguing that such assumptions were inadequate.[75] States, they pointed out, could no longer be considered hermetically sealed units whose only contact with the outside world
was through governmental representatives. Instead, the explosive growth
of international relationships has meant that their hard outer shells are
increasingly penetrated by individuals and organizations both below and

---

[72] Mann, "Chaos Theory and Strategic Thought," p. 65.
[73] Mann, "Chaos Theory and Strategic Thought," p. 65.
[74] For an early comparison of the transnationalist and traditional views of the international system see Martin J. Rochester, "The 'National Interest' and Contemporary World Politics," *The Review of Politics* 40 (January 1978): 77–96.
[75] The classic statement is in Robert O. Keohane and Joseph S. Nye, *Power and
Interdependence: World Politics in Transition* (Boston: Little, Brown, 1977).

above the level of national governments, making it more and more difficult for those governments to control the destinies of their own people. In this kind of a world, domestic and international politics are less and less separate spheres, and decisions affecting state interests are often made outside of government channels in settings like international organizations or private transnational associations where traditional forms of politico-military power may be irrelevant. Therefore, instead of a single hierarchy of power and issues where force dominates, the system is imagined as having a variety of hierarchies and power structures, depending on the nature of the issues being considered.

The implications of this transnationalist worldview for strategic analysis are profound. Strategists who adopt it must worry not just about the military balance at the top of the hierarchy but about power balances and their interactions in many different spheres simultaneously. They must exert their efforts, not only with other governments, but also in private organizations and international bodies that set rules for decisions affecting the nation's interests. They must study how transnational actors can affect the actions of governments, and they must plan how they can manipulate the domestic politics of other states for their own purposes while simultaneously resisting outside manipulation of their own domestic scene to influence them. The strategic interconnections and possibilities for influence may be far richer in such a world, but at the same time the web of interdependencies makes for a policy environment far more difficult to conceptualize and probably for a reduced ability of any one strategist to get his or her way. Even overwhelming power may fail to confer overwhelming influence.[76]

Because so many of these changes in the international *political* system are a result of changes in the international *economic* system, it is increasingly important for the foreign affairs strategist also to consider the shape of the international economic environment. The geographic structure of the world economy runs parallel to that of the international political system. Industrialized countries represented by the Organization for Economic Cooperation and Development (OECD) can be distinguished from the developing countries, oil producers from oil consumers, managed economies from *laissez faire* ones, and so on. Upon closer inspection, however, one finds that the more important economic relationships have little to do with the territoriality of nation-states. Functionally, one can perceive at least three global economic systems: a *trading system* for the exchange of goods and services; a *financial system* that handles the money transactions accompanying trade and investment; and an increasingly integrated *production system*, with individual products manufactured in many different countries and services emailed from wherever they can be done most cheaply. All three are coordinated and regulated by a fourth system: a

---

[76] For the difference, see Chapter 5.

growing network of international economic *treaties and institutions* that
provide economic governance on a global scale.[77]

Dramatic changes have been taking place in all of these systems as part
of a process generally called globalization. Here is the classic definition, by
New York Times columnist Thomas L. Friedman:

> globalization . . . is the inexorable integration of markets, nation-states
> and technologies to a degree never witnessed before – in a way that is
> enabling individuals, corporations and nation-states to reach around the
> world farther, faster, deeper and cheaper than ever before, and in a way
> that is enabling the world to reach into individuals, corporations, and
> nation-states farther, faster, deeper and cheaper than ever before.[78]

More simply, globalization can be defined as "the ever-freer movement of
goods, services, ideas, and people around the world."[79] Or to be more precise,

> contemporary globalization is a complex, controversial, and synergis-
> tic process in which improvements in technology (especially in com-
> munications and transportation) combine with the deregulation of mar-
> kets and open borders to bring about vastly expanded flows of people,
> money, goods, services, and information. This process integrates people,
> businesses, nongovernmental organizations, and nations into larger net-
> works.[80]

Interdependence has developed into globalization over the last two
decades as the result of the convergence of three great historical forces.[81]
First, *technological* advances have dramatically lowered transportation and
communication costs, while simultaneously spreading ever more capable
and inexpensive computers around the world and enabling them and their
software to communicate with each other. Second, *political* advances such
the end of the Cold War and the East Asian economic miracle have dis-
credited static economic models in the Third World and enabled some
three billion people there and behind the former Iron and Bamboo Cur-
tains to enter what is becoming for the first time a truly global market

---

[77] "National economies are becoming more integrated in four fundamental ways –
through trade, finance, production, and a growing web of treaties and institutions." Jeffrey Sachs, "International Economics: Understanding the Mysteries of
Globalization," *Foreign Policy* 110 (Spring 1998): 98.

[78] Thomas L. Friedman, *The Lexus and the Olive Tree.* Newly Updated and Expanded
ed. (New York: Anchor/Random House, 2000), p. 9.

[79] John Micklethwait and Adrian Wooldridge, "From Sarajevo to September 11: The
Future of Globalization," *Policy Review* 117 (February & March 2003): 51.

[80] Thomas W. Zieler's, "Globalization," in Alexander DeConde, Richard Dean Burns
and Fredrik Logevall, eds., *Encyclopedia of American Foreign Policy*, 2nd ed.,
vol. 2 (New York: Scribner's, 2002), p. 135.

[81] These three historical forces are adapted from Friedman's triple convergence,
described in Chapter 3 of *The World Is Flat: A Brief History of the Twenty-First
Century* (New York: Farrar, Straus and Giroux, 2005), pp. 173–200.

economy.[82] Third, *economic* changes – enabled by technology and driven by the new global competition – both empowered and forced people to learn how to finance, produce, and trade goods and services globally. "Clearly, it is now possible for more people than ever to collaborate and compete in real time with more other people on more different kinds of work from more different corners of the planet and on a more equal footing than at any previous time in the history of the world," writes Friedman. As a result the planet is shifting "from a primarily vertical (command and control) value-creation model to an increasingly horizontal (connect and communicate)" model, with profound strategic implications.[83]

The information revolution alone is having an important impact on both the structure and operation of the international system. One astute observer summarized its effects under eight headings: interconnection (by means of information flows), disaggregation/decentralization (replacing dominance and hierarchy), disintermediation (as individuals bypass middlemen and act directly), dislocation (as more and more things can be done from more and more places), acceleration (of information and decision cycles), amplification (as more and more people and assets come into play), virtualness (as the digitized world becomes able to do things that only the real world once could), and asymmetry (empowering small players to compete with large ones).[84] And in truth, the information revolution unleashes a myriad of contradictory trends that only begins with the struggle between global fragmentation and integration, anarchy and control:

> The revolution empowers individuals and elites. It breaks down hierarchies and creates new power structures. It amplifies the capacity to analyze, reduces reaction time to allow only for impulse and can be a tool for amplifying emotions or rationality. It offers both more choices and too many choices, better information and more questions about authenticity, greater insight and more fog. It can reduce the risk to soldiers in warfare and greatly increase the cost of conflict. It can make the United States so strong militarily that no one dares fight her in ways in which she is prepared to fight, while enabling opponents to take advantage of new options in asymmetrical conflict. It cedes some state authority to markets, to transnational entities and to non-state actors and, as a consequence, produces political forces calling for the strengthening of the state. It is the best tool for democrats and the best weapon for demagogues.[85]

[82] For the consensus on market economics, see Daniel Yergin and Joseph Stanslaw, *The Commanding Heights: The Battle between the Government and the Market Place That Is Remaking the Modern World* (New York: Simon and Schuster, 1998).

[83] Friedman, *The World is Flat*, pp. 8, 201.

[84] David Rothkopf, "Cyberpolitik: The Changing Nature of Power in the Information Age," *Journal of International Affairs* 51 (Spring 1998): 334–336. This is not to say that nonstate actors become more powerful than states, or that states lose power; instead, "the new world overlaps and rests on the traditional world in which power depends on geographically based institutions." Robert O. Keohane and Joseph S. Nye, Jr., "Power and Interdependence in the Information Age," *Foreign Affairs* 77 (September/October 1998): 82.

[85] Rothkopf, "Cyberpolitik," pp. 327–328.

However contradictory, globalization is clearly reflected in economic statistics, which now show a dramatically different picture for the three systems of international trade, finance, and production than they did for most of the twentieth century. The world's trade has grown much faster than its production, increasing as a percentage of gross world product from about 7 percent in 1950 to over 20 percent by the end of the century. This trend is especially pronounced for the United States, where the amount of gross domestic product (GDP) involved in international trade has historically been about 10 percent but had risen to 24 percent by the mid-1990s.[86] International financial flows have grown even more rapidly than trade; moreover, their form has changed, from portfolio to foreign direct investment (FDI) and, within portfolios, from long-term bonds to stocks and short-term notes traded electronically.[87] Perhaps most remarkable is the emergence of a globalized production system, characterized by international outsourcing, insourcing, open-sourcing, offshoring, and supply chaining, and used not only for the manufacturing of goods but also for the collaborative production of intellectual property and the worldwide provision of any service that can be digitized.[88] Finally, the governance of all three systems has so tightened that even a Republican president and Congress found themselves forced in 2004 to repeal export tax breaks for American industry rather than suffer retaliatory tariffs under a ruling of the World Trade Organization (WTO).[89]

Evaluating Globalization

Nevertheless, there is still considerable room for debate as to the extent and effects of globalization. Many observers point out that in some ways the world was more globalized a century ago, before World War I and the Great Depression, than today. Though world markets are now more integrated for trade, they are no more integrated for capital and are actually less integrated for labor than they were a century ago.[90] That the world is still essentially a collection of national economies is attested to by the fact that different nations have different interest rates, are often at different places in the business cycle, and have different monetary and fiscal

---

[86] Martin Wolf, "Will the Nation-State Survive Globalization?", pp. 179–180.

[87] Jeffrey Sachs, "Understanding the Mysteries of Globalization," p. 98.

[88] Freidman, *The World Is Flat*, Chapter 2.

[89] Under a WTO ruling in 2002, retaliatory EU tariffs against U.S. goods began in March 2004 at 5 percent and rose 1 percent each month. Congress passed repeal over the Columbus Day weekend in October 2004.

[90] Wolf, "Will the Nation-State Survive Globalization?", p. 181. Increased restrictions on labor mobility may not matter as much, however, since computerized and virtually free worldwide communications mean that many tasks can be done anywhere without workers having to move.

policies.[91] Indeed, large areas of the world have not even been touched by economic globalization: "Most of the world's citizens live on less than $10 a day; most don't have access to phones; four out of every five have never traveled further than 100 miles from home."[92] Even a country as globalized as the United States produces 90 percent of its goods and services for domestic use.[93] As to globalization's political effects, it is probably still true that "the most important events in international politics are explained by differences in the capabilities of states, not by economic forces operating across states or transcending them."[94]

Moreover, although many argue that globalization is inexorable, there is reason to question its future. For a decade now, the international trading system appears to show a slowing of global liberalization and an acceleration in the formation of regional trading blocs like the North and Central American Free Trade Associations (NAFTA and CAFTA), with the issue unresolved as to whether regional liberalization will lead the broader system to freer trade or become an impediment to it.[95] Financially, economists increasingly question whether current global imbalances can be sustained, now that foreign lending to the United States to finance its consumption of overseas goods and services has surpassed $3 trillion.[96] Certainly war or terrorist attacks with weapons of mass destruction would sharply curtail globalization for years or even decades; if they hit key transportation nodes, terrorists could shut down the flow of supplies that sustains globalized production.[97] Even short of apocalypse, history shows that "policy, not technology, has determined the extent and pace of international economic integration. . . . Globalization is not destined, it is chosen," and it is not hard to imagine circumstances in which governments might feel

---

[91] Robert M. Dunn, Jr., "Has the US Economy Really Been Globalized?" *The Washington Quarterly* 24 (Winter 2001): 53–66.

[92] Micklethwait and Wooldridge, "From Sarajevo to September 11," p. 52.

[93] Paul Krugman quoted in Kenneth N. Waltz, "Globalization and American Power," pp. 49–50.

[94] Waltz, "Globalization and American Power," p. 52.

[95] On the point of the destructive or benign impact of regional trading arrangements, contrast the views of Sidney Weintraub, "Regionalism and the GATT: The North American Initiative," *SAIS Review* (Winter-Spring 1991): 45–57, who fears the protectionist tendencies of regional trade blocs, with those of Peter M. Ludlow, "The Future of the International Trading System," *Washington Quarterly* 12 (Autumn 1989): 157–170, who sees in regional trading blocs a passage to a freer global system.

[96] Paul Blustein, "Foreign Investment's Flip Side: U.S. Trade Deficit Swells Along With Consumption, Debt," *Washington Post* (February 25, 2005): A1, 18; Zanny Minton Beddoes, "The Great Thrift Shift: A Survey of the World Economy," *Economist* 376 (September 24, 2005): 28.

[97] Niall Ferguson spins out various economic and political disaster scenarios in "Sinking Globalization," *Foreign Affairs* 84 (March/April 2005): 64–77. For the consequences of terrorist attack on transportation systems, see Chapter 2, "The Next Attack," in Stephen Flynn, *America the Vulnerable* (New York: HarperCollins, 2004), pp. 17–36.

compelled to choose more independence.[98] Indeed, some astute observers argue that the border-weakening processes of globalization inevitably give rise to boundary-strengthening pressures of localization, as people seek "the psychic comforts of close-at-hand, reliable support – for the family and neighborhood, for local cultural practices, for a sense of 'us' that is distinguished from 'them'" – not to mention relief from the unrelenting pressures of a competitive globalized market.[99] Of course, it may turn out that globalization feeds on itself, that "the more pervasive globalizing tendencies become, the less resistant localizing reaction will be to further globalization."[100] But it is also possible that domestic backlash will limit globalization well short of what technology and the market might allow.

The primary challenge for strategists, though, is not just to divine the character, extent and likely future of globalization, but to assess its significance. On the plus side, globalization is almost certainly good for growth. By extending the advantages of specialization in the use of labor and capital, it makes all the world's economies more efficient.[101] Although landlocked countries and natural resource producers may be exceptions, globalization is even good for developing countries and also for the poor people within them – and is recognized as such by its beneficiaries.[102] During the 1990s, for example, per capita GDP grew 5 percent a year in the most globalized developing countries while it shrunk 1 percent a year in the least globalized; assisted by multinational corporation (MNC) wages that are 1.5 to 2 times local pay scales, the income of the poorest tenth in the freest, most open countries was ten times that of the poorest tenth in the least free.[103] It seems incontestable that globalization increases global wealth, even among the poorest.

Moreover, a convincing argument can be made that state power in today's world requires modern information technology, that the productive use of the latter requires both domestic political freedom and integration with the leading democratic states, and that powerful states will therefore share democratic values that emphasize prosperity and peace.[104] Some

---

[98] Wolf, "Will the Nation-State Survive Globalization?", p. 182. Still, people in most countries affected by globalization think it is good for themselves and their countries, and although they think that job opportunities, work life, and inequality have recently worsened, they blame those problems on other causes. See Bruce Stokes, "Global Is Better," *National Journal* (June 7, 2003): 1762–1770.

[99] James N. Rosenau, "The Complexities and Contradictions of Globalization," *Current History* (November 1997): 362. See also Jean-Marie Guehenno, "The Impact of Globalisation on Strategy," pp. 8–9.

[100] Rosenau, "Complexities and Contradictions," p. 364. Original italics removed here.

[101] Sachs, "Understanding the Mysteries of Globalization," pp. 99–102.

[102] Bruce Stokes, "Global Is Better," pp. 1762–1770.

[103] Micklethwait and Wooldridge, "From Sarajevo to September 11," pp. 58–59.

[104] Gompert, "Right Makes Might: Freedom and Power in the Information Age," pp. 45–73.

advocates of globalization even claim that it will make war between economically integrated states less likely, simply because the disruption in the delivery of outsourced services or components would be so disruptive to an offshore business that it would be unlikely to reestablish commercial links once the war was over. Friedman therefore predicts that gains from economics will henceforth trump gains from geopolitics, and "no two countries that are both part of a major global supply chain . . . [like China and Taiwan] will ever fight a war against each other. . . ."[105] Still, strategists who realize that similar claims for "the silken strands of commerce" were made by the French *philosophes* in the seventeenth century and by Norman Angell in his famous book before World War I will have to decide whether twenty-first century globalization is more powerful in this respect than its predecessors.[106]

Even if globalization leads to a wealthier, more democratic, and more peaceful world, it also has some negative effects. As the localization backlash mentioned above attests, globalization is among those forces that are increasing economic inequality and insecurity, both within nations (as global competition restructures production, reducing the income of unskilled workers in developed countries and skilled ones in developing countries) and between nations (as globalized states pull ahead of non-globalized states).[107] Indeed, countries may engage in a race to the bottom, offering tax breaks and other incentives to MNCs but in the process impoverishing assistance to citizens disadvantaged by globalization along with national education and infrastructure.[108] More dramatic damage may be caused by global monetary instability now that Third World economies are open to computerized flows of hot money, as evidenced first in the 1994–95 Mexican peso crisis and then in the 1997–98 Asian financial meltdown, especially as it spread to Latin America and Russia.[109] Just as it facilitates legitimate businesses, making them much more efficient and widespread, globalization also empowers all kinds of criminal activities, including

---

[105] See "The Dell Theory of Conflict Prevention," Chapter 12 in *The World Is Flat*, pp. 419–429. Friedman provides evidence here that the India-Pakistan 2002 nuclear crisis resulted in Indian business pressure on New Delhi to stand down.

[106] On the philosophes, see Felix Gilbert, *To the Farewell Address* (Princeton, NJ: Princeton University Press, 1961), pp. 56–65. Norman Angell's book was *The Great Illusion* (New York and London, 1913).

[107] Sachs, "Understanding the Mysteries of Globalization," pp. 106–108.

[108] Gerald Epstein, James Crotty, and Patricia Kelly, "Winners and Losers in the Global Economics Game," *Current History* 95 (November 1996): 377–381. This process is probably limited, however, by the fact that companies search for levels of education and infrastructure that require a robust tax base.

[109] On macroeconomic instability, see Sachs, "Understanding the Mysteries of Globalization," pp. 102–106; on the Asian crisis, see Paul Krugman, "The Return of Depression Economics," *Foreign Affairs* 78 (January/February 1999): 56–74, and Barry Eichengreen, "The Asian Financial Crisis," Chapter 2 in *Great Decisions 1999* (New York: Foreign Policy Association, 1998), pp. 19–29.

illegal trade in narcotics, arms, intellectual property, people, and money.[110] Finally, those trying to manage these problems must deal with the democratic deficit in global governance, the concern that the international institutions needed to regulate globalization lack the accountability and actionable rights that citizens of democratic states find in their own legislatures, courts, and constitutions.[111]

Perhaps the greatest significance of globalization for strategists, though, is the additional complexity and volatility it introduces into their calculations. This is partly because globalization is more than an economic phenomenon. In fact, to economic globalization one should add at least three other dimensions: military, socio-cultural, and environmental.[112] Military globalization facilitates the actions of Al Qaeda as well as the extraordinary, information-based lethality of the American military. Social globalization encompasses everything from the spread of ideas to the homogenization of culture to the migration of peoples. Environmental globalization means global pollution, global warming, and global epidemics like AIDS and avian influenza. Integration in the economic, military, social, and environmental dimensions may proceed at different rates, advancing in some while remaining stagnant or even receding in others. Moreover, as globalization becomes "quicker and thicker," networks in these four areas increasingly interact with each other,

> which means that the effects of events in one geographical area or in the economic or ecological dimension can have profound effects in other geographical areas or on the military or social dimension. These international networks are increasingly complex, and their effects are therefore increasingly unpredictable. . . . As a result, globalization is accompanied by pervasive uncertainty.

In short, globalization seems to introduce into the international system many of the characteristics outlined in chaos theory. At a minimum, it means that strategists will increasingly "have to respond to issues that involve greater complexity, more uncertainty, shorter response times, broader participation by groups and individuals, and an uneven shrinkage of distance."[113]

Internal Pressures

Most of our discussion so far has dealt with assumptions regarding the *external* factors that affect state action; that is, we have assumed that the

---

[110] See Moises Naim, "The Five Wars of Globalization," *Foreign Policy* 134 (January/ February 2003): 28–37.

[111] Joseph S. Nye, Jr., "Globalization's Democratic Deficit," *Foreign Affairs* 80 (July/August 2001): 2–6.

[112] Robert O. Keohane and Joseph S. Nye, Jr., "Globalization: What's New? What's Not? (and So What?)," *Foreign Policy* 118 (Spring 2000): 104–119.

[113] Nye, *Paradox of American Power*, p. 87, 91.

pressures which motivate statesmen come from outside their own states, from configurations of power in the outside world or the characteristics of the international system itself. But it is quite possible that a country's foreign policy may be driven more by *internal* factors than by international ones, that its actions on the world scene may be determined not so much by its leaders' cold assessment of international affairs as by domestic political, economic, social, and cultural pressures. Indeed, with globalization opening nation-states more and more to outside influences, even international pressures may have their effects via states' domestic systems. As a result, one of the most important assumptions that a foreign affairs strategist must make concerns the balance between external and internal influences, between domestic and international causes of state actions.

Even in retrospect, it may be difficult to tell whether internal or international developments had the predominant influence on a given outcome. A war may be explained as arising out of the need to oppose a powerful threat, or as a result of leaders' efforts to distract the populace from domestic troubles (the so-called "foreign war panacea").[114] In 1998, for example, when President Clinton bombed Osama bin Laden's guerrilla camps in Afghanistan and a pharmaceuticals factory in Sudan three days after his grand jury testimony in the Monica Lewinsky case, was it to distract the country from the scandal and head off impeachment, or was it purely in retaliation for the bombing of U.S. embassies in Kenya and Tanzania two weeks earlier?[115] In the late 1960s, when China decided to open relations with the United States under the pressure of Soviet military attacks along its long, relatively undefended border, was it a classic balance of power move, or was it a result of factional infighting within the Chinese communist party during the Cultural Revolution?[116] Such questions often remain the subject of dispute among historians for decades.

Of course, it is likely that both external and internal pressures influence most decision makers' choices. But the major factor determining which will predominate seems to be perceptions of threat. When threats from the external environment are high they tend to capture decision makers' attention and motivation, whereas internal pressures have more sway when threats are low, even if opportunities abound.[117] As noted in Chapter 1, all kinds of domestic pressures frustrated foreign affairs strategy during

[114] In what is perhaps the most well known case, the option of declaring war on England or France was suggested by Secretary of War William Seward to President Lincoln in 1860 as a possible way of heading off the American civil war.

[115] Joe Klein, *The Natural: The Misunderstood Presidency of Bill Clinton* (New York: Broadway Books/Random House, 2002), p. 175.

[116] Robert O. Scalapino, "China and the Balance of Power," *Foreign Affairs* 52 (January 1974): 349–367.

[117] This pattern follows psychologists' understanding that pain is more urgent than pleasure. See Jack Levy, "Prospect Theory, Rational Choice, and International Relations," *International Studies Quarterly* 41 (March 1997): 100.

the Clinton years as the nation focused on economic issues and presidential scandals, and the salience of domestic issues seemed undiminished in the first months of the Bush administration.[118] But 9/11 captured the nation's attention as few foreign affairs issues ever have, and internal distractions were quickly set aside to deal with the new threat posed by mass terrorism.

Perhaps the most important assumptions to be made about the impact of internal influences on a state's international behavior have to do with its form of government. Extensive research into the incidence of war in recent world history demonstrates that democracies do not fight other democracies.[119] There are, of course, many examples of popular war fever operating to push democratic states into conflict, notably including the American declaration of war on Spain in 1898. But these instances do not really disprove the theory, since such popular movements often are fueled by the actions of nondemocratic opponents.[120] Moreover, even if democratic processes do occasionally lead states into war, there is no question that the most heinous aggressions of the twentieth century – whether of Nazi Germany, imperial Japan, communist North Korea and North Vietnam, or Saddam Hussein's Iraq, not to mention the adventurism of the USSR – were all perpetrated by totalitarian systems of government.

Still, the democratic peace hypothesis has its qualifications. Some argue that there is no convincing evidence of why democracies do not fight each other, or that "the number of wars between democracies is not statistically different from what random chance would predict. Both wars and democracies are [historically] rare, and that is why there are not many wars between democracies."[121] Others contend that peace only obtains between mature democracies; transitional, democratizing states are often more aggressive and war-prone even than stable autocracies.[122] It has also been pointed out that constitutional liberalism – meaning the rule of law and protection of the basic liberties of speech, assembly, religion, and property – does

---

[118] See Terry L. Deibel, *Clinton and Congress: The Politics of Foreign Policy* (New York: Foreign Policy Association, 2000). Also David Halberstam, *War in a Time of Peace* (New York: Scribner, 2001), esp. Chapters 15 and 19.

[119] "With only very marginal exceptions, democratic states have not fought one another in the modern era. This is one of the strongest nontrivial or non-tautological generalizations that can be made about international relations.... [A]greement on the condition of virtual absence of war among democracies...is now overwhelming...." Russett, *Controlling the Sword: The Democratic Governance of National Security*, p. 123.

[120] In the case of Spain, the monarchy's corrupt rule over Cuba and the appalling conditions there were the grist that the sensationalist American press used to whip up demands for war.

[121] David E. Spiro, "The Liberal Peace – 'And Yet It Squirms,'" *International Security* 19 (Spring 1995): 177.

[122] Edward D. Mansfield and Jack Snyder, "Democratization and the Danger of War," *International Security* 20 (Summer 1995): 5–38.

not always accompany popular elections, and that such "illiberal" democracies are likely to generate nationalism, conflict, and war. Thus, "the democratic peace is actually the liberal peace."[123] Even more problematical than democratization is the impact of spreading market economics, which often accompanies democratization. Modernization has long been thought to cause a dangerous erosion of societal traditions and values, leaving people in developing countries adrift without psychological support. Now it appears that the introduction of market values into such societies "can lead to illiberal and unstable democracy, military dictatorship, state failure, sectarian violence, or some combination thereof – and bitter anti-Americanism" conducive to the growth of terrorism.[124]

Whether market democracies really are less aggressive obviously makes a big difference to the proper concerns of foreign affairs strategy. For if one assumes that pressures from outside the state – generated by the operation of the international system and the need to amass power – are so demanding that any statesman would have to respond to them in similar ways, then one can argue that a state's internal form of government is irrelevant to its strategy.[125] This assumption leads to the conclusion that the way to change state behavior is to engineer external pressures and rewards and, in the case of potential aggressors, to construct countervailing balances of power. But if forms of government are critical to external behavior, and if market democracies are more peaceful, then strategists may decide to involve themselves in the internal affairs of other states, doing what they can to make other governments more liberal, market based, and democratic – a much more difficult assignment.

As the world's oldest democracy, the United States has always been sympathetic to other democracies, going back at least as far as the Greek civil war in the 1830s.[126] Woodrow Wilson, of course, remains the most prominent American statesman to argue that the way to make the world "safe for democracy" was to make its governments democratic. More recently, it was *glasnost*, the internal changes in the governance of the Soviet Union under Mikhail Gorbachev, that gave the West its best assurance that the "new thinking" in Soviet foreign policy during the late 1980s was fundamental and enduring rather than another tactical retreat on the order of numerous

---

[123] Fareed Zakaria, "The Rise of Illiberal Democracy," *Foreign Affairs* 76 (November/December 1997): 35.

[124] Michael Mousseau, "Market Civilization and Its Clash with Terror," *International Security* 27 (Winter 2002/03): 15.

[125] The result might be a statement like Henry Kissinger made when explaining the rationale behind the detente strategy of the Nixon administration: "we will judge other countries, including Communist countries, ... on the basis of their actions and not on the basis of their domestic ideology." *White House Years*, p. 192. If false, this assumption may be the most serious theoretical shortcoming of traditional realist thought. See Chapter 3 for a brief contrasting of realist and idealist views.

[126] See Chapter 4, section on value projection, for further details.

earlier Cold War thaws, likely to be reversed when it suited Soviet purposes. Then, during the 1990s, this assumption largely determined one's stance on whether U.S. post–Cold War strategy in Eurasia ought to concentrate on bolstering democracy within Russia or on strengthening the smaller states of Middle Europe as counterweights to Russian power.[127]

Today, American foreign policy is heavily mortgaged to the idea that the spread of democracy, along with capitalist economic arrangements, will make for an international environment more congenial to American interests, and that it is possible to shape such an environment. The Clinton administration made "enlargement" of market democracy one of three pillars of its national security strategy, and argued that democratic states were not only more peaceful but also better partners in trade and in protecting the environment.[128] Seeking an *ex post facto* justification for his war in Iraq, George W. Bush continued this tradition and made it the centerpiece of his second-term foreign policy, declaring in his second inaugural address that "the best hope for peace in our world is the expansion of freedom," and that therefore it would be "the policy of the United States to seek and support the growth of democratic movements and institutions in every nation and culture, with the ultimate goal of ending tyranny in our world."[129] Rightly or wrongly, it seems clear that American strategists of both political parties now assume that the internal form of government adopted in other nation-states is of critical interest to the United States.

The Role of Ideas

So far we have sought insight into the international environment for foreign affairs strategy by assuming that the external and internal pressures that bear on other states' leaders are controlling. But what about the leaders themselves? Do their ideas matter? If foreign statesmen are important figures on the world stage, the most important thing to know about the international environment may well be the kinds of ideas or principles that motivate them.[130]

---

[127] An interesting manifestation of this debate was the division in the early 1990s between Richard Nixon, who urged aid to Russia in support of democracy, and Henry Kissinger, who argued that the West should strengthen counterweights to Russian power. Compare Don Oberdorfer, "Nixon Warns Bush to Aid Russia, Shun 'New Isolationism,'" *Washington Post* (March 12, 1992): A1, A22, with Henry Kissinger, "Don't Resurrect an Empire," *Washington Post* (January 14, 1992): A19.

[128] "The successor to a doctrine of containment must be a strategy of enlargement—enlargement of the world's free community of market democracies." Anthony Lake, "From Containment to Enlargement," speech at the School of Advanced International Studies, Washington, DC, September 21, 1993. See also *A National Security Strategy of Engagement and Enlargement* (Washington, DC: The White House, February 1995), and Douglas Brinkley, "Democratic Enlargement: The Clinton Doctrine," *Foreign Policy* 106 (Spring 1997): 111–127.

[129] Text of address in *Washington Post* (January 21, 2005): A24.

[130] This way of thinking is of course a continuation of the shift begun in the previous section from the external to the internal contexts, *i.e.*, from causes of state

Quite apart from the personal proclivities of statesmen, of course, ideas may have a dramatic impact on the internal pressures statesmen face. These may be homegrown, like the ethnic or national identities that were so obvious during the 1990s in the Balkans and the successor states of the Soviet Union. Or, as suggested above, they may be imported from abroad, a phenomenon that appears to be growing as literacy rates advance worldwide, elites increasingly travel for study in foreign lands, publishing becomes a global enterprise, and modern communications technology beams ideas of all kinds across international frontiers. How else can one explain the worldwide spread of democratic forms of government in the post–Cold War era, or the global consensus against socialist economic arrangements? What other cause than the impact of television could lie behind the U.S. decision to intervene with force in 1992 to feed starving people in Somalia, a country without the slightest weight in the global balance of power? World public opinion was often adduced as a powerful force for good or evil in the early twentieth century, but it may well be only in today's world that it is coming into its own, creating pressures in societies that then have impacts on governments' behavior.

Indeed, some analysts argue that ideas are *all* that matter in today's international environment, that even national interests are the product of social and cultural norms.[131] In this view neither international anarchy nor the distribution of power determine state behavior.[132] More important is identity, which even in the society of states tells "you and others who you are and . . . you who others are" and implies a set of expected reactions to external pressures.[133] Identities, it is argued, are socially constructed – that is, determined by ideas, discourse, and practice within a social context. Therefore they can and do change as a result of experience or outside pressures, including the example of international institutions or global norms. Thus, militarist Japan can become a pacifist state after defeat in war and under the pressure of long-term occupation; Europeans can become so disillusioned with the state system after two world wars and the Great Depression that they create a supranational institution for Europe and even shift their personal identities in its direction. Moreover, norms themselves – what is "expected and required" in interstate behavior – can change rather quickly in an era of great power peace,

---

behavior originating outside the state to those coming from inside it. But we are still looking at the international environment because we are still concerned with how *foreign* strategists direct their states; Chapter 3 considers how the strategist deals with his own domestic environment.

[131] For a very brief overview of this school of thought, called constructivism, see Stephen M. Walt, "International Relations: One World, Many Theories," *Foreign Policy* 110 (Spring 1998): 40–41.

[132] Alexander Wendt, "Anarchy Is What States Make of It: The Social Construction of Power Politics," *International Organization* 46 (Spring 1992): 391–426.

[133] Ted Hopf, "The Promise of Constructivism in International Relations Theory," *International Security* 23 (Summer 1998): 175.

institutionalized diplomacy, and virtual pressure groups. While nationalism and regionalism are still strong in today's world, therefore, some believe
that we are also seeing a shift from internationalism, where cooperation
among states is valued but sovereignty is protected, toward cosmopoli-
tanism, where individuals are considered and consider themselves citizens
of the world who deserve protection even against the power of their own
governments.[134]

Standing against such imported changes, however, is the weight of culture, simply defined as "collectively held ideas, beliefs and norms."[135] Culture is partly a matter of objective elements like a common history, language, customs, institutions, and especially religion, which lead different
groups to "different views on the relations between God and man, the individual and the group, the citizen and the state, parents and children, husband and wife, as well as different views of the relative importance of rights
and responsibilities, liberty and authority, equality and hierarchy."[136]
Political culture is the subset of these elements that determines a nation's
style of political interaction and its form of government; the persistence
of political culture helps explain why a country like Russia has remained
authoritarian whether ruled by czars, the Communist party, or Vladimir
Putin, and why spreading democracy to Afghanistan or Iraq is so much
harder than just changing their constitutions. But culture is also partly
a matter of one's subjective identification as *belonging* to a particular
group – for example, being a Hispanic, Muslim, or Japanese. Samuel
Huntington has persuasively argued that, because such basic differences
are so difficult to compromise, culture will be the determining factor in
international conflict for the foreseeable future.[137] Certainly an inability to
concede is characteristic of religious differences, and religious revival is
currently sweeping the non-European world.[138] Still, there is also the
"tenacity of modernity and secularism," along with statesmen's readiness
to "see brotherhood and faith and kin when it is in their interest" and to
ignore them when it is not.[139] Culture and religion, then, may at times
generate pressures statesmen cannot ignore, while at other times they are
used by statesmen to advance their purposes.

---

[134] Coral Bell, "Normative Shift," *National Interest* 70 (Winter 2002/03): 5–20. See
also Samuel P. Huntington, "Dead Souls: The Denationalization of the American Elite," *National Interest* 75 (Spring 2004): 5–18, and James Kurth, "The Late
American Nation," *National Interest* 77 (Fall 2004): 117–125.

[135] Carole Pateman, quoted in Michael C. Desch, "Culture Clash: Assessing the
Importance of Ideas in Security Studies," *International Security* 23 (Summer
1998): 151.

[136] Huntington, "The Clash of Civilizations?" p. 25.

[137] Huntington, "The Clash of Civilizations?" pp. 22–49.

[138] Peter L. Berger, "Religion and the West," *National Interest* 80 (Summer 2005):
112–120.

[139] Fouad Ajami, "The Summoning: 'But They Said, We Will Not Harken'," *Foreign
Affairs* 72 (September/October 1993): 2–9.

In addition to whatever domestic pressures they may impose on states-men, world public opinion, constructed identities, ingrained culture, and religious beliefs may also directly affect leaders' *own* way of thinking. That is, a decision maker may not just respond to or manipulate the pressures of an Islamic society, which he leads; he may himself be a Muslim. Cer-tainly statesmen's personal moral codes can affect their decisions. "I know but one code of morality for men," wrote Thomas Jefferson, "whether acting singly or collectively."[140] Replied the unifier of Italy, Count Camilio Benso di Cavour, nearly a century later: "What rascals we would have been if we had done for ourselves what we did for Italy." Though some leaders may only apply whatever ethical scruples they possess to their own personal behav-ior, others clearly come to office with deeply ingrained moral positions on foreign policy issues. Jimmy Carter, for example, was a born-again Chris-tian whose strong religious views led him to adopt a vigorous human rights and anti-nuclear weapons policy, along with an active role as peacemaker in the Middle East. When asked whether he had discussed the Iraq war with his father, George W. Bush referred to a "higher father" he appeals to for strength.[141] More generally, it does seem that most statesmen habitu-ally rule out on moral grounds some actions they might otherwise take in the anarchical world of international politics, like the assassination of the leaders of other states – although after outlawing this practice in the late 1970s, the United States has used assassination against terrorists.[142] In this and many other areas, morality may have a subtle if mostly unseen effect on statecraft.[143]

But morality, if it is influential, is probably only one aspect of a states-man's idea set. On a more pedestrian level, ideas may have their effect through the application of principles to real-world cases. All statesmen like to be seen as acting from principle rather than self-interest, and har-ried decision makers often find precedent a compelling, even an essential tool for dealing with the complexities they face. Many Western decision makers have legal training which teaches them to apply law to cases, a mental process that may well carry over into their statecraft, and whatever

---

[140] Jefferson to James Madison, 1789 (Jefferson Papers, University of Virginia, ME7:449), at etext.virginia.edu/Jefferson.

[141] Bob Woodward, *Plan of Attack* (New York: Simon & Schuster, 2004), p. 421. On Bush's religious views, see also Alan Cooperman, "Openly Religious, to a Point," *Washington Post* (September 16, 2004): A1, A8.

[142] In November 2002, the CIA used a Hellfire missile fired from a Preda-tor UAV to kill an Al Qaeda leader in Yemen. For a summary of the law and opinion on the practice of assassinations, see "Assassination: Does It Work?," in *Terrorism Q&A* at the Council on Foreign Relations website-http://cfrterrorism.org/policy/assassination˙print.html.

[143] This discussion is not intended to apply to the ethics of officials as they participate in governmental decision making. Thus, it does not touch on Watergate or Iran-*contra* indiscretions. Rather, we are speaking here only of the degree to which morality affects the substance of policy positions.

proclivity leaders may have for thinking in legal terms is reinforced by the fact that modern states are bound by a dense network of treaty obligations and other international law. In addition, states are parts of international regimes, like the WTO and the International Telecommunications Union, that regulate many of their interstate contacts. All of these involvements require the application of law and other principles to the routine of foreign relations.

If they take the form of ideologies, ideas may play a much more direct and controlling role in statecraft. Until recently the leaders of many socialist and communist governments professed to be guided in foreign policy by Marxist-Leninist principles, and John Foster Dulles, Secretary of State to President Dwight D. Eisenhower, used to argue that he could predict Soviet behavior from his detailed knowledge of the works of Marx and Lenin.[144] Nor are such ideologies restricted to the socialist world of another era. In the United States, as noted at the beginning of this chapter, politicians have been elected on strongly ideological platforms of the left or right; Ronald Reagan, for example, condemned the Soviet Union and disparaged Third World states at least partly because he believed so strongly in democracy and *laissez faire* capitalism. Such leaders take power with a well-formed set of ideas that often have a very strong impact on policy, especially during their early days in office.

If ideas do play a role in foreign policy decisions alongside external and internal pressures, then strategists must obviously make different assumptions about state behavior. They might expect, for example, that international alignments would be based, not on the pattern of power, but on the pattern of ideas, so that ideologically compatible states would align against those of differing outlooks. If principles and morality are determinative, the strategist must study the broad ideas and moral codes that statesmen of other lands are likely to follow. If law or at least legal reasoning plays an important part, then legal advisors should perhaps have a greater role in strategy than simply attempting to justify what the statesman does. And if culture and religion rule, then strategists must calculate, for example, the effect on Indian and Arab foreign policies of Hindu and Islamic fundamentalism, respectively, as well as the broader cultural influences to which foreign statesman might be subject.

In the end, however, determining whether ideas or power move international politics is no easy undertaking. Although there is little doubt that the Soviet Union lost the Cold War, for example, there is considerable room for debate over what mechanisms were responsible for its defeat. Was it the power that the West brought to bear on the Soviets, the "unalterable counter-force" of containment: the troops in NATO, the war in Korea, the economic and military aid to allies worldwide, the superior Western technology in the arms race, the covert action used against Soviet clients,

[144] Gaddis, *Strategies of Containment*, pp. 136–137.

Tender-Minded	Tough-Minded
Rationalistic (Principles)	Empiricist (Facts)
Intellectualistic	Sensationalistic
Idealistic	Materialistic
Optimistic	Pessimistic
Religious	Irreligious
Free-willist	Fatalistic
Monistic	Pluralistic
Dogmatical	Skeptical

Figure 2.3: William James' philosophical temperaments.

the aid to the mujahedin in Afghanistan and to other armed groups battling Soviet-backed regimes?[145] Or was it the attraction of the idea of political liberty and the crisis of confidence in communist ideology, abetted by Radio Free Europe transmissions and personal contact with the West by elites from the Eastern bloc?[146] In a word, was Eastern Europe freed and the Soviet Union destroyed by the power of power or the power of ideas? Doubtless both played some role, but it is the strategist's job to formulate assumptions as to how each operates in contemporary international affairs.

Into the Subconscious

Although one would like to think that assumptions about the importance of power and principle as motive forces in the international environment would be made on the basis of long experience and careful study of world realities, it seems at least as likely that they turn on much deeper habits of mind. The American philosopher William James grouped many of these intellectual characteristics into two "temperaments" he called tender- and tough-minded (see Figure 2.3).[147] Three of James' characteristics, interrelated and implicit in much of the discussion so far, seem particularly important. One has to do with belief in free-will or determinism; another involves the strength of ethical imperatives; and the last relates to whether preferred patterns of reasoning are rationalistic or empiricist, deductive or inductive – that is, whether one reasons "down" from general principles to specific cases or "up" from the specific to the general. Tender-minded

[145] The quoted phrase is Kennan's from "The Sources of Soviet Conduct," *Foreign Affairs* 25 (July 1947): 566–582.

[146] For a provocative statement of this viewpoint, see Stanley Kober, "Idealpolitik," *Foreign Policy* 79 (Summer 1990): 3–24.

[147] William James, *Pragmatism* (Cleveland, Ohio: Meridian Books/World Publishing Co., 1955), pp. 19–28. James's temperaments correspond rather strikingly to those of today's foreign policy idealists and realists; see Chapter 3.

thinkers usually consider human beings free agents, have strong ethical tendencies, and tend to reason deductively. More specifically, they believe that statesmen are largely free to shape the international environment; hence there is little excuse for unethical behavior and much reason for them to follow moral precepts and other principles in their actions, decision making methods which accord with this school's preferred top-down method of reasoning. The tough-minded, on the other hand, find the answers to problems less in principles than in the particularities of cases and believe that the statesman is highly constrained by the environment in which he works. For this school the international environment along with facts on the ground are largely controlling, the dictates of power leave little room for maneuver, and the statesman can neither be expected nor afford to follow moral precepts.

Of course, no strategist, no statesman falls completely on one side or the other of this temperamental divide; we all lean at some times toward what we *want* to do and at others toward what we *can* do. Not surprisingly, these two tendencies bring us back to the two fundamental elements of strategy: intentions and capabilities, purpose and power, ends and means. To some degree, too, they encapsulate what may be the most important assumption of all: the extent to which leaders can shape reality to suit their purposes. Ironically, the predictability inherent in the assumption that the world's statesmen are weak relative to their environment would seem to make the strategist's views of the external context more useful, even as that same weakness restricts his or her ability to shape the future. The assumption that statesmen can change reality, by contrast, allows more room for strategic creativity but at the cost of a far less enduring, and, hence less useful, set of assumptions about the international environment.

3

The Domestic Context for Strategy

It is customary to think of foreign policy as happening "from the top down," as an exercise in which a few knowledgeable people at the top of the government formulate a foreign affairs strategy and then successfully market it in the policy process so that it determines the statements and actions of government. Indeed, that is the approach taken in this book, for foreign affairs strategy is primarily an intellectual enterprise undertaken by individuals in the Executive branch who are charged with running the government. But in a democracy, foreign policy also happens "from the bottom up," as the people express their own ideas of what should be done directly, through interest groups, and ultimately through their elected representatives in Congress. These determinations will rarely be as comprehensive or integrated – as strategic – as those of professionals in the Executive branch, but they may be very strongly articulated and can be backed by all the constitutional powers of Congress.

A successful strategy must therefore consider from the outset what can be sold to the public and on the Hill.[1] As generations of strategists have discovered, it does little good – and may cause much harm – to pursue what may otherwise seem to be rational or even essential objectives if such democratic support is lacking. During the late 1960s, for example, supporters of the Vietnam war complained that the United States could win if only public demonstrations against the war would stop. The comment was both plausible and absurd – plausible because such demonstrations *did* send strong signals to the enemy of the public divisions which would eventually end U.S. involvement in Vietnam and lead to victory by the North, absurd because any realistic strategy for a democracy at war had to take such manifestations of public disaffection into its calculus. If the war could not be won in spite of them, then the only logical alternative to curtailing democratic freedom of expression was to disengage. Such considerations doubtless lie behind the constitutional requirement for an outright

---

[1] "...history shows – a lesson most public officials have to learn and relearn – that to move ahead on important national issues without public support is to invite being undermined in the long run. Generating consensus, or at least public support, may not be easy to achieve. But in a democracy, it is necessary." Daniel Yankelovich, *Coming to Public Judgment* (Syracuse, NY: Syracuse University Press, 1991), p. 117.

declaration of war by the people's representatives, a procedure that might have spared the nation much grief had it been followed.[2]

Congressional support is not precisely equivalent to public support, but few would contest the proposition that over time the Congress will represent the will of the people on most issues. Foreign affairs strategy needs the support of Congress, not only because contrary political leadership from the Hill can cause the president serious problems with the broader public, but most directly because the Congress is given a major role in foreign policy by the Constitution, including treaty approval and provision of the instruments of statecraft essential to strategic success. Again, history shows that neither the importance of the goals strategists espouse nor the seriousness of the threats they see relieves them of the need to factor in this requirement. The classic case is that of Woodrow Wilson, who made the mistake of assuming that the League of Nations was so important to world peace that even a Senate dominated by the opposing party and ignored in its negotiation would have to approve it. The result was that Wilson destroyed himself in a belated effort to build public support, the League became a wrenching and divisive political issue, and the United States never joined the organization, with incalculable effects on the troubled interwar period and the origins of World War II.[3] Again, during the mid-1980s President Reagan argued that the United States simply could not tolerate the existence of a communist government like that of the Sandinistas in Nicaragua, and that everything short of outright American military intervention – including U.S. support of an armed insurgency known as the *contras* – had to be done to overthrow it. But although the President was able for a time to get some funding from Congress to support the *contras*, he was ultimately unable to convince the people that the objective was important enough or the *contras* worthy enough for that support to be sustained.[4] His refusal to recognize the importance of public support, and accordingly to change the objective, led straight into the Iran-*contra* affair and the most serious crisis of his presidency.

The foreign affairs strategist must also recognize that the Executive branch is itself an important constituency whose opinion is vital to strategic success. In the first place, of course, members of the bureaucracy are part of the broader public – indeed among its very best informed and most

---

[2] Perhaps as part of the lessons that the Vietnam syndrome taught, both George Bushes were careful to get formal congressional support (if not a declaration of war) before using American troops against Iraq. The controversy over the 2003 Iraq war has led some to propose reviving congressional declarations of war, a provision of the Constitution that has fallen into desuetude since 1941. Leslie H. Gelb and Anne-Marie Slaughter, "No More Blank Check Wars," *Washington Post* (November 18, 2005): A19.

[3] The classic account is Thomas A. Bailey, *Woodrow Wilson and the Great Betrayal* (New York: MacMillan, 1945).

[4] Reagan's explanation of his policies, and his admission of his lack of persuasiveness, are in *An American Life* (New York: Simon and Schuster, 1990), esp. Chapters 63 and 69.

politically engaged members. They also will have vested interests in the matters with which they are dealing, or at the very least a different, more narrowly focused perspective than that of the foreign affairs strategist who leads them. And they will form their own appreciation of what the broader public wants, often having more direct contact with it on the issues for which they are responsible than do higher-level decision makers. The result may be a set of opinions strongly at variance with official strategy on the part of the people charged with carrying it out, with serious results for policy implementation.[5] Perhaps the best example from postwar history is the India-Pakistan crisis of 1971, when the State Department sided with India while President Nixon and his National Security Advisor, Henry Kissinger, wanted to tilt toward Pakistan.[6] As Kissinger described it, the Department simply used its control over the machinery of execution to flagrantly disregard unambiguous presidential directives. It was able to do so through "a constant infighting over seeming trivial issues, any one of which seemed too lightweight or technical to raise to the President but whose accumulation would define the course of national policy."[7] The upshot was a foreign affairs strategy so weakened in the face it presented to the world that it lost whatever opportunity it might have had to head off a serious crisis in South Asia.

As the above examples demonstrate, a loss of domestic support inside or outside of the government can lead to strategic failures in two ways: first by disrupting execution of the strategy itself through methods as diverse as street demonstrations, an adverse vote in Congress, or Executive branch sabotage; and second by lowering perceptions of the nation's power on the part of those overseas who are the targets of strategy.[8] Once begun, however, a cycle of failure will not stop here. A president who fails abroad will

---

[5] It is in fact a myth to assume that, because they are headed by political appointees who serve at the President's pleasure, government agencies will automatically follow his direction. Presidents appoint officials because of some combination of knowledge in a given area, capability of action, constituency representation, and personal loyalty. Most will be skilled, energetic individuals with strong views, and unless the President can exercise vigilance (virtually impossible except on a few major issues), they will go their own way. Indeed, if the policy is strongly contested, even presidential decisions have only a short-term impact. This is why most policy disputes are never settled in Washington – until people on one or the other side leave office. See the memoirs of all recent presidents and national security advisors, as well as Richard E. Neustadt, *Presidential Power* (New York: John Wiley, 1980).

[6] State's bias had to do with an affinity toward India as a democracy and with revulsion at the atrocities committed by the Pakistani army in East Bengal, whereas Nixon and Kissinger saw Pakistan as the victim of Indian aggression, a key ally opposing the Soviet alliance with India, and critical to the ongoing secret opening to China.

[7] Henry Kissinger, *White House Years* (Boston, MA: Little, Brown & Co., 1979), pp. 863–864.

[8] Popular support for a president is a critical element of the nation's power. See Chapter 5.

lose the political strength that is essential to later foreign policy successes, to the future of his legislative program at home, and perhaps to remaining in office when election time rolls around. Success overseas will have the opposite effects. As a result, presidents can hardly separate matters of public, Congressional, and bureaucratic support for foreign policies from their larger need for public approval. Despite the popular cliché, they know intuitively that politics does not stop at the waters' edge; popularity and success at home and abroad are reciprocally linked.[9]

Foreign policy is thus inevitably and thoroughly entwined with domestic politics. As Yale political scientist Bruce Russett puts it, "The success or failure of international policy is in fact substantially driven by domestic political developments, and so, therefore, is the choice of policy by a leader who aspires to success."[10] Elaborating on this point, a leading text in international relations explains that

> international politics is a product of the normal pulls and tugs of domestic affairs, that leaders (not nations) make policy decisions and do so to maximize their prospects of staying in office, and that decisions, therefore, are strategic, taking into account expected responses by adversaries and supporters and designed to maximize the leader's (not the state's) welfare. I call this view the strategic perspective. The question of personal political power guides policy choices, and the cumulative effect of policy choices gives rise to what we call the international system. Therefore, domestic politics, foreign policy, and international politics are inextricably linked.[11]

The lesson seems clear. Although foreign affairs strategy is designed to influence the international environment, it is rooted in its domestic context. So even as foreign affairs strategists try to deduce how and how strongly other strategists are influenced by their own domestic environments, they have to deal with their own. Indeed, strategists' assumptions about their domestic context are just as vital as their assumptions about the international environment, and it is equally important that they be factored into strategic designs from the start.[12]

The "domestic environment" section of the assessment level in the model for foreign affairs strategy is the place to clarify and validate those

---

[9] It is of course also true that presidential failure or success in domestic policy will affect prospects for success overseas, a fact best demonstrated by Ronald Reagan's mastery of domestic politics (including Congress) during the first year of his presidency. See Chapter 5.

[10] Bruce Russett, *Controlling the Sword: The Democratic Governance of National Security* (Cambridge, MA: Harvard University Press, 1990), p. 7.

[11] Bruce Bueno de Mesquita, *Principles of International Politics: People's Power, Preferences, and Perceptions* (Washington, DC: CQ Press, 2003), p. xvi.

[12] Some argue they inevitably are: "...domestic groups, social ideas, the character of constitutions, economic constraints (sometimes expressed through international interdependence), historical social tendencies, and domestic political pressures play in important, indeed, a pivotal, role in the selection of a grand strategy...." Richard Rosecrance and Arthur A. Stein, eds. *The Domestic Bases of Grand Strategy* (Ithaca, NY: Cornell University Press, 1993), p. 5.

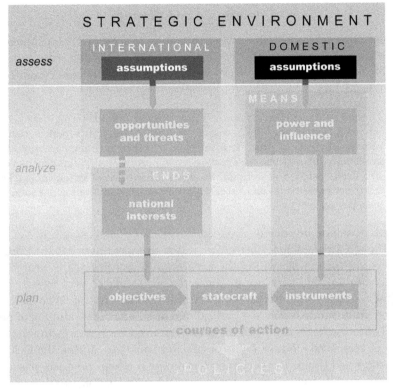

Figure 3.1: The domestic environment.

assumptions (see Figure 3.1). Here strategists should take note of char-acteristics of their own domestic political, social, and cultural setting – including the motivations of the actors inhabiting it – that will bear on the strategy under consideration but are not more specifically related to the categories in the following analysis section.[13] These features will usually include the shape of opinion among leaders and the public; the power and likely impact of parties and influence groups; the composition, structure, and operation of the legislature; and the views and capabilities of the fed-eral bureaucracy and the administration in power. In doing so, strategists should particularly consider how these factors will constrain or facilitate the kind of action they have in mind, both for the present and into the future. This chapter will focus particularly on American public opinion, the strategic culture that underlies it, the political and party structure through which it is expressed, and the domestic circumstances facing American strategists in the early twenty-first century.

---

[13] Common pitfalls in using this part of the model are either to focus on the domestic situation in the target country rather than the strategists' own, or to let the section grow into a long background or history dissertation. Keep it spare, limited only to those features of the home front that the strategist needs to keep in mind as the analysis proceeds.

Americans and Strategy

Most observers agree that, when it comes to foreign affairs, Americans are not natural strategists. To some extent this disability has to do with their form of government, as Alexis de Tocqueville famously pointed out 175 years ago:

> Foreign politics demands scarcely any of those qualities which are peculiar to a democracy; they require, on the contrary, the perfect use of almost all those in which it is deficient.... [A] democracy can only with great difficulty regulate the details of an important undertaking, persevere in a fixed design, and work out its execution in spite of serious obstacles. It cannot combine its measures with secrecy or await their consequences with patience.[14]

And, it might be added, *American* democracy is particularly deficient. Although the presidency has grown much stronger relative to the Congress since de Tocqueville wrote, the separation of powers at the heart of the Constitution still sets up an "invitation to struggle" over foreign policy that contrasts with fusion-of-power systems like that of Great Britain.[15] One unfortunate result is a cyclical and often disruptive shifting of power between the branches, with the perceived need for action giving the president increased clout in times of crisis or war (*e.g.*, during the Cold War or after 9/11) and the Congress reclaiming it when the crisis passes (as in the post-Vietnam era or the post–Cold War 1990s). In addition, U.S. federalism dilutes the centralized power found in strong presidential systems like France's, adding to the difficulty of maintaining strategic direction. In fact, it can be argued that, despite having an elected captain, the United States is not really a ship of state at all, for the crew is in command and each of its members reserves the right to decide where to sail every day.[16] Scholars often contend that most citizens do not possess the degree of knowledge and sophistication, nor democratic systems the flexibility, essential to the complex and ever-changing realm of foreign affairs. Foreign policy practitioners find the public unwilling, especially on national security issues, to accept either the compromises that are usually essential to successful negotiations or the cost and risk associated with forcing one's own way; they want victory without cost, a free lunch.[17]

[14] Alexis de Tocqueville, *Democracy in America*, Henry Reeve text as revised by Francis Bowen, now further corrected and edited with introduction, editorial notes, and bibliographies by Phillips Bradley (New York: Vintage Books, 1958), p. I, 243.

[15] "The Constitution ... is an invitation to struggle for the privilege of directing American foreign policy." Edwin S. Corwin, *The President: Office and Powers, 1787–1984* (New York: New York University Press, 1984).

[16] Edward N. Luttwak, Center for Strategic and International Studies, NWC lecture, August 6, 1987. Used by permission.

[17] Robert Gallucci, NWC Lecture, August 10, 2002. Used by permission.

George Kennan's image of the United States as an enormous dinosaur, normally oblivious to the outside world but likely to destroy everything in its vicinity when provoked, vividly sums up such skepticism about America's strategic temperament.[18]

But public opinion in the United States about foreign affairs is shaped by more than its form of government. Also under girding opinion on current policy is a set of foundational beliefs that predispose Americans to react in characteristic ways to overseas events and challenges. Some are held in common by most Americans and serve to unite them; others are held by different groups in society and can divide the country. Taken together, they can be considered the U.S. strategic culture.

To begin with, Americans are roughly twice as nationalistic as people in most other Western democracies, with over 90 percent glad to be Americans and over 70 percent very proud of their nationality.[19] American nationalism is also different than other countries' because it is based on political values rather than cultural or ethnic superiority. Since anyone can become an American, Americans generally believe that their values are universally applicable – and welcomed – outside their country.[20] American nationalism is also forward looking and triumphant rather than backward looking and aggrieved; where other countries remember defeats that must be redressed, Americans minimize past setbacks and are naturally optimistic about the future. Traditionally spared the destruction of war on their own soil, inhabiting a continent endowed with great natural resources, and enjoying considerable social and economic mobility, Americans expect to solve problems abroad as well as at home and are impatient with those who argue that some can only be managed.[21] Having

[18] "I sometimes wonder whether in this respect a democracy is not uncomfortably similar to one of those prehistoric monsters with a body as long as this room and a brain the size of a pin: he lies there in his comfortable primeval mud and pays little attention to his environment; he is slow to wrath – in fact, you practically have to whack his tail off to make him aware that his interests are being disturbed; but, once he grasps this, he lays about him with such blind determination that he not only destroys his adversary but largely wrecks his native habitat." George F. Kennan, *American Diplomacy, 1900–1950* (New York: Mentor, 1952), p. 66.

[19] Comments on American nationality in this paragraph come from Minxin Pei, "The Paradoxes of American Nationalism," *Foreign Policy* 136 (May/June 2003): 30–37. The comparable figures from other, similar counties range from the mid-30s to the mid-50s, with only Ireland, Poland, and India approaching U.S. levels. Ironically, Americans are so nationalistic because "promoting nationalism is a private enterprise" in the United States rather than state sponsored: "most of the institutions and practices that promote and sustain American nationalism are civic, not political; the rituals are voluntary rather than imposed; and the values inculcated are willingly embraced, not artificially indoctrinated." Pei, "Paradoxes of American Nationalism," p. 33.

[20] See the value projection component of the national interest in Chapter 4.

[21] "Americans tend to seek finality in international affairs. They want problems solved, threats eliminated." Robert Kagan, "Power and Weakness," *Policy Review* 113 (June & July 2002): 3–4.

established their nationhood by an act of willful separation from the old world, they see their nation as exceptional: separate, different, superior, exempt from the usual laws of rise and decline, and destined to lead world progress.[22] In the view of many critics, this unique nationalism and exceptionalism imparts a moralistic cast to American statecraft that engenders oscillation between "overinvolvement and isolationism "– repeated swings between crusades to save the world and withdrawal as too good for the world – while opening the country to charges of hypocrisy when it acts from obvious self-interest rather than its proclaimed moral standards.[23] American nationalism, exceptionalism, and moralism can also blind the country's decision makers to the very different nationalism, culture, and moral standards of other countries.

Former Secretary of Labor Robert Reich identifies four cultural parables or myths that further inform Americans' views in the public arena, both at home and abroad.[24] First is "the mob at the gates," the idea that the United States is a beacon of virtue in a world of tyranny and barbarism, a proper model for others but also at risk, because of its openness and naiveté, of having its fragile liberties swamped by forces of evil. The second is of "the triumphant individual," self-reliant and self-made, hard working, risk taking, and with the right stuff to succeed against the odds. Third and somewhat in conflict with this parable is that of "the benevolent community," a story of generosity and compassion, of "self-sacrifice, community pride, and patriotism." Finally, there is "the rot at the top," the idea that powerful elites in society, business, or government are decadent, corrupt, and conspiring against the public interest.

When juxtaposed against real-world events, these myths can help explain the country's debates and actions in foreign policy. Is the Third World, for example, part of the benevolent community or the mob at the gates? Are international organizations like the UN and the International Criminal Court rotten at the top, while at the same time somehow capable of imperiling a fragile American sovereignty? Does the United States have to go after terrorists overseas because its fragility and openness prevent successful defense at home? Must the country prevail in an individualistic, unilateralist way or does it need to draw on a benevolent international community to defeat its enemies? The answers Americans give to these and many other questions can depend on what role they assign themselves and various foreign actors in such national myths.

If these elements of strategic culture apply to all or most Americans, other belief systems may be held by some groups in society but not by

---

[22] Trevor B. McCrisken, "Exceptionalism," in Alexander DeConde, ed., *Encyclopedia of American Foreign Policy*, Vol. 2 (New York: Scribner's, 2001), pp. 63–80.

[23] Kissinger, *White House Years*, p. 65.

[24] Robert B. Reich, *Tales of a New America* (New York: Random House, 1987), pp. 8–13.

	REALIST	IDEALIST
Human nature	Fixed, aggressive, power-seeking	Flawed but perfectable
International system	Inevitable anarchy and conflict	Reformable
Focus on	What is	What could be
Key factor	Power, expediency	Morality, principle
Statesmen must	Do what works	Do what's right
Policy set by	External pressures	Internal political processes
International agencies	Tools of sovereign states	Can constrain or reform states
Key objective(s)	Balance or preponderance of power	Globalization, democratization, or institutionalization
History	Cyclical	Progressive

Figure 3.2: Characteristics of realism and idealism.

others. Perhaps chief among these is the division between realism and idealism, a feature of American foreign policy that runs from the debates between Jefferson and Hamilton in the 1790s to arguments between neo-conservatives and realists today (see Figure 3.2).[25] In a nutshell, realists believe that neither human nature nor the international system can be fundamentally changed, and that therefore strategists must focus on the real world as it is, not as they might like it to be. The reality of human nature, as

[25] For an outstanding summary of American realism and idealism, see Paul Seabury, "Realism and Idealism," in Alexander DeConde, ed., *Encyclopedia of American Foreign Policy*, Vol. 3 (New York: Charles Scribner's Sons, 1978), pp. 856–866. The modern debate began after World War II, when so-called "realists" like George Kennan attacked a "legalistic-moralistic approach to international problems" as the "most serious fault" in past American policy making. Kennan deprecated the fact that, "instead of taking the awkward conflicts of national interest and dealing with them on their merits," many Americans thought that "it should be possible to suppress the chaotic and dangerous aspirations of governments ... by the acceptance of some system of legal rules and restraints." George F. Kennan, *American Diplomacy, 1900–1950* (New York: Mentor Books, 1951), pp. 93–94. "Idealists" like Frank Tannenbaum counterattacked Kennan and other realists for trying to "persuade our people to abandon their humanitarian and pacific traditions and frankly adopt the doctrine of power politics and of the balance of power as the basis of their foreign policy," a doctrine he believed would "throw all morality and law out of the window" and "convert the United States into a centralized military empire" living from war to war. Frank Tannenbaum, *The American Tradition in Foreign Policy* (Norman, OK: University of Oklahoma Press, 1955), pp. xi-xiii.

realists see it, is aggression and power seeking; in the international system, it is anarchy and conflict between states. Regardless of the internal form of government a state might have, realists believe that these external realities of power dictate its statecraft. So however much statesmen might want to do what is *right*, they must instead do what *works*, eschewing morality for the pursuit of power (and the augmentation of power through alliances) if they wish to survive. Realists differ on whether statesmen aim at a preponderance or a balance of power, and on whether they pursue offensive or defensive strategies.[26] But history for them is cyclical, and grand schemes of global reform are but wishful and dangerous illusions.[27]

Idealists, on the other hand, believe that man is perfectible and the international system improvable, that conflict and war are not unavoidable but the result of statesmen's mistaken ideas and choices. Strategists should therefore focus less on power than on purpose, less on how the world is than on how it can be changed for the better.[28] Some idealists think that such fundamental change will result from growing economic interdependence, globalization, and the information revolution; others believe that states' lust for power (if not their sovereignty) can be curbed by stronger international laws and institutions; still others argue that internal factors are at the root of war and that the key to peace therefore lies in replacing war-prone dictatorships with peace-loving democratic forms of government.[29] But whatever the precise path forward, idealists believe in progress, rejecting the realist view that history is not merely "one damn thing after another" but often "the same damn thing over and over."[30]

It is likely, of course, that we are all idealists when we can be but realists when we have to be.[31] Still, many observers contend that Americans' optimism naturally leads them to idealism, and that it is only after their crusades to reform the world get them in trouble that they fall back on

---

[26] Stephen M. Walt, "International Relations: One World, Many Theories," *Foreign Policy* 110 (Spring 1998): 37.

[27] David Jablonsky, "Time's Arrow, Time's Cycle: Metaphors for a Period of Transition," *Parameters* (Winter 1997–98): 4–27.

[28] Idealism also includes a belief that, since doing foreign policy means applying principles, anyone can be a diplomat and public opinion can be trusted, while realists tend to fear popular passions and consider that the specialized knowledge foreign policy requires makes it properly an elitist vocation. In addition, idealists tend to favor cooperative solutions to world problems (including collective security as a solution to the problem of war) even where severe conflicts of interest are involved, whereas realists often stress defending national interests even at the expense of international agreements (see for example the differences over arms control with the Soviets in the late 1970s and early 1980s).

[29] Walt, "International Relations: One World, Many Theories," pp. 39–40.

[30] Benjamin Schwarz and Christopher Layne, "A New Grand Strategy," *Atlantic Monthly* (January 2002).

[31] The comment was by LTC Robert J. Vaughan, Army National Guard, NWC '92, in a seminar during August 1991.

realism to clean up the mess.[32] In this view, realism is a European import that is attractive on this side of the Atlantic only to some members of the policy elite.[33] As former Secretary of State Madeleine Albright put it,

> The debate between realism and idealism in foreign affairs moves back and forth like a pendulum because neither extreme is sustainable. A successful foreign policy must begin with the world as it is but also work for what we would like it to be. On a globe this complicated, even the purest of principles must sometimes be diluted. Still, we get up in the morning because of hope.... If all America stands for is stability, no one will follow us for the simple reason that we aren't going anywhere.[34]

While these two tendencies do begin to explain the divisions in American opinion over foreign policy, their application in the American experience requires a somewhat more detailed explanation. Walter Russell Mead has identified four deeply rooted, broad approaches to foreign policy that help to show how realism and idealism combine in Americans' policy preferences.[35] Named after the leaders who most vividly personified them, they are the Jeffersonian, Wilsonian, Hamiltonian, and Jacksonian traditions.

The Jeffersonian tradition combines a kind of minimal realism with elements of isolationism. Its adherents consider American liberty fragile, and while they are worried about the mob at the gates, they also fear that the real enemy will be us. Their primary goal in foreign policy is to preserve democracy at home against external forces that might disrupt or destroy it, and democracy in their view demands a weak and decentralized government along with controls on concentrations of economic power. In addition to foreign threats, Jeffersonians worry lest over-ambitious foreign policy goals imperil democracy *internally*. They therefore insist that foreign affairs be conducted in strict fealty to the Constitution and at the lowest possible cost and risk. Interests should be defined narrowly and means kept limited; the United States should "speak softly, and carry the smallest possible stick."[36] Americans should concentrate on being an exemplar of democracy at home, eschewing crusades for both security and human rights. Above all, Jeffersonians want to avoid war, which threatens liberty through a large military, a dangerously strong and secretive Executive

---

[32] For example, see Gideon Rose, "Get Real," *New York Times* (August 18, 2005): A25.

[33] This view is a theme of Henry Kissinger's *Diplomacy* (New York: Simon & Shuster Ltd., 1994), esp. Chapter 2, 18, 29 and 31, and is fully explained in Walter Russell Mead, *Special Providence: American Foreign Policy and How It Changed the World* (New York: Alfred A. Knopf, 2001).

[34] Madeleine K. Albright, "A Realistic Idealism," *Washington Post* (May 8, 2006): A19.

[35] Mead, *Special Providence*, pp. 86–87.

[36] Mead, *Special Providence*, p. 192.

branch, high costs, and crushing national debt.[37] After 9/11 Jeffersonians could have been expected to support strong defenses against terrorism, but they would have opposed the Iraq war and especially feared the USA Patriot Act and the Bush administration's surveillance of telephone conversations, banking records, and its citizens' travel.

Crusades, however, are just what Wilsonians want. They are idealists and exceptionalists who want to expand the benevolent community to include the whole world. In particular, Wilsonians believe that the United States should export its democratic values to other nations because democracies are more stable, peaceful, and prosperous, likely to be partners in solving the world's problems rather than adversaries. Spreading democracy is therefore a practical imperative, but it is also a moral duty: American power, in their view, should be used not selfishly but to promote universal good. Similarly, since technology has both intensified the destructiveness of modern wars and, along with the expansion of American interests, made it impossible for the United States to stay out of them, the country should lead the way in developing international laws and organizations to prevent war and control its ferocity. Wilsonians thus believe that conflict is not an unavoidable feature of the state system, that reform is possible as well as necessary. Indeed, they think that institutionalized cooperation with other countries is essential to solving the world's most serious problems.[38] One can surmise that Wilsonians would support American efforts to spread democracy, but they would excoriate George W. Bush's recourse to war in Iraq and his administration's principled opposition to the UN, the International Criminal Court, the Kyoto treaty on climate change, and other projects of world governance.

Hamiltonians, for their part, can be seen as commercial idealists but with an intellectual approach and an instinct for power that resembles realism.[39] Hamiltonians are realists in that they believe that American statecraft must be based on power and interest. But Hamiltonian power is more economic than military, and they see the free export of American goods and services as essential to that power. Therefore, Hamiltonians' primary interests are freedom of the seas and skies, an open door abroad for U.S. commerce, access to strategic materials overseas, and an integrated world financial system to support trade and investment. Hamiltonians want the United States to have a military adequate to support these interests, and they favor security alliances with other nations as needed to project American power and defend American trade.

---

[37] Mead, *Special Providence*, Chapter 6: "'Vindicator Only of Her Own,'" pp. 174–217.

[38] Mead, *Special Providence*, Chapter 5: "The Connecticut Yankee in the Court of King Arthur," pp. 162–166.

[39] Mead, *Special Providence*, Chapter 4: "The Serpent and the Dove," pp. 99–131.

But they also believe that U.S. interests need not be secured in conflict with other nations, because trade substitutes "the win-win strategy of commerce for the zero-sum game of war."[40] Indeed, free trade is a force for peace, and giving trade its proper place in American foreign policy should enable American diplomats to engage other countries on the basis of compromise and mutual advantage and to champion the international treaties and institutions necessary to support it. Thus, Hamiltonians marry the idealism of the Wilsonian stress on world order with realism's cold-eyed determination to secure American hegemony, defining both in economic terms. As enthusiasts for globalization, today's Hamiltonians would support the spread of market economic systems worldwide as well as measures to strengthen and maintain American dominance of international financial institutions like the IMF, World Bank, and WTO – along with efforts to put America's own economic house in order.

Finally, there is the Jacksonian school: partly realist, somewhat isolationist, thoroughly populist, and incorporating all of Reich's American myths in one way or another. Jacksonians are realist in their view that international politics is inevitably characterized by anarchy, conflict, and war, and that military power is the power that counts. Their quasi-isolationism begins with the view that the benevolent community is the family, extended to like-minded Americans and even the entire nation when it is threatened; but for them the whole rest of the world is the mob at the gates. Wilsonian crusades to reform world politics or Hamiltonian schemes to coordinate the global economy are therefore at best naïve, at worst dangerous. Indeed, the very idea of world government is an abomination, a threat to American sovereignty; Jackonians do not trust even their own government, seeing political and economic elites as inefficient, corrupt, and perverse – rotten to the core. Instead, they believe in the self-made man, the triumphant individual, with personal courage and honor his highest virtues. Similarly, Jacksonians consider commitment and credibility the United States' most vital interests. Although they normally do not pay much attention to international affairs, clear threats engage Jacksonians' martial patriotism and their insistence that every able-bodied man be ready to fight for his country. On these occasions they want the United States to use maximum force, to limit American casualties even if foreign civilians must die in greater numbers as a result, and to demand unconditional surrender, following the laws of war only if the enemy also plays by the rules.[41] Presumably, this group of Americans would not be surprised to find that the Bush administration had deceitfully tricked Americans into attacking Iraq, but they would also demand that the United States finish the job and

[40] Mead, *Special Providence*, p. 103. See Chapter 5 for an elaboration of the differences between political and economic power.
[41] Mead, *Special Providence*, Chapter 7: "Tiger, Tiger, Burning Bright," pp. 218–263.

pursue terrorists using whatever means are necessary, including illegal detention, no-holds-barred interrogation, covert action, and even nuclear weapons.[42]

Splits and Shifts in Public Opinion

Although far from complete, the above discussion of the United States strategic culture reveals some of the foundational elements upon which American public opinion is formed. Strategists who understand them should be better able to gauge how the public and Congress will react to ongoing events, as well as to their own strategic designs. But if public support is vital to the success of foreign affairs strategy, obvious questions remain as to whether and how strategists can best garner it. Must they simply estimate what kinds of policies the public will support and then conform to the popular will, or is public opinion malleable enough that they can lead rather than follow?[43] And if public opinion *can* be led, is its very changeability likely to become a liability over the long run, with people capable of turning against a strategy as easily as they were convinced to support it? Unfortunately, both the degree of stability of the popular will, and the nature of the constraints it imposes (or possibilities it offers) to foreign affairs strategy, are questions without easy answers.

Obtaining and maintaining adequate public support does seem to have become a much more difficult task for American strategists during the last several decades than it was during the first years after World War II. Before the late 1960s, a stable consensus existed within the United States in support of containment and anti-communism. There was, to be sure, vigorous debate during the massive policy shifts of the late 1940s, when the United States reluctantly abandoned its wartime alliance with the Soviet Union (along with its dreams of one world under the United Nations) and began the rebuilding of just-defeated Germany and Japan within an unprecedented network of anti-Soviet alliances. But by 1950 some 80 percent of the American people had concluded that containing the spread of communism worldwide was very important to the United States, and even more remarkably, an equal percentage were willing to go to war with the Soviet Union in the event of communist attacks on countries as distant as Germany or the Philippines.[44] More fundamentally, people

---

[42] Mead, "Braced for Jacksonian Ruthlessness," *Washington Post* (September 17, 2001): A27.

[43] Note that this is a parallel question to the one asked in Chapter 2 about the international context: Is the strategist relatively free to shape events, or are the pressures of the system controlling?

[44] Eugene R. Wittkopf, "Was There Ever a Foreign Policy Consensus in American Popular Opinion?" Chapter 6 in *Faces of Internationalism: Public Opinion and American Foreign Policy* (Durham, NC: Duke University Press, 1990), pp. 166–193.

tended to trust their government and to believe what it was saying to them about foreign policy, and at least 70 percent of them thought the U.S. should take an active role in world affairs.[45]

By the early 1970s, however, the trauma of the Vietnam war had broken or at least badly eroded this consensus. Trust in government fell from nearly 80 percent in the early 1960s to about 25 percent by the end of the 1970s, and relative unity gave way to three distinct belief systems, reflecting on the one hand a split of internationalists into two camps and on the other a marked strengthening of quasi-isolationist sentiment.[46] The first group, often labeled *Cold War* or *conservative internationalists*, tended to see the world in East-West terms and feared that the balance of power was dangerously, even irrevocably tilting against the West. Of realist mindset, members of this school viewed international relations as a zero-sum game based on raw power and the Soviet Union as a revolutionary, expansionist state whose threat to the United States could only be met by superior military counterforce. The second group, called by scholars *post–Cold War* or *liberal internationalists*, considered military balances and realpolitik viewpoints largely irrelevant and focused much more on North-South relations. Though still a threat, the Soviet Union was seen as an ordinary great power with whom the United States had some interests in common (like arms control), a country that could be dealt with through ordinary diplomatic means. Much more important than Soviet machinations were the Third World's problems of poverty and underdevelopment, as well as new global issues crying out for urgent attention.[47]

In retrospect, it seems possible that these two groups had really existed throughout the post-World War II era, forming distinct "security" and "equity" cultures within the broader consensus of containment. If so, the apparent Cold War consensus about American foreign policy in those years may actually have been a working *dissensus* between them, sustainable because of respect for the presidency and trust in government

[45] Ole R. Holsti, "Public Opinion and Containment," Chapter 2 in Terry L. Deibel and John Lewis Gaddis, *Containing the Soviet Union* (Washington, DC: Pergamon-Brassey's, 1987), p. 24; John E. Reilly, ed, *American Public Opinion and U.S. Foreign Policy 1991* (Chicago, IL: Chicago Council on Foreign Relations, 1991), p. 12.

[46] By the mid-1980s trust in government had recovered somewhat (to mid-40%), only to fall to nearly 20% in 1994. It recovered to almost 60% after 9/11, but fell again later that decade. See American National Election Studies, University of Michigan, at www.umich.edu/nes.

[47] The portraits of Cold War and post–Cold War internationalism here and that of semi-isolationism below, as well as those three terms, are drawn from Ole R. Holsti and James N. Rosenau, "The Three-Headed Eagle: Three Perspectives on Foreign Affairs," Chapter 4 in Holsti and Rosenau, eds., *American Leadership in World Affairs* (Boston, MA: Allen & Unwin, 1984), pp. 108–139. The reader will note the rough correspondence of these two internationalist schools with the views of the Reagan and Carter administrations presented at the beginning of Chapter 2.

and because the country was wealthy enough to avoid having to choose between being a global policeman or global philanthropist.[48] But whatever it was that dissolved under the pressure of budgetary stringencies and containment's failures, the increasing acrimony and divisiveness that characterized foreign policy debates among internationalists in the post-Vietnam era was exacerbated by the strengthening of a third group, variously called *semi-isolationists* or *noninternationalists*. Those following foreign affairs in this group believed that the Soviet Union lacked the intention and the Third World the capability to harm the United States; the only dangers they saw from the East lay in miscalculation and accidental war, from the South in entanglement. A partly Jeffersonian group, the semi-isolationists saw an activist foreign policy, particularly its military and covert aspects, as not only unnecessary and futile but also incompatible with a progressive, democratic system at home. The United States was faced with daunting domestic problems which demanded urgent attention, they argued; the country could best help the world by drastically slowing the arms race, cutting its own military forces to the minimum needed for continental defense, terminating its overseas alliances, and getting its own house in order so as to set a better example for other countries.[49]

This fragmentation of opinion after Vietnam might well persuade the strategist that public opinion is in fact quite unstable, even fickle. And in fact there is a good deal of evidence that would seem to support that view. First, virtually all opinion analysts agree that most Americans are poorly informed on foreign policy issues. For example, in 1964, 42 percent of the public did not know the U.S. was a member of NATO; in 1979 only a third could correctly identify the two countries involved in the headline-generating Strategic Arms Limitation Talks (SALT) negotiations; and throughout the 1980s only small minorities could keep good guys and bad guys straight among Sandinistas, *contras*, rebels, and other warring parties in Nicaragua and El Salvador.[50] Even after a conflict as widely reported on as the 2003 Iraq war, some 60 percent of Americans believed at least one of the following incorrect propositions: that the United States had found WMD in Iraq, that there was evidence of Saddam Hussein's links to Al Qaeda, or that most of the world's people had supported the war.[51] Second, as one might expect from these examples of ignorance, few among the general public are paying attention to foreign policy matters most of

---

[48] Thomas L. Hughes, "The Crack-Up," *Foreign Policy* 40 (Fall 1980): 33–60, esp. p. 53.

[49] Twenty-first century intellectuals in this group include Christopher Layne, "Offshore Balancing Revisited," *The Washington Quarterly* 25 (Spring 2002): 233–248, and Eugene Gholz, Daryl G. Press, and Harvey M. Sapolsky, "Come Home, America: The Strategy of Restraint in the Face of Temptation," *International Security* 22 (Spring 1997): 5–48.

[50] Russett, *Controlling the Sword*, p. 89; see also Wittkopf, *Faces of Internationalism*, p. 15.

[51] Steven Kull, Clay Ramsay, and Evan Lewis, "Misperceptions, the Media, and the Iraq War," *Political Science Quarterly* 118 (#4, 2003–2004): 575.

the time. Even after 9/11 only 26 percent of Americans polled were following foreign news "very closely," while 45 percent claimed to be unaffected
by international events.[52] The so-called "attentive public" is ordinarily put
by the experts at only 5 percent to 25 percent of the population, depending on the issue.[53] The conclusion to be drawn might well be that on most
issues, most of the time, strategists need not worry what the public thinks,
because it thinks very little.

   Given the public's inattention and ignorance, it is not surprising to find
that popular views about foreign affairs issues can change radically. For
example, in 1965 nearly 80 percent of Americans felt the United States
should play an active role in world affairs and just 16 percent that it should
stay out, whereas by 1982 the activists had dropped to nearly 50 percent
and the "stay outs" more than doubled to 35 percent.[54] Similarly, after
9/11 only 20 percent to 30 percent thought the United States could stay
out of world affairs, but by 2005 the Iraq war had convinced some 42 percent that the country should "mind is own business internationally."[55] An
even more striking example of volatility is the massive reversal in preferences on defense spending that took place in just two years from 1980 to
1982, when those in favor of increases dropped two-thirds from 60 percent to 21 percent while those backing cuts doubled from 12 percent to
24 percent.[56]

   Public opinion analyst William Schneider explains this kind of instability as a product of the interaction between the three post-Vietnam schools
of thought sketched earlier.[57] His model of public opinion argues that the
inattentive public – people who know or care little about foreign affairs and
who are often poor and poorly-educated – is not ideologically isolationist
but simply noninternationalist, that is, suspicious and distrustful of government in general and predisposed against U.S. involvement with other
countries in particular. If internationalism is the credo of the establishment, in other words, latent isolationism based on disinterest is a populist
sentiment.[58] Whereas internationalists take positions on one side or the
other of issues like cooperation or confrontation with other countries, these
noninternationalists are more responsive to matters like prosperity or corruption – so-called valence issues where everybody is on the same side but

[52] Poll done by Pew Center for the People and the Press in early 2002, quoted in
   Pei, "Paradoxes of American Nationalism," p. 37.
[53] Yankelovich, *Coming to Public Judgment*, p. 19. Ole Holsti puts opinion leaders
   at 5% of the population, the attentive public at 15–20%, and the mass public at
   75–80%. NWC Lecture, August 11, 1987. Used by permission.
[54] Holsti, "Public Opinion and Containment," p. 24.
[55] "Stop the world, we want to get off," *Economist* (November 19, 2005): 29.
[56] Reilly, *American Public Opinion and U.S. Foreign Policy 1991*, p. 32.
[57] William Schneider, "Conservatism, Not Interventionism: Trends in Foreign Policy
   Opinion, 1974–1982," in Kenneth A. Oye, Robert J. Lieber, and Donald Rothchild,
   eds., *Eagle Defiant: United States Foreign Policy in the 1980s* (Boston, MA: Little,
   Brown, 1983), pp. 39–43.
[58] Schneider, NWC lecture, August 27, 1990. Used by permission.

people differ as to how serious a problem has become or how important a desired quality is.

To internationalists, peace and strength are *positional* issues, with liberals backing peace and conservatives strength; but to noninternationalists they are *valence* issues, preferred according to which seems to be in short supply. When noninternationalists fear war, their desire for peace pushes them into alliance with liberal internationalists (who always favor cooperative approaches); when on the other hand noninternationalists see the United States being pushed around (as during the Iranian hostage crisis of 1980) or are disturbed by events that seem to threaten important American interests (like the 9/11 terrorist attacks), they join the conservative internationalists' fixed position in support of military strength or even armed intervention. In Schneider's view, volatility in public opinion is due to the fact that the noninternationalist group "swings left and right unpredictably in response to its current fears and concerns."[59]

> Peace and strength are the valence issues of surpassing concern to noninternationalists. As the relative salience of these two issues changes, so does the coalition pattern and the dominant ideological complexion of foreign policy opinion.[60]

What happens, of course, is not only that noninternationalists change their minds but that they become actively concerned with foreign affairs. In fact, whereas on most foreign policy issues policymakers can ignore the public's views much of the time, on some issues at some times the inattentive public becomes active enough that leaders need to pay attention. According to pollster Daniel Yankelovich, three factors are involved in determining how important public opinion will be on any given issue: "the size of the public majority in favor of or opposed to a particular policy, the intensity and urgency of its opinions, and whether it believes that the government is responsible for addressing them. Public opinion reaches the tipping point when a significant majority of the population feels strongly that the government can and should do something about a given issue."[61]

[59] Schneider, "Conservatism, Not Interventionism," p. 42.
[60] "Noninternationalists ally themselves with the left on questions of intervention because they see no point to American involvement in most of the world. They are against foreign aid, against troop involvement, against anything that smacks of foreign entanglement." But they also like "strength and toughness in foreign affairs because that increases our independence and makes us less likely to become involved in the business of other countries....The basic impulse is defensive;" they want to be strong not to intervene but to better stay out. "Thus, noninternationalists support the conservative elite on many issues having to do with defense and toughness. They support the liberal elite when it becomes a question of direct American involvement" that liberals oppose. Schneider, "Conservatism, Not Interventionism," p. 43.
[61] Daniel Yankelovich, "Poll Positions: What Americans Really Think About U.S. Foreign Policy," *Foreign Affairs* 84 (September/October 2005): 12–13.

Wars with high casualty rates are obviously such issues, as the Vietnam and Iraq wars proved.

Although recent research indicates that swings in public opinion are usually quite rational reactions to domestic or international events, they can obviously make life very difficult for presidents who happen to be in power when they take place. And dramatic changes in public opinion are as likely to occur shortly after as before presidential elections, so a president chosen during one phase of opinion may well find himself spending most of his time in office in a quite different climate.[62] Jimmy Carter, for example, was elected in the depths of the post-Vietnam trauma, when people were distrustful of all overseas involvement, concerned about the morality of American foreign policy, and out to tame the military and the Central Intelligence Agency (CIA). But by the middle of his presidency Americans were rapidly becoming alarmed over Soviet adventurism, worried about gasoline supplies and prices, ready to increase defense spending, and demanding that the government assertively defend American interests abroad. The result was that Carter was forced to choose between maintaining his initial policies despite fading public support, or changing course dramatically at mid-term and opening himself to charges of inconsistency (in fact, he did some of each). Ronald Reagan, for his part, was elected by the assertive mood that so discomfited Carter, only to find that public opinion had shifted back toward the center within a year or two of his inauguration. The confrontation with the Soviet Union and contempt for arms control which had been hallmarks of the early Reagan foreign policy then had to yield to more moderate approaches.[63]

Stability and Structure in Public Opinion

Much recent research, however, argues that these indications of volatility are only surface manifestations, and that underneath them all public opinion is really quite stable. Yale's Bruce Russett, for example, contends that to blame "volatile public moods and opinion changes" for instability in the foreign policies of democracies is "a serious misrepresentation of the facts: public opinion on major issues of security policy has not been terribly unstable either for individuals or for aggregate levels of opinion."[64] And foreign policy opinion analyst Eugene Wittkopf believes that Americans'

---

[62] For a more complete explanation of this argument, see Terry L. Deibel, *Presidents, Public Opinion, and Power*, Headline Series #280 (New York: Foreign Policy Association, 1987), pp. 10–19.

[63] Remembering Chapter 2, the reader will note that changing public opinion is the second force which pushed the Carter and Reagan administrations toward very different policies than those with which they began; the first was the displacement of ideological assumptions about the international environment by knowledge based on experience.

[64] Russett, *Controlling the Sword*, p. 115.

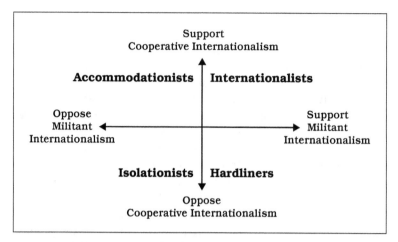

Figure 3.3: Wittkopf's model of public opinion.

attitudes not only are broadly stable over time but that "they exhibit both structure and ideological sophistication," a position hard to square with the widespread ignorance and inattention noted above.[65]

In support of this view, Wittkopf finds that public opinion on foreign policy in the United States is structured around peoples' differing acceptance of one of two kinds of internationalism: cooperative and militant. Whereas the liberal and conservative internationalists discussed above are differentiated by their fears and policy *ends*, these categories are defined principally according to the different *means* they favor. People in both profess a sense of global responsibility and a recognition that the vital interests of the U.S. are wide-ranging, but militant internationalists are far more willing to defend American interests assertively using the harder foreign policy tools (including armed intervention), while cooperative internationalists feel America's active role should be based on working with other countries.

In Wittkopf's scheme (see Figure 3.3), people fall into one of four clusters of belief depending on their position for or against these two "faces of internationalism":

- **internationalists** are *for* both approaches, cooperative and militant. They believe in active U.S. involvement with a mix of conciliatory and coercive strategies, and to some extent can be thought of as representing the pre-Vietnam internationalist consensus, the fusing of the equity and security cultures;
- **isolationists** *oppose* both kinds of internationalism, and with it any sort of active U.S. role overseas;
- **accommodationists** are *for* cooperative but *against* militant internationalism; and
- **hardliners** are *for* militant but *against* cooperative approaches to the world.

[65] Wittkopf, *Faces of Internationalism*, p. 14.

Using survey data compiled every four years by the Chicago Council on Foreign Relations, Wittkopf finds a remarkably steady one-quarter of the population in each of these groups going back to 1974. Three-fourths of the public thus appears resolutely internationalist.[66] However, two-thirds of these people are "split between the accommodationist and hardliner quadrants, which reflect[s] concern not with *whether* the United States should be involved abroad, but with *how* that involvement should be pursued."[67] For all Wittkopf's emphasis on stability, that division over the form of U.S. involvement in the world would seem to support Schneider's view of a non-internationalist swing group which could block foreign affairs strategies when energized, either by lining up with accommodationists against military interventions, or by joining with hardliners to oppose expensive or entangling cooperative actions.[68] One may surmise that 9/11 activated the inattentive public like few events in American history, pushing non-internationalists into alliance with hardliners in support of the wars in Afghanistan and Iraq; later, as casualties mounted in the latter conflict, it was their growing preference for peace over abundant and obvious strength that contributed to falling support for the war.

Other analysts have argued that to really understand the structure of public opinion one must separate two dimensions that are combined in Whittkopf's militant-cooperative scheme, that whether people approve of using military force must be differentiated from whether they think the United States should engage independently or cooperatively with other nations.[69] Doing so reveals (see Figure 3.4) that all isolationists are not the same, because some favor using force while others do not. It also shows that some unilateralists do *not* favor the use of military force, and

[66] Wittkopf finds interesting sociodemographic correlates to these four belief systems, arguing that Republicans and domestic conservatives are hardliners, Democrats are accommodationists or internationalists, low-income blue collar workers are isolationists or hardliners, and so forth. "Accommodationists are typically liberals and perhaps moderates with college educations who reside in the East. Hardliners, on the other hand, are conservatives who tend to have less than a college education, who, at least in the 1980s, are Republicans who tend to live in the Midwest or West. Finally, internationalists tend to be moderates, they may be Democrats and may be college-educated, but at least in the 1970s were better characterized as high school educated from various regions of the country other than the East." *Faces of Internationalism*, p. 49.

[67] Wittkopf, *Faces of Internationalism*, p. 27.

[68] Bruce Russett makes the point that, since the range of important issues strikes these four groups differently, it is impossible for a president to construct a single coalition to support his foreign affairs strategy. "If preferences are distributed over more than one dimension there can be *no stable majority coalition even if individual preferences remain fairly stable over time*. Rather, there will be shifting (technically, cyclical) majorities with different winning coalitions . . . ." *Controlling the Sword*, pp. 115–116. Italics in original.

[69] Ronald H. Hinckley, "Measuring National Security Attitudes," Chapter 3 in *People, Polls, and Policymakers* (New York: Lexington Books/Macmillan, 1992), pp. 17–28. See also William O. Chittick, Keith R. Billingsley, and Rick Travis, "A Three-Dimensional Model of American Foreign Policy Beliefs," *International Studies Quarterly* 39 (September 1995): 313–331.

International Involvement / Type of Involvement		Favor		Oppose
		Independent	Cooperative	None
		Unilateralist	**Multilateralist**	*Isolationist*
Use of Military Force Abroad	Y E S	*Hardliner*	*Internationalist*	Forceful
	N O	Soft	*Accomodationist*	**Restrained**

Figure 3.4: Revealing the unilateralist-multilateralist dimension.

so are hardly hardliners. These categories offer a more finely-grained look at opinion, but the numbers of people in each correspond roughly to Wittkopf's. About three-quarters of Americans favor and one-quarter oppose international involvement, and of those who favor it about a third are unilateralists and two-thirds multilateralists. In the unilateralist camp there are about twice as many hardliners as soft or antimilitary unilateralists; among multilateralists there are somewhat more internationalists than accommodationists; and isolationists are about evenly split between pro- and anti-military.[70]

These structural maps of public opinion obviously raise as many questions as they answer. How, for example, can one reconcile the stability and sophisticated belief systems that structure implies with the apparent volatility of opinion and widespread ignorance about foreign affairs? Indeed, how can people radically shift their opinions with the wording of questions while at the same time remaining definite and vociferous about what they will or will not allow a president to do in foreign policy? Yankelovich has suggested that the key to these paradoxes lies in the *quality* of public opinion on the issue at hand, which in turn depends on whether or not people have had the time, opportunity, and need to think through the matter, resolve their own conflicts and ambivalences about it, and come to what he calls "public judgment."

It is wrong, Yankelovich argues, to denigrate the validity of public opinion because it is uninformed or to attribute its volatility to ignorance. For although *expert* opinion is based on validated knowledge and should be as free as possible from human biases, *public* opinion is quite properly based on value judgments in which personal preferences are the major focus.[71] Therefore, the fact that the public lacks the detailed knowledge of

[70] Hinckley, "Measuring National Security Attitudes," p. 23.
[71] See Yankelovich, "Knowledge vs. Opinion," Chapter 4 in *Coming to Public Judgment.*

experts on a given subject may be of little consequence to the quality of opinion. More important is that people have the time to absorb an issue's significance, work through the conflicts among differing values (or between values and behavior) that it raises, and arrive at a set of views that are comprehensive, reasonably integrated, and responsible (in the sense that their logical consequences are understood and accepted).[72]

The faults of public opinion noted above may therefore be signs of mass opinion that has not yet arrived at public judgment. Mass opinion does tend to be shapeless and apathetic. It is also incoherent, with people thinking in a compartmentalized way about issues that are intrinsically related. And it is often volatile and mushy, in the sense that a change in the way a question is phrased or the pointing out of costs and risks will have dramatic effects on a respondent's reaction. Public judgment, by contrast, is steady, solid, and internally consistent.[73] Although the process of getting to public judgment may take years or even decades for some issues, it is essential to the healthy functioning of democracy.

Like foreign affairs strategy itself, so much of public opinion during the post-Vietnam era was related to the contest with the Soviet Union that one might well have expected radical changes with the end of the Cold War. In particular, many feared that with no threat to engage them, the American people would revert to their default pre–World War II position of isolationism and unilateralism.[74] Surprisingly, however, analysts found more continuity than change during the 1990s, testifying to the stability of public opinion.[75] Americans remained internationalist, with more than 60 percent wanting the United States to play an active role in the world. As during the Cold War, however, most did not want the United States to lead alone; instead, they favored cooperative action and burden sharing with other countries, particularly if military force was to be used.[76] Moreover, people's foreign policy priorities continued to address self-interested goals

[72] Three processes are therefore needed to arrive at public judgment: consciousness raising, working thorough (a psychological process in which individuals resolve conflicts), and final resolution. Yankelovich, *Coming to Public Judgment*, Chapters 5, 6, 10, and 13.

[73] See Yankelovich, "What is Quality in Public Opinion?," Chapter 2 in *Coming to Public Judgment*. Elite (and presumably more expert) opinion, in fact, is likely to be more volatile than this kind of public judgment, precisely because it is informed more by information than values and can therefore change with changing knowledge. Russett, *Controlling the Sword*, p. 117.

[74] See, for example, Arthur Schlesinger, Jr., "Back to the Womb: Isolationism's Renewed Threat," *Foreign Affairs* 74 (July/August 1995): 2–8.

[75] Eugene R. Wittkopf, "Americans' Foreign Policy Beliefs and Behavior at the Water's Edge," *International Studies Notes* 22 (Fall 1997):1–8; Ole R. Holsti, "Public Opinion and Foreign Policy," Chapter 2 in *Eagle Rules?*, Robert J. Lieber, ed. (Upper Saddle River, NJ: Prentice Hall, 2002), pp. 16–46.

[76] Steven Kull and I. M. Destler, "Putting the Puzzle Together," Chapter 12 in *Misreading the Public: The Myth of a New Nationalism* (Washington, DC: Brookings Institution Press, 1999), pp. 249–265.

of personal security, economic prosperity and social welfare.[77] Preventing the spread of nuclear weapons, stopping the flow of illegal drugs, protecting the jobs of American workers, combating international terrorism, and securing adequate supplies of energy were the public's top five foreign policy objectives in 1998, picked in that order as very important by 82 percent to 64 percent. And despite the country's freedom to shift from the negative goal of containment to positive foreign policy objectives, altruistic goals like spreading market democracy or improving poor countries' standards of living remained at the bottom of the list, embraced by no more than 25–35 percent of the public.[78]

What was different in the 1990s, however, was a drop in the overall importance of foreign affairs relative to domestic concerns (as noted in Chapter 1). There was a sharp falling off of interest in foreign news, and when asked to identify the most important problems facing the United States, only 2–3 percent of respondents in 2000 picked a foreign policy problem (as compared to 10–20 percent during the Cold War). If Americans were still internationalist, then, they were "apathetic internationalists" – and since politicians care less about how many people are on each side of an issue than about how intensely they feel about it, the results for the politics of American foreign policy were profound. Because there was little penalty for doing so, politicians were encouraged to neglect or politicize foreign policy; special interests able to offer rewards to them were empowered regardless of public approval of their programs; and presidents found it harder to lead in foreign affairs, sometimes even losing congressional votes (like approval of the Comprehensive Test Ban Treaty or the payment of UN dues) on which they had solid public backing.[79] In this atmosphere real spending on international affairs could be cut 40 percent from its mid-1980s peak and popular internationalist policies could be stalled indefinitely in the Congress, but at election time people voted on domestic issues, reelecting those who had demonstrably violated their foreign policy preferences.[80]

Opinion, Parties, and Polarization

It was, of course, predictable that the lack of serious perceived threats after the Soviet Union's collapse would cause the potency of internal influences on foreign policy to rise during the 1990s, accompanied by the reassertion of congressional prerogatives that were set aside during the long crisis of the Cold War. Predictably, too, the ranks of accommodationists or liberal

---

[77] William Schneider, "The New Isolationism," Chapter 2 in Robert J. Lieber, ed., *Eagle Adrift* (New York: Longman, 1997), pp. 27–28.

[78] John E. Reilly, ed., *American Public Opinion and U.S. Foreign Policy 1999* (Chicago, IL: Chicago Council on Foreign Relations, 1999), pp. 16–17.

[79] James M. Lindsay, "The New Apathy," *Foreign Affairs* 79 (September/October 2000): 2–8.

[80] Kull and Destler, "Putting the Puzzle Together," p. 259.

internationalists grew somewhat, as did those of noninternationalists and semi-isolationists. Hamiltonians successfully pushed commercial outreach in the increasingly globalized world of the Clinton years, while idealists on the left championed assertive multilateralism and humanitarian interventions, embracing use of the military instrument they had so often condemned during the Cold War. Meanwhile, Jacksonians and realists became cautious, not finding stakes in 1990s disputes commensurate with the cost and risk of arms. Republicans holding these latter views took over the Congress in 1994 and quickly challenged the Democratic president on his military interventions, multilateral peacekeeping, and cooperative diplomacy. Americans, it appeared, were not getting a return to isolationism, but neither were they experiencing a rebirth of bipartisanship in foreign policy. Instead, political parties that had grown more and more divided over domestic policy now came increasingly to embody foreign policy divisions as well.

This increasing partisanship means that twenty-first century foreign affairs strategists must not only understand something of the structure and content of American public opinion, but also get a sense of how those groups and ideas relate to the Democratic and Republican parties. In the United States, of course, people join parties mainly because of their stands on domestic issues. Many Americans are *liberal* or *conservative* on both economic and social policy, but some are liberal on economic issues yet conservative on social ones (call them *populists*), while others are conservative on economic issues but liberal on social ones (label them *libertarians*).[81] During the 1950s and early 1960s such divisions did not matter much to foreign affairs strategists because the major American political parties were "big-tent" organizations with considerable internal diversity on domestic policy. But in the decades after Vietnam the parties gradually became much more politically homogeneous, ideologically extreme, and geographically sectional – a development with profound effects on the domestic context for foreign affairs strategy.

Here, in a nutshell, is how it happened. The Democratic party had always been connected with the American labor movement, and its embrace of other disadvantaged groups in American society made it liberal on social as well as economic issues. But its liberalism had been diluted since the Civil War by the allegiance of the "solid South," and the loss of this generally conservative region to an increasingly conservative Republican party made the Democrats a party of the ideological left whose strength was concentrated in the urban Northeast, North, and coastal West. The Republican party, for its part, was always the party of business (including international commerce and finance), ensuring a conservative stance on economic issues. But it was only with the rise of evangelical Christianity at its grass roots and the advent of Ronald Reagan's ideological conservatism

[81] Ole R. Holsti, *Public Opinion and American Foreign Policy*, rev. ed. (Ann Arbor, MI: University of Michigan Press, 2004), p. 153.

at the top that the party moved strongly rightward on social issues. Most Midwestern progressives and Northeastern moderates parted company with the Republican party on these issues, making it a party of the right and one predominantly of the rural, no longer "solid" South and mountain West.

As these transformations were working themselves out, surveys of the nation's governmental and private sector leaders revealed increasingly strong correlations between domestic ideology and party identification. By the mid-1990s, for example, 78 percent of Republican leaders identified themselves as conservatives and only 4 percent as liberals; 68 percent of Democrats identified themselves as liberals, only 6 percent as conservatives.[82] "It has taken 40 or 50 years to work itself out," concluded Hans Noel, political scientist at the University of California at Los Angeles, "but the ideological division in America – which is not new – is now lined up with the party division."[83] At the same time, researchers have also found a close correspondence between domestic ideology and opinion on foreign policy. Thus, the dominant pattern in the foreign policy views of leaders in 1996 was

> one of very large differences between [domestic] liberals and conservatives, with populists and libertarians arrayed in the middle. The largest gaps are on such [foreign policy] goals as protecting the environment, international economic cooperation, combating hunger, arms control, strengthening the United Nations, improving the standard of living in developing countries, and human rights – all most highly ranked by the liberals – and military superiority, fighting drug trafficking and illegal immigration, goals given much higher priority by the conservatives.[84]

To put it another way, 68 percent of accommodationists were liberal on domestic issues, and 82 percent of hard-line leaders were conservative.[85] And since domestic ideological divisions also line up with partisan identification – that is, since most Democrats are liberals and most Republicans conservatives – these foreign policy divisions become Democrat–Republican divisions.[86] By 2005, in fact, pollster Yankelovich could write

---

[82] Ole R. Holsti, "Continuity and Change in the Domestic and Foreign Policy Beliefs of American Opinion Leaders," paper prepared for the American Political Science Association Annual Meeting, Washington, D.C., August 1997, p. 24, used by permission; see also Holsti, *Public Opinion and American Foreign Policy*, pp. 193–196.

[83] Quoted in David Von Drehle, "Political Split is Pervasive," *Washington Post* (April 25, 2004): A10.

[84] Holsti, "Continuity and Change," p. 22.

[85] However, the composition of internationalists and isolationists in terms of domestic ideology looked about the same.

[86] This also is a new development in the United States. In the decades immediately following World War II, differences over foreign policy did not align with party divisions; indeed, the parties' foreign policy positions were close enough to each other that independents usually stood to one side of them rather than in between. Ole R. Holsti, "Public Opinion and Foreign Policy," p. 35.

that "Americans are at least as polarized on issues of foreign affairs as they are on domestic politics."[87] Indeed, one comprehensive typology of attitudes and party identification found that support for an assertive foreign policy, including unilateralism and readiness to use force, was the single characteristic across *all* of foreign and domestic policy that best distinguished Republicans from Democrats.[88]

Partisan polarization has pernicious results for foreign affairs strategy. It has certainly increased the tension any president feels between the requirements of leading his party and those of leading the country in foreign affairs. To keep himself in power, a president must choose ends and means that appeal to his party's so-called "base" of activists, always more ideologically extreme than its rank and file. But to succeed in foreign policy he will usually need much broader support, obtainable only by adopting centrist strategies that may appeal to independents and moderates of the other party but will displease his closest supporters. Another result is a certain delegitimization of compromise as an honorable way to deal with policy differences. This problem is acute in the Congress and between it and the Executive, particularly so in the House of Representatives, where partisan gerrymandering has led to some outrageously configured electoral districts that are ideologically homogeneous. These constituencies attract candidates who are true believers and encourage them to appeal to the extremes; such men and women are hardly ready or able to accommodate other viewpoints when they get to Washington.[89] The replacement of moderates with extremists means that even presidents who want to lead the country rather than just their party in foreign affairs have a much harder time doing so with firm support from the legislative branch.

Nor is partisan division over foreign policy the whole of the story. For as the parties became more ideologically distinct, their identities, their *raisons d'etres* inevitably became more important to their members, as well as opposed to each other. Although party missions are usually more about domestic policy than foreign affairs, they also happened to run head-on into the realities of the post–Cold War world, posing acute (though different) dilemmas for each party that split each into two different foreign policy camps.[90] Partisanship thus became overlaid with factionalism.

---

[87] Yankelovich, "Poll Positions," p. 2.

[88] "Foreign affairs assertiveness now almost completely distinguishes Republican-oriented voters from Democratic-oriented voters." *Beyond Red Versus Blue: The 2005 Political Typology* (Washington, DC: Pew Research Center for the People and the Press, May 10, 2005), p. 1–5.

[89] "...party caucuses on both sides of the Capitol have become more cohesive internally and further apart from each other philosophically." David S. Broder, "Don't Bet on Partisan Niceties," *Washington Post* (January 1, 2003): A19. Also Brian Faler, "Redder Reds, Bluer Blues Tilting the Senate," *Washington Post* (January 9, 2005): A4.

[90] The following discussion is expanded somewhat in my chapter in Donald R. Kelley, *Divided Power: The Presidency, Congress, and the Formation of American Foreign Policy* (Fayetteville, AK: University of Arkansas Press, 2005), pp. 66–72.

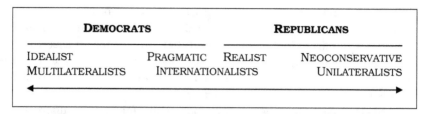

Figure 3.5: Foreign policy factions in the Democratic and Republican parties.

The Democrats' ideological mission, for example, is compassionate and redistributionist; people join the party because they want to use government to help the disadvantaged, to relieve human suffering, to uplift the downtrodden. The corollaries of this position are that government is part of the solution to national problems, and that its interference in the free market is necessary and desirable. But as a party based on compassion for the less fortunate, Democrats have a very difficult time distinguishing between the suffering of Americans and foreigners, all of whom are endowed by their creator with inalienable rights and should in their view be part of the benevolent community. The widespread suffering apparent in the post–Cold War world split these liberal internationalists in two, with an *idealist* faction wanting to apply the party's *raison d'etre* overseas in places like Somalia, Haiti, Rwanda, Bosnia, Kosovo, and East Timor, and another *pragmatist* faction that was more sensitive to the time and resource limitations of the government, the costly nature of interventions, and the Vietnam-like risk that military operations posed – all in conflict with critical domestic programs (see Figure 3.5). As the governor of a small southern state without much foreign policy experience or interest, Bill Clinton was driven by Carter-era idealists on his staff and in the Congress during his first years in office.[91] But once his large domestic programs were blocked and he turned his formidable intellect to foreign affairs, Clinton settled on a pragmatic approach, admitting that "we cannot become involved in every problem we really care about."[92]

The Republicans faced quite a different dilemma. Their mission is to promote equality of opportunity rather than results, to ensure a level playing field for the competitive meritocracy they consider essential to American greatness. The corollaries of this mission are that government is part of the problem, not part of the solution, and that its interference with the free market is both unnecessary and undesirable. In foreign affairs, Republicans traditionally tended to see the dynamics of international politics in the same way they saw the domestic polity: namely, as a competition in which the fittest survive. They played realist to the Democrats' idealism,

[91] For example, National Security Advisor Anthony Lake, Secretary of State Warren Christopher, and the congressional Black Caucus.

[92] Remarks by the President to the Nixon Center for Peace and Freedom, Mayflower Hotel, Washington, D.C., March 1, 1995.

seeing conflict based on power within an anarchic system as fundamental to international politics. But this view of how the world works left Republicans with the dilemma of how to deal with the powerful post–Cold War countertrend of growing globalization and economic interdependence, with its emphasis on cooperation rather than competition. Moreover, whereas the Democrats' divisions are matters of degree, the dilemma posed by the Republicans' mission, along with the fundamentally different orientation of the party's new members, resulted in a far more profound split. Indeed, it is almost as if there are two Republican parties. In domestic affairs, the division has to do with whether economic or social issues matter more and is between economic enterprisers and social conservatives.[93] In foreign policy, the split turns partly on realism versus idealism with regard to ends, partly on cooperative internationalism versus unilateralism with regard to means (see Figure 3.5).[94]

The old Republican party retains a realist's mindset. Skeptical that the world can be changed in any fundamental way, it is convinced that conflict can be managed and the nation protected by skilled statecraft and careful attention to husbanding American power. Being wary of ambitious, big government enterprises, its members are cautious in foreign policy, preferring to set objectives within a rather narrow view of what the national interest requires. Realist with regard to ends, they are cooperative internationalists when it comes to means, seeking strength from allies and willing to compromise somewhat on maximum American goals if the essentials can thereby be accomplished at less cost and risk. In short, they solve the dilemma posed by globalization in a Darwinian world through American leadership of the international system and its institutions. This kind of internationalist realism was the traditional Republican approach of the Nixon/Kissinger team and also of George H. W. Bush and his national security advisor Brent Scowcroft, who compromised American goals in the 1991 Gulf War to keep a broad international coalition together and because they believed that invading Iraq proper to depose Saddam Hussein would be more costly and risky than it was worth.[95]

The new Republican party, however, is idealist in ends and unilateralist in means. It is the party of Ronald Reagan and of Richard Cheney, Condoleezza Rice, and George W. Bush, who brought us the second Iraq war. Ironically, its distinctive approach to foreign policy was sharpened in the mid-1990s by unilateralist opposition from a Republican-controlled Congress to the Democrats' idealism of the left. These new Republicans

---

[93] This distinction is taken from Pew Center, *Beyond Red Versus Blue.*

[94] On the Republican split between realism and neoconservative idealism, see Gideon Rose, "Present Laughter or Utopian Bliss?" *National Interest* 58 (Winter 1999/2000): 41–47.

[95] For a recent exposition of the realist-internationalist worldview as found in Brent Scowcroft, see Jeffrey Goldberg, "Breaking Ranks," *New Yorker* (October 31, 2005): 54–65.

saw no particular reason for the United States to pursue an engaged foreign policy in a world without serious threats, and they were convinced
that international treaties and institutions were imperiling American
sovereignty. Moreover, as American power waxed during the 1990s they
became convinced that the United States was so powerful that it could
adopt a maximal view of what the national interest required and achieve
its goals without much help from other nations. They therefore cut drastically the nonmilitary instruments of statecraft and obstructed the Clinton
administration's cooperative efforts at peacekeeping and humanitarian
intervention.[96]

But the new Republican party is not only unilateralist in means; it is also
idealist in ends. So-called neoconservatives within the party have argued
that conflict management is not enough, especially not after 9/11, that
there are monsters loose in the world who pose mortal dangers to the
United States and must be destroyed. Moreover, these Republican idealists believe that the international system can be fundamentally changed to
create a peaceful world, and that the way to do it is to change the internal
forms of government in other states into democracies. They are Wilsonians
of the right, in other words, rejecting his emphasis on international institutions but determined to make the world safe through democracy, if necessary by military force.[97] As President George W. Bush put it in his second
inaugural address, "The survival of liberty in our land increasingly depends
on the success of liberty in other lands. The best hope for peace in our world
is the expansion of liberty in all the world."

Strategy Begins at Home

Such, then, is the domestic political context within which foreign affairs
strategists must operate, an environment of increasing polarization over
foreign policy *between* the parties and of factional splits *within* them. The
images of American politics and public opinion presented above suggest
that, at least on issues of major public concern, strategists must deal carefully with the domestic context, directing their foresight over the shoulder
of projected strategies to see whether enough of the people are likely to

---

[96] I trace these battles in some detail in *Clinton and Congress: The Politics of Foreign
Policy*, Headline Series 321 (New York: Foreign Policy Association, Fall 2000).

[97] Key sources on neoconservatism include Nicholas Lemann, "Without a Doubt,"
New Yorker (October 14 & 21 2002): 164–179; Elizabeth Drew, "The Neocons in
Power," *New York Review of Books* 50 (June 12, 2003); Francis Fukuyama, "The
Neoconservative Moment," *National Interest* 76 (Summer 2004): 57–68; Charles
Krauthammer, "An American Foreign Policy for a Unipolar World," *AEI Irving Kris-
tol Lecture* (February 10, 2004); James Mann, *The Rise of the Vulcans* (New York:
Viking, 2004); Henry R. Nau, "No Enemies on the Right," *National Interest* 78
(Winter 2004/05): 19–28; Francis Fukuyama, *America at the Crossroads: Democ-
racy, Power, and the Neoconservative Legacy* (New Haven, CT: Yale University
Press, 2006).

follow. Among other things, they must consider how the inattentive public might engage on a policy issue as events develop, and whether non-internationalists might shift into alignment with one or another school of internationalists to block (or support) their actions. They must think about how Jeffersonians, Wilsonians, Hamiltonians, and Jacksonians will react to events, and which elements of strategic culture are relevant to planned courses of action. They must ascertain on which matters the public has come to judgment and conform their approach to those considered opinions. They must certainly try to anticipate how factions within the parties will see their initiatives, what their strength is in Congress, and whether support can best be built on a partisan or cross-factional basis. Above all, they must understand that, when it cares about key issues, public opinion in democracies is ultimately rather effective in getting its way.[98] Even the most strenuous efforts by popular presidents can only move the polls 5–10 percent in their preferred directions; attempts at leadership by presidents with popularity ratings below 50 percent will generally be futile or even counterproductive.[99] As Abraham Lincoln put it, "Public sentiment is everything. With public sentiment nothing can fail, without it nothing can succeed."[100] Or in a modern version, "If the people lead, the leaders will follow."[101]

As a member of the minority that is attentive and politically active, the foreign affairs strategist should also recognize that opinion leaders as a group hold some views that are quite different from those of the broader public.[102] For example, for decades some 97–99 percent of leaders have favored an active U.S. involvement in the world, a much higher percentage than the public.[103] At the same time, "the world seems to be a much scarier place for the public than for leaders," particularly when it comes to threats to personal security and prosperity like terrorism, low-wage job competition, immigration, drugs, and environmental dangers.[104] Similarly, as to goals, leaders always put a lower priority than the

---

[98] "…long term differences between public opinion and official foreign policy are rare." Russett, *Controlling the Sword*, pp. 128, 157.

[99] Russett, *Controlling the Sword*, p. 102.

[100] From the Lincoln–Douglas debate of August 21, 1858. Quoted in Holsti, *Public Opinion and American Foreign Policy*, p. 34.

[101] A bumper sticker observed in the nation's capital, late 1992.

[102] These consistent patterns are revealed by two quadrennial series of leadership opinion polls that began in the mid-1970s. See the Holsti and Rosenau Foreign Policy Leadership Project (FPLP) polls in presidential election years since 1976, and the Chicago Council on Foreign Relations polls taken in the off years since 1974 and published the following years under the title *American Public Opinion and U.S. Foreign Policy*.

[103] Marshall M. Bouton, and Benjamin I. Page, *Worldviews 2002: American Public Opinion and Foreign Policy* (Chicago, IL: Chicago Council on Foreign Relations, 2002), p. 69.

[104] Bouton and Page, *Worldviews 2002*, p. 70.

public on domestic programs, and they are less interested (by as much as 50 percentage points) in using American foreign policy to serve the country's economic interests by protecting American jobs or supporting American business abroad; leaders are also consistently more pro–free trade than the public.[105] As to instruments, leaders tend to be much more supportive of foreign aid than the average American.[106] Interestingly, the more knowledgeable people are, the more their views align with those of leaders, suggesting that ignorance rather than values accounts for most of these differences.[107]

Overall, in fact, the most in-depth set of foreign policy polls taken over the last three decades has found that, while the public and leaders agree on much of foreign policy, "leaders have persistently been at odds with majorities of citizens on a fifth of survey questions and have significantly different positions on nearly two-thirds of the questions. One might conclude that leaders need to do a better job either educating the public or following their preferences."[108] Samuel Huntington has argued that American elites are becoming transnationalist and cosmopolitan, with those on the left wanting the United States to become like the world and those on the right determined to make the world over like the United States. Meanwhile, he contends, most ordinary Americans want the country to remain distinct, following its own cultural and moral standards.[109] Whether or not such sweeping generalizations are right, the persistent divergences between elites and the public sketched above should warn foreign affairs strategists not to confuse their own preferences with those of the nation.

At the same time, strategists should beware of assuming that the domestic context provides all constraint and no latitude. On the many issues where mass opinion remains unformed, a leader can help the country find the right course if he or she meets people on the terrain of their values and preoccupations, offers them real choices, and is able to allow them the time

---

[105] Bouton and Page, *Worldviews 2002*, p. 72; Kohut and Mead, *America's Place in the World 2005*, p. 29.

[106] Bouton and Page, *Worldviews 2002*, p. 71.

[107] In general, the more knowledgeable people are about world events the more internationalist they are and the more they favor a shared U.S. leadership role. Ignorance, on the other hand, correlates with seeing terrorism increasing and the world as threatening, wanting the U.S. to stay number one militarily, and placing emphasis on taking care of America first, especially by protecting American jobs. Andrew Kohut and Walter Russell Mead, *America's Place in the World 2005* (Washington, D.C., and New York, Pew Research Center for the People and the Press and Council on Foreign Relations, 2005), pp. 31–33.

[108] Bouton and Page, *Worldviews 2002*, p. 69.

[109] Samuel P. Huntington, "Dead Souls: The Denationalization of the American Elite," *National Interest* 75 (Spring 2004): 5–18. Huntington thus identifies three alternatives for the United States' relationship to the world – Cosmopolitan: America becomes the world; Imperial: The world becomes America; National: America remains America.

necessary for working through the issues involved.[110] And where the people have made up their minds, the resulting public judgment may be less a constraint on strategists than a solid foundation for action. For example, despite variations in the strength of internationalism and differences as to whether American engagement overseas should be pursued in a cooperative or unilateral, militant or restrained way, it appears that most people have come to judgment on the idea that "in today's interdependent world, the United States cannot afford to turn its back on the rest of the globe."[111] If so, the fact is important, for it means that oft-expressed fears of resurgent isolationism are unfounded, even now that terrorism has accentuated the cost of international involvement.[112]

Moreover, most analysts agree that the public allows the president more leeway in foreign than in domestic policy. For the most part, public opinion sets broad parameters for leaders in this realm rather than mandating action; people are reactive, not directive, judging what they like and dislike even if they have no idea what should be done.[113] By all accounts the relationship between opinion and foreign policy is an extremely complex and interactive one, in which people learn from the actions and words of politicians even as they set the limits of acceptable action, while policymakers simultaneously read public opinion and attempt to manipulate it. Perhaps all that can be said about who controls whom is that it depends. In these conditions, foreign affairs strategists will need to use their knowledge of public opinion to help set means as well as ends, to discover, not only *what* actions are possible, but also *how* to do what needs to be done in the most acceptable way. As Russett puts it:

> Public opinion sets broad limits of constraint, identifying a range of policies within which decision makers can choose, and within which they must choose if they are not to face rejection in the voting booths.[114]

> [Leaders therefore] put together specific policies from within some range of acceptable options which a majority is prepared to tolerate. Selection of the specific option is an exercise of political leadership, and statesmanship.[115]

Handling public and congressional opinion has not been easy for America's post-Vietnam presidents, and they have adopted very different strategies for dealing with it.[116] Richard Nixon, for example, took power

---

[110] Yankelovich, *Coming to Public Judgment*, Chapter 13.

[111] Yankelovich, *Coming to Public Judgment*, p. 157.

[112] On 9/11 heightening of the costs of an active foreign policy, see Stephen M. Walt, "American Primacy: Its Prospects and Pitfalls," *Naval War College Review* 55 (Spring 2002): 9–28.

[113] William Schneider, NWC Lecture, August 27, 1991. Used by permission.

[114] Russett, *Controlling the Sword*, p. 110.

[115] Russett, *Controlling the Sword*, p. 118.

[116] For a more complete sketch of these differing approaches, see Terry L. Deibel, "Grand Strategy Lessons for the Bush Administration," *Washington Quarterly* 12 (Summer 1989): 133–134.

just as the original Cold War consensus was disintegrating and had to deal with the most fractionated and superheated opinion of any recent president. He and Henry Kissinger also adopted a sophisticated foreign affairs strategy that encompassed both muscular containment and active negotiations, thereby mixing realist and idealist, hardline and accommodationist, Jacksonian and Jeffersonian elements. Since some of the boldest elements of this strategy (like the opening to China) also seemed to require secrecy, it was perhaps natural that the administration dealt with the chaos in public opinion by ignoring it, revealing its broad purposes but otherwise shutting out the Congress and even much of the foreign affairs bureaucracy. But the unfortunate result was that the Nixon administration exacerbated rather than assuaged opposition to its statecraft and found itself poorly positioned to sustain its strategy when the Watergate scandal destroyed the president's credibility.

Jimmy Carter, reacting to what he called the "lone ranger" style of the Nixon-Kissinger team, adopted quite a different approach.[117] Carter felt that the secrecy of his predecessor's foreign policy had been morally wrong, and he understood that foreign policy in a democracy required public support. "I believe we can have a foreign policy that is democratic," he said at Notre Dame in 1977. "We can also have a foreign policy that the American people support and, for a change, know and understand."[118] Unfortunately, though, Carter's technique for democratizing policy was to bring the post-Vietnam dissensus right into his administration at the highest levels, hiring people with such fundamentally different assumptions about how the world works as Secretary of State Cyrus Vance and National Security Advisor Zbigniew Brzezinski. Having little experience in foreign affairs strategy and few settled views of his own, this president found himself unable to bring conceptual coherence to their widely divergent advice. The result was an administration constantly at war with itself and an utter lack of strategic coherence.

Ronald Reagan stepped into this vacuum with a clear if ideological sense of what needed to be done and a formidable arsenal of communications skills, and he made a serious attempt to lead public opinion (as well as the Executive branch's own personnel) in his preferred directions. Compared to Carter, Reagan may well have been lucky in the international scene he inherited.[119] But in the domestic politics of foreign policy Reagan created his own success through carefully crafted speeches, a public-opinion minded White House staff, and a clear and consistent message – at least until the Iran-*contra* affair. While Carter was an earnest and sincere man

---

[117] Zbigniew Brzezinski, *Power and Principle* (New York: Farrar, Straux, Giroux, 1983), p. 8.

[118] Quoted in Seyom Brown, *The Faces of Power* (New York: Columbia University Press, 1983), p. 452.

[119] Michael Mandelbaum, "The Luck of the President," *Foreign Affairs: America and the World 1985* 64 (No. 3): 393–412.

who said what he felt and believed, Reagan was a performer who gave voice to whatever would have the intended effect on his audience. Known as the teflon president, he also showed how a president's personal popularity can rub off on his policies while insulating him somewhat from their shortcomings.[120]

George H. W. Bush was far more competent than his predecessor in the day-to-day handling of foreign affairs but lacked Reagan's communications skills or his clear vision of the nation's purposes abroad. Patrician and elitist by nature, Bush eschewed the wholesale Reagan approach to the domestic politics of foreign policy in favor of a retail style that emphasized personal relationships. In addition to his political experience in the Congress and the Republican National Committee, Bush had learned foreign policy as ambassador to the UN, head of the CIA, and minister to China; he knew the institutions of government intimately and was confident of his ability to work with them directly. So instead of leading public opinion and using its power to pressure Congress and the Executive like Reagan, he lobbied members of Congress personally and put in place a smoothly functioning team of foreign policy professionals to manage the bureaucracy.[121] While this style worked well for many policy issues, on those where broad public support was essential – as in the run up to the 1991 Gulf war or in dealing with the many issues posed by the post–Cold War revolution in international politics – the administration was severely handicapped by its inability to articulate a coherent and persuasive rationale for its actions.[122]

Bill Clinton, by contrast, was an extraordinary public communicator, albeit in a much different style than Ronald Reagan. Whereas Reagan did scripted speeches best, Clinton's strength was in spontaneous, empathetic interaction with people, where he was able to combine political savvy, intellectual brilliance, and the ability to make an emotional connection. Clinton had an unparalleled knowledge of domestic and economic issues and of how globalization connected the two. His administration also took campaign-style spin to new levels, establishing a rapid-response media operation dubbed the War Room.[123] However, his status as a plurality president, his lack of experience in foreign policy, his uneasy relationship with the American military, and his decision to concentrate on domestic

[120] Polling data indicated that Reagan was always more popular than his policies. Terry L. Deibel, "Why Reagan Is Strong," *Foreign Policy* 62 (Spring 1986): 108–125; also "Reagan's Mixed Legacy," *Foreign Policy* 75 (Summer 1989): 34–55.

[121] For a more complete description of Bush's approach and its successes, see Terry L. Deibel, "Bush's Foreign Policy: Mastery and Inaction," *Foreign Policy* 84 (Fall 1991): 5–6.

[122] Richard Morin, "How Much War Will Americans Support?" *Washington Post* (September 20, 1990): B1, B3; Dan Balz and Ann Devoy, "For Bush, Persian Gulf War Was Transforming Moment," *Washington Post* (March 3, 1991): A1, A36.

[123] Joe Klein, *The Natural: The Misunderstood Presidency of Bill Clinton* (New York: Broadway Books/Random House, 2002), p. 165.

affairs left him unsure of himself on security issues in the early years of
the administration and oddly reticent to sell his policies forcefully. Later,
when he turned his formidable intellect to foreign policy and had had time
to learn its nuances, Clinton became every bit as knowledgeable as he
was in the domestic arena, and he worked skillfully to curtail violence in
the former Yugoslavia, the Middle East, and Northern Ireland. But growing partisanship, factionalism and an impeachment scandal deprived this
president of the effectiveness with public opinion that his communication
skills might otherwise have allowed.

George W. Bush lacked both the communication skills of a Clinton and
the close knowledge of government of his father. Although not out of touch
with policy details like Reagan often seemed to be, Bush's fractured English
and stumbling delivery may explain his Reaganesque reluctance to engage
in spontaneous interaction with the public. He had fewer press conferences than any president in recent memory, preferring instead to appear
before audiences of carefully culled supporters or the military. His administration also continued and perfected Clinton's super-sophisticated spin
control operation, even extending it on occasion to include paying journal-
ists to spread proadministration information. Of course, Bush's popularity
was temporarily helped by a massive rally-round-the-flag effect after 9/11,
and as long as his party controlled Congress he faced a less difficult task on
the Hill than most of his predecessors – although his effectiveness was compromised by the administration's evident lack of respect for the legislative
branch. Still, by his second term the President's repeated over-optimistic
statements regarding the course of the war in Iraq had generated a credibility problem nearly as serious as Reagan's over the Iran-*contra* affair.[124]

The failure of so many presidents to master the domestic context of foreign affairs strategy stands as yet another warning to those who think that
statecraft need only assess the international context. Public opinion may
be ill-informed, volatile, and ambivalent, but it has an underlying culture,
structure, and logic. Moreover, its power in a democracy is undeniable;
Congress may not think strategically, but it and not the Executive branch
is Article I in the Constitution. If the domestic context is critical to the success of foreign affairs strategy, then assumptions about it must be carefully considered and find a prominent place in strategic logic. It seems that
strategy, like charity, begins at home.

The Domestic Context Since 9/11

What, then, does American public opinion look like in this post-9/11 age? A
brief review of current opinion on the concepts covered in this book will give
a sense of the domestic parameters within which the twenty-first century

---

[124] Richard Morin and Dan Balz, "Bush's Popularity Reaches New Low: 58% in Poll
Question His Integrity," *Washington Post* (November 4, 2005): A1, A5.

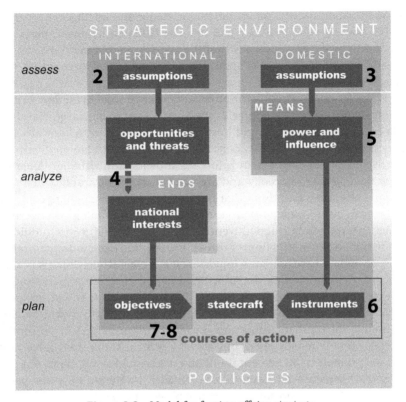

Figure 3.6: Model for foreign affairs strategy.

American foreign affairs strategist must work (see Figure 3.6 for the numbers of the chapters in which these concepts are discussed).

First, as noted above, the attacks of 9/11 refocused Americans' attention on international affairs.[125] In the Chicago Council on Foreign Relations (CCFR) quadrennial poll of 2002, 36 percent of the public picked terrorism as the biggest problem facing the United States, the first time since the CCFR polls began in 1974 that a foreign policy issue had displaced domestic concerns at the top of that list. Overall, foreign policy problems were chosen as most important by 41 percent of respondents, an increase of more than 35 percent since 9/11; interest in foreign news jumped by 20 percent.[126] Moreover, American internationalism was reaffirmed and strengthened by the attacks. In November 2001 a record 81 percent supported an active U.S. role in world affairs, and post-attack polls also

---

[125] Unless otherwise noted, data in this paragraph is from Bouton and Page, "Refocused Internationalism After 9/11," Chapter 1 in *Worldviews 2002*, pp. 10–14.

[126] In the CCFR 1998 poll, foreign affairs problems were chosen by just 7%; as noted above, in 2000 another poll put the figure at 3%.

showed strong support for spending on defense and intelligence.[127] By late 2005, however, the Iraq war had tempered this enthusiasm, persuading some 42 percent of Americans that the country should mind its own business internationally, a level about the same as in post-Vietnam 1976 and post–Cold War 1995.[128]

When Americans look at the international environment for foreign affairs strategy discussed in Chapter 2, the Middle East looms large. Saudi Arabia has joined Iran, Iraq, and North Korea as the countries toward which Americans are most hostile. Solving the Israel–Palestinian conflict is considered more important than before the attacks, and although Americans view the Palestinians coolly and are divided on the desirability of a Palestinian state, they also think that the United States must change its policy to be more even-handed toward the parties. With the fading of concern over America's economic competitiveness and a natural desire to huddle with traditional allies in this time of threat, Europe has risen in importance relative to Asia. There, Japan's importance is falling while China's is rising, but Americans now view Japan as friendly, practicing free trade and reliable in the war on terrorism, while China is seen as a threat, practicing unfair trade, and unreliable in counterterrorism.[129] As to the international economic environment, Americans believe by 56 percent to 27 percent that globalization is mostly good, but only 14 percent think the United States should promote it, 39 percent think America should slow it down or reverse it, and 29 percent – almost a third – consider it a threat. Fifty-one percent find globalization bad for American job security, so it is not surprising that Americans are more sympathetic to those who think tariffs are necessary (50 percent) than to those who want to eliminate them (38 percent). Still, a plurality of 44 percent think the North American Free Trade Agreement (NAFTA) was good for the United States, and 73 percent support free trade if government programs are in place to help displaced workers.[130] At the same time, more than 90 percent want trade agreements conditioned on other countries' promises to maintain minimal working conditions and environmental protections.[131]

The public ranks threats, the subject of Chapter 4, in three or four categories.[132] In the top tier are *terrorism-related threats*: international

[127] To keep things in perspective, however, readers should note that domestic problems were still picked as most important by most Americans, and even the support for increased spending on intelligence and defense was about 10% lower than that for more spending on health care, education, and combating crime.

[128] Shoon Kathleen Murray and Chris Spinosa, "Post 9/11 Shift in Public Opinion: How Long Will It Last?" Chapter 7 in Eugene R. Wittkopf and James M. McCormick, eds., *The Domestic Sources of American Foreign Policy* (Blue Ridge Summit, PA: Roman and Littlefield, 2003), p. 101.

[129] Bouton and Page, "The Changing Geopolitical Landscape," Chapter 6 in *Worldviews 2002*, pp. 46–58.

[130] Kohut and Mead, *America's Place in the World 2005*, p. 29.

[131] Bouton and Page, *Worldviews 2002*, pp. 39–40, 42.

[132] Unless otherwise noted, statistics on threats in this paragraph are from Bouton and Page, *Worldviews 2002*, pp. 15–17.

terrorism itself is picked as a critical threat by 91 percent, chemical and biological weapons by 86 percent, and nuclear weapons in unfriendly hands by 85 percent; Islamic fundamentalism is seen as a critical threat by 61 percent. Next are *threats to personal security* like epidemics (68 percent) and the influx of large numbers of immigrants (60 percent) – which 74 percent think the government could do a better job controlling – along with *geopolitical concerns* such as Arab–Israeli war (67 percent), North Korea's and Iran's nuclear programs (67 percent and 61 percent, respectively), and China's developing power (52 percent).[133] Third are *long-term problems*, like global warming (46 percent) and world population growth (44 percent). Finally, it is interesting to note that, since the 1990s, economic problems like financial crises overseas and competition from Japan, Europe, or low-wage countries have dropped to the bottom of the list, although 55 percent do think U.S. indebtedness to other nations is a major threat.[134]

With regard to power and influence, discussed in Chapter 5, 55 percent thought the United States was more powerful in 2002 than a decade earlier and "extremely influential" in the world, but by 2005 two-thirds of Americans feared that their country was less respected than in the past, mainly because of the Iraq war. Interestingly, two-thirds believe "economic strength is more important than military strength in determining a country's overall power and influence," but the same number also think maintaining superior military power is very important, and 50 percent want the United States to remain as the world's *only* military superpower.[135] Indeed, regarding the instruments of state power treated in Chapter 6, support for the use as well as funding of the military rose sharply after 9/11. In the 1990s, the deployment of ground troops in places like Bosnia, Haiti, Rwanda, and Kosovo garnered support of only about 30 percent of the public, but after 9/11 substantial majorities of Americans endorsed invading Afghanistan (65–75 percent) and Iraq (57 percent).[136] However, some analysts believe that the casualties incurred in Iraq have created an "Iraq syndrome," similar to the Vietnam syndrome, that will prevent the United States from using the military instrument for the foreseeable future except in response to a direct attack.[137] Indeed, Yankelovich believes that "the American public is beginning to feel that Washington has put too much emphasis on military responses to the challenges it faces and that the diplomatic, economic, political, and intelligence capabilities of the United

---

[133] Daniel Yankelovich, "Poll Positions," p. 15; Kohut and Mead, *America's Place in the World 2005*, pp.50–52.

[134] Kohut and Mead, *America's Place in the World 2005*, p. 20.

[135] Bouton and Page, *Worldviews 2002*, pp. 22–23; Kohut and Mead, *America's Place in the World 2005*, p. 53.

[136] Murray and Spinosa, "The Post 9/11 Shift in Public Opinion: How Long Will It Last?", pp. 102–105.

[137] John Mueller, "The Iraq Syndrome," *Foreign Affairs* 84 (November/December 2005): 44–54. But see, below, that a majority in late 2005 still favored preemptive attack.

States have neither received the attention they deserve nor been deployed skillfully."[138] Polling on foreign assistance does seem to show some potential for the expansion of this instrument despite the fact that about equal numbers say they want to cut it back as want to maintain or increase it, because most Americans support aid for humanitarian purposes and think the government spends vastly more helping other countries than it actually does.[139] As for international organizations as instruments of American policy, attitudes towards the UN have soured somewhat since the 1990s, but 48 percent of the American public retain a positive view of the organization, and 54 percent think the United States should cooperate with it fully.[140]

When it comes to goals for American statecraft, the subject of Chapter 7, 86 percent of Americans think *defense against terrorism* should be a top priority of the United States, followed closely by preventing the spread of WMD at 75 percent.[141] "Without question, combating the threat of international terrorism – characterized by President Bush and others as a 'war' on terrorism – has become, for most Americans, the centerpiece of U.S. foreign policy."[142] The next level of objectives has to do with Americans' *personal welfare*. Indeed, protecting the jobs of American workers at 84 percent is almost as important to the public as terrorism defense; then comes reducing the spread of AIDS and other diseases (72 percent), reducing dependence on imported energy (67 percent), combating the flow of illegal drugs (59 percent), and reducing illegal immigration (51 percent). Next in priority are traditional, *longer-range foreign policy goals*, like maintaining superior military power (50 percent), dealing with global climate change (43 percent), and strengthening the UN (40 percent). *Economic concerns* like warding off financial instability, reducing the trade deficit, and protecting business interests abroad are the next tier, chosen by about 50 percent of the people.[143] Finally, *idealist and altruistic goals* are chosen as very important by only a quarter to a half of the public. Although 42 percent of Americans would protect people in other nations against genocide, only 37 percent give top priority to defending human rights abroad, 31 percent to improving the standards of living in developing countries, and a meager 24 percent to the Bush administration's primary objective of promoting democracy overseas.

Finally, the public continues even after 9/11 to be very clear regarding *how* the United States should use its policy tools to achieve these goals,

---

[138] Yankelovich, "Poll Positions," p. 16.

[139] Bouton and Page, *Worldviews 2002*, pp. 43–44.

[140] Kohut and Mead, *America's Place in the World 2005*, pp. 27–28.

[141] Unless otherwise noted, statistics on goals in this paragraph are from the table in Kohut and Mead, *America's Place in the World 2005*, pp. 54–63. Unsurprisingly, the priority of goals parallels to a great extent the priority of threats discussed above.

[142] Bouton and Page, *Worldviews 2002*, p. 18.

[143] Bouton and Page, *Worldviews 2002*, Figure 2–2, p. 19.

the "ways" of statecraft also discussed in Chapter 7. For example, "asked whether the more important lesson of September 11 is that the United States needs to work more closely with other countries to fight terrorism or that the United States needs to act on its own more to fight terrorism, 61% say the United States needs to work more closely with other countries."[144] Indeed, just 12 percent think the United States should be the single world leader, whereas 74 percent endorse shared leadership; of the latter group, 46 percent want the United States to be no more or less assertive than other countries, and only 25 percent want it to be the most assertive.[145] At the same time, the public does favor aggressive tactics in the war on terror. Sixty-six percent of Americans endorse assassination of terrorists, 52 percent think preemptive attack on countries that seriously threaten the United States is often or sometimes justified, and 46 percent agree that it is at least sometimes acceptable to torture terrorism suspects.[146]

Future events will certainly affect American public opinion. One can expect that the terrorism-related attitudes noted above will gradually fade in the absence of another attack on the homeland, and that American enthusiasm for international engagement will again strengthen once the Iraq war is history. But it is remarkable that, from the Cold War through the wars on terrorism and Iraq, not only the structure of opinion has held firm but also certain ingrained attitudes. First among these is internationalism, the desire to play an active part in world affairs. Second is the preference for doing so in cooperation with other countries, using multilateral institutions and instruments if possible. Third, not surprisingly, is an affinity for cooperative and nonviolent instruments of statecraft, with the costly and risky military maintained as second to none but held in reserve unless absolutely necessary. Fourth is a persistent focus on foreign policy goals that serve domestic personal welfare, like protecting jobs, securing energy, and controlling drugs and immigrants, while downgrading efforts to spread American values overseas. Various groups of Americans may of course differ from these constants, and events may enable one or another of such groups to have their way for a time. But given their persistence over decades and across dramatic changes in American circumstances, it is likely that these are the public opinion parameters within which foreign affairs strategists will continue to work for many years to come.

The Role of Contextual Assumptions

We have now finished our overview of assumptions about the environment for strategy, both foreign and domestic. By now it should be obvious that

---

[144] Bouton and Page, *Worldviews 2002*, p. 31.

[145] Ten percent want the U.S. to exert no leadership at all. Kohut and Mead, *America's Place in the World 2005*, p. 53.

[146] Bouton and Page, *Worldviews 2002*, p. 23; Kohut and Mead, *America's Place in the World 2005*, pp. 24, 49–50.

they are among the most critical yet elusive of the conceptual elements
with which the foreign affairs strategist must deal. We have already noted
that the sense of constraint or possibility they provide is vital to the outcome of strategic thinking, and also that this very importance – along with
the fact that they so often reside in the background of strategic thought –
makes assumptions psychologically resistant to change even when the
environment itself is changing rapidly. We argued that the strategist must
counteract this tendency by maintaining a mental stance of provisional
agnosticism, a willingness to overlay all other assumptions with the additional assumption that knowledge is always insecure, along with a readiness constantly to reassess it in the light of available evidence.[147]

We have noted, too, some pathologies of strategic assumptions, two of
which are worth reemphasizing as we conclude. First is allowing ideological
thinking to interfere with clear-eyed views of the nation and the world. Ideology does have an important role in foreign affairs strategy, for within ideologies lie many of the values that inform definitions of the national interest.[148] Ideologies are also useful leadership tools, as Ronald Reagan proved;
they offer a compelling vision of what needs to be done that can be easily communicated to the public, Congress, and the Executive bureaucracy.
But because ideologies usually contain a highly generalized and abstracted
interpretation of history and are focused on the world as it is becoming
(and should become), they can interfere with a realistic appreciation of
the world as it is. The result can be a strategy blind to reality, ironically
unable to achieve the values ideology espouses. As Bayless Manning once
wrote,

> The relationship between a foreign policy that has some component of
> ideological preference and a foreign policy that is heavily ideologized is the
> relationship between normal cell activity and cancerous cell activity.[149]

To invert the medical metaphor, ideology is like a powerful medicine of
which a drop will cure but a teaspoonful will kill. Some ideology may be
essential to a sense of purpose in strategy, but too much can be deadly.

The second key pathology of assumptions is incoherence or inconsistency, that is, holding a set of assumptions that are mutually contradictory, or shifting one's views rapidly from one set to another. The Carter
administration is one obvious example of this problem in both dimensions.

---

[147] Henry Kissinger discusses the need for such reevaluation by asking why the
U.S. was surprised at the beginning of the Yom Kippur war in 1972. He concludes that the failure of intelligence in this case was "not administrative but
intellectual.... We had become too complacent about our own assumptions. We
knew everything but understood too little." *Years of Upheaval* (Boston, MA: Little,
Brown & Co., 1982), pp. 465–467.

[148] See Chapter 4.

[149] Bayless Manning, "Goals, Ideology, and Foreign Policy," *Foreign Affairs* 54
(January 1976): 278.

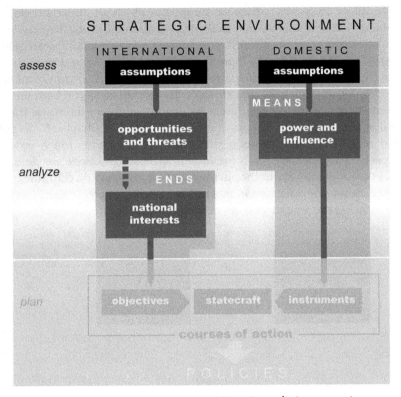

Figure 3.7: From assessing assumptions to analyzing concepts.

Brought up as a cold warrior but born again as a transnationalist, Carter constantly waffled between the two worldviews, while his administration moved steadily rightward as events propelled Brzezinski's influence upwards and Vance's down. The Clinton administration in its early years is another negative example. With little knowledge of or interest in foreign policy, this president allowed himself to be dragged by his Carter-era staff and liberal members of the Democratic-controlled Congress into policies on China, Haiti, Bosnia, and elsewhere without a careful assessment of their feasibility or cost, only later to fail or abandon them in public humiliation.

To specify coherence and consistency as important attributes of strategic assumptions is again to underline the difficulty all assumptions pose, since these very attributes seem to cut across the need for assumptions' constant reassessment. Moreover, neither the world nor the nation need actually *be* consistent or coherent. Thus the strategist must balance the requirement for a solid foundation for strategic planning with the chaos reality presents to his senses, and trade off the importance of reassessment in a rapidly changing world against the value of consistency over the life of long-range strategic enterprises.

In all of these ways, then, assumptions about the international and domestic context pose special challenges to strategic logic. They also relate directly to the concepts ahead, as the model for foreign affairs strategy illustrates (see Figure 3.7). The domestic environment is the source of the values that undergird national interests; the international environment is the source of the challenges that threaten those interests; and both environments may provide opportunities for advancing them. Interests, threats, and opportunities are discussed next, in Chapter 4. Chapter 5, on power and resources – the means of strategy – will of course touch on many aspects of the domestic context in which those resources are produced. Thus assumptions about the environment for strategy will continue to play a role even as our discussion moves from thinking about the real world to considering the analytical tools needed to deal with it.

Part II

Analyze

4. Interests, Threats, and Opportunities
5. Power and Influence

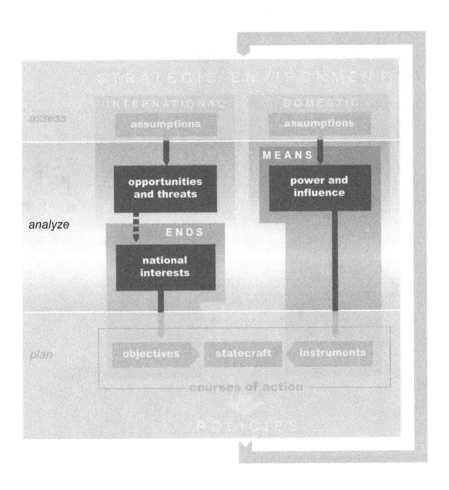

4

Interests, Threats, and Opportunities

Important as a clear understanding of the domestic and international context is for the strategist, it is still only the background for strategic thought. Strategy, after all, is not merely an intellectual but a performing enterprise; it exists for action and proves its value through results. Its first requirement is therefore a sense of direction through the informational morass presented by the environment it seeks to influence, a way of deciding what goals to pursue. Strategy must begin, in other words, with purpose; and purpose in foreign affairs strategy rests on the concept of the national interest.

The national interest's role in strategic logic is to justify the statesman's actions, to provide a standard of judgment against which goals can be measured. It is "an effort to describe the *underlying rationale* for the behavior of states and statesmen in a threatening international environment."[1] The strategist's sense of the national interest answers the question: Why are we doing this? Although it alone cannot offer a complete answer to that question, the national interest provides a first cut at the desirability of any given policy, a necessary if not sufficient condition for pursuing a goal.[2] If a policy cannot be justified on the basis of the nation's interests, then it should be abandoned. As former Congressman Lee Hamilton put it, "The basic test for judging any foreign policy decision is easy to state but hard to apply: Does it serve the American national interest?"[3]

Used in this way, the idea of national interest does not stand for any *particular* kind of foreign or national security policy. The national interest has long been denigrated by those who find policies based on it to be necessarily realist in nature, characterized (so the critics argue) by an excessive concern for power relationships and a lamentable disdain for moral

---

[1] Fred A. Sonderman, "The Concept of the National Interest," *Orbis* 22 (Spring 1977): 122. Italics added.

[2] The reason national interest alone cannot provide a complete justification for policy is that cost (including risk) also plays a role in determining desirability; if a goal is too costly it may become undesirable even if it is in the nation's interest. See Chapter 8.

[3] Lee H. Hamilton, "Defining the National Interest," *Christian Science Monitor* (March 30, 1998): 11.

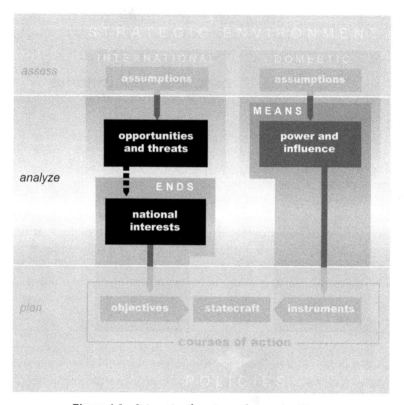

Figure 4.1: Interests, threats, and opportunities.

considerations.[4] Then, in the immediate aftermath of the Cold War, the national interest was interpreted by some as requiring drastically-reduced American involvement abroad, indeed as mandating a near-isolationist policy.[5] But the role of the national interest in strategic logic will accommodate any kind of content. It recognizes that a nation's interests may well be served by promoting its ideals. And although the concept of a standard of judgment against which to measure the desirability of objectives implies some restriction on purely capricious policies, the national interest is quite broad enough to encompass a deeply engaged, fully internationalist foreign policy.

With this chapter, we move from the first to the second level of the graphic model for foreign affairs strategy, that is, from assessing assumptions about the strategic environment to analyzing key strategic concepts (see Figure 4.1). National interests, along with threats and opportunities, are a product of that analysis, and they are therefore of a fundamentally

---

[4] For idealists, the national interest is often replaced by global interests. See the brief discussion of the realist-idealist debate in Chapter 3.

[5] See Alan Tonelson, "What is the National Interest?" *The Atlantic Monthly* 268 (July 1991): 35–39, 42, 44–46, 48–52.

different nature than the assumptions that were the subject of Chapters 2 and 3. Though threats and opportunities come *from* the international environment, they and interests are not reality but analytical interpretations placed on reality; they are artifacts of strategic thought. As Harvard political scientist Stanley Hoffmann writes, "The national interest is not a self-evident guide, it is a construct."[6] This point is important to remember, for if the interests, threats, and opportunities that drive critical strategic decisions can quite readily be conjured into or out of existence, then strategists must pay careful attention to the thought processes that formulate them. This chapter will first discuss the kinds of interests nation-states have and then define interests in strategic logic: distinguishing them from objectives, relating them to values, and considering the criteria on which they can be prioritized.[7] It will then similarly consider threats and opportunities, locating them in strategic logic, considering their relationship to interests, and discussing how recent administrations have conceptualized and responded to them.

Categories of Interest

The national interests of the United States, indeed of any state, seem to fall naturally into four broad categories (see Figure 4.2). First (and foremost) is *physical security,* meaning protection against externally-caused injury or destruction of life and property within the territory of the United States, and of American citizens or their possessions abroad. At its most basic this interest simply represents the imperative of survival, both of individuals protected by the nation-state and of the state itself. This category can thus include protection against imported diseases as easily as armed attack by another state. The term "security" also implies a *subjective* freedom from fear as well as *objective* safety from danger.[8] Under it governments strive to prevent or deter (if possible) and defend against (if necessary) a whole range of depredations, running from terrorism to thermonuclear holocaust.

---

[6] Stanley Hoffmann, "In Defense of Mother Teresa," *Foreign Affairs* 75 (March–April 1996): 172.

[7] There seems to be no consistency among authors who have attempted to define the national interest. Most speak of a vision, or future desired state of affairs, and often interests are equated with ends or objectives. Donald E. Nuechterlein defines the national interests of the United States as "the country's perceived needs and aspirations in relation to other sovereign states constituting its external environment." Nuechterlein, *America Overcommitted: United States National Interests in the 1980s* (Lexington, KY: University Press of Kentucky, 1985), p. 7. But no general description, especially not one as vague as "needs and aspirations," can do the strategist much good. That is why this term, like others in the framework on which this book is based, is defined operationally, according to the role the concept plays in relation to other concepts within the overall analytical scheme.

[8] This theme is developed in Arnold Wolfers, "'National Security' as an Ambiguous Symbol," *Political Science Quarterly* 67 (December 1952): 481–502.

1. PHYSICAL SECURITY
2. ECONOMIC PROSPERITY
3. VALUE PRESERVATION AT HOME
4. VALUE PROJECTION OVERSEAS

Figure 4.2: Categories of the national interest.

Naturally, their degree of success will vary widely with circumstances. After all, a nation's physical security can be either minimally accomplished through a successful if bloody resistance to an actual attack, or it can be fully achieved through a national security strategy that mitigates all dangers with a high degree of psychological comfort.[9] While it has taken on a special significance and caused the formation of a whole new department in the U.S. government since 9/11, security of the homeland and the people within it has always been the essential core of the security interest.

The second broad category of national interest is that of *economic well-being*, or more simply, *prosperity*. Of course, most of a government's activity to promote economic welfare takes place in the domestic arena under broader *national* strategies, but the globalization of the U.S. economy means that prosperity must also be promoted by foreign affairs strategy. Trade policy must be managed, the international financial and monetary system policed, exports of American manufacturers promoted and direct overseas investments safeguarded, and coordination attempted among the disparate economic policies of nations. Here too a range of achievement is possible, from an irreducible national interest in mere subsistence to the maximal interest in a very high, even luxurious standard of living.

A third category of interests comprises those directed toward the *preservation of the nation's internal system of government, values, and civic culture* against change coerced or imposed from outside.[10] Because values and forms of government are preeminently a matter of internal affairs it may seem difficult to think of how such interests relate to foreign policy, but the widespread abuse of narcotics and dangerous drugs is one example of a problem with international dimensions that strikes directly at the nation's internal value structure; so, potentially, is uncontrolled immigration. In addition, this category of interest asserts the nation's autonomy – its ability to maintain its political independence in the face of coercion by another government – a quality sometimes called self-sufficiency, sovereignty, or

---

[9] It will be remembered from Chapter 1 that the subset of foreign affairs strategies serving physical survival is termed national security strategies. See Figure 1.1.

[10] Alexander George and Robert Keohane specify three "irreducible" national interests that are very close to three of my four categories: physical survival, economic subsistence, and liberty. "The Concept of National Interests: Uses and Limitations," in George, *Presidential Decisionmaking in Foreign Policy: The Effective Use of Information and Advice* (Boulder, CO: Westview Press, 1980), p. 222.

even liberty.[11] Many consider this characteristic – indeed the whole category of value preservation – as an aspect of physical security; several of the official *National Security Strategies of the United States* have listed "the survival of the United States as a free and independent nation, with its fundamental values intact and its institutions and people secure" as a single interest.[12] But it is important for clear thinking to keep physical security and value preservation separate, indeed to list all interests independently of each other, since tradeoffs may need to be made between them (as will be seen later). The achievement of value preservation will also always be a matter of degree, since even the world's most powerful nations are not completely immune to foreign pressure. As Henry Kissinger once put it, "Countries that proclaim that they are unaffected by pressure are either bluffing or have had the good fortune never to be exposed to it."[13]

The fourth and final category of the national interest is the *projection of the nation's values and morality overseas*. For a variety of reasons, great nations and even some nonstate actors sometimes feel that they have a unique mission in the world, a duty to spread their vision of society to other lands, even to make the world over in their own image. The Soviet Union had its world socialist revolution; France has its *mission civilisatrice*; Al Qaeda wants to restore the caliphate; and the United States has its human rights policies, humanitarian concerns, and efforts to spread market economies and democratic political systems.[14] Of course, governments may well promote their values abroad in order to serve other categories of interest. Americans may believe that the spread of representative

---

[11] George and Keohane define liberty as "the ability of inhabitants of country to choose their own form of government and to exercise a set of individual rights defined by law and protected by the state." "The Concept of National Interest: Uses and Limitations," p. 224. I think they overstate the case, since many states have an interest in autonomy and preservation of their system of government but do not grant individual rights to their citizens. Osgood finds a similar interest he calls "self-sufficiency," defined as "the conduct of foreign relations without reference to other nations or to matters beyond unilateral national control." Robert Endicott Osgood, *Ideals and Self-Interest in America's Foreign Relations* (Chicago, IL: University of Chicago Press, 1953), p. 5.

[12] See, for example, the George H. W. Bush *National Security Strategy of the United States* (Washington, DC: GPO, August 1991), p. 3. Perhaps this conflation comes from the historic phrase "territorial integrity and political independence" coined by Secretary of State John Hay in the Open Door notes and incorporated in the League of Nations Covenant (Art. 10) and the United Nations Charter (Art. 2, para. 4). Strangely, in spite of his definition of self-sufficiency as a separate interest, Robert Osgood defines "survival or self-preservation" as encompassing political independence and the preservation of fundamental governmental institutions. Osgood, *Ideals and Self-Interest*, p. 5.

[13] Kissinger, *White House Years* (Boston, MA: Little, Brown & Co., 1979), p. 721.

[14] President Reagan often quoted John Winthrop's biblical invocation of the United States as a "citty [sic] upon a hill," and the Clinton administration proclaimed what it called the "enlargement" of market democracy abroad as a central purpose of its foreign policy. See remarks of Anthony Lake, Assistant to the President for National Security Affairs, "From Containment to Enlargement," Johns Hopkins University School of Advanced International Studies, September 21, 1993.

government around the world serves their physical security, since democracies rarely fight other democracies. Or they may think that market systems abroad will create an overseas demand for American exports and thus contribute to U.S. prosperity. But as used here this category of interest is meant to represent the promotion of values abroad for their own sake, simply because of an inwardly felt mission to do good in the world or to create an international environment which is more compatible with the internal culture and political system of the United States, a foreign policy ecosystem in which Americans can breathe easier. As such, value projection also includes humanitarian interventions to respond to natural disasters overseas, relieve human suffering, or halt mass murder.

Although universal in nature, the first three of these categories of interest are validated for Americans in their nation's founding documents. The Declaration of Independence lists as "unalienable rights" life (i.e., security), liberty (value preservation), and the pursuit of happiness (prosperity); while the Constitution was adopted to "provide for the common defense [security], promote the general Welfare [prosperity], and secure the Blessings of Liberty [value preservation]." Nowhere in these documents, however, is there mention of anything like value projection, perhaps because the founding fathers recognized that their fledgling nation could hardly afford the costs or controversy that supporting this interest so often engenders. As befits concepts imbedded in basic law, interests tend to endure; as Lord Palmerston famously asserted, nations do not have permanent allies or enemies, only permanent interests.[15] In reality, however, interests do change over time, though slowly. For example, the U.S. interest in Middle Eastern oil appeared only after the internal combustion engine revolutionized means of transport. But Palmerston was right in highlighting the lasting quality of interests. Their durability is one of the factors that enables them to provide a standard of evaluation for strategy itself.

Defining Interests

The categories of interest outlined above apply at the highest level of strategic analysis, applicable to the nation as it relates to its entire international environment. At this level they are universally applicable to any nation-state. But strategists usually make interests more specific than security, prosperity, value preservation and value projection by applying those categories to various regions, countries, and functional issues; indeed, global interests usually must be translated "downward" to more specific

[15] "We have no eternal allies, and we have no perpetual enemies. Our interests are eternal and perpetual, and those interests it is our duty to follow." Remarks of Henry John Temple, 3rd Viscount Palmerston (1784–1865), defending his foreign policy in the House of Commons, March 1, 1848; *Hansard's Parliamentary Debates*, 3d series, vol. 97, col. 122, as cited in Suzy Platt, ed., *Respectfully Quoted: A Dictionary of Quotations Requested from the Congressional Research Service* (Washington, DC: Library of Congress, 1989).

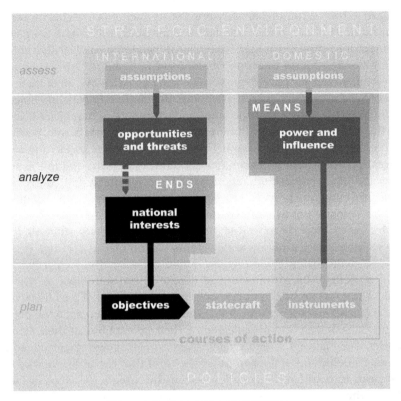

Figure 4.3: Interests and objectives.

locales and issues in order to make their strategic meaning clear. And as they become more specific, interests also become less universal, for while every country has an interest in, say, prosperity, the content of that interest will vary from country to country and from time to time. So, for example, the national interest of the United States in prosperity as applied to the Middle East would mean an adequate flow of oil from the region at reasonable prices and, in Saudi Arabia, political and economic stability (which in current terms means a strong Saudi monarchy). In such a hierarchy, each lower level interest depends on the related interest above it for legitimacy.

Objectives or goals, the purposes of strategy, are likewise justified by their relationship to interests at their own or a higher level – as noted earlier, justifying objectives is the primary function of interests in strategic thought. But interests are quite different from goals, and although many writers equate the two, there is an important analytical reason to distinguish between them (see Figure 4.3).[16] For interests should be set without

---

[16] Donald Nuechterlein, for example, begins a chapter on the national interest by saying that the term "has long been used by statesmen and scholars to describe the foreign policy goals of nation-states." *America Overcommitted*, p. 1. Stanley Hoffmann calls interests "the sum of the objectives that policymakers have set." "In Defense of Mother Teresa," p. 172.

regard to their attainability; they provide an anchor of stability for strategy but do not by themselves mandate action. Since every nation's power is limited, the objectives it can establish will generally fall well short of what the full extent of its interests would seem to demand.[17] In other words, governments never have the luxury of being able to serve all of their interests to the maximum degree. Therefore, to equate interests and objectives would require, either that the state underestimate and in effect lose sight of the full range of its real interests, or that it set goals well beyond its capabilities. In the first case it would be ill-equipped to identify serious threats or important opportunities should they appear, and in the second it would likely embark on actions that must inevitably fail. Moreover, an objective can quite properly serve more than one interest, a possibility that would be lost if the two are equated.

Interests, properly conceived, do not care about power. After all, to take an extreme case, a nation-state retains its interest in security even if it cannot avoid being conquered by a foreign army – indeed, right up to the moment of its extinction. And a poverty-stricken state in the Third World still has an interest in prosperity even if it cannot feed its own people. Yet statesmen's conceptions of their country's interests often defy this logical disconnect and are affected by their perceptions of their country's power (see Figure 4.4). More often than not, "as power expands, so does a state's definition of its own interests," and that expanded view of interests can in turn lead to a larger view of the threats the country faces.[18] These threats can then seem to make necessary the far-reaching objectives that ample power makes possible. Such reasoning can work in the opposite direction as well, with a constrained view of power leading to an underspecification of interests and threats. Either way, this causal chain of interest and threat conceptualization – namely, power → interests → threats → objectives – is a faulty application of strategic logic. Strategists should keep perceptions of their own power disconnected from their formulations of interests, consulting their capabilities only when setting objectives.[19]

Given the close relationship between interests and objectives, it is not surprising that statements of one often include items that are really the other. One obvious way to tell the difference is that objectives, being action items, need verbs, whereas interests are grammatical subjects, composed

---

[17] Those who speak of a gap between interests and commitments, like Walter Lippmann's classic statement in *U.S. Foreign Policy: Shield of the Republic* (Boston, MA: Little, Brown & Co., 1943), or between power and interests, are really speaking of an insufficiency of power to support the objectives they believe that the country needs to advance its interests or protect them against threats.

[18] Robert Jervis, "The Compulsive Empire," *Foreign Policy* 137 (July/August 2003): 83–87. See Chapter 5.

[19] See Chapter 7, Step 1, Ends, for a further discussion of the effect of perceptions of means on ends from the point of view of objective setting.

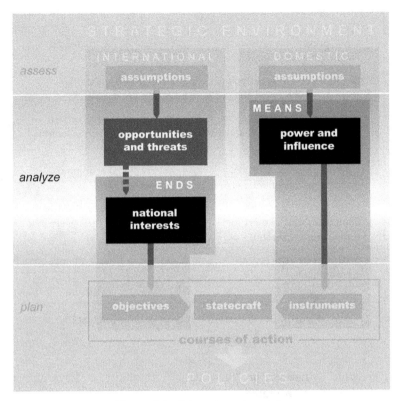

Figure 4.4: Interests and power.

of nouns and adjectives. Robert Art, for example, lists his six "overarching national interests" in two places (compared in Figure 4.5). The first time they read like objectives, whereas the second time most are clearly stated as interests, with no sense of whether or to what degree they are achievable.[20] Notice for example how the action item to "*prevent* great power Eurasian wars" becomes the end-state of "deep peace among the Eurasian great powers," or how the goal to "*preserve* an open international economic order" becomes an interest in "international economic openness."

Another recent example of confusion over what interests are and how to formulate them comes from the Commission on America's National Interests. Its report noted quite properly that "interests are analytically distinct from what a nation is prepared to do to protect those interests." But its summary table of five vital interests (see Figure 4.6) reads like a list of action items, of objectives that the country should work

[20] Robert J. Art, *A Grand Strategy for America* (Ithaca, NY: Cornell University Press, 2003), comparison of the list of "interests" on p. 7 with the list in Table 1.8 on p. 43. The first interest in the second column is the only exception; it should be phrased as "A secure homeland."

First, prevent an attack on the American homeland;	1. Defense of the homeland
Second, prevent great-power Eurasian wars . . . ;	2. Deep peace among the Eurasian great powers
Third, preserve access to a reasonably priced and secure supply of oil;	3. Secure access to Persian Gulf oil at a stable, reasonable price
Fourth, preserve an open international economic order;	4. International economic openness
Fifth, foster the spread of democracy and respect for human rights abroad;	5. Democracy's consolidation and spread, and the observance of human rights
Sixth, protect the global environment	6. No severe climate change

Figure 4.5: Robert Art's two versions of interests.

to "Prevent," "Ensure," or "Establish."[21] Similarly, a "favorable world order," though often stated as if it were an American interest, is really only an objective that serves the interests of security and prosperity.[22] After all, Americans do not want such a world for its own sake but because a disorderly world gives rise to threats to their security and disrupts the commerce that contributes to their prosperity. Many lists of interests also include items that are really *threats*, like the Commission's items 1 (WMD attacks) and 3 (hostile or failed states), perhaps because of the close relationship between interests and threats (discussed below). More difficult to explain but hardly unusual is when even *instruments* are included as interests, as the Commission has done in item 2. (Alliances, of course, are means of statecraft, not ends in themselves.)[23]

---

[21] Graham T. Allison and Robert Blackwell, *America's National Interests*, A Report from The Commission on America's National Interests, a joint project of the Kennedy School of Government at Harvard, the Nixon Center, and the RAND Corporation, 2000, pp. 17 (italics removed), 5.

[22] This mistaken interest is one of the four listed in Nuechterlein, *America Overcommitted*, p. 8. The other three interests listed there are defense of the homeland, economic well-being, and promotion of values.

[23] Here is another example: "Healthy, cooperative, and vigorous relations with allies and friendly nations" (*National Security Strategy of the United States*, 1991, p. 3). Mistaking allies as an interest or even as an objective risks clientitis, the sin of confusing one's own interest with that of another.

Vital US national interests are to:

1. Prevent, deter, and reduce the threat of nuclear, biological, and chemical weapons attacks on the United States or its military forces abroad;

2. Ensure US allies' survival and their active cooperation with the US in shaping an international system in which we can thrive;

3. Prevent the emergence of hostile major powers or failed states on US borders;

4. Ensure the viability and stability of major global systems (trade, financial markets, supplies of energy, and the environment); and

5. Establish productive relations, consistent with American national interests, with nations that could become strategic adversaries, China and Russia.

Figure 4.6: Commission on America's National Interest – summary of vital U.S. national interests.

These kinds of analytical errors warn strategists to be careful that their defined interests are *really* interests and not obviously some other strategic concept. Whether general and applied to the whole range of American foreign affairs strategy or specific and tailored to a particular problem or issue, interests are end-states, conditions one wants to preserve or attain, snap shots of a valued reality or hoped-for future. They are fundamental and enduring, not dependent on a particular international context. Most important, interests stand alone. They carry their own justification: they are desirable simply because they are desirable, because they are in accord with the nation's values. One wants to be secure, after all, simply because wholeness is obviously better than pain and injury and life seems better than death, to be prosperous simply because being rich is better than being poor.[24] Thus, a statement of interests is a wish-list that stands on its own terms; power and cost should be irrelevant to its formulation.[25]

[24] As Sophie Tucker once put it, "I been rich and I been poor. Rich is better."

[25] Power (the subject of Chapter 5) and cost (discussed in Chapter 8) are of course critical to strategic thinking, but they should not be incorporated into one's concept of interest. The distinctions drawn here between interests and objectives are revisited from the point of view of the latter in Chapter 7.

Values and Standards of Judgment

The fact that the national interest carries its own justification – that the desirability of interests cannot be validated by reference to some objective criterion – has caused many political scientists to condemn the concept as useless or even dangerous. Their argument is that the national interest is too subjective to provide any check on policymakers or to be useful in analysis, that the standard of judgment it purports to provide is nothing more than a cloak for the statesman's own preferences. This question – of how interests provide standards for evaluating goals and what kind of standards they are – is a complex one worth some reflection.

Certainly it is true that the national interest rests on nothing more substantial than value judgments.[26] Virtually all writers on the subject agree that "interests can be seen as applications of values in context" and that "when we speak of national interest, we speak of values."[27] Even its foremost critic considers it axiomatic that "the national interest is rooted in values," arguing that this characteristic is precisely what makes the concept "difficult to employ as a tool of rigorous investigation."[28] These viewpoints are different than those of many policy makers, who often speak of serving "interests *and* values" as if they were two different kinds of justification for decisions. Nor do they correspond exactly to Harvard political scientist Joseph Nye's idea that "values are simply an intangible national interest," to be differentiated from tangible or "strategic" interests.[29] Nye's colleague Samuel Huntington gets closer to the truth when he asserts that "[n]ational interests usually *combine* security and material concerns, on the one hand, with moral and ethical concerns, on the other."[30]

In fact, *interests – all interests – are simply what one values*. People value security, prosperity, and preservation of their domestic way of life, and Americans also value a world of market democracies where human suffering is minimized. The first three kinds of interests may not seem to be based on values simply because the values they engage – survival, prosperity, and liberty – are almost universally accepted, whereas the humanitarian and moral considerations related to value projection interests are

[26] Note that the word "values" is used here in a different way than when we discussed the two categories of preserving values at home and projecting them abroad. Here we mean valuation of what is best for society, the weighing of consequences for the community; earlier we were speaking of a specific constitutional order and moral codes to be protected or promoted.

[27] George and Keohane, "The Concept of National Interests," p. 221. Sonderman, "The Concept of the National Interest," p. 124. George and Keohane also argue that specifying interests "implies a choice among values standing behind those interests."

[28] James N. Rosenau, "National Interest," *International Encyclopedia of the Social Sciences* (New York: MacMillan/Free Press, 1968), Vol. II, p. 34.

[29] Joseph S. Nye, Jr., *The Paradox of American Power: Why the World's Only Superpower Can't Go It Alone* (New York: Oxford University Press, 2002), p. 139.

[30] Samuel P. Huntington, "The Erosion of American National Interests," *Foreign Affairs* 76 (September/October 1997): 35. Italics added.

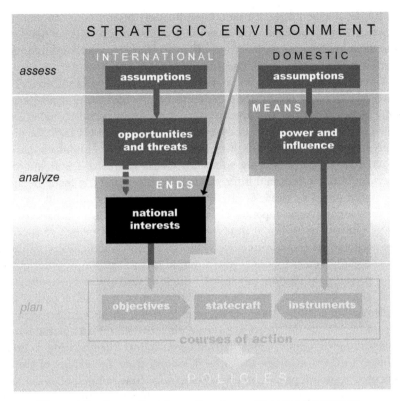

Figure 4.7: Connecting domestic values and national interests.

widely debated and often highly controversial. The controversy becomes especially acute when one attaches to this most debatable category of interests the most risky and costly form of response: military intervention.[31] Therefore, strategists must be particularly careful to be sure that the interests they identify in this category are really interests and really national, and that they have the support of public opinion, before launching enterprises to serve them. But controversial or not, the fact remains that *all* interests are expressions of national values – hence the diagonal arrow between the domestic environment, where values originate, and national interests in Figure 4.7.[32] Indeed, Huntington goes so far as to argue that "[n]ational interest derives from national identity. We have to know who we are before we can know what our interests are."[33] And although it may seem

---

[31] See the discussion of the Clinton humanitarian interventions at the end of this chapter.

[32] "I believe . . . that the distinction between interests and values is largely fallacious." Hoffmann, "In Defense of Mother Teresa," p. 172.

[33] Huntington, "The Erosion of American National Interests," p. 28. Note the difference of Huntington's view with Robert Art's contention that features of the international *environment* can be used "to identify America's national interests," as if interests were set outside the state. *A Grand Strategy for America*, pp. 42–43.

paradoxical given the frequent identification of the concept with hard-headed, realist policies, the national interest is precisely where values *should* come into the strategic equation (rather than, for example, by distorting assumptions about the international environment).

But does basing the national interest on values mean that no real standard of judgment exists, that the concept provides no restraint on decision makers? Part of the answer to this question relates to whether one believes that interests can be *objectively* determined by a thought process that would lead informed individuals to the same or similar conclusions, or whether they are entirely *subjective*, being whatever a statesman says they are.[34] If the national interest is subjective, then the issue belongs to the realm of policy process rather than strategic thought, and any check on decision makers depends on where sovereignty is located within the state. Obviously, national interests determined by a prince or a politbureau provide little assurance that national rather than personal values will prevail. But "in a democracy, the national interest is simply what citizens, after proper deliberation, say it is."[35] Such democratic subjectivity is quite a different enterprise than academic theorizing, and helps establish the legitimacy of a values-based concept of interest. For although the political theorist might be delighted to have an objective standard against which to measure foreign policy, most citizens would find it frightening to imagine a foreign affairs strategy that was detached from the values of the community it was supposed to serve. Being sure that public policy serves the nation's values (and mediating value conflicts where they exist) is hardly an illegitimate activity; it is instead the proper function of any democratic political process.

Insofar as the national interest can be determined objectively, on the other hand, the concept itself honestly applied does offer a dual check on mere personal preference.[36] First, being the "national" interest distinguishes it from the interests of various subgroups below the level of the nation-state – often termed "special interests" – on the one hand, and from supranational interests (or the interests of the so-called "international community") above the state level, on the other. American foreign affairs strategy must therefore be justified as serving the people of the United States as a group, *e pluribus unum*, and as serving their interests in preference to those of people subject to other political systems.[37] This requirement does

---

[34] Rosenau, "National Interest," pp. 34–40.

[35] Nye, *Paradox of American Power*, p. 139.

[36] Indeed, any logical scheme must eventually come to rest on a set of premises that cannot be proven within the scheme itself. Strategy is no exception.

[37] This again is considered by some critics to be an insuperable bar to the utility of the concept, since it is impossible to scientifically sum up the conflicting values of the special interests, and because the nation-state is supposedly becoming less and less the focus of people's loyalties or even of the goals of foreign policy. Rosenau, "National Interest," pp. 37–39.

not mean that global public goods like an open economic system, protected international commons, and strong international laws and institutions are not legitimate parts of the American national interest, or that the United States cannot serve the interests of other nations and peoples while serving its own.[38] Indeed, in a globalized, interdependent strategic environment it would seem that such considerations would have to be part of any sensible concept of American national interests. But being "national" does mean that political authorities must be able to find among the parochial interests of individuals and groups within society an aggregate set of interests that are truly nation-wide in scope, lest statecraft based on them lose its legitimacy.[39]

The second check on personal preference that an objectively-determined sense of interest can provide comes from the concept of "interest" itself, because it requires some long-term advantage for the community that might be quite different from what people want or would enjoy in the short run.[40] The issue of the U.S. federal budget deficit provides an excellent example. Whereas many Americans might have wished to continue the consumption binge of the 1980s into the 1990s, or might enjoy the continuation and expansion of the Bush tax cuts of the early 2000s, most also can understand the collective interest in reducing the federal budget deficit – even at the cost of current pleasures. Another example is a substantial federal gasoline tax, which would simultaneously lower the federal deficit, reduce American dependence on foreign oil (and with it the lopsided trade balance it helps generate), cut the flow of revenue to authoritarian regimes like those in Tehran and Moscow, and improve the environment. Although Americans may still have political difficulty cutting the deficit or enacting a gas tax, no reasonable person can deny that they are "in our interest." Thus, the national interest can be seen as the foreign affairs subset of the public interest, a concept which functions in the decision making process

---

[38] Nye, *The Paradox of American Power*, pp. 141–147.

[39] In the 1990s Samuel Huntington argued that parochial interests so dominated the United States government that it should do as little foreign policy as possible until the country could recapture a sense of truly national interest. "The Erosion of American National Interests," pp. 28–49. Peter Trubowitz believes that in the United States "there is no single national interest," only sectional interests driven by different economic rates of growth and relationships to the world economy. See his *Defining the National Interest: Conflict and Change in American Foreign Policy* (Chicago, IL: University of Chicago Press, 1998), p. 12.

[40] The restraining nature of the concept of interest is developed in Friedrich Kratochwil, "On the notion of 'interest' in international relations," *International Organization* 36 (Winter 1982): 1–30. On p. 6 Kratochwil makes the point that, even on the personal level, it often "makes sense to distinguish carefully something wanted or desired – like sitting down in a snowstorm due to exhaustion – from the interest involved – not doing so because of the danger of freezing to death. Thus, even on the simplest level, the interest argument requires some giving of reasons, a justification that goes beyond the mere indication of likes and dislikes."

"to justify claims and demands, and obliges members of a public to defer to such a decision even if they regard it as being contrary to their own preferences."[41]

Of course, the problem of specifying the content of the national interest does not thereby disappear; tough choices regarding the community's security, prosperity, and the preservation and projection of its values must still be made. These choices will often be controversial and (as demonstrated below) may differ somewhat from administration to administration. But making them on the basis of the national interest is quite different than merely following the impulse of whomever happens to control the machinery of government at a particular time. Imbedded in the logic of strategy, the national interest can function as an anchor against the erratic winds of emotionalism, able precisely because of its foundation in national values to protect the state, not against the just claims of morality, but against the whims of sentimental moralism.[42] As Henry Kissinger put it, looking back at the history of U.S. foreign policy as he took office,

> Moral exuberance had inspired both overinvolvement and isolationism. It was my conviction that a concept of our fundamental national interests would provide a ballast of restraint and an assurance of continuity.[43]

Prioritizing Interests

Not all interests, of course, are equally important. Statesmen traditionally label those of the greatest consequence "vital interests," but even deciding which interests are vital can be difficult. Nuclear strategist Bernard Brodie defined vital interests as those one is willing to fight for – a good definition for everyone except the strategist, whose problem is precisely to decide what interests *are* worth fighting for. Brodie gave an answer to that question, too; he argued that we should fight only for those issues deemed to affect the security of the nation against attack, thereby confining vital interests to the first of the four categories of interest set forth above.[44] Though physical security may be *primus inter pares* for any state, it seems unwise to assume that no economic interest could ever be vital or that interests of value preservation and projection are always of

---

[41] Kratochwil, "On the notion of 'interest,'" p. 6.

[42] This distinction is key to resolving the apparent paradox of how a hardheaded concept like the national interest can be based on something as squishy as national values. The national interest is often portrayed as being the opposite of morality, which in turn is equated with values; but in fact it incorporates the community's moral values. What it is the opposite of is not morality but moralism, that is, the kind of emotionalism that can lead to radical policy swings in a short period of time.

[43] *White House Years*, p. 65.

[44] Bernard Brodie, *Strategy and National Interests: Reflections for the Future* (New York: National Strategy Information Center, 1971), p. 12.

secondary consequence.[45] Perhaps for that reason Elmer Plischke broad-ened the definition of vital to include "that which a nation deems to be essential, which it will not willingly forsake, and for which if necessary it will fight – diplomatically, politically, and militarily."[46]

It makes little sense, in any case, to rank interests according to whether or not a particular instrument (in this case, the military) is to be used to protect or advance them. After all, a president may not need or be able to use force to defend every vital interest, and he may use the military to serve interests that are not vital.[47] In some cases armed force may simply be a very effective and low cost way to deal with a problem. In others, vital interests may be threatened in ways that would render an armed response futile or too dangerous to other interests, as the United States has learned in dealing with the nuclear threat from North Korea. Even in past examples, therefore, one must still assess the importance of interests *de nouveau*.

One might well ask, for example, whether the United States really had a vital interest in Lebanon during the early 1980s. Ronald Reagan declared that it did in 1983 and proved it by sending in the Marines; in 1984, though, after 241 of them died in a terrorist bombing of their barracks in Beirut, he apparently decided otherwise and pulled them out. Then there are the cases of Grenada, invaded by President Reagan in 1983, and Panama under General Noriega, invaded by President George H. W. Bush in 1989. The first was believed to harbor a Cold War security threat, the second a narcotics-related threat to American values, but in neither case does armed action prove a vital interest except in the mind of the deci-sion maker. Even harder are cases like the former Yugoslavia during the mid- to late-1990s. Here the military was used only late in the game and to address part of the problem, in a situation far away from the United States and seemingly remote from its interests, but one spawning terrible human atrocities and possibly carrying the seeds of a wider Balkan or even European war.[48]

Most countries, to be sure, do not have the luxury of worrying about interests that are remote in either a geographical, moral, or temporal sense. But great nations can aspire to a higher level of security, to a greater degree of prosperity, to a further advance of their values, and thus can set objec-tives that are much more expansive "in space, time, and even in conception"

---

[45] Hans J. Morgenthau, "Another 'Great Debate': The National Interest of the United States," *American Political Science Review* (December 1952): 973. Osgood, *Ideals and Self-Interest*, p. 5. See also Sonderman, "The Concept of the National Inter-est," p. 125.

[46] Elmer Plischke, *Foreign Relations: Analysis of Its Anatomy* (New York: Greenwood Press, 1988), p. 54.

[47] Nuechterlein, *America Overcommitted*, p. 12.

[48] Ronald Reagan gave one answer to these questions in 1986 when asked whether sending military helicopters into Bolivia to help in pursuing drug traffickers was in the national interest. "Anything we do," he said, "is in the national interest."

than less powerful countries.[49] Their perennial problem, as Brodie put it
so well three decades ago, "is to determine the outer boundaries of what
is truly vital"[50] – to avoid either over-defining their interests in ways that
might lead to unnecessary foreign entanglements, or under-defining them
and either settling for a lower level of well-being or inviting real but avoid-
able damage. In other words, they must not only decide *what* their interests
are but also arrive at some sense of how *important* they are.

Perhaps the most elaborate scheme for doing the latter was created
by Donald Nuechterlein, who offered a ranking scheme with four levels
of intensity: survival, vital, major, and peripheral.[51] *Survival* interests, as
the name implies, are those so important to the nation that their compromise would be catastrophic and their achievement is urgent; obviously,
most would fall within category 1, physical security. *Vital* interests, at a
slightly lower level, can also involve category 2 or 3, economic well-being
and protection of values. Here somewhat more compromise is possible and
decision makers have more time to work toward the interest's satisfaction.
Major interests are those that are considered to be "important but not crucial" to the nation. Hence, policymakers can settle for less than complete
achievement of these interests, and most issues concerning them will be
settled by negotiation. Finally, *peripheral* interests are essentially unim-
portant to the well-being of the whole United States (though they may be
to some Americans' private interests); issues involving them need not be
matters of priority attention.[52]

Most analysts opt for a simpler ranking scheme, limited to two or at the
most three levels. Former National Security Council staffer and ambassador Robert Blackwill lists vital, important, and peripheral; Robert Art

---

[49] Brodie, *Strategy and National Interests*, p. 13. Brodie's quote refers to expansive
interests, which I have changed to objectives for the reason already explained:
viz., a country's power should not affect its conceptualization of its interests, only
its setting of objectives.

[50] Brodie, *Strategy and National Interests*, p. 18.

[51] The purpose is to discover the "stake" of the nation in a given interest, or why
certain issues "may receive more attention from policy-makers at some times
than at others." See Chapter 1 in Nuechterlein, *America Overcommitted*, pp. 9–
14.

[52] As is hinted in this description of Nuechterlein's framework, much of the level
of intensity depends upon the urgency posed by the threats interests are under
at a given moment. The categorization thus depends on more than the intrinsic
value of the interest itself; indeed, one has the impression that the importance
of interests is being determined by threats. Thus, survival interests involve "an
imminent, credible threat of massive destruction to the homeland," such as the
1962 Cuban missile crisis, to which decision makers must react immediately;
vital interests are those "where probable serious harm . . . to the nation will result
if strong measures . . . are not taken within a short period of time;" major interests
involve "potential harm" if no action is taken; while peripheral interests risk "little
if any harm . . . if a 'wait and see' policy is adopted." This confusion of interest
and threat is typical of such treatments of national interests; the relationship
of the two is discussed at length below. Nuechterlein, *America Overcommitted*,
pp. 9–10.

- **Intrinsic value or importance**
  (benefit/cost calculations, inability to compromise)
- **Level of attainment** (how much of the interest is in hand)
- **Precedence or sequence** (required before other interests can be protected or advanced)
- **Urgency** (time that decision makers have to secure interest)
- **Threat or Opportunity** (level of danger to interest or opportunity to advance it)

Figure 4.8: Criteria used in ranking interests.

classifies interests as vital, highly important, and important; other analysts simply differentiate "vital" interests from "others."[53] Art bases his ranking scheme on three criteria: "the benefits if the interest is protected, and the costs if it is not; the sequence in which these interests can be achieved; and the manner in which military force can be used to support them."[54] The first of these criteria is simply an indication of the interests' value or importance, as is Nuechterlein's criteria of whether or not the interest can be compromised. The second assumes that interests can be completely attained and that some need to be fully in hand before others can even be addressed, whereas most of the time interests are pursued simultaneously and only partly achieved. The third adopts the idea of predicating an interest's importance on one of the instruments that might be used to pursue it, here as elsewhere an odd inversion of ends and means.

As these examples illustrate, ranking interests is a problematic exercise in strategic thought. Most of the criteria for doing so seem to wither under careful scrutiny (see Figure 4.8). To be sure, some interests do seem to be intrinsically more important; without survival, obviously, other interests quickly become moot. But beyond that minimal level of achievement, security may not be more important than prosperity. After all, people who are starving may well risk their lives to get food. Thus, how interests are ranked may depend as much upon their level of attainment, on how much of each the nation has, as on their intrinsic value. For similar reasons, sequence or precedence also can only be partially used to prioritize interests. Again, the pursuit of most interests requires some level of all the

---

[53] Robert D. Blackwill, "A Taxonomy for Defining US National Interests in the 1990s and Beyond," in *Europe in Global Change: Strategies and Options for Europe*, Werner Weidenfeld and Josef Janning, eds. (Gutersloh: Bertelsmann Foundation Publishers, 1993), pp. 411–418. Art, *A Grand Strategy for America*, pp. 45–47.

[54] Art, *A Grand Strategy for America*, p. 45.

others; perhaps only value projection interests are truly subordinate to those in other categories, but there are nevertheless countless examples of nation-states pursuing them even when their security or economic interests are far from fully achieved and even to the detriment of those supposedly more-important interests. Finally, Nuechterlein's criterion of urgency, the time a decision maker has to secure the interest in question, seems more related to the imminence of the threat an interest may face than to the interest itself.[55] Indeed, perceptions of threats may have the most significant impact of all on the ranking of interests – just one of the reasons why threat analysis is itself a subject worth serious study.

Threats, Challenges, and Resistance

Threat is an idea well-known to military strategists; to them it represents the possibility if not the probability of physical assault. But in the broader context of foreign affairs strategy, threats can come from many other sources than hostile military force. People routinely speak of the threat of trade retaliation, for example, while narcotic drugs are said to be a threat to the nation's youth. Almost any tool of state power, including hostile propaganda, trade policy, economic sanctions, control of important natural resources (like oil or water), and various kinds of covert action, can be used by one government to threaten another. In a negotiating context threats can consist simply of a government's unwillingness to accede to another government's demand in one area unless its negotiating partner yields in an area of interest to it. And there are also contextual threats, like global warming or the spread of disease, that are not directed by a foreign strategist but make the international environment less hospitable or even dangerous. As these examples demonstrate, nonmilitary or nontraditional threats (sometimes called "challenges") can endanger interests other than physical security.

Strategists, of course, encounter threats as both their originators and their recipients. On the one hand, a threat may be seen as an *active* undertaking by one state to influence another's behavior, an effort that is part of a nation's foreign affairs strategy.[56] On the other hand, it may be *passively* experienced by the targeted state as the result of such an undertaking, or thought of as the psychological condition of feeling threatened.[57]

---

[55] Interestingly, most of these problems disappear when one attempts to rank objectives rather than interests: in an action plan some things are more important than others, and steps need to be taken and goals accomplished in a precise sequence. The conclusion, as noted in Chapter 7, may be that strategists should devote their energies to prioritizing objectives rather than interests.

[56] See Chapter 7.

[57] These two ways of seeing a threat are elucidated by David A. Baldwin, "Thinking About Threats," Chapter 3 in *Paradoxes of Power* (New York: Basil Blackwell Inc., 1989), pp. 46–47.

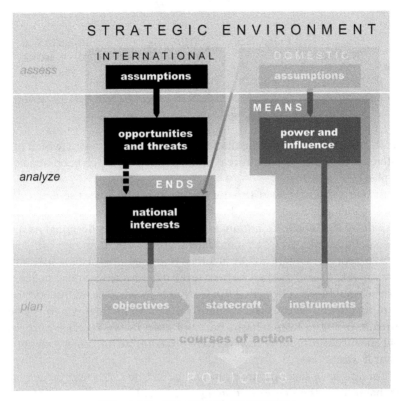

Figure 4.9: Threats and opportunities.

Distinguishing active from passive threats suggests the important possibil-ity that a state may attempt to threaten another without succeeding, or may find itself threatening another without wanting to do so. Whether active or passive, threats have two classic components: *intentions* and *capabilities*. That is, to make a threat that is creditable to its recipient, a state must have both the intent and the ability to do harm. Intentions and capabilities, of course, represent the ends-means equation of the threatening state, the combination of purpose and power necessary for any strategic enterprise.

In this chapter, "threats" are considered from the receiving end, from the point of view of the state being threatened. The arrow in the model for foreign affairs strategy (Figure 4.9) from "assumptions" about the interna-tional environment to "opportunities and threats" is to indicate that the latter come *from* overseas; indeed, unlike national strategy, foreign affairs strategy deals *only* with threats and opportunities from abroad. But the arrow from "opportunities and threats" to "national interests" has a quite different meaning: here the idea is that threats are *to* (and opportunities *for*) interests. Indeed, as will be seen below, threats are only threats if they jeopardize an interest, and opportunities only opportunities if they can help the state advance an interest. To ensure that those relationships exist,

EXTERNAL FORCES:	THREATS	RESISTANCE
INTEREST	**LESS<---STATUS QUO--->MORE**	
STRATEGY:	PROTECT	PROMOTE

Figure 4.10: Strategy and active resistance.

strategists should follow the discipline of explicitly showing which of their interests they believe each threat endangers (or to which each opportunity applies).

In one sense, received threats can be thought of as the active face of the broader phenomenon we have called resistance; in effect, *threats are resistance that takes the initiative.* If the status quo is accepted as a reference point of interest attainment (see Figure 4.10), then one can say that threats represent all the external forces that might reduce the fulfillment of any interest to *less* than its current level, whereas resistance applies to the forces brought into play when the state acts to advance an interest to *more* than its current level. A government will *protect* its interests in the face of threats, trying to keep what it has; but even in the absence of threats it will encounter resistance as it actively *promotes* its interests, striving to get what it wants.

Threats have several important characteristics. The first is *seriousness* or magnitude, the degree of damage that would be expected if the threat should materialize. If attributable to a threatening actor, this characteristic is obviously tied to its capabilities, or means. The second is *likelihood*, the probability that the threat will actually happen. It clearly relates to the opponent's intentions, or ends. Often these two characteristics are inversely related, with more damaging threats being less likely to materialize than less dangerous ones.[58] This relationship may also be true of different *levels* of damage from the same threat; global warming, for example, may be judged likely to produce a modest rise in temperature to which most countries can adapt, but there may also be some lesser probability that it will move past a tipping point where positive feedback loops create "practically a different planet."[59] A third characteristic, also tied to intent, is timing or *imminence*, how soon the feared development might occur: momentarily (like a nuclear attack in a crisis), in the months or years ahead (like the spread of a dreaded disease), or far in the future (like a powerful

[58] In risk (danger) analysis, exceedance probability curves look like the economist's standard demand curve, sloping to the right; thereby showing that higher losses usually have lower probability and lower losses, higher probability. Howard Kunreuther, "Risk Analysis and Risk Management in an Uncertain World," *Risk Analysis* (No. 22, 2002): 656–657.

[59] James Hansen, Director of NASA's Goddard Institute of Space Studies, quoted in Juliet Eilperin, "Debate on Climate Shifts to Issue of Irreparable Change," *Washington Post* (January 29, 2006): A1, A16.

yet still authoritarian China). Fourth might be called *tractability*, meaning the degree to which the threat can be dealt with, a characteristic critical to objective setting. Obviously, some threats can be mitigated or eliminated more easily than others, and there are some about which nothing can be done.

Threats that are serious, highly likely to materialize in the short term, and easily dealt with are the simplest for foreign affairs strategy, as are those that have a low probability of inflicting little damage, are far in the future, and about which little can be done anyway. It is threats whose characteristics make them neither essential to counter nor easy to ignore that pose the most difficult strategic challenges. Threats that would be catastrophic but are highly unlikely actually to happen (for example, a Cold War Soviet attack on Western Europe); those that are rather likely but not very serious (say, a terrorist attack with conventional weapons); potentially severe and likely threats whose impacts would be felt far off in the future and are difficult and expensive to counter (like global warming) – these are the kinds of threats that pose the worst strategic dilemmas.

Threats can be ranked or prioritized by seriousness, likelihood, imminence, or tractability, that is, according to any of the criteria just discussed or all of them somehow combined. William Perry and Ashton Carter created a three-level ranking system based on a shifting combination of seriousness, likelihood, and imminence. Their "A list" includes threats to national survival, like an all-out nuclear war or the rise of a powerful and hostile peer competitor. Their "B list" includes threats that are imminent but do not endanger survival, like the North Korean or Iranian nuclear programs. Their "C list" captures "contingencies that indirectly affect U.S. security but do not directly threaten U.S. interests," a formulation into which they put the humanitarian interventions of the 1990s, from Somalia and Haiti to Rwanda and the former Yugoslavia.[60]

When identifying threats, strategists must decide how to measure other states' capabilities and intent. Capabilities, of course, are relatively easy to judge, in spite of the fact that governments may attempt to conceal the full range and certainly the technological sophistication of, for example, their military forces. Intent is much more difficult to discern, since it requires that one step inside the mind of foreign decision makers to guess what they might do with whatever power they command. It is therefore quite tempting to infer intentions from capabilities, to assume (for example) that a country purchasing or manufacturing substantial levels of armaments would not do so unless it intended to use them. But such inferences can prove very costly, since lots of countries may have the ability to damage one's interests, and threats once identified tend to demand action. Moreover, such inferences may not be correct, since states take actions that may appear

---

[60] Ashton B. Carter and William J. Perry, *Preventive Defense: A New Security Strategy for America* (Washington, DC: Brookings Institution, 1999), pp. 11–15.

threatening for many reasons, including threat perceptions of their own. Indeed, it is of just such reciprocal threat assessments that arms races and even wars are occasionally made. Nor is the possibility of such damaging escalation limited to security interests. In the area of economic well-being, efforts to ensure fair trade may lead to protectionist action-reaction cycles that wind up hurting the nation's prosperity rather than advancing it. The obvious lesson is that strategists should always seek information on their adversaries' intentions independent of what is known about those adversaries' capabilities.

Inferring intentions from capabilities is not the only pattern of thought that can lead to an over-estimation of threats. John Mueller has pointed out that the reverse process can also take place, whereby loudly trumpeted intent to do harm – say, on the part of Nikita "We-Will-Bury-You" Khrushchev or Osama bin Laden – leads decision makers to infer capabilities that may not exist.[61] To those who point to 9/11 as proof of Al Qaeda's power, Mueller responds that such extreme events are often seen to be harbingers of worse to come but usually turn out to be aberrations. In addition to the harbinger fallacy, strategists need to guard against being more alarmed by occasional dramatic fatalities (say, the nearly 3,000 lost on 9/11) than steadily-mounting cumulative ones (like the 15,000 American children who succumb to preventable diseases year after year because they lack vaccinations); becoming unduly frightened by all dangers when informed about one; preferring to put themselves in a much more dangerous situation (such taking a car trip rather than flying) if there is an appearance of control over the danger; and reacting far more to threats if the focus is on those who might be hurt (the 5% who will die of avian influenza) rather than on those who will not (the 95% who will survive).[62] There are also, of course, institutional biases that pressure strategists to exaggerate threats: media for whom bad and sensationalistic news is good news, industry that profits from actions taken to deal with threats, and politicians who feel more comfortable warning about the many threats that will not materialize than being silent about the one that might.

It is also possible, of course, to underestimate threats, as some argue the United States did with regard to Al Qaeda in the late 1990s. There may simply be no knowledge of an actor's capabilities and/or intentions, intelligence on either may be so incomplete that a combination of the two sufficient to constitute a threat is not recognized, or a recognized threat may not rise to the level where it can successfully compete against other threats for the attention of the decision makers who must take action if anything

[61] Unless otherwise specified, this paragraph draws on John Mueller, "Simplicity and Spook: Terrorism and the Dynamics of Threat Exaggeration," *International Studies Perspectives* 6 (May 2005): 208–234.

[62] Paul Slovic, "Informing and Educating the Public About Risk," *Risk Analysis* 6 (No. 4, 1986): 403–415.

is to be done. Even if a threat is known, and its likelihood and seriousness fully appreciated, it may not be plausible enough until after it materializes to generate from the nation's political system the kind of resource reallocation necessary to do anything meaningful about it. Indeed, this last consideration seems particularly germane to the Clinton administration's policy towards Al Qaeda. One thing is certain: with so many factors conspiring to foster the over- or under-estimating of threats, getting the threat picture right remains a major strategic challenge.

As they address that challenge, strategists should remember that threats alone do not create danger for the state. Danger is the product of threat plus *vulnerability*, which can be defined as an openness or susceptibility to injury or loss.[63] Logically, both are necessary: vulnerability alone cannot create danger, but without it no threat is actionable. And the seriousness of the danger depends both on the nature of the threat and on the value of the vulnerable asset. Danger can thus be conceptualized as the product of the probability that a threat will materialize (based on the intent and capability of its originator), the probability that it will succeed (based on the targeted asset's vulnerability), and the consequences if the threat does materialize and succeed (based on the endangered asset's criticality or importance).[64] The requirement that both threat and vulnerability be present for danger to exist points to two very different ways of dealing with it. Strategists who feel endangered may respond *offensively*, by attempting to reduce or eliminate either the intent or capability of the threatening actor to do them harm, or they may respond *defensively*, bypassing the threat itself in favor of efforts to mitigate the vulnerability it seeks to exploit.

The possibility of taking defensive action to reduce vulnerability, instead of using offense to eliminate threats, can help solve the major dilemma strategists face when dealing with threats. For on the one hand, strategists must search out threats to specified interests assiduously and take them seriously, since "the statesman's test is not only the exaltation of his goals but the catastrophe he averts."[65] But on the other hand they must also have the courage not to counter all conceivable threats to the maximum degree, lest they do damage to other interests in the process (for example, hurting prosperity by overspending to protect physical security) or generate counteractions that will leave interests less protected or

---

[63] *Webster's II New Riverside University Dictionary* (Boston, MA: Houghton Mifflin, 1984).

[64] This 3-part definition of danger is adapted from a formula for risk management: $R = Pa \times Ps \times C$, where R is risk, Pa is the probability that an attack will occur, Ps is the probability of the attack's success, and C is the consequence of the attack. Paul Rosenzweig and Alane Kochems, "Risk Assessment and Risk Management: Necessary Tools for Homeland Security," *Backgrounder* No. 1889 (Washington, DC: Heritage Foundation, October 25, 2005), p. 3. I use the term "risk" differently and rather more broadly; see discussion in Chapter 8.

[65] Kissinger, *White House Years*, p. 55.

advanced than when they began. When it comes to national security they
must bear in mind the law of parsimony of enemies, which dictates that
one provoke as few opponents as possible.[66] Therefore, attaining the maximum possible level of security may require that strategists tolerate some
continued danger in the recognition that perfection cannot be attained even
by the most powerful, that all security interests cannot be completely protected. Similarly, attaining the maximum practicable level of prosperity
may involve accepting some level of trade discrimination against American products rather than engaging in retaliatory protectionism that may
do more harm than good. And even the most effective value projection
may need to include some restraint on the promotion of Western mores in
culturally different societies, lest they cause a backlash against American
influence. In all these areas, strategists must avoid pressing beyond what
Clausewitz called the "culminating point" of their efforts, the point at which
success begins to turn into failure.[67]

And what of opportunities? This concept is meant to identify special features of either the international or domestic environment that enable policy
makers to advance national interests in ways unique to the situation under
consideration or that usually are not available or likely to be successful.
Opportunities have many of the same characteristics as threats, including
magnitude or importance (the extent to which the opportunity might really
help advance the interest in question); imminence (whether the opportunity is available now or at some time in the future); and likelihood (if in the
future, whether it will be sustained or fade into unimportance).[68] Opportunities are not a perfect conceptual opposite of threats, however, because
opportunities require action on the part of strategists if they are to make
any difference, whereas threats are expected to have their impact if the
strategist does *not* act. For that reason opportunities are sometimes paired
not with threats but with "constraints," which also depend upon action
by recipients to be meaningful.[69] Certainly a comparison of opportunities
and constraints can be a useful exercise to help validate the strategist's

---

[66] See Frederick H. Hartmann, *The Relations of Nations*, 4th ed. (New York: MacMillan, 1973), p. 83.
[67] Michael Howard and Peter Paret, eds. and trans., Carl von Clausewitz, *On
   War* (Princeton, NJ: Princeton University Press, 1976), pp. 528, 566, 570–
   573. For a discussion of this aspect of the paradoxical logic of strategy, see
   Edward N. Luttwak, *Strategy: The Logic of War and Peace* (Cambridge, MA: Belk-
   nap/Harvard, 1987), especially Chapter 3.
[68] Opportunities do not have tractability, because if they cannot be grasped they
   do not exist. Michael M. Schmitt identifies the same three characteristics, but
   calls them variables used to assess opportunity and threat-based objectives.
   Schmitt, "Identifying National Objectives and Developing Strategy: A Process Oriented Approach," *Strategic Review* (Winter 1997): 24–37.
[69] For example: "International conditions...impose constraints on state action, as
   well as offering opportunities to exploit." Art, *A Grand Strategy for America*,
   p. 12.

assumptions regarding the net effect of the environmental forces that hinder or facilitate state action. Sometimes strategists will go so far as to see threats themselves as providing opportunities, for example by encouraging congressional action, increasing public support for measures they think necessary, or bringing allies on board. John Foster Dulles once noted that "fear makes easy the task of diplomats," and the Bush administration saw 9/11 as helping to facilitate both national defense and international cooperation.[70] But logically threats are not opportunities, and strategists must be wary of conjuring up threats that do not exist in order to facilitate action that would be unnecessary in their absence.

Interests and Threats

By now it should be obvious that the relationship between interests, on the one hand, and threats and opportunities, on the other, is one of the closest and most critical in all strategic thought. In the first place, both opportunities and threats depend in a sense upon interests, for in the logic of strategy, neither can meaningfully exist unless it affects one or more interests. In particular, if a feature of the international environment does not jeopardize an interest, then it is not a threat, however nasty it may be. Thus, while a state can have interests in the absence of threats, it cannot have threats in the absence of interests. Moreover, as noted earlier, the seriousness or magnitude of a threat depends in part on the value of the interest it endangers. Indeed, the very definition of a threat requires that one specify not only the anticipated damage but also its object. Terrorist detonation of a nuclear weapon in downtown Washington, for example, is a horrific threat not just because it would be a very big bang, but because it puts at risk the survival of hundreds of thousands of people along with the continued habitation and use of the nation's capital city. Clearly, threats are important because and to the extent that they jeopardize important interests.

Nor is the relationship between threat and interest necessarily an obvious, either-or kind of thing. Threats worth acting against may be at some remove in time and/or distance from the interests they might endanger, so the *connectivity* of a threat, its temporal and geographic proximity to an interest, is another important threat characteristic. Ambassador Robert Blackwill thinks strategists ought to ask themselves the following questions when deciding upon threats:

[70] Dulles quoted in John Lewis Gaddis, *Strategies of Containment*, Revised and Expanded ed. (New York: Oxford University Press, 2005), p. 142; "The events of September 11, 2001, fundamentally changed the context for relations between the United States and other main centers of global power, and opened vast, new opportunities." *National Security Strategy of the United States*, September 2002, p. 28.

How many steps can be discerned between X threat and major impact on US national security interests...? What are the individual links in that connectivity..., and what is the range of probability that one step will follow another...?

If the U.S. does not act at this stage on a particular external issue, what might then happen to bring the threat closer to a national security interest we care about? How plausible is the postulated chain of events, *and how long is the chain?*[71]

Connectivity, of course, reflects both a threat's likelihood and its imminence, as well as the degree of certainty that attends its assessment.

But not only do threats depend upon a connection with interests for their existence and importance; interests also depend upon threats (and opportunities) for the priority they assume in any strategic plan.[72] In fact, whereas interests really do change little if at all in the short run, recent American foreign affairs strategy demonstrates that what does change is the prioritization given them, based (as noted in Figure 4.8) on three principal criteria: (1) the value placed on an interest, (2) how much of it is already attained, and (3) what threats appear likely to challenge it (or what opportunities the international environment presents to advance it). The interplay of interests and threats is well illustrated by comparing the Cold War presidencies of Reagan, Carter, and Nixon, in which, despite the rather similar international environment each faced, the ranking of interests varied widely with valuation, level of attainment, and threat perceptions.

When Ronald Reagan took office in 1981, for example, his administration felt an extreme sense of threat from the USSR to the United States' physical security. Economic well-being, though the top priority for the administration during its first year in office, was initially seen as a domestic matter without much relevance to foreign affairs strategy. And although Reagan eventually transformed Carter's human rights policy into the modern American notion of spreading democracy around the world, he initially rejected the projection of American values overseas as a luxury the United States could not afford, fearing that efforts to protect human rights in nations like South Korea or the Philippines would jeopardize these allies' cooperation against the all-important Soviet threat and might even destabilize them, opening the door to communist takeovers. Physical security thus became the Reagan administration's foremost and nearly exclusive national interest.

For Jimmy Carter, by contrast, threats to the national interest were far more diffuse. Given his very different view of the nature of the regime in Moscow, Carter did not believe when he took office in 1977 that American physical security was significantly imperiled; as noted in Chapter 2, he

---

[71] Blackwill, "Taxonomy," pp. 405–406. Italics in original.

[72] This quality causes much confusion among writers who attempt to rank interests, as explained regarding Nuecterlein's ranking scheme in note 52 above.

thought that whatever danger existed came more from the massive nuclear capabilities of both sides than from malevolent Soviet intentions. But given high levels of inflation and sluggish economic growth, Carter felt that prosperity was an interest requiring major attention and that its sources often lay abroad, in raw materials and markets for American industry. Even more fundamental was the high value he placed on the projection of American values overseas, his conviction that morality required the United States to stop supporting authoritarian regimes and to insist that they respect the human rights of their citizens. Lacking Reagan's sense of threat from Moscow, Carter felt free to pursue value projection even at considerable cost to U.S. relations with Third World security partners and the Soviet Union itself.

By contrast, all evidence suggests that neither Richard Nixon nor Henry Kissinger gave any thought to the projection of American values overseas; they most certainly would have considered it at best a futile, at worst a dangerous idea. Prosperity also got little attention from Kissinger, at least until the 1973–74 oil embargo and price increases by the Organization of the Petroleum Exporting Countries (OPEC) demonstrated one of the international dimensions of American economic well-being. For this first post-Vietnam administration, like Reagan's after it, the security of the United States was thus the only interest worth much attention, and the Soviet Union was perceived as the major threat to be dealt with – albeit one that could be managed through a sophisticated strategy combining cooperative inducements with the counterforce of military containment.

As these examples illustrate, each administration has to prioritize and make tradeoffs among interests, either under pressure of perceived threats or because it finds some interests of greater value or in shorter supply than others. During the Great Depression of the 1930s President Franklin Roosevelt was willing to resort to unconstitutional legislation and extra-constitutional action (like packing the Supreme Court) to pull the country out of its economic crisis, thus compromising *value preservation* in order to get more *prosperity*. During the Cold War, on the other hand, most American presidents accepted less *economic well-being* as the price of both peacetime rearmament and the economic breaks given allies whose allegiance was needed to protect American *security*, though (as noted) President Carter stressed prosperity and especially value projection over security.[73] President Clinton, facing his own economic problems as he entered office and seeing no likely threats of military attack, similarly reduced physical *security* (by cutting military forces) in order to reap a peace dividend that served the interest of long-term *prosperity*. The George W. Bush administration, believing the nation to be under dire threat of military attack after 9/11, incurred massive federal budget deficits that

---

[73] Alfred E. Eckes, "Trading American Interests," *Foreign Affairs* 71 (Fall 1992): 135–154.

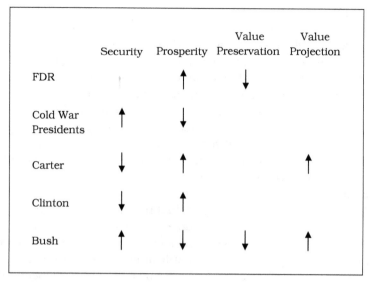

	Security	Prosperity	Value Preservation	Value Projection
FDR		↑	↓	
Cold War Presidents	↑	↓		
Carter	↓	↑		↑
Clinton	↓	↑		
Bush	↑	↓	↓	↑

Figure 4.11: National interest tradeoffs in recent American statecraft.

compromised the country's long-run *prosperity* in order to protect its *security*, and was also willing to forego some *preservation of internal values* (in the form of civil liberties and democratic openness) as the government tried to track down terrorists.[74] Each of these instances involved a different perception of threat, a different valuation of interests, and hence a different calibration of priorities (see Figure 4.11).[75] The fact that such tradeoffs need to be made is the reason why strategists should list interests separately from each other, for combining them makes seeing potential tradeoffs far more difficult.

Threat-Based versus Opportunity-Based Strategies

It is impossible, then, to determine the importance of interests without a sense of the threats and challenges arrayed against them, as well as the opportunities that are available for advancing them. Yet it makes a very big difference whether the strategist begins by assessing threats and opportunities or by determining interests. In particular, there are two

---

[74] Hence the strictures of the Patriot Act and the president's claim of authority to wiretap Americans without court approval. Lisa Rein, "Bush Defends Spying Program As 'Necessary' to Protect U.S.," *Washington Post* (January 2, 2006): A02; Carol D. Leonnig, "Administration Paper Defends Spy Program," *Washington Post* (January 20, 2006): A1, A10.

[75] "When you are in a country with order, you clamor for liberty. When you are in a country of violence and anarchy, you clamor for order." Alejandro Santos, editor of the Colombian weekly magazine *Semana*, quoted in Scott Wilson, "Colombia Tilts Right As Rebels Fight," *Washington Post* (January 31, 2002): A20.

logical flaws inherent in any strategy that identifies threats before being clear about interests.[76] First, such a strategy can leave the initiative largely in the hands of the adversary, allowing him in effect to determine one's own interests. This phenomenon may have been more obvious during the Cold War than in the war on terrorism, but in either case it can result in failing to meet the test of control that successful strategy demands. Second, and for that reason, such a strategy is often very costly, likely to bankrupt the state in an effort to meet the adversary at times and places of *his* choosing.[77] To be sure, there may be powerful psychological reasons, related to the credibility that is so important in the reassurance of allies and deterrence of enemies, not to yield even intrinsically worthless ground. On the one hand, there is the fear that if a nation does not act to stop an adversary in one instance, allies will conclude that it may not do so in another. On the other hand, there is the hope that acting even in a situation where one's interests are not vital will have a deterrent effect in situations where vital interests are engaged. Still, deciding in advance that anything threatened must be protected deprives strategy of its independence of choice.

There is thus a great deal of difference between a strategy that is entirely *centered* on threats, and one that takes *account* of threats to previously-established interests. Sound strategy requires that interests be determined first, independently, with the international environment searched for threats to them only later.[78] The same is true for opportunities, which also must not be allowed to create interests and whose pursuit in their absence might be just as wasteful, if less dangerous. For opportunities that do not benefit interests are no more real than threats that do not imperil them, and they set the stage for actions that are no more justifiable.

---

[76] John Gaddis develops these weaknesses at length for the historical examples of NSC-68 and flexible response, two strategies of containment in which threats were allowed to determine interests. See *Strategies of Containment*, Chapters 4 and 7.

[77] "If a government begins with a threat assessment before going through these earlier conceptual stages [to establish interests], it may react to a threat with major commitments and resources because it is severe... rather than because it is related to a vital US national security interest...." Blackwill, "Taxonomy," p. 404.

[78] Whittle Johnson has argued the contrary case in a lengthy indictment of Gaddis's approach. His view is that interests cannot be determined in the absence of an assessment of threats, since even if one decides which areas of the globe are vital because of their industrial capacity or accumulation of weaponry, one cannot determine which areas adjacent to them must also be defended in order to protect the primary areas unless one knows the threats to them. This kind of reasoning, referred to by Steven Walt as the uncomfortable tendency of strategic interests to develop interests of their own, seems to endow areas of only instrumental importance with primary value. It does not follow the role of national interest within the strategic logic outlined here, which is to justify strategic goals. But then, Johnson also rejects the whole idea of strategic logic. See "The Containment of John Gaddis," *National Interest* 6 (Winter 1986/7): 89–91.

Strategists will usually, of course, find *both* threats and opportunities that relate to valid interests. At first thought it might be assumed that all threats must be dealt with before taking advantage of any opportunity, but this precedence may not reflect sound strategic logic. Should one ignore truly extraordinary opportunities, either to address lesser threats or even to seek some additional safety against the most important ones? Should one protect a well-achieved interest of limited value, rather than advance one of greater importance that is only partially accomplished? Such reflections lead one to conclude that the ranking criteria discussed above should apply to opportunities as well as threats, and that only by considering the relationships between interests and opportunities alongside those between interests and threats can one acquire a sound sense of strategic priorities.

Too much emphasis on either opportunities or threats, then, can lead to illogical and dysfunctional strategies. However, the international environment may provide an abundance of one or the other in any category of the national interest, leading naturally to strategies that are primarily opportunity-based or threat-based.[79] The Clinton and George W. Bush administrations provide two final examples, both of focus on differing areas of the national interest, and of how opportunity- and threat-based strategies evolve.

Without the Soviet threat to deal with, the United States recovered a good deal of choice during the 1990s in determining which interests it wished to advance, a freedom that allowed Clinton to pursue post–Cold War opportunities.[80] As noted earlier, the Clinton team reduced the priority of the security interest in favor of prosperity. Clinton created a new National Economic Council to coordinate the international aspects of economic revitalization, while launching a comprehensive deficit reduction and public investment program in his first State of the Union Address.[81] He was also able to get NAFTA and the General Agreement on Tariffs and Trade's (GATT's) Uruguay Round approved by Congress before the Republicans took charge of both houses in 1995.[82]

But projection of American values abroad was the interest category that gradually began to dominate the Clinton statecraft, for reasons of both

---

[79] Some analysts use the term "interest-based" as the opposite of "threat-based," but the current discussion should make clear that all strategies must be interest-based, whether they emphasize opportunities for or threats to those interests.

[80] Michael N. Schmitt found two "striking features" in the Clinton national security strategy: "the move away from threat to opportunity and from security to well-being and value emphasis...." "Identifying National Objectives and Developing Strategy: A Process Oriented Approach," pp. 32–33.

[81] Ruth Marcus and Ann Devroy, "Asking Americans to 'Face Facts,' Clinton Presents Plan to Raise Taxes, Cut Deficit," *Washington Post* (February 18, 1993): A1, A22.

[82] Thereafter, however, Clinton lost momentum in trade policy, failing repeatedly to secure so-called "fast track" trade agreement authority from Congress. The story of all three trade issues is in Deibel, *Clinton and Congress*, Headline Series 321 (New York: Foreign Policy Association, Fall 2000), pp. 30–34.

opportunity and threat. On the one hand, the administration took advantage of the liberation of areas once dominated by the Soviet Union to proclaim "enlargement" of the circle of market democracies abroad as the new
central organizing principle of its foreign policy. On the other hand, it saw
the human suffering generated by ethnic and nationalist violence as a
threat to American values, and the administration followed its value projection instincts by intervening against that threat from Haiti to the former
Yugoslavia to East Timor. To be sure, such interventions were not easily
decided upon. The Clinton administration felt a moral imperative to redress
atrocities like the ethnic cleansing practiced by Serbian forces in Bosnia
and Kosovo or the genocide that struck Rwanda in 1994. But interventions
to end them could be extremely costly in dollars and lives, urgently raising
the question in each case of whether vital interests were truly engaged. As
Henry Kissinger wrote regarding Somalia:

> Whenever American lives are at stake, so is a conception of vital inter-
> ests – or else the sacrifice mocks the anguish of bereaved families....
> "Humanitarian intervention" asserts that moral and humane concerns
> are so much a part of American life that not only treasure but lives must
> be risked to vindicate them; in their absence, American life would have
> lost some meaning. No other nation has ever put forward such a set of
> propositions.[83]

During the 2000 presidential campaign the Republican party took full
advantage of the dilemmas that attend value projection to attack the
Democrats for their interventions, and the Bush administration came to
power determined to hew closely to more narrowly-defined concepts of
interest and to eliminate what it considered to be nonvital American interventions abroad. "U.S. intervention in these 'humanitarian' crises should
be, at best, exceedingly rare," wrote Condoleezza Rice. "Foreign policy in
a Republican administration will...proceed from the firm ground of the
national interest, not from the interests of an illusory international community."[84] Then came the attacks of September 11, 2001, and with them
a nearly exclusive focus on the terrorist threat. But if the Clinton administration moved from an opportunity-based to a threat-based strategy as it
increasingly pursued value projection, the Bush administration moved in
the opposite direction as it sought security from the threat of terrorism.

The initial Bush reaction to 9/11 was so focused on the threat that it was
overwhelmingly offensive in nature. Although it did include some defensive
elements, like strengthening cockpit doors on commercial airliners, the
administration argued that the multiplicity of targets and the need for a

---

[83] Henry Kissinger, "Somalia: Reservations," *Washington Post* (December 13, 1992):
      C7. For a strong statement of the dangers of humanitarian intervention, see
      Stephen John Steadman, "The New Interventionists," *Foreign Affairs: America
      and the World 1992/93* 72 (No. 1, 1993): 1–16.
[84] Condoleezza Rice, "Promoting the National Interest," *Foreign Affairs* 79 (January-
      February 2000): 62, 53.

free society like America's to maintain its openness would make efforts to reduce vulnerability insufficient.[85] And so it launched a global war against terrorism, ousted the Taliban and Al Qaeda from Afghanistan, and initiated war against Saddam Hussein in Iraq. By 2005, however, the high cost of these actions and the gradual discrediting of its publicly-expressed reasons for invading Iraq were taking their toll, and the administration gradually began emphasizing opportunities alongside threats. In particular, Bush followed Clinton's idea of enlargement, making the spreading of democratic governance worldwide the central organizing principle of his second term in office.

The threat-based and opportunity-based parts of the Bush strategy were in considerable tension, however, because the United States continued to need the cooperation of many countries in its war on terrorism, some of which were governed by authoritarian regimes that routinely violated their subjects' human rights. In a few cases, most notably Uzbekistan, the administration pushed its pursuit of democratic opportunities to the point of rupturing relations that were needed for its offensive against the terrorist threat; but in many more it soft-pedaled its objections against antidemocratic practices in order to preserve counter-terrorist cooperation.[86] How this tension plays out in the future will depend, as does so much of foreign affairs strategy, on the balance of threats and opportunities the United States finds in the international environment, and on how its leaders relate them to their concept of the national interest.

This comparison of threat- and opportunity-based strategies has begun to take us beyond the concepts of interest, threat, and opportunity into the consideration of strategic responses to them, reminding us that specifying national interests and identifying relevant threats and opportunities hardly completes the analysis of foreign affairs strategy. To do that, means must be brought into the equation alongside ends. Strategists must consider power and resources, the tools that the statesman can command, and the ways in which they might be applied to defend interests against threats or take advantage of opportunities to advance interests. Only then can they establish objectives with some confidence of their being accomplished. The role of power in strategic thought, and the instruments of statecraft that give it expression, are the subjects of the next two chapters.

---

[85] To reduce vulnerability airport security was greatly strengthened, airplane cockpit doors were hardened against forcible entry, and a new Department of Homeland Security was created.

[86] Peter Baker, "The Realities of Exporting Democracy," *Washington Post* (January 25, 2006): A1, A8. The survey of mixed results quotes a senior official as saying: "They come into conflict every day....The question becomes the weight given to the intangible interest in freedom versus the tangible interest in having a base in Uzbekistan, for instance."

5

Power and Influence

We have defined strategy as the relationship in thought and action between ends and means, as a systematic way of achieving objectives through the application of resources. Assessing interests (and the threats and opportunities that relate to them) is the first step toward purposeful statecraft, for the process of setting strategic objectives must begin with a clear view of the values strategy is designed to serve. But the strategist cannot even finalize his or her goals, let alone make progress toward their achievement, without also looking carefully at the other end of the ends-means equation.[1] Strategists must grapple, in other words, not only with interests, threats and opportunities, but also with the concept of national power.

Power is the motive force of statecraft, the capacity to act in foreign affairs.[2] It is necessary in order to get things done, to accomplish one's purposes, to carry out one's own will despite the resistance that accompanies all strategic endeavors.[3] But although power is vital to the successful conduct of statecraft, and despite the fact (as noted in Chapter 2) that states in an anarchic world have no choice but to seek power in order to survive, it is still possible to exaggerate its role. Some analysts even go so far as to conclude that power is itself a goal of policy, as in Hans Morgenthau's classic assertion "that statesmen think and act in terms of *interest defined as power.*"[4] But to see power as a goal is for most nation-states at most times fundamentally wrong, and it is always strategically illogical.[5]

---

[1] The process of setting objectives and choosing instruments is the subject of Chapter 7.

[2] This definition is the one used by Donald Puchala in *International Politics Today* (New York: Dodd, Mead & Co., 1971), p. 176, following the analysis of George Modelski, *A Theory of Foreign Policy* (New York: Praeger, 1962).

[3] "'Power' (Macht) is the probability that one actor within a social relationship will be in a position to carry out his own will despite resistance...." Max Weber, *The Theory of Economic and Social Organization* (Glencoe, IL: Free Press, 1957), p. 406.

[4] Hans J. Morgenthau, *Politics Among Nations: The Struggle for Power and Peace*, Fifth ed., Rev. (New York: Alfred A. Knopf, 1978), p. 5. Italics added.

[5] "Simply put, power is an instrument for promoting and achieving goals. As such, it is a mistake to think of the quest for power as the ultimate goal of foreign policy leaders or of the nation they represent. Rather, power is the servant of ambitious leaders... to advance the objectives they hold dear." Bruce Bueno de Mesquita, *Principles of International Politics: People's Power, Preferences, and Perceptions*

Although individuals may seek power for its own sake, governments seek power because they need it to achieve all their other goals. It is instrumental, like money in economic life.[6] To make power into a goal of statecraft is to confuse means with ends, with the result that strategic thinking becomes confused if not impossible.

On the other hand, there is a tendency among American practitioners of foreign policy, far more than among those of domestic policy, to overlook the role of power and assume that simple statements of intent will achieve important ends. The State Department, for example, may announce U.S. policy on trade discrimination, or democratization, or the spread of weapons of mass destruction, as if the statements were self-executing. Of course, the policy declarations of major countries like the United States do have a certain influence of their own, particularly if the country has a reputation for backing its statements with action. But that is precisely the point. The ship of state does not move very far through international waters without a propulsion system. And one of the major contributions of strategic thinking, with its emphasis on the "how" of policy, is to force decision makers to confront the need for resources to back their objectives, along with the implications of acquiring and using those resources.

Thus, the "power and influence" section on the "analyze" level of the model for foreign affairs strategy is the place to evaluate the availability and extent of resources to back statecraft – including the state of the national economy and federal budget – and to ask whether the nation's power is limited and fixed or ample and expandable (see Figure 5.1). It is also the place to analyze the influence that the United States is likely to have on the actors whose cooperation it needs to accomplish its objectives. As will be made clear in what follows, "power" should be distinguished from "instruments" of statecraft both conceptually and operationally; both are "MEANS" of strategy, but power as used here is latent or potential in nature, whereas instruments are the actual, mobilized *forms* of power. Instruments must be created from the nation's potential power and so are located below power and influence, and both are placed below the "domestic environment" because power flows from domestic attributes. This chapter explores both the meaning of power in the twenty-first century and its relationship to other strategic concepts.

(Washington, DC: CQ Press, 2003), p 15. See also Kenneth N. Waltz, "Realist Thought and Neorealist Theory," *Journal of International Affairs* 44 (Spring 1990): 34–36.
6   "Influence (an aspect of power) is essentially a means to an end. Some governments or leaders may seek influence for its own sake, but for most it is instrumental, just like money. States use influence primarily for achieving or defending other goals...." K. J. Holsti, *International Politics: A Framework for Analysis*, 6th ed. (New York: Prentice-Hall, 1992), p. 117.

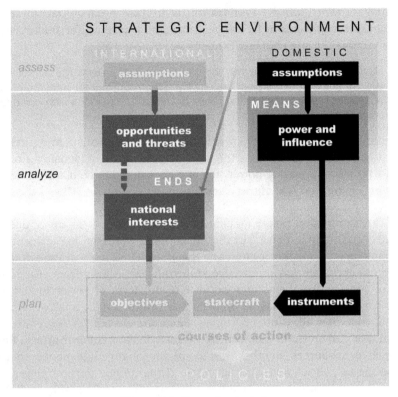

Figure 5.1: Power in strategy.

Power as Control over Resources

Power is not only one of the most important factors in statecraft but also one of the most central and elusive concepts in political theory.[7] Although political scientists are anything but agreed on its meaning, there are three basic ways of looking at power: first, as control over resources; second, as control over actors; and third, as control over outcomes.[8] Control over resources is the oldest and most widely used conceptualization – the oldest, that is, among scholars, and still the most widely used among statesmen

---

[7] A great deal of time and effort has been invested in attempting to understand and define power and its close correlates, such as strength, influence, authority, rule, persuasion, inducement, coercion, compulsion, compellence, deterrence, force, and so on. Alas, the literature reveals no agreement on terminology. See, for example, Robert A. Dahl, "Power," in David L. Sills, ed., *International Encyclopedia of the Social Sciences*, Vol. 12 (New York: MacMillan/Free Press, 1968), pp. 405–415.

[8] Jeffrey Hart, "Three Approaches to the Measurement of Power in International Relations," *International Organization* 30 (Spring 1976): 303.

and other practitioners.[9] Perhaps this is because viewing power as control over resources seems by far the most straightforward way of thinking about the subject. As one textbook explains it,

> Having power means having the wherewithal or *capacity* to act. Since the capacity to act stems from possessing, controlling, and directing resources requisite for action, power becomes synonymous with resource control.[10]

Being concrete, this view of power lends itself to observation, measurement, and comparison. It also has the considerable virtue of focusing attention on the actor possessing power, the one considered to be *powerful*, and its management and use of the resources at its command. This is the sense in which power is used in this book.

But thinking of power as control over resources – "as an undifferentiated quantifiable mass," in the disparaging words of one academic[11] – seems very unsatisfactory to many theorists. Their main argument is that the requirements for an effective statecraft vary widely from situation to situation, so that what may seem a useful form of power in one may be completely irrelevant or even counterproductive in another. Nuclear weapons, after all, cannot get one's candidate elected UN Secretary General, nor can a veto in the Security Council defeat a nuclear attack. Power assets or resources, in other words, are not fungible like money; they are specific to policies and contingencies. Thus, no one form of power – for example, military power – is inherently superior to all the others. Indeed, some analysts believe that nothing sensible can be said about power at all unless one knows over whom the power is to be exerted and for what purposes.[12]

Instead of viewing power as control over resources, then, most political scientists prefer to define it as a kind of causation, a variation on the venerable scientific theme of independent variables (the controlling factors) and dependent variables (those controlled).[13] Power thus becomes not a set of resources belonging to one actor but a relationship *between* actors in a

---

[9] "Because the ability to control others is often associated with the possession of certain resources, political leaders commonly define power as the possession of resources." Joseph S. Nye, Jr., *Bound to Lead* (New York: Basic Books, 1990), p. 26.

[10] Puchala, *International Politics Today*, pp. 172, 176.

[11] David A. Baldwin, "Power Analysis and World Politics: New Trends versus Old Tendencies," in Klaus Knorr, ed., *Power, Strategy, and Security* (Princeton, N.J.: Princeton University Press, 1983), p. 13.

[12] This analysis is based on the argument presented in Baldwin, "Power Analysis in World Politics," pp. 5–17.

[13] "...power terms in modern social science refer to subsets of relations among social units such that the behaviors of one or more units (the responsive units, R) depend in some circumstances on the behavior of other units (the controlling units, C)." Italics in original. Dahl, "Power," p. 407. "The closest equivalent to the power relation is the causal relation." Dahl, "Power," p. 410.

political system – a matter of control by one actor of another. As political scientist David Baldwin puts it, "a relational concept of power assumes that actual or potential power is never inherent in properties of A, but rather inheres in the actual or potential relationship between A's properties and B's value system."[14] Professor Robert Dahl's definition of power as the ability of A to get B to do something *which he would otherwise not do* is probably the most widely known definition of power as control over actors, but Hans Morgenthau obviously had such a definition in mind when he called power "man's control over the minds and actions of other men."[15] "Ultimately," as one recent international relations textbook put it, "power is about mobilizing resources to alter the behavior of others."[16]

Some political scientists take this approach one step further, and argue that it may be better to think of power not so much as control over *actors* as control over *outcomes*, that one should substitute a results-oriented definition for the behavioral one.[17] The reason, again, is that the kind of power varies – not only with the actor being influenced, but also with the issue in dispute. Thinking along these lines, Joseph Nye calls power "the ability to achieve one's purposes or goals," while A. F. K. Organski combines the actors and outcomes approaches by defining it as "the ability to influence the *behavior of others* in accordance with *one's own ends*."[18] The concept of power as control over outcomes has the advantage of being applicable to multilateral, mixed-motive relationships on multiple issues where patterns of control vary among actors according to the concerns being addressed; it also fits situations where resistance seems to come, not from another actor, but from the results of actions taken for other purposes (like global pollution) or even from forces of nature. By focusing on outcomes, this way of thinking about power also has a comforting finality about it: certainly controlling resources or other actors must be secondary to achieving results.[19]

---

[14] Baldwin, "Power Analysis in World Politics," p. 13. "Mere possession of resources does not guarantee power. To confer power, these resources must be used, and they must be used in such a way as to influence other nations, for power is the ability to determine the behavior of others." A. F. K. Organski, *World Politics*, 2nd ed. (New York: Alfred A. Knopf, 1968), p. 103.

[15] Robert Dahl, "The Concept of Power," *Behavioral Science* 2 (July 1957): 202. Italics added. Morgenthau, *Politics Among Nations*, p. 30. "Whatever the material objectives of a foreign policy, such as the acquisition of sources of raw materials, the control of sea lanes, or territorial changes, they always entail control of the actions of others through influence over their minds." Morgenthau, pp. 33–34.

[16] Bueno de Mesquita, *Principles of International Politics*, p. 15. See also Holsti, *International Politics*, p. 117: "power can thus be defined as the general capacity of a state to control the behavior of others."

[17] "Power can be thought of as the ability of an actor to get others to do something they otherwise would not do. . . . Power can also be conceived in terms of control over outcomes." Robert O. Keohane and Joseph S. Nye, *Power and Interdependence* (Boston: Little Brown, 1977), p. 11.

[18] Nye, *Bound to Lead*, pp. 25–26. Organski, *World Politics*, p. 104; italics added.

[19] Hart, "Three Approaches," pp. 296–297.

There is no question that conceptualizing power as control over actors or outcomes captures some compelling insights: that no one kind of power is inherently superior to any other in all situations, that different forms of power are needed to influence different actors and achieve different outcomes, that the impact of one's power depends on the actor being influenced – on its values and interests – as well as on one's own resources, and that for all these reasons nations can be powerful with some actors on some issues and weak on others. But it still makes sense for the strategist to restrict the meaning of power to control over resources, leaving these insights to be applied at other levels of strategic analysis.[20] For the trouble with the causal, relational definitions of power is that they progressively broaden the term until it subsumes virtually the whole of strategic logic, indeed of international politics.[21] They also lead to awkward terminology and semantic confusion.[22] It is more productive for strategic thinking to disaggregate, to define terms operationally, and to maintain a national rather than an abstract perspective.

Power should be seen, then, as describing the capabilities of an actor in international politics, the resources the actor controls. And if power is a characteristic of the initiator of a foreign affairs strategy, *influence* should be seen as the effect of that power on its intended targets. Influence may of course occur without its being intended by a powerful actor, but it always pertains to the recipient in a power relationship, to the actor upon which power is having its effect. Power exists independently of influence; it should neither be automatically assumed to confer influence nor automatically discounted if it fails to do so.[23] Strategists of the world's most powerful country court disaster when they confuse the two concepts, and

---

[20] In particular, the points made about the non-fungiblity of power are addressed by differentiating between potential and mobilized power, by specifying the strengths and weaknesses of the various instruments of policy grouped under the latter term (see Chapter 6), and by differentiating power from influence.

[21] Power as control over actors distracts attention from the user of power and his management of the resources necessary to strategic success; power as control over outcomes not only subsumes goals but virtually every other influence that may affect results. The trouble is that both causal definitions immerse one in the sea of variables that intervene between the exercise of one's power and the change in behavior or outcome that is desired. It is much cleaner analytically to consider those variables separately from one's own power to affect the behavior or outcome in question.

[22] Having equated power and influence, Baldwin and other writers are forced to use the awkward phrase "power bases," "power resources," "power assets," or "bases of influence" to describe the resources behind an actor's power. Far simpler to use the terms as laymen do, being clear that power and influence *are* different. David A. Baldwin, *Economic Statecraft* (Princeton, NJ: Princeton University Press, 1985), p. 9 note 6, pp. 20–24.

[23] "...power does not automatically equal influence." Robert J. Lieber, *The American Era: Power and Strategy for the 21st Century* (New York: Cambridge University Press, 2005), p. 19.

they must never forget that "it is influence, not power, that is ultimately most valuable."[24] Restricting the term power to control over resources will allow this chapter to focus on the still formidable variety of issues relating to the nation's management, husbanding, and use of its resources. For deciding to think about power as control over resources only begins the distinctions one must make before coming up with a concept of power that is useful for strategic purposes.

Latent or Potential Power

There are at least three dimensions of power-as-resources to which the strategist must be sensitive, each with its own important implications. The first is the distinction between latent and mobilized power, that is, between the potentiality for power that is inherent in a nation, on the one hand, and the power that is actually available to the strategist to conduct statecraft, on the other. Distinguishing between them is not just an academic exercise but one of the most fundamental of strategic choices.

Latent or potential power comes from national attributes that in themselves have nothing to do with foreign affairs – and this is why "power and influence" is located below the "domestic environment" in the model for foreign affairs strategy (see Figure 5.2).[25] A nation's *size or territorial extent* is certainly important, if only because it makes possible the massing of other elements of power. For example, although the fact that there are many countries larger yet far less powerful than Germany or Japan proves that size is not the only determinant of power, it is no accident that the superpowers of the Cold War era were the first and fourth biggest countries in the world. *Location and other geographical characteristics* (like climate and topography) may also be important; consider the radically different situations of the United States (still somewhat protected by oceans on two sides) and Poland (stuck on the invasion route between Russia and Germany without natural barriers to attack), or Afghanistan (both an historic invasion route and extremely mountainous), or Turkey (placed in a critical strategic location between Europe, Russia, and the Middle East/Persian Gulf/Central Asia). *Population* is also certainly an element of latent power – the USSR and U.S. were third and fourth most populous countries

[24] Stephen G. Brooks and William C. Wohlforth, "American Primacy in Perspective," *Foreign Affairs* 81 (July/August 2002): 32. See also Frederick Kempe, "A Question of Clout: America Has Never Been Stronger, But Its Global Influence is Waning," *Wall Street Journal* (October 17, 2005): "What's changed most [about the U.S. between 1990 and 2005] is the U.S. ability to translate muscle into clout, strength into influence."

[25] Treatments of the concrete elements of national power can be found in Morgenthau, *Politics Among Nations*; Organski, *World Politics*; Ray S. Cline, *World Power Trends and U.S. Foreign Policy for the 1980s* (Boulder, CO: Westview Press, 1980); and David Jablonsky, "National Power," *Parameters* (Spring 1997): 34–54.

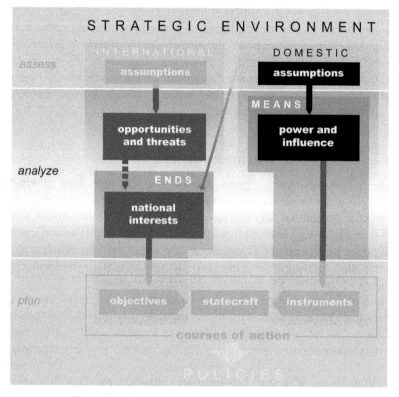

Figure 5.2: Power and the domestic environment.

during the Cold War – though a good deal depends on the ratio of people to landmass (population density) and on the education level and skills that the people possess. A country's *natural resources* contribute to its potential power, as the OPEC countries remind us by positive example and countless poverty-striken Third World states by negative; some would argue that energy resources and certain critical nonfuel minerals should be particularly noted as power factors because of their importance to economic health and military production.[26] But perhaps most important is the country's overall level of *economic sophistication* – its degree of industrialization, technological prowess, and overall wealth-generating capacity – for it is upon this foundation that mobilized power ultimately rests. As former U.S. Secretary of Defense Les Aspin once said, "In the short run U.S. security is protected by military power; in the long run it's protected by economic power."[27]

---

[26] See Ray S. Cline, *World Power Assessment: A Calculus of Strategic Drift* (Boulder, CO: Westview Press, 1975).

[27] Speech at the National Defense University, March 25, 1993.

Tangible factors:
Size or territorial extent
Location
Geographical characteristics
Population
Natural resources
Economic productivity
Intangible factors:
Social cohesion
Political stability
National character
Government and leadership
National will or morale
Intellectual quality

Figure 5.3: Attributes of latent power.

There are also certain intangible elements of power that should be considered under the heading of human, social, or qualitative factors (see Figure 5.3).[28] Some are inherent in society, others in its government, and some in the relationship between them. For example, there is little question but that a society must have a minimum of *social cohesion and political stability* if it is to be able to make use of the concrete elements of its power to effectively pursue foreign policy goals. A country that is plagued by deep ethnic or religious divisions, by significant domestic violence, or in the worst case by armed insurgency will have great difficulty applying its power or attention to foreign affairs. In addition, a nation's power is doubtless affected in a variety of ways by something called *national character*, a vague concept related to the cultural factors discussed in Chapters 2 and 3 that nevertheless remains useful to explain why some countries seem particularly good at statecraft while others with equal resources seem inept. The *quality of government and national leadership* – products of national character and the kind of political system a nation has – are also key determinants of its power, and the kind of relationship that exists between government and society can also be critical. A state with a solid bond of confidence and trust between leaders and led will be much more powerful, other things being equal, than one where the government is widely viewed as inept, dishonest, or illegitimate. The 2002 *National Security Strategy of the United States* summed it up as follows: "Ultimately, the foundation of American

---

[28] Organski and Jablonsky distinguish "natural" from "social" determinants of power; Morgenthau uses the term "qualitative" versus quantitative.

strength is at home. It is in the skills of our people, the dynamism of our economy, and the resilience of our institutions."[29]

Quality in society and government are manifest both in the motivation behind foreign policy and in the intelligence with which it is conducted. The former is sometimes called *national will or morale*, defined as a readiness to sacrifice, "a willingness by a large percentage of the individuals in a nation's population to put the nation's welfare above their own," or simply as "the degree of determination with which a nation supports the foreign policies of its government in peace or war."[30] In a nation-state, as in its military forces, morale may be most obvious in the ability to stand up under attack, but sacrifices may be called for in peacetime as well. One experienced American diplomat maintained that "determination may count as heavily as capabilities" in a nation's power, and spelled out its elements as the propensity to use capabilities, fortitude in the face of setbacks and sacrifices, and obstinacy in insisting on advantageous outcomes of its foreign undertakings.[31] The popular readiness to apply national resources to foreign affairs in general, and in particular to the foreign policy goals its government specifies, is just one of the ways in which public opinion and support becomes an aspect of national power.[32]

But the character of a state's government also affects its power through the *intellectual quality* that is brought to the conduct of foreign affairs. It is axiomatic that, even with the best of national will and morale, resources also have to be applied with brains if they are to have their intended effect. Strategic wisdom and tactical facility, the quality of statecraft and diplomacy, are therefore also vital to a nation's power, as is "the extent to which a state enjoys a reputation for well-informed, bold, and shrewd decision making by its government and national elites."[33] One need look no farther than the Carter administration or the early Clinton years to find excellent if unfortunate examples of the way in which strategic incoherence and tactical clumsiness can reduce a state's power in the world.[34]

The concrete or tangible elements of power discussed earlier can be thought of as additive or cumulative in nature, with the country's power generally expanding as each increases. In fact, many analysts have

---

[29] *The National Security Strategy of the United States of America* (Washington, DC: The White House, September 2002), p. 31.

[30] Sacrifice and relative welfare are discussed in Organski, *World Politics*, p. 184; support is Morgenthau's definition, *Politics Among Nations*, p. 140.

[31] Chas. W. Freeman, Jr., *Arts of Power: Statecraft and Diplomacy* (Washington, DC: U.S. Institute of Peace Press, 1997), pp 15–16.

[32] In the American political system, public opinion affects national power through its impact on resource allocation, by directly restraining what the President can do without congressional approval, by indirectly affecting his chances of reelection, and by affecting the perceptions of power held by those the president is trying to influence (see Chapter 3).

[33] Freeman, *Arts of Power*, p. 16.

[34] See Chapter 8.

attempted to quantify them and add up results, totaling territory in square miles, population in millions, gross national product in common currency values, and other factors to come up with a number representing total power that can be used to compare one nation's power with another's.[35] Such efforts are inherently unsatisfying, however, not only because they add up very dissimilar attributes, but also because they cannot include the intangible factors of policy motivation and intelligence. In fact, these intangible characteristics are probably best seen, not as among the power factors that can be added up to arrive at total power, but rather as multipliers of concrete power attributes. That is, their presence can increase a nation's power well beyond what its sheer resources might indicate, while their absence can reduce it to a fraction of what concrete resources would seem to make possible.[36]

Some analysts go so far as to include in potential power other intangible attributes that, like national character, have little to do with the intentionality of government. For example, the United States is arguably more powerful in today's information age simply because most Americans' native language is also the most widely used international language, a circumstance that contributes to the rapid diffusion of American culture and ideas throughout the global information net. If power means exercising influence over the minds as well as the actions of others this situation must count for something; the contrast with the difficult-to-learn Japanese or Chinese languages, for example, could hardly be more obvious. Similarly, the United States' ability to dominate international agencies and shape the agendas where key issues are decided – sometimes called *structural power* – can also greatly increase the chances it will achieve favorable outcomes.[37] Joseph Nye calls these kinds of attributes "soft power" and contrasts them with the "commanding method of exercising power":

[35] Organski reduces it all to GNP, which he believes represents power adequately all by itself; see *World Politics*, pp. 207–215. Steve Walt adds population and GNP to men under arms and defense spending, thus combining potential and mobilized power (see below); "Alliance Formation and the Balance of World Power," *International Security* 9 (Spring 1985): 42–43. Morgenthau does not attempt quantification, explaining that the process is subjective anyway; *Politics Among Nations*, pp. 156–160.

[36] Ray Cline offers the formula $Pp = (C + E + M) \times (S + W)$, where perceived power is equal to critical mass (population plus territory) plus economic and military capability, *times* strategic purpose and national will. Obviously, if there is no purpose or will, the concrete power factors count for nothing – at least in this equation. Cline also goes so far as to put a number on the intangible factors so that the whole equation can be used to produce a numerical rank. *World Power Trends*, pp. 1–23, 138–148, 166–178.

[37] See Holsti, *International Politics*, p. 128–130. "When you are looking for the effects of structural power, ask some of the following questions: Whose agenda is being discussed? Whose rules are being debated? Who established those rules? Who determines whether the 'playing field' is even? Who provides the referees? Whose standards are prevailing? Whose language do we use...?"

Hard power is the ability to get others to do what they otherwise would not do through threats or rewards. . . .

Soft power, on the other hand, is the ability to get desired outcomes because others want what you want. It is the ability to achieve goals through attraction. . . . It works by convincing others to follow or getting them to agree to norms and institutions that produce the desired behavior. Soft power can rest on the appeal of one's ideas or culture or the ability to set the agenda through standards and institutions that shape the preferences of others.[38]

In short, the universality of a country's culture and its ability to establish a set of favorable rules and institutions that govern areas of international activity are critical sources of power.[39]

Walter Russell Mead has characterized the economic side of U.S. soft power as "sticky power, which comprises a set of economic institutions and policies that attracts others towards U.S. influence and then traps them in it."[40] He argues that U.S. sticky power is built on the international monetary system, free trade, and economic integration – including even the huge amount of U.S. debt held by foreign governments, which forces them to defend their large stake in American prosperity.

Whether sticky or soft, however, these conceptualizations of power include very disparate phenomena, some of which are quite dependent upon control over concrete resources, whereas others do not pertain to actors at all. Structural power, for example, inheres more in the international system than in the nation; it may thus be more logically thought of as belonging to the global context affecting the constraints and possibilities within which states operate than as a kind of power possessed by nation-states themselves.[41] Furthermore, soft power may be mainly a vestigial reflection of a nation-state's past control over those resources rather than some new kind of present-day power. The United States, after all, controls the agenda and many of the institutions of world politics because it dominated the international system when they were established. It used its hard power as the victor in World War II to freeze some advantages for itself that it still enjoys, as well as to spread its culture and language worldwide.

[38] Robert O. Keohane and Joseph S. Nye, Jr., "Power and Interdependence in the Information Age," *Foreign Affairs* 77 (September/October 1998): 86.

[39] Joseph S. Nye, Jr., *The Paradox of American Power: Why the World's Only Superpower Can't Go It Alone* (New York: Oxford University Press, 2002), pp. 10–11; also *Bound to Lead*, p. 33. "The ability to establish preferences tends to be associated with the intangible power resources such as culture, ideology, and institutions. This dimension can be thought of as soft power, in contrast to the hard command power usually associated with tangible resources like military and economic strength." Nye, *Bound to Lead*, p. 32.

[40] Walter Russell Mead, "America's Sticky Power," *Foreign Policy* 141 (March/April 2004): 48.

[41] See Chapter 2.

Finally, power that springs from admiration of a country's institutions, values, and culture overseas is not in the control of governments and cannot be turned into usable instruments, like concrete resources can.[42] Despite these limitations, however, the concepts of soft and sticky power remind strategists to capitalize on the advantages and minimize the constraints of their position in the international system, and to conduct themselves so as to increase the latter and decrease the former.

Meanwhile, technology and globalization is changing the power advantages enjoyed by nation-states and nonstate actors. The information revolution has increased the power of nonstate actors by giving an unfiltered voice to individuals and allowing the formation of virtual, transnational interest groups that heretofore would have been too geographically dispersed to coalesce.[43] Information technology should also increase the power of democratic states more than authoritarian ones, both because their citizens are accustomed to using it and because their governments are not threatened by it.[44] When it comes to the size of states, however, the overall effect of globalization seems far less clear. On the one hand, small states able to take advantage of globalization may become more economically viable, and that diffusion of global wealth would in turn imply a long-term increase in their power relative to large states. The web-like architecture of modern interdependence, which should dilute the power of any single hub, may have a similar effect.[45] On the other hand, the cost of IT investments, economies of scale, and barriers to entry could keep smaller states out of the information age or well behind its leaders.[46] However these particular changes play out, evaluating shifts in the importance of various kinds of potential power and their impact upon the strength of various global actors will remain a critical part of strategic analysis.

Actual or Mobilized Power

All these elements of national power – from concrete resources like territory, population, and economic capabilities to the intangibles of society,

---

[42] Nye also at times confuses hard and soft power with coercion and co-optation, writing that soft power "co-opts people rather than coerces them" but also that "hard power can rest on inducements (carrots)" as well as threats (sticks). *The Paradox of American Power*, pp. 8–9. Hard power incentives, in my view, also co-opt. See Chapter 7.

[43] Keohane and Nye, "Power and Interdependence in the Information Age," p. 82.

[44] Keohane and Nye, "Power and Interdependence in the Information Age," pp. 93–94.

[45] Nye, *The Paradox of American Power*, pp. 91–95.

[46] "Contrary to the expectations of some theorists, the information revolution has not greatly decentralized or equalized power among states. If anything, it has had the opposite effect." Keohane and Nye, "Power and Interdependence in the Information Age," p. 89.

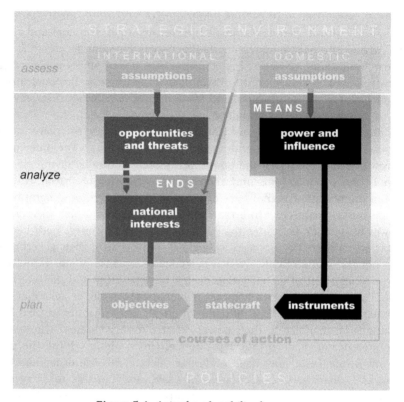

Figure 5.4: Actual and mobilized power.

culture, quality of government and other soft power attributes – represent the power which a nation-state can *potentially* bring to the conduct of its foreign relations. "On the relatively stable foundation of geography," as Hans Morgenthau put it, "the pyramid of national power rises through different gradations of instability to its peak in the fleeting element of national morale."[47] But from the point of view of foreign affairs strategy, power as we have been discussing it so far is only latent. Before it can be used for statecraft it must be mobilized by the government and converted into *actual* power, the tools or instruments of policy, like international radio transmitters, skilled diplomats, intelligence satellites, foreign aid dollars, and of course many kinds of military forces (see Figure 5.4).[48] The strengths and weaknesses of these instruments will be the subject of Chapter 6;

[47] Morgenthau, *Politics Among Nations*, p. 158.
[48] Analysts who recognize the distinction between potential and actual power use different terminology to express it: for example, gross national power versus externally projectable power (Puchala, *International Politics Today*, p. 176); national power versus governmental power (Modelski, *A Theory of Foreign Policy*, pp. 21–23).

once created, they are selected by the strategist as may be most appropriate to pursue immediate objectives that defend against actual threats
or take advantage of real opportunities. But the important points to grasp
here are that potential power must first be converted into actual power,
resources into instruments, and that there are important strategic choices
to be made concerning both the *balance* between these two forms of power
and the *kinds* of actual power to be created.[49]

Potential power is converted into actual power when the government
takes the assets of its citizens and turns them into instruments of statecraft. The confiscation may take the form of taxation, borrowing, or simply
printing money. But regardless of how it is done, since the same resources
can only be used once, the creation of actual power must be at the expense
of potential power.[50] Borrowing, for example, may seem to avoid the costs
to economic growth of taxation, but it will have similar and possibly more
profound effects through the capital markets via higher interest rates, just
as printing money will have its impact through inflation. Thus, no matter
how it is financed, buying the instruments of foreign policy can be thought
of as a kind of consumption, or short-term money in the pocket; whereas
building the nation's potential power is an investment in the future, like
money in the bank. The choice between latent and mobilized power, in
other words, is the classic economic choice between now and later, in this
case between having *some* usable power now and having the ability to get
more usable power later.[51] It is not a choice that is easily made. For while
potential power is fungible, it is not immediately usable; and though actual
power is ready for use, the instruments that comprise it are rather inflexi-
ble, specific in their influence over actors and outcomes. These characteristic differences between potential power and actual power (or instruments
of state power) are summarized in Figure 5.5.

---

[49] Many writers on the subject do not make a clear distinction between these two
forms of power. Writers as distinguished and as different as Morgenthau and
Nye mention military forces in the same sentence as economic power as if they
were on the same strategic level, or worse, as if there were not a strategic contradiction between them. To do so makes it virtually impossible to discuss power
intelligently from a strategic point of view.

[50] For example, "[b]y the 1970s, a negative relationship became evident between
the level of military expenditure and the change in industrial competitiveness:
the lower the level of military expenditure the stronger the competitive performance." James Kurth, "The Common Defense and the World Market," *Daedalus*
(Fall 1991): 216.

[51] One argument against this distinction is that buying defense hardware supports
the defense industrial base and that without the industrial base the country will
not be able to provide sophisticated weapons in the future, so spending on these
instruments supports potential power rather than detracting from it. But this
argument neglects the economic costs of confiscating the resources from whatever use they might have found in the civilian economy; it also fails to recognize
that investment in R&D can be done by the government as well as by the private
sector, on weapons as well as on civilian consumption products.

Power vs. Instruments

Resources	Tools
Money in a bank	Money in the pocket
Investment	Consumption
Fungible	Inflexible
Needs conversion	Immediately useable
Potential, latent	Actual, mobilized
Reflects timing of threat	Reflects kind of threat

Figure 5.5: Latent versus mobilized power.

From the long-term perspective strategists have no more important job than to husband and develop the potential power of the nation-state. Otherwise, they are in the position of a college plagued by declining enrollments that spends its endowment on salaries in order to avoid firing professors and staff; it can be done for a time, but such borrowing from the future eventually leads to disaster. In foreign affairs strategy the disaster will take the form of a slow erosion of the nation-state's future power and probably a deterioration of its relative position in the hierarchy of states. There is always a competition for resources in market economies between the government and the private sector, and then within government between expenditures on domestic and foreign policy. The strategist's long-term responsibility is to see that every dollar not needed for foreign affairs is either left to the private sector or used in domestic programs that will promote economic growth and development.

At the same time, strategists also have a short- to medium-term responsibility to advance the nation's interests and protect them against threats. To do that they need not just potential but actual power, or instruments. And the instruments to be bought must be appropriate to the threats and opportunities they see in the international environment. Since mobilized power is not fungible, it will do little good to have a national missile defense if the threat is a suitcase bomb, or an expensive military establishment if the available opportunity is to support market democracies abroad with foreign aid. The choice among these forms of mobilized power is made more difficult because considerable periods of time are required for a country to accomplish the conversion process: major weapons systems may take decades to design and build, and skilled diplomats are hardly created overnight. Decisions by one administration as to which instruments to buy thus will determine which forms of actual power it or its successor will have five, ten, fifteen, or even thirty years down the road. A mistake here will have consequences that are different, but every bit as disastrous, as those arising from a neglect of potential power: namely, a nation-state faced with a critical opportunity it cannot seize or with a serious threat it cannot counter.

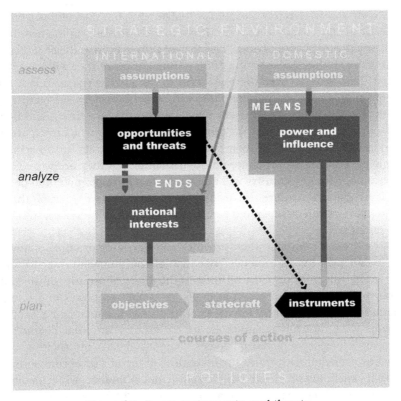

Figure 5.6: Power, instruments, and threats.

In their handling of power, then, strategists must strive for balance, not only between investing in potential power and having mobilized power, but also *among* the various instruments of power they might buy. And their choices in each case will be determined by the kinds of threats and opportunities they see in the future international environment, in relation to the national interests they have defined (hence, the dashed arrow in Figure 5.6 from "opportunities and threats" to "instruments"). As historian Paul Kennedy put it,

> Like an amateur athlete, the nation-state in times of peace ... has to balance many desiderata – earning its keep, enjoying its pleasures, *and* keeping fit and strong; but when the race (or a conflict) occurs, a far larger amount of energies and effort is given to winning and fighting, and the other elements are left until later. ...
>
> Grand strategy in war is, therefore, necessarily more military than it is in peace. The real task for the polity in question is to ensure that, in wartime, the nonmilitary aspects are not totally neglected ...; and that, in peacetime, the military aspects are not totally neglected.[52]

---

[52] Paul Kennedy, *Grand Strategy in War and Peace* (New Haven, CT: Yale University Press, 1991), p. 169.

Kennedy was focused on the military instrument, but the point is a broader one. Strategists who see a severe threat to their interests in the near future will buy the instruments necessary to deal with it, even at the cost of potential power. If they guess wrong and no threat appears they will have weakened their country over the long term to no good purpose. But if a different threat appears their jeopardy will be double, since the country will both lack the instruments needed to deal with the new threat and be less able to acquire them.[53] On the other hand, strategists who anticipate little threat will invest more of their country's resources in its future economic growth, reducing its purchases of instruments.[54] If they are wrong and a threat appears, the country will at least be in a stronger potential position as it struggles to acquire the needed policy tools.[55] It would seem that foreign affairs strategists should retain a presumption, therefore, in favor of potential power.

The Reagan administration provides an interesting example of how this logic can play out in practice. Because of the immediate nature of the threat he saw from the Soviet Union to the physical security of the United States, Ronald Reagan opted strongly for mobilized power and one particular form of it: military forces. Unfortunately, because he believed that means were radically expandable, he did so in a way that degraded the country's long-term, potential power. The huge federal budget deficits created by the administration's unwillingness to tax at a level commensurate with its spending programs crippled government finance, while its massive borrowing to finance the deficit (along with the tight money policy needed to counteract the inflationary forces unleashed by that fiscal stimulus) raised interest rates and sucked in capital from abroad, driving the exchange value of the dollar to historic highs. The credit crunch and the overvalued dollar hurt American manufacturing and turned the United States from the world's biggest creditor country into its biggest debtor, thereby afflicting two of the nation's most important sources of potential power: productive capacity and exportable capital.[56] As a result, one could argue, the

---

[53] David Baldwin argues that you cannot determine whether something is a power resource (meaning a usable instrument of statecraft) unless you know what context it is being used in: "What functions as a power resource in one policy-contingency framework may be irrelevant in another." Therefore, "preparing to deal with the worst contingencies may hinder one's ability to deal with less severe ones." "Power Analysis and World Politics," pp. 7, 16.

[54] Some analysts, called postclassical realists, make a similar point by arguing that statesmen usually focus on the *probability* rather than (as neorealists believe) the *possibility* of conflict, and that they will choose to serve longer range economic interests if the threat level is sufficiently low. Stephen G. Brooks, "Dueling Realisms," *International Organization* 51 (Summer 1997): 445–477.

[55] For example, Clinton may have insufficiently addressed the developing terrorist threat during the 1990s, but his successor would have faced a vastly more difficult situation in attempting to deal with those threats after 9/11 if Clinton had not fixed the deficit problem.

[56] Aaron L. Friedberg, "The Strategic Implications of Relative Economic Decline," *Political Science Quarterly* 104 (Fall 1989): 408–409.

United States moved into the post–Cold War era with a set of policy tools – military forces – that had only marginal relevance to the threats and opportunities of the 1990s, while it was deficient in the capital and competitiveness needed to take advantage of the Soviets having lost the Cold War.[57]

Absolute Power versus Relative Power

How powerful is the United States today? It seems clear from the discussion so far that the question has no simple answer. First, one has to distinguish between potential and actual power, and then decide within each category which elements or instruments are likely to be most important. For latent power, that answer depends on the nature of power in today's world; for mobilized power, the answer is much more tied to the uses to which instruments will be put. Second, one must ask, compared to what? Is the important metric over time, so that one is asking whether the United States is more or less powerful than before? Or is it in comparison to other global actors, so that one is asking whether the country is more or less powerful than another state or states?[58] If the first dimension of power-as-resources to which the strategist must be sensitive is that between latent and actual power, this question leads us to the second: that between absolute and relative power. A brief history of American power may help make the distinction, and the dilemma it contains, clearer.

Both in an absolute and a relative sense, the United States emerged from World War II in an unnaturally strong position.[59] The deficit spending and forced savings of the war effort had been a potent stimulus to its economy even as the productive capacities of virtually every other industrialized country were being destroyed by the fighting. The war also spurred technological advance, so the peace left American corporations in a position to market leading-edge products that had been kept from consumers first by the Great Depression and then by the war's insatiable demand for resources.[60] The United States was also in a position to establish the dollar as the world's reserve currency and write the rules for new financial

---

[57] See, for example, Brent Scowcroft's anguish over the paltry sums available for aid to newly liberated countries of Eastern Europe. George Bush and Brent Scowcroft, *A World Transformed* (New York: Alfred A. Knopf, 1998), pp. 138–140.

[58] As Robert Gilpin wrote: "the essential fact of politics is that power is always relative; one state's gain is by necessity another's loss." Robert Gilpin, *U.S. Power and the Multinational Corporation* (New York: Basic Books, 1975), pp. 22–25, 34.

[59] Paul Kennedy terms the power of the United States "artificially" high, while Joseph Nye calls this the "World War II effect." See Paul Kennedy, *The Rise and Fall of the Great Powers* (New York: Random House, 1987), p. 357; Nye, *Bound to Lead*, p. 5.

[60] In many industries, the U.S. was also able to build on sectoral advantages secured in wartime deals. The U.S. government divided airplane manufacturing with Britain, for example, so that British industry could build fighters while bomber aircraft were built here, giving the U.S. a lead in passenger airframes that persists among its high-tech advantages.

and trading systems favorable to its interests, based on institutions like the International Monetary Fund (IMF) and the GATT, putting in place the infrastructure of its soft power. Operating from a nearly autarchic position that involved less than 10 percent of its GNP in foreign trade, the United States produced and marketed almost half of the manufactured goods in the world of 1950.[61]

The intangible elements of America's potential power also were extremely favorable at this time. Victory over depression and war had given Americans a justifiable sense of self-confidence, and rapidly rising standards of living tended to blunt social, political, and even racial tensions. Successful governmental activism in the New Deal and the struggle against fascism gave Americans a very high level of trust in their government; as noted in Chapter 3, there was a broad consensus in public opinion behind containment as the most important goal of American foreign policy. With such high national morale, the United States readily took on foreign policy tasks from the Marshall Plan to the building of global alliances, and its views were accorded all the prestige that attached to the leader of the coalition that had won World War II.

The instruments of state power were also capable and in great abundance, many of them inherited from the war. Although demobilization was rapid and thorough, the United States carried into the peace the world's most powerful and modern military forces, deployed worldwide from a broad array of bases.[62] It alone possessed the atomic bomb, whose efficacy had just been demonstrated at Japan's expense. Its intelligence and diplomatic services were peopled with giants whose skills and reputations had been honed in the crucible of war, men like George Kennan, Chip Bohlen, Llewellyn Thompson, George Marshall, and Dean Acheson; even the Congress operated within a disciplined hierarchy of political power based on partisan loyalty and seniority principles. In 1947, contemplating an activist foreign policy unknown in earlier peacetime periods, the country completely reorganized its Executive machinery for national security decision making, establishing centralized agencies for defense and intelligence coordinated by a new National Security Council.[63]

By the third decade after the war ended, however, most of these power advantages had vanished. Many had gone because of changes in the world outside the United States, and ironically, some of those changes had been

---

[61] For a lucid portrayal of American economic supremacy in the postwar era, see Joan Edelman Spero, *The Politics of International Economic Relations*, 4th ed. (New York: St. Martin's Press, 1990). Also Kennedy, *Rise and Fall*, pp. 357ff.

[62] Many, of course, were acquired from Great Britain in the famous destroyers-bases deal, a good illustration of the point made earlier about how immediate threats can force a nation to trade potential for actual power.

[63] See David J. Rothkopf, "Greatness Thrust Upon Them," Chapter 3 in *Running the World: The Inside Story of the National Security Council and the Architects of American Power.* (New York: Public Affairs, 2005).

objectives of postwar American foreign affairs strategy. Assisted by the Marshall Plan and protected by the American military, Japan and Europe were now rebuilt and becoming real challengers to American economic primacy, shrinking the United States' share of world manufacturing output to the low 20 percents, where it has remained ever since. Successive rounds of tariff cutting under the American-engineered GATT were opening the U.S. economy to foreign trade, even as the depletion of domestic oil reserves left the country more and more vulnerable to foreign energy cartels. By 1971 the Nixon administration was forced to float the dollar, destroying the heart of the fixed exchange rate system the United States had created after the war, and in 1973 the U.S. suffered the first oil supply and price shocks administered by OPEC in retaliation for American support of Israel during its October War. Meanwhile the Third World had come into existence, to some extent as a result of long-standing American anticolonial policies, adding many new independent centers of power to an increasingly unwieldy international system. Most important in this relative decline of American power, though, was one change American strategy had fought to prevent: the reconstruction of the Soviet Union as an industrialized power and its emergence (after the humiliation of the 1962 Cuban missile crisis) as a military superpower.

But not all of the decline of American power that became apparent in the late 1960s and early 1970s was relative and a result of such changes in the external environment. In fact, these systemic changes were paralleled by a number of developments *within* the United States that reduced the country's absolute power. Not surprisingly, Americans' self-confidence suffered greatly as the country's economic, political, and military vulnerability was exposed, and national morale plummeted. At the same time, social cohesion was strained by slowing increases in standards of living, a facing up to long-deferred issues of racial and gender equality, and the arrival of the huge baby-boom generation at the age of independence (if not rebellion). The American political system too seemed to evolve in ways less able to deal with the nation's growing problems, as demands for democratization and the impact of television politics led to widespread use of primaries for choosing presidential candidates, a weakening of the roles of political parties, and a breakdown of mechanisms for maintaining discipline in Congress.

But by far the most corrosive of the internal developments affecting American absolute power were the manifold effects of the undeclared war in Vietnam. First, as noted in Chapter 3, the war and its conduct destroyed the foreign policy consensus backing containment and, along with the Watergate scandal, permanently reduced Americans' trust in their government to a quarter of its historic levels. Substantial numbers of them began to believe that the United States was a force for evil in the world, an attitude that not only reduced popular backing for foreign policy in general but also severely damaged the relationship between government and governed that is central to national power. Second, Vietnam cost the United States heavily in the instruments of foreign policy by so turning the American people against virtually all the harder tools of statecraft that they refused to fund a decade of military modernization and systematically ravaged their country's intelligence and covert action capabilities. Third, the Johnson administration's refusal either to abandon its Great Society programs or tax the country in order to pay for them along with the war was the first step toward the financial indiscipline that became chronic in the Reagan and Bush years. It led directly to inflationary pressures so strong that the Nixon, Ford, Carter, and early Reagan economic policies were dominated by efforts to contain them.[64] Finally, the spectacle of the United States caught in a war it would neither win nor leave, along with the other evidence of disarray in domestic and foreign policy, did great damage to American prestige in the world community, reversing the confidence in its leadership felt after the war by the subjects of American influence overseas and making its power that much harder to exercise.

The Economics of American Power

By the 1980s the impact of some of the country's self-inflicted wounds, like Vietnam and Watergate, had begun to fade. As noted above, Ronald Reagan declared that it was morning in America, adopted expansionary fiscal and contractionary monetary policies to deal with stagflation, and began the largest peacetime rearmament in American history. But the changes in the domestic social and political landscape described above, as well as increases in the power of other states, friendly and hostile, continued to affect America's absolute and relative power. Moreover, during the administration of George H. W. Bush the economy slipped into a recession, globalization began to make its negative effects felt on personal economic security, and Japan seemed to be an unstoppable economic powerhouse. Even after the collapse of the Soviet Union dramatically increased U.S. power in relation to its former principal adversary, many analysts thought that the economic basis of American power was deteriorating.[65]

As a result, a vigorous debate opened in the United States during the late 1980s and early 1990s about the decline of American power, a debate

---

[64] Nixon defied Republican ideology to impose wage and price controls, while Ford launched his ludicrous "Whip Inflation Now" campaign, complete with WIN buttons.

[65] As financier Robert Hormatz warned in the summer of 1991, "Unless the United States reinvigorates in this decade the economic roots of its international power, it risks an erosion of self-confidence and of its international leadership at the turn of the century. With a weak economy and a society in conflict over how to allocate slowly growing resources, this nation would find it increasingly difficult to achieve its essential global objectives." Robert D. Hormats, "The Roots of American Power," *Foreign Affairs* 70 (Summer 1991): 133–134.

that was at times more confusing than enlightening.[66] It is almost certain, for example, that the power of the United States was greater in *absolute* terms at the height of the declinist vogue in 1990 than it had been in 1950. Although some of the instruments of foreign policy may once have been in greater supply than they were in 1990, most of the tangible resources discussed above were far more robust in 1990 than they were even ten or fifteen years earlier. Certainly the American economy was bigger, more productive, and more technologically sophisticated than ever before. And yet virtually all observers would acknowledge that the power of the United States *relative* to its major allies (and, until the collapse of the Soviet Union, its major adversary) was less in the 1980s than it had been in the 1950s. This was so, of course, because relative power takes into account trends in *others'* power as well as one's own, and the United States, for a variety of reasons to be discussed later, was growing more powerful in the 1970s and 1980s at a slower rate than many other nation-states. "*Relative* decline" may therefore mean only "less rapid increase than others," not the downward movement in absolute power that the common-sense meaning of the term "decline" implies.

Unless it acquires more resources, the only way a nation-state can get wealthier over the long run is to improve the efficiency with which it uses what it has. Efficiency is best measured by the productivity of its labor force, the ratio of output produced to hours worked. Improving productivity requires investment: in research and development of new technology, in the capital equipment that turns out new products, in public infrastructure to grease the wheels of production and commerce, and in the skills of the labor force that manages all these processes. Investment in turn requires saving, and saving usually depends upon a willingness to defer at least some current consumption.[67] In sum, the path to wealth looks something like this: less consumption → more savings → more investment → more productivity.

We are back, in other words, to the choice between now and later, and statistics in the late 1980s and early 1990s indicated that the United States was increasingly choosing to consume and even to borrow for consumption rather than to save and invest for the future. Driven by huge dissavings in the federal budget and a reduction in personal savings rates, net national savings dropped from 8 percent of national product in 1950 to 1.7 percent in 1990.[68] The corresponding figures for net investment dropped from 7.7 percent to 3.4 percent, and with so little investment driving it, productivity growth fell from 3 percent annually to zero over the same

---

[66] The debate was triggered by an improbable historical best seller, Paul Kennedy's *The Rise and Fall of the Great Powers* (New York: Random House, 1987).

[67] Going into debt, of course, is negative savings, though the resources acquired by borrowing can be used for investment as well as for consumption.

[68] Hormats, "Roots of American Power," p. 145.

period.[69] Statistics showed that the U.S. role in the world economy also had deteriorated by the end of the Cold War. The U.S. share of world exports fell from 17 percent in 1950 to 10 percent in 1988, and its share of the global exports of science-based industries – that is, of world high-tech exports – dropped from 36 percent in the mid-1950s to 20 percent in the late 1980s.[70] Moreover, the American economy was itself far more penetrated by imports than ever before, many of them high-tech consumer and capital goods.[71] The share of patents granted by the United States to Americans declined more than 10 percent from 1970 to 1986.[72] Even U.S. monetary leadership waned, as the roughly half of the world's monetary reserves held in dollars in 1950 shrunk to just 9 percent by 1988.[73]

Faced with these dismal statistics, some foreign affairs strategists proposed international retrenchment, a shift in priorities from foreign to domestic needs. The danger that Yale historian Paul Kennedy pointed out under the rubric "imperial overstretch" was that the U.S. would feel so threatened by its declining position that it would sacrifice potential power in the effort to maintain its mobilized power:

> Past experience shows that even as the relative economic strength of number-one countries has ebbed, the growing foreign challenges to their position have compelled them to allocate more and more of their resources to the military sector, which in turn has squeezed out productive investment and, over time, led to a downward spiral of slower growth, heavier taxes, deepening domestic splits over spending priorities, and a weakening capacity to bear the burdens of defense.[74]

While it is certainly true that Japan or Germany, for example, spent a dramatically lower portion of gross national product on defense than the United States did during the Cold War and grew faster, few analysts found the imperial overstretch argument compelling.[75] After all, the share of

---

[69] As Theodore H. Moran put it in 1993, "If the relationship between consumption, savings, and investment proceeds unchanged, the United States will indeed follow, in its own way, the trajectory along which other great powers have slid." *American Economic Policy and National Security* (New York: Council on Foreign Relations Press, 1993), p. 70.

[70] Share of global exports: Nye, *Bound to Lead*, p. 2. Share of high-tech exports: Nye, *Bound to Lead*, p. 77; Moran, *American Economic Policy and National Security*, p. 33; Friedberg, "The Strategic Implications of Relative Economic Decline," p. 407. At the same time, the U.S. surplus of high-tech exports over imports shrunk from $6B in 1970 to $1B in 1987. Nye, *Bound to Lead*, p. 212.

[71] The overall import penetration ratio for the U.S. economy was 4.3% in 1965 but 13.5% in 1980. Friedberg, "The Strategic Implications of Relative Economic Decline," p. 405.

[72] From 65.7% in 1970 to 54% in 1986. Nye, *Bound to Lead*, p. 212.

[73] Nye, *Bound to Lead*, p. 2.

[74] Paul Kennedy, "The (Relative) Decline of America," *Atlantic* 260 (August 1987): 33.

[75] See Friedberg, "The Strategic Implications of Relative Economic Decline," pp. 410–411; Moran, *American Economic Policy and National Security*, p. 11; Nye,

American GNP devoted to the military did not increase during the Cold War but gradually decreased, from 8 percent during the years of the country's greatest post-World War II power advantage to 5 to 6 percent in the later Cold War years to 3 percent or less in the first post–Cold War decade. Moreover, the significant choice for potential power is not between spending on matters foreign or domestic but between consumption and investment, and defense spending was only a small part of overall American consumption, public and private.[76]

As noted earlier, the only way to increase potential power is to cut consumption in favor of savings and investment, to vote for more "later" and less "now." Since dissaving by the federal government was the largest component of the low American savings rate in the early 1990s, President Clinton understood that the way out of American relative decline was first to reduce if not eliminate the federal budget deficit, a task he accomplished by the mid-1990s.[77] With the government's escalating demands for capital suddenly thrown into reverse, interest rates fell just as American businesses were learning how to use the new information technology and beginning to reap the benefits of the restructuring that global competition had forced them to undertake. The economy roared ahead in the late 1990s, and after 1994 manufacturing productivity growth more than doubled from the rates seen in the 1980s and early '90s.[78]

As a result, the answer to the question "How powerful is the United States?" seems to have but one answer at the beginning of the twenty-first century: absolutely more powerful than it had ever been, and relatively more powerful than any foreseeable competitor. Considering the

---

Bound to Lead, pp. 9–10; and Hormats, "Roots of American Power," p. 137: "The danger for the United States at the end of this century is not imperial overstretch but domestic underperformance...."

[76] Joseph S. Nye, Jr., "What New World Order?" *Foreign Affairs* 71 (Spring 1992): 94.

[77] Clinton also wanted to "grow the economy" and add to potential power via federally-funded investments: in public infrastructure, R & D spending (through tax credits), and the education and training of workers. Moran, *American Economic Policy and National Security*, pp. 22, 28. Unfortunately, by increasing spending or lowering tax revenues, each of these latter moves worked against efforts to reduce the deficit, so the battle between deficit reduction and investment in economic growth became the principal economic policy struggle of the early Clinton years. For the history of this struggle, see Bob Woodward, *The Agenda: Inside the Clinton White House* (New York: Simon and Shuster, 1994). When push came to shove, Clinton chose deficit reduction.

[78] The average annual rate of change in output per hour in U.S. manufacturing was 2.9% from 1978–1993, 4.3% from 1994–1997, and 6.8% from 1998–2003. Author's calculations based on data in "International Comparisons of Manufacturing Productivity and Unit Labor Cost Trends, Supplementary Tables, 1950–2003," Table 1.2, U.S. Department of Labor, Bureau of Labor Statistics, February 2005. See also Evan Koenig, "Productivity Growth," Federal Reserve Bank of Dallas *Expand Your Insight*, March 1, 2000 http://www.dallasfed.org/eyi/usecon/0003growth.html

material attributes of potential power, the United States still has the fourth largest land mass of any country. It also retains many of the advantages of what Washington called its "detached and distant situation," including the ability to accumulate huge advantages in the hard instruments of power without automatically threatening other states and provoking them to balance against it.[79] The U.S. population, though a fraction of that in India or China, is far better educated – more than a third of all the colleges and universities in the world are located in America – and less plagued by rapid aging and impending shrinkage than Europe, Japan, or Russia.[80] The United States also retains many of its soft-power advantages: the attractiveness of its popular culture and political system, the worldwide use of its language, and its dominant position in international political, technical, and economic institutions.[81]

Most important in potential power, though, is the strength of America's economy. In absolute terms, the United States is much richer than ever before. In relative terms, its share of world output remains half what it was immediately after World War II, but the U.S. lead is still formidable.[82] Both the economy's size as measured by GDP and its spending on R&D are twice those of its closest rival, Japan.[83] Indeed, with R&D nearly equal to that of the next seven richest countries combined, the United States in the early twenty-first century is "continually expanding its lead in the innovation and application of new technology."[84] It publishes a third of the world's scientific papers, registers half its patents, and provides a third of its high-tech services.[85] Well-positioned to profit from globalization, the

---

[79] The phrase in quotes is from Washington's Farewell Address, 1796, as printed in Ruhl J. Bartlett, *The Record of American Diplomacy* (New York: Alfred A. Knopf, 1964), p. 87. The U.S. also benefits from the fact that most other states attempting to amass significant power would find themselves balanced by the neighbors they would unavoidably threaten before they could become powerful enough to challenge the U.S. William C. Wohlforth, "The Stability of a Unipolar World," *International Security* 24 (Summer 1999): 28–31.

[80] Thomas L. Friedman, *The World Is Flat: A Brief History of the Twenty-First Century* (New York: Farrar, Straus and Giroux, 2005), quoting Alan Goodman on higher education, p. 224; "Outside the United States, the population of the developed world is peaking now. By the early 2010s, assuming no change in fertility, it will decline by about one million people per year; by the late 2020s, by about three million people per year; and in the 2040s, by over five million people per year." Peter G. Peterson, "Riding for a Fall," *Foreign Affairs* 83 (September/October 2004): 124.

[81] Joseph S. Nye, Jr., "The Decline of America's Soft Power," *Foreign Affairs* 83 (May/June 2004): 16–20.

[82] U.S. share of world output is 22%. David H. Levey and Stuart S. Brown, "The Overstretch Myth," *Foreign Affairs* 84 (March/April 2005): 7.

[83] GDP: Brooks and Wohlforth, "American Primacy in Perspective," p. 22; R&D: Adam Segal, "Is America Losing Its Edge?" *Foreign Affairs* 83 (November/December 2004): 3.

[84] R&D: Brooks and Wohlforth, "American Primacy in Perspective," p. 23; quote from Levey and Brown, "The Overstretch Myth," p. 2.

[85] Papers and patents: Friedman, *The World is Flat*, pp. 269–270; services: Segal, "Losing Its Edge," p. 3.

U.S. economy is ranked consistently among the top three most competitive in the world and is by far the largest among them.[86]

When one turns to the instruments of statecraft, the United States' absolute and relative power seems even more commanding – especially in military strength. The country spends far more on its military forces than all meaningful competitors combined; in fact, some analysts rate American defense spending as equal to *the rest of the world's* put together.[87] The American dominance in conventional warfare has recently been demonstrated in Kosovo, Afghanistan, and twice against Iraq, in a now familiar pattern: devastating use of precision air attack, accompanied or followed by high-speed land assault when necessary, resulting in battlefield victory within a couple of months and with very limited casualties.[88] Other instruments of statecraft are less dominant than its military, but the *combination* of instruments that the United States possesses constitutes a unique fund of applicable power. Indeed, it is the massing of American leadership across the spectrum of potential as well as mobilized power that adds up to its remarkable dominance. Simply put, "the United States has no rival in any critical dimension of power."[89] "It is dominant by every measure: military, economic, technological, diplomatic, cultural, even linguistic...."[90]

There are, however, a number of caveats to this dominance that strategists would do well to note. First, while American geography may not have changed, 9/11 demonstrated that technology has eroded if not eliminated the invulnerability location once conferred. Second, although the United States still has a significant store of natural resources, its lackluster progress on energy conservation since the mid-'80s forces it to import more than half of the oil it uses, exposing the country to price and supply shocks that can be very significant.[91] Third, anti-Americanism, based on resentment both of the United States' relative status and the way the George W. Bush administration has chosen to use its hard power, has

---

[86] Lieber, *The American Era*, p. 17.

[87] Lieber, *The American Era*, p. 16. See Chapter 6 for a more complete description of these military capabilities.

[88] The 1991 Gulf War (where a month of aerial bombing was followed by land victory in 100 hours with 382 deaths), the 1999 Kosovo War (where air power alone did the trick in two months without a single American combat death), the 2001 Afghanistan war (where American special forces teamed up with the Northern Alliance to defeat the Taliban at a cost of only 69 deaths), and the 2003 Iraq war (where a combined air and land assault routed Iraq's military in three weeks with 139 lost). Lieber, *The American Era*, p. 22, and Thomas E. Ricks, "Where Does Iraq Stand Among U.S. Wars?" *Washington Post* (May 31, 2004): A16.

[89] Brooks and Wohlforth, "American Primacy in Perspective," p. 23.

[90] Charles Krauthammer, "The Unipolar Moment Revisited," *The National Interest* 70 (Winter 2002/03): 7.

[91] With oil use for heating and power generation declining and industrial use flat, the increase in oil usage comes entirely from transportation, putting the finger on relaxed fuel economy standards as the real culprit. James Fallows, "Countdown to a Meltdown," *Atlantic Monthly* 296 (July/August 2005): pp. 56–57.

eroded the country's soft power – another reminder that even the most powerful instruments cannot be counted on to buy influence. Finally, the American military's experience in Iraq demonstrates that it is far from solving the problems posed by insurgency and terrorism, however impressive it may be in conventional combat.

However, the most serious warnings regarding American power have to do with its sustainability, and particularly with the future of U.S. economic competitiveness. As it turned out, the economic boom of the late 1990s did nothing to improve the personal savings rate of American households, which from a historical level of 7 percent to 10 percent of disposable income has melted away to 5 percent in the mid-1990s, 2 percent in the early 2000s, and negative levels by mid-decade.[92] Although corporate savings have been high, the return of massive federal budget deficits under the George W. Bush administration has absorbed three-fourths of the economy's private savings and lowered the overall national savings rate to only 1.3 percent of national income.[93] Indeed, from a surplus of about 1 percent of GDP in 2000 the federal budget moved to a deficit of 5 percent in 2004, a massive swing in fiscal stance of 6 percent of GDP; projected surpluses of $5.6 trillion through 2011 have become projected deficits of $3 trillion.[94] The cause of these renewed deficits is partly the economic slowdown in the early Bush years and partly an increase in federal spending of 33 percent since 2001 for security, entitlements, and domestic discretionary spending (read "pork").[95] But the biggest single controllable cause, accounting for somewhere between 36 percent and 48 percent of the deficit, are the five major tax cuts enacted since 2001, totaling more than $2 trillion over a decade.[96] These cuts pushed federal revenue down to 16 percent of GDP, well below the 17.5–20 percent levels prevailing since the 1950s, and left the government with a chronic structural deficit.[97]

---

[92] Robert J. Samuelson, "A Nation of Big Spenders," *Washington Post* (August 17, 2005): A13; Sebastian Mallaby, "Do Seniors Need Saving?" *Washington Post* (October 31, 2005): A19; Nell Henderson, "Katrina Contributes To Drop In Spending," *Washington Post* (October 1, 2005): A8.

[93] Menzie D. Chinn, *Getting Serious About the Twin Deficits*, Special Report #10 (New York: Council on Foreign Relations, September 2005), p. 19; Lawrence H. Summers, "America Overdrawn," *Foreign Policy* 143 (July/August 2004): 47.

[94] Chinn, *Getting Serious*, p. 7; Jonathan Weisman, "The Tax-Cut Pendulum and the Pit," *Washington Post* (October 8, 2004): A1, A10.

[95] Sebastian Mallaby, "A Time for McCain," *Washington Post* (October 3, 2005): A17.

[96] "Since 2001, Bush has signed tax cuts of $1.35 trillion, $42 billion, $350 billion, $146 billion, and $143 billion over 10 years." Jonathan Wiesman, "President Signs Corporate Tax Legislation," *Washington Post* (October 23, 2004): A10. Thirty-six percent from CBO-based table in Weisman; forty-eight percent from CBO study cited by Fallows, "Countdown to a Meltdown," p. 53.

[97] Weisman, "Corporate Tax Legislation," and Fallows, "Countdown to a Meltdown," p. 53. It is noteworthy that these levels of taxation had not been seen since before enactment of the Great Society welfare programs, Medicare and Medicaid, whose expensive benefits the Republicans expanded via a prescription drug benefit.

When the federal government spends more than it collects in taxes and other revenue – the very definition of a deficit – the difference must be borrowed. And with Americans saving so little, the borrowing has come mainly from overseas. Borrowing to finance the budget deficit is part of a much larger capital inflow tied to two other deficits strategists need to worry about, the trade and current account deficits. Partly due to higher rates of growth (and therefore greater demand for goods and services) than its trading partners, the United States consumes more than it produces and imports more than it exports.[98] In fact, the United States now has a trade deficit approaching 6 percent of GDP, by far the highest of any major industrialized country in modern times; its current account deficit – the trade deficit plus what the U.S. earns on overseas assets – reached 7 percent of GDP in 2005, also "unprecedented for a major economy."[99] And this borrowing from foreigners is being used, not to finance investment by American businesses that would increase productivity or produce exports for sale abroad as it did in the 1990s, but for consumption: spending on consumer goods and housing has jumped from the usual two-thirds of American GDP to three-fourths, while foreign direct investment in American plant and equipment has plummeted in favor of purchases of securities.[100]

With the United States borrowing up to a trillion more dollars each year – $8 billion every working day – from abroad, it is not surprising that the proportion of total U.S. debt owned by foreigners is skyrocketing, from 18 percent in 1990 to 45 percent in 2005.[101] In fact, foreigners hold $8.1 trillion in American financial assets, about three-fourths of a year's GDP; when foreign assets held by Americans are netted out, the country's net international investment position (NIIP) comes in at about minus $3 trillion, a quarter of GDP.[102] Although the United States has for twenty years been the world's largest debtor, this rapid growth in foreign-held debt cannot help but weaken the country's economic leverage. Moreover, much of the debt is held in the form of U.S. currency and Treasury securities by ten or so mostly Asian central banks, who in 2004 alone accumulated $355.3 billion of such debt and thereby financed nearly that year's entire federal

---

[98] The resulting trade deficit is partly caused by the federal budget deficit, because tax cuts and government spending stimulate consumption, sucking in imports; while federal borrowing raises interest rates and drives up the value of the dollar, making exports more expensive and harder to sell abroad. Chinn, *Getting Serious*, pp. 7–8.

[99] Paul Blustein, "Foreign Investment's Flip Side," *Washington Post* (February 25, 2005): A1, A18; Brad Setser and Nouriel Roubini, "How Scary Is the Deficit?" *Foreign Affairs* 84 (July/August 2005): 194.

[100] Paul Blustein, "Foreign Investment's Flip Side."

[101] C. Fred Bergsten, "What's a Treasury Secretary to Do?" *Washington Post* (June 26, 2006): A21; Kempe, "A Question of Clout."

[102] Levey and Brown, "The Overstretch Myth," p. 3.

deficit of \$369.4 billion.[103] Asian countries use the inflow of dollars from sales of their exports to buy Treasury instruments because they want to prevent the normal consequence of a trade surplus: a rise in the value of their currency which would help correct the trade imbalance but in the process threaten employment in their export industries.[104] Of course, Asian employment comes at the expense of manufacturing jobs in the United States, which have fallen 16 percent since 2001.[105] But a potentially more serious result of the buildup of American debt in foreign hands is a new kind of American economic vulnerability.

All economists understand that the present situation is unsustainable, that foreigners will not continue indefinitely to accumulate American debt at these rates.[106] The only question is whether the adjustment will come sooner or later, and whether the landing will be hard or soft. Those expecting the latter argue that all players have "good reason to favor an orderly adjustment," which will be "unpleasant" but not catastrophic; after all, "a collapsing U.S. economy would inflict enormous, unacceptable damage on the rest of the world."[107] More fundamentally, the flow of capital into the United States is caused by what Federal Reserve Chairman Ben Bernanke called a "global saving glut," combined with the attractiveness of the United States as a place to lend.[108] Therefore, it can be argued,

> [i]t is a mistake to equate borrowing with a loss of power....Its net debtor status notwithstanding, the United States enjoys overwhelming dynamism and influence rooted in rapid productivity growth based on innovation at the technology frontier. Meanwhile, its serves as the "buyer of last resort," the primary source of technology transfer, and the global monetary anchor – the classic hegemon providing critical "public goods."[109]

> [Hence,] the dollar's role as the global monetary standard is not threatened, and the risk to U.S. financial stability posed by large foreign liabilities has been exaggerated....If anything, the world's appetite for U.S. assets bolsters U.S. predominance rather than undermines it.[110]

---

[103] Chinn, *Getting Serious*, pp. 8–9.

[104] Setser and Roubini, "How Scary Is the Deficit?"; Fallows, "Countdown to a Meltdown," pp. 54, 56.

[105] Chinn, *Getting Serious*, p. 12.

[106] See, for example, Bergsten's recommendations for U.S.-led major international effort to deal with "the precarious international financial position of the United States" through a Smithsonian- (1971) or Plaza- (1985) like agreement, in "What's a Treasury Secretary to Do?"

[107] Orderly adjustment: Levey and Brown's reply in Setser and Roubini, "How Scary Is the Deficit?" p. 199; unpleasant: Levey and Brown, "The Overstretch Myth," p. 6; collapsing U.S. economy: Mead, "Sticky Power," p. 52.

[108] Quoted in "The Great Thrift Shift: A Survey of the World's Economy," *Economist* (September 24, 2005): 3.

[109] Levey and Brown's reply in Setser and Roubini, "How Scary Is the Deficit?" p. 200.

[110] Levey and Brown, "The Overstretch Myth," pp. 2–3.

Still, those who fear this new vulnerability point out that "economic power usually flows to creditors, not debtors."[111] Moreover, the present situation is fundamentally unstable, since Asian central banks already see financing the U.S. deficit as a burden and only need to slow down their purchases of dollars to cause a sharp drop in the value of the currency and a sharp rise in interest rates (as the Fed tries to keep yields high enough for foreign lending to continue).[112] Faced with huge exchange rate losses as the dollar declines, foreign borrowers might then decide to dump U.S. securities, touching off a financial crisis, pushing interest rates even higher, and triggering a sharp global recession – in a word, "meltdown."[113] As former Secretary of the Treasury Larry Summers put it,

> the countries that hold U.S. currency and securities in their banks also hold U.S. prosperity in their hands. That prospect should make Americans uncomfortable.... having finally emerged from the Cold War's military balance of terror, the United States should not lightly accept a new version of mutually assured destruction if it can be avoided.[114]

Whether or not "the refusal of international investors to support out-of-control U.S. fiscal policies could become the defining event of Bush's second term," as the Dean of the Yale School of Management has warned, the more distant future holds even more serious challenges to American economic power.[115] Many of these have to do with the continuation and burgeoning of the current revenue-spending gap. First, there are the costs of the war on terrorism, including continuing stability operations in Iraq and Afghanistan running at least $1 billion a week, weapons procurement that is expected to rise to $100 billion a year by the end of the decade, and the huge costs of serious homeland security, including aid to first responders, public health improvements, and container and border security measures at tens of billions of dollars each.[116] Next, and even more daunting, comes the unfunded implicit liabilities of the entitlements promised in current law to retirees, which a recent report commissioned by the Treasury Department put at the astounding total of $45 trillion dollars – about two and half years worth of national output.[117] As a result,

---

[111] "While the United States roams the world looking to sweep up any spare savings to finance its huge deficits, China roams the world looking for new places to invest its surplus savings...." Setser and Roubini, "How Scary Is the Deficit?" p. 197. The current account deficit also tends to be self-perpetuating, since interest payments to foreigners add to the current account deficit and the debt.

[112] Setser and Roubini, "How Scary Is the Deficit?" p. 196.

[113] Chinn, *Getting Serious*, p. 23–25; Fallows, "Countdown to a Meltdown."

[114] Summers, "America Overdrawn," p. 48.

[115] Jeffrey E. Garten, "The Global Economic Challenge," *Foreign Affairs* 84 (January/ February 2005): 41.

[116] Peterson, "Riding for a Fall," pp. 112–116.

[117] Niall Ferguson and Laurence J. Kotlikoff, "Going Critical: American Power and the Consequences of Fiscal Overstretch," *National Interest* 73 (Fall 2003): 23.

For the first time in the post-World War II era, the United States faces a future in which every major category of federal spending is projected to grow at least as fast as, or faster than, the economy for many years to come. That means not just pension and health-care benefits for retiring "baby boomers," or increasing interest payments as deficits and interest rates rise, but also appropriated or "discretionary" spending for national defense, for foreign aid, and for domestic homeland security programs.[118]

It is possible, in fact, that the specter of "imperial overstretch" that was at the heart of the declinist debate in the late 1980s and early 1990s will be vindicated in the 2010s and 2020s, the consequence of a perfect fiscal storm of crippled revenues, inherited debt, security costs and, especially, spending on America's elderly. If so, "the decline and fall of America's undeclared empire will be due not to terrorists at our gates nor to the rogue regimes that sponsor them, but to a fiscal crisis of the welfare state."[119]

On the other hand, such dark scenarios might be obviated by outsized growth in the U.S. globalized, information-based economy. But here, too, many observers detect a "quiet crisis" in the technological basis of the economy that could lead to America "losing its edge." One problem is reduced spending on research and development, as federally funded R&D is curtailed by fiscal pressures and moves away from basic research to anti-terrorism, defense, and space; military R&D spending suffers under the pressure of weapons buying; and private industry (which spends only 10 percent of its R&D money on basic research) continues cutting R&D from 1 percent to 5 percent annually, as it did in the early 2000s.[120] Another is a steady decline in numbers of people qualified to do hi-tech R&D just as industry needs more of them. Public schools in the United States are doing a poor job of encouraging students to enter, and preparing them for, technology-based careers: for example, only 7 percent of U.S. eighth graders scored at the most advanced math level in a recent international study, compared to 38 percent and 44 percent in Taiwan and Singapore. Moreover, two-thirds of the American math and science teaching force will retire by 2010, but the number of Americans getting basic science degrees in college has slipped from third in the world in 1970 to seventeenth today, and graduate enrollment in science and engineering (S&E) programs peaked in 1993.[121] In addition, maintaining the 38 percent share of S&E Ph.D.s in the United States who were born abroad will be difficult given the pressure of terrorism-related visa restrictions, anti-Americanism, and growing career opportunities in their home countries. "If action is not taken now to change these trends," wrote the National Science Board in 2004, "we could reach 2020 and find that the ability of U.S. research and education

[118] Peterson, "Riding for a Fall," 117.

[119] Ferguson and Kotlikoff, "Going Critical," p. 31.

[120] Segal, "Is America Losing Its Edge?" pp. 3–4.

[121] Data above from Friedman, "The Quiet Crisis," Chapter 7 in *The World is Flat*, pp. 250–275.

institutions to regenerate has been damaged and that their preeminence has been lost to other areas of the world."[122] Meanwhile, the spread of market forms of economic organization, combined with the technological know-how that is transferred abroad in the normal process of American companies partnering with foreign firms, universities, and industry-government consortia, is creating centers of innovation overseas that will increasingly challenge U.S. leadership in science and technology in the years ahead.[123]

Absolute Wealth and Relative Power

It is not hard to think of policies that would reduce these economic dangers and strengthen United States potential power.[124] Underneath them all is the basic idea that will always be the key to increasing *absolute* American wealth and power: shifting resources from consumption to savings, from spending to investment, from now to later. But if the goal is to maintain or increase U.S. *relative* power, the strategist quickly runs into a dilemma. Because of the different ways in which international economic and political life are organized, ways that seem more and more divergent in the modern world, there is a growing tension between the steps needed to build economies as the basis of absolute power and those needed to increase relative power, a conflict between *mutual* and *competitive* gains.[125] To put it directly, it is increasingly difficult in today's world for any nation-state to increase its own wealth without at the same time making some contribution to the wealth and therefore the power of other countries. It is also increasingly difficult to increase a nation's wealth without increasing its economic vulnerability, thereby increasing the danger posed by other nations' power.

If the accumulation of power is the principal motivating factor in international politics, the accumulation of wealth provides a similar dynamic to the international economic system. But there is at least one very significant difference. In the anarchy of international politics, as we noted in Chapter 2, power tends to be wholly competitive in nature; since the contest is about relative power, it is what political scientists call a zero-sum game, where any player's gain is another's loss. Economic relationships are different in that they also include very strong elements of cooperation

---

[122] Quoted in Friedman, *The World is Flat,*" p. 258.

[123] Segal, "Is America Losing Its Edge?" pp. 4–6.

[124] See Chapter 9 for a discussion and recommendations.

[125] See Moran, *American Economic Policy*, pp. 42–43: "Even if macroeconomic policies were in long-term balance, and even if (backed by strong investment flows into plants, equipment, education and training) all American workers and firms were operating with maximum efficiency and high innovation, the globalization of the U.S. industrial base would continue." "...this has given rise to an agonizing dilemma between autarchy and efficiency....the autarchic route is not only expensive but leads rapidly to economic and technological (and therefore political) inferiority."

as well as competition. Indeed, since the demise of mercantilism, mainstream economic thinking has recognized the efficiency of building wealth through mutual gains. The theory of comparative advantage makes clear that free trade among nations benefits all by enabling each to specialize in the economic tasks it does most efficiently, an outcome demonstrated in practice over the past several decades as the world's wealth has mushroomed along with international trade. And as noted in Chapter 2, today's corporations are forming multinational productive and marketing arrangements that make exchange, cooperation, and teamwork even more important. The result is a more efficient use of the world's resources and more global wealth.

However, this intensified international economic cooperation and collaboration does not relieve foreign affairs strategists of concern for their country's relative power in a still-anarchic world of sovereign states. Even if all national economies and the trade between them were perfectly free it would still matter politically which ones got ahead economically, because changes in the relative economic standing of nation-states affect the balance of power between them. As it is, national economies are organized along widely differing lines, some of which give strong competitive advantages to their country's products internationally. In addition, nations may deliberately adopt predatory economic practices, engaging in a kind of geo-economic competition and using government-industry relationships and other elements of economic policy to stack the deck in favor of their producers.[126]

Despite intensified economic cooperation, in fact, comparative advantage itself seems to have shifted in an adversarial direction. What a country is most efficient in producing used to be thought of as related directly to its endowments of factors of production, like natural resources, that were unalterable by actions of society and government. But today's shrinking transportation and communications costs have meant that the major differences between countries lie in the quality of their workers and the equipment with which they have to work. In such an environment, nation-states create their own comparative advantages over time by educating a more productive workforce and by developing high-tech industries that themselves create market advantages.[127] Indeed, globalization has paradoxically made geography both less and more important – less important because material endowments no longer determine national productivity and wealth, more important because co-locating capital, entrepreneurship, and ideas for a particular technological niche is critical to success in the global marketplace.[128]

---

[126] Edward Luttwak, "From Geopolitics to Geo-Economics," *National Interest* 20 (Summer 1990): 17–23.

[127] Robert B. Reich, "Beyond Free Trade," *Foreign Affairs* 61 (Spring 1983): 782.

[128] Segal, "Is America Losing Its Edge?" pp. 2–8.

The intensified economic cooperation that is at the heart of globalization makes it increasingly difficult for nation-states to think and act as nation-states, to carry on their contest for power as distinct and autonomous entities. When many "American" companies are making products abroad and foreign corporations are employing and training large numbers of American workers in the United States, it is hard for a government to know who to protect, who to advantage and disadvantage; the whole concept of a national economy seems to slip between one's fingers.[129] Moreover, when the statesman reaches for economic instruments with which to influence another country, he is likely to find few that do not at the same time powerfully affect people in his own. Finally, there is a cost in power terms to the growing interdependence of the world economy itself, a loss of control over elements of productivity that may prove crucial to dealing with future challenges. This is true not only in defense industries but also in energy and across the gamut of high-tech companies that are at the core of a modern economy.[130] Yet political power is still territorially based, and national governments remain the highest decision structures for most purposes. Dealing with this mix of competition and collaboration, this contradiction between the imperative for national power in the international *political* system and the growing globalization of the international *economic* system, is without doubt one of the most difficult challenges faced by twenty-first century foreign affairs strategists.

When former Secretary of Labor Robert Reich used to ask his classes at Harvard whether they would prefer a future in which Americans were 25 percent richer but the Japanese (then the major economic competitor) were even wealthier than Americans, or one in which Americans were only 10 percent better off but still ahead of the Japanese, most students chose the later alternative, even though it would leave them absolutely 15 percent poorer than the former.[131] The foreign affairs strategist must take a similar position, and for two reasons. The first is found at the level of interests. If the only national interest were prosperity, one would certainly vote for the mutual gains known to produce greater wealth for all. But the nation-state must also defend and advance its interests in physical security and value preservation, and for those interests it must strive to maintain or improve its relative power position and therefore its wealth relative to other nation-states. The second reason why relative gains matter is that, even though a

---

[129] The classic on this point is Robert B. Reich, Todd Hixon, and Ranch Kimball, "Who Is Us?" *Harvard Business Review* (January/February 1990): 53–64, but see Ethan B. Kapstein, "We are US," *National Interest* 26 (Winter 1991–92): 55–62 for an opposing view.

[130] For an excellent discussion of the loss of American autonomy, see Aaron L. Friedberg, "The End of Autonomy: The United States after Five Decades," *Daedalus* 120 (Fall 1991): 69–90.

[131] Robert B. Reich, "What is a Nation?" *Political Science Quarterly* 106 (Summer 1991): 204.

strategy of mutual gains may increase wealth more in the short-run, one of relative gains may be important to securing wealth over the long run. A completely open and nonpredatory economic strategy may well maximize consumer welfare for the time being, but in a geo-economic world it may also result in the deterioration of those industries that are essential to building future comparative advantage and hence to the increase of wealth itself.[132]

At the same time, it would be disastrous to press the emphasis on relative gains to the point of autarchy. As the experience of the Soviet bloc conclusively proved, nothing would be so damaging to wealth and potential power as closing the nation's economy off from the pressures of global competition and the infusion of outside ideas and technology. Paradoxically, then, economic globalization mandates that today's solution to the relative power problem be an absolute wealth solution. The nation-state must compete for economic advantage, in so far as possible, within an environment that preserves the benefits of comparative advantage and the efficiencies of trade. Somehow, in other words, the foreign affairs strategist must strive for a balance between mutual and relative gains, trying to attain a nationally favorable distribution of increasing global wealth.

Such a balance would lean toward measures that can promote future domestic growth without interfering unduly with the efficiencies of either national or international markets. Steps like keeping the federal budget under control, helping to diffuse technological knowledge, encouraging civilian R & D and education and training, and adopting a consumption-based income tax would place few restrictions on the mutual gains available through global trade.[133] On the other hand, measures like relaxing antitrust laws to allow American firms to merge for better international competition, attempting through government political processes to pick and then subsidize commercial winners and losers, retaliating against unfair practices abroad that close foreign markets, and protecting American industries against foreign competition all have significant costs for the growth of the nation's absolute wealth and might well end up hurting the United States more than its economic rivals. There may be times when any or all are called for. But the strategist must always bear in mind that measures which promote *relative* gain – my gain at your expense – will often cut across the economic openness and market efficiencies that are central to *absolute* gain. That is the central tension in today's world between relative and absolute power.

---

[132] The specter is raised that simply allowing comparative advantage to play out will leave some countries in "a high-productivity, high-value-added, high-wage, high-innovation equilibrium and [others in] a lower-productivity, lower-skill, lower-wage, less innovative, and less technology-intensive equilibrium." Moran, *American Economic Policy and National Security*, p. 13.

[133] Sam Nunn and Pete Domenici, *The CSIS Strengthening of America Commission, First Report* (Washington, DC: Center for Strategic and International Studies, 1992), pp. 96–102.

Concrete Power versus Perceptual Power

Up to this point our discussion of power in foreign affairs strategy has treated the concept mainly as a matter of control over tangible, real assets, whether generalized and potential in nature (like the wealth-generating capacity of the national economy) or specific and actual in form (as in the various tools of statecraft).[134] But power is not only a matter of concrete resources; it is also and at the same time very much a psychological phenomenon, a matter of perceptions on the part of the statesman and those over whom he seeks influence. Hence the third distinction regarding power to which the strategist must be sensitive, in addition to those of potential versus actual power and absolute versus relative power: that between concrete and perceptual power.

"*Posse quia posse videntur*," ran the Roman phrase: he has power who seems to have power. Or as Thomas Hobbes put it, "the reputation for power *is* power." At first thought it might appear that perceptions and reality must converge, that impressions of a nation-state's power and the reality of its control over resources would be essentially the same. But that need not be the case. Many national assets may be hidden, either on purpose or inadvertently. Others, particularly the intangible ones, will be incalculable in any easily measured way. In the end, no one actually knows what a country's real power is, let alone how the power of several countries compares. The Australian scholar Geoffrey Blainey wrote that the only time the hierarchy of relative power is clear to all is right after a major war, when nations have just finished proving their ultimate strength.[135] Most of the time, strategists are left to their own very subjective calculations.

The possibility that perceptions of power can diverge significantly from the reality of power raises all sorts of interesting prospects. One is that the strategist's efforts to amass and mobilize power, even if successful, may not impress the appropriate foreign statesmen, rendering substantial expenditures of public funds useless and reminding us again that power does not necessarily produce influence. Another, however, is that a way might be found to alter perceptions of power in a positive way without having to engage concrete resources. What if the strategist could somehow avoid all of the difficulties, perplexities, and sacrifices involved in amassing concrete power and achieve the same effect through psychological means?

The ability to do so would profoundly alter the relationship between ends and means that lies at the center of all strategic thought (see Figure 5.7). The common sense view is that nation-states, like people, must have enough resources, enough power, to achieve all their objectives, that the quantitative relationship between ends and means is like a personal

---

[134] We did suggest that some elements of power were intangible, like social cohesion and national morale, but these too were seen as assets that the statesman can calculate and assess.

[135] Geoffrey Blainey, *The Causes of War* (New York: MacMillan/Free Press, 1973), pp. 112–118.

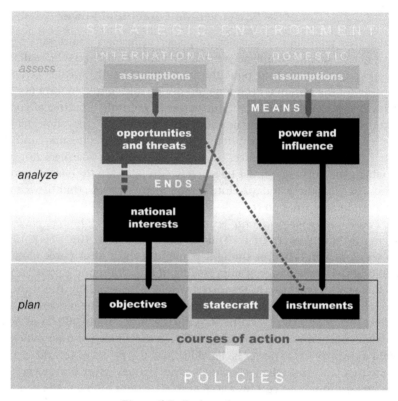

Figure 5.7: Ends and means.

budget, where income must eventually cover outlays. For the strategist to set goals beyond available resources would seem a highly risky enterprise that could quickly reduce statecraft to a species of bluff. As one writer put it, "few states have managed to operate beyond their foreign policy means for very long, and several that have attempted this have brought disaster upon themselves."[136] In an oft-quoted book written during World War II, Walter Lippmann defined solvency as the fundamental principle of foreign policy:

> . . . foreign policy consists in bringing into balance, with a comfortable surplus of power in reserve, the nation's commitments and the nation's power. The constant preoccupation of the true statesman is to achieve and maintain this balance.[137]

As the costs of the struggle with the Soviet Union intensified during the last decade of the Cold War, many observers began to worry anew about solvency. Indeed, a flood of books and articles appeared about the

---

[136] Puchala, *International Politics Today*, p. 188.

[137] Walter Lippmann, *U.S. Foreign Policy: Shield of the Republic* (Boston, MA: Little, Brown, 1943), p. 9.

gap in American policy between power and interests, and much of the declinist literature focused on this issue.[138] As noted above, the present-day combination of dramatic cuts in the U.S. government's revenue base with an extraordinarily expensive war on terrorism (including hot wars in Afghanistan and Iraq) makes this concern uncomfortably contemporary.[139]

But what if the strategist really could make up for a shortfall in concrete power resources by manipulating perceptions? Is it possible that the relationship between ends and means in strategy is not like a personal budget at all, but more like a bank's ledger, where reserves need only be a fraction of loans? If the numerous reports that the United States has been over-committed for decades are true, perhaps this is the way powerful states really operate, leveraging their clout for maximum effect. As in the world of finance, the strategic equation obviously becomes more and more risky as statecraft becomes more and more leveraged, more dangerous as the gap between ends and means grows along with the divergence between perceptions of power and its reality. Still, statesmen can hardly be expected minimize their power, and strategies to maximize the face it presents to the world would seem to make sense.

For some analysts the psychological impact of power goes by the name "prestige," which Robert Gilpin defined as "the reputation for power."[140] But the common sense notion of prestige goes beyond mere power to authority, denoting a sense of legitimacy based on the belief that power is rightfully possessed and exercised. In the anarchy of international politics such legitimacy is based in the first instance not on legal structures or electoral verdicts but on a nation-state's demonstrated capability, sound judgment, capacity for objectivity, even wisdom. More fundamentally, prestige springs directly from the character of a country itself: the attractiveness of its ideology, the universalism of its culture, and the acceptability of its institutions – soft power matters that its foreign policies can do little about. Thus, William Pfaff argued that the American victory in the Cold War resulted not so much from its strategies of containment as from the kind of society it was – "free, prosperous, and successful" – in contrast to the communist alternative.

---

[138] For example, Robert E. Osgood, "American Grand Strategy: Patterns, Problems, Prescriptions," *Naval War College Review* (September–October 1983): 5–17, wrote that "American foreign policy since World War II has been largely shaped and driven by repeated efforts to close the gap between ever-expanding security interests and persistently inadequate power to support them...." See also James Chace, *Solvency: The Price of Survival* (New York: Random House, 1981); and Eliot A. Cohen, "When Policy Outstrips Power – American Strategy and Statecraft," *The Public Interest* 75 (Spring 1984): 3–19.

[139] By mid-2006 the wars in Iraq and Afghanistan had cost the U.S. $409 billion in appropriated funds. "House Approves $94.5 Billion for Wars," *Washington Post* (June 14, 2006): A4.

[140] Gilpin, *War and Change in International Politics* (New York: Cambridge University Press, 1981), p. 31.

The great lesson of how the Cold War ended may be stated in these words: being is superior to doing. What a nation is, is essential. What it does can only express what it is.[141]

Historian Alan Henrikson has labeled the effects produced by prestige the "emanation" of power, and he points out that while states may exercise power through coercion (the actual use of force) or by threats and promises, a far more common way that power has its effect is through "nonphysical nonexplicit emission or radiation."[142] Of course, all successful political systems rely largely on consent, willingly or unwillingly obtained; as the revolutions in Iran in 1979 and Eastern Europe in 1989 showed, no amount of force can prevail if a sufficient number of people refuse.[143] Just as an evil empire can use the psychology of terror to repress far more people than its physical might could ever directly coerce, so a nation that can combine concrete power with virtue may be able to exceed material constraints.

> The ability to transcend the bounds of a nation's physical means – to radiate an *aura* of power beyond its national borders and material resources – may be the distinguishing mark of a civilization's greatness.[144]

It is possible, on the other hand, that efforts at psychological power projection may conflict with actions needed to attain international prestige and legitimacy. For example, the administration of George W. Bush set out to produce "shock and awe" by its invasion of Iraq, and the speed and effectiveness of the initial assault in March and April 2003 did produce respect and even fear of American power. But its inability quickly to defeat the insurgency in Iraq led to years of Americans humiliating and killing Arab Muslims, which when combined with the abusive treatment of prisoners at Abu Graib and elsewhere deeply tarnished the values that the United States claims to uphold and weakened its legitimacy in the region if not the world. Legitimacy may be more properly an attribute of influence, since it is confirmed by those subject to power rather than the powerful. But it requires that the latter exercise their power carefully and on behalf of ends endorsed by a broader audience than its own decision makers.

---

[141] William Pfaff, "Redefining World Power," *Foreign Affairs: America and the World 1990/91* 70 (No. 1, 1991): 48.

[142] Alan K. Henrikson, "The Emanation of Power," *International Security* 6 (Summer 1981): 155.

[143] "Unwilling consent" may seem like an oxymoron, but in fact that seems an accurate phrase to describe the sway held by totalitarian governments over Eastern Europe and the Soviet Union. The state apparatus of repression made the consequences of rebellion so horrific that people were ready to give the regime their behavioral consent, albeit unwillingly.

[144] Henrikson, "Emanation of Power," p. 152.

Power and American Strategy

The distinctions sketched above between potential and actual, absolute and relative, concrete and psychological power have played a major role in the foreign affairs strategies of recent American administrations. Whatever their other differences, both the Nixon–Kissinger team and Jimmy Carter believed that the decline of American power they observed in the late 1960s and 1970s was largely due to the systemic factors discussed above: the recovery of U.S. allies from the exhaustion of World War II, the end of colonialism and the birth of independent centers of power in the Third World, the maturation of Soviet military power, and the growing interdependence and vulnerability of the U.S. economy. Since these changes resulted from broad historical forces and were inherent in the very structure of the international system, they were seen as largely beyond American control. As Kissinger wrote of the late 1960s,

> we were becoming like other nations in the need to recognize that our power, while vast, had limits. Our resources were no longer infinite in relation to our problems; instead we had to set priorities, both intellectual and material.[145]

Still, Henry Kissinger and Richard Nixon were not at all sanguine about the effects of such decline; they recognized that less relative power would make every threat harder to counter, every interest harder to advance. Kissinger's coming of age as a Jew in Nazi Germany and Nixon's experiences in the rough and tumble of American politics had disabused them of the peculiarly American notion that, as Kissinger put it, "goodwill supplied its own efficacy."[146] Nixon and Kissinger thus feared the decline of American power and worked where they could to stop it; where they could not stop it, to manage and channel it in less rather than more destructive ways; and where they could not manage it, to disguise it so as to limit the effect of decline in the nation's concrete power on its perceptual power.

Indeed, all of the major elements of the Nixon–Kissinger foreign affairs strategy were designed to deal in one way or another with this central problem. First, the administration wanted to end the drain on American power represented by the war in Vietnam, but do so without causing a psychological collapse of confidence among U.S. allies. Second, Nixon's opening to China after two decades of hostility was designed to substitute a new balance of power against the Soviet Union for the waning preponderance of unilateral American power. Third, and simultaneously, the strategy of detente vis-à-vis the Soviets was intended to limit the most dangerous element of Soviet power, its nuclear weapons; although the negotiations were based on an explicit program of punishments and rewards whose efficacy depended on American strength, the attempt to move away from

---

[145] Kissinger, *White House Years* (Boston, MA: Little, Brown & Co., 1979), p. 57.
[146] Kissinger, *White House Years*, p. 230.

confrontation made sense for a country whose power then seemed to be declining in relation to its adversary. Fourth, in the Nixon Doctrine the administration unilaterally redefined its commitments throughout the world to exclude the use of American troops to defend allies, thus bringing ends into better balance with reduced means. And finally, the administration adopted "a style of diplomacy leaning toward the spectacular" in order to maximize the psychological impact of the power the country still had, with Kissinger engineering a series of secretly negotiated and dramatically unveiled diplomatic triumphs.[147]

Though Jimmy Carter agreed with the Nixon–Kissinger diagnosis of American power, he approached its decline from a very different perspective. For Carter, relative decline was almost to be welcomed, both for the United States in the world and for the office of the presidency in the American political system. Several elements seem to have combined to produce this attitude. For one thing, Carter's political experience had been much different than that of his Republican predecessors. He had come to office playing by the rules, and he seemed to lack an intuitive instinct for power, what Kissinger identified in Nixon as "an extraordinary instinct for the jugular."[148] Carter was also a born-again Christian who seemed to see power and morality as two opposing principles. He believed that after the turmoil of the late 1960s and early 1970s the country was in need of a period of "national repentance," that Nixon and Kissinger had conducted an amoral foreign policy, and that it was necessary to put values back in American statecraft.[149] For Carter, Vietnam and Watergate showed the consequences of the nation – and the president – having too much power and too little morality. Indeed, Carter considered the idea of limits the "subliminal theme" of his presidency and seemed to believe that lack of power engendered a kind of moral righteousness, telling his countrymen that "'more' is not necessarily 'better.'"[150]

For all these reasons, Jimmy Carter approached the use of American power far differently than Nixon and Kissinger. Where they had created an imperial presidency, Carter set out to make his office seem smaller than life in an effort to get closer to the people. By such symbolic steps as carrying his own luggage when traveling and dispensing with the traditional *Ruffles and Flourishes* in ceremonial appearances, however, Carter also sent psychological messages about his command of power to his political opponents and even to members of his own party. He sent similar signals of weakness in foreign policy as well, declaring that American strength should rest "not merely on the size of an arsenal but on the nobility of

[147] Kissinger, *Years of Upheaval* (Boston, MA: Little, Brown & Co., 1982), p. 126.

[148] Kissinger, *White House Years*, p. 163.

[149] Jimmy Carter, *Keeping Faith: Memoirs of a President* (New York: Bantam Books, 1982), pp. 19–20.

[150] Inaugural Address, Carter, *Keeping Faith*, p. 21.

ideas" and taking a number of early actions which seemed to indicate a disinclination to use military force, like cutting the defense budget 5 percent, announcing troop withdrawals from South Korea, canceling the B-1 bomber program, and deferring production of the neutron bomb.[151] Though Carter was a skilled negotiator and scored major triumphs in the SALT II and Panama Canal treaties, China recognition, peaceful transition in southern Africa, and especially the Middle East peace process, this president's method of negotiation involved painstaking efforts to identify areas of agreement between the parties rather than wielding threats or trying to force agreement. Where Nixon would send an aircraft carrier task force into the Bay of Bengal to warn India against overrunning Pakistan, or declare a nuclear alert to deter Moscow from sending troops into Middle East hostilities, Carter refused to send a flotilla off Somalia to keep Soviet-surrogate forces out of the Ogaden and decided that the United States need not send troops to rescue Zaire's Shaba province from attack by forces from Soviet-backed Angola.[152]

Ronald Reagan, for his part, was at least as attuned to the decline of American power as his predecessors and in full agreement with Nixon and Kissinger about the danger it presented to the United States. Indeed, his campaign attack on the Carter administration was precisely on the issue of its handling of American power: "Adversaries large and small test our will and seek to confound our resolve, but we are given weakness when we need strength; vacillation when the times demand firmness. . . ."[153] But Reagan differed from both of his predecessors in believing that decline could be reversed, that the United States could recover the kind of power advantage it had enjoyed during the 1950s. Again the reasons were diverse, and had much to do with this president's essential optimism about the United States and its future, a sense that "all would be well" that was decidedly anti-Kissingerian. More fundamentally, and unlike Carter or Kissinger, Reagan believed that the causes of American decline were not so much systemic as domestic, that they lay in the malfeasance of Watergate, in mistakes made in Vietnam, and in poor management of the economy. Believing that American power had been weakened by American failures, Reagan thought that it could be revived by American actions.

Reagan thus entered upon a four-part strategy to restore American power. Recognizing the importance of its economic component, his first priority was to break the stagflation afflicting the American economy by lowering the tax rates that he believed were responsible for sapping initiative in the private sector while encouraging the Federal Reserve to fight

---

[151] Carter, *Keeping Faith*, p. 21.

[152] Kissinger, *White House Years*, pp. 910–912; *Years of Upheaval*, pp. 587–588. Vance, *Hard Choices* (New York: Simon and Schuster, 1983), pp. 85–92; Brzezinski, *Power and Principle* (New York: Farrar, Straus, & Giroux, 1983), p. 189.

[153] Reagan acceptance speech, Republican National Convention, July 15, 1976, in *Vital Speeches* 42 (August 15, 1976): 643.

inflation with a tight money policy. The result of the Fed's actions was a
sharp recession in 1982, but the tax cuts combined with massive defense
spending to produce a classic Keynesian recovery albeit, as we have seen,
at the cost of severe budget and trade deficits. Second, Reagan sponsored
the greatest peacetime military buildup in American history, buying massive amounts of the form of mobilized power he considered most effective
to counter the Soviet threat and end the perception of American weakness abroad. Third, where Carter had refused to support dictators in the
Third World who violated the human rights of their citizens and American
moral standards, the Reagan administration set about restoring and
expanding American alliances worldwide as tools for aggregating free world
power.[154]

But perhaps the most remarkable feature of Ronald Reagan's emphasis
on restoring American power was his handling of its psychological components. As an actor, Reagan was well aware of the importance of perceptions,
and his multifaceted effort to refurbish the image of American power was
far more skillful than his effort to restore its reality. Reversing Carter, Reagan went out of his way during his first months in office to take actions
that would emphasize the power of the president and of the United States,
from firing Professional Air Traffic Controllers (PATCO) workers who had
engaged in an illegal strike, to shooting down Libyan warplanes when Moa-
mar Qadaffi challenged American rights in the Gulf of Sidra, to speaking
out dramatically about the Soviet "evil empire" and the possibility of using
nuclear weapons in a crisis. Huge World War II battleships were even refur-
bished and sent around the world to show the flag and fire their 16-inch
guns. At the same time, Reagan's domestic political successes, from ram-
ming his economic program through Congress to winning landslide reelection in 1984, reinforced his reputation as a determined leader who knew
what he wanted and how to get it. Even his personal qualities – the horse-
back riding, sagebrush clearing, wood-chopping Western persona, able to
survive an assassination attempt with his optimism undaunted – served
to enhance the psychological impact of American power.[155]

As in most efforts at psychological power projection, actions spoke
louder than words. The Reagan administration showed itself quite willing to use military power in a variety of situations, from Grenada to Beirut
to Benghazi and Tripoli. It kept constant pressure on the Sandinista government in Nicaragua, and under the Reagan Doctrine supported armed
insurgencies in Afghanistan, Angola, and Cambodia. Moreover, the world
saw Reagan's growing defense budgets well before the hardware they would
buy reached the armed forces. Indeed, it is likely that the Soviet fear of

---

[154] See Terry L. Deibel, "Hidden Commitments," *Foreign Policy* 67 (Summer 1987):
46–63.
[155] For more on Reagan's skills in this area, see Terry L. Deibel, "Why Reagan is
Strong," *Foreign Policy* 63 (Spring 1986): 108–125.

Reagan's strategic defense initiative, a program whose real effects were even farther out in the future, had a dramatic effect on the advent of Mikhail Gorbachev, *perestroika*, and *glasnost* – the beginning of the end of the USSR.

The bottom line regarding the Reagan administration's handling of the nation's power is thus a complex one. In the end, as noted earlier, Ronald Reagan had a negative impact on the United States' potential, concrete power. But he was a master at manipulating short-term perceptions of power to make up for shortfalls in concrete power – a specialist in psychological power projection. In that respect his impact both on American national morale and on other nations' judgments of American power was formidable.[156]

George H. W. Bush continued the emphasis on military and psychological power begun by his predecessor. He campaigned for the presidency in 1988 on a harder line toward the Soviet Union than President Reagan was then espousing, invaded Panama within a year of taking office, and went on not only to fight the Gulf War but also to deploy American military forces in Somalia for humanitarian purposes. Still, Bush's moderate political image made his efforts at psychological power projection far less convincing than Reagan's, the more so as Americans turned their attention from the waning Soviet threat to economic issues and dangers. Moreover, although this president understood the dangerous Reagan legacy in potential power – he admitted in his inaugural address, after all, that the U.S. had "more will than wallet" – his "no new taxes" pledge left him unable to work out a strategy for dealing with it. Bush hardly lost the 1992 election on foreign policy grounds, but his failure at the polls owed much to this inability to see that the challenge of power in the 1990s was not in psychological power projection or even in the use of actual power – the tools of statecraft – but rather in rebuilding the nation's long-term, potential power for the future.[157]

Although his motives had little to do with foreign policy, Bill Clinton understood better than any American post-war president the critical importance of economic performance to American power, as well as how globalization was changing the creation of national wealth. Just as Reagan had defeated Carter's quest for a second term by highlighting the Democrat's lack of understanding of American power and his failure to use its military component effectively, so Clinton's "It's the economy, stupid!" campaign and his ability to articulate how the American people could use globalization to restore the country's economic power was the basis of his successful challenge to an incumbent Republican president. Once in office,

---

[156] Terry L. Deibel, "Reagan's Mixed Legacy," *Foreign Policy* 75 (Summer 1989): 34–55.

[157] For a more complete treatment of the Bush foreign policy, see Deibel, "Bush's Foreign Policy: Mastery and Inaction," *Foreign Policy* 84 (Fall 1991): 3–23.

Clinton made the courageous choice to temporarily set aside his campaign promises of help for those hurt by globalization and instead put through Congress a program designed to fix the economic problems left by his pre-decessors, passing it without a single Republican vote.[158] As noted above, his action cleared the way for booming economic growth in the late 1990s, an end to the annual deficits of the Reagan and Bush years, and a start in reducing the national debt they left behind.

But while skilled in the husbanding of potential power, Clinton was much less certain in his use of actual power for foreign policy purposes. He was suspicious at first of military power, and he projected an image of uncertainty and vacillation that undermined the psychological component of power. Although his administration acted skillfully to deal with the threat of economic collapse in the 1995 Mexican peso crisis, it was only after the threat and then use of the military worked as an adjunct to diplomacy in Haiti and Bosnia that Clinton seemed to gain the necessary confidence in the use of American power on the international stage.[159]

George W. Bush, by contrast, made faith in the superiority of Ameri-can power, especially military power, the key to his foreign affairs strategy. From the outset, Bush adopted a swaggering leadership style that rejected most multilateral treaties and commitments in favor of unilateral action on maximum American terms. Rather than accommodating the interests of other nations and compromising somewhat on U.S. objectives in order to get their cooperation in securing vital American goals at less cost and risk, the younger Bush adopted a maximalist approach that assumed other nations would follow the United States simply because America's over-whelming power left them no other choice. After the terrorist attacks of 9/11, this view of power translated into a global war on terrorism that adopted a broad view of the threat and emphasized offensive, unilateral military actions over defense at home and cooperative intelligence and law enforcement abroad. Meanwhile, as noted above, Bush's economic program helped undo the Clinton legacy of responsible budgeting and plunged the country into annual deficits even larger than those of his Republican pre-decessors. Bush's confident use of and faith in the efficacy of hard power overseas was thus ironically paired with a failure to nurture its economic basis at home – a near mirror image of the Clinton approach.

As these case histories show, few factors are more important in the suc-cess or failure of foreign affairs strategy than coming to grips with the nature and uses of power. Strategists must remember that power is a mat-ter of control over concrete resources, but it is also a matter of shaping psychological perceptions. They must worry about furthering the nation's

---

[158] For the Clinton first year economic program, see Woodward, *The Agenda*.

[159] For a more complete discussion of Clinton's foreign policy, see Terry L. Deibel, *Clinton and Congress: The Politics of Foreign Policy*, Headline Series #321 (New York: Foreign Policy Association, Fall 2000).

absolute power, but also about maintaining and increasing its relative power. On the basis of a careful analysis of the international strategic environment and of the future threats and opportunities it presents, they must strike the proper balance between potential power and actual power. And in order to approach their toughest task, the specific matching of means to ends, they must not only master the macro aspects of power presented above but also possess a thorough knowledge of the instruments of policy themselves, their strengths and weaknesses. That task is the subject of Chapter 6.

Part III

Plan

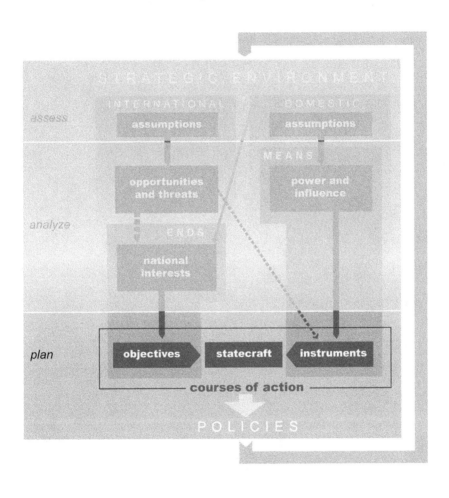

6

The Instruments of State Power

To operationalize foreign affairs strategy, statesmen need not just latent, potential power but actual, mobilized power: the instruments or tools of strategy. Critical choices for these instruments arise on two levels. First, strategists must decide which instruments to *buy* and in what quantities; these decisions turn largely on assumptions about the international environment and the threats and opportunities it holds for the future, as discussed in Chapters 2 and 4. Second, strategists must decide which of the available instruments to *use* to pursue their chosen objectives – to seize immediate opportunities or deal with clear and present dangers. This second kind of choice turns on the specific strengths and weaknesses of the instruments – the subject of this chapter – and on how those relate to strategic objectives, the contexts within which they must be pursued, and their targets – the subjects of Chapters 7 and 8.

Focusing on the tools through which strategy is implemented shifts our consideration of power from the general to the specific. In fact, the whole of foreign affairs strategy must now be seen from a slightly different perspective as the strategist moves from analysis to planning, from concept to detail – in short, from *thinking* about strategy to *doing* it. In the process, our attention will also shift from Washington to the field: to the effects various actions are likely to have on other actors, how they will react, how we will respond to their reactions, and so forth. Hence, this chapter and the next two will be pitched at a lower level of analysis than the first part of the book, a level on which generalization becomes more difficult because specifics of time and place are more controlling. Wisdom here will be couched less as theoretical construct than practical maxim, drawn from experience as much as from logic. And yet strategists need such maxims, such policy relevant generalizations, to guide their choices among the myriad of instruments and their varieties of use.[1]

"Instruments" are located on the "MEANS" side of the model for foreign affairs strategy because they are the tools statesmen use to accomplish their ends (see Figure 6.1). They are located below "power and influence" since they depend upon potential power for their creation and maintenance and because, used correctly, they generate influence for the state. As

---

[1] The term "policy relevant generalizations" is Alexander George's.

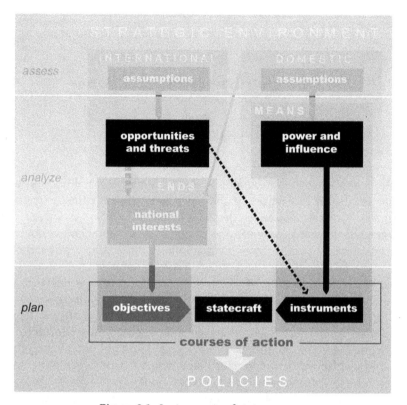

Figure 6.1: Instruments of state power.

noted in Chapter 5, the dashed arrow from "opportunities and threats" to "instruments" is drawn to indicate that the *quantity* of instruments strategists purchase with the country's potential power, as well as the *kinds* of instruments bought, will depend on their assessments of future threats and opportunities. Finally, "instruments" are next to "statecraft" because the latter term denotes the ways in which they are applied to objectives to create courses of action, the building blocks of foreign affairs strategy.

Strategists can begin to get a sense of the possibilities for action by grouping instruments according to their essential characteristics. On the simplest level, the tools of statecraft may be classified as political, informational, economic, or military in nature (see Figure 6.2). The main *political* instruments are negotiations, international law and organization, and alliances. *Informational* instruments include propaganda or public diplomacy (including informational, cultural, and exchange programs) in peacetime, and in wartime psychological operations and information warfare. *Economic* instruments include foreign aid (both economic and military), trade and financial policy, and sanctions. And the *military* instrument can be used either persuasively, as an adjunct to diplomacy (usually short

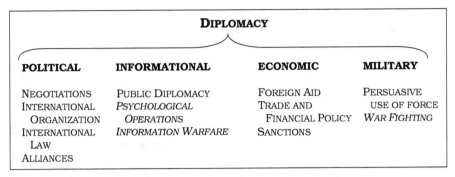

Figure 6.2: Instruments of state power.

of combat), or in outright warfare.[2] This kind of rough grouping is not intended to imply any restriction upon the nature of the *goals* to which these instruments might be applied. It is common practice, after all, to use economic or military instruments for political purposes, or political tools for economic goals.[3] It should also be noted that any one of these "instruments" can be subdivided into several more specific tools; trade policy, for example, includes preferences, subsidies, licensing, tariffs, and quotas, among others. So one can aggregate or differentiate instruments as seems most conceptually useful. Although Figure 6.2 lists the full range of instruments used in peace and war, this chapter will deal only with peacetime instruments of state power, leaving psychological operations, information warfare, and war fighting to the military strategist.

All of the instruments listed above can be thought of as having their effect within the broad context of the diplomacy that takes place constantly between states. Diplomacy may thus be considered the overarching tool of state power, the lead or coordinating instrument within which economic sanctions, military force, negotiations on specific issues, or any of the other

---

[2] At the end of World War II, Harold Lasswell specified four types of statecraft: propaganda, diplomacy, military force, and economic. Harold D. Lasswell, *World Politics Faces Economics* (New York: McGraw Hill, 1945), p. 9. David Baldwin adopts a four-part taxonomy that is very similar to that given here:
"1. Propaganda refers to influence attempts relying primarily on the deliberate manipulation of verbal symbols.
2. Diplomacy refers to influence attempts relying primarily on negotiation.
3. Economic statecraft refers to influence attempts relying primarily on resources which have a reasonable semblance of a market price in terms of money . . . .
4. Military statecraft refers to influence attempts relying primarily on violence, weapons, or force."
David A. Baldwin, *Economic Statecraft* (Princeton, N.J.: Princeton University Press, 1985), pp. 13–14.

[3] A good illustration of the use of economic rewards for political objectives is the 1991 Andean Trade Preference Act (ATPA), offered as part of a U.S. anti-narcotics program. Karen DeYoung, "4 Andean Ministers Plead for Trade Pact," *Washington Post* (February 13, 2002): A10.

instruments must be placed.[4] This view of diplomacy is supported by the fact that the lead role for foreign policy formulation and execution in most governments' capitals is played by the ministry of foreign affairs, while ambassadors are given authority in the field over the representatives of the agencies that manage the other policy tools within their embassies. Thus, in a practical sense diplomacy is the instrument that must attempt to provide real-time coordination of all the other instruments. Of course, "diplomacy" as used here includes not only the usual activity of diplomats as they interact with their counterparts from other countries, but also the *actions* of governments and nonstate actors that so often speak louder than words.[5] It is, in short, the outward expression of foreign policy.

The purpose of this chapter is to outline many of the essentials that strategists should know about each of these instruments in order to be prepared to choose among them when constructing a strategy. Undoubtedly, such knowledge is best gathered through long and varied experience in their use, either directly or through elaborated case studies. A single chapter purporting to cover them all can only try to define, describe, and illustrate each so that strategists have a more complete idea of what they are dealing with than simple terms like "public diplomacy," "foreign aid," or "military force" might suggest, in the process pointing out the major strengths or advantages (and weaknesses or disadvantages) of each instrument's use – characteristics that strategists will use to estimate the benefits and costs of their proposed courses of action.[6] Since strategy is fundamentally about relationships, these positives and negatives for each instrument will relate to the concepts in strategic logic that are specified in the model for foreign affairs strategy – that is, to the strategic context, to the threats and opportunities presented by that context, to national interests, to the nation's power and its influence on other international actors, to objectives, and to other instruments. Specific questions that capture these relationships are elaborated in Figure 6.3.

Political Instruments: Negotiation

If diplomacy encompasses all communications among nation-states and other international actors, negotiations – a more or less formal set of discussions about a particular issue or set of issues between two or more parties – can be seen as a specific tool governments use when everyday diplomacy seems insufficient. Some of the most noteworthy negotiations

---

[4] Hans Morgenthau defines diplomacy "in its widest meaning" as "comprising the whole range of foreign policy." *Politics Among Nations*, 5th ed. rev. (New York: Alfred A. Knopf, 1978), p. 529.

[5] See Thomas Schelling, *The Strategy of Conflict* (New York: Oxford University Press, 1963) for the view that states really communicate tacitly far more than verbally, since in international politics it can be dangerous to believe what another government says.

[6] See Chapter 8.

International Environment: What conditions in the international context are needed for this instrument to work successfully? What conditions should raise warning flags against its use? How robust, or effective across a wide range of environmental conditions, is the instrument?

Domestic Environment: What conditions in the domestic context are needed for this instrument to work successfully? What circumstances are typically needed to sustain public support for its acquisition and use?

Threats and Opportunities: Which threats is this instrument best used to counter? Which opportunities can it most readily take advantage of? On what kinds of threats and opportunities is it unlikely to be effective?

Interests: Which interests is this instrument most effective in supporting? Which interests can it not well serve?

Objectives: Is this policy tool usable only for one or a few kinds of strategic objectives, or can it be employed for a variety of purposes? Are there qualities of this instrument that will tend to undermine the pursuit of some other strategic objectives?

Power and Influence: What demands on the state's potential power – its resources – does this tool pose? How costly and risky is this instrument, and what can be done to minimize both? Which kinds of nation-state regimes and nonstate actors is this instrument most likely to influence?

Instruments: Does this instrument work best alone or in tandem with other policy instruments? If the latter, what is its optimal or necessary relationship with other tools? Are there certain qualities of this instrument that will tend to bolster or undermine other instruments?

Statecraft: In what ways can this instrument be used most effectively? *E.g.*, should it be overt or covert, broad or narrow, actual or prospective, gradual or total?

Figure 6.3: Questions on instruments of state power.

of the post-World War II era have been those between the United States and the Soviet Union over arms control; among the U.S. and other combatants about ending the Vietnam war; between the U.S. and China on normalization and recognition; between Israel, its Arab neighbors, and the Palestinian Liberation Organization (PLO) over autonomy, peace and mutual recognition; and among white minority regimes, black liberation movements and governments, and outside parties over armed intervention, independence, and majority rule in southern Africa.[7]

[7] These include the Lancaster talks giving birth to Zimbabwe, the multi-year effort led by U.S. Assistant Secretary of State Chester Crocker for the withdrawal of outside forces from Angola and the independence of Namibia, the UN's efforts to resolve the black-on-black civil wars in Angola and Mozambique, and the internal negotiations to bring majority rule to South Africa. Though often separate efforts

In addition to such classic efforts to resolve contentious issues, negotiations are constantly underway to solve international problems and set the technical parameters that guide the transnational interactions of individuals, corporations, and nation-states in an ever more integrated world. Like the decade-long conference on the Law of the Sea or the eight successive rounds of trade negotiations under GATT and its successor, the WTO, these are often carried out under the auspices of the UN or other international organizations and usually involve many nations. Although rarely as newsworthy as highly-charged political negotiations, such problem-solving discussions are far more common and in the long run may well be more important in affecting overall state behavior.

In many ways, international negotiations are similar to the domestic negotiations that take place routinely between labor and management, buyer and seller, plaintiff and defendant, or husband and wife. But they also have certain unique features. First, cultural and linguistic differences often intensify the conflicts of interest that usually underlie contentious issues. Moreover, although every negotiation assumes that the parties have ongoing relations with each other – otherwise there would be no need to negotiate – sovereign states living in distinct territories may find fewer common interests and a narrower range of interactions to pull them together than people living in the same society. Third, although customary international law or existing treaties may structure the context of an international negotiation, they often take place in the absence of norms or laws that bind the parties, so there may be no commonly accepted, overarching framework within which to work out differences and few restraints on the parties' behavior outside the negotiation process. Fourth, and most important, the lack of an international monopoly on the use of force means that organized violence is always present as an alternative to a negotiated agreement.

Considered by itself, then, negotiation is paradoxically both the weakest and the strongest of policy instruments.[8] It is the weakest because it relies solely on force of argument and emotion to change another actor's behavior. But it is the strongest because it is the only instrument really capable of *solving* international problems, of creating, registering, and codifying a genuine meeting of the minds on issues in dispute.[9] Thus, as the Duc

---

with different parties, these negotiations have been so linked to each other and to world events that they can fairly be said to have constituted a single negotiating process. See Chester A. Crocker, *High Noon in Southern Africa* (New York: W. W. Norton, 1992).

[8] Steven Mann, "The Interlocking Trinity," unpublished paper written at the National War College, November 5, 1990.

[9] This characterization assumes that the parties are using negotiation because of a genuine interest in dealing with the issues between them. Negotiations may also be employed by one or both of the parties with no thought of actual agreement, *e.g.*, for propaganda purposes, to satisfy intense domestic pressures, to buy time

deCallieres put it in his classic writings on seventeenth century European diplomacy, "the secret of negotiation is to harmonize the interests of the parties concerned":

> ... there is no durable treaty which is not founded on reciprocal advantage, and indeed a treaty which does not satisfy this condition is no treaty at all, and is apt to contain the seeds of its own dissolution. Thus the great secret of negotiation is to bring out prominently the common advantage to both parties of any proposal, and so to link these advantages that they may appear equally balanced to both parties.[10]

Because negotiation is the weakest of instruments, it is the most in need of support by the others. Economic sanctions, trade retaliation, foreign assistance, or the use of force can be expected always to be on or near the table; promises and threats, rewards and punishments can be expected to play a role in the negotiating process along with simple force of argument. But insofar as negotiation is the strongest of instruments, these other tools can only assist and never substitute for the genuine process of persuasion that lies at its heart. Otherwise, the "agreement" reached will prove no settlement at all, but quickly disintegrate in rancorous disputes over its implementation.[11]

Nor can the negotiator avoid this dilemma through dishonesty or stratagem. In warfare, to be sure, secrecy and surprise are valued tools, but there the objective is not to persuade but to coerce. Though Machiavelli wrote that "one who deceives will always find those who allow themselves to be deceived," and an old saw defines a diplomat as someone sent to "lie abroad" for his country, even so skilled a practitioner of power politics as Henry Kissinger warned that "in foreign policy one must never forget that one deals in recurring cycles and on consecutive issues with the same people; trickery sacrifices structure to temporary benefit."[12] Again, deCallieres perhaps put it best:

> ... a lie always leaves a drop of poison behind, and even the most dazzling diplomatic success gained by dishonesty stands on an insecure foundation, for it awakes in the defeated party a sense of aggravation,

or stall an unfavorable action by the other side, or to increase public pressures on it to compromise.

[10] DeCalliers, *On the Manner of Negotiating with Princes*, A F. Whyte trans. (Notre Dame, IN: University of Notre Dame Press, 1963), p. 110.

[11] "In a joint enterprise of sovereign states, only those agreements endure which both sides have an interest in maintaining." Henry Kissinger, *White House Years* (Boston, MA: Little, Brown & Co., 1979), p. 1081. This, of course, is the ultimate answer to the issue of enforceability and verification. If the settlement is genuine, and both sides have an interest in its execution, implementation will take care of itself. But if agreement was forced by the use of other instruments, enforceability and verification will require special attention.

[12] Niccolo Machiavelli, *The Prince*, Luigi Ricci/E. R. P. Vincent trans. (New York: Mentor/Penguin, 1980), p. 93; Kissinger, *White House Years*, p. 747.

a desire for vengeance, and a hatred which must always be a menace to his foe.... [O]ne negotiation successfully carried through by the honest and high intelligence of a diplomatist will give him a great advantage in other enterprises on which he embarks in the future.[13]

The delicacy of negotiation as an instrument of statecraft is revealed in the large number of conditions that must attend its successful use. In the first place, the timing of negotiations is vital. A dispute or problem must be "ripe" for settlement, a fact illustrated by the many negotiations pursued for years without success that move rapidly to conclusion once changes in conditions persuade all sides that an agreement on obtainable terms is better than a continuation of disagreement. For example, the Reagan administration tried fruitlessly for seven years to engineer a settlement in southern Africa; it was only in the eighth year – when radical shifts in Soviet foreign policy under Gorbachev, military exhaustion on the battlefield in Angola (and a perception by all combatants that they could not win by force), and the effect of economic sanctions and recession in South Africa all combined – that a series of accords on withdrawal of foreign forces from Angola and Namibian independence was quickly reached.[14] Similarly, the promise of the 1979 Camp David accords for Palestinian autonomy lay dormant for 14 years until a change of government in Israel, the end of Soviet backing for Arab intransigence, the financial starvation of the PLO following its support for Iraq in the Gulf War, the growing potency of Islamic fundamentalism in the occupied territories, and even the advancing age of key leaders like Shimon Perez and Yassir Arafat made mutual recognition possible and even urgent at Oslo in 1993.[15] But negotiations may well be productive for the long run even if they lack any short run prospect for success. Lacking ripeness, negotiators may spar for years over the shape of the table or who is a legitimate party to the talks, but the knowledge gained, the contacts made and the personal confidences developed can be essential to making the most of the opportunity for settlement when it comes along. Perseverance in the face of even apparently insurmountable obstacles may therefore be vital to eventual success.[16]

---

[13] DeCallieres, *On the Manner of Negotiating with Princes*, pp. 31–32.

[14] For details, see Pauline Baker, *The United States and South Africa: The Reagan Years* (New York: Ford Foundation and the Foreign Policy Association, 1989); Michael Clough and Jeffrey Herbst, "South Africa's Changing Regional Strategy," *Critical Issues* 4 (New York: Council on Foreign Relations, 1989); Chas. W. Freeman, "The Angola-Namibia Accords," *Foreign Affairs* 68 (Summer 1989): 126–141. Similar conclusions can be drawn regarding the settlement of the civil war in El Salvador. Terry Lynn Karl, "El Salvador's Negotiated Revolution," *Foreign Affairs* 71 (Spring 1992): 147–164.

[15] Daniel Williams, "As Much As Anything, Cold War's End Fostered Israel-PLO Deal," and David Hoffman, "Just 2 Professors, Writing a Book..." *Washington Post* (September 1, 1993): A1, A28. Alas, when some of these conditions were reversed in the late 1990s, the process descended once again into deadlock and violence.

[16] Some believe it unwise to begin a negotiation unless there is some prospect for success, since the simple agreement to talk confers a certain legitimacy on the

Successful negotiations also require careful attention to format and procedure; they are rarely just a product of appointed negotiators sitting down together and haggling out an agreement. The need to overcome or circumvent political pressures coming from the parties' constituencies and the requirement for top-level political decisions at various points in the process often lead to secret, back channel discussions behind the formal negotiating process; open covenants must sometimes be arrived at privately if they are to be concluded at all. Thus, Henry Kissinger made a habit of conducting his own secret negotiations on arms control "in the channel," often without the knowledge of the formal U.S. negotiating team.[17]

Negotiators also often require the involvement of outside facilitators or mediators, third parties whose role ranges from simply bringing the sides together, to operating as a conduit for their communications (in so-called "proximity talks" or shuttle diplomacy, where the parties refuse to deal directly with each other), to offering their own proposals for settlement. Here small powers can often provide neutral territory and a voice of impartiality free of interests in the matter at issue, but great powers have special capacities for bringing pressure and offering inducements for (or guarantees of) a settlement. Thus, after the Cold War only Washington and Moscow could use cutoffs of aid and diplomatic relationships with their former allies to drive political settlements in long-running Third World conflicts. Sometimes the two kinds of intervention can work together on different aspects of a settlement: while Norway could offer a secluded and neutral site for the PLO's 1993 talks with Israel, U.S. political backing and fund-raising efforts were critical to the prospects of the Palestinian autonomy experiment that followed.

Once enjoined, the process of negotiation depends critically on the skill of the negotiators in a game where few rules can be adduced for every situation. "The secret of negotiations," as Kissinger writes, "is meticulous preparation.

> The negotiator should know not only the technical side of the subject but its nuances. He must above all have a clear conception of his objectives and the routes to reach them. He must study the psychology and purposes of his opposite number and determine whether and how to reconcile them with his own. He must have all this at his fingertips because the impression of indecisiveness invites hesitation or intransigence.[18]

Often, negotiations proceed via salami tactics, with each side making marginal concessions in an attempt to elicit concessions from the other. In its effort to strike the best deal possible, each will try to discern the other's

other side, an initial concession one might not wish to give to a rogue state or an unsavory nonstate actor. On the other hand, a standing policy of willingness to talk to anyone, anytime, anywhere about anything might well be worth more in breaking down misunderstandings and facilitating diplomacy than it would cost.

[17] See, for example, *White House Years*, pp. 810–823.

[18] Kissinger, *White House Years*, p. 731.

minimum demands – the "resistance point" beyond which the other party simply will not settle – without revealing its own.[19] Often negotiators try to attain the equal balance of advantages deCallieres calls for by "linking" the issues at hand to outside matters which may at first have seemed totally extraneous to the discussion, but this tactic may as likely serve to complicate and widen areas of disagreement as help to resolve them. Moreover, many issues do not lend themselves to a split-the-difference approach, and the process of bargaining from such positions may never reach the sides' real minimum demands.

Often the only way out of such a stalemate is for negotiators to use their creativity to redefine the problem; success, as deCallieres writes, "may be most easily attained by abandoning the approach which caused the original dispute, and taking up the matter from another aspect."[20] Some experienced practitioners and a growing number of scholars argue that negotiators should set aside opposing positions altogether and focus on the underlying interests that must be satisfied.[21] Kissinger did this in his talks with China and Egypt by abandoning traditional salami tactics in favor of an approach later disparaged as preemptive concession, laying all his cards on the table and making the underlying interests so clear that each side could best judge how to satisfy the other's basic requirements. Scholars call this facing the problem rather than the people; the idea is to get the parties engaged in a common effort to identify options through which all can gain rather than remain pitted against one another in a struggle for advantage at the other's expense.

In the end, though, not all interests are reconcilable, not every dispute can be settled, not all problems can be solved. Negotiators must retain a clear view of their nation's interests and a sense of all the possible deals that would be worse than no deal at all; as fatal as a lack of creativity is the "common fault of those who have a lively imagination," namely, to "look at a matter on so many sides that they forget in which direction they are traveling."[22] This warning may be especially significant for American leaders, used to the give and take of democratic processes, who find it difficult "to accept the fact that in some conflicts opposing positions are simply irreconcilable."[23] Moreover,

> [i]n every negotiation a point is reached where both sides have gone too far to pull back. Accumulated mutual concessions create their own momentum; at some stage retreat puts into question the judgment of the negotiators.[24]

---

[19] Gordon A. Craig and Alexander L. George, *Force and Statecraft* (New York: Oxford University Press, 1995), pp. 160–161.

[20] deCallieres, *On the Manner of Negotiating with Princes*, p. 123.

[21] Roger Fisher and William Ury, *Getting to Yes* (New York: Houghton Mifflin, 1981).

[22] deCallieres, *On the Manner of Negotiating with Princes*, p. 30.

[23] Kissinger, *White House Years*, p. 349.

[24] Kissinger, *White House Years*, p. 1081.

Such momentum can carry diplomats beyond what a clear reading of the national interest requires, past what a genuine meeting of minds would involve. The overriding question of every negotiation is thus whether there is a commonality of interests sufficient for a deal. Sometimes the best that can be done is to fudge irreconcilable issues and settle for a limited agreement that will avert conflict, hoping that the passage of time will so change conditions that the impossible becomes possible – an approach used in the 1972 Shanghai communiqué on the thorny issue of the reunification of Taiwan with China in order to permit U.S.–Chinese rapprochement. At other times no amount of creativity or skill will avoid outright failure – though the coordinated use of other instruments of state power in the context of ongoing negotiations may well change a party's calculation of its interests (or of what its interests require) in ways that will lead to success.

Political Instruments: International Organization

Negotiations are often bilateral and ad hoc, with two governments coming together as needed to solve a problem or expand their cooperation. But sometimes ongoing efforts to regulate the affairs of many nations are called for. Beginning about two centuries ago, governments realized that such continuing, multilateral negotiations could be greatly facilitated by permanent organizations, with their own legal charters, established procedures, and standing facilities. Once created, such bodies required a new kind of multilateral diplomacy familiar to legislators in every democratic country: *parliamentary* diplomacy. And the proliferation of agencies created to deal with particular issues or problems eventually suggested the need for a universal organization intended to deal with multiple facets of international life, including issues of war and peace. The result after World War I was the League of Nations; after World War II, the United Nations.

Since the days when Woodrow Wilson fathered (and the Senate rejected) the League Covenant, U.S. policy toward international organizations has swung erratically between enthusiastic embrace and hostile repudiation. These shifts have reflected less the reality of international organizations than ambivalence within the American body politic, long divided between idealists or pacifists who expect miracles of peace from these agencies, and nationalists or isolationists who fear their encroachment on American sovereignty. Far from disappearing with the end of the Cold War, such divisions were brought more sharply into focus, as those who hoped for a new world order under a strengthened UN clashed with those who thought that such an organization would send its black helicopters to take over the United States.[25] The Clinton administration reflected this ambivalence: it

---

[25] See, for example, Jesse Helms, "Saving the UN," *Foreign Affairs* 75 (September-October 1996): 2–7; but also replies to his attack in "Letters to the Editor," *Foreign Affairs* 75 (November-December 1996): 172–179.

began life enunciating a doctrine of "assertive multilateralism," but after the loss of eighteen Americans who were supporting a UN mission in Somalia it quickly drew back into a posture that seemed more ready to blame than to strengthen multilateral organizations.[26] Meanwhile, Republicans in Congress withheld legally-binding dues to the UN, opposed U.S. participation in peacekeeping and nation-building, and railed against the prospect of American troops serving under foreign command. Their unilateralist suspicion of everything multilateral was essentially adopted by the administration of George W. Bush, which rejected the Kyoto treaty on climate change, attacked and obstructed the International Criminal Court, abrogated the Anti-Ballistic Missile Treaty, blocked an enforcement protocol to the Biological Weapons Convention, and went to war in Iraq without UN legitimization. So politicized a history emphasizes the importance of strategists acquiring a balanced view of the utility of international organizations as instruments of American statecraft, along with a sense of how U.S. parliamentary diplomacy can be most effective within them.

The UN, of course, is only the most prominent agency within a substantial universe of public intergovernmental organizations (IGOs), international agencies whose members are governments of nation-states.[27] Conceptually, that universe can be divided into two parts according to purpose. By far the largest number of these bodies and the vast preponderance of the funds cycling through this universe are devoted to advancing the economic welfare and social well-being of the world's peoples.[28] First among these are the so-called "specialized agencies" of the original UN system, created shortly after World War II and including such well-known organizations as the Food and Agriculture Organization (FAO), the International Civil Aviation Organization (ICAO), the International Telecommunications Union (ITU), and the UN Educational and Scientific Organization (UNESCO), along with the international financial institutions (IFIs) known as the International Monetary Fund (IMF), and the World Bank (composed of the International Bank for Reconstruction and Development, or IBRD, and the International Development Association, or IDA). Then there are a variety of funds and programs set up decades later via major multilateral conferences to provide continuing attention to issues which cross-cut the

---

[26] Michael Hirsh, "The Fall Guy," *Foreign Affairs* 78 (November/December 1999): 2–8.

[27] There is in addition, of course, a far greater universe of NGOs, or nongovernmental international bodies, whose members are individuals, companies, or private national associations.

[28] Looking at the UN system in 2001, for example, the assessed budgets of the UN proper plus peacekeeping activity was $3.8 billion, but the assessed and voluntary budgets of the specialized agencies, programs and funds came to $8.6 billion. This crude allocation probably exaggerates the proportion of funds going to peace and security functions, but even so the welfare side absorbs about 70 percent of the total. Figures from Global Policy Forum, table on Total UN System Estimated Expenditure, at www.globalpolicy.org/finance/tables/tabsyst.htm.

older specialized agencies' concerns, beginning with the UN Conference on Trade and Development (UNTAD) in 1964 and continuing with the UN Fund for Drug Abuse Control (UNFDAC), UN Environment Program (UNEP), UN Fund for Population Activities (UNFPA), and many others. And finally there are scores of smaller agencies, often regional rather than global in scope, managing everything from fisheries to river navigation. Regulation of the global commons (the high seas, airways, space, Antarctica and the airwaves); establishing trade laws, postal regulations and the like; dealing with global issues like population, food, and the environment; advancing the welfare of labor and children; and of course promoting the whole complex of activities known as development – all fall under this function of international welfare.

By far the most prominent goal of international organization, however, and the original and most profound purpose of global bodies like the UN is to promote international peace and security, indeed to eradicate war from the international system. At first, it was hoped that peace could be ensured through a system of collective security, based on the idea that, if states mutually guaranteed each other against any attack and agreed in advance to go to war to repel it, no aggressor would be so foolish as to take on the armed resistance of the entire world. At the least, it was hoped, wars would be brief and decisive; at the most, they would never occur. The trouble was that the promise of generalized response to aggression was never believed, because governments proved unwilling to spill their citizens' blood unless the breach of the peace posed the most direct threat to their own national interests. Moreover, what seemed simple in theory usually proved complex in practice: aggression was clouded and indirect, wars were internal as often as international, and IGOs tended to reflect the divisions between their members in waffling and paralysis. Decisive action was put off in favor of diplomacy, and military responses in favor of economic sanctions, while aggressors created situations on the ground that could be changed only by full-scale warfare. Collective security was always just out of reach, first a casualty of the weakness and divisions of states in the interwar period, then of the superpower deadlock during the Cold War.

With the Security Council stalemated for 45 years by 279 vetoes, the UN fell back on other efforts, like providing a forum for talking over problems and disputes, acting as a synthetic third party offering techniques of pacific settlement (such as good offices and mediation), attempting to control or reduce armaments, and – in a unique invention – stationing multilateral peacekeeping forces between the armies of hostile states to prevent conflict (*e.g.*, in the Middle East and Cyprus).[29] When the Cold War ended and President George H. W. Bush turned to the Security Council for legitimacy before the 1991 Gulf war, it was hoped that the organization might begin

---

[29] Boutros Boutros-Ghali, "An Agenda for Peace," United Nations SC Doc. S/24111 (June 17, 1992).

to function the way its founders intended, as a working collective security system at the heart of a new world order. Instead, however, the post–Cold War period saw a proliferation of nationalist and ethnic conflicts, internal wars for which the UN's interstate conflict prevention machinery had not been designed. The organization responded by adapting its Cold War peace and security services in directions as varied as monitoring chaos and providing relief supplies in a disintegrating Yugoslavia (UNPROFOR), relieving famine and pursuing warlords in Somalia (UNOSOM I and II), attempting to restore democracy in Haiti (UNSMIH), helping to end civil war in Sierra Leone (UNOMSIL), and searching for weapons of mass destruction in Iraq (UNSCOM and UNMOVIC).[30] There were calls for the organization to establish a system of "collective responsibility" in lieu of collective security, an integrated system "linking the different phases of action – from evaluation to pacific settlement to preventive measures to peace-keeping to enforcement...."[31] But by the time of the 9/11 attacks such ambitious schemes remained unrealized.

Short of becoming a world government, in fact, there are definite limits to what an international organization can do to square the circle of peace in a world of sovereign states. An international organization like the UN – with its "executive" Security Council, "legislative" General Assembly, and "judicial" International Court of Justice (ICJ), the so-called World Court – may bear a superficial resemblance to the institutions of nation-states, but the resemblance is *only* superficial. In a modern democratic country there is a complex legal system connected to a central monopoly on the use of overwhelming force. Laws are made on behalf of citizens by their representatives, and adjudications are enforced whether an individual likes it or not. But international law is not so fully elaborated, nor are sovereign states subject to it in the way that citizens are to the law of their own societies. The UN General Assembly cannot enact laws binding upon states, the ICJ does not have compulsory jurisdiction over state disputes, and those organs that attempt to execute international regulations – including the UN Security Council – must mainly rely on governments' voluntary cooperation.

---

[30] John M. Goshko, "U.N. Orders U.S.-Led Force Into Somalia," *Washington Post* (December 4, 1992): A1, A20; Julia Preston, "U.N. to Stay In Somalia Until 1995," *Washington Post* (September 23, 1993): A27–28; Julia Preston, "Haiti Embargo Revived," *Washington Post* (October 14, 1993): A1, A24; John M. Goshko, "U.N. Extends Peace Mission in Haiti," *Washington Post* (March 1, 1996): A23. See also Ramesh Thakur, "UN Peace Operations and U.S. Unilateralism and Multilateralism," Chapter 8 in David M. Malone and Yuen Foong Khong, eds., *Unilateralism and U.S. Foreign Policy: International Perspectives* (Boulder, CO: Lynne Rienner, 2003), pp. 153–179.

[31] "Collective responsibility" is a term of Edward C. Luck and Toby Trister Gati, "Whose Collective Security?" *Washington Quarterly* 15 (Spring 1992): 44; second quote is from former UN Undersecretary for Special Political Affairs Brian Urquhart, "The United Nations: From Peace-keeping to a Collective System?" in *New Dimensions in International Security*, Adelphi Paper 265 (London: IISS, Winter 1991/92): 24.

In spite of these shortcomings, many analysts fall into the habit of treating the United Nations as if it were an international actor in its own right. They recommend that "the United Nations" should do this or that, and blame it for failures here or there. In some areas of economic and social welfare, it is true, states have given organizations so-called "supranational" power, the power to decide issues over governments' objections; they have done so because the consequences to their interests of continuing disagreement are far more serious than those of agreement forced against those interests. A failure to set international radio bandwidths would cause chaos in the airwaves; a lack of international postal regulations would mean the end of international mail; and the collapse of the European Union (EU) would result in much lower standards of living on the continent if not near-term impoverishment. The concomitant of such power, though, is often a voting system that gives real weight to the manifest inequalities among nations; and (even in the EU) the possibility of a political decision by any state to withdraw – however costly – remains in the background. Still, states members of these welfare organizations *can* properly speak of them acting or not, of succeeding or failing, and must therefore make influencing their decisions a major objective of strategy.

But in matters of peace and security states are as yet simply unwilling to delegate such powers. Although the UN does have an international civil service headed by a Secretary General who can exhort states to behave and bring their representatives together, it utterly lacks the authority (or indeed the ability) to do anything but talk about international problems unless authorized by governments through the UN's political organs. Except for trained diplomats, international secretariats lack all of the other instruments of state power discussed in this chapter as well as the funds to obtain them; they can trade only in pure persuasion. Although UN members agree that the Security Council acts on their behalf when it finds threats to the peace, breaches of the peace, and acts of aggression under the Chapter VII enforcement provisions of the Charter, the Council is composed of governments, some of whom have vetoes.[32] As Ernest Lefever puts it:

> The United Nations is not and cannot be a political actor in a world of sovereign states....the Security Council is no substitute for alliances, ad hoc Great Power coalitions or unilateral foreign policy initiatives. The United Nations on occasion may be a useful instrument to serve the parallel interests of the United States and other major powers in addressing specific crises. But this consequential difference between actor and instrument has been frequently confused, especially since the Cold War's end.[33]

---

[32] The provisions of Chapter VII and Article 25 of the Charter. In fact, for the average, vetoless member of the UN, the Security Council does have supranational powers in this respect, but not for the Perm 5.

[33] Ernest Lefever, "Reining In the U.N.," *Foreign Affairs* 72 (Summer 1993): 17.

When it comes to peace and security, in other words, the United Nations is no more than the will of whichever Nations can be United, as the Bush administration's 2006 efforts to orchestrate international pressure on Iran over its nuclear program well illustrated. As a result, conceptualizing international organizations as actors in their own right is generally a fundamental error in thinking that can lead to serious errors in strategy. Strategists should never refer to the "United Nations," therefore, always to the "*members* of the United Nations."

Do IGOs, then, offer their member governments any specific capabilities they would not otherwise have? Or should one consider these organizations purely secondary instruments of statecraft? Perhaps international organizations should only be considered part of the modern context in which diplomacy takes place, a feature of the international environment discussed in Chapter 2. Relative to the world's great powers, certainly, the UN's weakness is far more obvious than its strength. States operate through IGOs, but to do so they must utilize their own policy tools. Governments may use them for multilateral negotiations, but it is still governments that do the negotiating. The Security Council may impose economic sanctions on a misbehaving country, but it is still states that do the sanctioning. In the 1991 Gulf War, the Council authorized military action, but it was the troops of the United States and its coalition partners that did the fighting and the dying. Having such examples in mind, one might even conclude that IGOs are not even *instruments* in their own right, let alone actors.

Closer examination, though, will reveal that intergovernmental bodies are more than derivative policy instruments, that they do provide states with modest capabilities that the latter would not otherwise possess. In the first place, international organizations like the UN in New York provide established forums for multilateral diplomacy. That is, they bring most of the world's governments together on a continuing basis so that states interested in doing business can be in touch rapidly, personally, and simultaneously with a wide range of other states. They thus can facilitate a quick reading of the world's pulse on a given issue or proposal, helping policymakers decide what it will take to bring a particular diplomatic effort to fruition. General Assembly resolutions, though not binding legislation, do offer a portrait of world governmental opinion on matters of international concern. And international organizations can be used to transmit as well as receive: Henry Kissinger found Secretary General Kurt Waldheim "a great gossip. One could be sure that he would convey what one was reluctant to say directly – veiled threats or plans for compromise too delicate to put forward under one's own name."[34] IGOs are also great platforms for public diplomacy, as when Adlai Stevenson released to the

---

[34] Henry Kissinger, *Years of Upheaval* (Boston, MA: Little, Brown & Co., 1892), p. 455.

world the Kennedy administration's information about Soviet missiles in Cuba during a Security Council session in October 1962, or when Secretary of State Colin Powell set forth the case for war against Iraq in February 2003.[35]

Second, and even more importantly, international organizations provide established machinery and legal frameworks to facilitate interstate cooperation, both in peace and security and in matters of global welfare. Calling the Security Council into session to deal with a crisis has a certain meaning that ad hoc conferences do not possess, and it meets under rules already worked out in the Charter. In particular, the prospects for economic sanctions, or other enforcement actions that depend for their success on near-universal observance, may be much improved by having a ready-made context for action. Regulatory or standards-setting decisions taken by organizations like the WTO or the World Meteorological Organization (WMO) are products of settled decision-making procedures and fit within an elaborated legal framework accepted in advance by the parties. Thus, time-consuming and politically debilitating efforts to decide how to decide can be avoided. Moreover, as products of recognized decision-making bodies, IGO decisions carry a certain international legitimacy that ad hoc enterprises might not, lessening the criticism and resistance states might face for the same actions taken unilaterally.[36] And by elaborating established bodies of law and precedent, individual decisions may add up to more than the sum of their parts.

Third among the advantages that international organizations can offer as instruments of state power are the additional resources they may command. If policymakers can persuade enough other states to back their objectives, IGOs can help accomplish the tasks on which governments agree. The assessed contributions of members are legally binding obligations under their charters (although some states – like the U.S. – have been chronically in arrears), and they add up to a considerable amount of resources. In FY 2004, for example, the assessed regular and peacekeeping budgets of the UN system totaled $6.7 billion; voluntary contributions to the system in 2001, the most recent year for which these data are available, totaled another $6.8 billion.[37] Moreover, the legitimacy provided by an IGO decision can provide the foundation for effective bilateral fund-raising

---

[35] "The Powell Presentation: 'A Policy of Evasion and Deception,'" *Washington Post* (February 6, 2003): A24–27.

[36] The U.S. spearheaded the establishment of the UN Fund for Drug Abuse Control in 1973 for exactly this reason: to gain entry for crop eradication and substitution programs to states like Burma that were big opium producers but with which the U.S. had poor or no bilateral relations.

[37] Data from Global Policy Forum, table on Total UN System Estimated Expenditures. They include spending under the UN regular budget, the peacekeeping operations budget, and UN specialized agencies, programs, and funds. For financial obligations, see the Charter, Art. 17, para. 2.

efforts, as Secretary of State James Baker understood when he passed the hat among U.S. Desert Storm allies before the allied counterattack in the 1991 Gulf War.[38] In addition, despite their lack of executive power, international secretariats do have resident expertise that states can tap as an in-kind resource for direct support of their objectives.

Finally, resort to the UN can also provide the foreign affairs strategist with political cover in the domestic context. George H. W. Bush was careful to get UN approval for Desert Storm before going to Congress for its approval, thereby confronting the lawmakers with the choice of going along with military action to rescue Kuwait or refusing to back what the international community had already agreed to; and though his son went to Congress (and eventually to war) without the UN's advance approval, he paid a steep price in domestic and international legitimacy. Harry Truman, in fact, believed that the UN Security Council's decision to intervene in Korea would be so persuasive to Americans that he did not go to Congress for permission to use American forces there at all. It is important to recognize, however, that the mere agreement of large numbers of nations to one's course of action does not necessarily make it more moral or democratic; after all, many governments seated at the UN do not reflect the will of their peoples.[39] Nor, as Truman discovered in Korea and Clinton in Somalia, does UN approval guarantee long-term support from the American people if military costs escalate.

There are, of course, some concomitant disadvantages of using international organizations as instruments of foreign affairs strategy. One is that their decision making processes often do not reflect the relative power of nations. Although the IFIs have weighted voting based on members' contributions and the Security Council gives its five permanent members vetoes, the legal fiction of the sovereign equality of states usually means that decisions are taken under one state, one vote rules. Members of an international body may thus decide that the organization will "do" things that are utterly unrealistic, and governments wishing to use them as instruments of national policy must use other instruments of statecraft to get decisions to come out as they prefer, for example by lobbying member governments in their capitals and using the full array of promises and threats. Indeed, it is at least possible that an effort to get the "right" IGO decision may consume more of the state's actual power than it adds to that power, especially if in the process the state has to reduce its objectives to the lowest common denominator sufficient for majority support.

---

[38] The result was a net cost to the United States of about $13 billion, compared with the 2003 war's costs of roughly $250 billion by 2006. "Paying for Iraq: Blood and Treasure," *Economist* (April 8, 2006): 33–34. The various estimates this article reviews place the second war's *eventual* costs somewhere between $410–630 billion, compared with perhaps $400 billion for ongoing containment.

[39] As Lefeber puts it, "The number of actors is morally irrelevant. It is the intention and consequence of the action that counts." "Reining in the U.N.," p. 19.

But this is not the only or even the most serious way that deciding to work through international organizations can dilute the autonomy of state action. For once objectives are agreed upon within an international coalition and put into writing in an approved resolution, it can be more difficult for national policy to go beyond or avoid them. Before the 1991 Gulf War, for example, the United Nations agreed only on the expulsion of Iraqi forces from Kuwait, not the destruction of Saddam Hussein's military machine nor the occupation of his country. Though President Bush had domestic political reasons for ending the counterattack when he did, there seems little doubt that the specter of the United States continuing with the war under a barrage of allied (including Arab) criticism was a major factor in his decision.[40] American interests, in other words, are rarely likely to be entirely the same as those of other countries, and multilateral action can extend only so far as interests coincide. Doing things through an international organization has a way of codifying and solidifying those constraints beyond what multilateral cooperation alone might engender, tying one's own instruments of power to the interests of the larger collectivity.

With all of their advantages, then, international organizations must be seen as constraints on, as well as enablers of, state action. They are part of the environment as well as an instrument, a stage more often than an actor. They offer legitimacy but can limit freedom of action, may share costs yet compromise objectives, and can provide opportunities to strengthen coalitions but also empower the weak, including adversaries. Above all, strategists must realize that they are not substitutes for painstaking efforts to coordinate the will of nations. Whether the issue is a technical one advancing international welfare or a matter of peace and security, the hard work of coalition building must still be done. Without a strong great power lead, in fact, international agencies usually do not work very well. As the leading American theorist of this instrument once put it,

> . . . timely and decisive action by multilateral bodies such as the United Nations is utterly dependent upon the determined leadership of a great power that has the resolution and audacity to move out front, to pull the majority along rather than to wait for it, to carry the lion's share of the burden while tolerating free riders, and to live with the inevitable criticism. Multilateralism is not the antithesis of unilateralism. It depends upon, and starts with, unilateralism.[41]

---

[40] Again, though, one must be careful not to attribute too much of this effect to the action of the IGO, for the criticism would probably have been forthcoming even if the coalition had been assembled outside the UN and would have been much more severe in the absence of any coalition at all.

[41] Inis L. Claude, Jr., "Collective Security After the Cold War," Chapter 1 in Gary L. Guertner, *Collective Security in Europe and Asia* (Carlisle Barracks, PA: U.S. Army War College, 1992), pp. 21–22.

Given strong leadership, however, international organizations can be essential tools to deal with today's most pressing problems. They offer many of the capabilities essential to combating terrorism, from multilateral intelligence sharing to nation-building and coordinated police work. They are also well-positioned to deal with transnational issues like narcotics trafficking, international crime, climate change, and the economic stresses of globalization. But IGOs are also human institutions, plagued by politicization, bureaucratization, inefficiency, corruption, and occasional scandal.[42] Strategists wishing to make use of their unique capabilities will need both to accept and help correct their shortcomings, and to give them the power needed to execute their tasks.

Political Instruments: International Law

Although international law is often made by and employed in the context of international organizations, and its creation is frequently the end-point of negotiations, it plays its own role – also as both an enabling instrument of statecraft and a constraining feature of the international environment. Traditionally, the term "international law" refers to rules purporting to regulate the behavior of nation-states, in peace or war, that emerge gradually from their customary practices or are stipulated by treaties they negotiate.[43] It recognizes that the sovereignty of nation-states precludes their being bound without their consent, although over time the practices of states can create customary, binding law.[44] But binding or not, as long as the world lacks a government, international law will be without an enforcement mechanism, or more precisely will be enforceable only by the political decisions of other sovereign states. Such characteristics make the law of nations quite different than the law applied within states and lead some to question whether it is law at all.

Nevertheless, that international law is useful to states should be obvious from the very fact that it exists. On the most basic level, rules that regulate behavior help make life predictable for everyone, creating a web of

---

[42] Especially since the Reagan years, various Congresses and administrations have waged campaigns to reform an institution bloated by political staffing and subject to majority budgeting at rich nations' expense. The organization has also been weakened by sex scandals in some peacekeeping operations, and by corruption in the pre-war Iraq oil-for-food program. See Colum Lynch, "U.N. Chief's Record Comes Under Fire," *Washington Post* (April 24, 2005): A14, A18.

[43] The ICJ, for example, can apply "international conventions...establishing rules expressly recognized by the contending parties;...international custom, as evidence of a general practice accepted as law;...the general principles of law recognized by civilized nations" and as subsidiary sources, "judicial decisions and the teaching of the most highly qualified publicists of the various nations ...." Art. 38, ICJ Statute.

[44] States can, of course, give consent in advance, as members of the UN did when they agreed that they would carry out decisions of the Security Council and pay assessed dues. UN Charter, Articles 25 and 17.

expectations that allows governments to go about most of their business without meeting resistance at every turn. Indeed, international law arose precisely because states needed to order their relations with one another, especially in places like the high seas where no state had sovereign control. More specifically, law can provide a framework for cooperation, helping to lock in the terms of dispute settlements or regulate transactions between parties. Courts applying international law can also be useful for dispute resolution, although the ICJ's lack of automatic compulsory jurisdiction makes litigation of serious political issues possible only if the parties have already agreed to it.[45] Conformance with the law can be used to legitimize state actions both at home and abroad, and arguments based on law may assist in routine diplomacy and specific negotiations, particularly if it can be shown that the behavior the diplomat is trying to elicit from another government is mandated by a treaty to which it is a party. In all these ways, international law is basic to the business of foreign affairs, and it is associated most closely, among the instruments of state power, with negotiations and international organizations.

International law does, of course, have some disadvantages of which strategists must be aware. Many stem from the inconvenient fact that law usually sets rules for the behavior of *all* states, not just *other* states. Governments must be careful, therefore, not to espouse or create rules that they themselves do not wish to follow, unless the benefits of others' conformance would be greater than the costs of their own.[46] This general applicability of law creates special problems for powerful countries, for since the law applies equally to all states, it reduces the advantages that the most powerful enjoy. Moreover, when they act in ways that take advantage of their superiority, like engaging in preventive war, great powers inevitably set precedents that may in time have legal effect, giving other states permission to act as they do. Democratic states may also be more constrained by international law than autocratic ones, finding it more difficult to take actions that seem manifestly outside its boundaries simply because the citizens of democracies tend to expect law-abiding behavior of their governments.

Indeed, some observers believe that powerful democracies like the United States have recently become endangered by what has been called the twentieth century's "great trend in international law: the increasing international regulation of more and more issues once typically seen as part of state domestic jurisdiction."[47] Although the traditional law of nations

---

[45] See Article 36, ICJ Statute. Obligatory adjudication mechanisms are sometimes built into treaties regulating trade or technical issues.

[46] Treaty law can of course make distinctions among classes of states, as does the Nuclear Non-Proliferation Treaty between nuclear and non-nuclear weapons states, imposing different rights and obligations on each.

[47] Steven R. Ratner, "International Law: The Trials of Global Norms," *Foreign Policy* 110 (Spring 1998): 66.

precluded interference in the internal affairs of states, so-called "new" international law has recently sought to reach into them in a variety of ways.[48] First, there is the development of so-called "soft law – precepts emanating from international bodies that conform in some sense to expectations of required behavior but that are not binding on states."[49] Resolutions of international conferences or the UN General Assembly, for example, can help solidify norms and thus more quickly lead to hard law, and they also may imply that policy on domestic issues like the death penalty or workplace safety should follow prevailing international standards.[50] Second, globalization has as so interlinked nations that many formerly domestic issues now require international coordination or have become connected to those that do; thus, environmental regulation now is tied to global warming, and domestic labor law has become connected to international trade and foreign investment.[51] Third, following the ethnic conflicts of the 1990s in Rwanda and the former Yugoslavia, a right of international humanitarian intervention has been asserted in order to prevent gross violations of human rights, the theory being that countries whose governments abuse or fail to protect their citizens forfeit their sovereign right to exclusive control over them.[52] Fourth, and most dramatically, there is a movement to make state officials directly accountable to international and foreign courts for criminal conduct, thereby giving a body of law that was traditionally applicable only to nation-states direct application to individuals within them.

To be sure, traditional international law recognized the ability of any state to try individuals suspected of having committed, *outside* state territory, crimes like piracy and the slave trade. In the last two decades this doctrine of "universal jurisdiction" has been expanded by prosecutors and legislatures in Spain, Belgium, and elsewhere to include a right to try officials of another state for crimes they committed *within* their own or other countries. Thus, despite the Chilean government's protests, the former Chilean dictator Augusto Pinochet was arrested in Britain for extradition to Spain where he was to be prosecuted for crimes committed within Chile, and cases were filed in Belgium under its 1993 war crimes law against American civilian and military officers for wartime acts of state against Iraq.[53] At

[48] The UN Charter, for example, precludes the organization from intervening "in matters which are essentially within the domestic jurisdiction of any state ...." Art. 2(7).

[49] Ratner, "International Law," p. 67.

[50] David B. Rivkin, Jr., and Lee A. Casey, "The Rocky Shoals of International Law," *National Interest* 62 (Winter 2000/2001): 37.

[51] Ratner, "International Law," pp. 74–75.

[52] Opening the 1999 UN General Assembly, Secretary General Kofi Annan declared that "massive violations of human rights will not stand." Quoted in Edward Luttwak, "Kofi's Rule," *The National Interest* 58 (Winter 1999/2000): 57–62.

[53] On Pinochet, see T. R. Reid, "Pinochet Decision Aids Rights Pacts," *Washington Post* (March 26, 1999): A21, and Jeremy Rabkin, "International Law *vs.* the

the same time, international courts have been created to try individuals, including government officials, for human rights violations. The European and Inter-American Courts of Human Rights had for some time allowed citizens to bring such cases against their own governments, and they were joined in the late 1990s by the International Criminal Tribunals for the Former Yugoslavia and Rwanda, which indicted and tried government officials as well as ordinary citizens for criminal acts in those countries.

Rather than continue to resort to ad hoc tribunals, the Rome Conference of 1998 negotiated a treaty that established an International Criminal Court (ICC) to try citizens of any nation for war crimes, crimes against humanity, genocide, and even aggression (once it could be defined).[54] Although the Clinton administration supported the idea of such a court, participated in its negotiation, and signed the Treaty of Rome, it decided not to ask the Senate's consent to ratification because the treaty gave international prosecutors the right to indict (and the ICC jurisdiction to try) American soldiers and other officials without their government's consent.[55] Remarkably, the Treaty of Rome extended prosecutorial jurisdiction even to nationals whose countries were not parties to it. Whereas Clinton hoped to modify these provisions, the Bush administration went into outright opposition, withdrawing the U.S. signature from the treaty, negotiating agreements with scores of countries giving U.S. officials blanket immunity, and signing an American Servicemen's Protection Act that empowered the president to use "all necessary means" to liberate citizens detained by the ICC.[56]

In the view of critics, the reaching of international law into states in these ways poses two dangers to the United States, and indeed to any

American Constitution," *National Interest* 55 (Spring 1999): 33–34; on Belgian law, see Glenn Frankel, "Belgian War Crimes Law Undone by Its Global Reach," *Washington Post* (September 30, 2003): A1, A15.

[54] Naomi Roht-Arriaza, "Institutions of International Justice," *Journal of International Affairs* 52 (Spring 1999): 475–483.

[55] Clinton had wanted prosecutions to be controlled by the UN Security Council, where the U.S. has a veto. Robert W. Tucker, "The International Criminal Court Controversy," *World Policy Journal* 18 (Summer 2001): 71–81. U.S. concerns arose partly because the Yugoslavia tribunal, at the request of Russian legislators, had considered charges against NATO for war crimes in its 1999 Kosovo campaign. Charles Truehart, "Taking NATO to Court," *Washington Post* (January 20, 2000): A15, A24.

[56] Peter Slevin, "U.S. Renounces Its Support of New Tribunal for War Crimes," *Washington Post* (May 7, 2002): A1, A18. By late 1994, some 96 countries had signed such Article 98 agreements. Colum Lynch, "Congress Seeks to Curb International Court," *Washington Post* (November 26, 2004): A2. In order to get them, the Bush administration has gone so far as to threaten or actually cut aid to Jordan, Columbia, and several nations who have sent troops to Iraq. See "For us or against us?" *Economist* (November 22, 2003): 27; Tom Malinowski, "Bush's Court Crusade," *Washington Post* (August 16, 2002): A25; and Jackson Diehl, "Allies and Ideology," *Washington Post* (November 24, 2003): A21.

constitutional, democratic country. First, since there is no elected and accountable international legislature, the creation of legal norms outside treaties violates the basic constitutional idea that there is no law without democratic representation; and in so far as it applies to individuals directly, such law bypasses the procedural guarantees of individual liberty embedded in the U.S. Constitution and its Bill of Rights.[57] Second, if it can bind the United States without its consent, the new international law can be used by other states as a way of constraining America's extraordinary power and limiting its ability to lead in the maintenance of world order.[58] The ICC's critics are right that law, whether international or domestic, is always about equalizing power, as noted above. But a country possessing the political, economic, and military capabilities of the United States hardly needs to fear courts that lack enforcement mechanisms.[59] More broadly, the principle of sovereign consent is so well supported by the realities of power that it is inconceivable that any of these developments, or all of them put together, could erase it.

Rather than focusing on the improbable, strategists might instead consider how the United States can encourage the development and strengthening of the traditional law of nations as a long-term tool to shape the international system in ways favorable to U.S. interests. Such a course would, it is true, require occasional tradeoffs of short-term for long-term interests, sacrifices of the immediate benefits of actions that counteract desirable norms in the hope that strengthening those standards through compliance will eventually work to shape other states' behaviors. Only strategists operating from a position of confident relative superiority and with a very distant time horizon are likely to be willing to field such policies, but they would certainly be possible for the United States today. Intelligently used, in fact, this instrument provides a long-range tool of statecraft quite unlike any other.

Political Instruments: Alliances

Alliances are long-term politico-military ties between two or more nation-states designed to improve their security.[60] Their explicit and enduring nature distinguishes them from alignments (a mere coming into line of states' objectives without any direct agreement between them), ententes (weak, broad understandings based on common policies or diplomacy), and

---

[57] This is the main theme of Rabkin, "International Law *vs.* the American Constitution."

[58] Rivkin and Casey, "The Rocky Shoals of International Law," p. 7.

[59] The ICC in particular includes several safeguards against politicization, including subordination to status of forces agreements, pre-approval of all prosecutions by a 3-judge pre-trial panel, prior jurisdiction by a citizen's own courts, and limitation to "wide-spread and systematic" atrocities. "Right to the Brink," *Economist* (July 6, 2002): 29.

[60] This definition, and much of the reasoning in this section, is adapted from Terry L. Deibel, "Alliance, Military and Political," *International Military and Defense Encyclopedia*, Vol. I (Washington, DC: Brassey's US, 1993), pp. 116–121.

coalitions (short-term relationships formed for a narrow, specific purpose, like fighting a war). Moreover, alliances must include a degree of commitment that binds the allies, compelling their action in some defined circumstances. Historically, such commitments were "if... then" clauses placed in treaties that obligated the parties to react if a given event (like an attack) took place, and the strength of the commitment depended on the specificity with which the triggering event and the response to it were defined. A traditional alliance, then, was "a treaty binding two or more independent states to come to each other's aid with armed force under circumstances specified in the *causes foederis* article of the treaty."[61] Today, some U.S. alliances (like NATO or the alliances with South Korea and Japan) have such treaties, but the commitments involved in other alliances (like those with Israel or Saudi Arabia) are based on other factors. Thus, modern alliances can be quite adequately defined simply as "formal or informal commitment[s] for security cooperation between two or more states."[62]

Alliances show a wide variety of characteristics. Although all by definition involve relatively long-term commitments, their duration may vary from years to decades and their commitments may be strong or weak, specific or vague. They may be formal and have elaborate machinery for cooperation and decision making, or be informal, rudimentary, and procedurally ad hoc. They may deal with a single threat or issue, or be very broad in scope. They may involve two, three, or many states, reaching across the globe (like the U.S.–Pakistan alliance) or, like most multilateral compacts, confining themselves to a geographic region (*e.g.*, the Organization of American States or the North Atlantic Treaty Organization). Members may be relatively equal or very dissimilar in power, and alliances may entail mutual rights and duties or be an asymmetrical guarantee of a small power by a great one. In sum, alliances are a malleable tool that states can shape to fit their needs and circumstances.

The strength of an alliance is, to be sure, somewhat dependent on factors beyond the allies' control. Most important among them is a common threat, but it helps also to have shared interests and objectives, similar systems of government, even a common culture and language. At the same time, alliances and the commitments that underpin them are created and maintained by their members using many of the other instruments of state power; in that sense they are a derivative instrument, quite unlike most tools treated in this chapter.[63] If the commitment is enshrined in a treaty, then the relevant instruments are primarily negotiation and international

---

[61] Paul W. Schroeder, "Alliances, 1815–1945: Weapons of Power and Tools of Management," in Klaus Knorr, ed., *Historical Dimensions of National Security Problems* (Lawrence, KS: University Press of Kansas, 1976), pp. 227–262.

[62] Stephen M. Walt, "Why Alliances Endure or Collapse," *Survival* 39 (Spring 1997): 157.

[63] For a complete description of these factors and explanation of their binding effects, see Terry L. Deibel, *Commitment in American Foreign Policy* (Washington, DC: NDU Press, 1980).

law. Although some alliances are secret, public diplomacy (or at least pub-
licity) can also be key to a commitment's force, because it raises the cost in
credibility of failing to honor the promise when the chips are down. International organization may be involved if a multilateral alliance is fully elaborated into machinery for planning, infrastructure, exercising, and decision,
like NATO; indeed, the division of labor that results from defense planning can itself have a powerful committing effect. Military forces may play
their role in commitment by being stationed in so-called "tripwire" positions
where they will be physically involved in any attack, as U.S. forces were in
Europe during the Cold War and are today in South Korea. International
trade and finance can have a committing effect if an ally supplies essential
commodities or has sizeable amounts of its partner's debt or foreign direct
investment (FDI), and economic and military aid used to strengthen the
capabilities of weaker allies also binds states together – for, as Machiavelli
recognized, "it is the nature of men to be as much bound by the benefits
that they confer as by those they receive."[64] Thus, virtually all the primary instruments of state power can be involved in creating this derivative
tool that, through its durability and obligations, becomes an instrument
in itself.

Nation-states create and maintain alliances to achieve a variety of benefits. Chief among them, as will be recalled from Chapter 2, is to increase
a state's capabilities artificially by aggregating the power of two or more
states (and making clear their intentions) in the face of a threat, the better
to deter attack or defend against it if deterrence fails. Alliances can help
states share the economic and military burdens of defense and deterrence,
and they can also fulfill the purely instrumental role of allowing a state to
build or use bases on the territory of another that it needs to project its
military power into distant regions. Quite apart from such military tasks,
alliances are also used by dominant states to help manage the international system and shape it to suit their purposes.[65] Giving a commitment
is an inexpensive way, at least in the short run, to get other states to do
what they would not otherwise do, and alliances can be used by powerful
states to co-opt weaker ones, reducing the risk that the latter will start
local conflicts or engage in balancing behavior against them. Indeed, as
primary elements in the balance of power, the long-term relationships that
alliances ratify and sustain help structure the international system itself.
Alliances can also provide legitimization for great power action on the world
stage by demonstrating that there is some degree of consensus behind it,
as NATO did in the 1999 Kosovo war.

But like other tools of statecraft, alliances also have their weaknesses,
disadvantages, and costs. Many of these relate to the commitments that
lie at the heart of any alliance, for to the extent that they bind states,

[64] Machiavelli, *The Prince*, p. 68.
[65] See Schroeder, "Alliances, 1815–1945."

commitments also limit their freedom of action. Alliances thus take their place with international law and organization as tools that constrain as well as enable. Especially for powerful countries like the United States, they may necessitate unwelcome compromises in objectives or even preclude certain actions altogether; at the very least they involve some degree of consultation and may require shared decision making. Moreover, although making promises may be a cheap method of influence, commitments may also fall due, confronting policymakers with an uncomfortable choice between paying the costs of upholding them or seeing their country's credibility disintegrate, with predictable effects on all its other international relationships. Honoring commitments may not be automatic, but they nevertheless pose a substantial risk that cannot be ignored: the risk of entrapment in an unwanted conflict.[66] Moreover, although they help structure and can be used to manage the international system, analysts since Woodrow Wilson have understood that alliances are exclusionary vehicles that may provoke counter-alliances and thereby set the world stage for war. Statesmen will hope that they can manage their alliances to avoid such unfortunate results, but there is no escaping the dilemma that the strength of a commitment, and hence its effectiveness in deterring enemies and reassuring partners, is directly related to the costs of creating it and the risks it carries if its promises fall due. Even short of catastrophe, the costs of sustaining an alliance in lost freedom of action, diplomatic attention, aid dollars, and the consumption of other instruments of statecraft may loom so large that the relationship appears to absorb more power than it generates.

Nor are the benefits of such compacts always evident. Politically, alliances hardly guarantee solidarity and support, as the United States discovered when several NATO members actively opposed its 2003 war in Iraq. Militarily, allied forces may not be very capable or useful, and the need to coordinate decision making with them during combat may slow and limit the effectiveness of force, lessons the U.S. learned in the 1999 Kosovo war and applied when it rejected allied help in Afghanistan in 2001.[67] Moreover, because the tools that create alliances are so many and varied, the calculus of commitment by all concerned is necessarily complex and uncertain.[68] Therefore, it is quite possible for one state to be committed to another in its own eyes but not in the eyes of its ally or enemies, or for a state considering itself free of obligations to be seen by others as committed. In other words,

---

[66] "The decisions of a great power will be shaped by the requirements of the national interest as perceived at the moment of decision, not only by abstract legal obligations whether vague or precise...." Kissinger, *White House Years*, p. 895.

[67] The intricacies of alliance leadership in Kosovo are described in Wesley K. Clark, *Waging Modern War: Bosnia, Kosovo, and the Future of Combat* (New York: Public Affairs, 2001).

[68] Bruce Russett, "The Calculus of Deterrence," *Journal of Conflict Resolution* 7 (June 1963).

there is no necessary correspondence between either the fact or the degree of commitment, on the one hand, and the existence or amount of related deterrence or reassurance, on the other. Indeed, given that commitments ultimately depend on human decisions made at the moment the triggering event occurs, it is quite possible that the leaders of committed states may themselves be unsure of their responses. For psychological factors unappreciated before the moment of decision will enter in, such as an unwillingness to write off sunk costs, worries about consistency and reliability, or the pull of transnational personal relationships, along with pressures from public opinion and interest groups. There is thus plenty of room for surprises all around.

As a country whose relatively isolated location encouraged the pursuit of security through freedom of action, the United States has been particularly sensitive to these disadvantages of alliances and wary of the commitments they entail. George Washington, after all, warned against "permanent" alliances and Thomas Jefferson against "entangling" ones, and although the country relied on an alliance with France to help win its independence, it quickly renounced that treaty and avoided any more like it for a century and a half.[69] Still, containing the Soviet threat led to three successive waves of American alliance building during the Cold War.[70] First to be established, during the Truman administration, were the NATO and Australia–New Zealand (ANZUS) treaties, strategic agreements with similarly advanced societies designed to aggregate power for the new bipolar struggle. Second were the very different Eisenhower-Dulles treaties with South Korea, Taiwan, and the Southeast Asian and Central Treaty Organization countries (SEATO and CENTO). These were tactical responses to breaches of containment in Korea, Vietnam, and Iraq that connected the United States to societies with very different cultures and governments; far from aggregating power, they were efforts to deter subversion and prepare for Soviet attack on weak, unstable nation-states that required massive American support. For both Truman and Eisenhower, however, the historic American preference for freedom of action resulted in treaties that did little in themselves to bind the United States, promising only that Washington would respond by taking "such action as it deems necessary" or acting "in accordance with its constitutional processes."[71] Instead, U.S. commitments came through the back door, from actions like putting

---

[69] Washington quote from the Farewell Address, in Ruhl J. Bartlett, *The Record of American Diplomacy* (New York: Alfred A. Knopf, 1964), p. 88; Jefferson, 1st Inaugural Address, 4 March 1801.

[70] These periods of American alliance building are described in some detail in Terry L. Deibel, "Alliances for Containment," in Deibel and John Lewis Gaddis, eds., *Containing the Soviet Union* (Washington, DC: Pergamon-Brassey's, 1987), pp. 106–115.

[71] "Such action" is from the North Atlantic Treaty; "constitutional processes" is the standard language used in the Pacific treaties of alliance (SEATO, ANZUS, Taiwan, Japan, Korea). See Roland A. Paul, *American Military Commitments Abroad* (New Brunswick, NJ: Rutgers University Press, 1973), p. 15–16.

American troops in tripwire positions on Europe's Fulda Gap and Korea's demilitarized zone (DMZ), participating in joint commands and organizations, doing multilateral planning and exercising, intensifying trade and other economic links, or building networks of official and sub-national contacts. And the third wave of Cold War alliance creation in the Carter and Reagan years did away with treaties entirely, building informal "security partnerships" to support the Carter Doctrine through facilities access and overflight rights, base construction, foreign aid dollars, diplomatic contact, executive agreements, and statements of intent. It was almost as if American decision makers thought that by keeping commitments inexplicit they could avoid their costs and risks while retaining their deterrent advantages.[72]

Since the demise of the Soviet Union, many observers have thought that these Cold War alliances would disappear; some even argue that alliances themselves are outmoded as tools of American state power. In fact, most of the Eisenhower–Dulles alliances were gone well before the Cold War ended, victims of changing threat perceptions, shifts in domestic politics, and the dynamics of the war against terrorism that have changed the cost-benefit ratio on all sides.[73] American partners may still value their access to military technology and to Washington's decision making that an alliance provides – not to mention the reassurance of its security guarantee – but the reduced level of threat leaves them less willing to tolerate treatment as junior partners or to follow Washington's lead when they disagree with it. The United States, for its part, may still value allies for burden sharing and peacekeeping in post-conflict situations, and it may still occasionally need bases near war zones or access to airspace and facilities. But technology allows the Pentagon increasingly to project power directly from the United States, and large permanent deployments of American forces tend both to cause local frictions and be less flexible than the ever-shifting terrorist threat demands. More than one observer contends that "[t]hese trends confirm the growing primacy of ad hoc and bilateral alliances over permanent and multilateral alliances," if not the obsolescence of alliances themselves.[74]

Still, one not need look far to discover trends that validate the continued utility of this venerable tool. The Carter–Reagan partnerships in the Middle East and Gulf have not faded but grown stronger as a result of oil politics and the Iraq wars, and both Bill Clinton and George W. Bush expanded NATO and strengthened the alliance with Japan as part of the United States hedging strategy against a resurgent Russia and a rising China. Such Cold War relics have persisted and prospered not only because their leader

[72] Terry L. Deibel, "Hidden Commitments," *Foreign Policy* 67 (Summer 1987): 22–45.
[73] By 1986 only the SEATO commitment to Thailand and the Korean treaty remained.
[74] Bruno Tertrais, "The Changing Nature of Military Alliances," *Washington Quarterly* 27 (Spring 2004): 135–150.

has been willing to bear a disproportionate level of costs, offer necessary inducements, and accommodate local concerns, but also in some cases because they have developed into genuine security communities based on shared values and identities – as well as the vested interests of elites.[75] In addition, since 9/11 the United States has embarked on a fourth wave of security partnerships, seeking cooperation in the war on terror along with the facilities and permissions needed to project its military power into Afghanistan and Iraq.[76] Although at least as informal as the third, Cold War wave created by Carter and Reagan, these relationships with states in Southwest and Central Asia will inevitably create commitments as diplomacy proceeds, aid is delivered, bases are built, combined exercises occur, and networks of personal contacts expand. Even multilateral alliances may find new utility, for a NATO-like structure might be just what the Pacific community needs to corral a strengthening China, and Persian Gulf security might be best served by the expansion and formalization of the Gulf Cooperation Council to include Iran as well as postwar Iraq. Therefore, although the formality of the era of treaty commitments may be gone, it seems likely that this flexible tool of state power will retain its strategic utility for some time to come.

Information Instruments: Public Diplomacy

Most diplomacy, whether bilateral or multilateral, is conducted directly with foreign governments. Public diplomacy differs in being aimed at foreign publics, particularly at opinion leaders who influence public opinion in their societies and thereby indirectly affect the policies of their governments. One American foreign service officer with thirty-five years in the public diplomacy business defined it as "the government's process of communicating with foreign publics to create understanding of U.S. ideas and ideals, institutions and culture, and current goals and policies."[77]

> [T]he core idea is one of direct communication with foreign peoples, with the aim of affecting their thinking and, ultimately, that of their governments. It embraces programs in both the government and private sectors, the latter often sponsored or inspired by the former. In practice it is concerned with publicly promoting U.S. policy interests abroad and with helping others gain an understanding of our people and society in the hope that our actions may be viewed sympathetically or that a degree of mutual understanding will be achieved.[78]

---

[75] Walt, "Why Alliances Endure or Collapse," provides a comprehensive list of such disintegrative and preservative factors.

[76] Alexander Cooley, "Base Politics," *Foreign Affairs* 84 (November/December 2005): 79–92.

[77] Hans N. Tuch, "Improving Public Diplomacy," *Foreign Service Journal* 67 (May 1990): 14.

[78] Gifford D. Malone, "Managing Public Diplomacy," *Washington Quarterly* 8 (Summer 1985): 199.

Though composed of a variety of informational, cultural, and educational programs, public diplomacy divides conceptually into two functional categories.[79] The first might be called the "policy information" or "advocacy" role, that of explaining and defending a government's policies to foreign audiences and, at the same time, factoring the likely reactions of foreign publics back into policy decisions by the government. For the United States this function is performed in Washington by the president, the secretary of state and other high officials, along with their press spokesmen and women; overseas it is performed by ambassadors, public affairs officers, and embassy press attaches. Though the communication is *to* people in other countries, the information comes *from* the U.S. government, so policy information and advocacy can be thought of as a *government*-to-people program. The second category of public diplomacy could be termed "cultural communications," or the portrayal of one country's culture and society to people in another. This function is orchestrated by the State Department's Bureau of Education and Cultural Affairs in Washington and by its public affairs officers and their cultural affairs staffs in embassies overseas. Since the source of the information here is clearly American society itself, cultural communications is essentially a *people*-to-people program, with the government in the role of facilitator and catalyst.

The differences between these two functions extend "from the objectives they serve to the messages they carry to the media they use.

> Policy information is a highly political function, moving from issue to issue on a day-to-day basis with the foreign policy of the government in power. Cultural communications is a long-range effort representing the nation (rather than the government) in all its stability and character. Policy information must advocate and defend; it is by nature partisan and biased. Cultural communications explains and portrays; it must give at least the impression of truthfulness in order to be credible and effective. Policy information uses the fast media, such as radio, TV, and the press. Cultural communications needs the slower books, exhibits, and films that provide the kind of visual and in-depth verbal treatment cultural subjects require. The source of policy information is of course the government, whereas the most authentic cultural materials come from the private sector they seek to portray.[80]

Although it is true that some media are more suited either to the cultural or to the policy function, most media can be and are used for either. United States Information Service libraries and American Centers or

---

[79] Christopher Ross, "Public Diplomacy Comes of Age," *Washington Quarterly* 25 (Spring 2002): 75–84. Paul Blackburn sketches 4 dimensions of public diplomacy: policy advocacy, broadcasting, educational exchanges, showcasing U.S. culture and society. Paul P. Blackburn, "The Post–Cold War Public Diplomacy of the United States," *Washington Quarterly* 15 (Winter 1992): 75–90.

[80] Terry L. Deibel and Walter R. Roberts, *Culture and Information: Two Foreign Policy Functions*, The Washington Papers 40 (Beverly Hills and London: Sage Publications, 1976), p. 57.

Corners abroad thus offer books and periodicals to foreign audiences on
U.S. foreign policy as well as the whole range of American society and
culture; periodicals produced by State and articles placed by its officers in
foreign newspapers and journals can be on either subject; television from
Worldnet and international radio broadcasts by the Voice of America (VOA)
include shows on American music and social life as well as interviews with
policymakers and "editorials" advocating policy positions; electronic feeds
of the so-called "wireless file" to posts overseas include news items on cultural topics as well as policy speeches and documents; American scholars sent abroad to lecture and international visitors brought to the United
States to learn may focus on either realm. Only a few kinds of vehicles, such
as exhibits, touring performing arts groups, and the Fulbright educational
exchange program seem usable exclusively for cultural communications
purposes.

Controversy has often surfaced over how separate these two functions
should be and how important each is in American foreign policy.[81] One
school of thought argues that a free society like the United States best
serves its interests by projecting an image of itself as free as possible of
government presence and interference. In this view, all public diplomacy
efforts should be completely untainted by propaganda, and American society should be presented as accurately as possible, warts and all. Therefore,
cultural communications and academic exchanges should be kept completely separate from policy influence, and some even argue that the VOA
should function like the Corporation for Public Broadcasting or the BBC
in England, covering even foreign policy positions of the government in the
same manner as would any other journalistic enterprise.[82] In any case, this
viewpoint considers foreign policy advocacy less important than the long-
term portrayal of American society, culture, and political and economic
systems, arguing that the latter kind of programs build mutual understanding that can transcend the policy issues of the moment and best
contribute to American interests over time.[83]

---

[81] This controversy is but one of the many ways that public diplomacy resembles
foreign aid as an instrument of statecraft, for analysts of foreign aid also divide
over whether aid should be firmly attached to the U.S. national interest and dedicated to political goals that serve it or wholly devoted to development overseas,
as noted below. Other similarities are that both programs take place in a field
crowded by exogenous and private sector actors and influences, both tend to be
very long-term in their effects, and the results of both are extremely difficult to
evaluate.

[82] As an example of this viewpoint, see Kim Andrew Elliott, "Too Many Voices of
America," *Foreign Policy* 77 (Winter 1989–90): 113–131, and Sanford J. Ungar,
"Pitch Imperfect," *Foreign Affairs* 84 (May/June 2005): 7–13. The BBC, of course,
also manages domestic broadcasts to Britain itself, whereas State is forbidden
by law to propagandize the American people.

[83] Helena K. Finn, "The Case for Cultural Diplomacy," *Foreign Affairs* 82 (November/
December 2003): 15–20.

The other view is that there is no point to any public diplomacy effort unless it serves official objectives, so even cultural communications programs should follow the priorities of strategists if they are to be funded by the taxpayer. Moreover, cultural communications may or may not build mutual understanding, and understanding may or may not lead to tolerance and greater receptivity on the part of foreign publics and governments of U.S. policies; like any kind of education, outcomes here are hard to predict. Proponents of this more skeptical view argue therefore that the role of cultural communications is primarily to provide the context within which "hard freight" policy messages can be most effectively communicated. Since both functions use essentially the same media, the separation of cultural communications from policy advocacy makes no more sense on operational than on philosophical grounds. Although policymakers should never bend the truth, people advocating a strong emphasis on current policy in U.S. public diplomacy would contend that not only VOA's editorials but also its selection and treatment of news items should be influenced by policy considerations, and even that Fulbright exchanges should at least be targeted on countries and subjects that support strategic objectives.[84]

Whether aimed at creating mutual understanding or promoting a specific U.S. foreign policy, both of these kinds of public diplomacy require the ability to communicate directly with foreign publics and assume that what the public thinks will eventually make a difference in the state's international conduct. In the radically different context of controlled information environments, by contrast, Western public diplomacy has taken on a third function: to open channels of communication to peoples whose governments actively try to prevent access to any independent sources of information. Here neither advocacy of one's own foreign policy nor communication of information about one's own country and its people seems most effective. Instead, U.S. government media like Radio Liberty and Radio Free Europe attempted to be surrogates for the free press that the Soviet Union and its satellites in Eastern Europe lacked, broadcasting the truth about *local* events; TV and Radio Marti and Radio Free Asia try to fulfill the same functions today in Cuba and in Asian countries like China and North Korea. Merely providing complete and unbiased news coverage can have a devastating impact on the credibility of governments that censor the news, and such efforts by international radio broadcasters are credited by dissidents in the former Soviet empire as being one of the major factors bringing about its disintegration.[85]

---

[84] It is interesting to note in this connection that even the BBC, cited as a model of unbiased news reporting, takes direction from the Foreign Office regarding languages and hours of broadcast. Elliott, "Too Many Voices of America," p. 125.

[85] Kevin J. McNamara, "Reaching Captive Minds with Radio," *Orbis* 36 (Winter 1992): 23–40.

Of course, such dramatic results are rare. Indeed, one of the reasons for the ongoing debate between policy advocacy and cultural communications is that all public diplomacy programs, and particularly cultural communications efforts, are intrinsically difficult to evaluate. It is relatively easy to obtain anecdotal information, such as that Mikhail Gorbachev was listening to the BBC and VOA at his Black Sea exile during the August 1991 coup attempt, or that Anwar Sadat was picked as a U.S.-sponsored international visitor to the United States when he was a young military officer and Egypt was firmly allied to the Soviet Union. Statistics can be gathered about how many copies of a magazine are distributed, how many column inches are placed in influential foreign newspapers, how many texts of policy speeches are delivered to columnists and editorialists, even how many listeners tune in to VOA broadcasts. It is much more difficult to determine what these people are thinking, whether their attitudes or views have been changed by public diplomacy activities, and then whether those changed views had any impact on governmental policies. Indeed, one of the obvious weaknesses of public diplomacy is the tenuous, indirect nature of the links between action and result, between impact and success.[86] Psychologists indicate that attitudes even among attentive and influential publics are generally resistant to change, so propaganda efforts have great difficulties unless they are focused on new or emerging policy issues or are simply used to reinforce (or move people to act on) established attitudes.[87] Even in retrospect, after the fall of a Berlin Wall or when a specific campaign succeeds in marshalling public support for a current policy initiative (as the United States did in Europe during the mid-1980s to support NATO's deployment of intermediate range nuclear missiles), it is difficult to know just what made the difference.[88]

Like all diplomacy, public diplomacy is an instrument that works best when used with other instruments, and it is particularly valuable as preparation for or an adjunct to government-to-government negotiations on a variety of subjects. When other tools are used in a cooperative way, public diplomacy can help maximize and attribute their effect, for example, by publicizing U.S. help in safeguarding a foreign country's cultural assets under the American ambassador's Fund for Cultural Preservation.[89] When other tools are used coercively, it can help minimize resistance, as when

---

[86] See Chapter 8 for discussion of the linkages between courses of action and success.

[87] For example, research indicates that it is six times more difficult and expensive to move someone who is undecided to soft support for a policy than to move a soft supporter to hard support. Peter G. Peterson, *et al, Finding America's Voice: A Strategy for Reinvigorating U.S. Public Diplomacy* (New York: Council on Foreign Relations, 2003), p. 69. See also the differences between public opinion and public judgment discussed in Chapter 3.

[88] David M. Abshire, *Preventing World War III* (New York: Harper and Row, 1988), pp. 191–192.

[89] Finn, "The Case for Cultural Diplomacy," p. 20.

Worldnet interviewed the leaders of the Caribbean nations during the 1983 invasion of Grenada to demonstrate that they had indeed requested U.S. intervention.[90] Of the broad categories of state interests, public diplomacy is perhaps best suited to value projection; indeed, it should probably be the primary instrument (along with technical and economic assistance) for spreading the gospel of democracy and market economic systems overseas. In this way it may also be useful in pursuing economic prosperity, an interest more directly advanced by using public diplomacy as an adjunct to advertising American-made products overseas. Finally, this instrument can make a contribution in many circumstances to security, both to refute slanderous disinformation about American policy or practices and as a tool for breaking down the credibility of authoritarian regimes and the isolation of their peoples.

Recent changes in the technological and political environment for communications pose new challenges and provide new opportunities for public diplomacy. First, there is the dramatically increased competition from the private media in a world where American music, American movies, and American networks (like CNN) proliferate. Although these phenomena add up to a very significant U.S. impact on global consciousness, they are not within the foreign affairs strategist's control, often portray a limited and unhelpful image of American society, and create a media density that dwarfs even the most substantial government effort. They make effective policy advocacy programs far more difficult, and they also put a premium on doing cultural communication via cooperative and facilitative efforts with the private sector. On the other hand, new technologies like direct satellite TV broadcasting and the Internet can be exploited for propaganda purposes – though the price for doing so may be very steep.

Second, although the opening up of formerly denied societies in the Soviet empire clearly reduces the overall need for some kinds of media and programs, it also has provided an exceptional opportunity to affect the course of developments in relatively-media poor societies where both the pace and significance of change are extraordinary. In these circumstances the ideal public diplomacy program mix shifts away from activities like international radio broadcasting toward vastly higher levels of people-to-people exchanges and technical assistance aimed at increasing the strength and competence of newly-freed local media.[91] At the same time, as the advocates of Radio Farda (to Iran) and Radio Marti (to Cuba) point out, there will still be a need to use public diplomacy to frustrate totalitarian regimes and crack open the doors of closed societies.

---

[90] K. J. Holsti, *International Politics: A Framework for Analysis*, 6th ed. (Englewood Cliffs, NY: Prentice-Hall, 1992), p. 170.

[91] Sanford J. Ungar, "Pressing for a Free Press," *Foreign Policy* 77 (Winter 1989–90): 132–153.

Finally, the post–Cold War reemergence of centuries-old animosities, together with the wave of anti-Americanism that swept the world following the 2003 U.S. invasion of Iraq, have emphasized the need for cultural communications in the post-9/11 era – along with the importance of American public diplomacy generally. Analysts from all sides of the political spectrum now recognize that the neglect of these programs after the Cold War ended was a serious mistake, and funding has begun to be restored, if slowly.[92] At the same time, the extreme improbability that the United States can win the policy argument in the Muslim world, along with recognition that terrorism is underpinned by deep-seated educational, religious, and societal attitudes, have put a premium on cultural communications between the Western world and the world of Islam.[93] American diplomat Helena Finn put the task in historical perspective:

> Throughout the postwar era, desperate and disenfranchised young people in developing countries sought solace in communism....American officials mounted a determined, and ultimately successful, ideological campaign in response....Today, the youth of the Muslim world, deeply confused about their identity and critical of their own corrupt and autocratic rulers, seek refuge in another extreme ideology that promises a better and more dignified life. The United States...must offer a more compelling alternative.[94]

Such an effort would inevitably use slower, in-depth media and would have to focus on the public as well as elites. It would also require improved cultural understanding in the United States, as well as broad and deep dialogue with the region, to counteract the impression that American power is unilateral and arrogant and to build networks of common humanity. Such efforts will not be easy or quick, as the failure of the initial post-9/11 round of commercialized, Madison Avenue public diplomacy programs demonstrated, and they are unlikely to lessen hostility to current American policies in the region.[95] But in an age of culturally- and religiously-driven terrorism, efforts to promote mutual understanding between radically

---

[92] Compare, for example, the reviews of analysts as disparate as these at Harvard's Kennedy School and the Heritage Foundation: Joseph S. Nye, Jr., "The Decline of America's Soft Power," *Foreign Affairs* 83 (May/June 2004): 16–20; Stephen Johnson, Helle C. Dale, and Patrick Cronin, *Strengthening Public Diplomacy Requires Organization, Coordination, and Strategy,* Backgrounder #1875 (Washington, DC: Heritage Foundation, August 5, 2005).

[93] Blackburn, "The Post–Cold War Public Diplomacy of the United States," pp. 83–84; Ramez Maluf, "How to Sell America," *Foreign Policy* 149 (July/August 2005): 74–79.

[94] Finn, "The Case for Cultural Diplomacy," p. 15.

[95] These included Radio Sawa, offering young people a mixture of popular American and Arab music with political messages mixed in, complemented by TV ads portraying the lives of Muslims in America and slick magazines about American culture. Howard Schneider, "A Little U.S. Pop-aganda for Arabs," *Washington Post* (July 26, 2002): A24.

different societies may be far more important to Americans' physical security and economic prosperity than any policy advocacy program, no matter how successful.

Economic Instruments: Trade and Finance

Whereas negotiations, international organizations and law, and public diplomacy rely on verbal symbols and the persuasive skills of those using them, economic statecraft is based on the manipulation of resources that have or can be given a market price.[96] Economic instruments can therefore have more "bite" than verbal ones and may offer the promise of greater effectiveness. Though economic statecraft is often defined as the use of economic instruments for political purposes, a more accurate description is the use of economic tools to support objectives that serve *any* category of the national interest, including that of economic welfare.[97]

Economic instruments naturally fall into the three categories of foreign aid, trade and financial policy, and sanctions. The first and last of these categories overlap the middle one, since aid involves *providing* goods, services, and finance across international boundaries while sanctions involve *disrupting* trade and financial relationships.[98] The middle category is still worth distinguishing, however, to denote ongoing policies that are usually adopted for domestic economic reasons but nevertheless have strategic implications and may on occasion be used to exploit them. In addition to these three categories, economic instruments can be distinguished according to whether they involve the exchange of goods and services or the transfer of money. Figure 6.4 groups economic policy tools horizontally on the real/financial axis and vertically according to whether they provide or withdraw economic benefits, or can do either – that is, according to the three categories of aid, trade and finance, and sanctions.[99]

As a group, economic tools have several distinctive advantages. One is their ability to effect a change in a target state's behavior through the mechanism of altered power relationships.[100] Strategists most often attempt to affect the behavior of other actors by influencing their *intentions*, but

---

[96] Adapted from Baldwin, *Economic Statecraft*, pp. 13–18.

[97] See Chapter 4. "Its fundamental characteristic is simply that economic policy be deliberately formulated so as to promote the foreign policy goals of the state – whatever those may be." Baldwin, *Economic Statecraft*, p. 77.

[98] Readers should note that positive and negative distinctions apply to the nature of the instrument itself, not to how it is used. Any instrument of statecraft can be used either co-optively or coercively. See Chapter 7.

[99] This table is based on Tables 2 and 3, "Examples of Economic Statecraft," in Baldwin, *Economic Statecraft*, pp. 41–42.

[100] Michael L. Brown lists five purposes for economic sanctions: "to enhance regional stability, to achieve leverage over the policies of other countries, to increase the capabilities of allies, to reduce the capabilities of adversaries, and to engage in signaling." "The Economic Dimensions of Strategy," *Parameters* 16 (Summer 1986): 36.

	Foreign Aid	**Trade and Financial Policy**	**Sanctions**
Exchanges of goods and services:	import/export subsidies	tariff policy (including MFN/PNTR)	embargo
	technical assistance	quota policy	boycott
	food/commodity grants	licensing policy	blacklist
		direct purchase	preclusive buying
			dumping
Exchanges of money:	grants	capital flow policy	asset freeze
	loans	taxation policy	expropriation
	investment guarantees	foreign investment policy	inducing inflation
		interest rate policy	debt expansion

Figure 6.4: Examples of economic statecraft.

because of the close connection of economic resources and national power discussed in Chapter 5, economic statecraft is particularly well-suited to affecting other states' *capabilities*.[101] Thus, economic measures can be used to weaken potential adversaries, to strengthen allies' capabilities, or even to bolster one's own economic position.[102] Such changes in relative power may not produce immediate changes in behavior, but they will alter the choices of targeted decision makers over time by reallocating the costs and benefits of their actions.

Another advantage of economic tools is that they occupy middle ground between political and military instruments in terms of impact, costs, and risks, particularly when used coercively. Because economic measures usually cost the state using them, either as a charge on the state's budget or because they hurt its citizens as well as their target, they send a powerful signal that its decision makers consider the issue a serious one, but they do so without the user having to play the ultimate card of military force. As Columbia University's David Baldwin points out:

> Economic techniques usually cost more than propaganda or diplomacy and thus tend to have more inherent credibility. Military techniques, of course, usually entail [still] higher costs and therefore [have] even more credibility; but their costs may be too high. Economic techniques are likely to represent an appealing combination of costs that are high enough to be effective yet low enough to be bearable.[103]

[101] These, of course, are the two fundamental dimensions of threat (see Chapter 4).
[102] James P. O'Leary, "Economic Warfare and Strategic Economics," *Comparative Strategy* 5 (No. 2, 1985): 203.
[103] Baldwin, *Economic Statecraft*, pp. 107–108.

For the United States, the world's largest economy, economic tools also have the advantage of being in plentiful supply. Trade, finance, and sanctions, moreover, can be used without direct cost to the federal budget, a characteristic that may recommend them to strategists in times of high federal deficits.

But economic statecraft also has its peculiar disadvantages and weaknesses. The economic nature and setting of these instruments demand extraordinarily subtle, complex, and difficult calculations on the part of the strategist. Because of the fungibility of money, even their economic effects are difficult to estimate. For example, it may seem obvious that withholding military items would weaken a country's military power, or that granting food aid would result in fewer people going hungry, but in fact quite opposite results may occur. If the target country is a high-cost food producer but a low-cost producer of military hardware, withholding food supplies may actually stunt its military development more than withholding weaponry.[104] On the other hand, for a country with the opposite cost structure, giving military hardware might result in fewer people going hungry than would offering food aid.[105]

But even if the strategist's economic *reasoning* is right, the economic *impacts* of his or her statecraft may still be problematical. Economic tools must have their effects through a vast network of transnational economic linkages that dwarf the financial power of any government. Indeed, the effects of economic tools may well be weakening as world product grows, because the clout that governments control can increasingly be overwhelmed by market forces.[106] And the fact that economic impacts tend to be slow and cumulative in nature allows plenty of time for exogenous factors to influence the outcome, some of which even the most knowledgeable planner could not be expected to anticipate.

Economic instruments are not only difficult to make effective; they are also politically hard for a democracy to use. Globalization has the paradoxical effect of making international economic affairs into domestic political issues, as perturbations in the international economy increasingly have

---

[104] Thus, strategic goods are not simply military items but "anything that is needed to pursue a given strategy and that is relatively inefficient to produce at home." Baldwin, *Economic Statecraft*, p. 215. To decide which goods are strategic one has to know the relative cost position of all economic outputs in the target country.

[105] Baldwin, *Economic Statecraft*, p. 304. Such counterintuitive results are due to the ways in which the exchange of goods alters countries' patterns of production at home. As noted in Chapter 5, trade benefits countries by allowing them to reshape production in ways that make better use of their resources; economic statecraft in the trade arena seeks to alter those benefits, either reducing them (for an adversary) or enhancing them (for a partner). Thus, sanctions should be designed to deprive a country of the goods it finds most inefficient to produce at home, whatever their character, while economic aid should offer those goods in ways or on terms better than those available in the market.

[106] Baldwin, *Economic Statecraft*, pp. 127–137.

economic effects at home. At the same time, Western governments and publics (and increasingly, governments elsewhere) have long accepted the idea that economic activity should be privately managed and the government's regulatory role kept as limited as possible. The result is not only that many of the tools of economic statecraft are beyond government control, but also that trying to bend market forces to the purposes of statecraft may require degrees of regulation that are politically unacceptable or practically unachievable.[107]

Economic tools can be used either for short-term reaction to particular crises or for long-term efforts to alter the international structure of power in one's favor.[108] Thus, foreign aid to the Third World can be used either as a quid pro quo for the allegiance of U.S. friends and allies or to foster economic development; economic sanctions can either be imposed as countermeasures to other countries' hostile acts (like Jimmy Carter's grain embargo against the Soviet Union following its invasion of Afghanistan) or be employed as long-term measures of containment (like the export controls imposed on Iraq after the Gulf War). The ample amounts of time necessary for most economic measures to make themselves felt, and the fact that they act directly on other states' capabilities but only indirectly on their intentions, usually makes them better suited to the longer-range kind of use. Certainly the direct use of economic tools to change the behavior of target nations (as in the effort to coerce Saddam Hussein's withdrawal from Kuwait before the 1991 Gulf war) is unlikely to deliver enough economic pain quickly enough to meet the needs of short-term crisis management.[109]

Foreign aid and sanctions are the most widely studied economic measures, simply because they are primarily used for foreign policy purposes. But before discussing them in detail, a few comments should be made about broader trade and financial policies, which have impacts on other countries and can therefore be used by strategists for their international effects. Tariff policies, including the granting or withholding of permanent normal trade relationships (PNTR), can be used to discriminate for or against a target state; one example was the periodic Congressional debate over granting most favored nation status to China, for years a major weapon in U.S. China policy. Quotas and licenses can be used to promote

---

[107] This point is particularly germane to the United States, usually seen as an example of a "weak state" economic model, at least in comparison with competitors like Germany or Japan. Its fractionated bureaucracy, dominant interest groups, and lassez-faire philosophy create an "inherent weakness of government control over the nation's economic life for purposes of statecraft." See G. John Ikenberry, David A. Lake, and Michael Mastanduno, "Introduction: Approaches to Explaining American Foreign Economic Policy," *International Organization* 42 (Winter 1988): 11.

[108] O'Leary, "Economic Warfare and Strategic Economics," p. 181. Economic tools thus play a shaping role in the international economy similar to that of alliances in world politics.

[109] O'Leary, "Economic Warfare and Strategic Economics," p. 201.

or prevent imports or exports, and direct purchases can support another state's economy or (in the case of preclusive buying) deny it needed commodities, as well as acquire important assets.[110] On the financial side, governments can influence international capital flows and foreign investment (both at home and of their nationals abroad), discriminate in taxation policies, and even manipulate domestic interest rates for their international economic effects (for example, to suck in foreign capital or export inflation). However, because these instruments are primarily for management of the domestic economy, they cannot be used as boldly by foreign affairs strategists as sanctions and foreign aid; domestic effects must usually take priority.

Since the Great Depression of the 1930s, the United States has led the world in reduction of trade barriers. Free trade policies have generally been adopted to serve the American interest in prosperity, but it is also widely understood that a prosperous world economy, furthered by ever-freer trade, is an essential component of American security – protectionism, after all, made a significant contribution to the Depression, and it in turn to the political turmoil leading to World War II. In fact, during the early decades of the Cold War American strategists granted trade concessions to security partners (such as the nascent European Common Market) in order to strengthen them against the Soviet threat, accepting less satisfaction of prosperity interests for more security. In recent decades the ability to export has also been seen as at least as critical as traditional foreign aid to economic development in Third World countries. Finally, trade concessions can be offered as *quid pro quos* to support any foreign policy purpose.

Strategists seeking to negotiate freer trade and to open foreign markets to American exports must choose between multilateral, regional, sectoral, and bilateral strategies.[111] Multilateral negotiations, like the eight rounds of talks held under the GATT and the current WTO-based Doha round, have the breadth that allows multiple bargains and hence the biggest rewards, along with enough visibility to get top politicians' attention and head off protectionist pressures. But they also are complex and unwieldy, tend to suffer dispiriting crises and breakdowns, require a great deal of political energy, and may last longer than an administration's time in office. Regional pacts, like the North and Central American Free Trade Areas

---

[110] Those who question the inclusion of direct purchase among techniques of economic statecraft would do well to consider the important contributions made by Jefferson's offer of money for Louisiana (instead of using, for example, military force to acquire it) or Seward's purchase of Alaska. A recent example of the utility of direct purchase has been the American buying of nuclear material from the formerly Soviet republics as an anti-proliferation measure.

[111] The following sketch of these strategies' advantages and disadvantages is largely from Gary C. Hufbauer and Jeffrey J. Schott, "Strategies for Multilateral Trade Liberalization," Chapter 7 in Geza Feketekuty, ed., with Bruce Stokes, *Trade Strategies for a New Era* (New York: Council on Foreign Relations, 1998), pp. 125–141.

(NAFTA and CAFTA), may be able to liberalize trade more than global ones and can therefore set benchmarks for them, but they also create trade-distorting preferences and conflicting rules. Sectoral agreements, like Clinton's landmark treaties on information technology and on financial services and telecommunications, are also effective in some circumstances, and bilateral pacts can be an important way of moving forward when other modalities fail.[112] But strategists will find none of these approaches effective unless they attend carefully to the domestic sources of protectionism, particularly domestic income inequality and job losses resulting from overseas competition, that otherwise can make trade liberalization politically untenable.

Along with free trade, the United States has also promoted what might be called free finance, the opening of all the world's economies both to foreign direct investment in plant and equipment and to portfolio (stock and bond) investments from overseas.[113] Spurred on by the electronic linking of investment and lending across borders, the opening of national financial markets allows the world's capital to move to places where it can be used most efficiently. Capital market liberalization helps rich country prosperity through increased opportunities for the sale of their financial services and for returns on investment, and it also supports development in Third World countries, which need private finance if they are to grow out of poverty.[114] Nevertheless, the 1994 Mexican peso crisis, and especially the emerging markets debacle that began in Thailand in 1997 and quickly spread to Malaysia, Indonesia, and South Korea (and then to Russia in 1998, Brazil in 1999, and Argentina in 2000), demonstrated that if liquid capital can flow *into* developing country markets easily it can also flow *out* in a panic, with devastating results for innocent local bystanders left unemployed and destitute, as well as severe consequences for governmental stability.[115] These episodes suggested that Third World capital markets should be liberalized only to the degree that other economic structures and policies are put in place, including strong regulation and limits on foreign currency borrowing, to limit the risk that free financial markets otherwise pose.[116] In this area then, if not in trade policy, American foreign

[112] Benjamin J. Cohen, "Containing Backlash: Foreign Economic Policy in an Age of Globalization," Chapter 14 in Robert J. Lieber, ed., *Eagle Rules* (Upper Saddle River, NJ: Prentice Hall, 2002), pp. 309–317.

[113] Cohen, "Containing Backlash: Foreign Economic Policy in an Age of Globalization," pp. 317–321.

[114] Robert Wade, "The Coming Fight over Capital Flows," *Foreign Policy* 113 (Winter 1998–99): 41–54.

[115] Paul Krugman, "The Return of Depression Economics," *Foreign Affairs* 78 (January/February 1999): 56–74.

[116] Alan S. Blinder, "Eight Steps to a New Financial Order," *Foreign Affairs* 78 (September/October 1999): 50–63. Many also believe that international financial institutions, especially the IMF, must improve their preventative and crisis response capabilities. But see also Kenneth Rogoff, "The IMF Strikes Back," *Foreign Policy* 134 (January/February 2003): 38–49.

affairs strategists must decide whether the long-term economic benefits of liberalization outweigh its short-term dangers for financial and political stability, security, and development.

Economic Instruments: Foreign Aid

Perhaps the simplest and most direct definition of foreign aid is the one written by political scientist Hans Morgenthau: "the transfer of money, goods and services from one nation to another."[117] For our purposes, however, Morgenthau's parsimony requires some elaboration. First, foreign aid as used here includes only publicly-funded economic resources. Substantial amounts of private money, goods, and services flow to other nations alongside official foreign aid; but the aid a strategist can use is that provided by *governments*, either directly or through intermediaries, to foreign governments or to private entities working in another country.[118] Second, the transfer of aid must be on concessional terms: that is, the money, goods, and services must be made available to the recipients at a cost below what they would have to pay to acquire them through normal commercial channels. Otherwise, their provision can hardly be considered "assistance" in any meaningful sense. Finally, foreign aid as used here is meant to include any transferred resource with a market value regardless of its nature or the purpose for which it is given or used. In particular, as we will see, aid as a tool of state power need not necessarily be used for purposes of development.

Aid can be classified in at least five ways: according to the type or kind of aid being given, the terms under which it is offered, the route by which it travels between countries, its destination country or region, or its purpose.[119] As Morgenthau noted, *types* of aid include *foreign exchange* (or the forgiving of debt owed from earlier aid), *goods* delivered in kind (like military equipment, food, or other commodities), or *services* that may accomplish needed tasks or impart important know-how (often referred to as technical

---

[117] Hans Morgenthau, "A Political Theory of Foreign Aid," *American Political Science Review* 56 (1962): 301. Kal Holsti defines it as "the transfer of money, goods, technology or technical advice from a donor to a recipient." *International Politics: A Framework for Analysis* (Englewood Cliffs, NJ: Prentice-Hall, Inc., 1992), p. 192. Paul Mosley's definition: "money transferred on concessional terms by the governments of rich countries to the governments of poor countries." Paul Mosley, *Foreign Aid: Its Defense and Reform* (Lexington, KY: University of Kentucky Press, 1987), p. 21.

[118] Aid from private sources in the U.S. runs about 43 percent of U.S. official development assistance (ODA). "Ranking the Rich 2004," *Foreign Policy* 142 (May/June 2004): 51, 53, also Robin Wright, "Aid to Poorest Nation's Trails Global Goal," *Washington Post* (January 15, 2005): A18.

[119] Most categorizations of aid tend to mix up these criteria with disconcerting results. U.S. budget categories are development assistance (purpose), multilateral assistance (route), and food, ESF, and military aid (type). Kal Holsti lists technical assistance (type), grants and commodity programs (terms and type), development loans (purpose and terms), emergency humanitarian assistance (purpose). *International Politics*, pp. 194ff.

	HUMANITARIAN ASSISTANCE	20%
	Migration, Refugee, Disaster Relief	7%
	Food Aid (PL-480)	7%
	HIV/AIDS initiative	6%
	DEVELOPMENT ASSISTANCE	34%
Economic	USAID, Peace Corps	4%
Assistance	DA, Millennium Challenge	23%
	Multilateral (contributions to IOs and IFIs)	7%
	POLTICALLY-ALLOCATED ECONOMIC AID	24%
	Eastern Europe/FSU programs	4%
	Narcotics, Law Enforcement	8%
Security	Economic Support Fund (ESF)	12%
Assistance	MILITARY ASSISTANCE	25%
	Foreign Military Financing (FMF)	21%
	International Military Training	
	and Education (IMET) and other SA	4%

Figure 6.5: FY2005 U.S. foreign aid.

assistance). As to *terms*, aid may take the form of either *grants* or *loans*, with the precise allocation varying markedly among various donors and across different time periods. Aid travels along *bilateral* or *multilateral routes*; that is, it may be provided directly to its recipients by the donor government or it may be given to an IFI like the World Bank and distributed by it along with funds provided by other governments. As to *destination* countries, a donor government may choose to concentrate its aid in a very few countries or to disburse its largesse widely, and it may pick countries on virtually any grounds it chooses. Finally, among the many *purposes* for which aid may be given, it is useful to distinguish between economic and political, short-term and long-term, and program and project aid (the former being aid to support the country's economic, social, or political *programs* as opposed to building a specific infrastructure *project* like a dam or a road).

Figure 6.5 provides a snapshot of the U.S. aid program in FY 2005.[120] This categorization scheme makes the purposes of aid clearer by differentiating the *uses* to which aid is put in a country from the *reasons* for giving it. Thus, resources provided by the programs listed under "Politically-Allocated Economic Aid" are used for development and humanitarian purposes, but the decisions as to who gets the money reflect not developmental

[120] Source: Author computations based on categorization scheme used in Lael Brainard, "Compassionate Conservatism Confronts Global Poverty," *Washington Quarterly* 26 (Spring 2003): 154, using FY 2005 actual appropriations (budget authority) as found in Table 27-1, Budget Authority and Outlays by Function, Category, and Program, *Budget of the United States Government for Fiscal Year 2007* (Washington, DC: GPO, 2006). Rounding errors result in a total over 100 percent.

needs but American political and security interests. If aid is grouped by the reasons for giving it, then one can distinguish aid for *development and humanitarian* purposes from *security* assistance by placing politically-allocated economic aid and military assistance in the latter category and development and humanitarian assistance in the former, each with about half the resources. Alternatively, if aid is grouped by the uses to which it is put, *economic* can be distinguished from *military* aid in a three-fourths/one-fourth split by placing politically-allocated economic aid in the economic category.

As this portrait implies, the American foreign aid program has always been an amalgam of high-minded, even altruistic goals having to do with other countries' and peoples' well-being, on the one hand, and self-interested goals related to the political, security, and economic objectives of the United States, on the other. These contrasting perspectives are reflected both in the government and the academic community as a struggle between altruistic idealists and self-interested realists, between those who believe in development for its own sake, and those who want to serve the national interest either by promoting development or by using aid to accomplish other objectives.

Officials in the U.S. Agency for International Development (USAID), for example, generally see their role as one of promoting development in Third World countries. Most believe that the development of poor countries supports American national interests, and some also understand and even appreciate the leverage that aid may provide in the service of political or security goals. Still, aid officials usually disparage short-term policy objectives that interfere with sound economic decisions on assistance flows and uses, accepting them only as a necessary but regrettable evil.[121] In the academic community, the close correspondence of aid with eleemosynary activity has produced far more extreme variants of this view. For as one scholar wrote, "Of all our foreign policy instruments, aid is the only one that places the most vulnerable individuals on the planet at its core."[122] Some idealist academics even argue that American aid should be strictly devoted to development and poverty alleviation overseas without any reference whatever to the national interest of the United States. Robert Curry, for example, notes with evident dismay that

> some officials and community members regard aid as a useful foreign policy tool because it provides the U.S. government with leverage over recipient-country policies in which the United States has a perceived interest. Others, among them this observer, advocate a more generous and forthcoming U.S. response to poorer countries' needs *that is not tied to U.S. interests.*[123]

---

[121] For example, see Thomas Carothers, "Democracy, State, and AID: A Tale of Two Cultures," *Foreign Service Journal* (February 2001).

[122] Ethan B. Kapstein, "Reviving Aid: Or Does Charity Begin at Home?" *World Policy Journal* 16 (Fall 1999): 35.

[123] Robert L. Curry, Jr., "A Review of Contemporary U.S. Foreign Aid Policies," *Journal of Economic Issues* 24 (September 1990): 822. Italics added.

Those adopting the aid-as-charity viewpoint often advocate dispensing all forms of aid through multilateral channels, believing (wrongly) that when so distributed it no longer gives its donors influence over recipient countries.[124]

On the other side of the issue are officials in the State Department and White House backed by realist scholars. From their perspective, the United States government has no business taking money from private citizens through the taxation power (or borrowing it at their expense) unless for purposes that serve the national interest. Alexander Hamilton expressed the philosophical underpinnings of this view when he wrote that "an individual may . . . meritoriously indulge the emotions of generosity and benevolence, not only without an eye to, but even at the expense of, his own interest. But a government can rarely, if at all, be justifiable in pursuing a similar course."[125] Political scientist George Liska applied Hamilton's principle directly to aid in a classic 1960 book on the subject:

> The sole test of foreign aid is the national interest of the United States. Foreign aid is not something to be done, as a Government enterprise, for its own sake or for the sake of others. The United States Government is not a charitable institution, nor is it an appropriate outlet for the charitable spirit of the American people.[126]

In line with this approach, State Department and foreign policy officials in the White House tend to see aid as a way of buying influence with foreign governments, its cutoff as a method of punishing behavior that harms American interests. And American ambassadors overseas like to engage in what has been called "checkbook diplomacy," using aid to reward foreign officials who support U.S. positions on important issues. Thus, Hans Morgenthau wrote that most aid is really given for political purposes like keeping failed but friendly governments afloat ("subsistence" aid), strengthening allies or engaging in a division of labor for better security ("military" aid), displaying one's power for psychological effect by building useless but visible white elephants ("prestige" aid), or simply paying the necessary price for political services rendered ("bribery").[127] In spite of its economic character, he argued, "foreign aid is no different from diplomatic or military policy or propaganda. They are all weapons in the political armory of the nation."[128]

---

[124] "The choice between multilateral vs. bilateral aid hinges largely on the relative priority of economic vs. political motives in donor aid strategy." Gordon Donald, *U.S. Foreign Aid and the National Interest* (Washington, DC: National Planning Association, 1983), p. 15.

[125] Cited in Steven W. Hook, *National Interest and Foreign Aid* (Boulder, CO: Lynne Rienner, 1995), pp. 119.

[126] George Liska, *The New Statecraft: Foreign Aid in American Foreign Policy* (Chicago, IL: University of Chicago Press, 1960), p. 127.

[127] Morgenthau, "A Political Theory of Foreign Aid," p. 302.

[128] Morgenthau, "A Political Theory of Foreign Aid," p. 309.

Strategically, Morgenthau's position is the correct one; considered as an instrument of statecraft, foreign aid must serve the national interest. Two caveats to this position must, however, be noted. First, the national interest can well justify the use of aid in ways other than the support of short-term attempts to influence other governments. Certainly it is broad enough to embrace the use of aid to promote genuine economic, social, and political development. After all, growing economies overseas are far more able than stagnant ones to contribute to American prosperity as purchasers of American goods and suppliers of materials for American industry, and prosperous countries are less likely to be narcotics traffickers, weapons proliferators, sponsors of terrorism, or senders of destitute migrants to American shores. The national interest will even accommodate development and humanitarian assistance as a variant of value projection – as a way of making the world more like us *for its own sake*, simply because we want to do good in the world or are more comfortable in such a world.

One must be wary, though, of asking too much from development on behalf of the national interest, or from aid on behalf of development. As Morgenthau put it more than forty years ago:

> ... the popular mind has established correlations between the infusion of capital and technology into a primitive society and its economic development, between economic development and social stability, between social stability and democratic institutions, between democratic institutions and a peaceful foreign policy. However attractive and reassuring these correlations may sound to American ears, they are borne out neither by the experience we have had with our policies of foreign aid nor by general historic[al] experience.[129]

Because development depends on a wide variety of economic, cultural, social and political factors well beyond the influence of outside actors, its success is extraordinarily difficult to engineer and predict. Gordon Donald, Stanton Burnett and other experienced practitioners have argued that aid for development should be seen not as a capital input but as a catalyst, "a way of inducing innovations," and as such an inherently risky enterprise.[130] Virtually all academic experts and practitioners now agree that only broad-based economic growth can alleviate poverty, and that aid can work to spur growth only if the country in question has an effective

---

[129] Morgenthau, "A Political Theory of Foreign Aid," pp. 304–5.

[130] Donald, *U.S. Foreign Aid and the National Interest*, pp. 9–10. "The real energy and commitment to improve economic performance must come from host-country leadership, local constituencies, and private investment. The role of aid, at best, can be to induce the receiving government to put its economic house in order and to foster an environment in which private enterprise can flourish." Stanton H. Burnett, *Investing in Security: Economic Aid for Noneconomic Purposes*, Significant Issues Series, Vol. 14, No. 8 (Washington, DC: Center for Strategic and International Studies, 1992), p. 8.

government accountable to its people and has adopted a free enterprise system open to international trade – highlighting the dilemma that the countries most able to benefit from aid are least in need of it, while those that need it most are least able to use it.[131] Morgenthau concluded that aid for development had a "very much smaller range of potentially successful operation" than generally thought, and that, even if successful in economic terms, its political results were unpredictable, uncontrollable, and as likely as not to be "counterproductive in terms of the political goals of the giving nation."[132]

But if development for national interest (as opposed to charitable) purposes is inherently difficult and problematic, using aid for political influence is fraught with its own grave difficulties, and these comprise the second caveat against too warm an embrace of foreign assistance as a tool to serve national interests.[133] In the first place, few governments are willing to embrace bribery or developmentally-useless prestige aid publicly, so economically sound uses are generally needed to justify whatever assistance is ultimately made available. In fact, USAID is directed by Congress to program all foreign aid in a way that makes economic sense, regardless of whether the aid was originally given for political/military reasons, and irrespective of the short-term goals its granting or withholding is supposed to secure.[134] Foreign aid used for political influence is thus usually a long-term proposition nestled uneasily within a short-term context. The steadiness and predictability needed for economic success run directly counter to the flexibility required to attach aid to political behavior. Indeed, the stop-and-go funding that short-term uses engender naturally tends to frustrate long-term developmental objectives, while the long-term

---

[131] Nancy Birdsall, Dani Rodrik, and Arvind Subramanian, "How to Help Poor Countries," *Foreign Affairs* 84 (July/August 2005): 143. "History has shown that nations that have embraced democracy combined with capitalism and participation in the global trading system have experienced the highest economic growth and generated the highest quality of life for their citizens." Rep. James Kolbe (R-Ariz.), "Lessons and New Directions for Foreign Assistance," *Washington Quarterly* 26 (Spring 2003): 194. See also Carol Graham and Michael O'Hanlon, "Making Foreign Aid Work," *Foreign Affairs* 76 (July/August 1997): 96–104; and Arvind Panagariya, "Think Again: International Trade," *Foreign Policy* 139 (November/December 2003): 20–22.

[132] Morgenthau, "A Political Theory of Foreign Aid," pp. 307–308.

[133] "Foreign aid is inherently an iffy business. What else can be expected when one sovereign nation tries to influence the behavior of another by giving it money and sending people over to say how the money should be spent? ... one should remain realistic about such a complex and risky endeavor." Ernest Graves, "Restructuring Foreign Assistance," *The Washington Quarterly*, Vol. 16, No. 3 (Summer 1993): 196.

[134] Morgenthau argued that since the real purposes for which aid is most often given are considered illegitimate, most aid is disguised as for economic and developmental purposes. The results often are to fool ourselves and invite either disappointment or disaster. Morgenthau, "A Political Theory of Foreign Aid;" see also Burnett, *Investing in Security*, p. 9.

investment of resources for development tends to preclude turning the aid spigot on and off for political purposes.

Even if one accepts that aid should be used as a tool of influence, then, certain guidelines need to be born in mind. First, there is little doubt that the further a goal is from the primary economic objective of the aid (like building a dam), the less likely it will be achieved. General economic goals like development are thus inherently less realizable than specific ones, and political goals less viable than economic ones. Second, experience indicates not only that non-economic goals jeopardize the importance of economic goals, but multiple objectives for the same aid program sharply reduce the chances for achieving all but the most immediate primary goal and may damage that one as well by diluting the effects of whatever influence aid offers. Third, influence on the receiving country with regard to any political goal is directly tied to the donor's willingness and ability to regulate the flow of aid in response to the recipient's behavior (what one study calls "spigot credibility.")[135] Unfortunately, that willingness tends to be inversely proportional to the importance of the relationship to Washington, leading to the fourth conclusion: that the effectiveness of U.S. influence is likely to decline as the interests at stake escalate. Paradoxically, only when the relationship is of little interest to Washington is the United States likely to have real aid leverage to accomplish its goals.[136] With regard to the success of influence attempts backed by aid, then, one could argue that

> the best odds obtain when the objective is economic; closely related to (or exactly the same as) the specific work to be carried out by the aid project; short-term; genuinely supported by the political leadership of the recip-ient country; not burdened with secondary objectives; and disbursed, delayed, or suspended according to a credible and tight connection to the donor's insistence on clear performance standards.... [137]

In addition to these inherent difficulties, there are some reasons to think that foreign aid is likely to be less effective as a political instrument in the years ahead. First, the United States is in a less commanding posi-tion as a donor, as Japan and Europe increase their giving and private aid providers proliferate.[138] More donors means that developing countries have more places to turn for aid; although they have lost the ability to play the superpowers off against each other that was so profitable during the Cold War, recipients can now diversify their aid, making a refusal or cutoff from one source less damaging.[139] Another reason why aid may be of declining

---

[135] This and the other lessons in this paragraph and the one above are adapted from Stanton H. Burnett, *Investing in Security*, pp. 2–16, 69ff.

[136] Baldwin, *Economic Statecraft*, p. 310.

[137] Burnett, *Investing in Security*, p. 16. Italics in original. See also pp. 69 ff.

[138] Robin Wright, "Aid to Poorest Nations Trails Global Goal," *Washington Post* (Jan-uary 15, 2005): A18.

[139] Holsti, *International Politics*, p. 194.

utility as a political tool is that it simply matters less to developing countries. Many of them are wealthier now, and aid has become a smaller part of their overall budgets.[140] At the same time, trade has eclipsed aid in its importance to Third World economic growth; indeed, the effect of ODA is swamped by trade, foreign investment, and debt repayment terms in its impact on LDCs.

Moreover, even among economic tools, aid is a particularly difficult instrument for American statesmen to use due to its peculiar status in the U.S. domestic environment. Aside from the use of military power in combat and possibly economic sanctions, foreign aid may be the most visible and controversial of foreign policy instruments; it is certainly the least popular. Whatever their personal generosity toward the unfortunate, Americans see foreign aid as a kind of social welfare program that contradicts cherished principles of self-help.[141] Though only about 1 percent of the federal budget goes for overseas aid, Americans think the proportion is 25 percent, and a plurality of 48 percent want it cut (only 14 percent want more, with 35 percent favoring current levels).[142] They tend to see foreign aid as a giveaway program and to find foreign needs less compelling than those at home in times of budgetary stringency; in one survey, "helping to improve the standards of living of less developed countries" was dead last among twenty foreign policy goals in the number of Americans who picked it as very important.[143] Moreover, the steady stream of famine, disaster, and conflict stories emanating from Third World locations seems to prove that aid does not work, or at least that the needs are so great as to be overwhelming and efforts to deal with them futile.[144] Reacting to such compassion fatigue, Congress has traditionally used its power of the purse to hobble aid with a variety of earmarks and restrictions – 274 were counted in 2002 – that reduces its value to the strategist even more.[145]

---

[140] As early as 1989, ODA was 2.2 percent of GNP in low income countries. Anne Krueger, *Economic Policies at Cross-Purposes: The United States and Developing Countries* (Washington, DC: Brookings Institution, 1992), p. 49.

[141] Hook, *National Interest and Foreign Aid*, p. 118.

[142] Marshall M. Bouton and Benjamin I. Page, *Worldviews 2002: American Public Opinion and Foreign Policy* (Chicago, IL: Chicago Council on Foreign Relations, 2002), p. 43–44.

[143] Bouton and Page, *Worldviews 2002*, p. 19.

[144] Curt Tarnoff and Larry Q. Nowels, *U.S. Foreign Assistance: The Rationale, the Record, and the Challenges in the Post–Cold War Era* (Washington, DC: National Planning Association, 1994), p. 2.

[145] Brainard, "Compassionate Conservatism Confronts Global Poverty," p. 166. Of course, Congress appropriates funds for all the instruments of statecraft. But once it buys a fighter aircraft, Congress' appropriation powers cannot control how or on what missions it is flown; once an ambassador is confirmed overseas, Congress cannot dictate what he says. Foreign aid is different, since it is a resource with a market value, and Congress' power over its employment is accordingly much greater.

Has this tool of policy then lost its *raison d'etre?* Aid for charity may be a-strategic, aid for development is hard to make effective, and aid for political influence is always problematical, but with all its limitations aid may still be the best means of achieving many foreign policy objectives. Military and economic aid will still be effective in strengthening an ally, gaining access to bases or ports overseas, or securing overflight rights, as the post-9/11 effort to establish American bases in Central Asia demonstrates. Aid can also be used simply to buy acquiescence on important security interests, for example, to fund dismantlement of the former Soviet nuclear arsenal and to reengage Soviet weapons scientists in productive work at home.[146] And there will probably continue to be cases, few in number but perhaps great in importance, in which threatened aid cutoffs can produce important political concessions that are totally unrelated to the aid in question.[147]

Foreign aid can also be used, and public opinion consistently demands that it be used, for commercial goals that support American prosperity.[148] Perhaps most directly, aid can be tied to purchases in the donor's market, thus creating jobs and an improved balance of payments. One estimate has it that a billion dollars in tied aid produces 20,000 jobs (although the cost to the recipient in inefficient use of the resources can run as high as 15–20 percent).[149] In some cases (*e.g.*, military aircraft) the survival of whole industries is dependant upon economies of scale that are only possible through aid-subsidized sales. Project aid can also be used to solidify trade relationships and bolster investment opportunities overseas, or act as a foot in the door for U.S. products by installing equipment that needs American parts and service or by setting up technical services on U.S. standards.[150] Nor should aid's role in crises be forgotten. The $25 billion dollar financial rescue package that the Clinton administration put together for Mexico in early 1995 worked brilliantly to prevent economic and political chaos in that country that could have directly threatened American prosperity, and once in place the leverage it provided was used by American diplomats to dissuade Mexico from leading forces opposed to the indefinite extension of the Non-Proliferation Treaty at its renewal conference later that year.[151]

[146] Jessica Mathews, "National Security Blunder," *Washington Post* (May 5, 1995): A25.

[147] For example, one of Ronald Reagan's critical messages to Ferdinand Marcos at the time he was being overthrown was that U.S. aid would be terminated if loyalist forces used U.S.-supplied weapons to keep him in power. George P. Shultz, *Turmoil and Triumph* (New York: Charles Scribner's Sons, 1993), p. 636.

[148] See Tarnoff and Nowels, *U.S. Foreign Assistance: The Rationale, the Record, and the Challenges in the Post–Cold War Era*, pp. 14–19.

[149] Krueger, *Economic Policies at Cross-Purposes*, pp. 56–58.

[150] Donald, *U.S. Foreign Aid and the National Interest*, p. 4.

[151] R. Jeffrey Smith, "Permanent Nuclear Treaty Extension May Be Approved by Consensus Vote," *Washington Post* (May 8, 1995): A7. Paid back within three years, it also generated a $580 million profit for the U.S. Treasury. Robert E. Rubin and Jacob Weisberg, *In an Uncertain World* (New York: Random House, 2003), p. 34.

American aid may also be critical to the management of global problems that increasingly seem to jeopardize American security and prosperity and which cannot be dealt with except in cooperation with other nations. For example, it is obviously in the interest of the developing as well as the industrialized countries for the former to grow with as little additional pollution as possible, but clean development will be more expensive and is unlikely to be LDCs' chosen path unless much of its additional costs are offset. Similarly, actions to save species from extinction are in the interests of developed and developing alike, but the rainforests are located in the South, whereas the resources needed to save them may be available only in the North. Other actions, such as those essential to counter narcotics trafficking, tend to be far more in the donor's than the recipient's interest, and aid given through multilateral contexts can often get essential work done that otherwise would be politically impossible.[152] When it comes to such challenges of globalization, in fact, aid can be used not only to persuade and fund government action to deal with transborder problems but also to pay for surveillance of transnational threats, support research to find solutions to them, and deal with sudden crises – as well as help poor countries take advantage of globalization's opportunities.[153]

Finally, as befits its long-range character, aid is particularly well-suited for actions intended to reshape the international environment in ways that will make the world more conducive to the accomplishment of American interests in the years to come. In the security arena, aid can be used to shift regional balances of power in one's favor, for example by strengthening the nation-states between Germany and Russia so that a power vacuum in Central Europe does not rekindle violent competition between them. In the economic area, as noted, it can help create growing, market-oriented, and equitable economies that will be purchasers of American exports. As to value projection, aid can take advantage of opportunities to spread democracy abroad by funding elections, training police, judges, and legislators, or supporting the development of civil society.[154] It is also obviously the primary tool available to react to humanitarian disasters. This last use, in fact, is likely to increase substantially in coming years, both because it is the one area of foreign aid that the American people wholeheartedly support, and because the number of natural disasters has been increasing since the turn of the millennium.[155]

---

[152] For example, the United States spearheaded the creation of UNFDAC (the UN Fund for Drug Abuse Control) in the early 1970s largely to make counternarcotics action possible in Burma, a major drug-producing nation that was impervious to American bilateral influence.

[153] Carol Lancaster, "Redesigning Foreign Aid," *Foreign Affairs* 79 (September/October 2000): 76–78.

[154] Lancaster, "Redesigning Foreign Aid," pp. 81–82.

[155] Sixty-one percent of Americans think combating world hunger should be a very important foreign policy goal, and 84 percent favor food and medical assistance to people in needy countries. Bouton and Page, *Worldviews 2002*, pp. 44–45.

Nor should one entirely write off the use of aid for purely altruistic reasons. For despite considerable controversy over whether aid really can spur development and alleviate poverty, Western governments and publics have recently expressed a revived interest in helping the poor abroad, both through broad development plans and targeted efforts to help the worst off.[156] Rock stars like Bono have been hosting fund-raising concerts, foundations like that of Bill and Melinda Gates are pouring huge amounts into conquering poor-country diseases, and academics like Harvard's Jeffrey Sachs are publishing books with titles like *The End of Poverty*.[157] Since the 2002 UN Summit on Global Poverty in Monterrey, Mexico, EU nations have pledged to increase their ODA to .7 percent of GDP by 2015; the G-8 have agreed to double aid to Africa by 2010 and to eliminate all debt owed by the world's twenty-seven poorest countries; and George W. Bush has pledged $10 billion over three years through a new Millennium Challenge Corporation to fund development in countries with governments best able to use it.[158] In addition to such utopian plans for ending world poverty, the Bush administration has launched targeted efforts to improve the lives of the neediest in countries that are not developing, pledging $15 billion over five years for the President's Emergency Plan for AIDS Relief and $1.2 billion over five years to fight malaria in Africa.[159] Of course, whether these pledges will materialize in dollars despite record budget deficits, and if so whether the funds will really accomplish their objectives, remains to be seen.

Economic Instruments: Sanctions

Economic sanctions are measures that use economic power to disrupt normal economic intercourse between or economic conditions within states for foreign policy purposes. They include a wide variety of actions, and although all sanctions have common advantages and disadvantages, their characteristic strengths and weaknesses can differ quite dramatically according to the kind of sanction being used. The most common sanctions

---

[156] Studies note, for example, that $558 billion in aid over 43 years failed to lift most of Africa out of economic stagnation, and that $1 trillion in aid to 80 countries over 45 years demonstrated no clear relationship between aid and growth. These dismal results are noted in William Easterly, "The Utopian Nightmare," *Foreign Policy* 150 (September/October 2005): 61, and Kolbe, "Lessons and New Directions for Foreign Assistance," pp. 192–193.

[157] Justin Gillis, "With Gates's Help, Immunization Initiative Surges," *Washington Post* (A1, A18; Jeffrey Sach's, *The End of Poverty: Economic Possibilities for Our Time* (New York: Penguin Press, 2005).

[158] Paul Blustein, "After G-8 Pledges, Doubts on 'Doing It'," *Washington Post* (July 10, 2005): A14; Blustein, "Debt Cut Is Set for Poorest Nations," *Washington Post* (June 12, 2005): A1, A23; Blustein, "U.S. Aid Plan Comes Up Short," *Washington Post* (June 22, 2003): A22.

[159] David Brown, "Progress on AIDS Is Focus of Assembly," *Washington Post* (May 31, 2006): A10; Peter Baker, "Bush Pledges $1.2 Billion For Africa to Fight Malaria," *Washington Post* (July 1, 2005): A1, A2.

are trade and financial, with *trade* being further divided into sanctions that interrupt exports (embargos) or imports (boycotts), and *financial* split into disruption of lending or investment. There are also *monetary* sanctions that aim to destabilize currency values (inducing inflation or deflation) in order to upset economic planning and cause psychological distress. And there are *asset* sanctions that freeze or transfer ownership of property, securities, or bank accounts held by the target state in other countries.[160] In addition to economic sanctions, some analysts also distinguish embargoes of arms and military equipment as "strategic" sanctions, and diplomatic and personal isolation of states and their leaders (for example, by closing embassies and preventing overseas travel) as "social" sanctions.[161]

With the exception of military force and possibly foreign aid, economic sanctions are the most studied and controversial of American foreign policy tools. Much of the debate revolves around an apparent paradox: that sanctions seem generally not to work, yet American statesmen continue to use them nonetheless. Certainly it is true that the United States has a fondness for economic coercion going back well before the Boston Tea Party and continuing through the various embargoes and boycotts before the War of 1812, King Cotton diplomacy during the Civil War, the embargo of strategic goods to Japan before World War II, and controls on exports to the Soviet empire, China, Cuba, and other communist states during the Cold War.[162] Sanctions were also a favorite tool during the 1990s, with five new sanctions laws passed by Congress just in the four years between 1993 and 1996.[163] But while there is little doubt that sanctions are a favorite tool of American statesmen, there is little agreement as to whether and under what circumstances sanctions work.

Most academic studies and many practitioners are strongly negative about sanctions' efficacy. One mathematical survey of over a hundred twentieth-century cases, with the revealing title "Fools Suffer Gladly," concluded that sanctions provided their users no bargaining advantage that was measurable in terms of favorable outcomes.[164] Another, "Why

---

[160] The above breakdown comes from Jonathan Kirshner, "The Microfoundations of Economic Sanctions," *Security Studies* 6 (Spring 1997): 36–40. Kirshner also notes an "aid" sanction, which I treat as simply a negative use of foreign assistance (see Chapter 7).

[161] Neta C. Crawford and Audie Klotz, *How Sanctions Work: Lessons from South Africa* (New York: St. Martin's Press, 1999) breaks anti-apartheid sanctions into these three categories.

[162] George A. Lopez and David Cartwright, "The Sanctions Era: An Alternative to Military Intervention," *Fletcher Forum* (Fall 1995): 65–85.

[163] These figures are from Jesse Helms, "What Sanctions Epidemic?" *Foreign Affairs* 78 (January/February 1999): 4. See also Richard N. Haass, "Sanctioning Madness," *Foreign Affairs* 76 (November/December 1997): 74–85, which cites a National Association of Manufacturing study claiming new American sanctions on 35 countries from 1993 to 1996.

[164] T. Clifton Morgan and Valerie L. Schwebach, "Fools Suffer Gladly: The Use of Economic Sanctions in International Crises," *International Studies Quarterly* 41 (March 1997): 42.

Economic Sanctions Do Not Work," found that there was little to no correlation between the degree of punishment sanctions inflicted and their success in obtaining concessions to a coercer's demands.[165] The most widely
used review of economic sanctions cases since World War I found that only
a third were "partially successful" and that their success rate had declined
sharply over time; it concluded that "although it is not true that sanctions
'never work,' they are of limited utility in achieving foreign policy goals."[166]

However, there is a problem with such studies of large numbers of cases:
the cases have to be abstracted to be aggregated, and they are so different one from another that everything depends on the judgments applied
when this "coding" is done. When looked at individually, recent cases seem
to have had mixed results. Sanctions on Panama and Haiti, two small
and economically vulnerable countries, failed in the late 1980s and early
1990s to change their policies or regimes until military force was used or at
least threatened; but sanctions do appear to have played an important role
in the decision of Libya to abandon its efforts to acquire nuclear weapons,
and they prevented Saddam Hussein from reconstituting his missile and
WMD programs for over a decade.[167] Therefore, although it depends might-
ily on how one defines success, the answer to the question of whether sanctions work seems to be that sometimes they do, and sometimes they do not.

The more important issue for foreign affairs strategists, then, has to
do with the purposes for which, and the conditions under which, various kinds of sanctions are likely to be (or not to be) effective. Immediately another paradox emerges: although (like most economic instruments)
sanctions are particularly suitable for long-term projects, they are often
used for short-term defensive or reactive purposes.[168] The Carter sanctions against Iran for the hostage taking and against the Soviet Union for
invading Afghanistan, Reagan's pipeline sanctions responding to the crack-
down in Poland, Bush's Iraqi asset freeze after the invasion of Kuwait, and
Clinton's sanctions on Haiti after the coup against President Bertrand Aristide were all crisis reactions to other nations' unacceptable actions. Such

[165] Robert A. Pape, "Why Economic Sanctions Do Not Work," *International Security* 22
(Fall 1997): 90–136. Write Morgan and Schwebach, "extreme costs are required
to produce relatively small changes in outcomes." "Fools Suffer Gladly," p. 45.

[166] Gary Clyde Hufbauer, Jeffrey J. Schott, and Kimberly Ann Elliott, *Economic Sanctions Reconsidered*, 2nd rev. ed., 2 vols. (Washington, DC: Institute for International Economics, 1990), pp. 1, 92–93, 105–106.

[167] David E. Weekman, "Sanctions: The Invisible Hand of Statecraft," *Strategic
Review* 26 (Winter 1998): 39–45 (on Haiti). Robin Wright and Glenn Kessler,
"Libya Vows to Give Up Banned Weapons: Two Decades of Sanctions, Isolation
Wore Down Gaddafi," *Washington* Post (December 20, 2003): A1, A18. George A.
Lopez and David Cortright, "Containing Iraq: Sanctions Worked," *Foreign Affairs*
83 (July/August 2004): 90–103.

[168] "Economic sanctions...have important reactive or second-strike characteristics
because such usage hinges on provocation, which better enables the United
States to overcome pre-existing political obstacles." Martin Shubik and Paul
Bracken, "Strategic Purpose and the International Economy," *Orbis* 27 (Fall
1983): 583.

short-term uses do have some benefits. They may satisfy domestic demands for a tough response at lower cost than using military force, and they can send a more powerful signal than diplomacy that another state's behavior is unwelcome. Indeed, their political impact may have rather little to do with the sanctions' economic effects on their intended target, thus neatly bypassing all the difficulties sanctions may have in causing real economic pain.

However, the long time needed for sanctions to inflict such damage ill suits them for use in a crisis if the goal is more than symbolic.[169] If they are intended to have any actual economic effect on another country, sanctions are better used by statesmen who have the patience to pursue changes in behavior or capabilities over the long-term.[170] And here sanctions that are designed to punish are more likely to succeed than those that aim to coerce, compel, or deter, for these latter changes in behavior leave the initiative in the hands of the target. If it decides not to yield, the sanctioning state is left with an unpalatable choice between giving up, continuing with a policy that is not working, or escalating to military force. Punishing, on the other hand, is a more modest goal that leaves the initiative with the sanctioner, who decides how much is enough. Thus, in many cases punishment becomes the fallback goal after more ambitious objectives have failed.[171]

Since sanctions need to have an economic impact if they are to change another state's behavior or capabilities, the most important condition required for success is that the target state be economically vulnerable. Figure 6.6 captures some of the more obvious characteristics of vulnerability – like high dependence on external trade and finance, or being at a low point in the business cycle – as well as some more surprising ones – like being a highly-developed, democratic, and industrialized market economy rather than a centralized, rural, and under-developed one.[172] If trade sanctions are contemplated, it helps for the sanctioner to have a near-monopoly on a commodity that the government or a large number of people believe they cannot do without, or one that is essential to an industry generating a large percentage of the people's or the government's income. It also helps if the sanctioning state is economically much more powerful than and closely linked to its target, so that it can both apply sufficient leverage and manage the costs of doing so. One survey indicates that successful sanctioners

---

[169] Richard N. Haass concluded that "Sanctions alone are unlikely to achieve desired results if the aims are large or time is short." Haass, ed., *Economic Sanctions and American Diplomacy* (New York: Council on Foreign Relations, 1998), p. 197. Original italics deleted.

[170] But Hufbauer, Schott, and Elliott also point out that excessively long sanctions efforts are usually failed ones, with failures averaging 8 years as compared with about 3 years for successes. *Economic Sanctions Reconsidered*, Executive Summary, p. 1.

[171] Haass, *Economic Sanctions and American Diplomacy*, p. 199.

[172] Table from Chantal de Jonge Oudraat, "Making Econonic Sanctions Work," *Survival* 42 (Autumn 2000): 116.

	More Vulnerable	Less Vulnerable

More Vulnerable   Less Vulnerable

Economic Characteristics

More Vulnerable	Less Vulnerable
Market economy	Centralized economy
Highly developed economy	Underdeveloped economy
Weak economy	Healthy economy
High dependence on exports and imports	Low dependence on exports and imports
High dependence on international capital markets	Low dependence on international capital markets

Social and Political Characteristics

More Vulnerable	Less Vulnerable
Industrial society	Rural society
Ethnically mixed	Ethnically homogeneous
Internally fragmented	Internally cohesive
Democratic regime	Authoritarian regime
Strong political opposition	Weak political opposition

Figure 6.6: Vulnerability to sanctions.

need to sustain at least a 2 percent impact on the target's GNP for three years, and that to do so they require a ten to one advantage in GNP along with at least a quarter of the target's trade.[173]

These considerations help explain why sanctions often work better against allies, which tend to have close economic connections, than against adversaries, which generally lack such ties and whose leaders might also fear establishing a precedent of yielding to a state with which they expect future conflicts. The ironic result is that "economic sanctions tend to be least effective against the few countries that the United States is most eager to coerce."[174] Indeed, foreign affairs strategists must be careful lest they overestimate a target's vulnerability; as one observer put it, "modern states are not fragile."[175] Sanctions can even wind up strengthening an adversary government's domestic position through a perverse manifestation of the rally-round-the-flag effect, as economic sectors hurt by sanctions give the government monopoly powers to defend against them, and the

---

[173] Lopez and Cartwright, "The Sanctions Era," 71–72. Hufbauer, Schott, and Elliott found that successful cases cost the targets 2.4% of GNP and took 2.9 years on average. They also found that the average sender's economy was 187 times larger than the average target's. *Economic Sanctions Reconsidered,* p. 1.

[174] Daniel W. Drezner, "Serious About Sanctions," *National Interest* (Fall 1998): 74. Note the parallel with aid, which tends to be least effective in the countries that most need it.

[175] Pape, "Why Economic Sanctions Do Not Work," p. 106.

government then uses those powers to redirect the costs of the sanctions onto its opponents.[176]

Assuming the target is sufficiently vulnerable, the next requirements for successful sanctions have to do with how they are applied. Since most goods and finance are available internationally and states' assets are often widely distributed, exploiting a target's vulnerability usually demands that sanctions be multilateral rather than unilateral in nature.[177] In the words of former U.S. Trade Representative Carla Hills:

> Unilateral sanctions never work....Multilateral sanctions may take a long time, as they did in [apartheid] South Africa, but you have a better chance.[178]

Some analysts argue that sanctions are particularly well-suited to coalitions, being the most effective measures on which states with vastly different interests can agree.[179] But such differences in interests also make sanctioning coalitions difficult to hold together for the long timeframes economic measures need to be successful, as costs to members rise and the lure of normal economic intercourse beckons.[180] Therefore, multilateral sanctions often need the additional glue of an international organization to sustain them. Such institutions can provide coordinating, monitoring, and enforcement machinery to increase the efficiency of the economic interruption, assistance to states paying a disproportionate share of the sanctions' cost, and collective or cooperative security against any retaliatory response, all while increasing the psychological and diplomatic pressure on the target.[181] Sanctioning through an international organization can also help legitimize the action and thereby maintain public support for it, an important consideration as sanctions-related hardships increase in the

---

[176] This is a principal conclusion of David M. Rowe, *Manipulating the Market: Understanding Economic Sanctions, Institutional Change, and the Political Unity of White Rhodesia* (Ann Arbor, MI: University of Michigan Press, 2001), cited in Jonathan Kirshner, "Economic Sanctions: The State of the Art," *Security Studies* 11 (Summer 2002): 160–179. See also Jean-Marc F. Blanchard and Norrin M. Ripsman, "Asking the Right Question: *When* Do Economic Sanctions Work Best?" *Security Studies* 9 (Autumn-Winter 1999/2000): 227–229.

[177] Haass concludes that unilateral sanctions are rarely effective, so multilateral support should be a prerequisite for using the tool. *Economic Sanctions and American Diplomacy*, pp. 200–201, 206–207.

[178] Quoted in Thomas W. Lippman, "U.S. Rethinking Economic Sanctions," *Washington Post* (January 26, 1998): A6. Brackets in original.

[179] Lopez and Cartwright, "The Sanctions Era," 67–68, 75.

[180] "'Sanctions fatigue' tends to settle in over time, and as it does, international compliance tends to diminish." Haass, *Economic Sanctions and American Diplomacy*, p. 205. Original italics deleted.

[181] Daniel W. Drezner, "Bargaining, Enforcement, and Multilateral Sanctions: When Is Cooperation Counterproductive?" *International Organization* 54 (Winter 2000): 73–102. Drezner finds that ad hoc coalitions are actually *less* effective than sustained unilateral sanctions, since early backsliding by members encourages targets to await the coalition's dissolution.

states applying them and the suffering of innocents in the target state is played back to domestic audiences, weakening their resolve.[182]

Whether unilateral or multilateral, the kind of sanctions applied can have a dramatic impact on their prospects for success. Trade sanctions are perhaps the most susceptible to circumvention via smuggling, for example, with financial sanctions somewhat less liable to workarounds. (Asset sanctions are least vulnerable to private sector avoidance since they are imposed through direct government seizure, but of course their feasibility depends on the assets' location.) Trade sanctions are also the most public of these measures, whereas monetary sanctions can be quietly imposed by central banks. Trade sanctions are slow to have their effects but may cumulate over time, whereas monetary sanctions have their effects quickly but degrade over time, with financial and asset sanctions in between with regard to speed and sustainability.[183] Financial sanctions may be more effective than trade sanctions because they can be more quickly imposed and targeted against the elites who are responsible for objectionable policies.[184] Indeed, targeted sanctions of all types seem to be the wave of the future, since they promise to have the most effect on those who have the power to change policy while avoiding widespread suffering on the part of people who, in an authoritarian regime, may have no influence whatever on their leaders. But since such leaders draw their economic sustenance from the societies they rule – and can sometimes even use sanctions to further enrich themselves – it is often doubtful whether such narrowly targeted measures can be strong enough to work.[185]

Once the kind of sanction is chosen, the strategist must decide how forcefully it ought to be applied. One knowledgeable specialist argues that partial, gradual sanctions (slow and soft) should be used with weak and vulnerable societies and/or when objectives are less ambitious, but comprehensive, immediate sanctions (quick and hard) will be needed with strong, less vulnerable states and/or far-reaching objectives.[186] Either approach has its disadvantages. Full immediate application may make

---

[182] Drezner, "Serious About Sanctions," p. 70. Such sanctions fatigue was so widespread that the George W. Bush administration's first effort against Iraq was to narrow and tighten the sanctions regime to keep it from falling apart.

[183] The preceding comments in this paragraph are from Kirshner, "The Microfoundations of Economic Sanctions," pp. 38–41.

[184] Lopez and Cartwright, "The Sanctions Era," p. 82. These authors find (pp. 71–72) that financial restrictions have had a 41% success rate, but trade restrictions only a 25% rate.

[185] For example, sanctions can make smuggling and other black market operations profitable by cutting off normal imports, offering predatory elites new opportunities to plunder. Although Haass recommends sanctions that focus on the responsible parties and the area of their misbehavior, he also notes that it is extremely difficult in most instances for such sanctions to pack a real punch. *Economic Sanctions and American Diplomacy*, pp. 202, 207–208.

[186] Oudraat, "Making Economic Sanctions Work," p. 117–118.

negotiated solution of the problem more difficult, or in rare instances call forth a retaliatory response. But gradual or partial use will give the target time to adjust and room to maneuver, as well as forfeit any psychological shock value. Most analysts therefore argue that, no matter what the circumstances, sanctions should be quick and decisive, as swift and purposeful as possible.[187] "If sanctions are to be effective in achieving their goal (i.e., halting objectionable policies by a particular nation), they must be harsh, comprehensive, immediate, and multilateral. The 'logic of the instrument' in its most effective state leans heavily toward a hard and fast policy."[188]

The need for decisive use puts a premium on coordinating sanctions with other instruments of state power. Certainly economic sanctions work better alongside other strategic and social sanctions that reinforce their effects, like arms embargos, withdrawal of diplomats, and terminating non-economic exchanges, in a package sometimes called compound sanctions.[189] Use of sanctions may poison the negotiating atmosphere, as noted above, but it may also be just what is needed to push a recalcitrant party toward a settlement of differences.

Most critical is the sanctions' relationship to military force. Although the military is often called upon to help enforce them, economic sanctions are considered by many as a substitute for force.[190] Even if they suspect that military force will be required to redress the problem, policy makers often turn to sanctions in situations where they hope to avoid the costs and risks of war, as did George H. W. Bush when Iraq invaded Kuwait in 1990. At the same time, sanctions often become a prelude to war, not because of retaliation by the target, but because the state using them gets frustrated with their ineffectiveness and decides to escalate means rather than abandon ends, as Bush did in 1990 and Clinton did in Haiti and Kosovo.[191] Some observers even believe that the use of sanctions may itself "increase the likelihood that the sanctioning state will ultimately resort to force. Policymakers may escalate in order to rescue their own prestige or their state's international reputation, and rhetoric used to justify sanctions can demonize the target regime, making publics willing to resort to more

---

[187] "Quick and decisive" is Hufbauer, Schott, and Elliott, *Economic Sanctions Reconsidered*, p. 1; "swift and purposeful" is Haass, *Economic Sanctions and American Diplomacy*, pp. 208–209.

[188] Lopez and Cartwright, "The Sanctions Era," p. 80.

[189] The term "compound sanctions" is from Blanchard and Ripsman, "Asking the Right Question," p. 225.

[190] Robert Pape argues that failing to control studies of sanctions' effectiveness for the use of force "is the most serious possible methodological error in a study of economic sanctions, because the principal policy usefulness claimed for economic sanctions is as an alternative to force." "Why Economic Sanctions Do Not Work," p. 106. See also on this point Daniel W. Drezner, "The Hidden Hand of Economic Coercion," *International Organization* 57, #3 (2003): 643–659.

[191] Drezner, "Serious About Sanctions," p. 72.

extreme measures if sanctions fail. Sanctions may even be the 'American way of war'...."[192]

But the relationship between economic and military coercion is far more subtle than this either-or thinking would suggest. First, economic sanctions are valuable to statesmen precisely because they lie "somewhere in between war and appeasement in terms of a continuum of 'toughness'" and draw on characteristics of each:

> Thus, they... are often intended to combine elements of appeasement and hostility, to demonstrate simultaneously both commitment and restraint. For this reason they are easily misunderstood. They are stronger than diplomatic protests but weaker than military attack. They are likely to appeal to reasonable but firm policy makers but not to cowards or jingoists. They are neither heroic nor saintly measures. They are often designed to deter and reassure simultaneously. Techniques that enable policy makers to demonstrate firmness while reassuring others of their sense of proportion and restraint can be highly useful....[193]

Sanctions may be a somewhat more risky instrument than political or informational ones, but they are less likely to provoke a military response than is the use of military force. Therefore, in situations where "applying pressure and avoiding the evocation of a violent response are both important goals, economic tools are likely to be especially attractive."[194] But sanctions are not just a useful alternative to force; like all nonmilitary coercion, they work best as part of an overall strategy that includes at least the threat of force in the background.[195] One reason is simply that using multiple tools is more effective: "Economic and military pressure can act together synergistically – just as naval and infantry forces usually work with air power – so that goals can be achieved at acceptable political, military, and economic cost."[196] Another has to do with credibility:

> ... in situations that are sufficiently serious and where the foreign policy objective is important, the possibility must be clearly communicated to the target that force will be used if necessary – to enforce the sanctions, to strategically buttress their effects, or as a last resort if sanctions fail. Sanctions imposed as an alternative to force because the political will to use force is lacking are not likely to be credible and therefore are not likely to be successful.[197]

---

[192] Robert A. Pape, "Why Economic Sanctions *Still* Do Not Work," *International Security* 23 (Summer 1998): 76–77.

[193] Baldwin, *Economic Statecraft*, pp. 104–105.

[194] Baldwin, *Economic Statecraft*, p. 110.

[195] ". . . economic sanctions . . . can be effective if they are part of comprehensive coercive strategies that include the use of force . . . ." Oudraat, "Making Economic Sanctions Work," p. 105.

[196] Kimberly Ann Elliott, "The Sanctions Glass: Half Full or Completely Empty?" *International Security* 23 (Summer 1998): 54.

[197] Elliott, "The Sanctions Glass: Half Full or Completely Empty?" p. 58. ". . . economic sanctions can be effective if all coercive options – including military

In sum, then, sanctions are most likely to work when:

- The target is economically vulnerable and much smaller than the sanctioner;
- The sanctioner and target have close trade and political relationships;
- Multilateral support is forthcoming, especially within an established international organization;
- Substantial amounts of time are available;
- Sanctions are applied fully and rapidly to maximize their economic impact, with the threat of force in the background; and
- Sanctioners avoid high costs to themselves.[198]

This last point is worth special emphasis, because the costs of sanctions, while substantial, are often hidden. They are born not by the sanctioning state's foreign affairs budget but by its economy, and consist not only of lost sales but also of lost economic opportunities and relationships. A study by the Institute for International Economics estimated that in 1995 U.S. sanctions cost American companies between $15 billion and $19 billion and affected 200,000 workers.[199] Sanctions can also impose huge costs on the populations of target countries, costs that may approach or exceed those of war but be far less obvious to the states using them. For example, some 2,300 civilians are estimated to have been killed in Iraq during the 1991 war, but UN studies concluded that 500,000 infants died from sanctions (and the Iraqi government's response to them) from 1991 to 1998.[200] Sanctions, in other words, are serious measures that need evaluation, both before and during their use, as careful as that which should generally attend the employment of military power.[201]

Military Instruments: Persuasive Use of Force

No one doubts that the United States is overwhelmingly the world's pre-eminent military power. Although it spends less than 4 percent of its GDP on military forces, its economy is so large that this amount is equal to that

force–remain open." Oudraat, "Making Economic Sanctions Work," p. 112. Thus, evaluating whether sanctions work only in isolation from other tools is fundamentally a-strategic. Like all instruments, sanctions should be judged successful if they *contributed* to objectives' achievement, rather than only if they *caused* them independently of the effect of other instruments.

[198] Most of these summary conclusions are adapted from Hufbauer, Schott, and Elliott, *Economic Sanctions Reconsidered*, Executive Summary, p. 1.

[199] Unpublished paper by Gary Clyde Hufbauer, Kimberly Ann Elliott, Tess Cyrus, and Elizabeth Winston, "U.S. Economic Sanctions: Their Impact on Trade, Jobs, and Wages," cited in Haass, *Economic Sanctions and American Diplomacy*, p. 203.

[200] Phillip S. Meilinger, "A Matter of Precision," *Foreign Policy* 123 (March/April 2001): 78–79.

[201] Haass, *Economic Sanctions and American Diplomacy*, is particularly effective in making this point, especially at pp. 205–206.

spent by the fifteen to twenty nations closest to it in military power, or more than the spending of all of the world's other significant military powers combined.[202] The capabilities this money buys are so formidable that the U.S. military alone can be fairly said to comprise not one but several instruments of statecraft. At one end of the spectrum of violence is the nuclear triad of submarine- and land-based intercontinental missiles and bombers, designed during the Cold War to deter Soviet attack and still capable of obliterating all life on the planet; at the other are rapidly-increasing numbers of special operations forces trained to conduct rescue attempts, coups d'etats, and counter-insurgency warfare right down to the level of hand-to-hand combat. The United States commands the seas with 37 Arleigh Burke class destroyers, 54 nuclear attack submarines, 12 aircraft carriers and a dozen VSTOL/helicopter carriers; it commands the air with hundreds of fighters and bombers, some of them invisible to radar, and with cruise missiles and unmanned reconnaissance drones; it dominates space with half of all the satellites circling the globe, including the GPS/NAVSTAR system and a hundred military satellites; it fights on land with 650,000 highly-trained, superbly-equipped Army and Marine Corps volunteers; and it is able to project power globally through forward-deployed forces and a network of bases inherited from the Cold War that has been expanded into the Persian Gulf and Central Asia, along with 10 brigades worth of equipment and munitions pre-positioned overseas, 20 roll-on roll-off transport ships, and a fleet of C-5 and C-17 cargo aircraft.[203] Of course, this thumbnail sketch hardly does justice to forces whose full capabilities would require a chapter or perhaps a book adequately to describe. As political scientists Stephen Brooks and William Wohlforth sum it up:

> The United States has overwhelming nuclear superiority, the world's dominant air force, the only truly blue-water navy, and a unique capability to project power around the globe. And its military advantage is even more apparent in quality than in quantity. The United States leads the world in exploiting the military applications of advanced communications and information technology and it has demonstrated an unrivaled ability to coordinate and process information about the battlefield and destroy targets from afar with extraordinary precision.... [On research and development it] spends three times more than the next six powers combined....

[202] General Peter J. Schoomaker, Chief of Staff of the U.S. Army, said that the administration's $440B defense budget request for FY2007 plus the ongoing costs of war in Afghanistan and Iraq (usually funded through supplemental appropriations) is 3.9% of the $13T economy. "General Defends Defense Spending," *Washington Post* (April 27, 2006): A7.

[203] This is roughly the description provided in Barry R. Posen, "Command of the Commons: The Military Foundation of U.S. Hegemony," *International Security* 28 (Summer 2003): 10–19, augmented by figures from *The Military Balance, 2003–2004* (London, UK: International Institute for Strategic Studies, 2003): 18–28.

No state in the modern history of international politics has come close to the military predominance these numbers suggest.[204]

The actual power that such military forces provide is impressive and in many ways unique. Certainly armed force is the most potent form of coercion; if decision makers are willing to use it, it can trump all other tools of statecraft. It is the only instrument that can take the decision on a foreign policy matter out of an opponent's hands entirely and into its user's, for it is the only one able to work not through influence but through brute force, by changing physical reality. Because military power trumps all other instruments, it is also the only tool that can deal decisively with military threats. And having so much and such a wide variety of it relative to any potential challenger gives the United States escalation control, the known ability to be able, if it is willing, to use enough and the right kind of force to prevail in the vast majority of conflicts. At least in the United States, the military also enjoys strong domestic support and the funding that goes with it; voting for military appropriations seems to be patriotic in a way that voting for foreign aid or for more and better diplomats is not.

But force in general, and American military power in particular, also has its weaknesses and limitations. Along with its superior power comes high cost and risk, and for this instrument both must be measured in lives as well as in dollars.[205] Nor does escalation control confer cost control; just because the United States possesses the military forces to prevail in most instances does not mean that its leaders or people will find the costs necessary for victory worth the stakes involved. High, possibly uncontrollable costs in turn mean that public support for the *use* of force is far more fickle than for its procurement and maintenance.[206]

Though it can trump the other tools of statecraft, military power is also a blunt instrument; it cannot create but only destroy. It may therefore be usable for a much smaller range of objectives than political, economic, or information instruments. Nuclear weapons, in particular, are good only for deterrence against other nuclear weapons. They are useless for the quintessentially military task of conquering territory, and they are so destructive that threats to use them are unconvincing except in response to their use by others.[207] Though all but unbeatable in full-scale traditional

[204] Stephen G. Brooks and William C. Wohlforth, "American Primacy in Perspective," *Foreign Affairs* 81 (July/August 2002): 21–22.

[205] "Military statecraft tends to be the most costly means of pursuing foreign policy goals." David A. Baldwin, "Success and Failure in Foreign Policy," *Annual Review of Political Science* 3 (#3 2000): 167–182.

[206] Indeed, the Vietnam syndrome that George H. W. Bush said the U.S. had "kicked...once and for all" on March 1, 1991, may be superceded by an Iraq syndrome following his son's war in Iraq. See E. J. Dionne Jr., "Kicking the Vietnam Syndrome," *Washington Post* (March 4, 1991): A1, A21; John Mueller, "The Iraq Syndrome," *Foreign Affairs* 84 (November/December 2005): 44–54.

[207] On this point see George F. Kennan, *Memoirs, 1925–1950* (Boston, MA: Little, Brown & Co., 1967), pp. 310, 472–474. The widespread deployment of tactical

warfare, America's conventional forces also have their limitations. Hi-tech warriors get progressively less invincible as they get closer to enemy territory, where effective weaponry (like automatic rifles and rocket-propelled grenades) is cheap and plentiful, and where local adversaries can take advantage of defensive positions, employ superior knowledge of and adaptation to climate and terrain, use their surplus of military-aged men, and have a bigger stake in the outcome.[208] Certainly the combination of high costs, public intolerance of casualties, and vulnerability to asymmetrical threats means that even the degree of military superiority the United States possesses is no guarantee of victory.

This brief discussion of strengths and weaknesses might lead one to think that military forces are useful only for combat, and many Americans do think of diplomacy and military power as alternative instruments, with diplomacy appropriate to peacetime and the military used exclusively for war. As Secretary of State George Shultz once wrote, however, "power and diplomacy are not alternatives. They must go together, or we will accomplish very little in this world."[209] Moreover, although the efficacy of the military's nonviolent roles depends to a large extent on its perceived effectiveness in combat, war remains the exception rather than the rule between states. Hence, the persuasive use of military force in peacetime is far more common and may well be more important than its war-fighting use. At least four non-war roles for the military are worth distinguishing.

The first includes a variety of tasks falling under the rubrics of humanitarian intervention and disaster relief, peace enforcement, peacekeeping, and nation building. Humanitarian intervention can be defined as "unsolicited interference by one state in the affairs of another" for the purpose of dealing with human suffering that its government is unable or unwilling to stop, in the best case, or is actually aiding, abetting, or perpetrating, in the worst.[210] Sometimes it takes the form of peace enforcement, where military forces are used to intervene in a violent situation within a foreign country in order to stop armed groups from causing havoc, or even to stop a civil war – an action that may well involve warfighting, albeit for altruistic reasons. Peacekeeping, in contrast, is the use of military forces with local parties' permission in a nonviolent environment. Such "soldiers without enemies" can keep antagonists apart or monitor contested

---

nuclear weapons in the 1950s and 1960s, the neutron bomb fiasco in the 1970s, and contemporary pressures to build bunker-buster earth-penetrating nuclear weapons do not convincingly change this conclusion. See William Arkin, "Not Just a Last Resort? A Global Strike Plan, With a Nuclear Option," *Washington Post* (May 15, 2005): B1, B5.

[208] Posen, "Command of the Commons," pp. 23–24.

[209] Secretary [George P.] Shultz, "Power and Diplomacy in the 1980s," *Current Policy No. 561* (Washington, DC: Department of State, April 3, 1984): 2.

[210] Quoted portion from Doris A. Graber, "Intervention and Nonintervention," *Encyclopedia of American Foreign Policy*, 2nd ed., Vol. 2 (New York: Scribner's, 2001), pp. 318–319.

	Economic Sanctions	Military Force
1945–1988	**2**	**3**
1989–2000	**15** (10)	**12** (10)

Figure 6.7: UN security council authorizations.

territory so that the parties will not feel driven by their need for self-protection to take actions that would generate conflict.[211] Nation-building uses military forces beyond peacekeeping to help a country rebuild after a war or in order to forestall one; here the military is really an instrument of foreign assistance, but one with a critical ability to protect itself and others in dangerous environments.

All of these tasks involve the active use of military forces, not primarily to fight, but to use their unique capabilities to resolve or prevent fighting by others or to deal with humanitarian emergencies. Where the action verges on warfare and is taken without a government's permission, it runs counter to the well-established legal principle of non-intervention in sovereign states' internal affairs and raises difficult questions of authorization. But the nationalist, ethnic, and civil conflicts of the post–Cold War era have generated an increasing need for this use of military power, and with it a growing sense that "states should not be allowed to hide behind the shield of sovereignty when gross violations of human rights occur on their territory...."[212] Indeed, eleven of the twelve cases of military intervention authorized by the UN Security Council during the 1990s were for humanitarian purposes (see Figure 6.7).[213]

A second noncombat use of military force is for presence and reassurance. This role is unlike those just discussed in being completely passive, at least in theory; its purpose is fulfilled simply through the existence of American armed force in other regions of the world. Left to themselves, states in Europe, Asia, or the Middle East might have to worry lest other countries in their regions become powerful enough to endanger their interests, and they could be expected to engage in competitive arms races, alliance building, struggles over disputed territory, and other destabilizing

[211] See Larry Fabian, *Soldiers Without Enemies* (Washington, DC: Brookings Institution, 1971).

[212] Chantal de Jonge Oudraat, "Humanitarian Intervention: The Lessons Learned," *Current History* 99 (December 2000): 420–421.

[213] Figure 6.7 compiled from data in Oudraat, "Humanitarian Intervention," p. 424. Figures in parentheses are the number of civil wars included in the bold-faced totals.

behavior. The United States, however, is both more powerful than any regional actor could hope to be and relatively disinterested as between them. Its interests in regional peace and security coincide with those of most if not all local states. As a distant, status quo power its military presence should be reassuring rather than threatening, especially to weaker and like-minded states; but even for powerful countries that do not share all its objectives, the U.S. military presence lessens the need to compete for top position.[214] Thus Germany, Saudi Arabia, and even China all welcome American forces in their regions, as do the smaller European states living in Germany's shadow, the Gulf sheikdoms subject to Saudi pressure, and Asian countries warily watching China's rise. Reassurance, of course, becomes the reciprocal of deterrence if an aggressor is identified, but in the post–Cold War world all states in key regions can be both deterred and reassured by America's forward presence – as long as the United States acts in a nonthreatening and relatively disinterested way.

A third noncombat function of American military power that reinforces the reassuring effects of America's forward-deployed military forces is military diplomacy augmented by training and combined exercises. The Pentagon organizes the world into five regional combatant commands, headed by commanders formerly called CinCs: the recently created Northern Command for homeland defense; the Central Command established in the Reagan years for the Middle East and Persian Gulf; and the much older Southern, Pacific, and European Commands for Latin America, Asia, and Europe. Except for SOUTHCOM, each of these commands is either located or has major bases and facilities in its region, and their diplomatic capabilities dwarf those of the Department of State. As *Washington Post* reporter Dana Priest described it,

> American generals and admirals, emissaries for fifty years of the world's strongest military, had long exercised independent influence abroad and competed with U.S. diplomats, corporations, and intelligence agencies to shape foreign policy. But during the 1990s, the sheer weight of their budgets and the heft of political authority handed them by the White House and the Pentagon had tipped the balance of power in favor of the CinCs and their institutions. In a decade when Congress significantly slashed money for diplomacy, the CinCs headquarters had grown to more than twice their Cold War sizes.[215]

By the early 2000s their staffs ran from the 1,100 of SOUTHCOM to 3,600 in PACOM, and their combined annual budgets approached $400 million. Most run adjunct academic institutes for research and international

---

[214] These arguments are adapted from Robert J. Art, *A Grand Strategy for America* (Ithaca, NY: Cornell University Press, 2003), pp. 140–145. Before the Afghan and Iraq wars sent even more troops abroad the U.S. stationed about a fifth of its forces overseas, a total of about 225,000 personnel.

[215] Dana Priest, *The Mission* (New York: W. W. Norton & Co., 2003), p. 71. The rest of this paragraph is based on her description of the commands' assets and operations, pp. 71–77.

conferences, as well as huge joint intelligence centers to track regional events. They administer the State Department's International Military Education and Training (IMET) program as well as the Pentagon's military training and combined forces exercises, enabling them to place American forces with local militaries worldwide. While State's small regional bureaus sit in Washington and only the Secretary has a dedicated aircraft and security entourage, all combatant commanders have long-range aircraft, helicopters, and a full staff and security complement for in-region travel. They use these assets and resources to move throughout their regions constantly, upstaging civilian U.S. diplomats at every stop with the sheer weight of their numbers, resources, and capabilities, along with their ability to reach into the power centers of many of the world's authoritarian regimes through military-to-military contact. Although one may wonder if this militarization of American diplomacy is wise over the long run, it does reinforce the military's reassurance and deterrence functions as well as prepare the ground both internally and externally for war fighting should that become necessary.[216]

The fourth nonviolent function of the U.S. military is to support the other, nonmilitary instruments of power, like economic sanctions and especially diplomatic negotiations. There is a delicate balance here, to be sure. If used unilaterally and indiscriminately, "sharp" military power can undercut other, "softer" instruments by alienating, offending, and frightening its targets.[217] But skillful use of force in peacetime can also support other tools of statecraft, giving them more clout than they might possess if used alone. Scholars are far from agreement on the *fungibility* of military force, that is, the degree to which it is usable in this way for a wide variety of purposes. As noted in Chapter 5, some believe that because the instruments that comprise mobilized power must be tailored to their objectives and targets, military forces can only do purely military tasks.[218] But others contend that military power is fungible in two ways. First, its use has spillover effects, somewhat like gravity, because security is so basic to the achievement of so many foreign policy objectives. When the United States provided security from the Soviet Union during the Cold War, for example,

---

[216] The primary peacetime role of the regional commands is to prepare military campaign plans, and their chiefs become the commanders of American forces during wars in their regions. See, for example, Wesley K. Clark's *Waging Modern War* (New York: Public Affairs, 2001), his memoir on the Yugoslav wars, or H. Norman Schwarzkopf, *It Doesn't Take a Hero* (New York: Bantam Books, 1992), his memoir of the Gulf war.

[217] For the argument that sharp power can undermine soft power, see Joseph S. Nye, Jr., *The Paradox of American Power: Why the World's Only Superpower Can't Go It Alone* (New York: Oxford University Press, 2002), p. 141. For "sharp" power, see Walter Russell Mead, "America's Sticky Power," *Foreign Policy* 141 (March/April 2004): 48.

[218] David A. Baldwin, "Force, Fungibility, and Influence," *Security Studies* 8 (Summer 1999): 177.

it created the context for the flourishing of the Western international economic system, an incredibly important byproduct.[219] The second form of fungibility is when military power is linked to other instruments:

> ... military power can be wielded not only forcefully but 'peacefully.' The forceful use of military power is physical: a state harms, cripples, or destroys the possessions of another state. The peaceful use of military power is intimidating: a state threatens to harm, cripple, or destroy, but does not actually do so....

> Lurking behind the scenes, unstated but explicit, lies the military muscle that gives meaning to the posturing of the diplomats. Especially for great powers, but for the lesser ones too, military power under girds the other instruments of statecraft.[220]

Such military intimidation can be done in three basic ways. First, it can be entirely implicit, a part of the overall situation that cannot be disowned or even ignored by either party. As George Kennan put it, "You have no idea how much it contributes to the general politeness and pleasantness of diplomacy when you have a little quiet armed force in the background."[221] Thus, as we have seen, some experts on economic sanctions believe that they work only when escalation to military instruments is at least left open as a possibility, and presidents engaged in coercive diplomacy often pointedly say that all options remain on the table. Second, military power can be openly linked to other tools in a negotiation, by threatening to use it but doing nothing beyond words to make the threat creditable. Third, statesmen can actually use military forces short of war to fortify their threats, engaging in what has often been called the political *use* of military force.[222] Here is the classic definition:

> A political use of the armed forces occurs when *physical actions* are taken by one or more components of the uniformed military services as part of a deliberate attempt by the national authorities to influence, or to be prepared to influence, specific behavior of individuals in another nation without engaging in a continuing contest of violence.[223]

This "use of discrete military moves to influence a particular situation" was seen during the Clinton years in examples as diverse as beefing up U.S. forces in Northeast Asia to help persuade North Korea to limit its

---

[219] Robert J. Art, "American Foreign Policy and the Fungibility of Force," *Security Studies* 5 (Summer 1996): 25–30.

[220] Art, "American Foreign Policy and the Fungibility of Force," pp. 9–10.

[221] After lecture remarks at the National War College, September 16, 1946, quoted in John Lewis Gaddis, *Strategies of Containment*, Revised and Expanded ed. (Oxford University Press, 2005), p. 39.

[222] Of course, Clausewitzian logic indicates that all use of the military is political, a continuation of politics by other means.

[223] Barry M. Blechman and Steven S. Kaplan, *Force Without War* (Washington, DC: Brookings Institution, 1978), p. 12. Italics removed except where seen.

nuclear weapons program, launching an airborne invasion force to help Haiti's junta appreciate that its days were numbered, or sending aircraft carriers into waters off Taiwan to indicate readiness to defend the island in the face of Chinese military intimidation.[224] The actual, demonstrative *employment* of force may also be undertaken for persuasive purposes, to show resolve or signal a willingness to escalate, as NATO did in 1995 when it bombed Serb positions in a successful effort to persuade Slobodan Milosevic to negotiate an end to the war in Bosnia.[225]

Such limited use of force with persuasive intent is generally called "coercive diplomacy."[226] Those who have studied it most carefully conclude that success can be facilitated by several conditions, including:

- leaders on both sides who are rational and really in control of their country's instruments;
- vital enough interests involved on the coercer's side to create a perceived asymmetry of motivation in its favor;
- clarity about objectives in the coercer's mind, to avoid unnecessary inflation or escalation of its demands;
- adequate domestic and international support for the coercer;
- use of force to check the target's military so that it is forced to rethink its policies, rather than to deflect pain on its population;
- a sense of urgency on the part of the target, enhanced by creditable threats of escalation that would leave the target less well off than acquiescence; and

---

[224] Quote from Blechman and Kaplan, *Force Without War*, p. 11. On Korea see Susan Rosegrant and Michael D. Watkins, *Carrots, Sticks, and Question Marks: Negotiating the North Korean Nuclear Crisis*, Parts A and B, Cases #C18–95–1297.0 and C18–95–1298.0 (Cambridge, MA: John F. Kennedy School of Government, Harvard University, 1995). On Haiti, see Ann Devroy, "Carter Swayed Clinton Into Bending in Talks," *Washington Post* (September 20, 1994): A1, A12. On Taiwan, see R. Jeffrey Smith, "China Plans Maneuvers Off Taiwan," *Washington Post* (February 5, 1996): A1, A18, and Dana Priest and Judith Havemann, "Second Group of U.S. Ships Sent to Taiwan," *Washington Post* (March 11, 1996): A1, A13.

[225] On the precursors to the Dayton conference on Bosnia, see Susan Rosegrant and Michael D. Watkins, *Getting to Dayton: Negotiating an End to the War in Bosnia*, Case #C125–96–1356.0 (Cambridge, MA: John F. Kennedy School of Government, Harvard University, 1996), and Richard Holbrooke, *To End a War* (New York: Random House, 1998).

[226] "Coercive diplomacy" is distinguished from "pure coercion. It seeks to persuade the opponent to cease his aggression rather than bludgeon him into stopping. . . . coercive diplomacy emphasizes the use of threats and the exemplary use of limited force to persuade him to back down. The strategy of coercive diplomacy calls for using just enough force to demonstrate resolution to protect one's interests and to emphasize the credibility of one's determination to use more force if necessary." Craig and George, *Force and Statecraft*, p. 189. I make a similar distinction between force and coercion as generic strategies in Chapter 7, broadening coercion to include nonviolent as well as military means.

- terms of settlement that are precise, giving the target confidence that it can definitively end the coercion in a nonhumiliating way.[227]

Even so, experience indicates that it is difficult to estimate the outcome of such efforts in advance and that, because motivation and will are more important than capability, military superiority is no guarantee of success.[228] Indeed, across twenty-two cases examined by scholars since 1938, U.S. efforts at military coercion have at best worked only about a third of the time, have failed outright nearly half the time, and have had ambiguous results the rest of the time.[229] The bottom line is that foreign affairs strategists considering the limited use of military force for persuasive purposes should leave their country a way out in case of failure – unless they are prepared to go to war.[230]

Conclusion: Instrument Priorities

Instruments are the tangible expression of priorities in a foreign affairs strategy. They are bought, as noted earlier, in order to be prepared for threats or opportunities that strategists see approaching in the international environment. The nation's potential power must be converted into actual or mobilized power, the tools of foreign policy, because potential power is not directly applicable to most of foreign affairs; to deal with threats or take advantage of opportunities, instruments must be in hand. Strategists must decide to buy those instruments well in advance of when they expect threats and opportunities to materialize because the process of acquiring them takes time, usually years and sometimes decades. But they do so with trepidation, because instruments' applicability comes at the price of their being quite situation-specific. As noted earlier, diplomatic assets cannot do what informational, economic or military tools can, just as nuclear warheads cannot do what special operations forces are capable of. Peering dimly into the future, foreign affairs strategists make their best, most educated guesses and then set their priorities into the concrete of people, training, equipment, and materiel, hoping their vision proves adequate to future circumstances.

Not all instruments have a cost to the federal budget, but for those that do the budget gives a snapshot of a government's foreign affairs priorities.

---

[227] Compiled from Alexander L. George and William E. Simons, eds., *The Limits of Coercive Diplomacy*, 2nd ed. (Boulder, CO: Westview Press, 1994), pp. 279–287, and Robert J. Art, "Coercive Diplomacy: What Do We Know?" Chapter 9 in Art and Patrick M. Cronin, eds., *The United States and Coercive Diplomacy* (Washington, DC: U.S. Institute of Peace Press, 2003), pp. 371–374, 387–402. I reserve the term "coercion" to include use of all instruments of state power, not just the military, in a coercive way. See Chapter 7.

[228] Art, "Coercive Diplomacy: What Do We Know?" pp. 402, 407.

[229] Art, "Coercive Diplomacy: What Do We Know?" pp. 385–387, 403.

[230] Art, "Coercive Diplomacy: What Do We Know?" pp. 408–410.

Conduct of Foreign Affairs	$7,424	1.7%
(Diplomacy and Negotiations)		
International Organizations	$2,279	.5%
Foreign Information and		
Exchange (Public Diplomacy)	$1,098	.3%
Foreign Assistance		
Development & Humanitarian	$14,953	3.4%
Security	$8,327	1.9%
Sub-Total: Nonmilitary	*$34,081*	*7.8%*
National Defense:		
Military Forces	$400,081	92.2%
Total Foreign Affairs	*$434,162*	*100.0%*

Figure 6.8: Funding of U.S. instruments in fiscal year 2005 ($ in millions).

Figure 6.8 shows how the instruments of American foreign affairs strategy were funded in fiscal year 2005, with the figures chosen so as to exclude as much as possible spending directly attributable to the wars in Afghanistan and Iraq.[231] These figures show that of the $434 billion appropriated for instruments of statecraft, some 92 percent went to military forces. The entire State Department, including its worldwide embassies and operations and the salaries of all the U.S. Foreign Service officers, was less than 2 percent of the total.[232] U.S. assessed contributions to international organizations to support their regular budgets and peacekeeping activities was less than a half percent, as was all of public diplomacy; and the entire foreign assistance budget, both development and security aid, was only a bit over 5 percent. In other words, the United States in 2005 dedicated almost twelve times as many resources to military power as to all the nonmilitary instruments put together. Among the nonmilitary instruments, foreign aid got two-thirds of the funding (split 64 percent development/humanitarian

[231] Data is FY 2005 actual discretionary budget authority taken from the U.S. FY 2007 federal budget. Information for the nonmilitary instruments comes from the 150 International Affairs account in Table 27–1, Budget Authority and Outlays by Function, Category, and Program, and budget authority rather than outlays are used because it excludes over $7B in Iraq reconstruction aid appropriated in an earlier year. Data for military forces comes from the Department of Defense table in *The Budget for Fiscal Year 2007* (Washington, DC: GPO, 2006), p. 76, exclusive of the supplemental used to pay for the wars in Afghanistan and Iraq.

[232] Although Secretary Colin Powell's leadership helped correct the situation to some extent, a spate of articles at century's end bemoaned the sorry state of American diplomacy. See Hans Binnendijk, "Tin Cup Diplomacy," *National Interest* (Fall 1997): 88–91; John Lancaster, "Panel Says 'State of Crisis' Near For Diplomatic Facilities Abroad," *Washington Post* (November 5, 1999): A31; Robert G. Kaiser, "Foreign Disservice," *Washington Post* (April 16, 2000): B1–2.

to 36 percent security), diplomacy about a fourth, international organizations 7 percent and public diplomacy just 3 percent.

One may well ask why the president and Congress picked this allocation of funds, and in particular why the military portion so overwhelms all the other instruments, or why public diplomacy and international organizations receive so small a share. The Department of Defense 2005 budget might be explained by the war on terrorism, or by Republican fondness for military tools, except that its relative size was almost exactly the same in FY 2000, at the end of the Clinton years and before 9/11.[233] One reason may be that although the effects of the American military on the country's influence are just as difficult to measure as those of its international radio broadcasting or the overseas interactions of its diplomats, military spending produces something tangible, like aircraft, ships, tanks and guns, that sending radio signals or diplomats abroad cannot match. The 9/11 attacks and the ensuing war on terrorism have helped restore funding across all instruments of statecraft that was sorely neglected during the 1990s. But they have not changed the overall dominance of the military, nor have widespread perceptions of anti-Americanism abroad and the shortcomings of unilateralism had much effect on the funding of public diplomacy or international organizations.

Whether this allocation of funding is the best one for future American foreign policy is a question affairs strategists would do well to ponder. For decisions on which instruments to buy must precede those on which instruments to use, and having the wrong instruments may render policymakers unable to deal with future threats or take advantage of future opportunities. Moreover, although strategists labor diligently to be certain that means follow ends, it is nearly unavoidable that the array of instruments they have at hand will help shape their foreign policy responses, if not their view of the international environment itself. To expand an old cliché, if all one has is a hammer, not only will one do a lot of pounding, but eventually every problem will begin to look like a nail. Moreover, whether or not policymakers facing a future crisis have the instruments they need, they will use the instruments they have. And the result may well be policy combining unnecessarily high costs and risks with an unnecessarily low prospect of success.

That said, it is time now to move from our discussion of potential and actual power to a consideration of how means are used to accomplish strategic ends. This long yet inadequate survey of the tools of statecraft has been designed, after all, to help prepare strategists for the real work of strategic planning. Up to now we have been looking at pieces of the strategic puzzle individually, exploring the characteristics of each, asking the

---

[233] FY 2000 appropriations were $294B for defense and $24B for international affairs. Historical Table 8.9, "Budget Authority for Discretionary Programs," *Budget of the United States Government* (Washington, DC: GPO, yearly).

questions they pose, but only briefly considering how each piece connects with the others. But now it is time to do more than just mention the most obvious relationships between these elements of strategy. Now we must focus directly on the connection between ends and means, and the way in which all the concepts treated above need to fit together if strategy is to achieve coherence. It is time, in other words, to look at the heart of strategic logic.

7

Linking Ends and Means

Defining the national interest, identifying threats and opportunities, validating assumptions about the strategic context, assessing domestic support, strengthening the nation's relative power and gauging its influence, buying instruments of statecraft and understanding their properties – all these are essential yet preliminary steps to the critical marriage of ends and means that lies at the heart of all strategy (see Figure 7.1). For after all these things are done, the strategist must still formulate specific objectives and decide exactly how to use instruments to achieve them.

Formulating such plans is the most difficult and important part of foreign affairs strategy, for it is the point at which limits must be recognized, costs and risks clarified, and priorities assigned. Trying to achieve one's chosen objectives, and doing so in particular ways, will have effects on other efforts to accomplish other objectives. These consequences must be weighed and the linkages between elements of strategy recognized and arranged, ideally in a manner that will cause the whole strategic construct to be more than the sum of its parts. Objective setting, in other words, is where everything comes together, where strategy either achieves coherence or fails to be strategy at all. Not surprisingly, it is where the enormity of the intellectual and practical challenge hits home.

In this chapter and the next, the focus will be on the "plan" level of the model for foreign affairs strategy (see Figure 7.2). "Objectives" are located on the "ENDS" side because they are the goals of strategy, the purposes to which it is directed. They are placed below "opportunities and threats" and "national interests" because objectives serve interests, either by protecting them against threats or by taking advantage of opportunities for their advancement. And "objectives" are next to "statecraft" and "instruments" because strategies require a combining of ends, means, and ways: the setting of objectives, the choice of instruments with which to pursue them, and the specification of how those instruments will be used. Those decisions result in the proposed "courses of action," or objective-instrument packages, that constitute the specific plans of a foreign affairs strategy.[1]

---

[1] Forty years ago Klaus Knorr similarly labeled the combination of military pressure and noncoercive influence "power packages," pointing to the importance of the skill with which they are designed. *On the Uses of Military Power in the Nuclear Age* (Princeton, NJ: Princeton University Press, 1966), pp. 167–168.

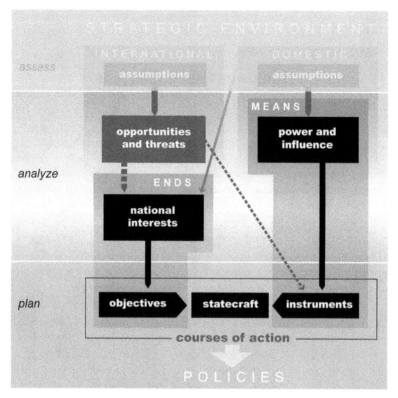

Figure 7.1: Ends and means.

Influence Attempts, Impacts, and Success

Before strategists can set objectives and choose instruments to pursue them, they need to be clear about what is really going on when the leaders of one nation-state or nonstate entity try to influence another. At their most fundamental, all strategies are efforts by an initiating actor (I) directed at a target actor or situation (T). Political scientists often refer to strategies as "influence attempts"; that is, attempts by I to get T to do what it would otherwise not do.[2] Since in most cases T has a choice in how it reacts to I's attempt to influence it, such attempts are essentially about changing the perceived costs and benefits of the alternatives T confronts so that it will choose to accede to I's demands.[3]

---

[2] This formulation, of course, is the commonly accepted definition of power among political scientists. Most people think of *power* as a characteristic that inheres in an actor; *influence* expresses the effect that power has on its intended target (see Chapter 5). Note also that, as will be seen below, some strategies do not rely on changing a target's behavior to achieve their purposes.

[3] These, of course, are the reciprocal of the cost-benefit analysis that must be done by strategists as they decide on objective-instrument packages, discussed in Chapter 8.

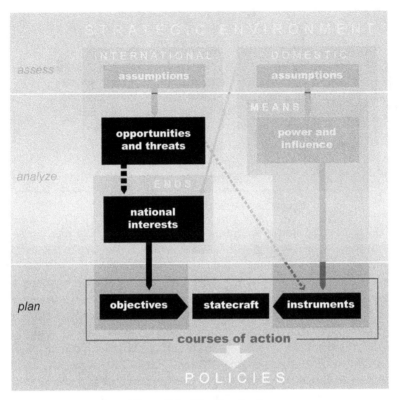

Figure 7.2: The plan level.

As the simple diagram I —> T implies, there are at least three elements to any influence attempt (see Figure 7.3). The first relates to I's *power* – in particular, to what it does to put the instrument or instruments it uses in motion. Here strategists need to know as much as possible about the characteristic strengths and weaknesses of the various instruments (the subject of Chapter 6), as well as which of them are available for the situation they face. The second element is the transmission link connecting I and T, represented by the arrow, an important consideration because many intervening factors may weaken or intensify the *impact* of an instrument on its recipient. Here the ways in which instruments are used and the environment in which they operate are critical considerations. And the third is the reaction of T, the target state or nonstate actor. Here the strategist needs to be familiar with the characteristics of its leaders and their likely responses, both to the impact of the instruments and to the objectives being sought. Obviously, to achieve *success* a strategy must include all three elements: the availability and employment of the instrument or instruments by I, an effective transmission link, and the intended reaction or choice by T. Each of them will require detailed treatment later in this chapter or the next.

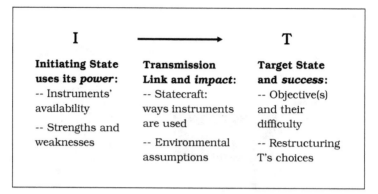

Figure 7.3: Anatomy of an influence attempt.

Of course, the simple diagram I —> T potentially subsumes a great deal of complexity that strategists need to untangle if they are to be clear about what they are undertaking. First, although usually the target that is the object of the influence attempt is also the recipient (R) of the instruments' effects, sometimes targets and recipients may *not* be the same.[4] Power being psychological as well as concrete in nature, strategists often undertake actions for their demonstration effects on individual or multiple third parties.[5] It has been suggested, for example, that George W. Bush's decisions to invade Afghanistan in 2001 and Iraq in 2003 were, at least partly, designed to shock other states into a realization that supporting terrorism does not pay.[6] Second, accordingly, there may be one recipient but multiple targets, multiple recipients but one target, or multiple recipients and multiple targets; the simple diagram of I —> T might instead look more like Figure 7.4, or some variation of it. Third, as is implied by differentiating recipients from targets, the power that underlies an instrument's success may not be that of the instrument itself. For example, T may yield to a demand backed by economic sanctions, not because of the economic pain they inflict, but because T fears that I will use its military tools if economic ones fail. Thus, it may be I's military power rather than the impact of its economic instruments that makes the sanctions work.

Nevertheless, arriving at a sense of whether an instrument will succeed ordinarily requires estimating its likely *impact*, the effect the instrument will produce on R across the transmission link (—>). The failure of an instrument to have an impact (or as powerful an impact as I intends) may be due to failures in the transmission link between I and R – for example,

---

[4] Where the recipient and target are the same, this discussion will use T to designate that actor; where they are different, R will represent the actor upon which the instrument has an impact, and T the actor that is the object of the influence attempt.

[5] On the psychological nature of power, see Chapter 4.

[6] John Lewis Gaddis, "A Grand Strategy of Transformation," *Foreign Policy* 133 (November/December 2002): 54.

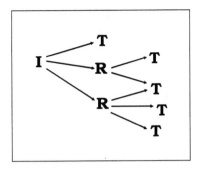

Figure 7.4: Multiple recipients and targets.

sanctions that are overwhelmed by outside suppliers, weapons that do not reach their targets, or a short wave signal too weak to be received – or it may have to do with lack of potency in the instrument itself, as it "arrives" at the recipient state – say, sanctions cast too narrowly to affect an exceptionally vibrant (or primitive) economy, a weapon that turns out to have little destructive effect, or a public diplomacy message that is unpersuasive to its audience. Either kind of failure may relate to the *ways* in which the instrument or instruments are used –that is, the *statecraft* employed– or to the strategic environment in which they are used, which may reduce their impact directly or offer R help in coping with their effects.

Even if an instrument causes real pain or delivers actual benefits, decision makers must be careful not to confuse that impact with its *success* in accomplishing objectives.[7] Foreign aid may be quite effective in building a dam or increasing agricultural productivity, for example, but as noted above the farther the real objective gets from such immediate, primary goals the more elusive success is.[8] Economic sanctions may inflict severe pain on a recipient country's people, causing widespread malnutrition or even completely wrecking the nation's economy (as was the case with sanctions on Haiti in the early 1990s) but still not remove entrenched leaders from power.[9] Armies may be victorious in battle, yet leave nothing but

[7] David Baldwin argues that success should be assessed across five dimensions: goal achievement, costs to the user and target, and stakes for the user and target. While I believe all these elements are important to instrument selection, I think it analytically more useful to define success more simply and narrowly as goal achievement. As discussed below, costs to the *user* of instruments must always be considered as a key element of goal feasibility and desirability, but imposing costs on the *target* should be considered part of success only if doing so is part of the policymaker's objective. David A. Baldwin, "The Sanctions Debate and the Logic of Choice," *International Security* 24 (Winter 1999/2000): 89–92.

[8] See Chapter 6, section on foreign aid.

[9] Douglas Farah, "Rural Haitians Reeling: Impact of Embargo Has Yet to Trickle Up," *Washington Post* (November 27, 1993), A1, A23 is just one of many newspaper articles from 1993 and 1994 detailing the devastating impact of the embargo on the average Haitian and its lack of impact on the junta of Raul Cedras.

destruction and chaos in their wake. Success requires a specified change on the part of the target government, a decision by human beings in reaction to all the inducements and pressures they face, including but hardly limited to those created by I's instruments. As a result, just as the use of an instrument by one country says nothing certain about its impact on another, so its impact on the recipient, however dramatic, says little about the initiating government's ability to achieve its objectives with the target of its influence attempt.

A Spectrum of Generic Strategies

When strategists put objectives and instruments together, they inevitably choose among four broad approaches, four generic strategies. These strategies naturally fall along a spectrum running from influence attempts that rely solely on argumentation, at one end, to actions that forcefully take the decision as to how to respond to I out of T's hands, at the other (see Figure 7.5).[10] Thus, at one end of the spectrum is *persuasion*, appeals to the mind and heart of the target government to get it to understand "why your demands are so important to you and why you think their demands are excessive."[11] Here force of argument is the only tool at the statesman's command, "to distill drop by drop into the minds of your competitors those causes and arguments which you wish them to adopt," and success often springs from the effort to identify larger common interests and to help the other government see the issue from a new and different perspective.[12] Persuasion may involve the transmitting of truthful or false information, but it changes only T's perceptions of the available alternatives, not the alternatives themselves.[13]

[10] The general idea of a spectrum was derived from the works of Alexander George on coercive diplomacy and diplomatic bargaining, of Holsti's discussion of how influence is exercised {*International Politics*, 6th ed. (New York: Prentiss-Hall, 1993), pp. 125–126}, and from Walter L. Barrows and Vincent D. Kern, "Superpower Statecraft in the Third World," *Harvard International Review* 8 (January-February 1986): 7. Holsti offers a five-spectrum model of how influence is exercised: persuasion, offer of rewards, granting of rewards, threat of punishment, infliction of nonviolent punishment, and force. His scheme combines my generic strategies with one of the ways discussed under statecraft below: the prospective/conditional versus actual/immediate use of instruments.

[11] Gordon Craig and Alexander George, *Force and Statecraft: Diplomatic Problems of Our Time* (New York: Oxford University Press, 1983), p. 163.

[12] "By this means your influence will spread gradually through their minds almost unawares." de Callieres, *On the Manner of Negotiating with Princes* (Notre Dame, IN: University of Notre Dame Press, 1963), pp. 121–122. See Chapter 6 section on "Political Instruments: Negotiation."

[13] This formulation is adapted from Robert A. Dahl's classic work, *Modern Political Analysis*, 3rd ed. (Englewood Cliffs, NJ: Prentice-Hall, Inc., 1976), Chs. 2–3. Dahl distinguishes three so-called "means" of influence: trained control, persuasion (either rational or manipulative), and inducement (using either rewards or the prospect of severe sanctions; only the latter, oddly, he calls "power," and

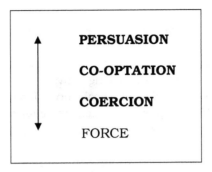

Figure 7.5: The spectrum of generic strategies.

Next along the spectrum lie two kinds of bargaining in which positive or negative inducements are added to pure persuasion, in the process changing T's alternatives or at least their costs and benefits.[14] Thus, the second stage in the spectrum is cooperative bargaining or *co-optation*, persuasive efforts that use *positive* incentives like offering or giving aid, providing security guarantees, lifting sanctions, or granting concessions on other issues. The Clinton administration called its use of this generic strategy *engagement*, roughly defined as the use of economic, political, or cultural incentives, either to influence problem countries to alter their behavior, or to cement relations with non-allies.[15] The third generic strategy is bargaining with *negative* inducements, or *coercion*, where the application or threat of economic sanctions, a cutoff in aid, the use of instruments covertly, or even military force may be employed.[16] There are several variants of coercive strategies, including containment, denial, deterrence, and compellence.

Like co-optation, coercion is still very much an attempt at influence, a characteristic in which it differs from *force*, at the far end of the spectrum. Usually of a military but occasionally also of an economic nature, force is

---

includes coercion as a subset within it). For Dahl, persuasion involves communicating information about alternatives, while inducement involves changing the alternatives themselves, with coercion apparently being a change such that all the alternatives are unsatisfactory or damaging to T. At any rate, the basic distinctions between pure persuasion, positive inducement, and negative coercion are clearly recognized.

[14] Craig and George, *Force and Statecraft*, p. 163. The authors make a distinction between persuasion and bargaining within specific negotiations that I have applied here to statecraft as a whole.

[15] For a brief discussion of the technique, see Richard N. Haass and Meghan L. O'Sullivan, *Engaging Problem Countries*, Policy Brief #61 (Washington, DC: Brookings Institution, 2000).

[16] The use of "coercion" here is similar to but slightly broader than "coercive diplomacy" as used by George and Craig in *Force and Statecraft*, p. 189. For them, coercive diplomacy focuses on the limited use of military force, and is distinguished from outright warfare, or "pure coercion." By contrast, coercion as used here may be generated by any instrument of state power, so long as it is used in an effort to persuade. And in my spectrum, George and Craig's "pure coercion" is labeled "force."

a strategy that does not expect or rely on decisions by its target. No influence attempt is really involved here: the statesman has at least temporarily
given up any effort to persuade or bargain and is reduced to forcing a direct
change in circumstances. The distinction made here between coercion and
force follows that of Thomas Schelling between the power to hurt as part
of a bargaining process and what he calls brute force, or the power to seize
and hold.[17] This final stop on the spectrum belongs more in the realm of
military than foreign affairs strategy and will therefore receive little attention in what follows.

The decision as to where on the spectrum of generic strategies a particular influence attempt should be placed is as difficult as it is consequential.
Under what conditions are governments or nonstate actors more likely to
respond to incentives, conciliation, inclusion, and cooperation? When, on
the other hand, should strategists use pressure, intimidation, exclusion
and isolation? Should strategists contemplating use of economic instruments prefer oxygen or asphyxiation?[18] Students of American diplomacy
disagreed for decades, for example, as to whether the continuing isolation
of Cuba was the best way to weaken Fidel Castro's regime or whether it simply drove him into the arms of the Soviet Union; this issue has taken on
even greater salience since Cuba's Soviet support ended, as some groups
advocate tougher sanctions to exploit the island's heightened economic
difficulties while others seek to increase exchange with the West so that
democratic ideas can subvert the regime from inside.[19] Even more difficult
are cases where the target country is in part supportive of, but in part hostile to, American interests. For example, American statecraft toward China
has shifted periodically from co-optive to coercive, and American strategy
after 9/11 must decide whether states that in some ways oppose and in
others support terrorists – like Pakistan, Syria, and even Saudi Arabia –
are best co-opted or coerced.

Considered in the abstract, co-optive strategies seem to have a variety
of advantages over coercive ones.[20] Coercion, after all, tends to generate
resistance on the part of the target's decision makers, to cause them stress
that may well interfere with rational decision making, and to strain relations between the two countries on other subjects where cooperation might
otherwise be possible. Among the target's public it engenders feelings of
hostility toward the coercing state, and may spark a rally-around-the-flag

---

[17]   Chapter 1, "The Diplomacy of Violence," in *Arms and Influence* (New Haven, CT:
       Yale University Press, 1966), pp. 1–34.
[18]   See Franklin L. Lavin, "Asphyxiation or Oxygen? The Sanctions Dilemma," *For-
       eign Policy* 104 (Fall 1996): 139–154.
[19]   For example, see Peter Slevin, "Pursuing an Opening to Cuba," *Washington Post*
       (March 9, 2002): A5.
[20]   The next two paragraphs draw heavily on David A. Baldwin, "The Power of Positive
       Sanctions," Chapter 4 in *Paradoxes of Power* (New York: Basil Blackwill Inc.,
       1989), pp. 58–81.

effect of support for leaders, even those otherwise seen as oppressive and dictatorial. Offering incentives, on the other hand, has opposite effects, engendering feelings of hope, reassurance, and attraction. Furthermore, it is likely that each kind of action tends to beget similar actions; therefore, threats and punishments may undermine overall stability in the international system, while promises and rewards may enhance it. In addition, co-optive actions and the cooperative relationships they often support tend to expose the other side's actions, automatically helping verification of agreements, while coercive actions put a premium on deception. Finally, co-optive strategies may more easily secure public support in I since they do not carry some of the risks of coercive moves.

Yet despite these advantages, coercion often seems to predominate in international relations. Part of the explanation may be that incentives seem to add direct expense (for example, in foreign aid dollars or trade concessions) that negative moves may not carry, since many of the instruments of coercive diplomacy have to be maintained anyway for defensive purposes.[21] In addition, powerful states (who disproportionately set the tone and the law of international relations) may use threats more since, given their relative power, they expect success – and successful threats, unlike successful promises, require no costly follow-through. Another reason for the prevalence of coercion may be the natural human tendency to react to danger by stiffening and threatening back, moves that seem more masculine and stronger than offers of reward for good behavior. Given the anarchy of the international system, states usually fear even to look weak lest they be taken advantage of.

Moreover, co-optive strategies are hard to arrange. They are a kind of transaction or exchange, wherein a benefit is offered by the initiator in return for a concession demanded from the target. If inducement and concession cannot be exchanged simultaneously, the target may refuse to make the concession first, fearing that the initiator may not deliver the promised benefit; or the initiator may refuse to give the inducement first, fearing that the target will simply pocket it and do nothing.[22] Moreover, it is hard for I to get the timing and balance between its carrots and T's concessions right, "neither offering too little too late or for too much in

---

[21] However, this factor is offset somewhat by the fact that the actual use of negative instruments tends to be more costly than their mere maintenance; certainly this is true of military force, while the costs of economic coercion in an ever more interdependent world increasingly boomerang on its originators.

[22] Sequencing problems of this kind have bedeviled the six party talks with North Korea in 2005–06. Said chief U.S. negotiator Christopher R. Hill, the DPRK "has not wanted to have all its obligations front-loaded with all of our obligations back-loaded." We need to "find a solution to the sequencing problem." Peter Baker and Glenn Kessler, "U.S. to Push Koreans On Nuclear Program," *Washington Post* (October 5, 2005): A20. For further discussion of timing and sequencing issues, see Step 3, "Statecraft," below.

return, nor offering too much too soon for too little in return."[23] Efforts at
co-optation also may give targets a kind of power that coercive strategies
lack – as Machiavelli shrewdly observed, "men love at their own free will,
but fear at the will of the prince."[24] For example, if initiators cannot easily observe the demanded concession being made, then targets can claim
that they made it but that other factors prevented the outcome the initiator wanted.[25] Even worse, using positive incentives may open a state
to blackmail by the target, as has so often been argued regarding U.S.
diplomacy with North Korea since negotiation of the Agreed Framework in
1994. Perhaps most important, the choice of using instruments co-optively
or coercively in an attempt to influence another state's *intentions* also has
an effect on its *capabilities* that the statesman cannot ignore.[26] Co-optive
incentives may add to the target state's ability to threaten or punish if the
influence attempt fails, whereas the coercive use of instruments is sure not
to augment its capabilities and may well decrease them.

Such considerations imply that the choice between co-optive and coercive diplomacy should be an either/or matter. However, just as tools of
different kinds are often used in combination, the two generic strategies
may well be mixed. American post–Cold War statecraft in both Europe and
the Far East seems to confirm this possibility, for it has nestled containment measures within broader policies of co-optation. Thus, attempts to
draw Russia into the Western community of nations have gone along with
expansion of the NATO alliance, while strategic cooperation with China has
proceeded in tandem with measures designed to strengthen American ties
to Japan, South Korea, and Taiwan. In both cases the coercive subpolicy
has been seen in part as a hedge against failure of the overall co-optive
strategy. However, coercive moves in both cases have also risked so antag-
onizing their targets as to jeopardize the broader strategies' chances of success. Such experience makes clear that, at the very least, mixing generic
strategies and the instruments that support them is a delicate operation

---

[23] Bruce W. Jentleson and Christopher A. Whytock, "Who 'Won' Libya?", *International Security* 30 (Winter 2005/06): 52. The authors argue the need for what they
call "reciprocity," a clear linkage in the target's mind between its concessions and
I's carrots.

[24] "and...a wise prince must rely on what is in his power, and not what is in
the power of others." Nicolo Machievelli, *The Prince*, trans. by Luigi Ricci, rev.
by E. R. P. Vincent (New York: New American Library/Oxford University Press,
1952), p. 91.

[25] The problems of low observability and non-simultaneous benefits are noted by
Daniel W. Drezner in "The Trouble with Carrots: Transaction Costs, Conflict
Expectations, and Economic Inducements," *Security Studies* 9 (Autumn-Winter
1999/2000): 188–218. Drezner therefore hypothesizes that inducements are
more likely to work between democracies and within the framework of international organizations, both of which help transparency, restrain leaders' capri-
ciousness, and (in the latter case) provide a forum in which benefit and concession can be make transparent and transaction failure punishable.

[26] See the discussion on the three kinds of objectives under Step 4 below.

that requires a high order of statesmanship, lest secondary instruments corrupt primary objectives. It also points out the need to ensure that the choice between cooperative and coercive approaches (or the mix of them) is clearly made, lest selection and use of means wind up determining ends.

What about sequential use of these two generic strategies? Although common sense would seem to recommend first using carrots, then sticks, the opposite sequence of inflicting pain while holding out the promise of assistance after demands are met has been a common pattern for American statecraft when seeking regime change. Indeed, coercion might be expected to *precede* co-optation with states seen as adversaries, because initiators need first to demonstrate their toughness (fearing the reaction should they seem weak), to weaken potential enemies, and to change opponents' cost-benefit calculations; only then can they risk strengthening an adversary with inducements, and only if stalemate or war are unacceptable. But coercion usually *follows* co-optation with allies, partly because allies will already be the recipients of inducements, which give the initiator leverage that it does not have with adversaries.[27]

There is another basic dimension of strategy that should be considered alongside its persuasive, co-optive, or coercive character, one that also fundamentally determines the relationship between I and T: namely, that of *offense* versus *defense*. In military strategy the distinction seems straightforward: an offensive strategy takes the initiative to attack the enemy, whereas a defensive strategy waits for an attack and prepares to repel it.[28] Clausewitz argued that defense is the strongest kind of war, because it does not need to move force over distances and benefits from interior lines of supply.[29] "In war," writes political scientist Jack Snyder, "the weaker side normally remains on the defensive precisely because defending its home ground is typically easier than attacking the other side's strongholds." Moreover, "the side defending its own homeland and the survival of its regime typically cares more about the stakes of the conflict than

---

[27] Drezner, "The Trouble with Carrots," pp. 188–218. Robert J. Art argues that positive inducements do increase the likelihood of success in coercive diplomacy, but only if they are offered after threatened or actual use of exemplary or limited force. "Coercive Diplomacy: What Do We Know?" Chapter 9 in Robert J. Art and Patrick M. Cronin, eds., *The United States and Coercive Diplomacy* (Washington, DC: U.S. Institute of Peace Press, 2003), pp. 388–389, 393–399.

[28] "What is the concept of defense? The parrying of a blow. What is its characteristic feature? Awaiting the blow. It is this feature...by which defense can be distinguished from attack in war." Carl von Clausewitz, *On War*, Michael Howard and Peter Paret, eds. and trans. (Princeton, NJ: Princeton University Press, 1976), p. 357.

[29] "What is the object of defense? Preservation. It is easier to hold ground than take it." Because it is the strongest form of war, Clausewitz argues, defense should be chosen by the weaker side; because it has a negative objective, however, he recommends it be abandoned as soon possible for the positive objective of offense. *On War*, p. 357–359.

does a would-be attacker," creating an asymmetry of motivation in favor of the defender.[30] An imbalance of legitimacy may also come into play if offense is equated with aggression, for the defender is protecting the status quo, usually recognized by law, whereas the aggressor is seeking change through force of arms.

Translating these ideas from military to foreign affairs strategy, it might be said that persuasive, co-optive, or coercive strategies are all offensive in nature because they are forward-leaning and active, taking the initiative to persuade, co-opt, or coerce rather than waiting for the target to act. Moreover, a strategy that takes advantage of opportunities to promote interests is inevitably one of offense, whereas a state in danger has the basic choice of offensively going after the intentions and/or capabilities of the threat it faces, on the one hand, or defensively working to reduce its own vulnerability, on the other.[31] Thus, offensive strategies will generally involve more contact with targets than defensive ones. At first thought, in fact, a defensive strategy may not seem like an influence attempt at all, but it should be remembered that a defense perceived as effective by a potential adversary may have a powerful deterrent effect. Though offense aims at changing and defense at preserving the status quo, the distinction between the two should not be misconstrued as that between an active and passive strategy, for a government may be very active indeed in preparing defenses. Nor should a defensive strategy be assumed to be less expensive than an offensive one; it all depends on the number of vulnerable targets to be defended and the size and vulnerability of the opponent.

Designing a Foreign Affairs Strategy

Once these basic choices between offense or defense and among generic strategies are made, foreign affairs strategists can begin to structure courses of action. To do so they set objectives, choose instruments to pursue them, and decide the kind of statecraft that will make best use of those instruments (see Figure 7.6). Like the application of concepts across the entire range of strategic thought, formulating strategy at the planning level is both a sequential and an iterative undertaking.[32] As noted in Chapter 1, there is a loosely ordered sequence of tasks strategists should follow as they begin the process, but doing each one puts the strategist in a better position to accomplish all the others, as well as to clarify the deeper assumptions and analysis on which the strategic construct rests. The steps in strategic planning thus should be thought of as layered on top of each other,

---

[30] Jack Snyder, "Imperial Temptations," *National Interest* 71 (Spring 2003): 31.

[31] See discussion of this point in Chapter 4.

[32] This point, which is common to all systematic decision making, is made explicit in Lewis G. Irwin, *The Policy Analyst's Handbook* (Armonk, NY: M. E. Sharpe, 2003), p. 24.

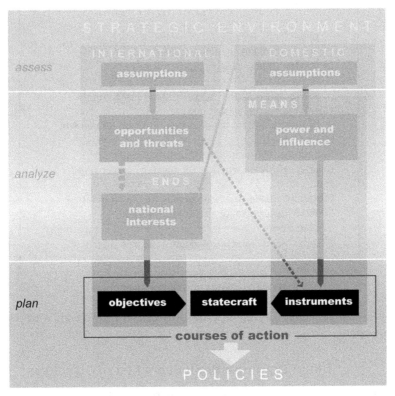

Figure 7.6: The plan level.

and the strategist should move among them freely, gradually sharpening assumptions, analysis, and plans as the work proceeds.

The rest of this chapter and the next are organized according to the eight-step process of strategy formulation summarized in Figure 7.7. It assumes that the strategist has already well begun the work described in earlier chapters, clarifying assumptions about the strategic environment at home and abroad, analyzing national interests and identifying related threats and opportunities, understanding the nature of power and influence the state has in the issue at hand. As he or she now proceeds to set objectives, however, interests will come more clearly into focus and may well need reformulation; as instruments and ways of using them are specified, one's sense of the nation's power and influence will be clarified; and as courses of action are assessed for cost, risk, and coherence (see Chapter 8), assumptions about the broader strategic environment and domestic support for the strategic enterprise will solidify. The process will become less sequential and more iterative, and eventually the strategist will achieve a high degree of confidence that all the bases have been touched, that all the key questions have been considered, and that the nation can commit its

1. **ENDS**: Draw up a preliminary list of <u>objectives.</u>
Check *desirability* against interests.
2. **MEANS**: Choose <u>instruments</u> to accomplish objectives.
3. **STATECRAFT**: Specify <u>ways</u> of using instruments. Check *feasibility* against power.
4. **IMPACT**: Estimate how courses of action (COAs) will affect recipients.
5. **SUCCESS**: Estimate how targets will react.
6. **COST**: Evaluate whether the strategy is worth its cost.
7. **RISK**: Consider that things may not go as planned. Recheck *desirability* against cost and risk.
8. **COHERENCE**: Check internal and external compatibility of ends, means, and ways; coordinate and prioritize.

Figure 7.7: Steps in strategy formulation.

power and prestige, its treasure and if necessary its blood, with its eyes wide open.

1. ENDS: Draw up a Preliminary List of *Objectives*

First, it is important to be clear about the nature of objectives themselves. Generally speaking, "a goal is a future state of affairs that someone considers desirable and worth spending some effort to achieve."[33] Because objectives are action items, they usually begin with verbs like "create," "develop," "promote," "protect," "ensure," "maintain," "deny," or "avoid." They mandate that the government *do* something, and not just anything that might seem momentarily attractive, but actions that will take advantage of opportunities to advance interests or protect them against threats. Hence, in a sound foreign affairs strategy, objectives must be linked *explicitly* to both independently identified interests and to the threats, or opportunities, that attend those interests (see Figure 7.8).

In the logic of foreign affairs strategy, then, objectives can be simply defined as *that subset of the national interest that the statesman decides to protect or promote.* As noted in Chapter 4, this close relationship between interests and objectives often leads to confusion as to which is which.[34] In

---

[33] A F. K. Organski, *World Politics*, 2nd ed. (New York: Alfred A. Knopf, 1968), p. 62.
[34] Organski, for example, cites power, wealth, cultural welfare, and peace as the major goals of states. Holsti lists security, autonomy, welfare, and prestige or status as the purposes all states seek. Wealth or welfare is of course the interest we have called economic prosperity, while cultural welfare and autonomy both fall under the interest of value preservation. Security is the same as our physical security, but power (as has been noted) is a means and not a goal, while prestige

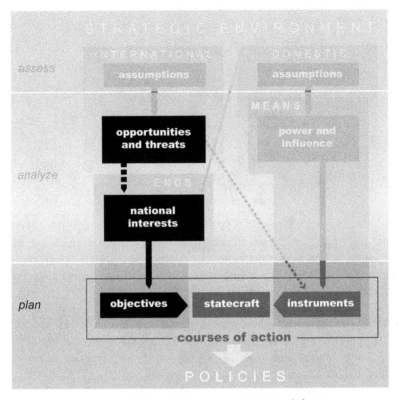

Figure 7.8: Linking objectives to interests and threats.

truth, the distinction between these two kinds of strategic ends *is* some-what arbitrary and fluid, like the lines between military strategy, opera-tions, and tactics. Still, the two are conceptually distinct in ways that go well beyond the tendency of objectives to be less general and more spe-cific than interests (see Figure 7.9). Interests are snapshots of reality and expressed grammatically as subjects, but the actionable nature of objec-tives and their role as parts of plans for maintaining or attaining that real-ity requires that they include verbs. Objectives derive their legitimacy by serving interests; interests, by contrast, are based on values and are self-justifying. Objectives can and often do serve more than one interest. They should and usually must be prioritized, whereas interests are difficult to rank except by reference to the threats and opportunities affecting them.

is a psychological dimension of power (see Chapter 5). Thus, among all the goals listed by these writers, only peace seems both a legitimate goal and one that is not in fact an interest in itself; it is a goal that directly serves the national interest in security but also supports prosperity and the protection and preservation of national values. Organski, *World Politics*, p. 63; K. J. Holsti, *International Poli-tics: A Framework for Analysis*, 6th ed. (Englewood Cliffs, NJ: Prentice-Hall, Inc., 1992), pp. 82–109.

Interests	Objectives
General	Specific
End-states	Action items
Subjects	Verbs
Based on values, self-justifying	Serve and are justified by interests
Power irrelevant	Power critical
Wish-list	What's doable
Cost irrelevant	Cost vital

Figure 7.9: Interests and objectives.

Most important, although interests can and must be identified without reference to the power necessary to protect or advance them, objectives cannot be set without careful consideration of the power they require. Objectives are what is doable within the wish-list of the nation's interests. They are not everything strategists need or want, just those things that can be sought at reasonable cost and risk.[35]

Though objectives are clearly on the ends side of the ends-means equation, then, objective setting takes place at the intersection of power and interests, the place where strategy becomes the art of the possible. Here the strategist must decide which interests can be advanced and which threats to interests can be countered, *given the power at the state's command*.[36] Like most strategic relationships, the one between objectives and perceptions of national power is interdependent: Each one has simultaneous influence on the other. On the one hand, the goals a government sets in foreign affairs determine its requirements for resources, since meaningful objectives must be backed by the tools necessary to achieve them. On the other hand, it makes no sense for a government to set goals unless it believes that it has or can develop the power their accomplishment requires. As a result,

---

[35] See Chapter 8, Steps 6 and 7.

[36] Arnold Wolfers suggested three categories of goals: those of *self-extension, self-preservation,* and *self-abnegation,* according to whether a state is a revisionist, status quo, or self-sacrificing power. Wolfers' categorization scheme is interesting because it reflects the amount of power or energy behind the goal in question, thereby making the all-important connection between objectives and resources. Organski captures a similar characteristic by distinguishing between *competitive* and *absolute* goals, the former achievable only by comparison with other states and therefore (in Wolfers' terms) self-extending rather than self-preserving in nature. Wolfers, "The Pole of Power and the Pole of Indifference," *World Politics* 4 (1951): 39–63, reprinted in James N. Rosenau, *International Politics and Foreign Policy* (New York: Free Press/MacMillan, 1969), pp. 177–178.

DESIRABILITY, DETERMINED BY REFERENCE TO:
- One's View of the National Interest
  (Chapter 4)
- Power and Resource Requirements
  (Chapter 5)

FEASIBILITY, DETERMINED BY REFERENCE TO:
- Availability of Instruments of Statecraft
  (Chapter 6)
- Assumed Characteristics of the Domestic
  and International Contexts
  (Chapters 2 and 3)

Figure 7.10: Characteristics of foreign policy objectives.

resource availability may influence or even determine a state's choice of international political goals. Not only are government demands for resources adjusted to match goals, but goals too are often adjusted to match resources available to governments.[37]

The first rule governing the logical relationship between ends and means, then, is that objectives cannot be set without an eye to instruments, to actual, mobilized power. This is so for two reasons. First, the *availability* of mobilized power is critical to the *feasibility* of the strategists' designs; obviously, if the wherewithal is not there, the objective will not be achieved and should not be adopted. But second and equally important, the *amount* of resources required is vitally important to the *desirability* of strategic goals; if an objective is too expensive the strategist probably will not want to do it, even if the needed power is available.[38] *How much* power will be needed will of course depend, not only on the nature of the objectives themselves, but also on the threats, constraints, and opportunities that the strategist has identified in the domestic and international systems. As noted in Figure 7.10, therefore, sound foreign affairs strategy must set goals that are *desirable* (in the sense both of serving the national interest and of being worth their expense) as well as *feasible* (that is, backed by sufficient power to have a reasonable chance of success, given the domestic

[37] Donald J. Puchala, *International Politics Today* (New York: Dodd, Mead, 1971), p. 185. Italics in original.

[38] This is the criterion of *worth*, and it reminds the strategist that goals' desirability cannot be established solely on the basis of their support of the national interest; they must also be worth the needed resources. At the very least, obviously, the value of the resources required to accomplish an objective should never exceed the value of the objective itself. See Chapter 8, Step 6, on Costs.

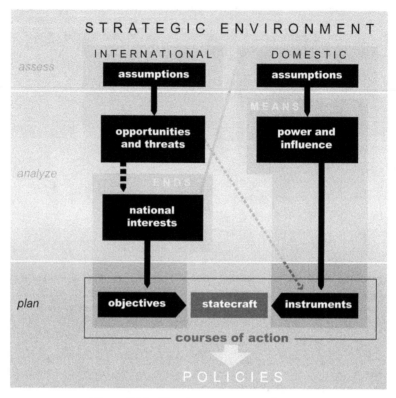

Figure 7.11: Objectives in strategic logic.

and international context).[39] Objective setting thus engages virtually every one of the central concepts in strategic logic: interests, opportunities and threats, power and influence (along with the instruments that make it effective), and the domestic and international environment (see Figure 7.11).

Given these considerations, objectives, earlier defined simply as actionable interests, can be more precisely defined as *the subset of interests that the strategist has the power to do something about – to promote or protect – at acceptable cost and risk and with a reasonable chance of success.*[40] Setting such objectives is a daunting challenge for governments, not only because of its sheer intellectual difficulty, but also because of the many uncertainties involved in assessing power and in coming to grips with the domestic and international circumstances in which it will be applied. Still, the strategist can be helped by understanding the logic sketched above,

---

[39] That objective setting engages all the other concepts in strategic logic is illustrated in Figure 7.10 via the inclusion of chapter numbers for each desiderata. The point is that objective setting simply cannot be done without being clear about all the other concepts.

[40] Success, cost and risk are discussed at length in Chapter 8 under strategy formulation Steps 5, 6 and 7.

because applying these standards results in a successively narrower and narrower window for adoptable goals to squeeze through.

The American involvement in Vietnam is as good an example as any to show how the analysis outlined in Figure 7.10 works and what can happen if it is not done carefully and continuously. Although the Johnson administration's declared purposes in Vietnam varied over time, the practical objective of American involvement was always to prevent Communist North Vietnam from forcibly taking over South Vietnam. It is relatively easy to agree that this goal met the first test of desirability, namely, that it was in accord with the United States' national interest. Even decades later there is little doubt that the projection of American values was set back by the fall of South Vietnam in 1975, and those who believed in the domino theory – that the bipolar balance of power was in unstable equilibrium – could also make a case that keeping South Vietnam out of the Soviet orbit, even if only for a decade, was important to American physical security down the road.

But if one then asks whether the South's defense was feasible, an affirmative answer becomes more difficult. The first test here is whether sufficient resources could have been made available by the American political system in the circumstances of the developing public opposition to the war, a judgment that depends upon one's assumptions about the *domestic* context. The second important test of feasibility is the many constraints on American action that were inherent in the *international* context: the North's superior morale and determination as it fought on home turf (while the United States was at best fighting a secondary war on the theory that it might prevent a bigger one), the North's nearby sources of supply (while the United States had to fight half way around the world), and the fear that China might intervene against the United States as it had during the Korean War.

Obviously these considerations made the objective of defending South Vietnam far more problematical. But even if the strategist can agree that the goal was feasible as well as in accord with the national interest, there is still the second test of desirability: whether preserving the South was worth the resources it consumed. And here one must add up not only hundreds of billions of dollars and over fifty thousand American lives, but also the social disruption at home, the damage to the nation's financial soundness, the loss of a decade of military modernization, the injury to the nation's prestige abroad, and the opportunity cost of all the other foreign policy goals that were not achieved because of the ongoing struggle in Southeast Asia. It was this third test that the war finally failed to pass in the court of public opinion and the reason that the American political system finally brought U.S. involvement to an end.

The first rule, then, concerning the relationship between ends and means in foreign affairs strategy is that objectives can only be set after the strategist has made the best possible estimate of the amount and kinds of mobilized power – the instruments of statecraft – needed to accomplish them; only after this is done can a determination be made as to whether they are feasible or even desirable. The second rule, ironically, is a warning against the first. It is that the strategist must not fall into the trap of letting resources *determine* objectives, for that would be to commit the most elemental sin of strategic logic: allowing means to determine ends rather than the other way around. In particular, if lack of power may make it impossible to do something important and inadvisable to try, the mere availability of resources should never persuade the strategist to set goals that are otherwise unnecessary or undesirable. Thus, even though the George W. Bush administration had the power to topple Saddam Hussein in 2003, the goal appears in retrospect to have been both unnecessary (given Iraq's lack of WMD or support for terrorist attacks on the United States) and undesirable (on grounds of its great expense, both in resources consumed and in its opportunity cost of energies diverted from the assault on Al Qaeda). This warning is similar to the one noted in Chapter 4 regarding the relationship of interests and threats. Threats bring interests to the attention of statesmen and help establish their priority, but must never be allowed to *create* interests; hence the proper relationship between interests and threats is one of mutual interdependence, but also one of clear predominance by interests. Similarly, the role of power in objective setting is critical, but it must be kept subordinate to the requirement that objectives first serve the national interest.

Unfortunately, this is often not what happens. Anyone experienced in bureaucratic politics knows how often budgetary considerations seem to drive out substantive reasoning. Disturbing evidence that this mechanism operates at the highest level of strategy was provided by historian John Lewis Gaddis, who concluded that the most profound influence on the different strategies of containment fielded by Washington during the Cold War was change not in perceptions of the threat posed by Moscow or in the values administrations brought to determining the U.S. national interest but in their perceptions of national power.[41] If administrations believed that the means available to them were expandable, either through the application of Keynesian economics (in the late Truman and Johnson administrations) or via the Laffer curve of supply side economics (in the Reagan and George W. Bush years), they tended to adopt *symmetrical* strategies – that is, strategies which required that the United States be able to meet each adversary capability with an equal or superior American capability. Such strategies required massive expenditures on a wide range of policy instruments in an effort to be ready to meet every plausible threat on its own level.

---

[41] John Lewis Gaddis, *Strategies of Containment* (New York: Oxford University Press, 1982), p. 355. Gaddis also noted that means-expansive administrations tended to define American interests more broadly and therefore to see more threats as critical, while means-limited administrations tended to define interests more narrowly and to consider a smaller range of threats as dangerous. Post-1980 examples in this paragraph were added by present author.

Officials who considered means to be limited (like those in the Eisenhower or Nixon administrations), on the other hand, searched hard for *asymmetrical* strategic formulas, ways of dealing with perceived threats that pitted the country's natural advantages and strengths against the adversary's weaknesses and therefore demanded fewer resources.

In fact, the relationship between means and ends in foreign affairs strategy is often eccentric, with the expansiveness of objectives swinging far more dramatically than actual power shifts would seem to allow or require. The reason is that statesmen living through good or bad times cannot tell how profound or long-lasting their experiences will eventually prove to be. Denied the benefits of hindsight, they are more impressed than they should be with current trends and react accordingly, allowing real interests to go unsupported in times when power appears to be shrinking, then broadening goals beyond what the nation's interests would justify in times when power seems to be expanding.[42] For example, although the economic downturn known as the Great Depression appears in the great sweep of the twentieth century to have been a mere interruption in the steady expansion of American wealth, at the time many feared it had exposed fatal flaws in market-based economic systems. Operating under its influence, President Franklin D. Roosevelt has been criticized by some historians for underestimating what the United States could do to resist the spread of armed aggression in the world of the 1930s and to prevent a second world war. At the other extreme, the high real growth rates of the 1960s produced in Lyndon Johnson what Senator J. William Fulbright (R-Ark.) famously called an arrogance of power, leading to the belief that it would be possible to preserve his Great Society at home while simultaneously undertaking expensive operations like the war in Vietnam abroad. As Johnson put it, "We are the richest nation in the history of the world. We can afford to spend whatever is needed to keep this country safe and to keep our freedom secure. And we shall do just that."[43] In the end, Johnson's overestimation of American power led to the morass of Vietnam, the end of his presidency, and the most severe single setback to American power in the postwar era, outcomes as damaging to the country's real interests as FDR's earlier restraint.

If too strong a reaction to trends in the nation's power cause defective strategies, a keen sense of resource limitations is usually good for strategy.

---

[42] Historian Melvin Leffler argues that *threat* causes "the mobilization of power; power, then, tempts the government to overreach far beyond what careful calculations of interest might dictate." "9/11 and American Foreign Policy," *Diplomatic History* 29 (June 2005): 395–96. My argument (following Gaddis) is that the process often begins, not with real threats, but with expansive *perceptions* of power which lead to larger perceptions of interests, and a broader sense of interests naturally generates more threats. Countering perceived threats to perceived interests then seems to make necessary the objectives that ample power makes possible.

[43] Remarks at the Pentagon, July 21, 1964. *Public Papers of the President: Lyndon B. Johnson* (1964), p. 875. Cited in Gaddis, *Strategies of Containment*, p. 205.

Facing a world of threats and with lots of attractive interests to promote, it is natural that statesmen feel hard pressed to do what seems even minimally required. The contrary sense that power is ample or expandable often leads to a sense that close attention need not be paid to strategic logic and hence to a relaxation of the discipline sound strategy needs to hold it together. Like Lyndon Johnson, for example, Ronald Reagan believed that defense was one area where budgetary constraints must not apply, that the nation had to spend whatever was needed. The result, as noted earlier, was a spending binge on military instruments of statecraft that seriously (if temporarily) weakened the country's potential power.[44] Similarly, the administration of George W. Bush operated under the assumption that the American economy could sustain massive increases in spending on multiple wars against "terrorists and tyrants" along with deep structural tax cuts, and it presided over increases in the annual federal budget deficit greater than any in the post–World War II era, as described in Chapter 5.[45] The result was a high-cost strategy that added the dangers of economic disaster to those of terrorist attack.[46] History thus indicates that, uncomfortable though it may be, the discipline of limited power helps strategists set achievable objectives and spend whatever resources are available wisely.

2. MEANS: Choose *Instruments* to Accomplish Objectives

These broad considerations regarding the proper influence of means on choosing ends form the backdrop for the next step in strategy formulation: choosing instruments that seem likely to achieve one's objectives (see Figure 7.12). The choice will turn, of course, on how the various instruments' characteristics fit the strategist's objectives and situation.[47] Unlike potential power, it will be remembered, instruments are usable only for some objectives; and as noted above, objectives are only potential goals until suitable instruments are found. In fact, so close is the relationship

---

[44] In his memoirs, Reagan says that whenever during the campaign he expressed the view that, if a choice had to be made between deficits and national security he would choose security, "the audience roared" its approval. Ronald Reagan, *An American Life* (New York: Simon and Schuster, 1990), p. 235. His OMB director relates that Reagan repeatedly said that defense was not a budget issue: "'You spend what you need.'" David A. Stockman, *The Triumph of Politics* (New York: Avon Books, 1986), p. 307.

[45] George W. Bush, cover letter to *The National Security Strategy of the United States of America*, September 2002. Jonathan Weisman, "Deficit is $521 Billion In Bush Budget," *Washington Post* (February 2, 2004): A1, A10.

[46] For example, see Niall Ferguson and Laurence J. Kotlikoff, "Going Critical: American Power and the Consequences of Fiscal Overstretch," *National Interest* 73 (Fall 2003): 22–32, and James Fallows, "Countdown to a Meltdown," *Atlantic Monthly* 296 (July/August 2005): 51–54, 56–58, 60–64.

[47] The variety here is so extraordinary that little can be said in advance to help direct the choice beyond the strengths and weaknesses of the instruments surveyed in Chapter 6. Everything will be situation- and objective-specific, so only the broad parameters of choice are discussed in what follows.

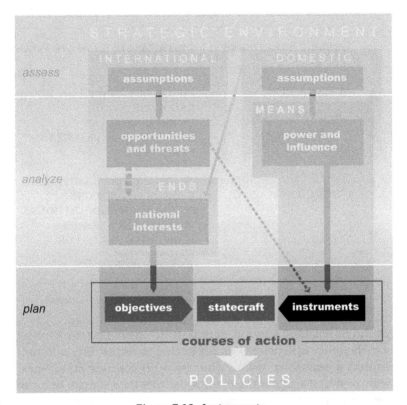

Figure 7.12: Instruments.

between ends and means that the very nature of a goal itself will remain unclear until the instruments to be used in its pursuit (and the *ways* they are to be used – Step 3) are specified. It is virtually impossible, for example, to know what is meant by the objective of spreading democracy overseas unless one knows whether it is to be done by information programs, technical assistance, or sending in the Marines. Similarly, a decision as to whether to adopt a goal of regime change might well turn on whether the means to be employed are multilateral diplomacy and diplomatic pressure, economic sanctions and military containment, covert action and special military operations, or full-scale invasion. In these and most other cases, the nature of the means used is so critical to the course of action being proposed that one can hardly define objectives without also specifying instruments.

To a large extent, the kinds of instruments selected will depend upon whether the generic strategy being pursued is persuasive, co-optive, or coercive. Indeed, the policy instruments discussed in Chapter 6 may seem at first glance to fit naturally into one of the generic strategies sketched above. Public diplomacy, for example, seems obviously persuasive, as does international law and organization (if one thinks of these instruments as

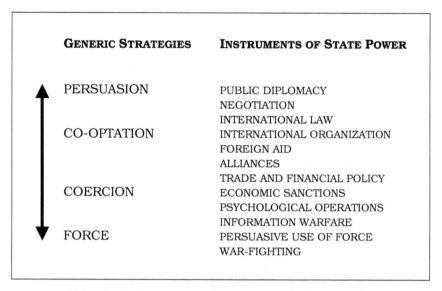

GENERIC STRATEGIES	INSTRUMENTS OF STATE POWER
PERSUASION	PUBLIC DIPLOMACY
	NEGOTIATION
	INTERNATIONAL LAW
CO-OPTATION	INTERNATIONAL ORGANIZATION
	FOREIGN AID
	ALLIANCES
	TRADE AND FINANCIAL POLICY
COERCION	ECONOMIC SANCTIONS
	PSYCHOLOGICAL OPERATIONS
	INFORMATION WARFARE
FORCE	PERSUASIVE USE OF FORCE
	WAR-FIGHTING

Figure 7.13: Generic strategies and associated instruments.

legal and multilateral forms of persuasion). Negotiation can certainly use any of the other instruments as bargaining elements, but is in itself also essentially a persuasive tool. By contrast, other instruments are inherently positive or negative in nature, *in the sense that their use can be expected to leave recipients better or worse off than before*. Thus, offering foreign assistance is positive but imposing economic sanctions, using military coercion and fighting wars are negative. While some instruments (like trade policy or financial manipulation) can be either, then, the inherently positive or negative character of most indicates that their typical use is for co-optive or coercive purposes.[48] As a result, they lend themselves to a particular position along the spectrum, as indicated in Figure 7.13.

It is important to remember, however, that these are only the typical uses of these instruments. In reality, any of them can support any of the generic strategies. The reason is that their co-optive or coercive character depends not on whether T will be *objectively* better or worse off than before their use but on T's *perceptions* of how they are being used by I, and that depends in turn on T's expectations in its relationship with I and how I's actions affect the interests T values. Since the game is all about influencing T, in other words, what matters is how T sees the instruments' use; and in

[48] In his *Economic Statecraft* (Princeton, NJ: Princeton University Press, 1985), pp. 40–41, Baldwin lists economic tools as positive and negative, despite his insistence that any instrument can be used in either a cooperative or coercive manner. To some extent, these positive and negative characteristics are semantic artifacts, the result of how narrowly we choose to define instruments. As noted in Chapter 6, for example, trade policy can be split into more specific actions that are positive or negative in character.

some circumstances the use of a positive instrument can be seen (and/or be meant to be seen) as coercive, or a negative instrument as co-optive. For example, the gradual lifting of U.S. economic sanctions against Libya during 2004–2006 as it abandoned efforts to build weapons of mass destruction might have been viewed as coercive by the Libyans if they expected a more rapid end to their international isolation.[49] Or the use of targeted, partial sanctions might be seen as accommodating by T if I was being strongly pushed by its domestic public opinion to impose a complete trade cutoff. As these examples demonstrate, therefore, the whole relationship between I and T rather than the positive or negative nature of the instruments being used will determine whether the strategy is a co-optive or coercive one.

Regardless of their overall strategy, it seems obvious that statesmen can only apply the instruments at hand. Certainly harried decision makers will want to avoid spending precious time and energy debating the use of tools that are not available, as Richard Nixon did when he enthusiastically reviewed the qualifications of former New York governor and presidential candidate Tom Dewey to be the first secret U.S. envoy to China. "Unfortunately," Kissinger dryly notes in his memoirs, "Dewey was no longer available, having died a few months previously."[50] But determining availability is a surprisingly complex undertaking, requiring the answers to several difficult questions.

The first necessity is to determine which instruments exist. Because of the time needed to create most tools of statecraft, decision makers often have only those left behind by their predecessors.[51] This point is obvious when it comes to specific military instruments, public diplomacy assets, or adequate foreign aid dollars. But even instruments that exist outside the state (like international law and organizations) will have been strengthened or weakened by the actions of prior administrations; and while negotiations are always an available tool, success in diplomacy requires resources like skilled personnel and a creditable reputation. Moreover, some instruments "exist" only for some situations. The U.S. war against the Taliban in Afghanistan, for example, could be begun soon after the 9/11 attacks only because the CIA already had working relationships in the area; the prior efforts of the Clinton administration against Osama bin Laden were essential in creating the instruments that made the CIA director's presentation of a covert campaign plan to President Bush so

[49] Robin Wright, "U.S. Opens Libya Interest Section, Plans Other Steps," *Washington Post* (February 11, 2004): A26; Glenn Kessler, "U.S. Restores Full Diplomatic Ties With Libya," *Washington Post* (May 16, 2006): A1, A14.

[50] Henry Kissinger, *White House Years* (Boston, MA: Little, Brown, & Co., 1979), p. 715.

[51] Whether time allows the creation of new tools of statecraft is one of the distinctions to be made between the short- and long-term. See discussion in Chapter 8, Step 8, Coherence.

persuasive.[52] Similarly, economic levers may exist for a given objective only if preexisting trade and monetary flows support them.

Moreover, as this last example suggests, some instruments must already be in use in order to "exist" for certain strategic purposes. Thus, foreign aid must already be flowing in order to be cut off, economic sanctions must already be in place to be lifted, military attacks must be under way to be stopped. Ending the use of already-employed instruments may be a powerful part of an influence attempt, but the requirement that they already *be* in use obviously limits the opportunities for terminating or withdrawing them. For that reason decisions on instruments' employment may quite rationally be based at least partly on preserving such options for the future, as when foreign aid is continued after a revolution in an attempt to "preserve influence" with the new regime.

A given instrument or set of instruments, of course, can usually be used only in one place and time. This limitation particularly applies to military assets and foreign aid dollars, but it also may apply to public diplomacy in some circumstances. This tool can be used to deliver multiple messages to the same audience, but only if the messages are compatible; in addition, the delivery even of information is subject to physical limitations like transmitter time in radio broadcasting.[53] Certainly all experienced human resources can be used only in one time and place, as became evident at the end of the Cold War when cuts in the State Department budget coincided with the need to open embassies in formerly Soviet countries. Often, therefore, a decision to do one thing may necessitate a decision to stop doing something else, simply because (at least in the short run) there is only one set of means to cover all ends.[54]

Finally, the strategist needs to ask whether the decision maker really can command the tools in question, along at least two dimensions.[55] The first stems from the fact that the instruments of statecraft are scattered among the various departments and agencies of government: negotiation with the Department of State, military tools with the Department of Defense, foreign aid with the Agency for International Development, trade policy with United States Trade Representative and the Commerce department, monetary policy with Treasury, paramilitary assets with the CIA, and so forth. Although one might assume that the president can control the use of these tools since he appoints the top officials of the Executive branch departments, everything we know about how the government really works indicates that

---

[52] Bob Woodward and Dan Balz, "At Camp David, Advise and Dissent," *Washington Post* (January 31, 2002): A13.

[53] In the information age public diplomacy finds it difficult to avoid giving the same message to multiple audiences, but this is more often a liability than an asset.

[54] This unfortunate fact is only one manifestation of the broader concept of opportunity cost, treated more fully in Chapter 8.

[55] Both dimensions of command depend on the domestic environment, discussed in Chapter 3.

presidents actually have a very difficult time doing so. In fact, presidential memoirs are suffused with concern about how to control the instruments of state power so that their *strategies* are reflected in official government *policies*.[56] If an objective is controversial, like Nixon's tilt toward Pakistan in the India–Pakistan crisis of 1971 or Reagan's support for the *contras* in Central America during the mid-1980s, agencies can almost be expected to ignore White House direction and field their own statecraft with the tools at their disposal.[57] So the president has to determine whether, for the instruments and the case in question, he can *actually* control the departments and agencies under his nominal command.

The second element of presidential command has to do with legal issues and the wider American society, where cooperation is often needed to use instruments effectively. Although presidents have successfully asserted broad authority to employ military forces without congressional approval (in spite of the Constitution and the War Powers Act), laws must be in place or obtainable to allow the president to use most policy tools in most situations.[58] Furthermore, such laws and the way they are applied must not be too far out of line with public perceptions of what might be called "policy correctness," at least on highly visible issues, lest they be unenforceable. Particularly when it comes to economic instruments, the American traditions of individualism and *laissez faire* economics make it very difficult for government to control the private actions of millions of Americans, even if adequate laws are on the books. Two centuries ago the effort to enforce economic sanctions against popular passions before the War of 1812 led even that icon of democracy, Thomas Jefferson, to ask Congress for draconian measures restricting civil liberties; and in modern times, American longshoremen made unnecessary the imposition of a formal boycott after the 1983 Soviet destruction of a South Korean airliner and its passengers by simply refusing to offload Soviet vessels.[59] Such examples should remind American decision makers that they have to be sure policy actions can be taken and enforced at home before they can hope for effectiveness abroad.

[56] See the discussion of the difference between strategy and policy in Chapter 1.

[57] See Kissinger, *White House Years*, pp. 842–918 on the India-Pakistan war; on Central America in the Reagan years, see Shultz, *Turmoil and Triumph* (New York: Charles Scribner's Sons, 1993), pp. 285–322, 400–428, 783–878, 901–924, and Constantine C. Menges, *Inside the National Security Council* (New York: Simon and Shuster, 1988). The importance of Executive branch support for a president's strategies is discussed in the introduction to Chapter 3.

[58] Flouting them can be politically disastrous, as Reagan found out in what became known as the Iran-contra affair.

[59] Secretary of State George P. Shultz told Moscow to keep its ships out of American ports until passions cooled, warning that the U.S. government could not guarantee their safety. Shultz, *Turmoil and Triumph*, p. 365. On the unenforceability of Jeffersonian sanctions, see Bradford Perkins, *Prologue to War: England and the United States, 1805–1812* (Berkeley, CA: University of California Press, 1961), pp. 158–165.

Assuming the necessary means exist and can be mobilized, it remains essential that strategists be willing to commit resources, and enough resources, to have a reasonable chance of achieving their objectives. The wars ongoing at this writing in Iraq and Afghanistan are obvious cases in point. Despite its enormous costs, the war in Iraq had not at this writing received the numbers of troops or amount of reconstruction funding necessary for success. And although Secretary of State Rice said in 2006 that the United States was "not going to tire" or "leave" Afghanistan, the administration halved reconstruction aid that year to $622 million, while in Helmand, an opium-producing province the size of West Virginia, it had but a hundred soldiers.[60] Although it is always difficult to know how much is enough, grossly under-resourced strategies are unlikely to succeed. The *sine qua non* of sound foreign affairs strategy remains a proper balance between ends and means.

3. STATECRAFT: Specify *Ways* of Using Instruments

In addition to choosing among the available instruments, strategists also must decide *how* they will be employed. Decisions on the *ways* tools are used – on *statecraft* – are as consequential as the choices of tools themselves, for they will go far to determine those instruments' impact on their recipients (see Figure 7.14).

Just as availability limits the tools the strategist can use, the ways instruments can be applied are usually restricted by the organization, equipment, and training of the officials who field them. As Graham Allison pointed out four decades ago in his classic study of the Cuban missile crisis, the standard operating procedures (SOPs) of an organization can severely constrain decision makers' ability to apply instruments in the ways they think would be most effective.[61] Within those constraints, there are several major dimensions involved in deciding how instruments will be used. In no particular order, they have to do with conditionality, secrecy, breadth, number, and order (see Figure 7.15).

Conditionality

First, an instrument can actually *be* used to produce its effect, or a foreign government can be told that the instrument *will* be used unless (or if) it conforms its behavior to the strategist's objectives. In the latter case, the use of the instrument is prospective and conditional, contingent on how T responds to the influence attempt. Thus, depending on the generic strategy being used, instruments can be employed for co-optive purposes either as mere promises or as actual rewards, and coercively as threats or punishments (see Figure 7.16). The use of instruments in

---

[60] "A Geographical Expression in Search of a State," *Economist Special Report on Afghanistan* (July 8, 2006): 23.

[61] Graham T. Allison, "Conceptual Models and the Cuban Missile Crisis," *American Political Science Review* 63 (September 1969): 689–718.

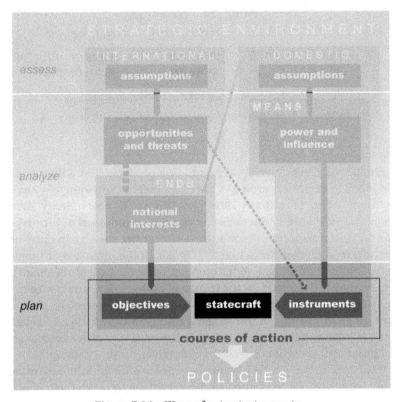

Figure 7.14: Ways of using instruments.

these ways will be seen quite differently from T's point of view (assuming T is the recipient of the instrument's impact), as shown in Figure 7.17. Thus, threats will generate dangers for T, punishments will impose costs on T, promises will be seen as opportunities by T, and rewards will be benefits for T.

- **Conditionality:**
  actual vs. prospective
  (ultimata)
- **Secrecy:** overt vs. covert
- **Breadth:** society,
  government, groups,
  individuals
- **Number:** individual or
  multiple
- **Order:** sequencing and timing
  (pre-emption and prevention)

Figure 7.15: Ways of using instruments.

310   Foreign Affairs Strategy

	CO-OPTIVE	COERCIVE
PROSPECTIVE	**PROMISE**	**THREAT**
ACTUAL	**REWARD**	**PUNISHMENT**

Figure 7.16: Bargaining characteristics of policy instruments.

Should statesmen use instruments prospectively first – that is, should one promise before rewarding or threaten before punishing – or are there occasions when immediate, direct application is best? Henry Kissinger wrote that "the stuff of diplomacy is to trade in promises of future performance," and prospective use may be desirable because it can delay or may even avoid altogether the actual application of the promised or threatened instruments.[62] One might, for example, achieve the benefits of alliance with a mere promise to defend, or the results of a battle via a threat without having to fight.[63] But when instruments are employed coercively, prospective use also gives warning to the targeted state, allowing it time to better prepare to withstand the threatened punishment if it is disinclined to change its behavior in accordance with the influencing state's demands.

If they are to exploit the advantages threats offer for influence attempts, foreign affairs strategists must understand how to make them effectively. Stanford's Alexander George has argued that an effective threat must be *potent relative to the demand* the threatening state is making, so that the target's leaders believe they will be worse off if they defy the demand than if they acquiesce.[64] Potency is a product of the *content* of the threat, what the initiator says it will do if its target does not acquiesce, and of the threat's *credibility*, the likelihood that the threatener will actually do it if the target does not acquiesce.[65] And credibility is in turn a function both of the *character* of the threat (including its urgency and the tangible actions the threatener takes to back it up, like demonstrative force) and the *context* in which it is issued (including public and Congressional backing, international support, the historical precedents set by prior threats and their follow through, and the initiating statesman's reputation for making good

[62] *Years of Upheaval* (Boston: Little, Brown, 1982), p. 1160.
[63] As Sun Tzu famously said about military strategy, "To subdue the enemy without fighting is the acme of skill." *The Art of War*, Samuel B. Griffith trans. (London, UK: Oxford University Press, 1971), p. 77.
[64] Demands, of course, are the initiating state's objectives, and making threats is simply a specific way of doing what all influence attempts try to do: changing the perceived costs and benefits of the alternatives T confronts so that it will accede to I's demands. For a discussion of objectives and choice see Chapter 8, Step 5.
[65] Content and credibility correspond to seriousness and likelihood, two characteristics of received threats discussed in Chapter 4.

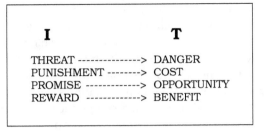

Figure 7.17: Effects of contingent or actual use on targets.

on his threats).[66] For example, the United States' failure to follow through on its threats in the three decades following the Vietnam war may have made it much more difficult for presidents to threaten effectively. Fearing a lack of public support, they may be reluctant to make big threats; but watching U.S. withdrawals from Vietnam, Lebanon, and Somalia, foreign leaders may also require much more potent threats relative to American demands before they will cave. The result could be that the United States has been forced to use outright punishments (and to incur their costs and risks) far more often than might otherwise have been the case.[67]

Similarly, it is likely that American credibility is affected by failure to follow through on promises made during the crisis *du jour* but forgotten when the next crisis comes along, a problem that has bedeviled U.S. post-intervention policy in Panama, Haiti, the former Yugoslavia, and to some extent in Afghanistan. As Kissinger puts it, "a nation that systematically ignores its pledges assumes a heavy burden; its diplomacy will lose the flexibility that comes from a reputation for reliability; it can no longer satisfy immediate pleas from allies by promises of future action."[68] Lacking credibility, decision makers will have actually to deliver rewards to get the job done, increasing costs and moving them up front. As George Shultz put it:

> A reputation for reliability becomes, then, a major asset – giving friends a sense of security and adversaries a sense of caution. A reputation for living up to our commitments can in fact make it less likely that pledges of support will have to be carried out.[69]

When they are tempted to use instruments conditionally, therefore, decision makers in a democracy must be sure they will really be ready and able to apply them if their promises are called due or their threats fail.[70]

---

[66] This model of threat potency is taken from Barry M. Blechman and Tamara Cofman Wittes, "Defining Moment: The Threat and Use of Force in American Foreign Policy," *Political Science Quarterly* 114 (Spring 1999): 6–11.

[67] For example, in the 1991 Gulf War, in Haiti, and in the former Yugoslavia. Blechman and Wittes, "Defining Moment," pp. 5, 26–28.

[68] Kissinger, *White House Years*, p. 895.

[69] George P. Shultz, "Power and Diplomacy in the 1980s," Address before the Trilateral Commission, Washington, D.C., April 3, 1984.

[70] The late Clinton and early Bush administrations both faced this problem with regard to regime change in Iraq, a goal they embraced ever more publicly while

Ultimata are a special case of prospective application in coercive strategies. The point of an ultimatum is to add a sense of urgency to the influencing state's demands that will help persuade decision makers in the targeted state to comply.[71] But ultimata may also intensify an impression of bluff if the attached punishment is not credible, may make the target less willing to comply by adding an element of humiliation to its yielding to demands, or may result in partial or qualified compliance that puts the initiating state in an extremely awkward position (since the very nature of ultimata rarely leaves states issuing them any ambiguity within which to maneuver).[72] On the other hand, ultimata can be used without any expectation of the targeted state yielding, simply to make clear to third parties that all nonforceful alternatives have been exhausted. As early as the morning of September 12, 2001, President Bush decided to deliver an ultimatum to the Taliban with demands that he specified in his speech to Congress on September 20 and repeated in his war message of October 7: "Close terrorist training camps. Hand over leaders of the al Qaeda network, and return all foreign nationals, including American citizens unjustly detained in your country."[73] The administration also delivered an ultimatum to Pakistan containing seven specific demands for cooperation.[74] Interestingly, the two ultimata were delivered with opposite expectations of success, both of which proved accurate.

Secrecy

When actually used, instruments may be overt or covert; that is, employed in ways that either are or are not attributable to the initiating government.[75] Covert action was defined in the National Security Act of 1947 as "an activity or activities of the United States Government to influence political, economic, or military conditions abroad, where it is intended that the role of the United States Government will not be apparent or

apparently lacking (or being unwilling to embrace) the means to give it effect – at least until 2002. Walter Pincus and Karen DeYoung, "Anti-Iraq Rhetoric Outpaces Reality," *Washington Post* (February 24, 2002): A1, A18.

[71] Craig and George argue that a "full-blown ultimatum has three components: a specific, clear demand on the opponent; a time limit for compliance; and a threat of punishment for noncompliance which is both credible and sufficiently potent. ... " The first element being essential to any influence attempt, and the last being essential to any workable threat, we are left with the middle requirement as the defining characteristic of an ultimatum. Gordon R. Craig and Alexander L. George, *Force and Statecraft*, p. 197.

[72] These are among the possible outcomes considered by an NSC group in 1990 before the Gulf War. Alexander L. George, *Bridging the Gap* (Washington, DC: U.S. Institute of Peace Press, 1993), pp. 80–81.

[73] Bob Woodward and Dan Balz, "'We Will Rally the World,'" *Washington Post* (January 28, 2002), p. A10; Bush's Address to the Nation, *Washington Post* (October 8, 2001): A6.

[74] Woodward and Balz, "We Will Rally the World,'" p. A11.

[75] The effects of covert action are visible; clandestine is the term given to actions whose effects as well as sponsorship are hidden.

acknowledged publicly."[76] Such activity is so distinctive in its characteristics that it is often discussed as an instrument in itself, but as the law indicates, it actually encompasses the hidden forms of all four categories of instruments noted in Chapter 6: political, informational, economic, and military. *Political* actions intervene directly in the political process of a target country by funneling money or equipment to political parties, supporting or disrupting political rallies, manipulating local political actors, or using an agent of influence to directly affect a government's decisions. *Information* actions can involve planting truth or lies in the target country's press on any subject from local political activity to prominent individuals' private lives, or it might consist of supplying false or misleading information directly to key actors.[77] *Economic* action means interference with commercial or economic activities, for example by scrambling bank records, surreptitiously destroying crops, or introducing counterfeit currency. *Military* action runs all the way from hostage rescue, sabotage, assassination of key political figures, or a coup d'etat to paramilitary operations that train and equip large armed groups or insurgencies.

Covert action has advantages that have commended it to leaders virtually since government began. First, some things just cannot be done openly, either because the target government will not allow them or because the initiating government is entirely denied access to the target's territory or people. Second, some actions that *could* be done openly would not be effective if their sponsorship were known – for example, foreign aid to political parties might discredit them in the eyes of the electorate they need to attract.[78] Third, some things done openly that *would* be effective might invite devastating retaliation with which the initiating state could not deal. Arguably, in fact, there are only two kinds of situations in which instruments should be used covertly: those in which effectiveness would be fatally compromised, or in which risks would greatly increase, if the instrument's initiator were known.[79] But covert action can also appeal to strategists because it does not require building the kind of domestic support that a public policy demands and because it is often much cheaper than the overt use of instruments. These characteristics take advantage of secrecy to allow a lessening of the resistance all strategies face both at home and abroad.

---

[76] PL 80–253, Sec. 503(e).

[77] Whether true or false, propaganda can be white (correctly attributed), grey (unattributed), or black (falsely attributed).

[78] This may be the reason that USAID chose not to reveal its $2 million program to support Fatah in the January 2006 Palestinian parliamentary elections. Scott Wilson and Glenn Kessler, "U.S. Funds Enter Fray In Palestinian Election: Bush Administration Uses USAID as Invisible Conduit," *Washington Post* (January 22, 2006): A1, A20.

[79] Bruce Berkowitz and Allan Goodman, "The Logic of Covert Action," *National Interest* 51 (Spring 1998): 38–46. Of course, this is close to saying that instruments should be used covertly only when that would increase benefits or reduce costs, criteria that presumably should apply to all ways of using instruments. See Steps 6 and 7 in Chapter 8.

However, these last comments also point to the disadvantages covert action carries, particularly in a democracy. Its anonymous nature may convince decision makers that they can act unaccountably, tempting them to do things they might not otherwise try and take risks they would otherwise shun. At the same time, its secrecy sharply limits participation by knowledgeable staff and debate as to the wisdom of proposed actions within and outside government, greatly increasing the possibility of poor strategic thinking or simple miscalculation. It seems highly unlikely, for example, that the Rube Goldberg nature of Jimmy Carter's Iran hostage rescue mission could have survived wider intergovernmental staffing, or that Oliver North could have connected Iran policy and the Nicaraguan *contras* – the two most controversial issues in Reagan's foreign policy – with an illegal funds transfer had it been proposed in public. In addition to the likelihood of spawning bad strategy destined for failure, covert action also risks "blowback" – the possibility that the initiator's own personnel will also be deceived by the secret policy, with disastrous results. And if failure comes and hidden sponsorship is exposed its costs are likely to be much worse, both for the initiator and overseas collaborators, than would a policy that was overt from the outset.[80]

Still, covert action is a way of using instruments that is unlikely to be eliminated, and the disadvantages sketched above suggest some guidelines for effective use. First, strategists contemplating covert action need to consider carefully whether a balance can indeed be struck between maintaining secrecy, on the one hand, and involving enough people to design a course of action with a reasonable chance of success, on the other. Internal dissent, either among agencies in Washington or between them and field operatives, is particularly difficult to resolve and especially damaging in covert enterprises. Second, decision makers must be careful lest they be tempted to hide an instrument's use for domestic political reasons, such as avoiding congressional opposition or a public debate, remembering that the need for public and congressional support discussed in Chapter 3 does not disappear simply because statecraft is hidden. Third, covert use of instruments needs to be in accord with any overt policy on the issue rather than in opposition to it, as was the case when the Reagan NSC staff covertly delivered arms to Iran while the rest of the U.S. government was engaged in Operation Staunch, lobbying other governments to embargo arms shipments to Tehran.[81] Indeed, using instruments covertly does not exempt them from the rule that instruments work best together, and tools used covertly often work best in tandem with those used overtly. Fourth, covert

[80] Again, the 2006 USAID covert aid to Fatah stands as an example: its revelation in the last days before the vote probably contributed to the unexpected victory of Hamas, whose campaign slogan was "America and Israel say no to Hamas...What do you say?"
[81] Shultz, *Turmoil and Triumph*, pp. 237, 785.

action should be used early, not as a desperate last resort when overt policy is failing, as the Nixon administration discovered while attempting to head off the election of Salvador Allende as president of Chile; secrecy and nonattribution are not quick fixes or magic bullets.[82] At a minimum, covert instruments, like overt ones, need infrastructure in place to have a chance of success, and it is not often that an initiating country has preexisting exploitable assets at a meaningful level within a target country's executive, legislature, political parties, labor unions, religious groups, armed forces, internal security organizations, or émigré and dissident groups. These guidelines can be simply summarized by noting that covert action must be part of a well-considered strategy, not a substitute for it.

Breadth

Whether covert or overt, instruments may be so designed that the direct recipient of their impact is either another state's *government* or its *society*, especially its influential public (including nonstate actors). As discussed in Chapter 6, among political instruments this characteristic is so important that it gives rise to a separate tool called public diplomacy, whose purpose is to affect the public and elite opinion of a foreign society in ways that will facilitate changes in its government's policies. In addition, many economic instruments work by having effects on the target state's economy and people, to which (it is hoped) the government will respond. But economic sanctions can be directed more narrowly, at a particular industry or even individual companies (as in the case of U.S. nonproliferation sanctions against certain Chinese corporations), or at governmental leaders (as the Bush administration applied in the March 2002 Zimbabwean elections) – the latter often called "smart sanctions." Indeed, one sanctions study distinguishes five "sites of influence" for this economic instrument: elite decision makers, government structures that need resources, the economy (meaning businesses and the general population), civil society, and third parties outside the state.[83]

As these examples show, this third way of using instruments is basically a question of how broadly or narrowly the instrument is applied. Military action, for example, could mean a war against a country's armed forces, a coup against its government, or an assassination of an individual leader. During the 1999 Kosovo War, air attacks were directed not only against Serbian war-making potential but against the economic assets of the dictator's family and cronies.[84] A presumption in favor of the narrower, governmental targeting of instruments would seem to be indicated by at least two considerations. First, for coercive instruments it is in conformity

---

[82] Kissinger, *White House Years*, pp. 658–678.

[83] Neta C. Crawford and Audie Klotz, "How Sanctions Work: A Framework for Analysis," Chapter 2 in *How Sanctions Work: Lessons from South Africa* (New York: St. Martin's Press, 1999), p. 31.

[84] David Halberstam, *War in a Time of Peace* (New York: Scribner, 2001), p. 474.

with the laws of war to avoid hurting civilians (although doing so may well be necessary to achieve one's objectives). Thus, the collateral damage caused by broad sanctions (and its corrosive effect on the coalition applying them) has often caused American statesmen to move from broad to narrow application.[85] Second, directing instruments against the public of a foreign country lengthens the transmission link, putting one more step between initiation and success – the step of the societal impact influencing the government.

Number

Fourth among ways, the strategist must decide how *many* instruments are to be used. One keen practitioner summed it up by saying that two requirements must be met when using instruments: first, "correctly matching the instrument to the problem, the means to the end," and second, "skillfully orchestrating the instruments of national power so that they reinforce each other."[86] In most cases, a combination of instruments will work better than one instrument working alone. Political scientist David Baldwin argues that "any technique of statecraft works poorly in isolation from the others," and Robert Art flatly states that "no single instrument of statecraft is ever sufficient to attain any significant foreign policy objective."[87] In Art's view, the need for multiple instruments arises because any important objective is multifaceted and because (assuming a coercive strategy) the targets of influence attempts will use their strongest instruments to counter the initiating state's strategy, quickly driving the interaction beyond any single tool.

American practice seems to endorse the advantage of multiple instruments. In the 1994 Haiti case, ousting the junta required sanctions, vigorous public diplomacy, use of international organizations, offers of economic aid, intensive negotiations by the Carter/Nunn/Powell team, and a very visible demonstration of the readiness to use military force.[88] The Dayton accords on Bosnia required the actual use of force (aerial bombing of Serb positions), sanctions, multilateral diplomacy, international legal indictments, and skilled bilateral negotiations.[89] Rebuilding Afghanistan and Iraq has required that the United States provide military and police security, massive foreign aid, the lifting of sanctions, trade preferences,

---

[85] This was the pattern in Haiti and Kosovo; Secretary of State Colin Powell was in the process of narrowing sanctions against Iraq to make them more effective when the 9/11 attacks occurred and the Bush administration opted for war instead.

[86] Steven R. Mann, "The Interlocking Trinity," unpublished student paper, National War College, November 5, 1990.

[87] Baldwin, *Economic Statecraft*, p. 143; Robert J. Art, "American Foreign Policy and the Fungibility of Force," *Security Studies* 5 (Summer 1996): 24.

[88] For an analysis of the combination of tools used, see David E. Weekman, "Sanctions: The Invisible Hand of Statecraft," *Strategic Review* 26 (Winter 1998), pp. 39–45.

[89] Susan Rosegrant and Michael D. Watkins, *Getting to Dayton: Negotiating and End to the War in Bosnia*, Kennedy School Case C125-96-1356.0 (Cambridge, MA: President and Fellows of Harvard College, 1966); Richard Holbrooke, *To End a War* (New York: Random House, 1998).

robust public diplomacy, legal assistance, and mobilization of international organizations. In the case of containment during the Cold War, all the instruments were used, from negotiations to trade policy to alliances and proxy warfare, although the emphasis and precise mix varied substantially from administration to administration.[90]

Order

Finally, assuming the use of multiple instruments, strategists must decide on their optimal timing and sequencing. Timing has to do with when to use how much of each instrument. If a tool is to be used *prospectively*, a decision must be made as to whether the maximum promise or threat will be employed at the outset or reserved for later use; if an instrument is to be used *immediately*, the decision will focus on whether to reward or punish gradually or all at once. It is natural in a bargaining situation to want to see how cheaply one's purposes can be accomplished, and like prospective use, gradual application may seem to lower costs and risks. But gradualism also has some of the same disadvantages as prospective use: for example, the gradual application of economic sanctions can give the target state time to adjust to their impact, while gradual escalation of military pressure may simply lessen the surprise and shock of all-out attack while lengthening the conflict and increasing casualties on both sides. In a co-optive strategy, like the Nunn-Lugar Cooperative Threat Reduction Program that seeks to secure nuclear materials in the former USSR, gradual use of aid will lower year-to-year costs and give time for various measures to be tested and prove their worth. But it may also allow threats to persist longer than necessary or opportunities to escape being fully taken advantage of.

Timing issues are particularly contentious with regard to military force, used either for coercive strategies or war. Beneath the ultimatum, political scientist Alexander George identifies two graduated variations of the use of force in coercive diplomacy: the "turning of the screw," in which the target is subject to "an incremental progression of increasingly severe pressure," and the "try-and-see" variant, in which modest threats or demonstrative use are followed, if necessary, by other modest threats or action.[91] The escalation resulting from such actions, of course, may or may not accomplish its purposes short of war. When it comes to using the military in combat, the conventional wisdom is that force should be a last resort because of its cost and risk, used after other instruments have been exhausted. But former Secretary of State George Shultz argues that "[t]he use of force obviously should not be taken lightly, but better to use force when you *should* rather than when you *must; last* means *no other*, and by that time the level of force and the risk involved may have multiplied many times over."[92]

---

[90] Gaddis describes these changes through 7 administrations in *Strategies of Containment*.

[91] George, *Bridging the Gap*, p. 80.

[92] Shultz, *Turmoil and Triumph*, p. 345. Italics in original.

A case also can be made for early or immediate use. Preemption and prevention may be seen as extreme cases of immediate use of instruments,
essentially the opposite of an ultimatum. Here I makes no threat at all
against T but simply undertakes direct use of instruments; the general idea
is to do unto others as they would do unto you, but do it first. As applied to
military instruments, *preemption* generally means attacking first to disrupt
an imminent attack by the other side; it is justified by the law of self-defense
when the threat is so immediate and overwhelming that it leaves no choice
of means and no moment for deliberation.[93] *Preventive* military action is
much more difficult to justify than preemption, as the Bush administration
discovered in the Iraq War of 2003, since by definition it is taken against
a gathering threat, when time pressures are not so great as to prohibit the
use of defensive or nonmilitary means. By putting a premium on the initiation of conflict, military prevention and preemption risk serious third party
and system effects that the strategist must weigh against the peril being
faced.[94] But preventive action of a nonmilitary kind – for example, taking
early diplomatic or economic action to forestall a developing conflict – may
be among the most cost-effective of foreign affairs strategies. The value of
such early action was recognized by Machiavelli, who compared many of
the threats statesmen face with "those hectic fevers, as doctors say, which
at their beginning are easy to cure but difficult to recognize, but in course
of time... become easy to recognize and difficult to cure."[95] Here the problem is usually that of garnering sufficient domestic support to take on the
burdens of acting before the dangers of the developing crisis have become
obvious.

Employing multiple instruments provides the opportunity for using
some prospectively and others immediately, some gradually and others
all at once, reducing the application of some while intensifying others over
time as their impact is assessed – all depending, of course, on the degree
of flexibility each instrument allows. Recent American coercive strategies show a variety of timing and sequencing patterns. In the 1994 Haiti
case, the Clinton administration (after long-standing economic sanctions
and failed multilateral diplomatic efforts) made increasingly explicit public warnings that military action was possible, probable, then imminent,
followed by the actual launching of an invasion to push ongoing bilateral negotiations over the top. Both Bushes followed a similar approach
in the months before launching their wars against Saddam Hussein's Iraq.

---

[93] This is the classic definition of self-defense, by Secretary of State Daniel Webster
in the 1835 *Caroline* case. Herbert W. Briggs, ed., *The Law of Nations*, 2nd ed.
(New York: Appleton-Century-Crofts, Inc., 1966), p. 985. Webster also noted that
the act must involve "nothing unreasonable or excessive; since the act, justified
by the necessity of self-defense, must be limited by the necessity, and kept clearly
within it."

[94] See discussion of risks under Step 7 in Chapter 8.

[95] *The Prince*, p. 39.

Before the 1991 Gulf War, George H. W. Bush deliberately turned the screw on Saddam, declaring the goal ("this will not stand") at the outset, then using diplomatic pressure, economic sanctions, and military deployments followed by an ultimatum in his unsuccessful effort to get the Iraqi dictator to withdraw from Kuwait without a war.[96] Similarly, before the 2003 Iraq War George W. Bush used gradually escalating verbal pressure, including Iraq in an "axis of evil" and warning that the U.S. "will not stand by as peril draws closer and closer," while intensifying air attacks under the Southern and Northern Watch campaigns and orchestrating international pressure (including the reintroduction of arms inspectors) through the United Nations, all against the background of a more than decade-long sanctions regime which it had earlier worked to narrow and tighten.[97] By contrast, the elder Bush followed quite a different approach in Panama in 1989, as had Reagan in Grenada in 1983, avoiding explicit threats of military action in order to achieve maximum surprise when the attack came.

The more instruments there are to be orchestrated, of course, the more complex such decisions about timing and sequencing become. As the cases noted above show, the usual movement in coercive strategies seems to be from prospective to actual use of each instrument, and from softer to harder instruments (e.g., from diplomacy to economic sanctions to military action). One could imagine situations, however, in which some instruments are directly applied while others are threatened or promised, in which some are used all at once and others gradually, or in which negative instruments are followed by positive ones rather than vice versa. Note, however, that this latter shift may be more consequential than mere instrument sequencing. It may really signal a shift of generic strategies from coercion to co-optation, bringing one back full circle to that most basic of strategic choices. Finally, strategists must remember that greater complexity inevitably means greater uncertainty, more opportunities for things to go wrong. As political scientist Richard Betts warns, "complex strategies with close tolerances are riskier than simple ones with few moving parts, and strategies that project far ahead and depend on several phases of interaction are riskier than ones with short time horizons."[98]

---

[96] "[Our goal was] the undoing of Iraq's invasion of Kuwait by the pursuit of a policy of coercive diplomacy against Saddam Hussein. We would begin with diplomatic pressure, then add economic pressure, to a great degree organized through the United Nations, and finally move toward military pressure by gradually increasing American troop strength in the Gulf." James A. Baker III, *The Politics of Diplomacy* (New York: G. P. Putnam's Sons, 1995), p. 277.

[97] State of the Union address, *Washington Post* (January 30, 2002): A16; Alan Sipress, "Powell: No Plans Now For War With 'Axis'," *Washington Post* (February 13, 2002): A20, and "U.S. Options On Iraq Still Undecided," *Washington Post* (February 19, 2002): A1, A8.

[98] Richard K. Betts, "Is Strategy an Illusion?" *International Security* 25 (Fall 2000): 20.

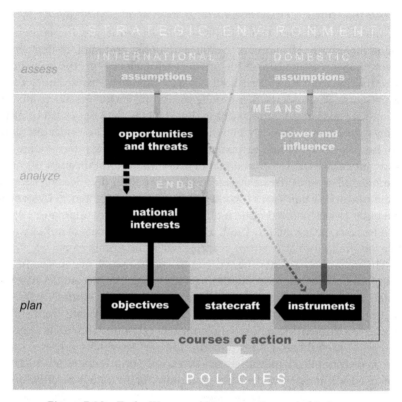

Figure 7.18: Ends, Ways, and Means as Courses of Action.

These first three steps in strategy formulation – which define objectives and link them to particular instruments via detailed statecraft – are
designed to produce strategic courses of action (see Figure 7.18). Just as
each objective in a strategic plan should be explicitly connected with the
interests it serves (and the threats or opportunities it addresses), so each
objective must also have its own instruments and ways of using them specified. At the planning level, in other words, strategists should proceed horizontally, connecting ends (objectives), ways (statecraft), and means (instruments) for *each* objective. The resulting strategy may be a single package,
with complementary courses of action designed in so far as possible to
protect and promote all of the interests at stake in the area the strategy
addresses. Or it may be in the nature of an options paper for an author-
itative decision maker, offering alternative and perhaps even conflicting
courses of action from which he or she will choose. Either way, each objective will meet the first test of desirability in that it serves the national interest, protecting it against a threat or taking advantage of an opportunity to
advance it; and each will also meet the second test of feasibility, since
it is connected to the instruments the strategist deems necessary for its
accomplishment used in the ways most likely to lead to success.

Nevertheless, creating such objective-instrument packages completes only the first three steps toward a finished strategic plan. Next, the strategist must evaluate and will probably refine the courses of action he or she has created. Several questions remain to be asked. How can one be sure that the means and ways chosen will have an *impact* on their recipients? Will that impact be sufficient to offer a fair prospect of *success*, that is, to cause the target of the strategy to do, suffer, or achieve what the initiating state wants so that I can accomplish its objectives? And once these questions are satisfactorily answered, there are still others that await. What will the proposed strategy *cost*? What *risks* does it pose, either of unanticipated costs or failure to achieve its objectives? And how *coherent* is the strategy? If it is an overall foreign affairs strategy, how well do its pieces fit together; and if it is a strategy dealing with a particular issue, country, or region, what effect will an effort to implement it have on other strategies designed to protect or promote other interests? These questions are addressed in Steps 4–8 of the process of strategic planning; exploring them will be the subject of Chapter 8.

8

Evaluating Courses of Action

Selecting objectives, choosing instruments, and fashioning the statecraft that connects them may seem to complete strategic planning, but these tasks really just begin it. For the courses of action created by that initial selection of ends, ways, and means require two kinds of evaluation before they can be finalized. First, strategists must think hard about how and to what degree the *benefits* of their proposed strategy will materialize, about whether their instruments as applied will have an impact that leads to success. These are Steps 4 and 5 in the strategy planning process (see Figure 8.1). Second, strategists must soberly consider the potential *downsides* of the actions they propose, including the costs and risks their proposed courses of action may engender, their compatibility with each other, and their effect on other foreign affairs strategies that serve other important interests. These are the concerns of Steps 6, 7, and 8 in the process.

4. IMPACT: Estimate How Courses of Action (COAs) Will Affect Recipients

How should strategists go about deciding whether their courses of action are likely to work, whether the ways and means chosen *will* in fact accomplish their objectives? First, it is necessary to estimate the proposed instruments' ability to *impact* their recipients – that is, to actually inflict punishment or a powerful fear of it, or to provide rewards or a confident expectation of them. As one experienced American diplomat put it, "The degree to which an opponent feels an injury or inducement applied to it through a capability gauges that capability's *impact*."[1] Impact has a lot to do with I's power – that is, with the strengths and weaknesses of the instruments, discussed in Chapter 6, that the strategist has chosen in Step 2. It also, obviously, has much to do with statecraft, the ways in which the strategist uses those instruments – whether their application is prospective or actual, broad or narrow, overt or covert, individual or multiple, sequential or simultaneous, gradual or all at once – discussed under Step 3.

---

[1] Chas. W. Freeman, Jr., *Arts of Power: Statecraft and Diplomacy* (Washington, DC: U.S. Institute of Peace Press, 1997), p. 19.

1. ENDS: Draw up a preliminary list of <u>objectives</u>.
Check *desirability* against interests.
2. MEANS: Choose <u>instruments</u> to accomplish
objectives.
3. STATECRAFT: Specify <u>ways</u> of using instruments.
Check *feasibility* against power.
4. IMPACT: Estimate how courses of action (COAs)
will affect recipients.
5. SUCCESS: Estimate how targets will react.
6. COST: Evaluate whether the strategy is worth
its cost.
7. RISK: Consider that things may not go as planned.
Re-check *desirability* against cost and risk.
8. COHERENCE: Check internal and external
compatibility of ends, means, and ways; coordinate
and prioritize.

Figure 8.1: Steps in strategy formulation.

If the strengths and weaknesses of instruments are attributes of the initiating state's power, its statecraft dramatically affects the transmission link between I and T, and the integrity of that link is critical to an instrument's impact. As illustrated in Figure 8.2, the transmission link depends not only upon the ways instruments are used but also on the strategic environment within which the influence attempt takes place. All of the assumptions about how the world works discussed in Chapter 2 become relevant here, for they set the parameters within which instruments will have their effects. The impact of an instrument might be quite different, for example, if states bandwagon rather than balance, if nonstate entities are numerous and powerful actors in the international system, or if the mechanisms governing world politics are chaotic or organic rather than Newtonian. Economic instruments will be dramatically affected by the operations of the international economic system, especially the degree to which globalization compromises states' independence. Perhaps the most important environmental consideration is what third parties might do to offset the impact of instruments on a recipient or target, for example, providing support to counter military threats, sending terrorists to disrupt nation-building efforts, or offering economic aid to ameliorate shortages caused by sanctions. Together, these environmental characteristics can be seen as constraints and enablers or even multipliers for the various objective-instrument packages being evaluated, operating to restrict or facilitate their impact.[2]

---

[2] A discussion of multipliers and limitations is provided by Michael N. Schmitt, "Identifying National Objectives and Developing Strategy: A Process Oriented Approach," *Strategic Review* (Winter 1997): 31–32.

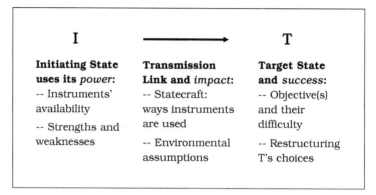

Figure 8.2: Estimating impact.

Assuming the transmission link is solid, strategists also need to study the characteristics of the recipient or target in order to determine which generic strategies and instruments are likely to have an impact. A strategy of pure persuasion, for example, would require a target government that was willing to enter a dialogue in good faith, open to reason, and likely to follow through on commitments made. Governments whose actions seem to violate prior agreements, like Japan in the diplomacy leading to World War II or North Korea and Iran today, can destroy their negotiating abilities by becoming unable to commit themselves believably to the other side.[3] If the strategy is co-optive in nature, one would need a sense that the target state was in a position to benefit from the available inducements, able (for example) to make good use of foreign assistance or trade concessions. If on the other hand one's strategy is coercive, the question becomes whether the tools at hand can inflict real pain on the target state, a question of its vulnerability. Here the precise questions to be asked are instrument-specific. Economic vulnerability will depend on such matters as how autarkic the target state's economy is, how dependent it is on imports or overseas markets. Vulnerability to information efforts will vary with the society's openness and its government's responsiveness to public opinion. Military vulnerability will depend on factors like the state's defensive systems and the quality of the military targets it offers.[4]

By thinking through the strengths and weaknesses of their instruments, the ways they are to be employed, the environment within which they must operate, and the characteristics of their recipients/targets, strategists can

---

[3] On Japan's diplomacy, see Paul W. Schroeder, *The Axis Alliance and Japanese-American Relations, 1941* (Ithaca, NY: Cornell University Press, 1958).

[4] At the opening of the war on terrorism in Afghanistan, for example, American strategists lamented that the state had few targets of value to bomb, rendering much of the United States high-tech standoff weapons systems useless. Bob Woodward and Dan Balz, "'We Will Rally the World'," *Washington Post* (January 28, 2002): A9.

get some sense of the kind of impact they might have. However, as noted earlier, the deployed instruments' impact does not directly lead to the ultimate success of a strategy; impact is a necessary but not sufficient condition for success. For example, sanctions may keep Iran's economy in the doldrums indefinitely, or the West may credibly offer massive economic aid to North Korea, but it is still quite possible (if not likely) that neither state's ruler will give up its nuclear weapons programs. To arrive at some estimation of success, strategists must consider how targets are likely to react to the impact they or other recipients see or feel.

5. SUCCESS: Estimate How Targets Will React

The characteristics of the target are therefore even more important when estimating the probabilities of success than when predicting the degree and likelihood of impact. But in order to construct successful objective-instrument packages, strategists simultaneously need to consider the nature of their objectives.[5] For it is I's objectives that determine the kind of demands it makes and therefore the range of alternatives T will face, and it is T's choice among those alternatives that will determine whether and to what degree I's influence attempt succeeds. Strategists must at this point therefore reconsider their objectives, this time not from the viewpoint of their *own* interests and power, but from that of their *targets'* interests and power.

Perhaps the most important characteristic of objectives to consider when trying to forecast success is how far-reaching, ambitious, and therefore difficult of achievement they are.[6] In this regard, at least three broad kinds of objectives are worth distinguishing. The first is the classic influence attempt, the effort to change a *government's intentions* or ends, its policies or behavior. Quite different are objectives intended to change a *state's capabilities*, its means; these may have a secondary effect of changing governmental policies, but success for such objectives can be said to have been achieved if capabilities alone are affected. (Not surprisingly, these two kinds of objectives correspond to the two components of threats – intentions and capabilities – with which strategies must deal.)[7] Third is the objective of overthrowing another state's government altogether, of *regime change*, not properly thought of as an influence attempt in many cases, since the

---

[5] "The single most important step in capability analysis is establishing who is trying to get whom to do what." David A. Baldwin, *Economic Statecraft* (Princeton, NJ: Princeton University Press, 1985), p. 149.

[6] For example, the most widely cited book on economic sanctions argues that "[t]he success rate importantly depends on the type of policy or governmental change sought." Gary Clyde Hufbauer, Jeffrey J. Schott, and Kimberly Ann Elliott, *Economic Sanctions Reconsidered*, 2nd. ed., Vol. 1 (Washington, DC: Institute for International Economics, 1990), pp. 92–93.

[7] See Chapter 4.

mechanism of changing behavior is to change the actors themselves rather than the intentions of an existing set of actors.[8]

If the objective is to change a target government's behavior – its objectives or the ends of its strategy – then it is critical for decision makers to estimate that government's interests with regard to the change. Difficult though it is to get inside the mindset of other statesmen, the initiating government must somehow come to an accurate view of how strongly the target government values the behavior to be changed, how deeply it is invested in the objectionable policy, and how tenaciously it would resist the new behavior that the influencing state wants it to adopt. Strategists must imagine themselves as leaders of T, using the strategic logic described in this book to divine the *other* side's strategy. For the influence attempt will succeed only if avoiding the desired change is valued less by those leaders than acquiring the benefits offered or ending the pain inflicted by the instruments that the strategist proposes to use.[9] Success, in other words, requires some proportionality "between the scope and nature of the objectives being pursued and the instruments being used in their pursuit."[10]

I's attempts to restructure T's alternatives or force its leaders to revalue them can follow several possible paths as it tries to ensure that "the costs of noncompliance it can impose on, and the benefits of compliance it can offer to, the target state are greater than the benefits of noncompliance and costs of compliance."[11] One is to lower the probability and raise the costs of successful resistance to I's demands; the former can be done by showing T that I is more credible and more highly motivated or that T lacks the ability to resist, the latter by making a bigger or more creditable threat, including of unacceptable escalation. Another path is to raise the probable benefits or lower the costs of acquiescence, by making a bigger or more creditable promise or by being ready to bargain and leaving T a way out of the situation I's strategy has created. Either way, the initiator wants to create a favorable asymmetry of both *motivation* (the strength of purpose or intent) and *capability* (the balance of power), an advantage in both ends and means that is perceived as such by the target state.[12] In the best case,

---

[8]   "Quite obviously, the more ambitious the demand on the opponent, the more difficult the task of coercive diplomacy becomes." Alexander George, "Coercive Diplomacy: Definition and Characteristics," Chapter 1 in George and William E. Simons, *The Limits of Coercive Diplomacy*, 2nd ed. (Boulder, CO: Westview Press, 1994). pp. 8–9. Certainly the same could be said for co-optive or persuasive diplomacy as well.

[9]   "A given sanction will be successful . . . largely depending on the target's ranking of the [relative] value of defiance and the cost of the sanction." Jonathan Kirshner, "The Microfoundations of Economic Sanctions," *Security Studies* 6 (Spring 1997): 34.

[10]   Bruce W. Jentleson and Christopher A. Whytock, "Who 'Won' Libya?", *International Security* 30 (Winter 2005/06): 51.

[11]   Jentleson and Whytock, "Who 'Won' Libya?", p. 51.

[12]   In coercive diplomacy, for example, George argues that I needs to estimate the relative motivation of the two sides: "*Motivation* in this context refers to each side's conception of what it has at stake in the dispute, the importance each side

I wants to make some choices so unattractive to T that they drop off the list of T's options, while making others attractive enough to be added to T's list for serious consideration and evaluation.

Objectives requiring change in another actor's behavior have a wide range of difficulty, from altering a UN General Assembly vote on a minor issue to stopping an ongoing military invasion. One well-established distinction worth noting is that between compellence and deterrence. *Deterrence* is an attempt to head off a feared action by another state, to prevent it from doing something it is not yet doing; whereas *compellence* is an effort to change an actor's ongoing course of action, either to stop something I finds intolerable or make it do something I finds essential.[13] Both the power of inertia and the need of T not to be seen bowing to I's demands should make compelling a state to initiate a new course of action intrinsically more difficult than preventing a change in its ongoing behavior.[14] Cutting a bit more finely, one can hypothesize at least five gradations of difficulty in intent or behavior-changing objectives (see Figure 8.3), for it would seem somewhat harder to prevent a state from repeating an action it had already taken than one it had never taken, harder still to get it to stop short of its objective in an ongoing action, even harder to get it to undo a completed action, and perhaps hardest of all to get it to do something it otherwise would not do at all.[15] Another important distinction affecting an objective's difficulty is whether it involves external, foreign policy behavior

attaches to the interests engaged by the crisis, and what level of costs and risks each is willing to incur on behalf of those interests. If the coercing power demands something that is more important to it than to the adversary, then the coercer should benefit from what may be called an *asymmetry of interests*." George and Simons, *Limits of Coercive Diplomacy*, p. 15.

[13] Robert J. Art, "The Four Functions of Force," in Robert J. Art & Kenneth Waltz (eds.), *The Use of Force: Military Power and International Politics* (Lanham: University Press of America, 1996, 4th ed.), pp. 3–11; Robert H. Dorff and Joseph R. Cerami, "Deterrence and Competitive Strategies: A New Look at an Old Concept," *Small Wars and Insurgencies*, Special Issue on *Deterrence in the 21st Century* (Autumn 2000): 109–123. Art argues elsewhere that logically, there are only "three fundamental outcomes of any attempt at influence," the third being defense, defined as taking steps to minimize the damage from what T is doing or may do; but unlike deterrence and compellence, the latter is not an influence attempt, since (although it may produce deterrence) its basic purpose is not to change T's behavior but protect against it. *A Grand Strategy for America* (Ithaca, NY: Cornell University Press, 2003), p. 6.

[14] On the deterrence/compellence distinction, see Thomas Schelling, *Arms and Influence* (New Haven, CT: Yale University Press, 1966), pp. 69–91; but also see David A. Baldwin, "Power Analysis and World Politics," Klaus Knorr, ed., *Power, Strategy, and Security* (Princeton, NJ: Princeton University Press, 1983), pp. 30–34.

[15] This chart is assembled from lists and ideas found in George and Simons, *Limits of Coercive Diplomacy*, pp. 8–9; Robert J. Art, "Coercive Diplomacy: What Do We Know?" Chapter 9 in Art and Patrick M. Cronin, eds., *The United States and Coercive Diplomacy* (Washington, DC: U.S. Institute of Peace Press, 2003), pp. 389–390 (which finds, however, no clear relationship between success and type of objective demanded, p. 401); and Schelling, *Arms and Influence*, pp. 69–91.

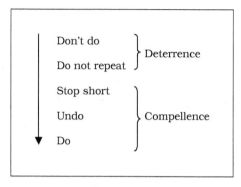

Figure 8.3: Increasing difficulty of intent-changing objectives.

or what is traditionally called the "internal affairs" of the target state. One can assume that the latter kind of goal will be more difficult to accomplish than the former, because internal matters will probably be both harder for outside policy instruments to reach (and therefore less likely to register impact) and more highly valued by foreign leaders.[16]

Status quo objectives like containment are often adopted by states when they believe that, for reason of its relative power or the strength of its values, a target state is unlikely to accede to more onerous demands at acceptable cost and risk. As practiced toward the Soviet Union during the Cold War and against Saddam Hussein's Iraq between the wars of 1991 and 2003, containment is a strategy designed to prevent the expansion or blunt the threat of an opponent, and it is used when one fears to send the very best – that is, when outright war is too costly relative to the interests at stake.[17]

In some strategies, though, the use of foreign policy tools may not directly aim at changing a government's behavior at all. The objective may instead be one of changing another state's *capabilities*, the means backing its strategy. Here the instruments' role is that of weakening the other state or, alternatively, of helping to strengthen its capabilities in order to make its government secure and effective. The latter kind of objective has been attempted by the United States following wars in Bosnia after 1995, Kosovo after 1999, Afghanistan after 2001, and Iraq after 2003, and it has become so important to twenty-first century American statecraft that offices to manage it have been created in the Departments of State and Defense. Reducing a foreign actor's power may be accomplished by destroying or taking away capabilities it already has, or it may be done less dramatically through a denial strategy, designed to weaken or prevent the growth of an

---

[16] This, of course, is one of the burdens that idealists must carry, since they believe that the internal structure of states is the key determinant of their foreign policy choices.

[17] Barton J. Bernstein, "Containment," in *Encyclopedia of American Foreign Policy*, 2nd ed., Vol. 1 (New York: Scribner's, 2001), pp. 345–364.

adversary's power by denying it control of territory, goods, or services.[18] Containment as practiced by the West against the Soviet Union during the Cold War included a healthy dose of denial, for it was designed not only to change Moscow's policy intentions – mainly, to discourage it from overseas adventures – but also (via export controls) to weaken its capabilities for such adventurism and its ability to threaten the United States. Specifically, when the Soviets invaded Afghanistan, the sanctions used by the Carter administration (and Reagan's later support for the mujahedin there) were intended to make the USSR pay a high price for its adventure, not only to deter further such actions but also to weaken and tie down its military capabilities.[19]

Weakening another state may not, however, be as straightforward as it might appear. For example, one might think that imposing costs on an adversary as part of a coercive strategy would always be to I's benefit, but in a non-zero sum interaction that is not always the case; as is usual in strategy, it all depends on T's reaction.[20] Nobel laureate Thomas Schelling has pointed out that making a threat with which T must deal is like raising the price of an item T will consume if it undertakes a particular course of action, and that as a result a mechanism similar to what economists call price elasticity of demand will come into play as T decides what to do.[21] T may indeed divert resources from capabilities that endanger I in order to defend against I's threat, although in the process it may construct so effective a defense that the bargaining value of the threat is lost. But it is also possible that T will consider *any* effective defense too costly and

---

[18] See Charles B. Shotwell, "Export Controls: A Clash of Imperatives," in Richard L. Kugler and Ellen L. Frost (eds.), *The Global Century: Globalization and National Security*, Vol. I (Washington: NDU Press, 2001), pp. 335–354.

[19] Zbigniew Brzezinski, *Power and Principle* (New York: Farrar, Straus, Giroux, 1983), p. 430; Jimmy Carter, *Keeping Faith* (New York: Bantam Books, Inc., 1982), pp. 472, 476; George P. Shultz, *Turmoil and Triumph* (New York: Charles Scribner's Sons, 1993), pp. 570, 692.

[20] By contrast, in a zero-sum situation, Schelling argues, "any costs that the enemy is obliged to incur have a positive value to our side, just as the costs we incur ... must be valued negatively." If the analyst is looking at the *whole* strategic situation, such costs do not need to be separately taken into account, since costs are by definition the reciprocal of gains. It is when the analyst is looking at only *part* of the strategic problem, at a "local" (say, a regional, country, or functional) issue, and considering "resources that might have been allocated instead to other arenas, or resources that can be saved and used later in different arenas, that we need to make specific allowance for costs. . . . [In this kind of zero-sum case] costs are simply the measure of consequences, or payoffs, that occur outside the boundaries of our local problem. They are the external economies that any partial or local analysis needs to take into account." Thomas C. Schelling, "The Strategy of Inflicting Costs," in Schelling, ed., *Choice and Consequence* (Cambridge, MA: Harvard University Press, 1984), pp. 272–273.

[21] Elasticity of demand is the measure of how sensitive purchasers are to a change in a commodity's price, that is, to how big relative to a change in price the change in the quantity bought will be.

instead use its resources to counter-threaten I in some other area, leaving the latter worse off than before it made the original threat. After all, it is of such reactions that arms races are made. It all depends on how responsive T is to the costs that I is imposing on it. As a result, the costs that T winds up paying may bear no relationship in either magnitude or direction to I's benefits.[22]

Instead of changing a government's behavior or capabilities, however, the objective may be to change the government itself, as in U.S. policy toward Hudson Austin in 1983, Manuel Noriega in 1989, Raul Cedras in 1994, Saddam Hussein after 1998 and, after the attacks of 9/11, the Taliban government in Afghanistan. In most cases it is impossible to negotiate a government out of power, since no instrument, at least none aimed at the state rather than its leaders, can inflict enough pain or offer enough benefit to offset what is being lost; outright or covert warfare will usually be required. Still, there are exceptions. The negotiations by the Reagan administration with Panama's Noriega in 1988 and under Clinton with Haiti's Cedras junta in 1994 are examples, and as the latter case demonstrates, they may succeed if it is possible to convince the offending government that its removal is inevitable and that a negotiated departure will be on better terms than a forcible one.[23] What happened in Haiti was simply that the United States restructured the junta's choices, convincing its members that they no longer included the option of staying in power.

More often, of course, governments change by less dramatic means. And since states are not unitary actors, strategists must calculate the effects of their actions not just on "the government" but on the factions that may be discerned within it, and not just on those in power but on various claimants to power. For elites in or out of government can act either as "circuit breakers" to buffer or interrupt the political effects of I's instruments, or as "transmission belts" between those instruments' impact and success.[24] Moreover, in a democratic state or even one whose government changes through palace or elite politics, actions by foreign governments can have an effect on the political prospects of various factions and parties. If the United States, for example, publicly stigmatizes Iran as part of an "axis of evil" when its president is a relative moderate, it may destroy the argument of Iranian moderates that their country's restraint will lead to benefits in its relationship with the West and thereby help radicals replace them in positions of power.[25] Similarly, when the government of Israel refuses to

[22] Schelling, "Strategy of Inflicting Costs," pp. 280–289.

[23] On Noriega, see Shultz, *Turmoil and Triumph*, Ch. 48; on Haiti, see David E. Weekman, "Sanctions: The Invisible Hand of Statecraft," *Strategic Review* 26 (Winter 1998): 39–45.

[24] Jentleson and Whytock, "Who 'Won' Libya?", p. 55.

[25] President Mohammad Khatami tried during his eight years in power to encourage a "dialogue between civilizations," but "'especially after Iran was branded in the axis of evil, these guys [hardliners] turned to the leader and said, 'What has

grant significant concessions in negotiations with a Palestinian Authority led by the relatively moderate Fatah party but validates Hamas-led violence against Israelis by withdrawing unilaterally from Gaza, it should not be surprised if Hamas takes votes from Fatah in a free and fair election.[26] Thus, in assessing the prospects of success for any course of action, strategists must look within the international actor they are trying to affect and focus on the human beings who control it or who may control it in the future, for it is their decisions that will ultimately matter.

Although most of the above discussion assumes that only a single objective is in play, strategists' influence attempts often have multiple objectives. Achieving several goals in the same target state is difficult, however, because T knows that I is unlikely to deliver on threats or renege on promises if its highest priority goal is being met. For example, as long as Soviet troops remained in Afghanistan during the 1980s, the government of Pakistan knew that the United States' primary goal would be the continuance of aid to the forces fighting them. Islamabad thus largely ignored Washington's demands that it restore democracy, abandon efforts to acquire nuclear weapons, and curb the drug trade – and the Reagan and Bush administrations continued foreign assistance anyway, despite the fact that the pursuit of all those secondary objectives was required by the laws governing the use of foreign aid. Only the departure of the Soviets from Afghanistan and the advent of a democratic government in Islamabad under Benazir Bhutto allowed the U.S. to place its nonproliferation objectives at the top of its agenda, resulting in the termination of aid when Pakistan's ongoing nuclear program became too obvious for the Bush administration to ignore.[27] Thus, when they are pursuing multiple objectives with a single target, it is crucial for strategists to be clear about which have the highest priority, and not allow secondary objectives to get in the way of primary ones.

Strategies may also, of course, have multiple and differing objectives in an array of targets, as noted in Chapter 7. For example, courses of action that appear to constitute an influence attempt directed at T may be undertaken at least as much to reassure ally X as to coerce T. They

Khatami gotten us?'" Iranian political analyst quoted in Karl Vick, "Iran Calling Wider World to Its Side," *Washington Post* (February 1, 2006): A18. Partly as a result Khatami's successor was Mahmoud Ahmadinejad, who restarted Iran's uranium enrichment program, denied the reality of the Holocaust, and repeatedly pledged to wipe Israel off the map.

[26] "Israel's departure from Gaza was designed to be a unilateral step, depriving Abbas [leader of Fatah and the PA] of a negotiated peace victory he could claim; instead, Hamas asserted it had driven the Israelis out with its uncompromising approach." Glenn Kessler, "U.S. Policy Seen as Big Loser in Palestinian Vote," *Washington Post* (January 28, 2006): A16.

[27] Terry L. Deibel, *Pakistan in the Bush Years: Foreign Aid and Foreign Influence*, Pew Case Studies in International Affairs No. 365 (Washington, DC: Institute for the Study of Diplomacy, Georgetown University, 1995).

may be designed to deter X from bandwagoning with T while simultaneously attempting to compel T to stop acting against X's interests, and they may quite possibly have a greater chance of success in the former than the latter. In such cases, whether I's strategy has "succeeded" or "failed" will depend on which goals with which targets are most important to I. The question for strategists is therefore not only whether particular instruments will work to change a particular target's behavior, but whether using them improves the state's *overall* strategic position.[28] To answer it in the case of multiple objectives and multiple targets, decision makers need at the very least to be clear as to which objectives are to be pursued with regard to which targets and what constitutes acceptable success in each case. And they must not only be clear in their own minds but also clearly and credibly communicate their goals to each of the target governments, so that those governments know what they must do to maintain or acquire proffered benefits or to avert or end inflicted pain.[29]

Whatever their objectives, strategists should not expect absolutes in either degree or probability when thinking about success. In the first place, success in foreign affairs strategy is rarely total.[30] Some courses of action may misfire, either from inadequate design or partial implementation, and others may not hit home, either from a failed transmission link or inadequate power relative to the objective demanded. But fortunately, total success is rarely necessary. It is important, therefore, for the strategist to consider what *degree* of goal achievement various instruments might deliver with various targets, and whether that degree of success is acceptable. Second, success to whatever degree is never certain. Research indicates that coercive influence attempts short of war, whether pursued with economic or military tools, work less than a third of the time at best (see Figure 8.4).[31] Indeed, there is perhaps no more important lesson for a foreign affairs strategist to learn than that influencing other nation-states is difficult. They are not called "sovereign" for nothing, and none of the instruments of state power is particularly effective when used for objectives that are aimed at important interests. So in making their calculations it is also important for strategists to come to some idea of likelihood, some sense

---

[28] Kirshner, "The Microfoundations of Economic Sanctions," p. 34, note 3.

[29] Two of Alexander George's eight conditions for success in coercive diplomacy are clarity about objectives and about the precise terms of settlement. See Chapter 6 section on military instruments.

[30] "Success is usually a matter of degree" is one of Baldwin's guidelines for decision makers. *Economic Statecraft*, p. 371.

[31] Figure 7 compiled from Table 5 in Art, "Coercive Diplomacy: What Do We Know?" pp. 403–405, and Kevin Lang and James Lee Ray, "Beginners and Winners: The Fate of Initiators of Interstate Wars Involving Great Powers Since 1495," *International Studies Quarterly* 38 (March 1994): 139–154. As David Baldwin points out in "The Sanctions Debate and the Logic of Choice," *International Security* 24 (Winter 1999/2000): 93–94, the figures on success for initiators of war are probably inflated by the dichotomous rating of wars as either victories or defeats.

Economic Sanctions	25–33%
Military Coercion	32%
War Initiation	40–72%

Figure 8.4: Comparative success rates for negative instruments.

of the *probabilities* attached to various degrees of success. In the process they may well decide to revisit Steps 1–3: to revise their objectives to make them more likely of achievement to an acceptable degree, to augment the instruments they have chosen, or to change the ways specified for their use.

At the same time, strategists should be aware that some objectives require complete implementation lest they leave the initiating state worse off than before. One example is U.S. control of its border with Mexico, where partial efforts have failed to stem massive illegal immigration but still had the perverse effects of persuading many migrants to stay in the United States rather than periodically returning home (because the return trip is so difficult) and of causing far more deaths among migrants (by forcing them onto more hazardous desert routes). Moreover, there is no benefit to half-hearted implementation. As Henry Kissinger remarked,

> once a great power commits itself, it must prevail. It will acquire no kudos for translating its inner doubts into hesitation. However ambivalently it has arrived at the point of decision, it must pursue the course on which it is embarked with a determination to succeed. Otherwise, it adds a reputation for incompetence to whatever controversy it is bound to incur on the merits of its decision.[32]

6. COST: Evaluate Whether the Strategy Is Worth Its Cost

All strategy, it bears repeating, is about ends and means. Ends are the upside of strategy: success in accomplishing objectives is the benefit strategists hope to achieve when they implement courses of action. Means, on the other hand, are the downside of strategy. Acquiring and using instruments is a cost, and beyond costs there are risks, the possibility that events will turn out worse than expected. Any sound strategy requires a positive balance between benefits on the one hand, and cost and risk on the other. While strategists are creating provisional courses of action and coming to some judgment as to their likely impact and success, therefore, they must

---

[32] Henry Kissinger, *Years of Upheaval* (Boston, MA: Little, Brown & Co., 1892), p. 520.

look hard at the downside, evaluating their proposed strategy for cost and risk, as well as its internal coherence and compatibility with other foreign affairs strategies.[33]

Cost is popularly defined as whatever must be given, sacrificed, suffered or forgone to secure a benefit or accomplish a result, the necessary loss or deprivation related to something gained, or the unavoidable penalty of an action.[34] More specifically, it is simply the amount paid for anything bought – the price.

> Every international objective carries a price tag marked "cost in terms of national resources." In a very rough sense, one could say that in international politics governments spend national resources in attempts to buy foreign policy objectives.[35]

Economists define the cost of something as "the value of what must be given up in order to acquire the item," or "the highest-valued opportunity necessarily forsaken."[36] Note that *value* as used in these definitions is independent of cost. Value is an inherent, not a comparative quality; all goods, services, or events have both desirable and undesirable attributes, and their value is the net of the former over the latter.[37] In foreign affairs strategy, an objective whose undesirable features equaled or exceeded its desirable ones would have zero or negative value and should not be formulated in the first place. The decision maker's problem is to choose among objectives that *all* have value. If she chooses the one with the *highest* value, its cost will be the goal or goals with the *next* highest value, the second-best objective(s) she cannot pursue because she's using the resources it would require on her chosen objective.[38]

---

[33] Staffers often provide decision makers with pros and cons of various courses of action; here it is suggested that the strategist himself construct a similar set of evaluative comments, either to refine the choice another may make or to lead him to an optimal final strategy.

[34] *Webster's New International Dictionary of the English Language*, 2nd ed., unabridged (Springfield, MA: G & C Merriam Co., 1960).

[35] Donald Puchala, *International Politics Today* (New York: Dodd, Mead & Co., 1971), p. 172.

[36] First quote from William J. Baumol and Alan S. Blinder, *Economics: Principles and Policy* (Fort Worth, TX: Harcourt Brace & Co., 1994), p. 7 (original italics removed); second from Armen A. Alchian, "Cost," in David L. Sills, ed., *International Encyclopedia of the Social Sciences*, 3rd ed. (New York: MacMillan/Free Press, 1968), p. 404.

[37] "The decision maker must choose among events that are amalgams of 'goods and bads.' He cannot choose all events whose desirable features more than offset their undesirable ones, given the limited resources at his disposal. A comparison among all the available options (each consisting of an amalgam of good and bad) yields for each option a rank-indicating measure of value. The cost of one amalgam is the best of the forsaken amalgams." Alchian, "Cost," p. 404.

[38] Comparing one low-cost and one high-cost objective, therefore, is not really fair. The valid comparison is between the high-cost objective and *all* the other low-cost objectives that might be achieved with the resources that the high-cost objective requires. Herbert A. Simon, *Administrative Behavior*, 4th ed. (New York: Free

The concept of cost is therefore an unavoidable element of choice itself. In fact, the idea of cost is meaningless without choice, and choices cannot rationally be made without regard to cost. As David Baldwin explains,

> Because resources are scarce, people cannot have everything they want. They must therefore choose among alternative uses of such resources. In doing so, they give up some valued alternatives in order to gain others. All concepts of costs...refer to this basic choice situation....From this perspective, all costs are opportunity costs.[39]

It is precisely because the resources applied to one objective are generally not available to advance others that the *relative* costs of various instruments matter.[40] Other things being equal, strategists should choose instruments that cost less because choosing unnecessarily expensive instruments to pursue an objective may well mean that some objectives of nearly equal desirability cannot be pursued as effectively, or indeed at all. In other words, each objective-instrument package or course of action should be not just *effective* but *efficient*, "acting effectively with minimal waste," so that as few resources as possible are consumed.[41]

This kind of thinking assumes, of course, that power is fungible – that resources not applied to one objective can in fact be applied to other, possibly very different objectives. As noted in Chapter 5, fungibility depends first on whether resources are in the form of potential power or specific instruments.[42] The former is by definition fungible, but its applicability in a given strategic situation depends on the time available to convert it into the necessary tools of statecraft. Instruments, on the other hand, are so specific in their capabilities that their fungibility will vary dramatically with the nature of the objectives to which they would be moved. Another characteristic that complicates cost calculations is that not all of them impact government budgets. As noted in Chapter 6, some instruments (like trade action)

Press, 1997), p. 256. In short, "it is imperative that the strategist assess what other objectives will not be met if the strategy under consideration is adopted." Schmitt, "Identifying National Objectives and Developing Strategy," p. 30. Thus, the prioritization of objectives will depend in part upon the costs of the instruments needed to achieve them.

[39] David A. Baldwin, "The Costs of Power," in *Paradoxes of Power*, Baldwin, ed. (New York: Basil Blackwell, 1989), pp. 83–84.

[40] The best strategies, of course, aim precisely at making this kind of magic happen, by setting objectives that will serve multiple interests and taking actions that support multiple objectives – the "two birds with one stone" approach. See below, Step 8.

[41] *Webster's II New Riverside University Dictionary* (New York: Houghton Mifflin Co., 1984).

[42] The fungibility debate is obscured by scholars' failure to distinguish between these very different categories. For example, see Robert J. Art, "American Foreign Policy and the Fungibility of Force," *Security Studies* 5 (Summer 1996): 7–42; David A. Baldwin, "Force, Fungibility, and Influence," *Security Studies* 8 (Summer 1999): 173–182; and Robert J. Art, "Force and Fungibility Reconsidered," *Security Studies* 8 (Summer 1999): 183–189.

impose most of their costs directly on society, and therefore do not immediately reduce the governmental resources available for use elsewhere. That characteristic may either recommend them to decision makers, or cause special wariness because of their possible political ramifications.

Efficiency is a characteristic of an individual course of action, comparing inputs to output, capturing its balance of ends and means. But strategists must eventually choose among multiple courses of action that have each presumably been made as efficient as possible. Having arrived at a sense of the value of each package's objective, in other words, they must then evaluate the *whole* outcome, including both the goal's accomplishment *and* the loss of the resources necessary to achieve that success.[43] For certainly strategists should choose among proposed courses of action based not just on their comparative *effectiveness* or *efficiency*; instead, they should net the value of the needed resources, the anticipated cost of each package's objective, against the value of that objective to get a sense of overall satisfaction for each package that can then be used to compare them.[44] In the end, in other words, strategists want to choose the courses of action that have the highest cost-effectiveness, the most favorable cost-benefit ratios.[45]

Choosing strategies based on comparative cost-benefit analysis leads to the startling conclusion that less effective tools of statecraft may actually be preferable to more effective ones if their cost is sufficiently lower.[46] Even in situations where force would work best, for example, statesmen may rationally choose political, informational, or economic instruments rather than military ones – necessarily scaling back their objectives in the process – simply because the more effective military strategy may not be worth its costs.[47] To revisit an earlier example, perhaps the United States can get an adequate degree and probability of success in spreading democracy by

---

[43] Economists call a favorable relationship of this kind a *consumer surplus*, the net gain in total utility that a purchase brings, comparing it to the profit of a firm, which is the net of total revenue minus total expenses of generating that revenue. Baumol and Blinder, *Economics: Principles and Policy*, p. 195.

[44] David Baldwin makes this point strongly in most of his recent writings. See *e.g.* "Evaluating Economic Sanctions," *International Security* 23 (Fall 1998): 192–194; "The Sanctions Debate and the Logic of Choice," pp. 83–86. He even argues in the latter (p. 90) that "[t]echniques of statecraft that involve excessive costs should not be viewed as successful, no matter what their effects are." I disagree; success should be achievement to some degree of whatever objectives decision makers set, and its common usage is equivalent to goal accomplishment.

[45] "...in choosing policy, statesmen must compare the costs, both political and economic, of introducing specific techniques with the benefits of expected outcomes." Kirshner, "The Microfoundations of Economic Sanctions," p. 34.

[46] David A. Baldwin, "Success and Failure in Foreign Policy," *Annual Review of Political Science* 3 (2000): 167–182.

[47] See the relationship of power and objectives under Step 1 in Chapter 7 for discussion of the two criteria of an objective's desirability: service to the national interest and worth.

using exchange of persons and technical assistance, rather than military invasion. Therefore, strategists cannot arrive at rational decisions by comparing just the benefits of different courses of action. Nor can they do so by just comparing their costs, or by comparing their costs to I with the costs they inflict on T (the so-called "balance of pain"). What they must compare is the cost-effectiveness, or cost-benefit ratios, of their potential objective-instrument packages *with each other*.[48] "In order to make rational policy decisions, policy makers need to ask how effective a policy instrument is likely to be, with respect to which goals and targets, at what cost, and in comparison with what other policy instruments."[49]

Such comparisons are extraordinarily difficult. For one thing, they include a staggeringly wide variety of elements that, on both the cost and benefit side, go well beyond material things.[50] If the course of action includes military force, for example, costs would have to include not only operating expenses for the engagement, replacement costs of destroyed equipment, and long-run costs of supporting veterans for the rest of their lives, but also the highly subjective value of lives lost, material and human resources temporarily unavailable elsewhere (including policy attention and energy at the top of government), and even the political capital expended on securing support of the action in the domestic environment. If I is making a promise or threat, there are as many as four distinct kinds of costs to be considered: those of communicating it, of making it credible, of monitoring T's activities to see whether it is effective, and (if necessary) of carrying it out as reward or punishment.[51] Anticipated costs also should include any collateral effects of a course of action that compromise other interests or other strategies.[52] Since there is no commonly accepted standard of political value that can play the role of money in economic life, adding up such costs, as well as the benefits of the objectives they attempt to purchase, is a highly subjective enterprise.[53] Although the disciplines of cost-benefit and multi-attribute analysis can help to quantify the values gained and lost in a strategic enterprise, they can do

---

[48] The balance of pain is irrelevant because it does not matter if I's action hurts it more than T, as long as I can tolerate the pain more than T can. See Baldwin, *Economic Statecraft*, Chs. 6, 7, and 9 for a wide-ranging discussion of costs.

[49] Baldwin, "Success and Failure," pp. 181–182.

[50] "By 'costs' we mean not just financial burdens but all reductions in valued things, and all increases in things valued negatively." Knorr, *On the Uses of Military Power in the Nuclear Age* (Princeton, NJ: Princeton University Press, 1966), p. 11.

[51] This final factor must be weighted for the probability that it will succeed, along with the probabilities that I will follow through on the promise or threat or that I will execute it regardless of what T does. Baldwin, "The Costs of Power," pp. 82–99.

[52] The issue of coordination is discussed under Step 8 below.

[53] Baldwin, "Power Analysis and World Politics," p. 8; Knorr, *On the Uses of Military Power in the Nuclear Age*, p. 9.

little to alleviate the intrinsic difficulty of assigning those values in the first place.[54] In the end, determining whether foreign affairs strategy is worthwhile is not like a business, where one can calculate a bottom line, but depends on the judgment of decision makers.

Adding to the difficulty, of course, is that cost estimates largely depend upon, and therefore must be based on guesses about, the reaction of the target to the influence attempt being made. Not surprisingly, recent history indicates that it is notoriously hard to know how long or how intensively instruments must be used in a given situation before success will occur. Even in so powerful a coercive influence attempt as the Kosovo war of 1999, for example, two months of NATO bombing produced few signs until the last couple of weeks that Serbian leader Slobodan Milosevic would actually capitulate. Similarly, a year of escalating threats and troop movements in 2002–03 did not persuade Saddam Hussein to yield. On the co-optive side, the American effort to help Afghanistan after the 2001–02 war faced obstacles from continued Taliban attacks, irrepressible warlordism, an economy based largely on opium production, and endemic poverty worsened by decades of war and oppression, with costs that were almost impossible to calculate in advance; the costs of restoring Iraq in the face of a stubborn insurgency and nascent civil war are even more indeterminate.[55] Nor were the oil deliveries and light water reactors promised to North Korea in 1994 enough to prevent it from embarking on a uranium enrichment program.

The strategists' sense of cost will thus be only an estimate, and like those of targets and objectives, cost estimates will depend greatly on the situation. Still, a few general statements can be made about the costs of various strategies and instruments. First, costs can be expected to increase as one goes down the spectrum of generic strategies from the purely persuasive to the co-optive to the coercive, with a major cost break occurring between persuasive strategies and the other two.[56] Furthermore, co-optive and coercive strategies that use instruments prospectively have different, indeed opposite, cost implications if they succeed or fail, for promises need be carried out only if they succeed, and threats only if they fail.[57] Logically, then, one criterion for the selection of generic strategies ought to be a cold-eyed estimate of which outcome is likely. The rule might be that, *ceteris*

---

[54] For a succinct description of these two decision making tools, see Lewis G. Irwin, *The Policy Analyst's Handbook* (Armonk, NY: M. E. Sharpe, 2003).

[55] This fact, of course, does not excuse the Bush administration from deliberately ignoring the well-considered opinions of many government studies and outside experts that the costs would likely run into the hundreds of billions of dollars. See James Fallows, "Blind into Baghdad," *Atlantic Monthly* (January/February 2004): 52–54, 56–58, 60, 62–66, 68–70, 72–74 for a survey of these. Strategists have an obligation not to let their ideology influence their cost estimates, no matter how important an objective may seem.

[56] For the spectrum of generic strategies, see Chapter 7.

[57] Thomas C. Schelling, *Strategy of Conflict* (Cambridge, MA: Harvard University Press, 1960), p. 177.

paribus, if success is expected, then threaten; if failure is likely (but not so likely that the influence attempt should be abandoned), then promise. Costs can also be expected to vary widely *within* these strategic categories according to which instruments are used and the statecraft with which they are employed.[58] Diplomacy, whether bilateral, multilateral, or public is cheaper than economic instruments; economic instruments are often less costly than military ones. Narrower and gradual use of instruments is bound to be cheaper in the short run than broad or full use, and covert action is well-known by decision makers as an inexpensive alternative to the open use of instruments.

It is important, finally, to note that costs are not necessarily just a negative factor in selecting objective-instrument packages; incurring them may also be critical to success. For accepting costs shows resolve, and resolve may be vital to the credibility of an influence attempt.[59] In the Afghan war, which in its early months relied mainly on Afghan troops, the use of American ground forces to lead the battle at Shahikot in early March 2002 – even the death of eight soldiers from hostile fire – was said by many analysts to be an important demonstration of U.S. commitment to victory in the war.[60] In contrast, the failure of the United States to put forces on the ground in Kosovo, along with President Clinton's public statements ruling it out, were widely seen at the time as among the reasons why Milosevic refused for so long to surrender.[61] Thus, the effectiveness of tougher, more coercive policy tools may be due not only to their impact on the target state but also to the commitment they demonstrate by the initiating state. Robust, sustained use of positive instruments as part of a co-optive strategy may have similar effects. If so, it is possible that the attempt to calculate costs should not be so much for the purpose of minimizing them as for that of arriving at *the most effective amount* of costliness.

---

[58] See Chapter 7 discussion of means and ways, Steps 2 and 3.

[59] "The ability to incur costs is inextricably linked with the ability to make binding commitments. In a cost-free world, no one could ever demonstrate resolve." Baldwin, *Economic Statecraft*, p. 283.

[60] "It gives lie to the belief that Americans can only fight from 35,000 feet," said retired Marine Lt. Gen. Bernard Trainor. Thomas E. Ricks, "Battle Sends Broader Message of U.S. Resolve," *Washington Post* (March 5, 2002): A15.

[61] Although the argument remains unsettled, many argue that Clinton's public change in that position, the Alliance's discussion of the need for ground forces, and the early preparations for their use were among the principal factors that led to the war's successful outcome. As General Clark wrote, "Planning and preparations for ground intervention were well under way by the end of the campaign, and I am convinced that this, in particular, pushed Milosevic to concede." Wesley K. Clark, *Waging Modern War* (New York: Public Affairs, 2001), p. 425. See also Barton Gellman, "'A Doctrine of Immaculate Coercion'," *Washington Post* (March 28, 1999): A1, A30; John F. Harris and Bradley Graham, "Clinton Is Reassessing Sufficiency of Air War," *Washington Post* (June 3, 1999); and William Drozdiak, "The Kosovo Peace Deal: How It Happened," *Washington Post* (June 6, 1999): A1, A22.

7. RISK: Consider that Things May Not Go As Planned

Despite the difficulties of estimating them, the world of costs and benefits still appears as a world of relative certainty: one chooses to spend a
specified amount of resources to achieve a given objective. But strategists
operate in a world where costs and benefits are problematical, a world in
which many unknowable factors affect the outcomes of influence attempts,
in which the interactions over extended periods of time of systems that are
themselves composed of interactive systems make most predictions highly
uncertain. They must therefore also deal with the concept of risk, the possibility that future reality may diverge from planners' expectations.

Usually, risk is thought of in negative terms. The dictionary defines it
as the possibility of loss, injury, disadvantage or destruction – all highly
negative outcomes.[62] After his security cabinet had considered the options
for responding to the 9/11 attacks, for example, President Bush pressed
his advisors to think about "the worst cases. . . . What are the real downside
risks?"[63] But to be risky, outcomes cannot just be negative; they must also
have less than a 100 percent likelihood of happening. For the idea of risk
captures both negative outcomes and their probability of occurrence.[64] In
the words of political scientist Rose McDermott,

> Risk is about the chance of loss. Thus, risk involves two components, the
> chance and the loss. Chance is fundamentally about probability. . . . Loss
> is critically a function of magnitude.[65]

Moreover, though the terms are often used interchangeably, risk technically differs from uncertainty in having a *known* probability of occurrence.[66] And uncertainty affects *both* the likelihood and the degree of loss,
for usually neither probabilities nor magnitudes can be precisely determined in advance.[67] Strategists, alas, operate in a world both risky and
uncertain.

---

[62] *Webster's New International Dictionary of the English Language.*
[63] Bob Woodward and Dan Balz, "At Camp David, Advise and Dissent," *Washington Post* (January 31, 2002): A14.
[64] "Risk is brewed from an equal dose of two ingredients–probabilities and consequences." Paul Slovic, "Informing and Educating the Public About Risk," *Risk Analysis* 6 (No. 4, 1986): 412.
[65] Rose McDermott, *Risk-Taking in International Politics: Prospect Theory in American Foreign Policy* (Ann Arbor, MI: University of Michigan Press, 1998), p. 6.
[66] "'Risk-taking' refers to . . . probability. . . . 'Uncertainty,' on the other hand, refers
to the degree to which the probability . . . is unknown." Bruce Bueno de Mesquita,
The War Trap (New Haven, CT: Yale University Press, 1981), p. 33. See also Jack
S. Levy, "An Introduction to Prospect Theory" and "Prospect Theory and International Relations: Theoretical Applications and Analytical Problems," in Barbara
Farnham, ed., *Avoiding Losses/Taking Risks: Prospect Theory and International
Conflict* (Ann Arbor, MI: University of Michigan Press, 1994), pp. 8–9, 129.
[67] Howard Kunreuther, "Risk Analysis and Risk Management in an Uncertain
World," *Risk Analysis* (No. 22, 2002): 656–657.

In strategy, risk is often felt as danger, the danger that a *threat* will exploit a *vulnerability*.[68] Risk as danger is passive; it is created by the prospective actions of others, or by the objective conditions of the international environment, and is present whether or not strategists are aware of it. But strategists can also incur risk as a result of their *own* actions, when they take the initiative to promote interests or protect them against threats. Risks of this kind will at least be different, and should presumably be less probable and/or consequential, than the dangers the strategy may have been created to deal with.[69] Such active risk is properly considered a subset of cost – technically as a cost whose probability of occurrence is less than 50 percent.[70] So artificial a dividing line between cost and risk may not seem very useful for foreign affairs strategists; after all, we are talking about a continuum rather than two distinct things. But distinguishing the two concepts makes the key point that costs must be evaluated for probability, that even likely costs are not certain, and that some costs are improbable enough as to properly be considered risks. One experienced U.S. diplomat summed it up with as much precision as may be useful by saying that costs are losses you *expect* to incur if things go according to plan, while risks are losses you expect to avoid but *may* incur if they do not.[71]

Risk further complicates the calculations that strategists make when evaluating and choosing among objective-instrument packages. It forces strategists to choose the courses of action, not that are *for sure* the most cost-effective, but that they *anticipate* will have the most favorable costs-benefit ratios. Rationality in such choices is therefore usually defined in terms of *expected utility*: the idea that individuals estimate the benefits and costs that will flow from each of the options before them and then choose among those options based partly on their net subjective value (or utility) and partly on their probabilities (or expectations of how likely they think each set of costs and benefits is to materialize).[72] As will be seen below, expected utility may not be how decision makers always choose, but it is

---

[68] See Chapter 4 discussion of threat.
[69] I use the phrase "may have" since risky strategies can also be formulated to take advantage of opportunities.
[70] "In general, risks are an important class of costs." Knorr, *On the Uses of Military Power in the Nuclear Age*, p. 12.
[71] Robert Gallucci, speech to NWC Class, August 31, 1999. Used by permission.
[72] Economists use the term utility to mean the subjective satisfaction that someone would get by acquiring a given set of goods or services. As applied to strategy, utility defined in this way would apply to an achieved objective and *only* that objective, regardless of its cost; it captures, in other words, a sense of gross rather than net satisfaction. However, political scientist Klaus Knorr *includes* costs in his formula for utility, $U=V-C$, writing that "utility depends on the difference between aggregate values and aggregate costs." *On the Uses of Military Power in the Nuclear Age*, p. 9. Expected utility follows Knorr's definition.

widely accepted as the way in which they ought to choose, building in risk as an aspect of their cost-benefit calculations.

At first thought, one would expect strategists making such decisions to try to avoid or reduce risk as much as possible. Certainly they try to minimize danger. Unfortunately, unless ways can be found through smarter statecraft to spend resources more efficiently, doing so will inevitably generate greater costs, because the strategist will need to buy and/or use instruments to reduce vulnerabilities or eliminate threats. Indeed, one can consider instruments as a kind of insurance, seeing danger or passive risk as threatened vulnerabilities that are not "protected" by instruments.[73] Therefore, as strategists' continuing scan of the international environment picks up more or more immediate threats, they must either devote more resources to countering and defending against those threats (thereby increasing costs) or see the level of danger to the nation-state rise (bearing increased passive risks); the same thing will happen in a constant-threat environment if the strategist must or wants to cut expense.[74] Cost and risk thus appear to be inversely related.

Falling or steady spending on implements of national defense may or may not, therefore, mean rising levels of danger; as illustrated during the 1970s and the 1990s, it all depends on levels of threat. The antimilitary bias of American public opinion in the immediate post-Vietnam years resulted in a static real defense budget during that decade of a little over 5 percent of GNP.[75] But those were years in which Soviet military capabilities grew relentlessly, while aggressive Soviet intentions were dramatized by a variety of interventions by Moscow and its clients in Angola, Ethiopia, Cambodia, Central America, and Afghanistan. Given this rising level of threat, there is little question that the failure of American defense costs to rise also resulted in a higher level of risk for the United States, and the resulting sense of danger was one that Ronald Reagan capitalized on during the 1980 presidential campaign. The defense cuts of the 1990s, however, took place in a much different international context, one in which the Soviet Union had ceased to exist and the somewhat higher level of intra-state violence posed a much smaller danger to American national interests. As a result, it was possible to cut the defense budget substantially without

---

[73] Catherine M. Deibel alerted me to the fact that the analogy is not exact, because fire insurance (for example) does not protect against fire damage itself but against the financial consequences of that damage.

[74] John Lewis Gaddis, "Containment and the Logic of Strategy," *National Interest* 10 (Winter 1987–88): 27–38. The choice strategists face here is between minimizing cost through an asymmetrical strategy or minimizing risk through a symmetrical one, as noted in Chapter 7 under Step 1. Alternatively, if the environmental scan identifies additional opportunities for advancing interests, strategists must decide how much cost and risk they wish to incur in order to pursue them.

[75] Economist Daniel Gaske has done calculations that indicate a real defense budget of $216B in 1974 and $214B in 1980, with an average budget across the period of $217B. Unpublished NWC paper.

increasing the nation's risk, though of course the precise level of spending needed to deal with new kinds of post–Cold War threat remained a matter of judgment.

But to say that cost and risk are inversely related tells only part of the story. For strategists actively trade costs and risks against each other as they create courses of action and relate means to ends in the design of objective-instrument packages. They can usually drive the risks of an influence attempt down by spending more, thereby raising its costs.[76] If resources are unavailable, or strategists prefer to use them somewhere else, they may have to tolerate the risks they face. Sometimes, as Henry Kissinger noted, "leaders must make boldness substitute for assets."[77] Or, since that risk can be visualized as a gap between instruments and objectives, means and ends, the strategist may also attempt to control it by narrowing or reducing objectives.[78] After all, fitting instruments and ways of using them to objectives is not just a matter of finding the best instruments for preexisting objectives. As noted in our Chapter 7 discussion of objectives under Step 1, goals themselves must be tailored so as to be achievable with the available instruments; both ends and means remain on the table.[79] However, adopting a less ambitious strategy may be impossible if the interests at stake are too important and the threat to them too great – or the opportunity for achieving them too tempting. Then statesmen may find the risk involved unavoidable – or actually desirable. Indeed, strategists who set objectives that seem unsupported by sufficient resources may simply be attempting to improve their cost-benefit ratios, leaving more to chance than some might think prudent. They find a higher degree of active risk preferable to spending more to lower it, either because it makes possible the pursuit of additional goals despite limited power, or because the resources needed to reduce it are valued more than what they can buy in risk reduction.

---

[76] For some objectives in some situations, of course, risk may be impossible to reduce no matter what strategists are willing to spend.

[77] Henry Kissinger, *White House Years* (Boston, MA: Little, Brown & Co., 1979), p. 899.

[78] The reader will recall this kind of policy risk from the discussion of leverage regarding the psychological nature of power, Chapter 5. Active risk, as a gap between instruments and *objectives*, can be distinguished from passive risk, defined above as a gap between instruments and *threats*. The difference is that threats are passively discerned, whereas objectives are an active response to them.

[79] This characteristic of strategic thinking bothers David Baldwin, who argues that "[i]f success is defined in terms of the degree to which an undertaking achieves a given set of goals, the recipe for success cannot take the form of 'change your goals.'" "The Sanctions Debate and the Logic of Choice," p. 88. True enough as a matter of theoretical comparison, but decision makers ought to be – and in fact are – free to change goals as they evaluate courses of action, since some objectives may well be unachievable or not worth their costs and risks no matter which instruments are chosen.

Risk, therefore, can have a positive as well as a negative face; it may be embraced rather than shunned. Sometimes it refers to gambles, courses of action where the variation in possible outcomes, best to worst, is simply wider than that of other courses of action.[80] People take on risky investments because they offer the prospect of greater returns, take the risks involved in job change in order to advance in their careers, and speed on the highway in order to get somewhere sooner. All these risk-takers know that they are exposing themselves to the possibility of greater loss, but they take the risk anyway as an inevitable concomitant of the opportunity to get a benefit at reduced cost. Similarly, strategists may expose their nations to the possibility of greater loss in the pursuit of problematical gains. If the status quo is sufficiently unsatisfactory, they may decide to shake it up in the expectation that the result is likelier than not to leave the country better off than before.[81] This kind of risk is not passive but positive and active, even entrepreneurial. It embraces uncertainty *and* a greater possibility of loss in order to access the possibility of gain.[82]

So just as strategists may reduce objectives in order to bring ends into line with means and thereby reduce risk, they may also expand their objectives in the hope of risky gains, gains that have a less than 50 percent chance of happening. Obviously, expanded objectives will be more difficult to achieve, assuming that the amount of resources devoted to them is not increased, and therefore the likelihood of success of such a strategy will be less than that of one with more limited objectives. This is another sense in which the concept of risk is used: namely, to denote a strategy with a low probability of success, of accomplishing its objectives. "By definition, risk implies some fear of losing an important value *or failing to obtain some desired goal.* ... [It can be] seen in terms of losses (costs or fears) *and gains* (opportunities or greed)."[83] But this is merely to look at the same situation from the other side, since the lower probability of success is a *result* of the relative lack of resources applied, and it is the increased possibility of failure due to low cost now that makes for the possibility of higher cost later on. If more resources were used, the strategy's objectives would be less

---

[80] David Pervin, "Why Take Risks?" *SAIS Review* 19 (Winter-Spring 1999): 252–255. " ... the choice of an act may be construed as the acceptance of a gamble that can yield outcomes with different probabilities." Daniel Kahneman and Amos Tversky, "Choices, Values, and Frames," *American Psychologist* 39 (April 1984): 341.

[81] John Lewis Gaddis argues the Bush administration did just this after 9/11, but judges that "the assumption that things would fall neatly into place after the shock was administered was the single greatest mis-judgment of the first Bush administration." "Grand Strategy in the Second Term," *Foreign Affairs* 84 (January/February 2005): 15.

[82] To repeat, one can define risk taking as "the probability of success that a decision maker demands before pursuing a course of action. 'Uncertainty,' on the other hand, refers to the degree to which the probability of success of a course of action is unknown." Bueno de Mesquita, *The War Trap*, p. 33.

[83] McDermott, *Risk Taking in International Politics*, p. 1. Italics added.

risky of accomplishment, but the cost would be higher. So the strategist is trading the certainty of paying more now against some possibility of paying much more later. Again, higher cost leads to lower risk and lower cost to higher risk, either of additional, unexpected costs or of failure to achieve objectives.

The 2003 U.S. war to oust Saddam Hussein's regime in Iraq illustrates several aspects of the relationship between cost and risk and how strategists may make different tradeoffs between them at different levels of their strategy. At the level of the United States overall foreign affairs strategy the war can be seen as part of an aggressive, forward-leaning, offensive approach to terrorism, part of a *high-cost, risk-minimizing* strategy. That is, the Bush administration's stated rationale for taking on the costs of the war was that removing Saddam Hussein would lower the danger (or passive risk) of the U.S. being attacked by terrorists. Those costs *included* several active risks that were possible consequences of initiating war, such as battlefield failure, high casualties, the exposure of American troops and civilians to attack in the region, negative shifts in Arab/Muslim opinion of the U.S. leading to the recruitment of more terrorists, radical takeovers of moderate Arab countries (one of which has nuclear weapons), entrapment of the U.S. in a high-cost open-ended occupation, and damaging the prestige and hence the power of the United States. These local or operational risks can be seen as necessary to access the gain the war hoped to secure: not only a lowering of the danger of attack on the homeland, but also (if the administration's rhetoric is to be believed) the prospect of democracy's spread in the region. At the same time, they could have been mitigated by raising the costs of the war, especially by using more troops and/or equipment, but also by providing better protection to Americans in the region, funding robust public diplomacy efforts, or offering additional aid to support moderate Arab governments. Since the administration did little of these things, the Iraq war could itself be fairly characterized as a *high-risk, cost-minimizing* strategy. When Vice President Cheney said in August 2002 that "the risks of inaction are far greater than the risk of action," he presumably meant that the danger or passive risk of terrorist attack on the United States, which the war was expected to reduce, was greater than the active, operational risks that the war would engender, given the balance of costs and risks that the administration chose in fighting it.[84]

Like much of George W. Bush's statecraft, the 2003 Iraq war was an example of a largely unilateral strategy. This characteristic (or its multilateral opposite) strongly affects the initiator's cost and risk. By definition,

---

[84] Speech to Nashville, TN, VFW, quoted in Dana Milbank, "Cheney Says Iraqi Strike Is Justified," *Washington Post* (August 27, 2002): A1. Even more interesting, it is possible that comprehensive high-cost risk-minimizing strategies inevitably spawn high-risk cost-minimizing substrategies, simply because their ambition spreads resources thinly among such substrategies.

unilateral strategies favor tools that can be used by a nation-state acting alone, and very often those instruments are used for coercive purposes.[85] But the distinction between unilateral and multilateral statecraft is not the same as that between coercive and co-optive strategies. The defining characteristic of a unilateralism is the belief that the nation's own power is sufficient to accomplish its purposes, that it therefore does not need to augment that power by enlisting the help of other states, and that it consequently need not accommodate its objectives to the interests of those states. Unilateral statecraft may be driven by the judgment that some objectives are both absolutely necessary and so contrary to the interests of other significant international actors that they would never receive their approval, but the result is a strategy setting maximum objectives *and* bearing very high costs, precisely because other states will not be contributing to their pursuit.

By contrast, a *multilateral* approach may have to set more modest objectives that accommodate the interests of other actors to some extent in order to enlist their support, thereby reducing the resources that must be expended by the initiating state without increasing (and probably even lowering) its risks. By effectively augmenting the power of the initiating state, multilateralism, like more formal coalitions and alliances, can thus provide some relief from the cost-risk dilemma all strategy faces. If the Iraq war of 2003 is an example of unilateral statecraft, the Gulf war of 1991 is an excellent example of multilateralism. The warfighting coalition of major American allies and most Arab states assembled by the administration of George H. W. Bush dramatically reduced the financial costs of the war, along with the risk that Saddam could portray it as a war of an infidel West against Islam.[86] In return, Bush kept the war's objectives within the parameters set by the UN Security Council, which allowed the expulsion of Iraq's army from Kuwait but not the overthrow of Saddam's regime.

The trading of cost and risk, as well as adjustment of goals and hoped-for benefits, implies an ability to estimate future probabilities with some degree of accuracy. However, because of the uncertainty of foreign resistance, third party actions, or domestic support, one can hardly expect

---

[85] Though a characteristic of strategy, unilateralism can also be considered a characteristic of instruments or of how they are applied. It obviously excludes instruments that require the cooperation of other nations (like multilateral diplomacy, international law and organizations, and alliances), but the other instruments can be used cooperatively as well as unilaterally.

[86] The net financial costs to the United States of the 1991 Gulf war have been variously estimated at about $13 billion, compared to well over $300 billion at this writing for the 2003-present Iraq war. The casualty rates are similarly different, though not in as great a ratio. Jonathan Weisman, "Projected Iraq War Costs Soar," *Washington Post* (April 27, 2006): A16–17; also, see Amy Belasco, *The Cost of Iraq, Afghanistan, and Other Global War on Terror Operations Since 9/11* (Washington, DC: Congressional Research Service, September 22, 2006).

strategists to make an exact correlation between objectives and resources, or to set the ideal balance of cost and risk, before undertaking a foreign enterprise. There is always the chance for failure, and the statesman usually cannot wait for certainty. "To shape events," as Henry Kissinger puts it, "one must act on the basis of assessments that cannot be proved correct when they are made."[87] Some experienced decision makers even go so far as to assert that leaders should take action when they know as little as 20 percent of what they think they need to know to make the decision; otherwise, they will act too late. Even in retrospect, it is difficult to know if the failure or success of highly leveraged strategies was a matter of the quality of strategic thought and action or simply the luck of breaking events.

After the army coup of September 30, 1991, in Haiti, for example, the administrations first of George H. W. Bush and then Bill Clinton announced as their objective the return to power of the constitutional, elected government of Jean Bertrand Aristide. They tried a variety of non-military instruments, including harsh economic sanctions, without success, and eventually Clinton was trapped by his own rhetoric into using military force. For over a year Clinton's strategy had seemed to lack the means to accomplish its objectives, while the sanctions had an extraordinarily severe impact on the country's already impoverished population. One might argue that the United States should never have declared such a goal without first being certain that the means were available to achieve it, but careful analysis before the event might well have concluded that the nonviolent instruments envisioned would in fact work.[88] Until the documents on Haiti are opened, then, we will not know if the risks were carefully (if mistakenly) assessed in a plausible strategic concept or if Haiti was a case of policy without strategy.

The May 1993 elections in Cambodia are an example of the opposite type. Although the United Nations peacekeeping effort in Cambodia was of unprecedented scope and expense, many commentators argued that, unless the parties (and especially the Khmer Rouge) were fully disarmed, the UN was taking enormous risks that the elections would be disrupted. Khmer Rouge attacks in the weeks leading up to the balloting certainly gave credence to that argument and to the view that the organization's members had fatally underestimated the amount of resources that would be necessary to secure a free and fair vote. In the event, however, the KR opposition seemed to evaporate, and nearly 90 percent of the Cambodian people participated in their first multiparty election since 1951, proving either that the UN estimated the needed resources accurately or that it

---

[87] Kissinger, *White House Years*, p. 914.

[88] The very weakness of the Haitian economy, and its close economic ties to the U.S., would have seemed to forecast that sanctions would have a strong impact (Step 4); but what was missing was the political connections that were needed for success (Step 5).

took great risks and won its gamble.[89] A decade later the UN lost a similar gamble in East Timor, when premature disengagement by members eager to cut costs led to battles among rogue security forces that severely imperiled the new nation's democratic future.[90]

American policy in the 1980s toward Nicaragua illustrates both negative and positive outcomes for risky strategies. President Reagan's approach – to arm the *contras* as a way of overthrowing the Sandinista government – seems a clear case of a policy objective without the means to support it. Given Soviet and Cuban aid to the region's largest army, Reagan's own refusal to send American military forces to do the job, and the slim chance that any government with a choice would negotiate itself out of power, it was relatively easy to deduce that the means were unavailable to achieve this objective – particularly after the Congress refused Reagan's request to fund the *contras*.[91] To its credit, the administration of George H. W. Bush recognized that the policy had reached a dead end. Secretary of State James Baker was able to strike a deal with Congress essentially giving up Reagan's objective for the new one of holding free and fair elections in Nicaragua, elections that most observers assumed the Sandinistas would win. In a different way, Bush's policy was as risky as Reagan's. But his risks paid off when the Nicaraguan people voted the Sandinistas out of power – just as the "new thinking" of President Gorbachev was bringing Soviet bloc aid to the region to an end.[92]

As these examples illustrate, the appropriate degree of risk (like the level of cost) will vary widely with different situations. The uniqueness of each scenario makes it impossible to offer specific guidelines for assessing risk, but clearly strategists need to think through the consequences of proposed courses of action along three ever-widening dimensions. First, and most important, they must systematically consider how T will react to I's actions, what I will then do in response to T's reactions, what T will next do in response to I's response, and so forth across the wide variety of plausible actions and reactions. If strategy has basically to do with "getting from where you are to where you want to go . . . in the face of resistance in some form," and if the resistance is provided by other strategists, then the use of the tools of state power will unavoidably be an interactive enterprise.[93] The fact that the resistance is intelligent is part of what makes the prediction of instruments' effects so difficult. Nevertheless, one element of risk reduction involves attempting to predict how the interactive behavior of the two parties will play out.

---

[89] William Branigin, "Voter Turnout Deals 'Historic Defeat' to Khmer Rouge, Sihanouk Declares," *Washington Post* (May 27, 1993): A42.

[90] Alan Sipress, "In E. Timor, an Optimistic Enterprise Turns to Ashes," *Washington Post* (June 2, 2006): A13, A16.

[91] Shultz, *Turmoil and Triumph*, pp. 292–297, 305–322, 402–426.

[92] James A. Baker, III, *The Politics of Diplomacy* (New York: G. P. Putnam's Sons, 1995), pp. 47–60.

[93] Gaddis, "Containment and the Logic of Strategy," p. 29.

Second, in an interdependent world almost any influence attempt is bound to affect the interests of third parties. It is not surprising that the most serious downside risk that U.S. decision makers identified in their 2001 decision to go to war in Afghanistan was the implosion of Pakistan, a vital third party to the Afghan conflict that was being pressured by the United States to reverse a foreign policy backed by strong institutional and religious interests. Similarly, sanctions or military action against one country (like Iraq or Serbia) may severely damage the economies of its neighbors, preferences offered to one trading partner inevitably discriminate against goods from others, public diplomacy (like the "axis of evil" speech) meant to threaten American adversaries upsets American allies, military action against one Muslim regime causes demonstrations and riots that threaten the stability of others – the list of possibilities seems endless. Yet strategists must systematically analyze the list lest they become so absorbed with the interactions between themselves and the target of their strategy that they lose sight of risks from other quarters.

Third, strategists need to look beyond both target and third country reactions to estimate broader effects on the strategic environment. The conduct of a state as powerful as the United States has profound effects on global norms, so it is not unlikely that its choice of instruments, and its decisions on how they are to be used, will affect the international security and economic environments of the future in ways that may be more – or less – benign for American interests. The use of nuclear weapons in a regional conflict, for example, with a resulting crumbling of the firebreak between nuclear and conventional arms, is one risk the United States has so far not been willing to run.[94] Institutionalist writers have suggested that whether the United States uses instruments unilaterally or multilaterally may well have substantial effects on its ability to protect its interests after its power advantage has faded, an argument that has increased salience given the strong unilateralist preferences of the George W. Bush administration.[95] Choices of instruments and ways of using them may also affect the domestic environment, particularly the level of support an administration can sustain for a foreign policy objective.[96] This fact is well understood (if not always heeded) with regard to the use of military force, but the loss of public (and through it congressional) support is also a major risk in the use of covert action, since public support cannot be built for it in advance. The economic damage caused by sanctions, or by concessional trade policies, can also pose domestic risks for an administration using them,

---

[94] Before the Gulf war, Gen. Powell explicitly considered the role nuclear weapons might play, showed the analysis to Secretary Cheney and had it destroyed. "The results unnerved me," he later wrote. Colin Powell, *My American Journey* (New York: Random House, 1995), p. 486.

[95] On the institutionalist view, see G. John Ikenberry, "America's Liberal Hegemony," *Current History* (January 1999): 23–38 and especially "Getting Hegemony Right," *National Interest* 63 (Spring 2001): 17–24.

[96] See Chapter 3.

while the use of aid funds provides opportunities for scandals that can erode the always-limited domestic support for this instrument.

As strategists consider these three situational levels, they should note that some strategies and instruments are likely to incur more risk than others. Coercive strategies would seem more risky than cooperative ones, since they increase tensions and may lead to retaliation.[97] Outright war is certainly the riskiest instrument, but even here the risks depend greatly on the target: invading Grenada or Haiti carries vastly different downside possibilities than invading Afghanistan, Afghanistan than Iraq, and Iraq than Iran. Deploying military force to support diplomacy or using economic sanctions incurs some escalatory risk, but states rarely go to war by accident, and the most draconian economic sanctions seldom elicit a military response.[98] More often, decision makers in the initiating state become frustrated by the failure of limited military actions, sanctions, or even diplomacy and move on to other instruments without carefully reevaluating the new costs and risks they present, as some believe happened to U.S. statecraft in Somalia, Haiti, Kosovo, and the 1991 Gulf war.[99] Acting covertly may seem to avoid some of the risks inherent in the underlying instrument (whether informational, economic, or military) because the lack of attribution does not engage national prestige, but its covert nature obviously presents risks of its own, the risks of exposure.

Although strategists may be aware of such considerations and attempt to factor them into their thinking, they are still human beings. And because cost and risk are about the downside of strategy, a product of uncertainty and negative consequences, people have a hard time dealing with them. Psychological experiments indicate that people suffer more from pain than they enjoy an equivalent amount pleasure.[100] Similarly, "losing hurts more than a comparable gain pleases," for people value what they have more than what they might get and therefore tend to see out of pocket costs (losses) as more significant than opportunity costs (gains foregone).[101] Hence the often-noted tendency to throw good money after bad and the

---

[97] As noted above, the most obvious risk with cooperative tools is that of blackmail.

[98] Geoffrey Blainey, "War As an Accident," Chapter 9 in *The Causes of War* (New York: MacMillan/Free Press, 1973), pp. 127–145. The only notable example of a military response in the long history of U.S.-imposed sanctions is Japan's Pearl Harbor attack of 1941.

[99] In Haiti and the Gulf war unsuccessful but effective economic sanctions led to military action; in Kosovo the refusal of the Serbs to yield at Rambouillet led to the decision to bomb.

[100] Amos Tversky and Daniel Kahneman state that "pain is more urgent than pleasure," and that "the asymmetry of pleasure and pain is the ultimate justification of loss aversion...." "Loss Aversion in Riskless Choice: A Reference Dependent Model," *Quarterly Journal of Economics* (#41, 1991): 1057.

[101] McDermott, *Risk Taking in International Politics*, p. 29. The overvaluing of what one has is called the endowment effect. For example, experimental subjects are more distressed by losing a $20 bill than they enjoy finding one.

unwillingness to write off sunk costs, a tendency particularly evident among statesmen caught in long wars (think of Richard Nixon taking five years to liquidate the American position in Vietnam, or the contrary example of Ronald Reagan's rapid 1984 withdrawal from Lebanon).[102]

These characteristics render decision makers likely to choose differently depending on whether they see the issue as one involving losses or gain. Specifically, individuals are risk averse when a gain is in prospect but risk acceptant when it comes to avoiding or trying to recover losses. The magnitude seems to matter less than the fact of a loss, so even losses that are small relative to a state's overall position may induce behavior that risks losing a great deal more.[103] Thus, near-pacifist Jimmy Carter authorized a highly complex military operation to rescue the American hostages in Tehran, and Bill Clinton risked war to stop killing in the former Yugoslavia. Both of them adopted risky strategies, against the objections of American allies, to rescue a situation they thought was deteriorating.[104]

Of course, whether a change in circumstances is seen as recovering a loss or obtaining a gain depends on where the observer places his or her mental reference point between the two.[105] And because they overvalue losses relative to gains, people tend to adjust or "renormalize" the reference point of their perceived status quo more quickly if gains are made than if losses are suffered; that is, they tend to pocket their gains quickly (and adjust their mental status quo accordingly) but nurse their sense of loss, feeling that the old, more desirable status quo is the way things really ought to be.[106] This means that if an exchange of people, property, or even prestige has taken place between two parties in an international dispute, they may perceive different status quos on the same issue. *Both* may believe they need to recoup or prevent losses and therefore be willing to take great risks, setting up an extremely dangerous situation.[107] Indeed, states are

[102] Robert Jervis, "Political Implications of Loss Aversion," in Farnham, ed., *Avoiding Losses/Taking Risks: Prospect Theory and International Conflict*, pp. 24, 26–27.

[103] Levy, "Prospect Theory and International Relations: Theoretical Applications and Analytical Problems," pp. 123.

[104] On Carter, see Rose McDermott, "Prospect Theory in International Relations: The Iranian Hostage Rescue Mission," in Farnham, ed., *Avoiding Losses/Taking Risks*, pp. 73–99; on Bush and Clinton, see Stephen Sestanovich, "American Maximalism," *National Interest* 79 (Spring 2005): 13–24.

[105] "Prospect theory posits that individuals evaluate outcomes with respect to deviations from a reference point rather than with respect to net asset levels, that their identification of this reference point is a critical variable, that they give more weight to losses than to comparable gains, and that they are generally risk-averse with respect to gains and risk-acceptant with respect to losses." Levy, "An Introduction to Prospect Theory," in Farnham, ed., *Avoiding Losses/Taking Risks*, p. 7.

[106] Robert Jervis, "Political Implications of Loss Aversion," pp. 35–36; Levy, "Prospect Theory and International Relations: Theoretical Applications and Analytical Problems," p. 124.

[107] Levy, "Prospect Theory and International Relations: Theoretical Applications and Analytical Problems," pp. 123–124.

"more often pushed into war by the fear that the alternative to fighting is a serious deterioration in their position [a loss] than pulled in by the belief that war can improve a situation that is already satisfactory [a gain]."[108] Fear seems more powerful than hope.

Because people find uncertainty and loss so distressing, they may also unknowingly resort to mental tricks that artificially devalue or eliminate them. For example, they will often value a reduction in risk from 10 percent to 0 percent, one that changes uncertainty into certainty, much more highly than a reduction in uncertainty from 50 percent to 40 percent, even though both represent a 10 percent risk reduction.[109] Moreover, when probabilities get close to certainties, people will often accept them as such, considering a 5 percent probability as impossible or a 95 percent probability as inevitable.[110] Their behavior then can reverse, becoming risk averse when faced with very likely losses ("resistance is futile") and risk seeking at the prospect of very likely gains ("a sure thing"). They may therefore find themselves completely unprepared when the "certain" does not happen or the "impossible" does. Similarly, people so hate losses that decision makers will more readily accept spending resources on instruments that may well never be used if the purchase is thought of as the cost of protection against possible threats rather than as an uncompensated loss, a phenomenon that partly explains why it is hard to buy instruments of statecraft in a low-threat environment.[111] Loss aversion also may bedevil negotiations, as each side weights the value of its own prospective concessions more strongly than equivalent gains offered by the other side.[112]

Strategists should recognize the operation of these kinds of psychological mechanisms and guard against them as they do their work, for example, by being mindful of where their reference point is and whether proposed courses of action are couched as seeking gains or recovering losses.[113] These mechanisms should also be recognized (and may perhaps be exploited) as strategists try to use instruments prospectively to alter the cost-benefit structures of the choices faced by the targets of their

---

[108] Robert Jervis, "Political Implications of Loss Aversion," p. 29. This was certainly true at Pearl Harbor, where the U.S. oil embargo convinced Japan that it was losing power relative to a United States it believed it would inevitably fight, and George W. Bush went to war against Iraq to attack the threat of Saddam's WMD rather than to grasp the opportunity of spreading democracy in the Middle East.

[109] "A change from impossibility to possibility or from possibility to certainty has a bigger impact [on people's sense of value] than a comparable change in the middle of the scale." Kahneman and Tversky, "Choices, Values, and Frames," p. 344.

[110] Slovic, "Informing and Educating the Public About Risk," p. 405.

[111] Kahneman and Tversky, "Choices, Values, and Frames," p. 349.

[112] Jervis, "Political Implications of Loss Aversion," p. 37; Levy, "Prospect Theory and International Relations: Theoretical Applications and Analytical Problems," p. 126.

[113] Indeed, in order to avoid these framing effects, options should be presented in both positive and negative terms: for example, that a certain course of action has a 20% chance of succeeding *and* a 80% chance of failing. McDermott, *Risk Taking in International Politics*, p. 26.

influence attempts, understanding that threats motivate more strongly than promises, that losses and uncertainty will be resisted and even denied, and that an opponent will be more inclined to risky behavior when reacting to a threatened loss than to a proffered gain.

Still, however uncomfortable it may be, all strategies have costs and risks. The first obligation of the strategist is to be aware of them and make an explicit effort to estimate them. Strategists should weight downside risks according to their probabilities and include them in their cost estimates. Equally important, strategists estimating the cost-effectiveness of various objective-instrument packages must also weight the benefits of the objectives by their probability of accomplishment. Just as strategists should be wary of the natural tendency to minimize downside risks, those embracing entrepreneurial risks in the hope of gain must be careful not to exaggerate the likelihood of those gains materializing. Good strategies will set objectives that have a reasonable chance of accomplishment and will try to keep costs and risks proportional to the interests at stake, as well as to the seriousness of the threats being countered or the importance of the opportunities being grasped. In situations where goals seem less than critical to the national interest, and where uncertainties are overwhelming or resources obviously not commensurate with the task, they will elect to conserve the nation's power and prestige for more vital and more certain projects.

8. COHERENCE: Check Internal and External Compatibility of Ends, Means, and Ways

Once the costs and risks of instrument-objective packages are assessed, the final step is to consider their compatibility with each other and with courses of action in other strategies. Here strategists must consider their schemes' coherence and face the necessity for strategic coordination and prioritization.[114] Feasibility alone argues strongly for focused, prioritized strategies that direct the bulk of resources to the few most essential objectives. After 9/11, for example, if the most important goal was to disrupt and destroy Al Qaeda and to capture or kill Osama bin Laden and his top lieutenants in Afghanistan, strategic focus should have ruled out launching other wars that would inevitably pull resources from the main event – as did the 2003 war in Iraq.[115] The same principle applies to a particular issue with a given country or region. If an administration's real concern with Iran is its behavior in Iraq, for example, then the United States may need to tolerate Iranian support for terrorism and/or its nuclear programs,

---

[114] After the course of action for each objective is developed, the strategist "should now step back and take a broad look at the overall package to determine whether it is internally consistent. Does it represent a coherent approach to international policy?" Schmitt, "Identifying National Objectives and Developing Strategy," p. 32.

[115] Barton Gellman and Dafna Linzer, "Afghanistan, Iraq: Two Wars Collide," *Washington Post* (October 22, 2004): A1, A14.

objectionable as both are, in order to obtain its highest priority objective. Strategists must discipline themselves, always keeping the one or the very few most important objectives foremost.

Prioritization is also required to preserve the coherence of strategic effort. Potential conflicts exist on several levels. First, objectives can be incompatible when they run into the real world; that is, the achievement of one may directly detract from or obstruct the achievement of another. During the Cold War years, for example, supporting human rights abroad and protecting the nation's security were often incompatible goals, since many of the security partners whose cooperation the United States needed to help contain Soviet power were ruled by authoritarian governments that routinely violated their citizens' human rights. An uncomfortable choice was therefore necessary. The United States could promote human rights in countries like South Korea, Taiwan, or the Philippines at the cost of close defense relationships with their governments, or it could nurture productive security ties with those governments at the cost of appearing to condone (or at least of not taking strong actions against) their human rights violations. The United States has faced a similar problem since 9/11, and Washington has noticeably moderated its criticism of China's actions in Tibet, Russia's in Chechnya, and many of the Central Asian states' human rights and democratic practices in order to better secure their cooperation in the war on terrorism – although it did choose to criticize Uzbekistan at the cost of an airbase there.[116] Indeed, security and intelligence assistance, one of the major tools the Bush administration used to promote cooperation against terrorism, also increased these governments' capacity to effectively repress internal dissent.

Second, as this last point implies, strategists must be careful that the instruments they choose to execute one strategy do not undercut objectives in another, especially objectives serving interests of equal or greater importance. The Clinton administration fell into this trap in 1993–94 when it decided to use the threat of revoking China's most favored nation (MFN) status to promote human rights there. The administration's prior emphasis on economic growth and revitalization in the United States argued powerfully against actions that would damage American businesses operating in China and Hong Kong. Yet revoking MFN would have done just that, demonstrating a conflict between this instrument of *foreign affairs* strategy and higher priority goals of *national* strategy. In addition, terminating MFN would also clearly have weakened both the human and the economic forces in China that were most supportive of democracy, for China's budding capitalists are among the most resistant to the rigidities of its authoritarian political system. Thus the very nature of this particular tool undercut not only other, more important objectives but its *own* objective as well.

---

[116] Robin Wright and Ann Scott Tyson, "U.S. Evicted from Air Base in Uzbekistan," *Washington Post* (July 30, 2005): A1, A15.

Third, strategists must be sure that instruments do not work against each other or against other instruments being used simultaneously to pursue other objectives. For example, one of the persistent problems facing U.S. mediation in the Middle East peace process is that its military aid program provides Israel with American weapons that Tel Aviv uses against Palestinians, undercutting the negotiating tool by discrediting the United States as an honest broker. Harmonizing instruments is particularly difficult if covert action is involved, since the very secrecy of such efforts makes it difficult for decision makers to see the contradictions they may present. The need for instrument compatibility can also preclude using positive and negative instruments on the same target, like aid and sanctions.

The need to coordinate and prioritize foreign affairs strategy, then, stems from a variety of potential conflicts. Not only are all its efforts drawing on the same pool of resources, but objectives may conflict with objectives, instruments may counteract instruments, and instruments used to promote one goal may directly undercut other goals.[117] Therefore, even the possession of overwhelming relative power, like that of the United States in the early twenty-first century, does not by itself solve the problem of coordination. For even in an ideal situation, where one's power might seem to make all things possible, the comprehensiveness of foreign affairs strategy requires one to pick and choose carefully. Relationships up, down, and sideways must be set for myriads of strategies on a variety of levels, for scores of countries and across hundreds of issues. Otherwise the likely result will be great efforts at cross purposes and ultimate failure.

The problem of coordination is all the more complex because of the breadth of foreign affairs strategy and the multiplicity of levels on which it operates. One can imagine a massive inverted tree, beginning with the four categories of interest described in Chapter 4 and branching out in a wide range of both geographic and functional areas to comprise successively more detailed goals and the ways and means needed to pursue them. Since each course of action will be specific to a country or a particular issue, there is a need to integrate (or at least consider the relationship of) each with all those under consideration for other locales or subjects. But the problem is still more complex, because a strategy to serve one objective may well require a series of subsidiary objectives which themselves have resource implications, affect other areas of policy, and require their own implementation strategies.

The fact that strategies tend to beget strategies leads to one of the most confusing aspects of strategic logic: the apparent reversibility of ends

---

[117] Robert Art endorses this step in cases where commitments seem to call for new supporting commitments: "ask whether the policies being implemented to support them all are mutually supportive, or are instead contradictory." *A Grand Strategy for America*, p. 170.

and means.[118] Like the relationship between strategy and policy discussed in Chapter 1 or the confusion of interests and objectives considered in Chapters 4 and 7, this intellectual challenge requires strategists frequently to step back and consider carefully the whole strategic construct lest they lose their way. On the one hand, since *objectives* are often set in the service of higher goals, it is easy to begin thinking of them as *means* to other ends. Though such objectives *are* subsidiary if one is looking up the strategic construct toward higher levels, that they are not means can be quickly reaffirmed if one keeps in mind the definition of means as power or resources. On the other hand, like power generally, specific *instruments* of statecraft can be so critical to goal achievement that the strategist is compelled to set their acquisition as a prior *goal*, necessary of accomplishment before the real objective can be pursued. As time passes, the pursuit of the means in question can become an end in itself, incurring costs far out of proportion to its value and distorting the whole strategic design. In the Kosovo war of 1999, for example, Americans were so focused on keeping NATO together that they arguably fought less effectively, despite the fact that the alliance had been created as a means to *more* effective war fighting. Their priorities were not necessarily wrong, because the alliance was indeed a valuable asset worth preserving for future use. But it was necessary to focus on the true nature of NATO as a means rather than an end in order to balance alliance preservation with the need for battlefield success. Confusions caused by the apparent reversibility of ends and means in either direction can be greatly ameliorated if strategists keep the whole enterprise in mind and are clear about whether they are facing up or down the strategic tree.

Though such illustrations show the challenge of strategic integration to be a daunting one, the interrelationships of issues and countries also provide the strategist with an opportunity to structure their actions in positive ways, to link goals and actions so that each helps rather than hinders the others' achievement. Henry Kissinger defined linkage in two ways:

> first, when a diplomat deliberately links two separate objectives in a negotiation, using one as leverage on the other; or [second] by virtue of reality, because in an interdependent world the actions of a major power are inevitably related and have consequences beyond the issue or region immediately concerned.[119]

---

[118] "Means-ends analysis is complicated by the fact that very few ends are ultimate or final values; most are intermediate or instrumental in some sense. Thus, the same activity may be viewed as a means in one context and a goal in another." David Baldwin, *Economic Statecraft*, p. 16. "When we use the language of means and ends, we say that means can themselves be ends and that ends can be means." Vernon Van Dyke, "Values and Interests," *American Political Science Review* (September 1962): 568. Also, see Fred A. Sondermann, "The Concept of the National Interest," *Orbis* 22 (Spring 1977): 128.

[119] Kissinger, *White House Years*, p. 129.

Real, causal linkage connects situations of strength with strength and weakness with weakness, but artificial, bargaining linkage is an attempt to overcome weakness on an issue by linking it with strength.[120] In prioritizing objectives, strategists will use both. They will look for ways to turn the inherent linkages of world politics and economics discussed in Chapter 2 to their advantage, "to create incentives or pressures in one part of the world to influence events in another."[121] They will also try to set objectives that serve more than one interest, and to use instruments in ways that support two or more objectives – to kill at least two birds with one stone. Such techniques hold the promise of moving strategy beyond coordination to coherence, beyond simply deconflicting its various parts to establishing positive interrelationships that will magnify a state's power and expand its range of achievable objectives.

Of American postwar foreign affairs strategies, the Nixon administration's approach was perhaps the most explicitly interlinked in this sense. As noted in Chapter 5, the administration's major goals were to open a new relationship with the People's Republic of China, get arms control and political agreements with the Soviet Union that would reduce the dangers of the superpower confrontation, and withdraw from the Vietnam war without defeat. Based on triangular geopolitics, all three were interrelated and mutually supportive. The opening to China supported Vietnam withdrawal by reassuring Nixon that the application of military force needed to back the latter goal would not cause the PRC to intervene as it had in the Korean War, and Moscow's fear of U.S.–Chinese rapprochement also put pressure on the Soviets to negotiate seriously with the United States on arms control and rules of geopolitical engagement. Negotiations with Moscow provided opportunity to make Soviet restraint in its support of Vietnam a condition of arms control agreements, while reinforcing Kissinger's leverage in his negotiations with Hanoi as well as in those with China. Finally, U.S. moves toward withdrawal from Vietnam reassured both Moscow and Beijing as to American intentions. When, in April 1971, the arrangements for the secret Kissinger visit to China were finally set and it looked as though both a Soviet SALT agreement and a Chinese summit were likely, the National Security Advisor told the president that they "had, in fact, linked the various strands of our policy as we had intended: 'We have done it now, we have got it all hooked together.'"[122]

Although prioritization has been used so far to denote importance, to distinguish things done from things not done, the term is often also used in a temporal sense to mean things done *first*. Precedence is also an essential part of any strategic construct, influencing not only the sort of micro decisions considered in Step 3 on the ways instruments will be used (like

---

[120] Art, "American Foreign Policy and the Fungibility of Force," pp. 30–31.
[121] Kissinger, *White House Years*, p. 31.
[122] Kissinger, *White House Years*, p. 716.

which of any concessions will be made first in a negotiation, or when various economic sanctions should be applied) but also macro decisions on which foreign affairs enterprise will be undertaken before another. In the late 1960s and early 1970s, for example, Nixon and Kissinger spent a great deal of effort considering whether moves toward detente with Russia or normalization with China should come first, and the Carter administration also debated intensely the timing of recognition of China in relation to the SALT II negotiations.[123] Timing is also of critical importance to the maintenance of political support at home for policy, because (as we noted in Chapter 3) a president's success in one political endeavor will increase his power in later ones. Although he eventually won Senate approval of the Panama Canal Treaties, for example, Jimmy Carter's decision to place such a controversial item first on his political agenda is widely seen as among the most consequential of his presidency, for the long political battle that ensued contributed far more to an image of presidential weakness than of strength.[124]

Timeframes must be considered, then, not only with regard to the intrinsic nature of the moves being coordinated, but also in relation to the constraints and opportunities presented by the domestic and international environment. Indeed, environmental changes provide a reference point for usefully distinguishing between short-term and long-term timeframes. "Short-term" can be seen as a period too abbreviated to reasonably expect or work toward consequential changes in either the domestic or the international contexts that will affect the likelihood of strategic success, while the "long-term" will accommodate such transformations. Internationally, such changes might include major shifts in the balance of power like that caused by the disintegration of the Soviet empire, reversals of alliances like that which took place on the Horn of Africa in 1977, or changes in foreign governments, like those during 1979 in Iran or Nicaragua or the 1992 shift from coalition to Labour governments in Israel that allowed the Middle East peace process to resume. Domestically, such shifts could include a gain (or loss) of seats in the Congress by the president in power, an economic recovery or recession that markedly increases or decreases the nation's potential power, or the delivery of new instruments of statecraft that the administration or its predecessors had bought some years earlier.

The strategist must not only anticipate how such conditions might change but also prioritize objectives over time to take advantage of their interrelationships. Very often, the accomplishment of one objective will pave the way for the achievement of another. Presidents who succeed in one area of foreign affairs, or even in domestic affairs, will find greater domestic support for their next and possibly more risky foreign venture. Such image

---

[123] Brzezinski, *Power and Principle*, p. 223ff; Cyrus Vance, *Hard Choices* (New York: Simon & Schuster, 1983), pp. 113–119.
[124] Vance, *Hard Choices*, pp. 156–157.

building also works overseas, as the discussion of psychological power projection in Chapter 5 noted. Foreign governments will not only be impressed with a successful foreign policy, but a carefully orchestrated statecraft will be able to build positions of strength that can contribute to downstream goals. Negotiators may shift their bargaining strategies depending upon the kind of international future they anticipate. Thus, strategists must seek to integrate their courses of action not only horizontally and vertically, but also in the fourth dimension, and they must coordinate their strategies with designs in the sphere of domestic policy as well. For these reasons, foreign affairs strategy finds its place as a subset of national strategy.[125]

The Uses of Foreign Affairs Strategy

The eight steps described in this and the prior chapter provide a systematic approach to the planning of foreign affairs strategy. Having completed them, strategists should not only have created courses of action that connect objectives, instruments, and statecraft in the service of national interests. They should also have created strategies that are efficient as well as effective, made choices based on a careful juxtaposition of anticipated benefit and cost, and set priorities to at least deconflict their proposed actions and if possible mutually reinforce them. In the process they will have made decisions about how much cost and risk they wish to bear and the balance between them, tailoring objectives to their power as well as their interests.

Governments often put their strategies in writing, both as a necessary exercise to clarify thinking and because of the need to communicate intended actions to those who must carry them out. In the U.S. government, broad foreign affairs strategies are often generated within the National Security Council system by an elaborate interagency review and decision process early in an administration, with more specific regional, country, and issue strategies following in later months and years.[126] Although the tone and format of these documents varies widely, most include the elements of strategy discussed in this book: some overview of assumptions about the international (and perhaps also the domestic) context, a discussion of the national interest and threats to it, consideration of power relationships and the nation's influence internationally, a review of the various instruments needed and desired by the administration, and a broad plan of action describing the statecraft through which they will be applied to overall objectives. The public document closest to a written U.S. foreign affairs strategy is the *National Security Strategy of the United*

---

[125] See Chapter 1.

[126] NSC-68, NSC 162/2, PRM 10, and other more recent papers are the best known examples of the former. See Aaron Friedman, "The Making of American National Strategy, 1948–1988," *National Interest* 11 (Spring 1988): 65–75.

States, put out by the White House periodically. The State Department has its own Strategic Plan supporting the National Security Strategy, and the Pentagon its *Military Strategy of the United States.*

But to speak of foreign affairs strategy as a written plan should not be taken to mean that any strategy will be implemented just as it is written. One experienced observer spoke of having been appalled upon reading the various color and rainbow plans that were written by the American military during the 1930s for conducting the next war; he felt they would have been a disaster for the country if implemented. But to take them literally was quite beside the point, he argued, because the captains and colonels who wrote them became the admirals and generals who fought and won World War II.[127] The process of strategy formulation, in other words, was far more important than the product; it focused and sharpened their thinking so that real strategies could emerge when the circumstances of the world war presented themselves. "Plans may be useless," as General Eisenhower once put it, "but planning is indispensable."[128]

The point of doing foreign affairs strategy, then, is not to get between blue covers a plan that can then be slavishly followed in day-to-day state-craft, nor should the image of strategy be that of any written document. The idea is rather to bring intentionality into one's statecraft, to infuse in decision makers' minds ways of thinking about policy and a sense of direction that will sustain them through the inevitable vicissitudes of foreign relations. Indeed, the chronic uncertainty with which strategists must deal argues for robust rather than optimal strategies, that is, strategies that may not be the best for any particular future but will work well enough for a wide range of plausible futures.[129] As former ambassador to NATO David Abshire once wrote:

> A plan, if it is fixed and stereotyped, is in fact the opposite of a truly good strategy. Strategy involves having a concept, priorities, and a direction – ones that are flexible and adaptable to changing situations – for the rational and disciplined allocation of resources to achieve specific objectives.[130]

Good strategies are rarely the product of committees, and they cannot be expected to result from the policy process. Indeed, any official statement of a government, regardless of its title, is by definition a policy, whatever its strategic content.[131] Rather, strategies are most often brought into government in the minds of key decision makers, who then must exert every effort to impose them upon the decision making process and see that they

---

[127] Ray S. Cline, remarks before the National War College class, late 1970s.

[128] Quoted by Shultz, *Turmoil and Triumph*, p. 83.

[129] Steven W. Popper, Robert J. Lempert, and Steven C. Bankes, "Shaping the Future," *Scientific American* (April 2005): 69.

[130] David M. Abshire, *Preventing World War III* (New York: Harper and Row, 1988), p. 12.

[131] See the distinction drawn between strategy and policy in Chapter 1.

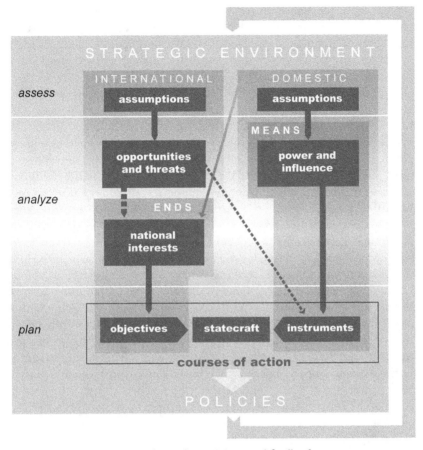

Figure 8.5: Implementation and feedback.

prevail in policy. Henry Kissinger wrote that government teaches decision making, not substance; statesmen consume the intellectual capital they bring to office rather than adding to it.[132] The best foreign affairs strategies thus exist in statesmen's minds rather than on paper, so that they can be adapted and applied as circumstances demand by those who know them intimately as their creators.

In practice, therefore, strategy formulation and revision proceeds in parallel with policy implementation. As described in Chapter 1, a president's foreign affairs strategy must struggle with competing strategic visions for control over policy, the statements and actions of government. No president wins all of these struggles in all areas of his strategy, so much of the time foreign *policy* will only partially reflect his foreign affairs *strategy*. Nevertheless, it is policy that affects the future strategic environment, both international and domestic, as the feedback arrow running around the right side of the model in Figure 8.5 illustrates; and it is those environments

---

[132] Kissinger, *White House Years*, p. 27.

that in turn determine future threats and opportunities, as well as the power and influence that will be available to address them. Strategists must therefore constantly take note of how closely policies conform to their strategies and watch to see how policies are affecting the environment at home and abroad. They must then alter their assumptions, and the strategies on behalf of which they fight future policy battles, accordingly.

Recent administrations have varied quite dramatically in their ability to see the interconnectedness of strategic logic, formulate a coherent foreign affairs strategy, impose its requirements on the government, and adapt their strategy as circumstances require. As indicated above, the most sophisticated strategy of the post-Vietnam era was that of Richard Nixon and Henry Kissinger, unique among recent administrations in the breadth of their knowledge of international politics and the essential agreement of their assumptions about how the world works. The administration of Jimmy Carter, on the other hand, represented the opposite extreme in strategic coherence. Characterized as a pious engineer who believed in fifty things but no one thing, Carter seemed to lack an overall sense of how strategy fits together, and (as we noted in Chapter 3) he compounded the problem by bringing the post-Vietnam dissensus right into his administration at the highest levels.[133] Unable to make up his mind consistently between his widely differing advisors, this president not only shifted his approach radically over time but found himself unable at any given time to set priorities among broadly differing objectives. The result was confusion and efforts at cross-purposes, with human rights efforts undermining security goals and Pyrrhic victories demonstrating presidential weakness.[134]

Ronald Reagan's approach, often characterized as peace through strength, depended upon changes in Soviet leadership which even Reagan himself doubted would ever take place.[135] For most of his administration, Reagan assumed that negotiation could succeed, not when two states have interests (albeit limited interests) that coincide, but simply when American

---

[133] Ward Just, "The Pious Engineer," *The New Republic* (December 6, 1982): 28–30; James Fallows, "The Passionless Presidency," *Atlantic* (May 1979): 33–46f.

[134] National Security Advisor Brzezinski in fact developed a list of 10 goals for the new administration that were quickly picked up by the engineer-president and used to measure progress. The goals book was in no particular order of priority and lacked any effort to highlight the relationships between goals. In spite of Brzezinski's claim that the goals book proved the administration did have a strategy, this lack of prioritization and interrelationship seems to support the opposite conclusion. Brzezinski, *Power and Principle*, pp. 53–57.

[135] "Somewhere in the Kremlin, I thought, there had to be people who realized that the pair of us standing there like two cowboys with guns pointed at each other's heads posed a lethal risk to the survival of the Communist world as well as the Free World. Someone in the Kremlin had to realize that in arming themselves to the teeth, they were aggravating the desperate economic problems in the Soviet Union, which were the greatest evidence of the failure of Communism.

"Yet, to be candid, I doubted I'd ever meet anybody like that." Ronald Reagan, *An American Life* (New York: Simon and Schuster, 1990), p. 268.

power overwhelms its adversaries. The Soviets, he wrote, would have to "sue for peace," the Sandinistas to cry "uncle."[136] Still, whatever its simplicities, Reagan had a consistent and coherent worldview and a much better sense of the need to set priorities than Carter. If nothing else, the American people – including those working for him in government – knew where he stood and where he was headed, at least until the Iran-*contra* affair seemed to contradict the simple truths on which his strategy was based.[137] And in spite of his ideological approach, Reagan was willing to change his assumptions when conditions warranted, able to seize the opportunity for dramatic, negotiated settlements when the opportunity appeared.[138]

George H. W. Bush came to the presidency as an Executive branch insider, bringing to the office a unique combination of foreign policy competence and direct personal involvement. Perhaps as a result, his foreign policy team adopted a pragmatic approach that favored continuity over change and was far more focused on expert management of individual problems than on broad strategic coherence. Thus, on the liberation of Eastern Europe, the reunification of Germany, and the collapse of Soviet power, as well as Central America and Angola, the administration helped avoid a violent end to the Cold War and skillfully wrapped up longstanding East-West problems. Most impressively, in the 1991 Gulf war Bush brilliantly assembled and led a broad international coalition to reverse the Iraqi invasion of Kuwait, securing critical American objectives at far less cost and risk than the unilateral path his son took on Iraq a dozen years later.

But although the elder Bush's administration boldly proclaimed a new world order, it adapted poorly to the radical changes that took place in the global environment during its watch and was unable to find a strategic concept that could integrate American statecraft in the post–Cold War era. It conducted policy toward China after the Tiananmen massacre as if the United States still needed Beijing to balance Soviet power, was slow and inadequate in its support for Gorbachev's reforms and for newly-established market democracy in Eastern Europe, failed to follow through on its military and political successes in Panama and Nicaragua, and did little to right the crippling budget deficits left by its predecessor. The federal government's constrained fiscal situation, the administration's political need to hide its centrism as the Republican Party shifted to the right, and the president's habitual caution, readiness to compromise, and

---

[136] Reagan, *An American Life*, p. 295.

[137] Simple truths like not dealing with terrorists, or standing up to nations like Iran which had humiliated the United States. Iran-*contra*'s seeming demonstration that Reagan (like other recent presidents) was not genuine, that he could say one thing and do something quite contrary to his declared principles, was the major reason why this minor scandal so weakened his presidency.

[138] For a more complete analysis of Reagan's foreign affairs strategy, see Terry L. Deibel, "Reagan's Mixed Legacy," *Foreign Policy* 74 (Summer 1989): 44–47.

tendency to rely on a small circle of like-minded advisors – all combined to produce "foreign policy without strategy, management without leadership, a kind of competent drift."[139] In the end, the administration of the first George Bush turned out to be very good at dealing with foreign affairs, but not very good at foreign affairs strategy.

Bill Clinton faced perhaps the toughest circumstances in which to seek strategic coherence of any president in the last half-century. His was the interregnum between the Cold War and 9/11, a decade during which American hegemony was still being consolidated and one that appeared to lack a central organizing threat. As noted earlier, Clinton's approach initially emphasized improving U.S. economic competitiveness and supporting democracy and human rights abroad. In the first, economic area he was quickly able to secure congressional approval of NAFTA and the Uruguay round of trade liberalization, adopted a Big Emerging Markets strategy to capitalize on the opportunities provided by globalization, and took courageous action to end the chronic budget deficits left by his Republican predecessors.[140] But in the second, value projection area Clinton's inexperience in foreign affairs and his determination to focus on domestic issues left him open to influence by liberals in Congress and advisors recruited from the idealist wing of the Carter administration. Under their tutelage he adopted expansive goals in Somalia, China, Haiti, and Bosnia without carefully considering the availability and cost of the means necessary to their accomplishment, leading to embarrassing policy reversals and humiliating defeats.

Meanwhile the administration veered from assertive multilateralism to enlargement to commercial promotion to humanitarian intervention to a doctrine of "indispensability" plus "do-ability" without ever finding a central organizing concept that could reconcile economic self-interest with humanitarian altruism. Though he grew more competent with experience, the best Clinton could do by way of strategy was to adopt a kind of restraining pragmatism that fell well short of coherence. Under that rubric he did some useful peacemaking in Bosnia, North Korea, the Middle East, and Northern Ireland, and succeeded in a major humanitarian gamble in Kosovo. But, confronted with the World Trade Center bombing, the destruction of U.S. embassies in two African countries, the millennium plots, and the attack on the USS Cole, the Clinton administration failed to engage decisively the gathering terrorist threat to the country's physical security.[141]

---

[139] For an expanded version of this critique, see Terry L. Deibel, "Bush's Foreign Policy: Mastery and Inaction," Foreign Policy 84 (Fall 1991): 3–23.

[140] Joe Klein, "Eight Years," New Yorker 76 (October 16–23, 2000): 188ff and The Natural: The Misunderstood Presidency of Bill Clinton (New York: Broadway Books/Random House, 2002). See also Bob Woodward, The Agenda: Inside the Clinton White House (New York: Simon and Schuster, 1994).

[141] For an expanded overview of the Clinton administration's foreign policy, see Terry L. Deibel, Clinton vs. Congress: The Politics of Foreign Policy, Headline Series 321 (New York: Foreign Policy Association, Fall 2000), Chapter 2.

And that brings us to George W. Bush, who came to office determined to set aside the frivolities of Clinton's humanitarian endeavors and focus his administration's energies on core national interests.[142] Adopting the unilateralist approach championed by Republican conservatives when they took over Congress six years earlier, Bush terminated Clinton's peacemaking efforts, denounced treaties and international organizations from the Kyoto environmental accords to the ABM treaty and from the UN to the International Criminal Court, and made building a national missile defense its top foreign affairs priority. While 9/11 did not erase these initial predilections, it established a new central organizing threat at the heart of American statecraft and stimulated the production of a new foreign affairs strategy based fundamentally on faith in American power and values. An explanation and critique of that approach, along with the formulation of a quite different alternative foreign affairs strategy, is the subject of our final chapter.

[142] Condoleezza Rice, "Promoting the National Interest," *Foreign Affairs* 79 (January-February 2000): 45–62.

9

Conclusion: American Foreign Affairs Strategy Today

Despite the many illustrative examples found throughout its pages, the emphasis in this book has been on *how* to think strategically about foreign affairs, not *what* to think about American foreign policy. Those who would succeed in foreign policy have been advised to begin with a clear conception of the national interest based on the nation's values, and then to scan the international environment for threats to those interests and opportunities for advancing them, while carefully checking their assumptions about how the world works against reality. They have been urged to think carefully also about the means available to them from the domestic context, including both material resources and public support, and to consider shrewdly what influence they may garner, both with the targets of their strategies and with third parties who may affect their success. They have been counseled to choose objectives that are both desirable and feasible, to marry them with instruments suitable for their achievement, and to select ways of using those instruments that will render their statecraft efficient and effective at reasonable cost and risk. In short, it has been argued that success in foreign policy begins with a sound foreign affairs strategy, strategy that must then be implemented through the policy process.

Such advice does not, of course, by itself a strategist make. Here there is no substitute for practice, for just as one cannot apply the concepts in strategic logic successfully without understanding them, so one cannot understand those concepts fully without applying them to the real world and using them to discipline one's thinking. Application can be done at three levels of difficulty. First, one can observe and analyze *past* strategies to see how others have applied (or not applied) strategic logic and what the results were. Second, one can critique *current* strategies whose outcomes are yet unknown, searching for sound and faulty assumptions, logical brilliance or error, clear or ideological thinking. Third, one can attempt to construct a *future* foreign affairs strategy, either for a specific country or regional relationship or a functional problem, or for all of them put together in the overall foreign affairs strategy of a nation. To be most productive these three levels of application should proceed in tandem, for it is in critiquing past and present strategies that one often finds the keys to better ones for the future.

This chapter will illustrate how strategic logic can be applied to current U.S. foreign affairs strategy by analyzing and critiquing the strategy of the George W. Bush administration. With any administration, of course, one sees mainly policy; the underlying strategy must be inferred from such words as are available and such actions as are observable. The Bush administration has not published a foreign affairs strategy, but the centrality of the war on terror in the Bush foreign policy makes *The National Security Strategy of the United States*, first published in September 2002 and updated in March 2006, the key document.[1] What follows, then, begins with an analysis of that strategy designed as an extended illustration of the concepts and logic discussed in earlier chapters. It is summarized in Figure 9.1, using a format based on the graphic model for foreign affairs strategy used throughout this book. This chapter will then critique the Bush strategy and, building on that critique, will suggest the outlines of an alternative American foreign affairs strategy.

Modeling the Bush National Security Strategy

The Bush National Security Strategy is most widely known at home and abroad for its emphasis on preemption, a doctrine that in application has meant a readiness to wage unilateral preventive war in Iraq. Of course, preemption is not an objective, an interest, or even an instrument; it is rather an aspect of statecraft, a *way* of applying instruments – in this administration, especially the military instrument. So to understand the Bush strategy one must start not with preemption, where the strategy ends, but with where it begins. And the Bush strategy is based on two fundamental conceptions about means and ends: first, that the United States has an overwhelming power advantage in today's world; and second, that American values are universal.

Here is the first sentence of the 2002 strategy's first chapter: "The United States possesses unprecedented – and unequalled – strength and influence in the world."[2] It is a formulation that equates power with influence, thereby bridging without comment a chasm through which many a strategy has fallen. Moreover, the administration's actions during its first term demonstrate a belief that the means available for foreign affairs were essentially unlimited. The obvious explanation for this perception of

---

[1] *The National Security Strategy of the United States of America* (Washington, DC: September 2002 and March 2006), hereinafter referred to as "2002 NSS" and "2006 NSS." Regarding the March 2006 version, National Security Advisor Stephen J. Hadley said "I don't think it's a change in strategy; it's an updating of where we are with the strategy...." Peter Baker, "Bush to Restate Terror Strategy," *Washington Post* (March 16, 2006): A1, A4.

[2] 2002 NSS, p. 1.

Strategic Environment

International	Domestic
- democracy is long-run cure for all the world's ills: terrorism, war, poverty, etc. - market economy is "the single most effective economic system" - political, religious, and economic liberty are indivisible, advance or fall together - American values are universal, non-negotiable, "right and true for all people" - key to peaceful, prosperous world is changing internal governance of other states - great powers motivated by common interests and common threats - U.S. hegemony is conducive to peace, welcomed by other nations - deterrence is doubtful against terrorists and weak against rogue states	- tax cuts will create a strong economy (supply side economics) - public will support deep, costly, lengthy engagement (9/11 a "transforming" event) - Congress will be Republican, compliant

National Interests	Threats & Opportunities	Power & Influence
- security of homeland - democracy and market economies abroad - prosperity and economic growth at home - unfettered U.S. sovereignty, freedom of action	- radicalism (terrorists, rogues) + technology (WMD) - regional conflicts - failed, undemocratic 3rd world states - economic stagnation in Europe and Japan - command and control economies in Third World - *lack of antagonism among great powers* - *spread of democracy: "freedom on the march"*	- U.S. possesses "unequalled . . . strength and influence" - means are unlimited - power is basically military in nature, backed by economic prosperity, democracy, and international support

Objectives (idealist)	Statecraft	Instruments (unilateralist)
1. prevent WMD attack on U.S. (V) 2. defeat terrorists – and tyrants (V) 3. encourage free and open societies on every continent (I) 4. build great power relations; head off peer military competitors (I) 5. promote economic growth and freedom (I) 6. defuse regional conflicts to prevent failed states, terrorist bases (S)	1. non-proliferation, deterrence, pre-emption 2. kill/capture, disrupt support 3. condemn and punish despots; support and aid democratizers 4. encouragement for democracy 5. external incentives for reform, debt relief, fighting disease 6. conflict resolution, intervention, stabilization and reconstruction	1. bilateral and multilateral diplomacy, New Triad, national missile defense 2. military, financial action, coalitions, and alliances; public diplomacy, foreign aid 3. diplomacy, public diplomacy, sanctions, international organization, foreign aid and investment 4. diplomacy, aid; military dominance 5. free trade, economic aid, IFI reform 6. diplomacy, military and economic aid

Figure 9.1. The Bush national security strategy.

unlimited means can be found in one of its oft-repeated assumptions about the domestic context: that tax cuts would create a strong economy while at the same time actually increasing the revenues necessary for foreign affairs. Parallel to this assumption about economics was another about politics: that the attacks of 9/11 would steel the American people to support long, costly wars, and that the public would therefore make available whatever resources were needed, whether dollars or lives, for foreign policy purposes. The 2006 strategy, however, seemed to reflect a somewhat chastened view of American power, for it mentioned only in its concluding paragraphs that the United States has "enormous power and influence," adding that, although "the times require an ambitious national security strategy," the country must recognize "the limits to what even a nation as powerful as the United States can achieve by itself."[3]

The Bush administration's expansive view of power was matched by its idealist assumptions about how American values play in the international environment. Although the 2006 version of the National Security Strategy was less strident than its predecessor on the correctness and universality of American values, the president wrote that "the ideals that inspired our history – freedom, democracy, and human dignity – are increasingly inspiring individuals and nations throughout the world," and the strategy asserted that "the desire for freedom lives in every human heart."[4] Indeed, the 2006 strategy was perhaps even more idealist than its predecessor, finding "moral imperatives" for everything from preventing genocide to promoting economic freedom to helping the world's poor.[5] More significantly, both strategies made clear that exporting American values to other nations was not only possible but essential, adopting the idealist assumption that the key to a peaceful world lies in changing the internal governance of other countries along American lines. As Secretary of State Condoleezza Rice put it, "The fundamental character of regimes now matters more than the distribution of power among them."[6] The 2006 strategy also assumed that political, religious, and economic freedom are "indivisible" and mutually reinforcing, noting that economic freedom creates a demand for and supports political freedom by "creating diversified centers of power" and expanding the "free flow of ideas," while economic failure can imperil democracy.[7]

These assumptions about American values have grown ever stronger over the life of the Bush administration. Once its intelligence on Iraq's

---

[3] 2006 NSS, p. 49.

[4] 2006 NSS, Bush prefatory letter; p. 3.

[5] 2006 NSS, pp. 17, 27, 31. The first substantive chapter of both strategies discusses how to "Champion Aspirations for Human Dignity."

[6] Condoleezza Rice, *Remarks* (Washington, DC: Georgetown University, January 18, 2006). In the 2006 NSS, on p. 1, the second sentence is repeated but hedged by replacing "more than" with "as much as."

[7] 2006 NSS, pp. 4, 27.

weapons of mass destruction and ties to Al Qaeda proved wrong, spreading democracy in the Middle East and Persian Gulf became retroactively the rationale for the U.S. invasion of Iraq, and as noted earlier the president made fostering freedom overseas the primary objective for the whole of his second term foreign policy.[8] In the 2006 strategy, spreading democracy was touted as the long-term cure for virtually every problem America faces, from terrorism to regional conflicts and from poverty to the downside of globalization.[9] New attention was given to the need to "help newly free nations build effective democracies" after "tyrannies give way," and Secretary Rice's "transformational diplomacy" at the State Department aimed to make American diplomats "more involved with the challenges *within* other societies."[10] In practice, however, the administration shaded its support for democracy, tailoring its policies to each country's importance to the war on terror, to other American interests, and to the administration's perceptions about what kind of government might follow American destabilization of an existing, authoritarian one.[11] Thus, the United States has been tough on Uzbekistan, Syria, and Iraq, but easy on Egypt, Saudi Arabia, and Pakistan – to say nothing of China and Russia.[12] Also, despite the rhetoric, funding for democracy promotion was stagnant except in the Middle East/Persian Gulf, and even in Iraq democratization funding was in decline by 2006.[13] Perhaps to justify this treatment the 2006 strategy discovered that "freedom cannot be imposed; it must be chosen," and warned that the administration would balance promoting freedom with "other interests that are also vital to the security and well-being of the American people."[14]

The Bush strategy's faith in power and values amounted to a strong implied assumption about American hegemony: that it would be both welcomed by other nations and conducive to peace. These were, of course, judgment calls both on other nations' motivations and also on what makes for a peaceful international order.[15] Although the 2002 strategy repeatedly

[8]   See his second inaugural address, the operative sentence of which is reproduced as the first sentence of the 2006 NSS, p. 1.
[9]   2006 NSS, pp. 3, 10–11, 15, 48.
[10] 2006 NSS, p. 4.
[11] This concern was heightened by the results of elections in Iraq and Palestine during the winter of 2005–06, which brought religious Shiites linked with Iran to power in Baghdad and a terrorist movement, Hamas, to power in Jericho.
[12] "Beyond its focus on Iraq, Washington has stepped up pressure on repressive regimes in countries such as Belarus, Burma and Zimbabwe – where the costs of a confrontation are minimal – while still gingerly dealing with China, Pakistan, Russia and other countries with strategic and trade significance." Peter Baker, "The Realities of Exporting Democracy," *Washington Post* (January 25, 2006): A1, A8.
[13] Peter Baker, "Funding Scarce for Export of Democracy," *Washington Post* (March 18, 2005): A1, A12; Baker, "Democracy in Iraq Not a Priority in U.S. Budget," *Washington Post* (April 5, 2006): A1, A18.
[14] 2005 NSS, pp. 5–6, 44. Italics added.
[15] See discussion of these points in Chapter 2.

spoke of a "*balance* of power that favors freedom," it clearly assumed other powers would not in fact balance the United States. In fact, the distribution of world power the Bush strategy favored was not balance but hegemony; there is little question that the administration wanted, and believed it could maintain, a clear hierarchy of power with the United States on top. As the president wrote in 2006, "we must maintain and expand our national strength...."[16]

Turning from environmental assumptions to analysis, the *interests* upon which the Bush national security strategy was based have to be inferred because, unlike most of their predecessors, the Bush strategies stated goals but not interests. Still, Bush's introductory letters to both strategies made clear that security was the most important interest, particularly a secure homeland: "Defending our nation against its enemies is the first and fundamental commitment of the federal government," he wrote in 2002, and his 2006 prefatory letter highlighted "our most solemn obligation: to protect the security of the American people."[17] The president was equally clear about *threats* to the homeland: "The gravest danger our nation faces lies at the crossroads of radicalism and technology."[18] Radicalism, of course, meant terrorists of global reach and rogue states; technology meant weapons of mass destruction. As should be clear from the assumptions sketched above, the next interest (of almost equal importance) was one of value projection: a world full of states based on American values, which almost by definition was threatened by failed, undemocratic states (that were also breeding grounds for the terrorism that threatened homeland security) and regional conflicts (that also endangered security and prosperity). The administration's third interest appeared to be prosperity and economic growth, because both strategies contained whole chapters on pursuing them in both the developed and developing worlds. Here the threats were lagging growth in the industrialized countries and the failure of the Third World to adopt the "single most effective economic system" offered by the United States, the model of unconstrained market capitalism – another American value that the strategies argued could and must be exported.[19] Last, one can infer a value preservation interest in autonomy, in unfettered U.S. freedom of action, from the 2002 strategy's stress on power and the administration's manifest fear of the threats to sovereignty posed by international laws and institutions.[20]

[16] Bush prefatory letter, 2006 NSS.
[17] Bush prefatory letters to the 2002 NSS and 2006 NSS.
[18] Bush prefatory letter to the 2002 NSS.
[19] 2006 NSS, p. 25; the 2002 version in Bush's letter was "a single sustainable model for national success: freedom, democracy, and free enterprise."
[20] The 2002 NSS contained an outright attack on the International Criminal Court (p. 31); as noted below, the 2006 version appeared to recognize that international institutions can be an adjunct to American power.

Though essentially threat-based, the strategies also identified some important *opportunities* from their assessment of the international environment. One was "the advance of liberty," which offered "an unprecedented opportunity to lay the foundations for future peace."[21] The other was the lack of antagonism among the great powers since the end of the Cold War, reinforced by shared (read: American) values and by fear of terrorism. Indeed, the administration initially believed that great power cooperation would be possible largely due to the transformative effect of 9/11, and in 2006 it continued to argue that "the struggle against militant Islamic radicalism . . . finds the great powers all on the same side."[22]

Moving to the planning level, one can find six *courses of action* through which the strategy purported to protect these interests against these threats.[23] *Preventing WMD attack against the homeland* obviously must be ranked as the most important objective, because that was the "gravest danger" to the most important interest.[24] Within it, nuclear weapons were singled out as posing the "greatest threat to our national security" because of their "unique" ability to cause massive casualties instantaneously.[25] *Defeating terrorists and tyrants* was the second objective because of the last assumption listed in Figure 9.1 about how the world works: namely, that deterrence would probably not stop terrorists and was weak against rogue states.[26] These first two objectives captured the forward-leaning, aggressive, and offensive approach of the Bush strategy: "The fight must be taken to the enemy, to keep them on the run."[27]

A variety of instruments were discussed under these two objectives, including foreign aid, public diplomacy, financial sanctions, and coalitions. However, the 2002 strategy made clear that the favored instrument was military power, contending that "[i]t is time to reaffirm the essential role of military strength," and that "[t]he goal is to provide the President a wider range of military options."[28] Such statements left little doubt that the administration saw power as essentially military in nature; for example, the chapter on instruments gave the military six paragraphs, intelligence four, and diplomacy just one. In addition to minor roles like counterproliferation and its use to quell regional conflicts, the military was assigned three key

---

[21] Bush prefatory letter, 2006 NSS.

[22] 2006 NSS, p. 36.

[23] In Figure 9.1, objectives are *roughly* linked to instruments by being placed under same number. Type face links each interest with the primary threat to it, as well as each objective with the primary interest it serves; objectives, instruments, and statecraft are linked by number. Objectives are ranked as vital (V), important (I), or secondary (S).

[24] 2002 NSS, Bush prefatory letter; this objective rates its own chapter, separate from the one on defeating terrorism.

[25] 2006 NSS, p. 19.

[26] 2002 NSS, defending the peace in Bush prefatory letter; deterrence on p. 15.

[27] 2006 NSS, p. 8.

[28] 2002 NSS, pp. 29–30.

tasks in the 2002 strategy: first, to preempt terrorist attack (Objective 1); second, to fight preventive war against terrorists and tyrants (Objective 2); and third, to dissuade peer military competitors by maintaining an overwhelming margin of superiority (see Objective 4), an idea that parallels a leaked draft of the Defense Guidance written in 1992 for Paul Wolfowitz under then-Secretary of Defense Dick Cheney.[29]

The 2006 strategy, however, had a wider view of the instruments necessary for these two security objectives and the ways of using them. Preventing WMD attack (Objective 1) was now to be accomplished through a combination that added nonproliferation and even deterrence to preemption. Nuclear nonproliferation emerged as essentially a multilateral effort, involving shutting down the production of new fissile material by closing loopholes in the Non-Proliferation Treaty and keeping existing materials out of the hands of terrorists and rogue states via the Global Threat Reduction Initiative. Deterrence was rehabilitated to some extent, for the 2006 strategy admitted that a defense that prevents successful attacks, along with consequence management (to limit and quickly repair attacks' damage) and forces configured to go after terrorists, could provide "tailored deterrence" of both state *and* nonstate actors.[30] The strategy thus spoke of a "New Triad" of nuclear and conventional strike systems, active and passive defenses (including missile defenses), and "responsive infrastructure" backed by "enhanced command and control, planning and intelligence systems."[31] Finally, the strategy emphatically reaffirmed the statecraft of preemption,

> the use of force before attacks occur, even if uncertainty remains as to the time and place of the enemy's attack. When the consequences of an attack with WMD are potentially so devastating, we cannot afford to stand idly by as grave dangers materialize. This is the principle and logic of preemption. The place of preemption in our national security strategy remains the same.[32]

Indeed, several conditions that restricted preemption in the 2002 strategy were dropped in 2006, perhaps because most were conspicuously ignored by the administration in the run up to the Iraq war. These included better intelligence than is necessary for post-attack retaliation, closer coordination with allies, precision in military strikes, and intent to "eliminate a *specific* [and presumably limited] threat."[33]

[29] Patrick E. Tyler, "U.S. Strategy Plan Calls for Insuring No Rivals Develop," *New York Times* (March 8, 1992): 1, 14.
[30] 2006 NSS, pp. 22, 43. Oddly, though, the strategy retains its doubts about deterrence via military retaliation alongside its enthusiasm about preemption, despite the likelihood that the intelligence needed to facilitate counterterrorist military action will be far better after than before an attack takes place.
[31] 2006 NSS, p. 22.
[32] 2006 NSS, p. 23.
[33] 2002 NSS, p. 16. Italics added.

Defeating global terrorism (Objective 2) involved tracking down, killing, and capturing hard core terrorists; cutting off their support networks; denying them control of areas they might use as safe havens; and dealing with supportive rogue states as if they were terrorists (we "make no distinction" – they are "equally guilty of murder").[34] These muscular, short-term techniques were largely inherited from the 2002 strategy, but the 2006 version greatly expanded long-term measures against terrorism. It also elaborated terrorism's deeper causes and argued that democracy (again) was the cure, for it would empower the "faithful followers of Islam" to denounce terrorist ideologies.[35] The United States needed therefore to engage in a battle of ideas, using public diplomacy to confront hostile propaganda quickly, tell America's story clearly, and facilitate dialogue with Muslim leaders.[36]

Encouraging *free and open societies on every continent* must be judged the strategy's third objective, a ranking supported by Bush's designation of it as one of two "inseparable priorities" along with "fighting and winning the war on terror."[37] This goal supported the interest in value projection, both for its own sake and also to drain the terrorist swamp and foster prosperity. It was sometimes called Wilsonian by those who forgot that Wilson's major accomplishment was the League of Nations, whereas Bush's idealism was part of a strategy that was notoriously suspicious of international institutions. Spreading democracy was to be accomplished by diplomacy (*e.g.*, organizing pro-democracy partnerships), public diplomacy (speaking out against autocrats and in support of reformers), sanctions (targeted against oppressive regimes), international organizations (both intergovernmental and NGOs), free trade and investment (with democratizing countries), and foreign aid (aimed at democracy promotion); despite the latter-day rationale for the Iraq war, the strategy did not list military force as an instrument for this objective.[38]

The strategy's fourth objective had to do with the world's great powers, both friendly and potentially hostile, and had therefore both a positive and negative aspect. Its positive side pledged to take advantage of the supposed values consensus and lack of conflicts among major countries in the post–Cold War world to *build strong relations among great powers*, with the purpose of preserving the peace and making American statecraft more effective, admitting that "there is little of lasting consequence that we can accomplish in the world without the sustained cooperation of our allies and partners."[39] This remnant of the realist policies the administration had championed before 9/11 may help explain its accommodating attitude toward the great non-democracies, Russia and China, despite repression of their own people and frequent opposition to American diplomatic efforts.

[34] 2006 NSS, pp. 9, 12.
[35] 2006 NSS, pp. 9–11.
[36] 2006 NSS, p. 45.
[37] 2006 NSS, Bush prefatory letter.
[38] 2006 NSS, pp. 6–7.
[39] "Preserving the peace" from the 2002 NSS; quote from 2006 NSS, p. 37.

At the same time, the 2006 strategy was quite explicit about authoritarianism in China and Russia, noting vaguely that the U.S. would encourage both to build democracy instead.[40] Indeed, despite its hope for cooperative great power relations, the strategy reiterated American readiness to act alone if necessary and warned that the United States would hedge its policies of friendship "in case states choose unwisely."[41] As noted above, in the 2002 strategy such hedging was cast in the form of an explicit negative great power objective: to keep American military forces so powerful as to *dissuade potential peer competitors* from attempting "a military build-up in hopes of surpassing, or equaling, the power of the United States."[42] This formulation was quietly dropped in the 2006 updating, which actually said rather little about the instruments or statecraft to be used to accomplish its fourth objective.

The strategies' fifth goal was to *promote economic growth and freedom*, an objective that mainly served America's interest in prosperity but was also aimed at mitigating the despair that leads to terrorism. It hoped to promote prosperity through a combination of global, regional, and bilateral free trade agreements and local free market reforms. The latter, yet another idealist effort to change other countries' forms of governance, were patterned after domestic Republican economic principles like cutting taxes, deregulation, shrinking the public sector, and opening markets to trade.[43] This objective also included reform of the international financial system and strengthening its institutions, although it looked forward to the time when private sector markets could "supplant" the IMF as the mainstay of financial stability.[44] The 2006 strategy also included a section on energy security that called for diversifying and reducing U.S. reliance on foreign sources of supply through a dramatic expansion of nuclear energy and investment in alternative fuels. Devoted entirely to increasing supply, the section nowhere even mentioned conservation.[45] For the developing world, the strategy emphasized battling infectious diseases, providing debt relief, and meeting basic human needs. The main instrument was foreign aid, made more effective by tying it to the local free market reforms that the administration believed were essential for economic growth.[46] Indeed, aid was the second most favored instrument in the Bush strategy (after military force), used for five of its six objectives.[47]

---

[40] 2006 NSS, pp. 39, 41–42.
[41] 2006 NSS, p. 36, 42.
[42] 2002 NSS, p. 30.
[43] 2002 NSS, p. 17; 2006 NSS, pp. 27–29.
[44] 2006 NSS, pp. 29–30.
[45] 2006 NSS, pp. 28–29.
[46] 2006 NSS, p. 33.
[47] 2006 NNS, p. 32. As noted in Chapter 6, some of the administration's most visible foreign affairs programs were assistance related, like the HIV/AIDs initiative and the Millennium Challenge Account, and aid funding nearly doubled in size by the end of Bush's first term.

The sixth and final objective was *defusing regional conflicts*. This goal supported the American interest in security (conflict could lead to "ungoverned areas that can become safe havens for terrorists") and also its interest in value projection, at least in avoiding humanitarian disasters.[48] In the 2002 strategy, a document suffused with boasting about American power and global mission, this objective stood out for being full of caveats about how limited U.S. resources were and how important it was for local parties to be ready to settle.[49] That defeatist tone disappeared by 2006, but the strategy still noted that "outsiders generally cannot impose solutions on parties that are not ready to embrace them.... "[50] Three strategies were proposed to defuse regional conflicts: prevention and resolution, intervention, and post-conflict stabilization and reconstruction. Though in its first term the Bush administration broke off the Clinton mediation efforts in the Middle East, Northern Ireland, and elsewhere, it here admitted that good offices and other outside assistance could help resolve conflicts if there was "bold and effective local leadership."[51] After starting life denouncing peacekeeping and terming the international community "illusory," moreover, it discovered by 2006 that the community did not have enough high-quality peacekeeping forces.[52] And after overthrowing the Iraqi government without a plan to run the country, it eventually established a State Department office to coordinate the "hard work" of reconstruction, admitting that military intervention would bring lasting peace and stability "only if follow-on efforts to restore order and rebuild are successful."[53]

As should be apparent from this review, the Bush national security strategy as set down in 2006 was still recognizably the same as that adopted a year after the attacks of 9/11. It had become, if anything, even more idealist than before, reemphasizing that spreading democracy and market economics worldwide was the key to peace and prosperity. It was also still unilateralist, reaffirming the country's readiness to go it alone, and it restated the role of preemption, "the same" as in 2002. But the 2006 "updating" had a very different feel to it, a workaday rather than missionary tone. The whole approach was that of an administration that had gotten its hands dirty and was thoroughly immersed in the nuts and bolts of statecraft; the contours of the original strategy were unchanged and still very visible, but the rough ideological edges seemed worn down by hard experience. Thirty-one pages had become forty-nine. The cocky assertions of superior American power and influence were gone, replaced by a strategy that was self-consciously "idealistic about goals, and realistic about

[48] 2006 NSS, p. 15.
[49] 2002 NSS, pp. 9–11.
[50] 2006 NSS, p. 14.
[51] 2006 NSS, p. 16.
[52] "Illusory" was the adjective used by Condoleezza Rice, "Promoting the National Interest," *Foreign Affairs* 79 (January-February 2000): 62.
[53] 2006 NSS, p. 16.

means."[54] Deterrence was partially rehabilitated, conflict management got serious attention, leadership replaced fear and loathing as an attitude toward international institutions, and bilateral, multilateral, and public diplomacy were more in evidence. Indeed, among the tools of state power only the exhausted American military was less prominent than in 2002.

Critiquing the Bush Strategy

In ends, then, the Bush strategy remained overwhelmingly idealist, and though means were expanded to include multilateralism, it retained a unilateralist default. Though emphasizing new opportunities to spread freedom it retained its focus on threats and kept much of its skepticism regarding deterrence, hoping instead to defend against and (if possible) preempt the immediate threats it identified while dissuading others seen as farther in the future. It was hegemonistic at its core – based, that is, on the perception and maintenance of superior American power – and was coercive more than co-optive in nature. It combined a Wilsonian effort to spread democracy and a Hamiltonian concern for free trade and market systems with Jacksonian militarism, but it utterly lacked Wilson's belief that international institutions and law must be at the center of world order and ignored Jeffersonian worries that war abroad can endanger democracy at home. Overall, the strategy was a high-cost effort to minimize the security dangers to the nation, symmetrical in its determination to meet every challenge on its own level.

Especially in its 2002 version, the Bush national security strategy had the considerable virtue of clarity and coherence; its parts fit together, with objectives that protected implied interests against identified threats, and instruments connected to their objectives. But it also had several features that demand scrutiny, including its assumptions about how the world works, its view of the nature of power, its conclusions about the seriousness of the threats to American interests, and its courses of action to deal with those threats.

As noted, the strategy's view of American *power* was central to its whole approach. Certainly it was correct regarding American primacy, especially in military power.[55] But the utility of that primacy was less clear, and the strategy's failure to distinguish power from influence left it in a poor position to assess how hegemony could work to protect and promote American interests. Did the power advantage of the United States confer influence over the actors and outcomes that mattered to it? Experience seemed to prove that often it did not. This issue was at play from the strategy's top to its bottom and was especially well illustrated in Iraq, from the extent to which major allies would bandwagon with the administration's unilateral

---

[54] 2006 NSS, p. 49.
[55] See Chapter 6, pp. 268–271.

actions rather than balance against them, to the utility of high-technology military forces in an urban insurgency and nascent civil war.

Even more questionable was the strategy's view that means were essentially expandable, even unlimited. Under George W. Bush the United States ran the largest trade and budgets deficits in its history, saved less than nothing domestically, and was dependent upon foreign borrowing to sustain its consumption of goods and services. In fact, the consistent failure of Republican supply side economics had caused the parties to switch places after 1980 with regard to fiscal probity.[56] Until the 1970s, Democrats' belief in Keynesian economics made them the party of expandable means, of "tax and spend." But after Ronald Reagan became president, Republicans became the party of expandable means, of "borrow and spend," accumulating trillions of dollars in national debt.[57] Thus, it was the Democrats under Bill Clinton who put the budget in surplus, and it was George W. Bush and a Republican-dominated Congress who accumulated nearly $3 trillion in additional debt during his first five years in office.[58] Simultaneously the United States stretched its military forces to the breaking point, whether measured by the impossibility of taking on other major contingencies or their difficulty in meeting recruitment and readiness goals. For a strategy that rested on military and economic hegemony, these were extremely significant weaknesses.

Indeed, the administration's belated realization that its means were not really unlimited was probably the principal reason that the 2006 national security strategy toned down the triumphalist boasting about American power that suffused the 2002 document. The dramatic drop in available financial and military power also goes far to explain the administration's turn toward diplomatic, even multilateral means in its second term, a move

[56] As to supply side economics, according to economists Gregory Mankiw (former chair of George W. Bush's Council of Economic Advisors) and Matthew Weinzierl, tax cuts on labor return roughly 17 cents on the dollar, on capital 50 cents on the dollar; therefore, between 50 and 83 percent of pre-tax cut revenue is permanently lost when taxes are cut. Moreover, the additional borrowing that deficit spending requires reduces investment by about a third of *its* value. "Cocktail-bar Calculations," *Economist* (August 20, 2005): 22–23; Sebastian Mallaby, "The Return of Voodoo Economics," *Washington Post* (May 15, 2006): A17.

[57] According to the Treasury Department's Bureau of the Public Debt, the national debt just before Reagan took office was just under $1T; when the elder Bush retired after 12 years of Republican rule it was about $4T, a $3T increase. During Clinton's time in office the debt initially increased and then fell somewhat after he brought the budget into surplus, for a net gain in 8 years of about $1.7T, making a total of $5.7T when the younger Bush took over. But by the end of fiscal 2005 the nation's debt had risen to nearly $8T. Republican administrations thus added $5.3 of the $7T overall increase since 1980, about 75 percent of the total, or $312B year (as opposed to Clinton's $212B a year). Data from http.//www. publicdebt.treas.gov/opd/opdhisto4.htm.

[58] Jonathan Weisman and Sailagh Murray, "Congress Raises Ceiling for Borrowing," *Washington Post* (March 17, 2006): A1, A4.

signaled by the departure or exile of key neoconservative officials and the appointment of the president's principal foreign policy advisor as Secretary of State.[59] Even in its responses to the apparent nuclear weapons programs of Iran and North Korea – two nations that President Bush once grouped with Iraq as part of an "axis of evil" – the administration came to multilateral diplomacy, using ad hoc groups of Asian and European countries and even including the UN Security Council as the ultimate forum of last resort. For if military solutions to either the Iranian or North Korean problem are either infeasible or would be outrageously costly, diplomacy is cheap.[60] Thus does the iron linkage of ends and means, the heart of all strategy, continue to have its way – even with an administration that did its best to ignore it.

Some of the strategy's central assumptions about the international and *domestic environment* also deserve scrutiny. In the absence of a new terrorist strike, one may well ask whether the trauma of the 9/11 attacks will remain powerful enough at home to sustain a strategy with so high a cost in dollars and lives. Perhaps because the shock of 9/11 was fading by 2006, the president found it necessary to begin his introductory letter to the updated strategy by saying that "America is at war. This is a wartime national security strategy...."[61] And so it was. At this writing, the country has surpassed three thousand American deaths in an Iraqi war that the substantial majority of its citizens believed was not worth its cost, casualties in Afghanistan were mounting in the face of increasing Taliban and Al Qaeda attacks, and the defense budget was rising each year even though it did not include the costs of those wars.[62] Moreover, it is unlikely that demands for domestic spending can be indefinitely deferred, to say nothing of the exploding costs of currently legislated entitlements that will hit the budget as the baby-boomers retire.

Just as questionable were some of the strategy's key assumptions regarding the *international environment*. First among them is the belief that American values are universal. Although some of the most basic American

---

[59] Leading neoconservatives Paul Wolfowitz and Douglas Feith left the Defense Department, while John Bolton was exiled to the UN. Secretary of State Condoleezza Rice, of course, has all the closeness to Bush that her predecessor Colin Powell lacked.

[60] In Iran, most authorities believe that the nuclear weapons program is so well protected that mere air strikes would only slow it somewhat, while conquering and occupying the country would be three to four times as difficult as the Iraq war proved. In 1994, it was estimated that a second war between North and South Korea would kill a million civilians in the vicinity of Seoul simply from the North's long range artillery, to say nothing of nuclear weapons use.

[61] 2006 NSS, Bush prefatory letter.

[62] War costs were instead funded through supplemental appropriations, and by early 2006 they had totaled nearly $400 billion. Weisman and Murray, "Congress Raises Ceiling for Borrowing," pp. A1, A4. By May 2006 nearly two-thirds of Americans, including a third of Republicans, believed the Iraq war was not worth its costs. Richard Morin and Dan Balz, "Confidence In GOP Is At New Low in Poll," *Washington Post* (May 17, 2006): A1, A4.

values may be widely shared, many are culturally determined products of the Western Enlightenment and as such utterly foreign to other cultures. Certainly many of the values of Islam as widely practiced in Southwest Asia are repugnant to Western mores: for example, the place of women in Sharia law and society. The determination of Afghanis to execute a Muslim man for converting to Christianity in 2006 spoke volumes about such fundamental differences. As one cleric, identified as a moderate, explained, "... ours is the complete and final religion. If you leave it, that is like throwing God away.... if you leave Islam, our law says you must be killed."[63] Another highly questionable assumption is that other nations would welcome U.S. hegemony rather than try to balance against the United States. Although America's power advantage currently precludes any forceful resistance to its hegemony, many observers saw "soft balancing" at work in the actions of its major allies before the Iraq war, and since then there have been countless examples of the Russians, French, Chinese, and others pushing their own political and economic agendas against those of Washington.

Perhaps the most central question regarding the Bush threat-based strategy has to do with its identified *threats*. Of singular importance here is whether terrorism was so serious that it deserved to take the place occupied by the USSR during the Cold War as the central organizing threat for all of American statecraft. Certainly it is possible that terrorists might cause even more horrific damage than they did in 2001 if they could get the proper weaponry in the proper position, whether by attacking American container terminals with dirty bombs or mounting a biological attack in a major city. But weapons of mass destruction are either very hard to make (nuclear), dangerous to their users and difficult to control (biological), or not especially capable of mass destruction (chemical).[64] For over five years, at least, 9/11 had not proved a harbinger; no followon attack occurred. Is the Bush administration giving the terrorist threat a lot more credit – not to say attention and resources – than it deserves while neglecting more important trends that have at least as much likelihood of affecting equally important interests? Even if the threat is as critical as claimed, it is fundamentally a-strategic to so emphasize any threat that one loses track of the costs and risks of the courses of action undertaken to deal with it, losses that may well add up to more – perhaps far more – than those that might have been caused by the original threat materializing. As the Iraq war proves, some cures are indeed worse than the disease.

Finally, as this last comment indicates, there are questions about the *courses of action* that the Bush strategy specifies for what it calls the Global War on Terrorism (GWOT). First, one can ask whether we are fighting

---

[63] Abdul Rauf, as quoted in Pamela Constable, "Afghan's Uneasy Peace With Democracy," *Washington Post* (April 22, 2006): A15.

[64] John Mueller, "Simplicity and Spook: Terrorism and the Dynamics of Threat Exaggeration," *International Studies Perspectives* 6 (May 2005): 217–219.

this war primarily with the wrong instruments in the wrong way, namely, with the military rather than diplomacy, intelligence, and law enforcement, and unilaterally rather than multilaterally. Should the United States forge ahead unilaterally when its closest allies object, or should it see such resistance as *prima facie* evidence that it might be wrong and reexamine its ends and/or means? Should military force be the primary instrument, or should it play a much more restricted and limited role? Then Secretary of Defense Donald Rumsfeld said that, in dealing with terrorism, "the best and in some cases the only defense is a good offense"; and the administration's national security strategies analyzed above were aggressive, forward-leaning documents that stressed suppressing the threat at its source.[65] Unfortunately, however, aggressive efforts to eliminate the threat may backfire by inciting more terror than they prevent. Despite Secretary Rumsfeld's comment, in other words, the best defense may be (at least in part) to *give no offense*, to avoid policies that make the recruiting of terrorists easier.[66]

Second, one can ask whether we are fighting the wrong war – that is, fighting a war against *terrorism*, a technique of the powerless, rather than against specific *terrorists* who have done the United States harm. It has been pointed out that wars against common nouns (like inflation or poverty) usually are not successful because such phenomena cannot be eliminated.[67] Declaring such a war usually broadens the enterprise beyond what can be sustained, raising costs and risks to unacceptable levels. There is, in other words, a significant difference between a "Global War on Terrorism" and a "War on Global Terrorists"; the former is open-ended in breadth and duration, whereas the latter is bounded by an objective that has at least a chance of being achieved.[68] How different American statecraft might look today if the Bush administration had sought a congressional declaration of war against Al Qaeda and Afghanistan after 9/11, like President Franklin D. Roosevelt did against Japan and Germany after Pearl Harbor. At the same time, one can ask whether the anti-terrorism effort should be a war at all, rather than mainly a police action against criminals, albeit particularly heinous ones. Given the importance of collaborative intelligence work to this struggle, it can well be argued that patient police work rather than military invasions and occupations is in most instances the most cost-effective way to handle it.

---

[65] Defense Department Transcript, "Secretary Rumsfeld Speaks on 21st Century Transformation of the U.S. Armed Forces," address to the National Defense University, January 31, 2002.

[66] In a famous leaked memo, Rumsfeld himself questioned whether the United States was capturing and killing more terrorists than Al Qaeda was recruiting.

[67] Grenville Byford, "The Wrong War," *Foreign Affairs* 81 (July–August 2002): 34–43.

[68] For an excellent critique of the GWOT along these lines, see Jeffrey Record, *Bounding the Global War on Terrorism* (Carlisle, PA: U.S. Army Strategic Studies Institute, December 2003).

None of this is to argue that terrorism is not important, or that the government should not do its utmost to prevent another 9/11. It is rather to point out that the morass in Iraq was the utterly predictable result of a strategy founded on an expansive, essentially unlimited view of means and an idealist approach to ends.[69] As demonstrated by NSC-68 and flexible response during the Cold War, such strategies usually lead to a broad and absolutist view of interests – such as that the homeland must be completely protected against any and all attacks – along with a wide definition of threats – comprising, in this case, all terrorists and rogue states everywhere. Then, to protect those interests against those threats, objectives are set that have not been carefully vetted for cost and risk and that demand far more resources than will be deliverable by the domestic political system over the long term – for example, that all terrorists everywhere must be eradicated and the governments of foreign countries transformed into democracies, even if the result of such objectives is several simultaneous full-scale wars.

It is true that, with regard to Iraq, a combination of failed interagency coordination and sheer incompetence added to the friction one would normally expect any ambitious strategy to encounter. But most of these shortcomings were built into the strategy from the outset. Believing that American values were universal, for example, neoconservative ideologues in the Department of Defense assumed that once Saddam's dictatorship was toppled, democracy would spring up of its own accord. This view not only excused them from the obvious requirement to plan effectively to run the country once its government had been destroyed, but even persuaded Vice President Cheney to forbid the defense officials who would be responsible for Iraq from using the expertise generated by a year's careful planning in the State Department.[70] Meanwhile, Secretary Rumsfeld's determination to demonstrate the validity of his theories of how military power should be "transformed" imposed on the military services a fast-moving but light-weight attack force that fielded too few troops to control the postwar situation.[71] And as National Security Advisor Condoleezza Rice failed

---

[69] Having brilliantly demonstrated these relationships in strategic logic in his work on the Cold War, John Lewis Gaddis has found the failings of the Bush strategy almost entirely in the realm of friction and poor implementation. See his "A Grand Strategy of Transformation," *Foreign Policy* 133 (November/December 2002): 50–57; and "Grand Strategy in the Second Term," *Foreign Affairs* 84 (January/February 2005): 2–15.

[70] In particular, Cheney ordered through Rumsfeld that Jay Garner fire from his staff Thomas Warrick, who had headed up the year-long State Department Future of Iraq project that predicted most of the difficulties the United States faced in the occupation. James Fallows, "Blind into Baghdad," *Atlantic Monthly* (January/February 2004): 72.

[71] "The military's fundamental argument for building up what Rumsfeld considered a wastefully large force is that it would be even more useful after Baghdad fell than during actual combat" to assert unmistakable control. "The heart of the

in her signal duties, both to coordinate all available governmental expertise on the problem, and to sufficiently warn the president that the very efficiency of Rumsfeld's *military* strategy would severely imperil the administration's *political* objectives – a classic Clausewitzian disconnect of ends and means.[72] Thus, it is hardly surprising that the Bush strategy led the U.S. into an open-ended military commitment that, like the Vietnam war, threatened to destroy the very objectives it was designed to serve.

Assessing Today's Interests, Threats, and Opportunities

It should be possible for a country as powerful and satisfied as the United States to construct a foreign affairs strategy that will adequately serve its interests at lower cost and risk than the Bush strategy. Such a strategy would put the terrorist threat in perspective and shift to a more defensive and multilateral approach to managing it. It would husband American power and realign its uses to recapture the support of like-minded nations, understanding that a status quo power need not alienate so many around the world, thereby multiplying the resistance that strategy inevitably faces, to protect and promote its interests. It would adequately fund nonviolent instruments and reduce the role of the American military to one of containment, deterrence and reassurance, except in unambiguous cases of actual or truly imminent attack. It would construct efficient and cost-effective courses of action and prioritize them so as to accomplish what is needful with a comfortable store of power in reserve. An outline of the major elements in such a foreign affairs strategy is presented in Figure 9.2.

The first interest such a strategy must protect is a reasonable level of security for the American homeland and for Americans abroad. This vital interest deserves to be first, not only due to its intrinsic value and its indispensability to the achievement of other interests, but also because of the continuing threat posed to it by Islamist terrorists, especially a decentralized Al Qaeda. But it is qualified as a "reasonable" level of security to remind us that security is never absolute, that the United States already enjoys substantial security despite the terrorist threat, and that the effort to make security total imperils prosperity and value preservation while quickly driving costs and risks to unsustainable levels. In the short term this interest requires a mix of defensive and offensive actions to contain and manage the terrorist threat. In the long term security may also encompass a set of end-states much more difficult to achieve, including peace among the

---

Army's argument was that with too few soldiers, the United States would win the war only to be trapped in an untenable position during the occupation." Fallows, "Blind into Baghdad," pp. 64–65.

[72] Of course, we are not privy to Rice's private conversations with Bush; but if she did so warn him, it was ineffective. Fallows' months of postwar interviews found Rice "conspicuously absent" from pre-war deliberations. "Blind into Baghdad," p. 72.

	Strategic Environment	
	International	**Domestic**
	• internal governance of foreign countries matters to peace and prosperity, but is exceedingly difficult to influence • other cultures are profoundly different from that of the West • market democracy good, but may not be exportable everywhere • hegemonic war is best prevented by a clear hierarchy of power • overwhelming power tends to generate resistance, balancing	• growing income inequality, political polarization • de-legitimization of compromise in Congress • internal cohesion deteriorating due to homogeneous immigration and language, ethnic, and religious divisions • public support requires positive cost-benefit ratio
	National Interests — **Threats & Opportunities**	**Power and Influence**
	• Reasonable homeland security • Stable climate, controlled warming • Great powers, key regions at peace • An open international economy • Sufficient oil at reasonable prices • Domestic liberty, unity, autonomy • A world of better governance, fewer and less-destructive disasters	• terrorist attack with nukes or germs • fear of and over-reaction to attack • greenhouse gas emissions • huge budget deficit and foreign debt • dependence on unstable oil market • terrorist blackmail, illegal migration • corrupt, oppressive regimes • *technology growth, global markets*	• means are limited, despite unipolarity and U.S. primacy • Influence with important actors not automatically conferred by power • power is both hard and soft • U.S. legitimacy is in tatters • imbalances in potential vs. actual power, military vs. non-violent tools
	Objectives — **Statecraft (Ways)**	**Instruments**
	1. Secure loose nukes and materials in FSU and elsewhere worldwide (V) 2. Emplace prioritized, layered defense of homeland (V) 3. Enact serious energy/climate policy (V) 4. Reduce budget and trade deficits (V) 5. Prevent major interstate conflict (I) 6. Restore U.S. legitimacy (I) 7. Control and diversify immigration (I) 8. Encourage market democracy (S) 9. Relieve worst suffering overseas (S)	1. set standards, co-optation 2. harden facilities & improve rebound (deter); control public fear 3. conservation, clean fuel; international leadership 4. fair taxation, entitlement reform 5. selective engagement 6. dialogue, multilateralism 7. border barriers, employer sanctions 8. exemplar, not missionary 9. multilateral cooperative action	1. bilateral and multilateral diplomacy, IAEA, aid, alliances, military 2. regulation, aid, market incentives 3. law, incentives; diplomacy, aid 4. tax and global trade policy with TAA 5. diplomacy, alliances, military 6. diplomacy. alliances, military presence to deter, reassure 7. public diplomacy, policy shifts 8. diplomacy, law enforcement 9. diplomacy, public diplomacy, aid 10. economic and military assistance

Figure 9.2. An alternative American foreign affairs strategy

major Eurasian powers, stability in other regions critical to American interests, and a stable global climate.

The most obvious threat to the security interest remains terrorist attack, especially with nuclear or biological weapons. But it is a threat that must be kept in perspective, because the second most important threat to our security is our own fear of and over-reaction to any attack that may – or may not – occur. In general, the likelihood of any individual American dying in a terrorist attack is extremely low. The total number of Americans killed by international terrorism since the late 1960s, including those who died on 9/11, is about the same as the total killed over the same period by lightning, automobile collisions with deer, or allergic reactions to peanuts.[73] It would be foolish to dismiss the catastrophic damage of an attack with WMD; authorities as knowledgeable as former Secretaries of Defense Robert McNamara and William J. Perry believe that there is a better than 50 percent chance of a nuclear strike in the U.S. within a decade.[74] But even this worse case would hardly "do away with our way of life," as one top military officer warned.[75] America's economy, military, and political culture are robust and resilient. Though a horrific catastrophe, such an attack would be localized, and life would go on in these United States.

More dangerous to our way of life would be our likely reaction to such an attack, whether it be closing off our interdependence with the global economy, sending our military to destroy the government of another Islamic state that may well be controlling local terrorists better than we could, or drastically curtailing civil liberties at home. As its name implies, terrorism works by provoking terror. Therefore, as political scientist John Mueller points out, "anything that enhances fear effectively gives in to them. Indeed, very often the costs of terrorism come much more from hasty, ill-considered, and over-wrought reactions ... to it than anything the terrorists have done." Bin Laden has explicitly predicated his strategy on "bleeding America to the point of bankruptcy" through overreaction.[76] Even today we are paying huge amounts "for a small reduction in probabilities that are already extremely low" and for measures that reassure "but do little to change the actual risk."[77] As statistician David L. Banks has written, "If terrorists force us to redirect resources away from sensible programs and future growth, in order to pursue unachievable but politically

---

[73] John Mueller, "Simplicity and Spook," p. 220.

[74] Robert S. McNamara, "Apocalypse Soon," *Foreign Policy* 148 (May/June 2005): 35.

[75] Quote from Gen. Richard Myers, then Chairman of the Joint Chiefs of Staff, quoted in Mueller, "Simplicity and Spook," p. 225.

[76] Mueller, "Simplicity and Spook," pp. 221–222.

[77] Howard Kunreuther, "Risk Analysis and Risk Management in an Uncertain World," *Risk Analysis* 22 (No. 4, 2002): 662–663.

popular levels of domestic security, then they have won an important victory that mortgages our future."[78]

Keeping control of our emotions is equally required because of the hard
truth that terrorism cannot be completely eradicated. As *Atlantic Monthly's*
James Fallows writes,

> This "war" will never be over.... There will always be a threat that some-
> one will blow up an airplane or a building or a container ship. Technology
> has changed the balance of power; it is easier for even a handful of people
> to threaten a community than it is for the community to defend itself. But
> while we have to live in danger, we don't have to live in fear. Attacks are
> designed to frighten us even more than to kill us. So let's refuse to mag-
> nify the damage they do. We'll talk about the risk only when that leads to
> specific ways we can make ourselves safer. Otherwise we'll just stop talk-
> ing about it, as we do about the many other risks and tragedies inevitable
> in life. We will show that we are a free, brave people by controlling our
> fears.[79]

Using the term "war" to describe anti-terrorist policies is misleading, therefore, because it implies that there will be a moment of victory. Instead, success will mean reducing the frequency and destructiveness of attacks, not
definitively eliminating the threat that they might happen. And statements
by government officials that heighten fear give Americans a false sense of
*in*security; they are simply self-inflicted wounds, unless they lead to concrete actions.[80] As RAND's Bruce Hoffman, one of America's most seasoned
terrorism experts, put it, "terrorism is just another fact of modern life. It's
something we have to live with."[81] And we can, because its worst consequences, however horrific, are not like the Soviet nuclear threat during the
Cold War; they would not pose an existential threat to the United States of
America, much less to life on planet earth.

Nonstate actors like Al Qaeda may have grown in importance in the
modern international system, but states still possess unique potential to
harm American security. In the short term the states of most concern are
Iran and North Korea. Iran is the lesser of the two, because it is reportedly still five to ten years from developing nuclear weapons and, although
a sponsor of terrorism, knows that giving America's enemies weapons of
mass destruction would risk events that could expose Iran to catastrophic
retaliation. North Korea, on the other hand, already has a growing nuclear
arsenal, is prone to reckless international behavior, and has a history of

---

[78] David L. Banks, "Statistics for Homeland Defense," *Chance* 15 (No. 1, 2002): 10.

[79] Fallows, "Success Without Victory," *Atlantic Monthly* (January/February 2005):
82.

[80] False sense of insecurity: Leif Wenar, University of Sheffield, UK, quoted in
Mueller, "Simplicity and Spook," p. 221; self-inflicted wound: Benjamin Friedman, quoted in Fallows, "Success Without Victory," p. 83.

[81] Quoted in Siobhan Gorman, "Fear Factor," *National Journal* 35 (May 10, 2003):
1463.

irresponsibly selling anything to anyone for a profit. Nor are military threats to the United States necessarily only short term. Even in the far less interdependent world of the twentieth century the United States was twice drawn into interstate world wars that began in Europe, and the Cold War spawned hot wars in Korea and Vietnam, plus scores of lesser military actions. It is hard to imagine that the United States in the twenty-first century could stay aloof from similar conflicts, so what Robert Art has called "deep peace among the Eurasian great powers" must remain a key American interest.[82] From the U.S. perspective, that peace is probably best assured by a clear hierarchy rather than a balance of power, with the United States on top. In addition, important American interests in other key regions of the world could be threatened by a hostile regional hegemon or simple instability. Peace and a favorable balance of power in those regions is therefore also a key American interest.

Finally, there is one major existential threat to American security (as well as prosperity) of a nonviolent nature, which, though far in the future, demands urgent action. It is the threat of global warming to the stability of the climate upon which all earthly life depends. Scientists worldwide have been observing the gathering of this threat for three decades now, and what was once a mere possibility has passed through probability to near certainty. Indeed, not one of more than 900 articles on climate change published in refereed scientific journals from 1993 to 2003 doubted that anthropogenic warming is occurring. "In legitimate scientific circles," writes Elizabeth Kolbert, "it is virtually impossible to find evidence of disagreement over the fundamentals of global warming."[83] Evidence from a vast international scientific monitoring effort accumulates almost weekly, as this sample of newspaper reports shows:

- an international panel predicts "brutal droughts, floods and violent storms across the planet over the next century";
- climate change could "literally alter ocean currents, wipe away huge portions of Alpine snowcaps and aid the spread of cholera and malaria";
- "glaciers in the Antarctic and in Greenland are melting much faster than expected, and . . . worldwide, plants are blooming several days earlier than they did a decade ago";
- "rising sea temperatures have been accompanied by a significant global increase in the most destructive hurricanes";
- "NASA scientists have concluded from direct temperature measurements that 2005 was the hottest year on record, with 1998 a close second";

---

[82] Robert J. Art, *A Grand Strategy for America* (Ithaca, NY: Cornell University Press, 2003), p. 43.
[83] Elizabeth Kolbert, "The Climate of Man – III: What Can Be Done?" *New Yorker* 81 (May 9, 2005): 61.

- "Earth's warming climate is estimated to contribute to more than 150,000 deaths and 5 million illnesses each year" as disease spreads;
- "widespread bleaching from Texas to Trinidad . . . killed broad swaths of corals" due to a 2-degree rise in sea temperatures.[84]

"The world is slowly disintegrating," concluded Inuit hunter Noah Metuq, who lives 30 miles from the Arctic Circle. "They call it climate change, . . . but we just call it breaking up."[85]

From the founding of the first cities some 6,000 years ago until the beginning of the industrial revolution, carbon dioxide levels in the atmosphere remained relatively constant at about 280 parts per million (ppm). At present they are accelerating toward 400 ppm, and by 2050 they will reach 500 ppm, about double pre-industrial levels. Unfortunately, atmospheric CO_2 lasts about a century, so there is no way immediately to reduce levels, only to slow their increase. We are thus in for significant global warming; the only debate is how much and how serious the effects will be. As the newspaper stories quoted above show, we are already experiencing the effects of 1–2 degree warming in more violent storms, spread of disease, mass die offs of plants and animals, species extinction, and threatened inundation of low-lying countries like the Pacific nation of Kiribati and the Netherlands. At a warming of 5 degrees or less the Greenland and West Antarctic ice sheets could disintegrate, leading to a sea level of rise of 20 feet that would cover North Carolina's outer banks, swamp the southern third of Florida, and inundate Manhattan up to the middle of Greenwich Village. Another catastrophic effect would be the collapse of the Atlantic thermohaline circulation that keeps the winter weather in Europe far warmer than its latitude would otherwise allow.[86] Economist William Cline once estimated the damage to the United States alone from moderate levels of warming at 1–6 percent of GDP annually; severe warming could cost 13–26 percent of GDP.[87]

But the most frightening scenario is runaway greenhouse warming, based on positive feedback from the buildup of water vapor in the atmosphere that is both caused by and causes hotter surface temperatures. Past ice age transitions, associated with only 5–10 degree changes in

---

[84] Cites for these quotations from the *Washington Post* between each semicolon, in order, are: Philip P. Pan, "Scientists Issue Dire Prediction on Warming," January 23, 2001: A 1, A14; Eric Pianin, "U.N. Report Forecasts Crises Brought On by Global Warming," February 20, 2001: A6; Juliet Eilperin, "Climate Talks Bring Bush's Policy to Fore," December 5, 2004: A1, A17; Eilperin, "Severe Hurricanes Increasing, Study Finds," September 2005: A1, A20; Eilperin, "Study Confirms Past Few Decades Warmest on Record," June 23, 2006: A3; Eilperin, "Climate Shift Tied To 150,000 Fatalities," November 17, 2005: A20; Eilperin, "Debate on Climate Shifts to Issue of Irreparable Damage," January 29, 2006: A1, A16.

[85] Doug Struck, "Inuit See Signs in Arctic Thaw," March 22, 2006: A1, A16.

[86] Eilperin, "Debate on Climate Shifts to Issue of Irreparable Damage."

[87] William Cline, *The Economics of Global Warming* (Washington, DC: Institute of International Economics, 1992), pp. 131–133.

average global temperatures, took place in just decades, even though no one was then pouring ever-increasing amounts of carbon into the atmosphere. Faced with this specter, the best one can conclude is that "humankind's continuing enhancement of the natural greenhouse effect is akin to playing Russian roulette with the earth's climate and humanity's life-support system."[88] At worst, says physics professor Marty Hoffert of New York University, "we're just going to burn everything up; we're going to heat the atmosphere to the temperature it was in the Cretaceous, when there were crocodiles at the poles. And then everything will collapse."[89] During the Cold War, astronomer Carl Sagan popularized a theory of nuclear winter to describe how a thermonuclear war between the United States and the Soviet Union would not only destroy both countries but possibly end life on this planet.[90] Global warming is the post–Cold War era's equivalent of nuclear winter, at least as serious and considerably better supported scientifically. Over the long run, it puts dangers from terrorism and traditional military challenges to shame. It is a threat not only to the security and prosperity of the United States, but potentially to the continued existence of life on this planet.

In addition to a reasonable level of security, Americans also have a vital interest in continued prosperity and steady economic growth. The specific interests in this category are essentially two: engagement with an open international economy, and the importation of sufficient oil at reasonable prices. The first of these figures into what Harvard professor Joseph Nye has called a strategy based on global public goods, defined as "something everyone can consume without diminishing its availability to others":[91]

> We gain doubly from such a strategy: from the public goods themselves, and from the way they legitimize our power in the eyes of others. That means we should give top priority to those aspects of the international system that, if not attended to properly, would have profound effects on the basic international order and therefore on the lives of large numbers of Americans as well as others.[92]

In addition to an open international economy, Nye lists among these goods open international commons (the seas, atmosphere and climate, space, and cyberspace) and strong international regimes, laws, and institutions.[93]

---

[88] Art, *A Grand Strategy for America*, p. 78.

[89] Quoted by Colbert, "The Climate of Man – III," p. 57.

[90] The seminal scientific article was R. P. Turco, O. B. Toon, T. P. Ackerman, J. B. Pollack, and Carl Sagan, "Nuclear Winter: Global Consequences of Multiple Nuclear Explosions," *Science* 222 (December 23, 1983).

[91] Joseph S. Nye, Jr., *The Paradox of American Power: Why the World's Only Superpower Can't Go It Alone* (New York: Oxford University Press, 2002), p. 142.

[92] Nye, *Paradox of American Power*, pp. 143–144.

[93] Nye, *The Paradox of American Power*, pp. 144–147. He also lists a balance of power in important regions (a security interest), economic development (an economic interest), and resolution of international disputes (another security interest); all are stated as objectives.

Of course, these interests have security as well as economic implications. The primary threats to American engagement with an open international economy are both protectionist sentiment exacerbated by the stresses of globalization and the unsustainable current imbalances in the American economy: large budget deficits, accompanying current account deficits, and buildup of foreign-held U.S. debt.[94]

The U.S. interest in energy is again expressed in moderate rather than absolute terms, as a *sufficiency* of supply. Since the burning of hydrocarbons is the primary cause of global warming, this economic interest is in obvious conflict with our security interest in a stable climate. The amount of oil deemed "sufficient" must therefore take that interest as well as prosperity into account and be dramatically if gradually reduced. Reasonable pricing is also a mixed interest. After all, high prices are the most effective means of reducing demand for oil and hence the amount of CO_2 pumped into the atmosphere. But high prices hurt prosperity through their inflationary pressure and, if they originate at the source, also provide resources to some of the world's most serious troublemakers, like Iran. Indeed, columnist Thomas Friedman has pointed out that not only is the United States paying for both sides of the war on terrorism (Congressional appropriations for our troops and foreign aid, plus oil revenue for those who fund the terrorists), but also that one can find a nearly perfect correlation between the price of oil and the capacity of conservatives in Iran to amass power and make trouble for the West.[95] Moreover, Friedman argues that "the price of oil and the pace of freedom always move in opposite directions in oil-rich petrolist states."[96] Threats to energy supplies thus spring both from American dependence on oil as a large percentage of its energy needs, and from the fact that the supply of foreign oil comes from unstable or hostile areas of the world like Africa, Venezuela, and the Persian Gulf.

In addition to its interests in security and prosperity, the United States also has interests in value preservation at home and value projection abroad. To a large extent, preserving the American way of life and governance in an age when the most immediate threat is from terrorism is a Jeffersonian concern, a matter of keeping the terrorist threat in perspective so that Americans do not compromise their civil liberties in a futile effort to become totally secure. In addition, distinctively American values might someday be imperiled by the surge in illegal immigration from Mexico and other Latin American countries, because its lack of diversity has created a

---

[94] For an extended explanation of these threats, see Chapter 5.

[95] Thomas L. Friedman, *The World Is Flat: A Brief History of the Twenty-First Century* (New York: Farrar, Straus and Giroux, 2005), pp. 283, 411, 460. Friedman's point is partially that the availability of oil revenues allows tyrannical predatory regimes to exist.

[96] Thomas L. Friedman, "The First Law of Petropolitics," *Foreign Policy* 154 (May/June 2006): 28–36.

competing cultural and linguistic bloc that appears to resist assimilation.[97] Third, there is some possibility that American autonomy could be compromised by terrorists who have (or could credibly claim to have) emplaced weapons of mass destruction on American soil, facing the president with a choice between meeting a terrorist demand or putting millions of his countrymen's lives at risk.[98] Such a scenario would be a more plausible, present-day equivalent of the Committee on the Present Danger's claim during the 1980 campaign that the Soviets were on the verge of attaining a military superiority sufficient to take over Washington without firing a shot. It is an unlikely threat to this vital interest, but one with the most serious potential consequences.

Finally, it can be argued that the United States has an important value projection interest in a world of better governance with fewer and less destructive man-made disasters. Again, the interest is stated in moderate terms. Other cultures are profoundly different in many ways from that of the West, and while market democracy has proven itself as the key to the good life in many of the world's regions, it is not exportable everywhere. A more reasonable end-state for the world than American-style market democracy would be simple good governance, in accordance with local norms and traditions. Liberal democracy may be the key to good governance, but liberal autocracy is certainly preferable to illiberal democracy.[99] The threat here is corruption and oppression, the determination of a ruler to remain in power regardless of popular will and to use the state to enrich himself and his associates regardless of the level of oppression or economic damage to the country. One illustration of this threat is Robert Mugabe, "elected" dictator of Zimbabwe, who has effectively destroyed the democratic opposition and economy of one of the potentially richest countries in Africa; another is in Somalia, where for years marauding warlords preyed upon the people and made central government impossible; still others are North Korea, Burma, Belarus, and Uzbekistan. Such governmental systems often interact with nature to produce horrific man-made disasters, causing tens or hundreds of thousands of deaths and untold misery. Though difficult to influence, they are threats that not only offend American values but may eventually endanger U.S. security as well.

---

[97] Samuel P. Huntington, "The Hispanic Challenge," *Foreign Policy* 141 (March/April 2004): 30–45.

[98] Stephen Flynn, *America the Vulnerable* (New York: HarperCollins, 2004), pp. 31–32.

[99] Fareed Zakaria, "The Rise of Illiberal Democracy," *Foreign Affairs* 76 (November/December 1997): 22–43. Again, this argument finds its Cold War predecessor in the warning by Jean Kirkpatrick that the United States should not destabilize authoritarian societies lest ineradicable communism take them over. Jean Kirkpatrick, "Dictatorships and Double Standards," *Commentary* 68 (November 1979).

Domestic Support, Power, and Influence

What can we say about the capacity of the United States to protect and advance these interests? Chapter 5 discussed in some detail both the tangible sinews of the United States' commanding relative power, as well as its economic vulnerabilities; these need not be repeated here. Of course, since its economy is critical to any nation's power, all the threats discussed above to the United States' interest in prosperity are also threats to the country's potential power. But there is also a variety of trends that may erode the *intangible* elements of American power in the years ahead, including growing income inequality, partisan political polarization, and social division following record levels of homogeneous immigration.

Diversity is an enormous source of strength for the United States, enabling it better to interact with the world because in part it *is* the world. But beyond some unknowable point, homogeneous immigration might become a source of political and economic division that imperils American political cohesion. At this writing there are estimated to be 11 to 12 million undocumented immigrants living in the United States, three-quarters of them Mexicans and other Latin Americans who have come across a largely unsecured border; they represent roughly 5 percent of the American labor force.[100] Two-thirds of the 400,000 to 500,000 who come across the border each year lack even a high-school education; with a net worth about 9 percent of non-Hispanic whites, Hispanics account for about 90 percent of the increase in people living in poverty in the United States, and they increasingly cluster in Hispanic-majority neighborhoods.[101] Rather than making a contribution to American diversity, their numbers and homogeneity are such that there is some risk they could become a parallel society and culture within the country. If the sheer mass of illegal Mexican-Americans and their descendants in the United States causes assimilation to fail, the entire United States will follow Florida and the Southwest to become a bicultural and bilingual society.[102] The unassimilated can be expected to have consistently different attitudes on issues of foreign affairs than other Americans, and foreign diasporas can reproduce overseas conflicts within the American political system, making coherent strategy more difficult. One must be careful, to be sure, not to exaggerate such effects. Still, governmental control of a defined population within a defined territory remains the very definition of sovereignty.

Partisan political polarization can have equally deleterious effects on U.S. intangible power by delegitimizing compromise as an art essential to

---

[100] These estimates from the Pew Hispanic Center, cited in S. Milton Kalita, "Illegal Workers' Presence Growing," *Washington Post* (March 8, 2006): A6.

[101] Legal immigration into the United States is estimated at from 750,000 to a million each year, so illegals are roughly a quarter of the total inflow. Robert J. Samuelson, "Build a Fence – And Amnesty," *Washington Post* (March 8, 2006): A19.

[102] Huntington, "The Hispanic Challenge," pp. 44–45.

governing in foreign as well as domestic policy. Perhaps the single most important measure that can be taken to reduce it is to end the gerrymandering of congressional districts, either through mandating some sort of geometrical contiguity or by moving the redistricting decision from State legislatures to nonpartisan bodies. For as noted in Chapter 3, districts that are politically homogeneous put a premium on candidates who run to the political extremes; once elected, they are unsuited by both temperament and politics to cooperate with similar extremists across the aisle.

Adding its effects to both cultural division and partisan polarization is the growing income inequality in American society, which also saps social cohesion and with it the foundations of American power. The United States is now more unequal in income and wealth than any other major industrialized country, and American economic inequality is increasing.[103] Decades ago Robert Reich pointed out that globalization was driving economic elites away from the rest of the country, making them more cosmopolitan than national in both outlook and behavior.[104] As the attitudes of elites and the government they control become more divorced from those of ordinary Americans, the latter have responded with heightened distrust of government, falling participation in the nation's political life, and efforts to take political decisions into their own hands.[105] All three of these trends make public support for coherent, sustained strategic enterprises harder to obtain.

Whatever its foundation, the outward expression of American power in the twenty-first century is both hard and soft, and the two need to function in a reinforcing rather than contradictory manner. Overwhelming power creates resistance and engenders balancing against it, unless it is itself balanced by an obvious intent to safeguard the interests of those subject to it. In recent years both the substance of American policies and the unilateral way they have been executed has sapped the legitimacy on which of much of the country's soft power rests, enlarging the gap between U.S. power and the influence it confers. Anti-Americanism surged after the war in Iraq, both in Muslim countries and in Europe.[106] For example, from the beginning of the decade to 2003, favorable views of the U.S. fell from 62 percent to 43 percent in France, 78 percent to 45 percent in Germany, and 50 percent to 38 percent in Spain; and from 52 percent to 15 percent in Turkey, 75 percent to 15 percent in Indonesia, and 23 percent to

---

[103] In the two decades from 1980 to 2001, earnings by the top fifth of families jumped about 50 percent from 7.7 to 11.4 times those of the bottom fifth; wealth disparities are even worse. Sebastian Mallaby, "Class Matters" and "Reward of the Hereditary Elite," *Washington Post* (November 14, 2005): A21 and (June 5, 2006): A15.

[104] Robert Reich, "What is a Nation?" *Political Science Quarterly* 106 (Summer 1991): 193–209.

[105] Samuel P. Huntington, "Dead Souls: The Denationalization of the American Elite," *National Interest* 75 (Spring 2004): 5–18.

[106] Andrew Kohut, *Anti-Americanism: Causes and Characteristics* (Washington, DC: Pew Research Center for the People and the Press, December 10, 2003).

13 percent in Pakistan.[107] In Muslim countries these abysmal figures recovered somewhat into the 20–40 percent range by 2005, helped in South and Southeast Asia by U.S. relief efforts following the late-2004 tsunami and in the Middle East by the Bush administration's calls for democracy, but in Europe they stayed virtually the same.

So far as we can tell, the causes of persistently unfavorable views of the United States on the part of majorities in so many countries are partly structural (*i.e.*, resentment of U.S. power by those frustrated with their own political and economic circumstances), partly cultural (including the ubiquity of America's popular culture such as movies and fast food, clashes between the values of American conservatives and those of modern Europe, and religious-secular differences), and partly policy-related (over the war in Iraq or the Palestinian issue).[108] More specifically, they are due primarily to low regard for President Bush, followed by opposition to the Iraq war, perceptions that the United States acts unilaterally without taking into account the views of other nations, and (in Muslim countries) widespread fear that U.S. military power could be turned against them.[109] Anti-Americanism not only fosters the recruitment of terrorists, thereby directly endangering American security, but also makes far more difficult the cooperation that the United States needs from other countries to accomplish its goals.[110]

More concretely, the overemphasis on the immediacy of the terrorist threat has led to an excess of actual power at the expense of potential power, while the decision to cast the struggle against terrorism as a war has tilted the balance among the instruments of state power sharply toward the military. Both imbalances need to be redressed. To fortify its potential power, the United States first needs to move as rapidly as fiscal prudence will allow to correct its structural budget deficit, reversing tax cuts favoring the wealthiest Americans in order adequately to fund the government and reduce the country's economic vulnerabilities.[111] As former director of

---

[107] The Pew Global Attitudes Project, *American Character Gets Mixed Reviews: U.S. Image up Slightly, but Still Negative* (Washington, DC: Pew Research Center for the People and the Press, June 23, 2005), Table, p. 1.

[108] Peter G. Peterson, *et al, Finding America's Voice: A Strategy for Reinvigorating U.S. Public Diplomacy* (New York: Council on Foreign Relations, 2003), pp. 23–25.

[109] Pew, *American Character Gets Mixed Reviews*, pp. 16, 23, 26–27, 31. On p. 16: "Among the publics around the world, a low regard for President Bush is more heavily correlated with an unfavorability [sic] rating for the United States than is any other attitude or opinion ...."

[110] See "Why Anti-Americanism Matters," in Peter G. Peterson, *et al, Finding America's Voice: A Strategy for Reinvigorating U.S. Public Diplomacy*, pp. 20–23; and Joseph S. Nye, Jr., "The Decline of America's Soft Power," *Foreign Affairs* 83 (May/June 2004): 16–17.

[111] The cost of the Bush tax cuts in 2005 alone was projected at $215 billion, 70 percent of it going to the top 20 percent of income earners, 22 percent to the top 1 percent. As a share of GNP, federal revenue is at its lowest level in 25 years. Isaac Shapiro, "Deficit Dance," *Washington Post* (January 11, 2005): A15.

the Congressional Budget Office Robert D. Reischauer aptly put it, "you can't run a twenty-first century government on a 1950s revenue base," and as noted in Chapter 5, the effort to try courts financial disaster.[112] The United States then needs to create a national technology fund and agency to increase research and development spending; relax visa controls keeping foreigners out of American universities; embark on a crash program to improve science and engineering education in American primary and secondary schools; and implement other sensible policies to supercharge future American productivity, which is the basis of economic growth and therefore of governmental revenue.[113] Also vital to retaining American solvency over the long run is some intergenerational agreement on a package of changes in benefits and taxation for Social Security, Medicare, and Medicaid, to reduce at least somewhat the enormous discrepancy between future revenues and obligations of the government. American power will remain limited despite these measures, but they would certainly help safeguard and increase it for the future.

At the same time, the government needs to redirect a portion of those resources it continues to spend on the instruments of state power away from the military and toward nonviolent tools, correcting the current militarization of American foreign policy. The Bush administration's increases in foreign aid are a good start, but the funding available to the State Department for the conduct of diplomacy should be at least tripled, and that for public diplomacy (especially exchange of persons) quadrupled.[114] Instead of funding for the military being a dozen times that for all the other tools of statecraft combined, as noted in Chapter 6, the United States should aim for a ratio of perhaps five to six times larger.[115] And this shift of funding

---

[112] Quoted in Jonathan Weisman, "Republicans on Hill Resist Party Leaders' Spending Cuts," *Washington Post* (March 14, 2006): A8, A9.

[113] Finland's technology agency and R&D fund, Tekes and Sitra, have raised the country's R&D to 3.5 percent (compared to 2.6 percent in the U.S.), an example of what can be done by free people who trust their government. Robert G. Kaiser, "Innovation Gives Finland a Firm Grasp on Its Future," *Washington Post* (July 14, 2005): A21. The crash educational program was suggested by Thomas L. Friedman, *The World Is Flat*, p. 275.

[114] Even in post-9/11 2003, for example, the U.S. was spending the grand sum of $150 million on all public diplomacy in the Middle East. Nye, "The Decline of America's Soft Power," pp. 16–20. Comparisons with the private sector are equally shaming. The U.S. government spends $5–10 million a year polling foreign publics, whereas American business spends $6 billion, and *individual* American-led multinational corporations spend more advertising abroad than the entire U.S. public diplomacy budget. Peter G. Peterson, *et al, Finding America's Voice: A Strategy for Reinvigorating U.S. Public Diplomacy*, p. 35.

[115] The Bush budget for FY 2007 gives 85 percent of the funding for national security to the Pentagon, 6 percent to diplomacy and economic aid, 9 percent to homeland security. Gordon Adams, "A Cry for Help from the Pentagon," *Baltimore Sun* (February 16, 2006).

should be matched by a determination to *use* diplomacy, in particular to drop the idea that American agreement to talk with actors whose ideology or conduct we find objectionable somehow confers on them unwarranted legitimacy, along with the often associated demand that they make substantive concessions merely to get the United States to the table. Within the military, the shift toward a concentration on fighting low-intensity wars against insurgency that began as a result of experience in the Iraq war and was ratified in the 2006 Quadrennial Defense Review should continue, with significant offsetting cuts made in weapons and training for full-scale conventional warfare.[116] Such cuts can be justified because, unlike threats from terrorists, traditional military threats from a peer competitor will appear on the horizon in sufficient time to reconstitute the forces needed to fight an old fashioned full-scale war.[117] Sacrificing some of that capacity now while beefing up the nonmilitary instruments will provide a mix of tools better suited to the objectives of twenty-first century statecraft.

Assembling Courses of Action

Having considered American interests and the threats to them, as well as what is needed to maintain and expand the country's power and influence in the world, we are now prepared to put together objective-instrument packages that have a reasonable chance of protecting those interests against those threats at acceptable cost and risk. The strategy proposes nine objectives, of which four are vital, three important, and two secondary.

Security

The highest priority courses of action must be to protect American security against terrorism. Because the most devastating kind of terrorist attack would probably require nuclear weapons, one vital objective should be to keep those weapons and the fissile materials necessary to make them out of the hands of terrorists (Objective 1). The most likely source of such materials and know how is the former Soviet Union, where a huge nuclear arsenal is inadequately secured and thousands of weapons scientists are poorly employed. Since 1991 the United States has sponsored the Nunn-Lugar Cooperative Threat Reduction Program in the FSU to dismantle nuclear weapons, secure nuclear weapons and materials, and employ nuclear scientists so they will not sell their expertise elsewhere. Though it was slow to act, the George W. Bush administration eventually embraced Nunn-Lugar, expanded it for use outside the FSU, and convinced the G-8 to match the

---

[116] On changes in the U.S. Army and Marine Corps, see Thomas P. M. Barnett, "The Monks of War," *Esquire* 145 (March 2006): 214–223.

[117] In naval power, for example, Robert Art argues that the United States needs a 3–5 power standard, not the 9–15 power standard it has today. *A Grand Strategy for America*, p. 242.

$1 billion annual U.S. funding of the program for a decade; it also set up a Global Threat Reduction Program in the Department of Energy to reduce and control high-risk nuclear and radiological materials abroad.[118] Still, Bush hardly made control of nuclear weapons and materials in other countries his top priority – the 9/11 Commission gave the government's performance of this objective a grade of D in late 2005 – and he continued even in his second term to take actions that ran counter to it, like torpedoing an inspection regime for the Fissile Materials Cut-off Treaty (FMCT), or offering nuclear fuel to India despite its refusal to put its entire nuclear production program under International Atomic Energy Agency (IAEA) safeguards or pledge to stop creating fissile materials.[119] Moreover, the administration's reluctance to reduce the United States' own nuclear arsenal, and its obvious interest in developing new nuclear weapons to support a "global strike" option as part of its preemptive strategy, undercut U.S. diplomatic efforts to corral the nuclear materials and weapons of others.[120]

Nevertheless, this most serious immediate threat to American security is preventable, at least in theory. As Harvard political scientist Graham Allison points out, "without fissile material, you can't have a nuclear bomb. No nuclear bomb, no nuclear terrorism."[121] Three steps are urgently needed: to dismantle excess Soviet-era weapons and secure the remainder, to rigidly control all existing fissile materials, and to keep any new fissile material from being produced. Allison estimates that these goals could be accomplished within three years at a cost of $30 billion, or about 7 percent of the U.S. annual defense budget.[122] Doing so would require close cooperation with Russia to establish a new international security standard mandating total control of all nuclear weapons and materials; a global "cleanout campaign" to extract all dangerous nuclear materials from non-nuclear weapons states; and serious enforcement measures, beginning with the IAEA but possibly encompassing carefully chosen military measures if needed, to prevent production of new fissile material and the creation of new nuclear weapons states.[123] Such steps are the most important things

---

[118] Richard G. Lugar, "Committed to Containing Nukes," *Washington Post* (October 23, 2004): A23; Peter Slevin, "Plan Launched to Reclaim Nuclear Fuel," *Washington Post* (May 26, 2004): A21.

[119] Dafna Linzer, "U.S. Shifts Stance on Nuclear Treaty," *Washington Post* (July 31, 2004): A1, A20; Jim VandeHei and Dafna Linzer, "U.S., India Reach Deal on Nuclear Cooperation," *Washington Post* (March 3, 2006): A1, A14; "National Security Report Card," *Washington Post* (December 9, 2005): A29.

[120] Walter Pincus, "Plan to Study Nuclear Warheads Stirs Concern," *Washington Post* (April 6, 2005): A2; William Arkin, "Not Just a Last Resort?" *Washington Post* (May 15, 2005): B1, B5.

[121] Graham Allison, "How to Stop Nuclear Terror," *Foreign Affairs* 83 (January/February 2004): 64.

[122] Fallows, "Success Without Victory," p. 90.

[123] Allison's strategy is based on the three no's: "no loose nukes, no new nascent nukes, and no new nuclear weapons states." "How to Stop Nuclear Terror," pp. 69–73. Because coercive strategies are only likely to reinforce the

the United States can do to prevent the most serious immediate security threat it now faces and should be given top priority in American strategy.

More broadly, the United States should more narrowly target its military offense against terrorism and shift the emphasis of its counterterror strategy to layered homeland defense and enhanced consequence management and recovery (Objective 2). Despite the conventional wisdom that there are too many potential targets in a modern Western society to protect them all, a democratic society can defend itself with a high degree of effectiveness and still remain both internally free and open to the world.[124] To do so, it must first undertake a nation-wide vulnerability study to identify likely targets, like transportation (especially trains and container ports), food and water supply, chemical industries, the electrical grid and other important infrastructure systems. It should then prioritize funding for defense based on those vulnerabilities.[125] Existing facilities should be protected with layered defenses, because even where no single kind of defense may be very effective, several different kinds layered on top of each other can provide very high levels of protection.[126] For new infrastructure, government should prod industry to set standards for (and require it to build in) the necessary security measures, which are much more efficient and effective when planned from the outset than added on later. Arranging with shippers to inspect containers destined for American ports in return for expedited processing on arrival even in a crisis is particularly essential. Rebound capacity and consequence mitigation capability must also be markedly improved, for defense is unlikely to be perfect.[127] Again, the end-state is the reasonable level of security that is doable, not perfect security that is impossible to achieve.

Layered defense is expensive – one study estimated its governmental costs at $45 billion annually and private sector costs at $10 billion

---

determination of Iran and North Korea to acquire or keep nuclear weapons in order to deter a threatening United States, the West should at least consider an entirely incentive based, co-optive approach in these two cases; at the very least, if the primary objective of American strategy is indeed non-proliferation, all conflicting objectives (and especially regime change) should be renounced. At the same time, dealing with these two weaponizing states is probably less important to reducing the terrorist threat than cleaning up fissile materials elsewhere in the world.

[124] As Steven Flynn writes, "security, pursued intelligently, can be achieved in ways that are fully supportive of civil society and individual rights." *America the Vulnerable*, p. 60.

[125] Fallows, "Success Without Victory," pp. 84–85. This would be a change from the original distribution formula, according to which per capita federal funding to low-risk states exceeded it to many high-risk ones.

[126] Flynn notes that anti-terrorism is like home security, where "statistically, five 60-percent measures when placed in combination will raise the overall probability of preventing a burglary to 99 percent." *America the Vulnerable*, p. 69.

[127] Flynn, *America the Vulnerable*, is the indispensable source for these measures, esp. Chapters 4, 6, and 7.

annually – and will take years if not decades to accomplish.[128] But it has several advantages over the offense. First, whatever its cost in dollars, its cost in the lives of American troops is certain to be lower than additional Iraqs. Second, it will not have boomerang effects that destroy the United States' reputation overseas or cause young Muslims to dedicate their lives to killing Americans. Third, it can have a deterrent effect, by denying terrorists the kind of mass death and destruction they seek by attacking. Fourth, and critically, much of it will have positive results even if another major terrorist attack never takes place. For example, defensive infrastructure improvements could also prevent electrical blackouts from natural causes like the one that paralyzed the northeast and parts of Canada in August 2003, could make the public health service better prepared to handle a serious epidemic, or could simply improve a sector's ability to manage everyday anomalies (like a traveler who breaches airport security trying to recover a forgotten laptop) without prolonged interruption to the services it provides.

Emphasizing defense does not mean abandoning offense, or even preemption. Diplomatic, intelligence, financial, and law enforcement cooperation to disrupt, disable, capture, and kill terrorists should continue, and military preemption will remain an option in the unlikely event of an imminent attack that is detected. Targeted, usually covert action by special forces and precision weapons should certainly be undertaken when high value terrorist targets are identified. But preemption should not be the centerpiece of a long-term anti-terrorist strategy, either in practice or rhetoric, and preventive war should never be undertaken without substantial international consensus as to its necessity. Sensible measures to reduce the risk and severity of terrorist attack will also require what homeland defense expert Stephen Flynn has called "security maturity," an understanding by ordinary Americans of the facts noted above: that "terrorism is simply too cheap, too available, and too tempting ever to be totally eradicated," and that "one can at best seek to reduce its frequency and destructiveness so that people feel reasonably – but never perfectly – safe from it."[129] Opinion leaders and politicians must contribute to this kind of maturity by refraining from scare mongering. Instead, they should "stress that any damage terrorists are able to accomplish likely can be absorbed, and that, while judicious protective and policing measures are sensible, extensive fear and anxiety . . . is misplaced, unjustified, and counterproductive."[130]

Over the longer run, the United States must work to sap the virulence of the Islamist movement as part of a broader public diplomacy effort to

---

[128] Michael O'Hanlon, *et al.*, *Protecting the American Homeland: A Preliminary Analysis* (Washington, DC: Brookings Institution, 2002), p. 131.

[129] First two quotes from Flynn, *America the Vulnerable*, p. 59; last quote from Mueller, "Simplicity and Spook," p. 223.

[130] Mueller, "Simplicity and Spook," p. 226.

restore America's international legitimacy (Objective 6). While not vital, this important objective needs massive increases in funding – as well as a better product to sell. In the Middle East, that means a policy that supports justice as well as liberty.[131] On the Palestinian issue, for example, the United States must be as critical of Israel as the Palestinians, when appropriate, and as supportive of the Palestinians as of Israel, when that is appropriate. Even the outlines of such a policy lie well beyond the scope of this study, and it would be difficult to pull off given the poor quality of Palestinian governance, but it requires above all a divorce of the United States, its money, and its equipment from illegal Israeli settlement activity in the occupied West Bank and from military attacks on Palestinians. Also important in the Middle East will be the eventual liquidation of the American occupation of Iraq, and a diplomacy toward the Iranian problem that garners the support of most governments in the Western and Muslim world. In addition, a serious energy policy like that discussed below would lessen the need to support repressive regimes that guarantee the flow of oil from the Persian Gulf, thereby cleaning up some of the slick of hypocrisy that coats American statecraft.

On the basis of such changes a long-range public diplomacy effort must promote educational reform in the region, using teacher training, curriculum development, and book translation to promote critical thinking and independent thought in contrast to the rote memorization that dominates Islamic religious indoctrination.[132] It must also open up dialogue on a scale that matters, mixing Americans with influential Muslims in both locations and restoring, even augmenting, the pre-9/11 flow of young Muslims to universities in the United States. Muslims need to see American society for what it is, rather than what their media represents it to be, and both sides need personal contact in order to feel the common humanity that unites rather than divides the two cultures.[133]

Globally, successful public diplomacy will also need policy changes. Any effort to restore American legitimacy will have to be based on a statecraft whose default position is multilateral and co-optive, rather than unilateral and coercive. The United States will have to convince other countries that it takes their interests into account whenever possible along with its own, and that it will at least consider their adamant objections as *prima facie* evidence that the policy being protested ought to be looked at more carefully. It will need to hold top officials accountable when its actions fail to live up to its values, and drop the crusader for the exemplar approach to spreading American values, as described below. Above all, the United

---

[131] Fallows, "Success Without Victory," p. 86.

[132] Helena K. Finn, "The Case for Cultural Diplomacy," *Foreign Affairs* 82 (November/December 2003): 18.

[133] As one U.S. ambassador to a Gulf state pointed out even before the 2003 Iraq war, only face-to-face contact with Americans can break through the hostility now generally felt by Muslim Arabs toward the United States.

States needs to put some energy behind telling its story to the world, to make the war of ideas a serious priority. Although it may be impossible to reestablish the separate, generally well-run United States Information Agency (USIA) that gave these programs focus until it was foolishly abolished in 1999, much more should be done to give public diplomacy visibility and clout within the State Department.[134] And if not all the programs decimated by budget cuts in the 1990s should be restored, most should be, including reviving VOA English-language broadcasting, reopening American Centers and libraries to foreign publics, and increasing the numbers of cultural and educational exchanges to at least their Cold War levels.[135] As professor Stephen Walt writes: "The United States is in a global struggle for hearts and minds, and it is losing. If anti-Americanism continues to grow, Washington will face greater resistance and find it harder to attract support."[136]

As for traditional military threats to its security, the United States can relax, at least for the moment. Such threats require states as launching platforms, and states, including rogue states, can be deterred because they have return addresses. Even if North Korea develops missiles that can reach the United States with nuclear warheads, there is scant reason to believe that the regime in Pyongyang wishes to commit national suicide. Although research and development should continue, deployment of national missile defense is therefore a low-priority use of huge resources that could be far better assigned to homeland defense, public diplomacy, and other nonviolent tools of statecraft. As to future peer competitors, the United States should disabuse itself of the illusion that it can prevent their emergence. China, the most pertinent case in point, continues its extraordinary economic growth, but its political system remains authoritarian and it is vigorously augmenting its military forces. Rather than building the wrong kind or amounts of military power in a futile effort to dissuade others' military programs, the United States would do better to strengthen international law and institutions and bring possible peer competitors into those regimes, binding them to an ever-stronger world order and strengthening their stake in its maintenance. A co-optive strategy thus designed to shape putative adversaries' intentions rather than a coercive effort calculated to stunt their capabilities is more likely to succeed across the decades,

---

[134] This change would involve not only establishing new coordination machinery and moving boxes on the organization chart but also changes in training, assignment, and promotion of personnel. See the recommendations of Peter G. Peterson, *et al*, *Finding America's Voice: A Strategy for Reinvigorating U.S. Public Diplomacy*, and Stephen Johnson and Helle Dale, *How to Reinvigorate U.S. Public Diplomacy*, Report #1645 (Washington, DC: Heritage Foundation, April 23, 2003).

[135] See recommendations of Finn, "The Case for Cultural Diplomacy," pp. 15–20, and Sanford J. Ungar, "Pitch Imperfect," *Foreign Affairs* 84 (May/June 2005): 7–13.

[136] Stephen M. Walt, "Taming American Power," *Foreign Affairs* 84 (September/October 2005): 117.

and it will help the United States reshape its own military programs to deal with far more likely and immediate threats.

Meanwhile, the United States should continue to rely on the strategy elegantly described by Robert Art as selective engagement in order to prevent and deal with interstate conflict that would endanger American security and prosperity (Objective 5).[137] Selective engagement concentrates resources on the three regions of the world that are most important to the United States for reasons of trade, investment, oil supplies, great power location, and potential WMD acquisition: Europe, East Asia, and the Persian Gulf. It requires the continuation of current security commitments, institutional alliances, and sufficient forward-deployed forces to deter conflict, reassure friendly states, and obviate the need for regional powers to balance local rivals via arms races or other destabilizing behavior. Its ability to buffer regional instability rests on a combination of power sufficient to deal with any situation yet far enough away and backed by benign enough intent not to appear threatening itself, making the United States the least unacceptable balancing power in these three regions. The strategy's success depends on the United States generally avoiding war except when its most vital interests require it, while demonstrating through deft and normally multilateral diplomatic leadership that its own interests correspond to a large extent to those of most regional powers.

Finally, the American interest in security requires urgent, serious action to halt global warming that could be leading the planet into catastrophic climate change (Objective 3). To say that this vital objective will not be easy would be an outrageous understatement. In 2004 about 7 billion metric tons of carbon were released into the world's atmosphere, 20 percent of it by the United States. As noted above, these emissions have already caused significant warming, and the yearly amount of emissions is expected to double or worse by mid-century. The UN-sponsored Intergovernmental Panel on Climate Change states that no less than a two-thirds cut in carbon emissions is needed by 2100 just to stabilize the level of atmospheric carbon at 550 parts per million, about double its pre-industrial levels.[138] Some authorities argue that the costs of adapting to a warmer climate would be

---

[137] Robert J. Art, *A Grand Strategy for America*, Chapter 4, "Selective Engagement." Although his excellent book lays out a national security strategy directed primarily at developing a rationale for U.S. military spending and deployments, Art's broad definition of American interests and his recognition that his strategy's success depends upon diplomatic and other nonmilitary factors brings him out very close to the foreign affairs strategy outlined here. Indeed, his "political policies" – avoiding excessive ambition and unilateralism, doing more to lock down WMD material in the FSU, lessening reliance on fossil fuels, encouraging European defense capabilities, dealing with inequality at home, and treating the political causes of terrorism (pp. 234–238) – capture many of the courses of action advocated here.

[138] Timothy E. Wirth, C. Boyden Gray, and John D. Podesta, "The Future of Energy Policy," *Foreign Affairs* 82 (July/August 2003): 137.

lower than those of minimizing climate change, but that would only be true at lower levels of warming, and it ignores the existential threat of self-feeding catastrophic change, to which adaptation would be impossible.[139]

Leading scientists are not sure this problem is solvable, but the range of plausible rates and consequences of warming is wide enough that all-out efforts even at this late date might still work. At home, the United States must abandon the Bush approach of voluntary restraint aimed merely at improving greenhouse gas "intensity" – a measure of efficiency that does nothing to control overall CO_2 emissions – and put in place a strategic energy policy like that described below. And because 80 percent of carbon emissions come from outside the United States and those emissions are growing faster in the developing than in the developed world, it must also stop obstructing meaningful international action from the G-8 to the 2005 Montreal conference, work to improve and ratify the Kyoto protocol, and assume leadership of an international effort to address this critical problem.[140]

> These steps require unparalleled leadership by the world's great powers, ... [including] a level of international cooperation never yet achieved in modern history. . . . Global warming presents a potentially severe, even catastrophic threat to the United States. In order to stabilize the world's average global temperature, it is the United States that must lead.[141]

Prosperity

In addition to these security objectives, the United States needs to serve its vital interests in prosperity and continued economic growth. The first goal here must be the restoration of fiscal sobriety: namely, the elimination of the federal government's outsized structural budget deficits (Objective 4). This vital objective requires a fair taxation policy that restores the government's revenue base while simultaneously narrowing income inequality, the historic purpose of progressive taxation of income. Eliminating the budget deficit and beginning to reduce the country's more than $8 trillion national debt can be expected to have all the economic benefits it had when Clinton did it as a mainstay of the 1990s economic boom. It would also help redress the country's trade balance, as would the energy strategy described below (since petrodollars are about a third of the U.S. current account deficit).[142] And reduction of the trade deficit would lessen the

---

[139] Art, *A Grand Strategy for America*, pp. 75–79.

[140] For examples of the deleterious effect of Bush policies internationally, see Juliet Eilperin, "U.S. Pressure Weakens G-8 Climate Plan," *Washington Post* (June 17, 2005): A8; Eilperin, "U.S. Won't Join in Binding Climate Talks," *Washington Post* (December 11, 2005): A1, A27.

[141] Art, *A Grand Strategy for America*, pp. 78–79.

[142] Based on 2005 deficit of about $800 billion, with 12 billion barrels of oil imports a day at $60 a barrel or $262 billion a year in petrodollar outflow. See Michael Kinsley, "'Oil Tax' Greases Wheels of Rich," *Washington Post* (June 20, 2005): A15.

vulnerability the U.S. economy faces from the large and growing amount of American debt held by foreigners. The other major action needed to reduce the trade deficit is a continued reduction of trade barriers, pursued most recently through the global negotiations under the WTO known as the Doha round. Success in such negotiations must be coupled with standards for labor, energy, and environmental policy abroad, and buffered by sufficient trade adjustment assistance at home at least to prevent the resulting displacement of low-wage workers from increasing U.S. income inequality. A sensible immigration policy as described below will also help by tightening the market for unskilled labor.

Equally vital, the United States needs a serious energy policy, not only to safeguard its prosperity but also to deal with global warming, one of the key challenges to its security (Objective 3). President Bush has said that the United States is addicted to oil, and so is the world.[143] The American transportation sector is the most hooked, being 95 percent dependent on oil. In 2005, 59 percent of the oil consumed in the United States was imported from overseas, and that is expected to increase to 68 percent by 2025.[144] This kind of dependence leaves the United States economy vulnerable to supply disruptions and price spikes, which may constitute the primary short-term threat to American prosperity. Indeed, every economic recession in the last four decades has been preceded by a significant rise in oil prices; altogether, according to study by the Oak Ridge National Laboratory, oil market upheavals have cost the American economy an astounding $7 trillion over the past 30 years.[145] As long as oil keeps its place in U.S. energy demand, there is no way to end dependence on foreign sources of supply, for even if domestic production could be more than doubled to meet the country's entire demand, doing so would burn through U.S. reserves in just four to five years.[146] Similar if longer-range fears of total depletion are held by most observers of the world's oil supply. Former Secretary of Energy Jim Schlesinger points out that, having already consumed a third of the three trillion barrels of oil originally thought to be in the earth's crust and currently burning thirty billion barrels each year (rising to 40 billion by 2025), the world will reach a plateau in oil production over the next couple of decades. "Even present trends are unsustainable. Sometime in the decades ahead, the world will no longer be able to accommodate rising energy demand with increased production of conventional oil."[147]

---

[143] George W. Bush, "'America Is Addicted to Oil'," State of the Union Address, *Washington Post* (February 1, 2006): A14–15
[144] Justin Blum, "No Way Found to Cut Need for Foreign Oil," *Washington* Post (December 22, 2005): A10; Philip J. Deutch, "Energy Independence," *Foreign Policy* 151 (November/December 2005): 20.
[145] Study cited in Wirth, Gray, and Podesta, "The Future of Energy Policy," p. 134.
[146] Deutch, "Energy Independence," p. 20.
[147] James Schlesinger, "Thinking Seriously: About Energy and Oil's Future," *National Interest* 82 (Winter 2005/06): 21.

Nor should it want to. Indeed, given the realities of global warming, the deeper worry is not that the world will fail to meet its energy demands with oil production, but that it will succeed, for fossil fuels account for 60 percent of climate warming emissions globally and 85 percent of them in the United States.[148] In the short term, as noted above, the United States needs a stable supply of oil imports at reasonable prices; every addict needs his fix. Keeping that supply secure will continue to require the kind of outsized military investment symbolized by CENTCOM and the two major wars already fought in the Persian Gulf. Nor should the country go cold turkey. The infrastructure of oil, indeed of all hydrocarbon energy, is too deeply embedded, built into capital goods that have useful lives of years if not decades – in fact, it is the very difficulty of switching to other sources of energy that creates this vulnerability. But for the long run, the United States must kick its oil habit and get its overall hydrocarbon consumption under control. It is well past time – about three decades, in fact – for the Executive and Congress to set aside petty wrangles over ANWAR drilling and CAFE standards and enact a strategic energy policy that would have the twin goals of drastically reducing both dependence on foreign oil and the emission of atmospheric carbon dioxide.

How can this be done? Theoretically, there are three ways: cutting demand for carbon-producing energy (say, making cars twice as efficient or driving them half as much), finding non-CO_2 producing energy supplies (like solar, wind, geothermal, biomass, or nuclear power), or preventing the carbon produced by burning hydrocarbons from getting into the atmosphere (say, by capturing and storing it in deep geological formations).[149] Conservation measures to lower demand are the most immediately doable and significant actions. Japan has shown the world how, cutting energy consumption per person to almost half that in the United States, so that Japan now imports 16 percent less oil than in 1973 to fuel an economy double the size.[150] The simplest and surest way to encourage conservation of oil is a sliding tax that would maintain a minimum price per gallon of gasoline that gradually rose from $3 to maybe $6-$10 (depending on the world price of oil), with its regressive taxation effects offset by credits for lower income citizens. This measure would mitigate the economic trauma of oil price swings, and it has the added advantage that the purchasers' money flows into the U.S. Treasury, where it can contribute to deficit reduction rather than financing overseas corruption, repression, anti-American Islamism, and terrorism.[151]

---

[148] Wirth, Gray, and Podesta, "The Future of Energy Policy," p. 136.

[149] Kolbert, "The Climate of Man – II," p. 55.

[150] Anthony Failoa, "Japanese Putting All Their Energy Into Saving Fuel," *Washington Post* (February 16, 2006): A1, A18.

[151] Such a tax has been recommended by economist Robert J. Samuelson, "Cheap Gas is a Bad Habit," *Washington Post* (September 14, 2005): A31, and neoconservative Charles Krauthammer, "Pump Some Seriousness Into Energy Policy," *Washington Post* (November 11, 2005): A25.

But these demand reduction measures are only the beginning. *New York Times* columnist Thomas Friedman has called for a "crash program for alternative energy and conservation" that "in one fell swoop . . . would dry up revenue for terrorism, force Iran, Russia, Venezuela, and Saudi Arabia onto the path of reform – which they will never do with $50 a barrel oil – strengthen the dollar, and improve" America's international prestige.[152] More specifically, Timothy Wirth, Boydon Gray, and John Podesta have proposed a bipartisan program to accomplish three 25-year goals: cutting U.S. oil consumption by a third, reducing its carbon emissions by a third, and developing and disseminating clean energy technologies worldwide.[153] They argue that these objectives can be accomplished through government incentives that will energize private industry to create the needed technology, market mechanisms to make the transition as efficient as possible, and regulations that combine allowing the time needed for innovation with long-range planning certainty.

> Three elements are necessary to begin. First, there should be an initial, modest restriction on carbon emissions, coupled with an aggressive emissions-trading program. . . . Second, governments should create a transition period of 10 to 15 years, during which they provide incentives for the development and use of low- and no-carbon technologies. Finally, it must be established with absolute certainty that at the end of the transition period, the limits on carbon will turn sharply and rapidly downward . . . [154]

Wirth, Gray, and Podesta propose government-labor-industry-environmentalist partnerships that would rapidly spread hybrid automotive technology throughout the fleet, commercialize ethanol production from agricultural waste, develop new coal power plants that capture and store the carbon dioxide they produce, rewire the electrical grid with computers to efficiently and reliably provide the current needed for a digital economy (also a defense against terrorism), and issue global development bonds to finance the spread of clean energy technology into the Third World. Indeed, although the feasibility of many of these technologies remains to be demonstrated, it is at least plausible that the congruence of the maturation of clean energy technology, including biotechnology, with the worldwide need for new carbon-neutral energy capital goods constitutes an extraordinary economic opportunity that can generate millions of jobs and billions of dollars in profits for the countries that capitalize on it in the century ahead.

Value Preservation and Projection
As noted above, the American way of life is far more endangered by political polarization, economic vulnerabilities, and the prospect of a drastic

[152] Thomas L. Friedman, *The World Is Flat*, p. 283.
[153] Wirth, Gray, and Podesta, "The Future of Energy Policy," p. 140.
[154] Wirth, Gray, and Podesta, "The Future of Energy Policy," pp. 142–143.

curtailment of civil liberties in an ill-conceived reaction to another terrorist attack than from any foreign coercion. But there is one important foreign affairs objective that serves American value preservation interests: the control of immigration (Objective 7). Arguing for controlled immigration is easily stigmatized as immigrant-bashing or racist, but it would modestly serve several American interests while helping preserve the nation's intangible power resources. A combination of physical control at the border, sanctions that are actually enforced on employment of undocumented immigrants by American businesses, and a regularized visa policy for essential guest workers would help to avoid a permanent cultural, linguistic, and economic underclass. Moreover, it would actually add to the country's diversity by making possible the entry of a wider range of cultures through the legal immigration process. Second, physical control at the border is also important to security – as essential as control and inspection of container shipping arriving at our ports – to ensure that terrorists lack easy routes to import weapons of mass destruction. Third, border control will also help reduce the importation of narcotics and other dangerous drugs, another threat to American value preservation. Finally, controlling illegal immigration would help raise the wages of the poorest Americans and legal immigrants, partly redressing the problem of income inequality by exploding the myth that there are some kinds of jobs Americans will not do regardless of salary.[155] None of these several benefits is in itself crucial, but taken together they make a compelling case for this course of action.[156]

Security, prosperity, and value preservation at home are intrinsically more important for the American people than remaking the world in our own image or acting to relieve the suffering of non-Americans; therefore, value projection should never be elevated to the central concern of U.S. foreign policy. Indeed, its objectives are decidedly secondary to those serving other interests. When value projection takes on the idealist form of spreading democracy worldwide it becomes especially problematical, for a variety of reasons. First, there is the question of whether a world moving rapidly toward market democracy would actually serve American interests in security and prosperity, as is so often claimed. From an overall, theoretical perspective, the answer would seem to be unambiguously positive. As noted earlier, democracies rarely fight each other, and therefore are conducive to peace; their governmental processes are more transparent and reliable, making them more adept at diplomacy and at building and using international law and organizations; and they trade more with and

---

[155] Robert J. Samuelson, "We Don't Need 'Guest Workers,'" *Washington Post* (March 22, 2006): A21. Samuelson points out that unemployment clusters in precisely those social groups with whom illegals compete, and that they drive down wages up to 10 percent.

[156] As noted in Chapter 8, the fact that real border control does not fix any single problem but instead partially serves several interests does not mean that we can do just some of it; for this objective, partial success is worse than doing nothing.

invest more in each other, and so should be more prosperous. Therefore, argues one democratizer, "Washington has promoted democracy whenever possible not only because it is right, but also because it serves U.S. interests."[157]

However, when one looks more closely, it appears that the spread of democracy may not serve American interests always and everywhere. For example, in places where public opinion is strongly anti-American, like the Middle East, there is every reason to believe that truly democratic governments would represent that opinion and act vigorously against American interests. Nor is democracy necessarily an answer to the threat of terrorism, at least in the short run. Italy's Red Brigades, Ireland's Provisional IRA, the Japanese Red Army, Germany's Baader-Meinhof Gang, Spain's ETA, and Oklahoma's Timothy McVeigh turned to terrorism, not because they lived under a repressive regime that suppressed their views, but because a majority of free people in these democracies overwhelmingly *rejected* their views.[158] And not only may democracy prove a mixed blessing, but the promotion of democratization itself can be long and difficult. It is, after all, an assault on value preservation in nondemocratic countries, a most egregious interference in a target state's internal affairs that will be strongly resisted. Many experts contend that it requires cultural attributes (like tolerance, acceptance of the rule of law, and a belief in the equality of all persons) that take a long time to develop.[159] Even the adoption of capitalism and the free market followed by rapid economic growth may not do much in the short run to foster political democratization if clever authoritarian rulers are careful to withhold rights that allow people to coordinate their political activities, as is most notably evident in today's China.[160]

That democratization takes time and is difficult to pull off is significant. Even if it works, newly democratizing countries are often highly volatile and unstable, hardly making the kind of reliable partners that mature democracies offer. And if it does not work, aggressive promotion of democracy can undercut diplomatic efforts to deal with regimes that remain in power and hold the keys to American interests, whether those involve fighting terrorism or stopping nuclear proliferation in countries like Iran and North Korea. As political scientists David Hendrickson and Robert Tucker point out:

[157] John M. Owen, IV, "Democracy, Realistically," *National Interest* 83 (Spring 2006): 35–38.

[158] F. Gregory Gause III, "Can Democracy Stop Terrorism?" *Foreign Affairs* 84 (September/October 2005): 70, 67.

[159] Irving Louis Horowitz, "The Struggle for Democracy," *National Interest* 83 (Spring 2006): 115–116.

[160] Bruce Bueno de Mesquita and George W. Downs, "Development and Democracy," *Foreign Affairs* 84 (September/October 2005): 77–86.

It is the necessary consequence of making the "end of tyranny" your aim that all tyrannical regimes . . . are converted into an enemy. States have immemorially set aside differences in regime type and negotiated with adversaries across those boundaries, because it is the only way to reach the goal of security they have set for themselves. . . . One cannot seek to delegitimize regimes and make their demise a declared objective of U.S. foreign policy, and then hope to reach agreements with them on vital issues.[161]

These realist arguments do not mean that the United States should stop promoting democracy, for a world of democracies is still more likely than a world of dictatorships to be prosperous and peaceful. But they should affect how the United States goes about democratization, the statecraft with which it promotes its values. First, as the Bush administration has admitted despite its soaring rhetoric, this goal should be carefully tailored, applied only when it does not conflict with more important objectives and where favorable outcomes look most consequential and likely. As Francis Fukuyama writes:

By definition, outsiders can't "impose" democracy on a country that doesn't want it; demand for democracy and reform must be domestic. Democracy promotion is therefore a long-term and opportunistic process that has to await the gradual ripening of political and economic conditions to be effective.[162]

Second, the cost and risk of democracy promotion must be kept under control. At a minimum, if Americans have learned nothing else from Iraq, it should be that democracy promotion is not worth war. Third, accordingly, the United States should move a good distance from its current messianic style of democracy promotion toward an exemplar style; that is, instead of forcing democracy on others, it should concentrate on perfecting its own democracy at home as an example to others and inviting them to experience it.[163] The tools employed should be restricted to diplomacy, rhetoric, exchange of persons, and aid to indigenous democratic groups and governments that request it – if they can be effectively helped and are expected to support American values and policy. Moreover, the United States should not push for the forms of democratic government unless and until the culture and civil institutions necessary to support it are in place, lest it wind up promoting illiberal democracy or helping radical movements seize power

---

[161] David C. Hendrickson and Robert W. Tucker, "The Freedom Crusade," *National Interest* 81 (Fall 2005): 19.

[162] Francis Fukuyama, "After Neoconservatism," *New York Times Magazine* (February 18, 2006).

[163] The messianic and exemplar styles are discussed in Trevor B. McCrisken, "Exceptionalism," *Encyclopedia of American Foreign Policy*, 2nd ed., Vol. 2 (New York: Scribner's, 2001), pp. 63–80. See also Robert W. Tucker, "Exemplar or Crusader? Reflections on America's Role," *National Interest* 5 (Fall 1986): 64–75.

through the ballot box.[164] "Our true mission," as Daniel Webster summed it up, is "not to propagate our opinions or impose upon other countries our form of government by artifice or force, but to teach by example and show by our success, moderation and justice, the blessings of self-government and the advantages of free institutions."[165]

Humanitarian intervention is the other, equally secondary objective of value projection, and here as in democracy promotion the guiding principle should be caution (Objective 9). The world is full of practices that violate American sensibilities, but American foreign policy should serve the interests of those in distress overseas only to the extent that it does not substantially compromise the interests of the American people. Because there is no objective need for altruism, public opinion rather than expert analysis should be controlling; the nation should project its values in this way only to the extent that the people, not their leaders, wish it to.[166] A statesman's role in this area of statecraft is therefore to discern the people's will and act on it – if effective action is possible in the circumstances, and if sufficient power is available given the press of competing objectives – while at the same time limiting the cost and risk of intervention to levels the people can be expected to support over the long run. For if public opinion is the proper foundation for U.S. entry into a humanitarian crisis, it must not drive America out prematurely lest the engaged prestige and power of the United States suffer. This is also an activity that cries out for broad international support and legitimization. If American values truly are universal, then others will feel compelled to help in any crisis that really demands and allows it. But if there is no international consensus, then American decision makers should probably conserve their country's power for more compelling threats and opportunities.

Evaluating Strategies for the Twenty-First Century

The outline of a U.S. foreign affairs strategy for the twenty-first century presented above is far from complete, and it is obviously based on the circumstances extant at its writing. Still, its implementation would involve a marked change from the Bush administration's statecraft. It would put primary energy and resources behind four objectives – securing (and stopping production of) nuclear material and weapons, building layered homeland

---

[164] President Bush has this exactly backwards, saying "Elections start the process. . . . you follow elections with institution building and the creation of civil society." Speech to the Freedom Forum as quoted in Baker, "Democracy in Iraq Not a Priority in U.S. Budget," p. A18.

[165] Hendrickson and Tucker, "The Freedom Crusade," p. 14.

[166] If the crisis engages interests other than value projection, as did the 1990s crises in the former Yugoslavia, then intervention may be decided upon on those other grounds; this discussion is only to establish that the value projection component of an intervention is not analytically specifiable.

defenses, adopting a strategic and climate-friendly energy policy, and restoring fiscal sanity in government finance – of which only two are even partly goals of current foreign policy and none are priorities. Based on a different set of assumptions about the domestic and international environments, it would involve an overall switch from coercion to cooptation and from default unilateralism to routine multilateralism, along with a rebalancing in anti-terrorism of offense and defense. Potential power and influence would be more advantaged relative to actual power, and nonviolent tools stressed more than military ones. But this proposed strategy remains to be evaluated. What are its likely costs and risks? Do its courses of action contradict or reinforce each other? And can Americans be expected to support them? Given limitations of space, answering such questions can be no more conclusive than the strategy itself, but the following speculations may serve to complete this extended illustration of foreign affairs strategy.

Although quantitative calculations are beyond the scope of this study, the proposed strategy includes some obvious savings as well as targeted expenses. The new emphasis on defense in the struggle against terrorism should preclude additional major wars unless a significant new homeland attack occurs, and that alone will be an enormous saving when compared, for example, to the dollars and lives spent in Iraq since 2003. Postponing national missile defense deployment will also be a huge savings. On the other hand, the accelerated effort to get loose nukes under control will be an added expense, yet over only two to three years – the whole idea is to get it done as soon as humanly possible. The cost of layered defense against terrorist attack will be vastly higher, but it will be borne mainly by the civilian economy and over a very considerable period of time. Moreover, as noted, a great deal of it will have positive payoffs unrelated to protection from terrorist attack, both for individuals and the economy, so some portion of the spending should be considered as directed not at foreign affairs but domestic welfare.

Such complex cost calculations apply to the rest of the strategy as well. The proposed strategic energy policy, for example, will certainly have short-term costs for the economy and will demand considerable government spending to jump start the development of clean energy technology. However, the latter can be financed through gas and carbon taxes and should be considered an investment that over the long term will reinforce economic stability and catalyze a commercial bonanza, to say nothing of possibly heading off the potentially astronomical economic costs of climate change. Getting the nation's fiscal house in order will require increased taxation, but the overall impact of balancing the federal budget on interest rates and productivity of capital (to say nothing of the trade deficit) should again be positive, as in the 1990s. Reallocating funding of the instruments of national power should not require overall increases, because small percentage reductions in military spending can fund huge increases in spending for nonviolent tools. Finally, multilateralism is generally less costly than unilateralism, since others are undertaking part of the effort, while the restoration of American legitimacy is an influence multiplier that should reduce the cost of objectives' achievement across the whole of policy. Overall, then, it appears that the proposed strategy should not be much more costly in the short run than the one it replaces, and over the long run should more than pay for itself.

What would be the effect of the proposed strategy on risk? The whole point of the strategy's four main components is to take decisive action to reduce the major dangers faced by the United States, especially those with the most horrific consequences: a nuclear explosion in an American city, destruction of the planet's life support system, and economic crises caused by financial imbalances or oil cutoffs. And the courses of action mandated by the strategy generally contain far less active risk than those they would replace. For example, quite apart from their effectiveness in reducing danger, defensive measures against terrorism are unlikely to destabilize friendly governments, lead to open-ended commitments, or generate new attacks in the way that even a skillfully-executed offensive strategy might. The shift away from routine use of the military, the riskiest instrument, should also help lower the prospect of unanticipated costs, while multilateral action spreads whatever intrinsic risk a course of action carries across multiple parties, thereby lowering potential costs for any one of them. There is some risk to prosperity from the tax increases that will be needed to balance the budget, but these can be offset to some degree by relaxation of monetary policy. All in all, then, the proposed strategy seems likely to trade some increase in short-term costs for a reduction in risks and the prospect of long-term economic gain.

The strategy is also free of major internal contradictions; indeed, several of its courses of action support multiple interests and are mutually reinforcing. Though the primary objective of the strategic energy policy is climate control, for example, it will also help cut the budget deficit by reducing military expenditures to defend oil supplies and reduce the trade deficit by curtailing oil imports, which in turn will help limit the amount of U.S. debt held by foreigners and dry up revenue to authoritarian regimes and terrorists seeking WMD. Getting control of immigration serves value preservation, provides additional security against importation of WMD, and reduces income inequality by raising the wages of less skilled Americans in a tightened labor market. The defensive, co-optive, and lower-cost approach to dealing with terrorism will also help restore American legitimacy, bolster its soft power, and reduce the budget deficit, as will replacing the missionary with an exemplar approach to spreading market democracy. These synergies should help the strategy be more than the sum of its parts, lowering its costs while enhancing its prospects for success.

There is, however, one critical shortcoming of this proposed strategy that cannot be ignored. That is its doubtful prospect of public and political support, and therefore of being implemented. Could a strategy of the sort outlined above ever make it through the American policy process? This is, after all, a strategy that promises at least some curtailment of government spending, especially on entitlements, along with increases in taxation on wealthier Americans to balance the budget. It mandates increases in the cost of energy, partly through a gasoline tax that will permanently end the cheap energy Americans love and encourage the use of more expensive, smaller, and less powerful cars, and partly through building infrastructure (like wind turbines and nuclear power plants) that many Americans find objectionable.[167] It requires that Americans accept some risk of attack on the homeland so that the country can reallocate resources to more efficient and productive ways of dealing with terrorism. It suggests an evenhanded approach to the Palestinian–Israeli dispute that might require tough action against Israel, even a curtailment of the roughly two-and-a-half billion dollars in military aid given by the United States each year. Perhaps the only part of the strategy that would get popular support is Objective 6 on immigration, since 75 percent of Americans think the government is not doing enough to secure the nation's borders – although the growing political power of those opposing such measures was also made vividly evident in 2006 by mass immigrant demonstrations in American cities.[168]

Indeed, the strategy outlined above expects the polarized American political system and the Congress to do things, like fixing social security and Medicare, passing a serious energy policy, and establishing and maintaining fiscal discipline, that they have repeatedly and conspicuously failed to do. It requires a quality of leadership that has recently been absent from the American political scene. More generally, it prescribes action now to deal with threats that lie far in the future, despite the fact that democratic "political systems do not allocate much effort to dealing with distant threats – even when those threats have a probability of 100 percent."[169] The demands the strategy makes on the American people and their elected representatives cannot be ignored, for any realistic foreign affairs strategy must take into account its prospects for enactment. Otherwise it risks the fate of many a spider's web – hanging ignored in a corner of the nation's strategic attic, hardly worth the effort to clear it away.

Readers can judge for themselves whether the strategy outlined above has any chance of implementation, and if not, how it might be altered to improve its prospects without losing its potential. But the extraordinary difficulty of making any sound foreign affairs strategy into actual foreign policy underlines the broader point that, in the end, most of the failings of American statecraft can be found at home rather than abroad.

---

[167] Anne Applebaum, "Tilting at Windmills," *Washington Post* (April 19, 2006): A17.
[168] Jonathan Weisman, "Senators Back Guest Workers," *Washington Post* (March 28, 2006): A5.
[169] James Schlesinger, "Thinking Seriously," p. 24.

Psychologists say that all life's important battles are fought within the self; negotiators frequently find the bargaining within their own government harder than that with their international counterparts; and in strategy, too, the real enemy is often us. The strategic grammar and logic presented in these pages is intended to help provide an intellectual framework for a foreign affairs strategy equal to the challenges of the twenty-first century, and perhaps the logic of such a strategy would be powerful enough that charismatic leaders could unify the nation and integrate the government behind it. After all, Americans have enormous assets with which to face the future: a vibrant economy, a free and stable political system, and pre-eminent power. There is no material reason why they should not enjoy a "good" – which is to say a strategic – foreign policy.

APPENDIX A

Definitions of Grand Strategy, National Security Strategy, and Statecraft

"...the nation's plan for using all its instruments and resources of power to support its interests most effectively."[1]

"...the coordinated direction of all the resources, military and nonmilitary, of a nation (or alliance) to accomplish its objectives."[2]

"...the art and science of employing national power under all circumstances to exert desired degrees and types of control over the opposition through threats, force, indirect pressures, diplomacy, subterfuge, and other imaginative means, thereby satisfying national security interests and objectives.

"'Military strategy' and 'grand strategy' are interrelated, but are by no means synonymous. Military strategy is predicated on physical violence or the threat of violence. It seeks victory through force of arms. Grand strategy, if successful, alleviates any need for violence. Equally important, it looks beyond victory toward a lasting peace. Military strategy is mainly the province of generals. Grand strategy is mainly the purview of statesmen. Grand strategy *controls* military strategy, which is only one of its elements."[3]

"...must be firmly rooted in broad national interests and objectives, supported by an adequate commitment of resources, and integrate all relevant facets of national power to achieve our national objectives."[4]

"[grand strategy]...where all that is military happens within the much broader context of domestic governance, international politics, economic activity, and their ancillaries."

[1] Robert E. Osgood, "American Grand Strategy: Patterns, Problems, and Prescriptions," *Naval War College Review* (September-October 1983): 5.
[2] Gregory D. Foster, "Missing and Wanted: A U.S. Grand Strategy," *Strategic Review* 13 (Fall 1985): 15.
[3] John M. Collins, *Grand Strategy: Principles and Practices* (Annapolis, MD: Naval Institute Press, 1973), p. 15.
[4] *National Security Strategy of the United States* (Washington, DC: The White House, January 1987), p. 1.

"...at the level of grand strategy, the interactions of the lower, military levels...yield final results within the broad setting of international politics, in further interaction with the nonmilitary transactions of states: the formal exchanges of diplomacy, the public communications of propaganda, secret operations, the perceptions of others formed by intelligence official and unofficial, and all economic transactions of more than purely private significance."[5]

"...as war and society have become more complicated...strategy has of necessity required increasing consideration of nonmilitary factors, economic, psychological, moral, political, and technological. Strategy, therefore, is not merely a concept of wartime, but is an inherent element of statecraft at all times. Only the most restricted terminology would now define strategy as the art of military command. In the present-day world, then, strategy is the art of controlling and utilizing the resources of a nation –or a coalition of nations– including its armed forces, to the end that its vital interests shall be effectively promoted and secured against enemies, actual, potential, or merely presumed. The highest type of strategy –sometimes called grand strategy– is that which so integrates the policies and armaments of the nation that the resort to war is either rendered unnecessary or is undertaken with the maximum chance of victory."[6]

"By 'strategy,' I mean quite simply the process by which ends are related to means, intentions to capabilities, objectives to resources."[7]

"...strategy, as I understand it, is nothing more than 'the calculated relation of ends and means.'...several qualifications should accompany this definition. First, it is meant to be generic: it can apply to any situation in which you face the task of getting from where you are to where you want to go on the basis of the resources and the determination you have available, but in the face of resistance in some form. Second, it refers to ends and means in general, not exclusively to military ends and military means. It therefore encompasses –and indeed can hardly be separated from– the realms of politics, economics, psychology, law and morality...; those dimensions of strategy are every bit as important as its military components. Third, the inclusion of the adjective 'calculated' is meant to imply a deliberate as opposed to an accidental, inadvertent, or fortuitous connection between ends and means: luck may enhance or impede the attainment of strategic objectives, but is not strategy itself.

[5] Edward C. Luttwak, *Strategy: The Logic of War and Peace* (Cambridge, MA: Belknam Press/Harvard, 1987), pp. 70, 179.

[6] Edwin Mead Earle, *Makers of Modern Strategy* (Princeton, NJ: Princeton University Press, 1943), p. viii.

[7] John Lewis Gaddis, *Strategies of Containment* (New York: Oxford University Press, 1982), p. viii.

"What, then, is 'grand strategy?' To my mind, it is simply the application of strategy as here defined, by states acting within the international state system, to secure their interests: it is what leads, if all goes well, to statecraft."[8]

"...the way in which you marshal all the forces at your disposal on the world chessboard. I mean not only the military forces you have, although that is very important, but all the political forces."[9]

"...a politico-military, means-ends chain, a state's theory about how it can best 'cause' security for itself."[10]

"...I will speak separately of foreign policy, of economic policy, and of military strategy in the classic sense. Yet...all three must operate in the end within one and the same framework, whether we call that framework simply international relations or, in fancier language, the transnational fabric of the world today. The goals that any nation, or group of nations, sets for itself must be consistent over all the three fields. They must, in short, be guided by a unifying concept, and this is what is meant by a Grand Strategy."[11]

"In the simplest terms, a state's grand strategy is its plan for making itself secure. Grand strategy identifies the objectives that must be achieved to produce security, and describes the political and military actions that are believed to lead to this goal..."[12]

"...the role of grand strategy – higher strategy – is to coordinate and direct all the resources of a nation, or band of nations – towards the attainment of the political objective of the war – the goal defined by fundamental policy."[13]

---

[8] John Lewis Gaddis, "Containment and the Logic of Strategy," *National Interest* 10 (Winter 1987–88): 29.

[9] George F. Kennan, "Soviet Diplomacy," Lecture of October 6, 1947, in Giles D. Harlow and George C. Merz, *Measures Short of War* (Washington, DC: NDU Press, 1991), p. 258.

[10] Barry R. Posen, *The Sources of Military Doctrine: France, Germany, and Britain Between the World Wars* (Ithaca: NY: Cornell University Press, 1984), p. 13.

[11] Helmut Schmidt, *A Grand Strategy for the West* (New Haven, CT: Yale University Presss, 1985), pp. 5–6.

[12] Stephen M. Walt, "The Case for Finite Containment," *International Security* 14 (Summer 1989): 6.

[13] B. H. Liddell Hart, *Strategy*, 2nd rev. ed. (New York: Meridian, 1991), p. 322.

"American grand strategy ... is measured not by military forces alone but by their integration with all those other elements (economic, social, political, and diplomatic) that contribute toward a successful long-term policy."[14]

"Statecraft has traditionally been defined as the art of conducting state affairs ... more often it refers to the selection of means for the pursuit of foreign policy goals.... To study statecraft, as conceived here, is to consider the instruments used by policy makers in their attempts to exercise power, i.e., to get others to do what they would not otherwise do."[15]

"... statecraft embraces all the activities by which statesmen strive to protect cherished values and to attain desired objectives vis-à-vis other nations and/or international organizations."[16]

"... the organized actions governments take to change the external environment in general or the policies and actions of other states in particular to achieve the objectives that have been set by policymakers."[17]

"The problem with governmental practitioners ... is that few of them understand what strategy really is. Originally it was a military subject concerned with using the instruments of war to achieve victory. Today, however, the dimensions of strategy have expanded, and it must be a peacetime pursuit.... Many people think a strategy is simply a plan. I disagree vehemently. The term was derived from the Greek *strategos*, meaning the 'art' of the general, not the 'plan' of the general. Art is an arrangement of elements in a manner that creates a whole that is far greater than the sum of its elements. This is just as true of peacetime strategies as of wartime ones. A plan, if it is fixed and stereotyped, is in fact the opposite of a truly good strategy. Strategy involves having a concept, priorities, and a direction – ones that are flexible and adaptable to changing situations – for the rational and disciplined allocation of resources to achieve specific objectives.

"What of grand strategy? Today more than ever, security is both military and economic, and the two must be interrelated in a grand strategy. Western grand strategy, however, must do even more. It must embrace political and diplomatic, technological, and even cultural and moral factors. It must

---

[14] Paul Kennedy, "The (Relative) Decline of America," *Atlantic Monthly* (August 1987): 29.
[15] David A. Baldwin, *Economic Statecraft* (Princeton, NJ: Princeton University Press, 1985), pp. 8–9.
[16] Harold and Margaret Sprout, *Toward a Politics of the Planet Earth* (New York: Van Nostrand Reinhold Co., 1971), p. 135.
[17] K. J. Holsti, "The Study of Diplomacy," in James N. Rosenau, Kenneth W. Thompson, and Gavin Bond, eds., *World Politics* (New York: Free Press, 1976), p. 293.

be a comprehensive way to deal with all the elements of national power, matching ends and means, relating them to commitments and diplomacy, and ensuring that they work in harmony."[18]

"...statecraft involves a process of reconciling what we want (objectives) with the resources available (capabilities) to meet these wants."[19]

"...concerned with situations...in which the best course of action for each participant depends on what he expects the other participants to do.

"Pure conflict, in which the interests of two antagonists are completely opposed, is a special case; it would arise in a war of complete extermination, otherwise not even in war. For this reason, winning in a conflict does not have a strictly competitive meaning; it is not winning relative to one's adversary. It means gaining relative to one's own value system; and this may be done by bargaining, by mutual accommodation, and by the avoidance of mutually damaging behavior. If war to the finish has become inevitable, there is nothing left but pure conflict; but if there is any possibility of avoiding a mutually damaging war, of conducting warfare in a way that minimizes damage, or of coercing an adversary by threatening war rather than waging it, the possibility of mutual accommodation is as important and dramatic as the element of conflict. Thus strategy is not concerned with the efficient application of force but with the *exploitation of potential force*. It is concerned not just with enemies who dislike each other but with partners who distrust or disagree with each other. It is concerned not just with the division of gains and losses between two claimants but with the possibility that particular outcomes are worse (better) for both claimants than certain other outcomes."[20]

"Some employ a restrictive definition of grand strategy that specifies only the threats to a state and the military means to deal with them. Others use a broader definition that specifies the threats to a nation's security and then details the military, political and economic means to meet them...I employ the term grand strategy in neither of these senses. Rather I use it, first, to specify the goals that a state should pursue, including both security and non-security goals, and, second, to delineate how military power can serve these goals. Unlike the first definition, mine includes goals other than simply security; unlike the second, my purview is restricted to military means. Non-military means are as important to statecraft as the military one, but I do not treat them as part of grand strategy, because

[18] David M. Ahshire, *Preventing World War III: A Realistic Grand Strategy* (New York: Harper and Row, 1988), pp. 12–13.

[19] COL Charles M. Fergusson, Jr., "Statecraft and Military Force," *Military Review* 46 (February 1966): 70.

[20] Thomas C. Schelling, *Strategy of Conflict* (Cambridge, MA: Harvard University Press, 1960), pp. 4–5.

I wish to preserve the useful distinction between grand strategy and foreign policy, which includes all of the goals and all of the instruments of statecraft.[21]

"The crux of grand strategy lies ... in the capacity of the nation's leaders to bring together all of the elements, both military and non-military, for the preservation and enhancement of the nation's long-term (that is, in wartime *and* peacetime) best interests.[22]

"Statecraft, from the days of Richelieu to those of Nixon, has consisted in the identification of national interests, the realistic assessment of available resources, and the alignment of both in an appropriate relationship within the context of the interests and resources of rival states.[23]

" ... most political strategy, whether local, national, or international, is nothing more than common sense – the transformation of ideas into action in light of certain realities and in pursuit of specific goals.

"When you enter government, you do so with certain beliefs and values, and your task is to turn them into enduring realities consistent with your interests."[24]

"Some say that foreign policy is to diplomacy what strategy is to war, but I prefer a broader conception of strategy as the overall game plan for achieving our goals through the coherent use of all available resources and delivery systems. Strategies are built around a clear sense of priorities, a precise analysis of the sequence and timing for using power and influence, and a laser-like focus on getting the job done. Diplomacy needs power behind it to be effective, but even when diplomacy is backed by power, it is unlikely to be effective *unless there is an overarching strategic framework.*"[25]

[21] Robert J. Art, "A Defensible Defense," *International Security* 15 (Spring 1991): 6–7.

[22] Paul Kennedy, *Grand Strategies in War and Peace* (New Haven, CT: Yale University Press, 1991), p. 5.

[23] Michael Howard, "The World According to Henry," *Foreign Affairs* 73 (May–June 1994): 133.

[24] James A. Baker III, *The Politics of Diplomacy* (New York: G. P. Putnam's Sons, 1995), p. 39–40.

[25] Chester Crocker, "Contemporary Challenges for the Foreign Policy Strategist," in *The Role of Allies in U.S. National Security Strategy*, Inaugural Lectures for the James R. Schlesinger Program in Strategic Studies, Institute for the Study of Diplomacy, School of Foreign Service (Washington, DC: Georgetown University, 1998), pp. 2–3.

"Grand strategies are really bundles of security, economic, and political strategies based on assumptions about how best to advance national security and build international order."[26]

"'Grand Strategy'...is the process by which a state matches ends and means in the pursuit of security. In peacetime, grand strategy encompasses the following: defining the state's security interests; identifying the threats to those interests; and allocating military, diplomatic, and economic resources to defend the state's interests.

"In concrete terms, the debate over U.S. grand strategy is being played out almost daily with respect to NATO enlargement, China, U.S.-Japan relations, Bosnia, U.S. policy with respect to the proliferation of weapons of mass destruction, trade policy, and the defense budget. These are not discreet issues. The function of grand strategy is to weave them into a coherent framework."[27]

"What are U.S. interests; what are the threats to those interests; what are the appropriate remedies for those threats? In short, what is to be the new grand strategy of the United States?"[28]

"Grand strategy represents a road map delineating our most important foreign policy goals and the most effective instruments and policies for achieving those goals. It contains a vision for America's role in the world based in part on America's domestic needs and in part on the international challenges the country faces. It thus establishes priorities and gives focus to an otherwise volatile foreign policymaking process...In this sense, it also adds an important element of predictability and stability for other countries."[29]

"At its best, grand strategy is a form of economics: a way of establishing priorities given competing international goals and thus of determining the best use of scarce resources."[30]

"Central among my convictions is that international politics is a product of the normal pulls and tugs of domestic affairs, that leaders (not nations) make policy decisions and do so to maximize their prospects of staying

---

[26] G. John Ikenberry, "American Grand Strategy in the Age of Terror," *Survival* 43 (Winter 2001–02), p. 25.

[27] Christopher Layne, "Rethinking American Grand Strategy," *World Policy Journal* (Summer 1998): 8.

[28] Barry Posen and Andrew L. Ross, "Competing U.S. Grand Strategies," Chapter 5. in Robert J. Lieber, *Eagle Adrift* (New York: Longman, 1997), p. 100.

[29] Sherle R. Schwenninger, "Revamping American Grand Strategy," *World Policy Journal* 20 (Fall 2003): 25.

[30] Schwenninger, "Revamping American Grand Strategy," p. 32.

in office, and that decisions, therefore, are strategic, taking into account expected responses by adversaries and supporters and designed to maximize the leader's (not the state's) welfare. I call this view the strategic perspective. The question of personal political power guides policy choices, and the cumulative effect of policy choices gives rise to what we call the international system. Therefore, domestic politics, foreign policy, and international politics are inextricably linked. We cannot make sense of international relations without considering all three.[31]

"'Strategy' traditionally referred to the planning and employment of military resources . . . to achieve victory in war itself. . . . Basil Liddell Hart broadened this conception when he realized that military victory might be insufficient. . . . [i]f it left the nation weaker and vulnerable. . . . He wrote, 'It is essential to conduct war with constant regard to the peace you desire.' . . . American nuclear strategists after World War II generalized this insight to include 'deterrence' or the prevention of war. . . .

'Grand strategy,' however, represented a still more inclusive notion: it went beyond mere generalship in war or deterrence in peacetime to include 'the policy governing [the use of military force] and combining it with other weapons: economic, political, psychological.' In modern terms, grand strategy came to mean the adaptation of domestic and international resources to achieve security for a state. Thus grand strategy considers *all* the resources at the disposal of the nation (not just military ones), and it attempts to array them effectively to achieve security in both peace and war."[32]

"Statecraft seeks through strategy to magnify the mass, relevance, impact, and irresistibility of power. It guides the ways the state deploys and applies its power abroad."[33]

"*Grand Strategy* is the term used to describe how a country will employ the various tools it possesses – military, economic, political, technological, ideological, and cultural – to protect its overall security, values, and national interests."[34]

[31] Bruce Bueno de Mesquita, *Principles of International Politics: People's Power, Preferences, and Perceptions* (Washington, DC: CQ Press, 2003), p. xvi.

[32] Richard Rosecrance and Arthur A. Stein, "Beyond Realism: The Study of Grand Strategy," Chapter 1 in Rosecrance and Stein, eds. *The Domestic Bases of Grand Strategy* (Ithaca, NY: Cornell University Press, 1993), pp. 3–4.

[33] Chas. W. Freeman, Jr., *Arts of Power: Statecraft and Diplomacy* (Washington, DC: U.S. Institute of Peace Press, 1997), p. 3.

[34] Robert J. Lieber, *The American Era: Power and Strategy for the 21st Century.* (New York: Cambridge University Press, 2005), p. 40.

APPENDIX B

A Linear Design for Foreign Affairs Strategy

LEVEL 1: Assumptions about the Nation and the World

- controversies over *facts* and *intelligence*
- constraints and opportunities in the international *system*, including motivations of major actors
- constraints and opportunities in the *domestic* system
- projections of future *trends*

LEVEL 2: The National Interest(s), Threats, and Opportunities

- national *survival*
- national *welfare* and *prosperity*
- preservation of national *value* system at home
- projection of national values overseas
- assessment of *threats* to those interests and *opportunities* for advancing them
- ranking interests and countering threats: the concept of *risk*

LEVEL 3: Foreign Policy Objectives

- *desirability*, determined by reference to:
  - one's view of the national interest (Level 2)
  - cost considerations (Level 4)
- *feasibility*, determined by reference to:
  - availability of mobilized power (Level 4)
  - constraints and opportunities in the domestic and international contexts (Level 1)

LEVEL 4: Power and Resources

- *assessment of latent or potential power*, including all of the factors that bear on national power (economic capacity, natural resources, population, territorial extent and location, etc.)
- *availability of actual or mobilized power*, according to investments in usable policy tools or instruments (such as military forces, covert action, information and exchange programs, foreign aid, etc.)
- *cost of using resources*, both in terms of absolute expenditures and of opportunity costs, *i.e.*, the impact on other domestic and foreign policy goals

LEVEL 5: Plans and Priorities

- *the relationship of ends to means*, of power to objectives; degree of leveraging and role of psychological power projection
- *the plans of action*: in terms of this model, how one applies available resources (Level 4) to achieve strategic objectives (Level 3) that serve the national interest (Level 2) in the assumed environment (Level 1); how the instruments of foreign policy are to be used
- *timeframe*: *short run*, defined as the life of an administration, vs. *long run*, defined as the time it takes to generate significant new resources (Level 4) or effect/anticipate changes in the international system (Level 1)
- *priorities*: setting geographic and functional interrelationships at all levels of policy to minimize contradictions and maximize effectiveness.

Explanatory Note: This framework has five levels, beginning with basic assumptions about the domestic and international context, continuing with the key concepts of interests, threats, objectives, and power, and tying them together with specific plans for the application of means to ends. The term "priorities" is there to remind us that almost any strategy tends to be functional or geographically specific, raising the need to integrate (or at least consider the relationship of) each course of action with all those under consideration for other locales or subjects. Thus, the model (or pieces of it) must be repeated for each policy area and geographic region. Moreover, while the process may look sequential, every part really depends on every other part; all the relationships must somehow be assessed. And the process is further complicated by the fact that the levels are three-dimensional: *i.e.*, a strategy to serve one objective may well establish a series of subsidiary objectives which themselves have resource implications, impact on other areas of policy, and require implementation strategies.

Index

CPSIA information can be obtained
at www.ICGtesting.com
Printed in the USA
LVHW010802220920
666732LV00001B/1

9 780521 692779